THE WEALTH OF NATIONS
VOLUME II

AN INQUIRY INTO
THE NATURE AND CAUSES OF

The Wealth of Nations

BY

ADAM SMITH

Edited by EDWIN CANNAN, M.A. LL.D.

Volume II

METHUEN & CO LTD
36 ESSEX STREET · STRAND · WC2

This edition first published September 1904
Second edition 1920
Third edition 1923
Fourth edition 1925
Fifth edition 1930
Sixth edition 1950
Reprinted in this size 1961
Printed and bound in Great Britain
by Butler & Tanner Ltd, Frome and London
Catalogue No. 2/5163/10
6.2

Contents

Book IV

Book V

Of the Revenue of the Sovereign or Commonwealth

[From 'Introduction and Plan of the Work' in vol. i. to 'Public Debts' above, the Contents are printed in the present edition as they appeared in eds. 3–5. Eds. 1 and 2 neither enumerate the chapter 'Conclusion of the Mercantile System,' nor divide Bk. V., ch. i., Pt. iii., Art. 1st into sections, since the chapter and one of the two sections appeared first in ed. 3. Eds. 1 and 2 also read 'Inequalities in Wages and Profits arising from the Nature of the different Employments of both' at Bk. I., ch. x., Pt. 1.]

BOOK IV

CHAPTER IV

Of Drawbacks

Merchants demand encouragements to exportation. Merchants and manufacturers are not contented with the monopoly of the home market, but desire likewise the most extensive foreign sale for their goods. Their country has no jurisdiction in foreign nations, and therefore can seldom procure them any monopoly there. They are generally obliged, therefore, to content themselves with petitioning for certain encouragements to exportation.

Drawbacks of duty paid on domestic produce are reasonable, as they preserve the natural distribution of labour. Of these encouragements what are called Drawbacks seem to be the most reasonable. To allow the merchant to draw back upon exportation, either the whole or a part of whatever excise or inland duty is imposed upon domestic industry, can never occasion the exportation of a greater quantity of goods than what would have been exported had no duty been imposed. Such encouragements do not tend to turn towards any particular employment a greater share of the capital of the country, than what would go to that employment[1] of its own accord, but only to hinder the duty from driving away any part of that share to other employments. They tend not to overturn that balance which naturally establishes itself among all the various employments of the society; but to hinder it from being overturned by the duty. They tend not to destroy, but to preserve, what it is in most cases advantageous to preserve, the natural division and distribution of labour in the society.

So are also drawbacks of duty paid on goods imported. The same thing may be said of the drawbacks upon the re-exportation of foreign goods imported; which in Great Britain generally amount to by much the largest part of the duty upon importation.[2] By the second of the rules, annexed to the act of parliament,[3] which imposed, what

---

[1] [Eds. 1 and 2 reads 'go to it'.]
[2] [The next four pages are not in eds. 1 and 2; see below, p. 7, note.]
[3] [12 Car. II., c. 4.]

3

Under the old sub-sidy a drawback of one-half is allowed. is now called, the old subsidy, every merchant, whether English or alien, was allowed to draw back half that duty upon exportation; the English merchant, provided the exportation took place within twelve months; the alien, provided it took place within nine months. Wines, currants, and wrought silks were the only goods which did not fall within this rule, having other and more advantageous allowances. The duties imposed by this act of parliament were, at that time, the only duties upon the importation of foreign goods. The term within which this, and all other drawbacks, could be claimed, was afterwards (by 7 Geo. I. chap. 21. sect. 10.) extended to three years.[1]

Of more recent duties the whole is generally allowed, The duties which have been imposed since the old subsidy, are, the greater part of them, wholly drawn back upon exportation. This general rule, however, is liable to a great number of exceptions, and the doctrine of drawbacks has become a much less simple matter, than it was at their first institution.

and in some cases the whole even of the old subsidy is allowed. Upon the exportation of some foreign goods, of which it was expected that the importation would greatly exceed what was necessary for the home consumption, the whole duties are drawn back, without retaining even half the old subsidy. Before the revolt of our North American colonies, we had the monopoly of the tobacco of Maryland and Virginia. We imported about ninety-six thousand hogsheads, and the home consumption was not supposed to exceed fourteen thousand.[2] To facilitate the great exportation which was necessary, in order to rid us of the rest, the whole duties were drawn back, provided the exportation took place within three years.[3]

We still have, though not altogether, yet very nearly, the monopoly of the sugars of our West Indian islands. If sugars are exported within a year, therefore, all the duties upon importation are drawn back,[4] and if exported within three years, all the duties, except half the old subsidy, which still continues to be retained upon the exportation of the greater part of goods. Though the importation of sugar exceeds, a good deal, what is necessary for the home consumption, the excess is inconsiderable, in comparison of what it used to be in tobacco.

[1] [Henry Saxby, *The British Customs, containing an Historical and Practical Account of each branch of that part of the Revenue*, 1757, pp. 10, 308.]
[2] [These figures are also quoted above, vol. i., p. 395, and below, p. 117.]
[3] [Saxby, *British Customs*, p. 12.]   [4] [*Ibid.*, p. 11.]

In the case of some prohibited goods there is no drawback. Some goods, the particular objects of the jealousy of our own manufacturers, are prohibited to be imported for home consumption. They may, however, upon paying certain duties, be imported and warehoused for exportation. But upon such exportation, no part of these duties are drawn back. Our manufacturers are unwilling, it seems, that even this restricted importation should be encouraged, and are afraid lest some part of these goods should be stolen out of the warehouse, and thus come into competition with their own. It is under these regulations only that we can import wrought silks,[1] French cambrics and lawns,[2] callicoes painted, printed, stained, or dyed, &c.

French imports generally are allowed a smaller drawback on re-exportation. We are unwilling even to be the carriers of French goods, and choose rather to forego a profit to ourselves, than to suffer those, whom we consider as our enemies, to make any profit by our means. Not only half the old subsidy, but the second twenty-five per cent. is retained upon the exportation of all French goods.[3]

Wines have been peculiarly favoured, By the fourth of the rules annexed to the old subsidy, the drawback allowed upon the exportation of all wines amounted to a great deal more than half the duties which were, at that time, paid upon their importation; and it seems, at that time, to have been the object of the legislature to give somewhat more than ordinary encouragement to the carrying trade in wine. Several of the other duties too, which were imposed, either at the same time, or subsequent to the old subsidy; what is called the additional duty, the new subsidy, the one-third and two-thirds subsidies, the impost 1692, the coinage on wine, were allowed to be wholly drawn back upon exportation.[4] All those duties, however, except the additional duty and impost 1692,[5] being paid down in ready money, upon importation, the interest of so large a sum occasioned an expence, which made it unreasonable to expect any profitable carrying trade in this article. Only a part, therefore, of the duty called the impost on wine,[6] and no part of the twenty-five

---

[1] [6 Geo. III., c. 28; 11 Geo. III., c. 49.]

[2] [Above, vol. i., p. 496.]

[3] [7 and 8 W. III., c. 20; 1 Geo. I., c. 12, § 3; Saxby, *British Customs*, p. 45; above, vol. i., p. 496. The first 25 per cent. was imposed in 1692, the second in 1696.]

[4] [Saxby, *British Customs*, pp. 13, 22, 39, 46. 'The additional duty' was imposed in 1703. For the 'impost 1692' and the subsidies see above, vol. i., pp. 496, 497, and below, pp. 409, 410. 'The coinage on wine' was the duty levied under 18 Car. II., c. 5, for defraying the expenses of the mint.]

[5] [Saxby, *British Customs*, pp. 13, 38.]

[6] [1 Jac. II., c. 3, and continuing Acts: £8 a tun on French and £12 on other wine.

pounds the ton upon French wines,[1] or of the duties imposed in
1745,[2] in 1763,[3] and in 1778,[4] were allowed to be drawn back upon
exportation. The two imposts of five per cent., imposed in 1779 and
1781, upon all the former duties of customs,[5] being allowed to be
wholly drawn back upon the exportation of all other goods, were
likewise allowed to be drawn back upon that of wine. The last duty
that has been particularly imposed upon wine, that of 1780,[6] is
allowed to be wholly drawn back, an indulgence, which, when so
many heavy duties are retained, most probably could never occasion
the exportation of a single ton of wine. These rules take place with
regard to all places of lawful exportation, except the British colonies
in America.

*especially when
exported to the
American colonies,*
The 15th Charles II. chap. 7. called an act for the
encouragement of trade,[7] had given Great Britain
the monopoly of supplying the colonies with all the
commodities of the growth or manufacture of Europe; and consequently with wines. In a country of so extensive a coast as our
North American and West Indian colonies, where our authority
was always so very slender, and where the inhabitants were allowed
to carry out, in their own ships, their non-enumerated commodities,
at first, to all parts of Europe, and afterwards, to all parts of Europe
South of Cape Finisterre,[8] it is not very probable that this monopoly
could ever be much respected; and they probably, at all times,
found means of bringing back some cargo from the countries to
which they were allowed to carry out one. They seem, however,
to have found some difficulty in importing European wines from
the places of their growth, and they could not well import them
from Great Britain, where they were loaded with many heavy duties,
of which a considerable part was not drawn back upon exportation. Madeira wine, not being a European commodity,[9] could be

[1] [7 and 8 W. III., c. 20, § 3; 1 Geo. I., st. 2, c. 12, § 3.]

[2] [18 Geo. II., c. 9; Saxby, *British Customs*, p. 64: £8 a tun on French and £4 on other wine.]

[3] [? 1762. 3 Geo. III., c. 12: £8 a tun on French and £4 on other wine.]

[4] [18 Geo. III., c. 27: £8 8s. on French and £4 4s. on other wine.]

[5] [*I.e.*, 5 per cent., not on the value of the goods, but on the amount of the previously existing duties; 19 Geo. III., c. 25, and 22 Geo. III., c. 66.]

[6] [20 Geo. III., c. 30: £8 a tun on French and £4 on other wine.]

[7] [The colonial part of the Act is said in its particular preamble (§ 5) to be for the purpose of 'maintaining a greater correspondence and kindness between' the colonies and mother country, and for keeping the colonies 'in a firmer dependence'.]

[8] [All this is dealt with in greater detail below, pp. 89–92.]

[9] [The framers of the Act were not so sure about Madeira being non-European. They excepted wine of the Madeiras and Azores by special provision, § 7 of 15 Car. II., c. 7, § 13.]

imported directly into America and the West Indies, countries which, in all their non-enumerated commodities, enjoyed a free trade to the island of Madeira. These circumstances had probably introduced that general taste for Madeira wine, which our officers found established in all our colonies at the commencement of the war which began in 1755, and which they brought back with them to the mother-country, where that wine had not been much in fashion before. Upon the conclusion of that war, in 1763 (by the 4th Geo. III. Chap. 15. Sect. 12.), all the duties, except 3 l. 10 s. were allowed to be drawn back, upon the exportation to the colonies of all wines, except French wines, to the commerce and consumption of which national prejudice would allow no sort of encouragement. The period between the granting of this indulgence and the revolt of our North American colonies was probably too short to admit of any considerable change in the customs of those countries.

though the export of other foreign commodities to those colonies was discouraged. The same act, which, in the drawback upon all wines, except French wines, thus favoured the colonies so much more than other countries; in those, upon the greater part of other commodities, favoured them much less. Upon the exportation of the greater part of commodities to other countries, half the old subsidy was drawn back. But this law enacted, that no part of that duty should be drawn back upon the exportation to the colonies of any commodities, of the growth or manufacture either of Europe or the East Indies, except wines, white callicoes and muslins.[1]

Drawbacks were originally granted to encourage the carrying trade, which was absurd, but they are reasonable enough. Drawbacks were, perhaps, originally granted for the encouragement of the carrying trade, which, as the freight of the ships is frequently paid by foreigners in money, was supposed to be peculiarly fitted for bringing gold and silver into the country. But though the carrying trade certainly deserves no peculiar encouragement, though the motive of the institution was, perhaps, abundantly foolish, the institution itself seems reasonable enough. Such drawbacks cannot force into this trade a greater share of the

[1] [From the words 'duty upon importation' at the end of the first sentence of the third paragraph of the chapter to this point is new matter, which appears first in Additions and Corrections and ed. 3. Eds. 1 and 2 read in place of it simply, 'Half the duties imposed by what is called the old subsidy, are drawn back universally, except upon goods exported to the British plantations; and frequently the whole, almost always a part of those imposed by later subsidies and imposts'. The provision of 4 Geo. III., c. 15, taking away drawbacks, is quoted below, p. 96.]

capital of the country than what would have gone to it of its own accord, had there been no duties upon importation. They only prevent its being excluded altogether by those duties. The carrying trade, though it deserves no preference, ought not to be precluded, but to be left free like all other trades. It is a necessary resource for those capitals which cannot find employment either in the agriculture or in the manufactures of the country, either in its home trade or in its foreign trade of consumption.

The revenue gains by their existence when they do not amount to the whole of the duty paid. The revenue of the customs, instead of suffering, profits from such drawbacks, by that part of the duty which is retained. If the whole duties had been retained, the foreign goods upon which they are paid, could seldom have been exported, nor consequently imported, for want of a market. The duties, therefore, of which a part is retained, would never have been paid.

They would be justified even if they always did amount to the whole duty paid, These reasons seem sufficiently to justify drawbacks, and would justify them, though the whole duties, whether upon the produce of domestic industry, or upon foreign goods, were always drawn back upon exportation. The revenue of excise would in this case, indeed, suffer a little, and that of the customs a good deal more; but the natural balance of industry, the natural division and distribution of labour, which is always more or less disturbed by such duties, would be more nearly re-established by such a regulation.

but only to independent countries, not to those in respect of which there is a monopoly of trade. These reasons, however, will justify drawbacks only upon exporting goods to those countries which are altogether foreign and independent, not to those in which our merchants and manufacturers enjoy a monopoly. A drawback, for example, upon the exportation of European goods to our American colonies, will not always occasion a greater exportation than what would have taken place without it. By means of the monopoly which our merchants and manufacturers enjoy there, the same quantity might frequently, perhaps, be sent thither, though the whole duties were retained. The drawback, therefore, may frequently be pure loss to the revenue of excise and customs, without altering the state of the trade, or rendering it in any respect more extensive. How far such drawbacks can be justified, as a proper encouragement to the industry of our colonies, or how far it is advantageous to the mother-country, that they should be exempted from taxes which are paid by all the rest of their fellow-subjects, will appear hereafter[1] when I come to treat of colonies.

They give rise to frauds. Drawbacks, however, it must always be understood, are useful only in those cases in which the goods for the exportation of which they are given, are really exported to some foreign country; and not clandestinely re-imported into our own. That some drawbacks, particularly those upon tobacco, have frequently been abused in this manner, and have given occasion to many frauds equally hurtful both to the revenue and to the fair trader, is well known.

[1] [Below, pp. 96–98.]

CHAPTER V

Of Bounties

Foreigners cannot be forced to buy our goods, so it is proposed to pay them to do so. Bounties upon exportation are, in Great Britain, frequently petitioned for, and sometimes granted to the produce of particular branches of domestic industry. By means of them our merchants and manufacturers, it is pretended, will be enabled to sell their goods as cheap or cheaper than their rivals in the foreign market. A greater quantity, it is said, will thus be exported, and the balance of trade consequently turned more in favour of our own country. We cannot give our workmen a monopoly in the foreign, as we have done in the home market. We cannot force foreigners to buy their goods, as we have done our own countrymen. The next best expedient, it has been thought, therefore, is to pay them for buying. It is in this manner that the mercantile system proposes to enrich the whole country, and to put money into all our pockets by means of the balance of trade.

Bounties are not demanded for any but losing trades, Bounties, it is allowed, ought to be given to those branches of trade only which cannot be carried on without them. But every branch of trade in which the merchant can sell his goods for a price which replaces to him, with the ordinary profits of stock, the whole capital employed in preparing and sending them to market, can be carried on without a bounty. Every such branch is evidently upon a level with all the other branches of trade which are carried on without bounties, and cannot therefore require one more than they. Those trades only require bounties in which the merchant is obliged to sell his goods for a price which does not replace to him his capital, together with the ordinary profit; or in which he is obliged to sell them for less than it really costs him to send them to market. The bounty is given in order to make up this loss, and to encourage him to continue, or perhaps to begin, a trade of which the expence is supposed to be greater than the returns, of which every operation eats up a part of the capital employed in it, and which is of such a nature, that, if all other trades resembled it, there would soon be no capital left in the country.

and their effect is to force trade into disadvantageous channels. The trades, it is to be observed, which are carried on by means of bounties, are the only ones which can be carried on between two nations for any considerable time together, in such a manner as that one of them shall always and regularly lose, or sell its goods for less than it really costs to send them to market. But if the bounty did not repay to the merchant what he would otherwise lose upon the price of his goods, his own interest would soon oblige him to employ his stock in another way, or to find out a trade in which the price of the goods would replace to him, with the ordinary profit, the capital employed in sending them to market. The effect of bounties, like that of all the other expedients of the mercantile system, can only be to force the trade of a country into a channel much less advantageous than that in which it would naturally run of its own accord.

Charles Smith forgets the cost of raising the corn upon which the bounty is paid. The ingenious and well-informed author of the tracts upon the corn-trade[1] has shown very clearly, that since the bounty upon the exportation of corn was first established, the price of the corn exported, valued moderately enough, has exceeded that of the corn imported, valued very high, by a much greater sum than the amount of the whole bounties which have been paid during that period. This, he imagines, upon the true principles of the mercantile system, is a clear proof that this forced corn trade is beneficial to the nation; the value of the exportation exceeding that of the importation by a much greater sum than the whole extraordinary expence which the public has been at in order to get it exported. He does not consider that this extraordinary expence, or the bounty, is the smallest part of the expence which the exportation of corn really costs the society. The capital which the farmer employed in raising it, must likewise be taken into the account. Unless the price of the corn when sold in the foreign markets replaces, not only the bounty, but this capital, together with the ordinary profits of stock, the society is a loser by the difference, or the national stock is so much diminished. But the very reason for which it has been thought necessary to grant a bounty, is the supposed insufficiency of the price to do this.

---

[1] [Charles Smith, *Three Tracts on the Corn Trade and Corn Laws*, 2nd ed., 1766, pp. 132–138.]

The fall in the price of corn since the establishment of the bounty is due to other causes. The average price of corn, it has been said, has fallen considerably since the establishment of the bounty. That the average price of corn began to fall somewhat towards the end of the last century, and has continued to do so during the course of the sixty-four first years of the present, I have already endeavoured to show. But this event, supposing it to be as real as I believe it to be, must have happened in spite of the bounty, and cannot possibly have happened in consequence of it. It has happened in France, as well as in England, though in France there was, not only no bounty, but, till 1764, the exportation of corn was subjected to a general prohibition.[1] This gradual fall in the average price of grain, it is probable, therefore, is ultimately owing neither to the one regulation nor to the other, but to that gradual and insensible rise in the real value of silver, which, in the first book of this discourse, I have endeavoured to show has taken place in the general market of Europe, during the course of the present century.[2] It seems to be altogether impossible that the bounty could ever contribute to lower the price of grain.[3]

The bounty keeps up the price both in years of plenty and of scarcity. In years of plenty, it has already been observed,[4] the bounty, by occasioning an extraordinary exportation, necessarily keeps up the price of corn in the home market above what it would naturally fall to. To do so was the avowed purpose of the institution. In years of scarcity, though the bounty is frequently suspended, yet the great exportation which it occasions in years of plenty, must frequently hinder more or less the plenty of one year from relieving the scarcity of another. Both in years of plenty, and in years of scarcity, therefore, the bounty necessarily tends to raise the money price of corn somewhat higher than it otherwise would be in the home market.

It has been supposed to encourage cultivation and so to lower price. That, in the actual state of tillage, the bounty must necessarily have this tendency, will not, I apprehend, be disputed by any reasonable person. But it has been thought by many people that it tends to encourage tillage, and that in two different ways; first, by opening a more extensive foreign market to the corn of the farmer, it tends, they imagine, to increase the demand for, and consequently the production of that

---

[1] [Above, vol. i., pp. 217–220.]

[2] [Above, vol. i., pp. 219–234, and cp. p. 458.]

[3] [These three sentences beginning with 'It has happened in France,' appear first in Additions and Corrections and ed. 3.]

[4] [Above, vol. i., p. 219.]

commodity; and secondly, by securing to him a better price than he could otherwise expect in the actual state of tillage, it tends, they suppose, to encourage tillage. This double encouragement must, they imagine, in a long period of years, occasion such an increase in the production of corn, as may lower its price in the home market, much more than the bounty can raise it, in the actual state which tillage may, at the end of that period, happen to be in.[1]

The addition to the price of corn at home caused by the bounty is a heavy tax on the people, which restrains population and industry and in the long run tends to diminish the consumption of corn. I answer, that whatever extension of the foreign market can be occasioned by the bounty, must, in every particular year, be altogether at the expence of the home market; as every bushel of corn which is exported by means of the bounty, and which would not have been exported without the bounty, would have remained in the home market to increase the consumption, and to lower the price of that commodity. The corn bounty, it is to be observed, as well as every other bounty upon exportation, imposes two different taxes upon the people; first, the tax which they are obliged to contribute, in order to pay the bounty; and secondly, the tax which arises from the advanced price of the commodity in the home market, and which, as the whole body of the people are purchasers of corn, must in this particular commodity, be paid by the whole body of the people. In this particular commodity, therefore, this second tax is by much the heaviest of the two. Let us suppose that, taking one year with another, the bounty of five shillings upon the exportation of the quarter of wheat, raises the price of that commodity in the home market only sixpence the bushel, or four shillings the quarter, higher than it otherways would have been in the actual state of the crop. Even upon this very moderate supposition,[2] the great body of the people, over and above contributing the tax which pays the bounty of five shillings upon every quarter of wheat exported, must pay another of four shillings upon every quarter which they themselves consume. But, according to the very well informed author of

---

[1] [Eds. 1 and 2 read (beginning at the third line of the paragraph) 'But it has been thought by many people, that by securing to the farmer a better price than he could otherwise expect in the actual state of tillage, it tends to encourage tillage; and that the consequent increase of corn may, in a long period of years, lower its price more than the bounty can raise it in the actual state which tillage may at the end of that period happen to be in.' The alteration is given in Additions and Corrections. The next two paragraphs appear first in Additions and Corrections and ed. 3.]

[2] [It is really anything but a moderate supposition. It is not at all likely that the increase of demand caused by the offer of a bounty on exportation would raise the price of a commodity to the extent of four-fifths of the bounty.]

the tracts upon the corn-trade, the average proportion of the corn exported to that consumed at home, is not more than that of one to thirty-one.[1] For every five shillings, therefore, which they contribute to the payment of the first tax, they must contribute six pounds four shillings to the payment of the second. So very heavy a tax upon the first necessary of life, must either reduce the subsistence of the labouring poor, or it must occasion some augmentation in their pecuniary wages, proportionable to that in the pecuniary price of their subsistence. So far as it operates in the one way, it must reduce the ability of the labouring poor to educate and bring up their children, and must, so far, tend to restrain the population of the country. So far as it operates in the other, it must reduce the ability of the employers of the poor, to employ so great a number as they otherwise might do, and must, so far, tend to restrain the industry of the country. The extraordinary exportation of corn, therefore, occasioned by the bounty, not only, in every particular year, diminishes the home, just as much as it extends the foreign market and consumption, but, by restraining the population and industry of the country, its final tendency is to stunt and restrain the gradual extension of the home market; and thereby, in the long run, rather to diminish, than to augment, the whole market and consumption of corn.

The enhancement of price would encourage production if it was an enhancement of real price, but it is not; This enhancement of the money price of corn, however, it has been thought, by rendering that commodity more profitable to the farmer, must necessarily encourage its production.[2]

I answer, that this might be the case if the effect of the bounty was to raise the real price of corn, or to enable the farmer, with an equal quantity of it, to maintain a greater number of labourers in the same manner, whether liberal, moderate, or scanty, that other labourers are commonly maintained in his neighbourhood. But neither the bounty, it is evident, nor any other human institution, can have any such effect. It is not the real, but the nominal price of corn, which can in any considerable degree be affected by the bounty.[3] And though the tax which that institution imposes upon the whole body of the people, may be very burden-

---

[1] [C. Smith, *Three Tracts on the Corn Trade*, 2nd ed., p. 144.]

[2] [This and the preceding paragraph are not in eds. 1 and 2. See above, p. 13, note 1.]

[3] [See above, vol. i., pp. 34–43. It does not occur to Smith that the additional corn might require greater labour to produce it than an equal quantity of the old.]

some to those who pay it, it is of very little advantage to those
who receive it.[1]

it is only a
degradation of the
value of silver,
The real effect of the bounty is not so much to raise
the real value of corn, as to degrade the real value
of silver; or to make an equal quantity of it exchange for a smaller quantity, not only of corn, but of all other
home-made commodities: for the money price of corn regulates
that of all other home-made[2] commodities.

for corn regulates
the money price of
labour,
It regulates the money price of labour, which must
always be such as to enable the labourer to purchase
a quantity of corn sufficient to maintain him and
his family either in the liberal, moderate, or scanty manner in which
the advancing, stationary or declining circumstances of the society
oblige his employers to maintain him.

of all rude produce, It regulates the money price of all the other parts
of the rude produce of land, which, in every period of improvement, must bear a certain proportion to that of corn, though this
proportion is different in different periods. It regulates, for example,
the money price of grass and hay, of butcher's meat, of horses, and
the maintenance of horses, of land carriage consequently, or of the
greater part of the inland commerce of the country.

and of almost all
manufactures.
By regulating the money price of all the other parts
of the rude produce of land, it regulates that of the
materials of almost[3] all manufactures. By regulating the money price
of labour, it regulates that of manufacturing art and industry. And
by regulating both, it regulates that of the complete manufacture.
The money price of labour, and of every thing that is the produce
either of land or labour, must necessarily either rise or fall in proportion to the money price of corn.

So farmers and
landlords are not
benefited by the
increased price due
to the bounty.
Though in consequence of the bounty, therefore,
the farmer should be enabled to sell his corn for
four shillings the bushel instead of three and six-
pence, and to pay his landlord a money rent proportionable to this rise in the money price of his produce; yet if,
in consequence of this rise in the price of corn, four shillings will
purchase no more home-made[4] goods of any other kind than three

---

[1] [In place of this and the preceding sentence eds. 1 and 2 read only 'It is not the real
but the nominal price of corn only which can be at all affected by the bounty.' The
alteration is given in Additions and Corrections.]

[2] ['Home-made' here and in the line above is not in eds. 1 and 2.]

[3] ['Almost' is not in eds. 1 and 2.]   [4] [Eds. 1 and 2 do not contain 'home-made'.]

and sixpence would have done before, neither the circumstances of the farmer, nor those of the landlord, will be much[1] mended by this change. The farmer will not be able to cultivate much better: the landlord will not be able to live much[2] better. In the purchase of foreign commodities this enhancement in the price of corn may give them some little advantage. In that of home-made commodities it can give them none at all. And almost the whole expence of the farmer, and the far greater part even of that of the landlord, is in home-made commodities.[3]

A worldwide degradation of the value of silver is of little consequence, That degradation in the value of silver which is the effect of the fertility of the mines, and which operates equally, or very near equally, through the greater part of the commercial world, is a matter of very little consequence to any particular country. The consequent rise of all money prices, though it does not make those who receive them really richer, does not make them really poorer. A service of plate becomes really cheaper, and every thing else remains precisely of the same real value as before.

but degradation confined to one country discourages the industry of that country. But that degradation in the value of silver which, being the effect either of the peculiar situation, or of the political institutions of a particular country, takes place only in that country, is a matter of very great consequence, which, far from tending to make any body really richer, tends to make every body really poorer. The rise in the money price of all commodities, which is in this case peculiar to that country, tends to discourage more or less every sort of industry which is carried on within it, and to enable foreign nations, by furnishing almost all sorts of goods for a smaller quantity of silver than its own workmen can afford to do, to undersell them, not only in the foreign, but even in the home market.

In Spain and Portugal gold and silver are naturally cheaper than in the rest of Europe, It is the peculiar situation of Spain and Portugal as proprietors of the mines, to be the distributors of gold and silver to all the other countries of Europe. Those metals ought naturally, therefore, to be somewhat cheaper in Spain and Portugal than in any other part of Europe. The difference, however, should be no more than the amount of the freight and insurance; and, on account of the great

---

[1] [Eds. 1 and 2 read 'in the smallest degree'.]

[2] [Neither 'much' is in eds. 1 and 2.]

[3] [This and the two preceding sentences from 'in the purchase' appear first in Additions and Corrections (which reads 'of even' instead of 'even of') and ed. 3.]

value and small bulk of those metals, their freight is no great matter, and their insurance is the same as that of any other goods of equal value. Spain and Portugal, therefore, could suffer very little from their peculiar situation, if they did not aggravate its disadvantages by their political institutions.

but by the hindrances to exportation they are made still cheaper, Spain by taxing, and Portugal by prohibiting the exportation of gold and silver, load that exportation with the expence of smuggling, and raise the value of those metals in other countries so much more above what it is in their own, by the whole amount of this expence.[1] When you dam up a stream of water, as soon as the dam is full, as much water must run over the dam-head as if there was no dam at all. The prohibition of exportation cannot detain a greater quantity of gold and silver in Spain and Portugal than what they can afford to employ, than what the annual produce of their land and labour will allow them to employ, in coin, plate, gilding, and other ornaments of gold and silver. When they have got this quantity the dam is full, and the whole stream which flows in afterwards must run over. The annual exportation of gold and silver from Spain and Portugal accordingly is, by all accounts, notwithstanding these restraints, very near equal to the whole annual importation. As the water, however, must always be deeper behind the dam-head than before it, so the quantity of gold and silver which these restraints detain in Spain and Portugal must, in proportion to the annual produce of their land and labour, be greater than what is to be found in other countries. The higher and stronger the dam-head, the greater must be the difference in the depth of water behind and before it. The higher the tax, the higher the penalties with which the prohibition is guarded, the more vigilant and severe the police which looks after the execution of the law, the greater must be the difference in the proportion of gold and silver to the annual produce of the land and labour of Spain and Portugal, and to that of other countries. It is said accordingly to be very considerable, and that you frequently find there a profusion of plate in houses, where there is nothing else which would, in other countries, be thought suitable or correspondent to this sort of magnificence. The cheapness of gold and silver, or what is the same thing, the dearness of all commodities,

---

[1] [Spain's prohibition of exportation of gold and silver had only been abolished at a recent period. The tax was 3 per cent. till 1768, then 4 per cent. See Raynal, *Histoire philosophique*, Amsterdam ed. 1773, tom. iii., pp. 290, 291. As to the export of gold from Portugal, see below, p. 56, note 1.]

which is the necessary effect of this redundancy of the precious
and agriculture and metals, discourages both the agriculture and manu-
manufactures are factures of Spain and Portugal, and enables foreign
thereby discouraged. nations to supply them with many sorts of rude,
and with almost all sorts of manufactured produce, for a smaller
quantity of gold and silver than what they themselves can either raise
or make them for at home. The tax and prohibition operate in two
different ways. They not only lower very much the value of the
precious metals in Spain and Portugal, but by detaining there a
certain quantity of those metals which would otherwise flow over
other countries, they keep up their value in those other countries
somewhat above what it otherwise would be, and thereby give
those countries a double advantage in their commerce with Spain
and Portugal. Open the flood-gates, and there will presently be less
water above, and more below, the dam-head, and it will soon come
to a level in both places. Remove the tax and the prohibition, and
as the quantity of gold and silver will diminish considerably in Spain
and Portugal, so it will increase somewhat in other countries, and
the value of those metals, their proportion to the annual produce of
land and labour, will soon come to a level, or very near to a level,
in all. The loss which Spain and Portugal could sustain by this
exportation of their gold and silver would be altogether nominal
and imaginary. The nominal value of their goods, and of the annual
produce of their land and labour, would fall, and would be expressed or represented by a smaller quantity of silver than before:
but their real value would be the same as before, and would be
sufficient to maintain, command, and employ, the same quantity of
labour. As the nominal value of their goods would fall, the real
value of what remained of their gold and silver would rise, and a
smaller quantity of those metals would answer all the same purposes
of commerce and circulation which had employed a greater quantity before. The gold and silver which would go abroad would not
go abroad for nothing, but would bring back an equal value of
goods of some kind or another. Those goods too would not be all
matters of mere luxury and expence, to be consumed by idle people
who produce nothing in return for their consumption. As the real
wealth and revenue of idle people would not be augmented by this
extraordinary exportation of gold and silver, so neither would their
consumption be much augmented by it. Those goods would, probably, the greater part of them, and certainly some part of them,

consist in materials, tools, and provisions, for the employment and maintenance of industrious people, who would reproduce, with a profit, the full value of their consumption. A part of the dead stock of the society would thus be turned into active stock, and would put into motion a greater quantity of industry than had been employed before. The annual produce of their land and labour would immediately be augmented a little, and in a few years would, probably, be augmented a great deal; their industry being thus relieved from one of the most oppressive burdens which it at present labours under.

The corn bounty acts in the same way; The bounty upon the exportation of corn necessarily operates exactly in the same way as this absurd policy of Spain and Portugal. Whatever be the actual state of tillage, it renders our corn somewhat dearer in the home market than it otherwise would be in that state, and somewhat cheaper in the foreign; and as the average money price of corn regulates more or less that of all other commodities, it lowers the value of silver considerably in the one, and tends to raise it a little in the other. It enables foreigners, the Dutch in particular, not only to eat our corn cheaper than they otherwise could do, but sometimes to eat it cheaper than even our own people can do upon the same occasions; as we are assured by an excellent authority, that of Sir Matthew Decker.[1] It hinders our own workmen from furnishing their goods for so small a quantity of silver as they otherwise might do; and enables the Dutch to furnish their's for a smaller. It tends to render our manufactures somewhat dearer in every market, and their's somewhat cheaper than they otherwise would be, and consequently to give their industry a double advantage over our own.

it discourages manufactures without much benefiting farmers and country gentlemen. The bounty, as it raises in the home market, not so much the real, as the nominal price[2] of our corn, as it augments, not the quantity of labour which a certain quantity of corn can maintain and employ, but only the quantity of silver which it will exchange for, it discourages our manufactures, without rendering any considerable service[3] either to our farmers or country gentlemen. It puts, indeed, a little more money into the pockets of both, and it will perhaps be somewhat difficult to persuade the greater part of them that this is

[1] [*Essay on the Causes of the Decline of the Foreign Trade, consequently of the Value of the Lands of Britain, and on the means to restore both*, 2nd ed., 1750, pp. 55, 171.]

[2] [Eds. 1 and 2 read 'not the real but only the nominal price'.]

[3] [Eds. 1 and 2 read 'the smallest real service'.]

not rendering them a very considerable service.[1] But if this money sinks in its value, in the quantity of labour, provisions, and home-made[2] commodities of all different kinds which it is capable of purchasing, as much as it rises in its quantity, the service will be little more than nominal[3] and imaginary.

It is essentially serviceable only to the corn merchants. There is, perhaps, but one set of men in the whole commonwealth to whom the bounty either was or could be essentially serviceable.[4] These were the corn merchants, the exporters and importers of corn. In years of plenty the bounty necessarily occasioned a greater exportation than would otherwise have taken place; and by hindering the plenty of one year from relieving the scarcity of another, it occasioned in years of scarcity a greater importation than would otherwise have been necessary. It increased the business of the corn merchant in both; and in years of scarcity, it not only enabled him to import a greater quantity, but to sell it for a better price, and consequently with a greater profit than he could otherwise have made, if the plenty of one year had not been more or less hindered from relieving the scarcity of another. It is in this set of men, accordingly, that I have observed the greatest zeal for the continuance or renewal of the bounty.

The country gentlemen established the duties on the importation of corn, and the bounty, in imitation of the manufacturers, Our country gentlemen, when they imposed the high duties upon the importation of foreign corn, which in times of moderate plenty amount to a prohibition, and when they established the bounty, seem to have imitated the conduct of our manufacturers. By the one institution, they secured to themselves the monopoly of the home market, and by the other they endeavoured to prevent that market from ever being overstocked with their commodity. By both they endeavoured to raise its real value, in the same manner as our manufacturers had, by the like institutions, raised the real value of many different sorts of manufactured goods. *without attending to the essential difference between corn and other goods.* They did not perhaps attend to the great and essential difference which nature has established between corn and almost every other sort of goods. When, either by the monopoly of the home market, or by a bounty upon exportation, you enable our woollen or linen manufacturers

---

[1] [Eds. 1 and 2 read 'a very real service'.]
[2] ['Home-made' is not in eds. 1 and 2.]
[3] [Eds. 1 and 2 read 'will be merely nominal'.]
[4] [Eds. 1 and 2 read 'could be really serviceable'.]

to sell their goods for somewhat a better price than they otherwise
could get for them, you raise, not only the nominal, but the real
price of those goods. You render them equivalent to a greater quantity of labour and subsistence, you increase not only the nominal,
but the real profit, the real wealth and revenue of those manufacturers, and you enable them either to live better themselves, or
to employ a greater quantity of labour in those particular manufactures. You really encourage those manufactures, and direct towards them a greater quantity of the industry of the country, than
what would probably go to them of its own accord. But when by
the like institutions you raise the nominal or money-price of corn,
you do not raise its real value. You do not increase the real wealth,
the real revenue either of our farmers or country gentlemen. You
do not encourage the growth of corn, because you do not enable
them to maintain and employ more labourers in raising it. The
nature of things has stamped upon corn a real value which cannot
be altered by merely altering its money price.[1] No bounty upon
exportation, no monopoly of the home market, can raise that
value.[2] The freest competition cannot lower it. Through the world
in general that value is equal to the quantity of labour which it can
maintain, and in every particular place it is equal to the quantity of
labour which it can maintain in the way, whether liberal, moderate,
or scanty, in which labour is commonly maintained in that place.
Woollen or linen cloth are not the regulating commodities by
which the real value of all other commodities must be finally
measured and determined; corn is. The real value of every other
commodity is finally measured and determined by the proportion
which its average money price bears to the average money price of
corn. The real value of corn does not vary with those variations in
its average money price, which sometimes occur from one century
to another. It is the real value of silver which varies with them.

All the expedients
of the mercantile
system force industry
into less advantage-
ous channels; boun-
ties on exports force
it into actually
disadvantageous
channels; the bounty
on corn does not
Bounties upon the exportation of any home-made
commodity are liable, first, to that general objection which may be made to all the different expedients of the mercantile system; the objection of
forcing some part of the industry of the country
into a channel less advantageous than that in which
it would run of its own accord: and, secondly, to

---

[1] [Eds. 1 and 2 read 'a real value which no human institution can alter'. Cp. p. 14.]
[2] [Ed. 1 reads 'raise it'.]

encourage its the particular objection of forcing it, not only into
production. a channel that is less advantageous, but into one
that is actually disadvantageous; the trade which cannot be carried
on but by means of a bounty being necessarily a losing trade. The
bounty upon the exportation of corn is liable to this further objection, that it can in no respect promote the raising of that particular
commodity of which it was meant to encourage the production.
When our country gentlemen, therefore, demanded the establishment of the bounty, though they acted in imitation of our merchants
and manufacturers, they did not act with that complete comprehension of their own interest which commonly directs the conduct
of those two other orders of people. They loaded the public revenue
with a very considerable expence; they imposed a very heavy tax
upon the whole body of the people; but they did not, in any sensible
degree, increase[1] the real value of their own commodity; and by
lowering somewhat the real value of silver, they discouraged, in
some degree, the general industry of the country, and, instead of
advancing, retarded more or less the improvement of their own
lands, which necessarily depends upon the general industry of the
country.

A bounty on pro- To encourage the production of any commodity,
duction would be a bounty upon production, one should imagine,
more effectual than would have a more direct operation, than one upon
one on exportation exportation. It would, besides, impose only one tax
and would lower upon the people, that which they must contribute
the price of the
commodity,
in order to pay the bounty. Instead of raising, it would tend to
lower the price of the commodity in the home market; and thereby,
instead of imposing a second tax upon the people, it might, at least
in part, repay them for what they had contributed to the first.
but such bounties Bounties upon production, however, have been
have been rare, very rarely granted.[2] The prejudices established by
the commercial system have taught us to believe, that national
wealth arises more immediately from exportation than from production. It has been more favoured accordingly, as the more immediate means of bringing money into the country. Bounties upon

---

[1] [Eds. 1 and 2 read 'They loaded the public revenue with a very considerable
expence, but they did not in any respect increase'. The alteration is given in Additions
and Corrections.]

[2] [In place of this and the two preceding sentences (beginning 'It would besides') eds.
1 and 2 read only 'It has, however, been more rarely granted.' The alteration is given
in Additions and Corrections.]

production, it has been said too, have been found by experience
more liable to frauds than those upon exportation. How far this is
true, I know not. That bounties upon exportation have been abused
owing to the interest to many fraudulent purposes, is very well known.
of merchants and But it is not the interest of merchants and manu-
manufacturers. facturers, the great inventors of all these expedients,
that the home market should be overstocked with their goods, an
event which a bounty upon production might sometimes occasion.
A bounty upon exportation, by enabling them to send abroad the
surplus part, and to keep up the price of what remains in the home
market, effectually prevents this. Of all the expedients of the mercantile system, accordingly, it is the one of which they are the
fondest. I have known the different undertakers of some particular
works agree privately among themselves to give a bounty out of
their own pockets upon the exportation of a certain proportion of
the goods which they dealt in. This expedient succeeded so well,
that it more than doubled the price of their goods in the home
market, notwithstanding a very considerable increase in the produce. The operation of the bounty upon corn must have been
wonderfully different, if it has lowered the money price of that
commodity.

The herring and Something like a bounty upon production, how-
whale fishery ever, has been granted upon some particular
bounties are in part occasions. The tonnage bounties given[1] to the
given on production. white-herring and whale-fisheries may, perhaps, be considered as
somewhat of this nature.[2] They tend directly, it may be supposed,[3]
to render the goods cheaper in the home market than they otherwise would be.[4] In other respects their effects, it must be acknowledged,[5] are the same as those of bounties upon exportation. By
means of them a part of the capital of the country is employed in
bringing goods to market, of which the price does not repay the
cost, together with the ordinary profits of stock.

They are supposed But though the tonnage[6] bounties to those fisheries
to augment the do not contribute to the opulence of the nation, it
number of sailors may perhaps be thought that they contribute to its
and ships.

[1] [Eds. 1 and 2 read 'The encouragements given'.]
[2] [The whale fishery bounty under 11 Geo. III., c. 38, was 40s. per ton for the first five years, 30s. for the second five years, and 20s. for the third.]
[3] ['It may be supposed' is not in eds. 1 and 2.]
[4] [Eds. 1 and 2 read 'would be in the actual state of production'.]
[5] ['It must be acknowledged' is not in eds. 1 and 2.]
[6] ['Tonnage' is not in eds. 1 and 2.]

defence,[1] by augmenting the number of its sailors and shipping. This, it may be alleged, may sometimes be done[2] by means of such bounties at a much smaller expence, than by keeping up a great standing navy, if I may use such an expression,[3] in the same way as a standing army.[4]

In granting the herring bounties Parliament has been imposed on, since (1) the herring buss bounty is too large, Notwithstanding these favourable allegations, however, the following considerations dispose me to believe, that in granting at least one of these bounties, the legislature has been very grossly imposed upon.

First, the herring buss bounty seems too large.

From the commencement of the winter fishing 1771 to the end of the winter fishing 1781, the tonnage bounty upon the herring buss fishery has been at thirty shillings the ton. During these eleven years the whole number of barrels caught by the herring buss fishery of Scotland amounted to 378,347. The herrings caught and cured at sea, are called sea sticks.[5] In order to render them what are called merchantable herrings, it is necessary to repack them with an additional quantity of salt; and in this case, it is reckoned, that three barrels of sea sticks, are usually repacked into two barrels of merchantable herrings. The number of barrels of merchantable herrings, therefore, caught during these eleven years, will amount only, according to this account, to 252,231⅓. During these eleven years the tonnage bounties paid amounted to 155,463 l. 11 s. or to 8 s. 2¼ d. upon every barrel of sea sticks, and to 12 s. 3¾ d. upon every barrel of merchantable herrings.

The salt with which these herrings are cured, is sometimes Scotch, and sometimes foreign salt; both which are delivered free of all excise duty to the fish-curers. The excise duty upon Scotch salt is at present 1 s. 6 d. that upon foreign salt 10 s. the bushel. A barrel

[1] [Eds. 1 and 2 read 'they may perhaps be defended as conducing to its defence'.]
[2] [Eds. 1 and 2 read 'This may frequently be done'.]
[3] [Eds. 1 and 2 read 'in time of peace' here.]
[4] [The next four pages, to foot of page 28, are not in eds. 1 and 2, which read in place of them: 'Some other bounties may be vindicated perhaps upon the same principle. It is of importance that the kingdom should depend as little as possible upon its neighbours for the manufactures necessary for its defence; and if these cannot otherwise be maintained at home, it is reasonable that all other branches of industry should be taxed in order to support them. The bounties upon the importation of naval stores from America, upon British made sail-cloth, and upon British made gunpowder, may perhaps all three be vindicated upon this principle. The first is a bounty upon the production of America, for the use of Great Britain. The two others are bounties upon exportation.' The new paragraphs, with the two preceding paragraphs as amended, are given in Additions and Corrections.]
[5] [In Additions and Corrections the term is 'seasteeks,' as in the Appendix.]

of herrings is supposed to require about one bushel and one-fourth of a bushel foreign salt. Two bushels are the supposed average of Scotch salt. If the herrings are entered for exportation, no part of this duty is paid up; if entered for home consumption, whether the herrings were cured with foreign or with Scotch salt, only one shilling the barrel is paid up. It was the old Scotch duty upon a bushel of salt, the quantity which, at a low estimation, had been supposed necessary for curing a barrel of herrings. In Scotland, foreign salt is very little used for any other purpose but the curing of fish. But from the 5th April 1771, to the 5th April 1782, the quantity of foreign salt imported amounted to 936,974 bushels, at eighty-four pounds the bushel: the quantity of Scotch salt delivered from the works to the fish-curers, to no more than 168,226, at fifty-six pounds the bushel only. It would appear, therefore, that it is principally foreign salt that is used in the fisheries. Upon every barrel of herrings exported there is, besides, a bounty of 2 s. 8 d. and more than two-thirds of the buss caught herrings are exported. Put all these things together, and you will find that, during these eleven years, every barrel of buss caught herrings, cured with Scotch salt when exported, has cost government 17 s. 11¾ d.; and when entered for home consumption 14 s. 3¾ d.: and that every barrel cured with foreign salt, when exported, has cost government 1 l. 7 s. 5¾ d.; and when entered for home consumption 1 l. 3 s. 9¾ d. The price of a barrel of good merchantable herrings runs from seventeen and eighteen to four and five and twenty shillings; about a guinea at an average.[1]

(2) the bounty is not proportioned to the fish caught, Secondly, the bounty to the white herring fishery is a tonnage bounty; and is proportioned to the burden of the ship, not to her diligence or success in the fishery; and it has, I am afraid, been too common for vessels to fit out for the sole purpose of catching, not the fish, but the bounty. In the year 1759, when the bounty was at fifty shillings the ton, the whole buss fishery of Scotland brought in only four barrels of sea sticks. In that year each barrel of sea sticks cost government in bounties alone 113 l. 15 s.; each barrel of merchantable herrings 159 l. 7 s. 6 d.

(3) the bounty is given to busses, Thirdly, the mode of fishing for which this tonnage bounty in the white herring fishery has been given

---

[1] See the accounts at the end of the volume. [In Additions and Corrections they are printed in the text.]

whereas the fishery ought to be carried on by boats, (by busses or decked vessels from twenty to eighty tons burthen), seems not so well adapted to the situation of Scotland as to that of Holland; from the practice of which country it appears to have been borrowed. Holland lies at a great distance from the seas to which herrings are known principally to resort; and can, therefore, carry on that fishery only in decked vessels, which can carry water and provisions sufficient for a voyage to a distant sea. But the Hebrides or western islands, the islands of Shetland, and the northern and north-western coasts of Scotland, the countries in whose neighbourhood the herring fishery is principally carried on, are everywhere intersected by arms of the sea, which run up a considerable way into the land, and which, in the language of the country, are called sea-lochs. It is to these sea-lochs that the herrings principally resort during the seasons in which they visit those seas; for the visits of this, and, I am assured, of many other sorts of fish, are not quite regular and constant. A boat fishery, therefore, seems to be the mode of fishing best adapted to the peculiar situation of Scotland: the fishers carrying the herrings on shore, as fast as they are taken, to be either cured or consumed fresh. But the great encouragement which a bounty of thirty shillings the ton gives to the buss fishery, is necessarily a discouragement to the boat fishery; which, having no such bounty, cannot bring its cured fish to market upon the same terms as the buss fishery. The boat fishery, accordingly, which, before the establishment of the buss bounty, was very considerable, and is said to have employed a number of seamen, not inferior to what the buss fishery employs at present, is now gone almost entirely to decay. Of the former extent, however, of this now ruined and abandoned fishery, I must acknowledge, that I cannot pretend to speak with much precision. As no bounty was paid upon the outfit of the boat-fishery, no account was taken of it by the officers of the customs or salt duties.

(4) the bounty has raised, or at any rate not lowered, the price of herrings. Fourthly, in many parts of Scotland, during certain seasons of the year, herrings make no inconsiderable part of the food of the common people. A bounty, which tended to lower their price in the home market, might contribute a good deal to the relief of a great number of our fellow-subjects, whose circumstances are by no means affluent. But the herring buss bounty contributes to no such good purpose. It has ruined the boat fishery, which is, by far, the best adapted for the supply of the home market, and the additional bounty of 2 s. 8 d.

the barrel upon exportation, carries the greater part, more than two thirds, of the produce of the buss fishery abroad. Between thirty and forty years ago, before the establishment of the buss bounty, sixteen shillings the barrel, I have been assured, was the common price of white herrings. Between ten and fifteen years ago, before the boat fishery was entirely ruined, the price is said to have run from seventeen to twenty shillings the barrel. For these last five years, it has, at an average, been at twenty-five shillings the barrel. This high price, however, may have been owing to the real scarcity of the herrings upon the coast of Scotland. I must observe too, that the cask or barrel, which is usually sold with the herrings, and of which the price is included in all the foregoing prices, has, since the commencement of the American war, risen to about double its former price, or from about three shillings to about six shillings. I must likewise observe, that the accounts I have received of the prices of former times, have been by no means quite uniform and consistent; and an old man of great accuracy and experience has assured me, that more than fifty years ago, a guinea was the usual price of a barrel of good merchantable herrings; and this, I imagine, may still be looked upon as the average price. All accounts, however, I think, agree, that the price has not been lowered in the home market, in consequence of the buss bounty.

Profits in the business have not been high. When the undertakers of fisheries, after such liberal bounties have been bestowed upon them, continue to sell their commodity at the same, or even at a higher price than they were accustomed to do before, it might be expected that their profits should be very great; and it is not improbable that those of some individuals may have been so. In general, however, I have every reason to believe, they have been quite otherwise. The usual effect of such bounties is to encourage rash undertakers to adventure in a business which they do not understand, and what they lose by their own negligence and ignorance, more than compensates all that they can gain by the utmost liberality of government. In 1750, by the same act which first gave the bounty of thirty shillings the ton for the encouragement of the white herring fishery (the 23 Geo. II. chap. 24), a joint stock company was erected, with a capital of five hundred thousand pounds, to which the subscribers (over and above all other encouragements, the tonnage bounty just now mentioned, the exportation bounty of two shillings and eight pence the barrel, the delivery of both British and foreign salt duty free) were, during the space of fourteen years, for every hundred pounds which they subscribed and paid into the stock of the society, entitled to three pounds a year, to be paid by the receiver-general of the customs in equal half-yearly payments. Besides this great company, the residence of whose governor and directors was to be in London, it was declared lawful to erect different fishing-chambers in all the different out-ports of the kingdom, provided a sum not less than ten thousand pounds was subscribed into the capital of each, to be managed at its own risk, and for its own profit and loss. The same annuity, and the same encouragements of all kinds, were given to the trade of those inferior chambers, as to that of the great company. The subscription of the great company was soon filled up, and several different fishing-chambers were erected in the different out-ports of the kingdom. In spite of all these encouragements, almost all those different companies, both great and small, lost either the whole, or the greater part of their capitals; scarce a vestige now remains of any of them, and the white herring fishery is now entirely, or almost entirely, carried on by private adventurers.

Bounties for manu-factures necessary for the defence of the country are not unreasonable. If any particular manufacture was necessary, indeed, for the defence of the society, it might not always be prudent to depend upon our neighbours for the supply; and if such manufacture could not other-wise be supported at home, it might not be unreasonable that all the other branches of industry should be taxed in order to support it. The bounties upon the exportation of British-made sail-cloth, and British-made gun-powder, may, perhaps, both be vindicated upon this principle.

It is less absurd to give bounties in times of prosperity than in times of distress. But though it can very seldom be reasonable to tax the industry of the great body of the people, in order to support that of some particular class of manufacturers; yet in the wantonness of great prosperity, when the public enjoys a greater revenue than it knows well what to do with, to give such bounties to favourite manu-factures, may, perhaps, be as natural, as to incur any other idle expence. In public, as well as in private expences, great wealth may, perhaps, frequently be admitted as an apology for great folly. But there must surely be something more than ordinary absurdity, in continuing such profusion in times of general difficulty and distress.[1]

---

[1] [The ten paragraphs ending here are not in eds. 1 and 2. See above, p. 24, note 4.]

Some allowances called bounties are, properly speaking, drawbacks. What is called a bounty is sometimes no more than a drawback, and consequently is not liable to the same objections as what is properly a bounty. The bounty, for example, upon refined sugar exported, may be considered as a drawback of the duties upon the brown and muscovado sugars from which it is made. The bounty upon wrought silk exported, a drawback of the duties upon raw and thrown silk imported. The bounty upon gunpowder exported, a drawback of the duties upon brimstone and saltpetre imported. In the language of the customs those allowances only are called drawbacks, which are given upon goods exported in the same form in which they are imported. When that form has been so altered by manufacture of any kind, as to come under a new denomination, they are called bounties.[1]

Prizes to successful artists and manufacturers do not divert industry to less advantageous channels, but encourage perfection. Premiums given by the public to artists and manufacturers who excel in their particular occupations, are not liable to the same objections as bounties. By encouraging extraordinary dexterity and ingenuity, they serve to keep up the emulation of the workmen actually employed in those respective occupations, and are not considerable enough to turn towards any one of them a greater share of the capital of the country than what would go to it of its own accord. Their tendency is not to overturn the natural balance of employments, but to render the work which is done in each as perfect and complete as possible. The expence of premiums, besides, is very trifling; that of bounties very great. The bounty upon corn alone has sometimes cost the public in one year more than three hundred thousand pounds.[2]

Bounties are sometimes called premiums, as drawbacks are sometimes called bounties. But we must in all cases attend to the nature of the thing without paying any regard to the word.

Digression concerning the Corn Trade and Corn Laws[3]

The corn bounty and corn laws are undeserving of praise. I cannot conclude this chapter concerning bounties, without observing that the praises which have been bestowed upon the law which establishes the

---

[1] [Eds. 1 and 2 read 'When that form has been altered by manufacture of any kind, they are called bounties.']

[2] [Above, vol. i., p. 222.]   [3] [This heading is not in ed. 1.]

bounty upon the exportation of corn, and upon that system of regulations which is connected with it, are altogether unmerited. A particular examination of the nature of the corn trade, and of the principal British laws which relate to it, will sufficiently demonstrate the truth of this assertion. The great importance of this subject must justify the length of the digression.

There are four branches of the corn trade; The trade of the corn merchant is composed of four different branches, which, though they may sometimes be all carried on by the same person, are in their own nature four separate and distinct trades. These are, first, the trade of the inland dealer; secondly, that of the merchant importer for home consumption; thirdly, that of the merchant exporter of home produce for foreign consumption; and, fourthly, that of the merchant carrier, or of the importer of corn in order to export it again.

I. The Inland Dealer, whose interest is the same as that of the people, viz., that the consumption should be proportioned to the supply available. I. The interest of the inland dealer, and that of the great body of the people, how opposite soever they may at first sight appear, are, even in years of the greatest scarcity, exactly the same. It is his interest to raise the price of his corn as high as the real scarcity of the season requires, and it can never be his interest to raise it higher. By raising the price he discourages the consumption, and puts every body more or less, but particularly the inferior ranks of people, upon thrift and good management. If, by raising it too high, he discourages the consumption so much that the supply of the season is likely to go beyond the consumption of the season, and to last for some time after the next crop begins to come in, he runs the hazard, not only of losing a considerable part of his corn by natural causes, but of being obliged to sell what remains of it for much less than what he might have had for it several months before. If by not raising the price high enough he discourages the consumption so little, that the supply of the season is likely to fall short of the consumption of the season, he not only loses a part of the profit which he might otherwise have made, but he exposes the people to suffer before the end of the season, instead of the hardships of a dearth, the dreadful horrors of a famine. It is the interest of the people that their daily, weekly, and monthly consumption, should be proportioned as exactly as possible to the supply of the season. The interest of the inland corn dealer is the same. By supplying them, as nearly as he can judge, in this proportion, he is likely to sell all his corn for the highest price, and with the greatest profit; and his knowledge of the state of the crop, and of his daily, weekly, and monthly sales, enable[1] him to judge, with more or less accuracy, how far they really are supplied in this manner. Without intending the interest of the people, he is necessarily led, by a regard to his own interest, to treat them, even in years of scarcity, pretty much in the same manner as the prudent master of a vessel is sometimes obliged to treat his crew. When he foresees that provisions are likely to run short, he puts them upon short allowance. Though from excess of caution he should sometimes do this without any real necessity, yet all the inconveniencies which his crew can thereby suffer are inconsiderable, in comparison of the danger, misery, and ruin, to which they might sometimes be exposed by a less provident conduct. Though from excess of avarice, in the same manner, the inland corn merchant should sometimes raise the price of his corn somewhat higher than the scarcity of the season requires, yet all the inconveniencies which the people can suffer from this conduct, which effectually secures them from a famine in the end of the season, are inconsiderable, in comparison of what they might have been exposed to by a more liberal way of dealing in the beginning of it. The corn merchant himself is likely to suffer the most by this excess of avarice; not only from the indignation which it generally excites against him, but, though he should escape the effects of this indignation, from the quantity of corn which it necessarily leaves upon his hands in the end of the season, and which, if the next season happens to prove favourable, he must always sell for a much lower price than he might otherwise have had.

The interest of a monopoly might perhaps be to destroy a portion of the crop, but corn cannot be monopolised where the trade is free. Were it possible, indeed, for one great company of merchants to possess themselves of the whole crop of an extensive country, it might, perhaps, be their interest to deal with it as the Dutch are said to do with the spiceries of the Moluccas, to destroy or throw away a considerable part of it, in order to keep up the price of the rest.[2] But it is scarce possible, even by the violence of law, to establish such an extensive monopoly with regard to corn; and, wherever the law leaves the trade free, it is of

---

[1] [Not a misprint for 'enables'. There are two knowledges, one of the state of the crop and the other of the daily sales.]

[2] [Above, vol. i., p. 177; below, p. 152.]

all commodities the least liable to be engrossed or monopolized by the force of a few large capitals, which buy up the greater part of it. Not only its value far exceeds what the capitals of a few private men are capable of purchasing, but supposing they were capable of purchasing it, the manner in which it is produced renders this purchase altogether impracticable. As in every civilized country it is the commodity of which the annual consumption is the greatest, so a greater quantity of industry is annually employed in producing corn than in producing any other commodity. When it first comes from the ground too, it is necessarily divided among a greater number of owners than any other commodity; and these owners can never be collected into one place like a number of independent manufacturers, but are necessarily scattered through all the different corners of the country. These first owners either immediately supply the consumers in their own neighbourhood, or they supply other inland dealers who supply those consumers. The inland dealers in corn, therefore, including both the farmer and the baker, are necessarily more numerous than the dealers in any other commodity, and their dispersed situation renders it altogether impossible for them to enter into any general combination. If in a year of scarcity therefore, any of them should find that he had a good deal more corn upon hand than, at the current price, he could hope to dispose of before the end of the season, he would never think of keeping up this price to his own loss, and to the sole benefit of his rivals and competitors, but would immediately lower it, in order to get rid of his corn before the new crop began to come in. The same motives, the same interests, which would thus regulate the conduct of any one dealer, would regulate that of every other, and oblige them all in general to sell their corn at the price which, according to the best of their judgment, was most suitable to the scarcity or plenty of the season.

Dearths are never occasioned by combination, but always by scarcity, and famines are always caused by the supposed remedies for dearths applied by government. Whoever examines, with attention, the history of the dearths and famines which have afflicted any part of Europe, during either the course of the present or that of the two preceding centuries, of several of which we have pretty exact accounts, will find, I believe, that a dearth never has arisen from any combination among the inland dealers in corn, nor from any other cause but a real scarcity, occasioned sometimes, perhaps, and in some particular places, by the waste of war, but in by far the greatest number of cases, by the fault of the seasons; and that a famine has never arisen from any other cause but the violence of government attempting, by improper means, to remedy the inconveniencies of a dearth.

Scarcities are never great enough to cause famine.   In an extensive corn country, between all the different parts of which there is a free commerce and communication, the scarcity occasioned by the most unfavourable seasons can never be so great as to produce a famine; and the scantiest crop, if managed with frugality and œconomy, will maintain, through the year, the same number of people that are commonly fed in a more affluent manner by one of moderate plenty. The seasons most unfavourable to the crop are those of excessive drought or excessive rain. But, as corn grows equally upon high and low lands, upon grounds that are disposed to be too wet, and upon those that are disposed to be too dry, either the drought or the rain which is hurtful to one part of the country is favourable to another; and though both in the wet and in the dry season the crop is a good deal less than in one more properly tempered, yet in both what is lost in one part of the country is in some measure compensated by what is gained in the other. In rice countries, where the crop not only requires a very moist soil, but where in a certain period of its growing it must be laid under water, the effects of a drought are much more dismal. Even in such countries, however, the drought is, perhaps, scarce ever so universal, as necessarily to occasion a famine, if the government would allow a free trade. The drought in Bengal, a few years ago, might probably have occasioned a very great dearth. Some improper regulations, some injudicious restraints imposed by the servants of the East India Company upon the rice trade, contributed, perhaps, to turn that dearth into a famine.

Governments cause famines by ordering corn to be sold at a reasonable price.   When the government, in order to remedy the inconveniencies of a dearth, orders all the dealers to sell their corn at what it supposes a reasonable price, it either hinders them from bringing it to market, which may sometimes produce a famine even in the beginning of the season; or if they bring it thither, it enables the people, and thereby encourages them to consume it so fast, as must necessarily produce a famine before the end of the season. The unlimited, unrestrained freedom of the corn trade, as it is the only effectual preventative of the miseries of a famine, so it is the best palliative of the inconveniencies of a dearth; for the inconveniencies of a real scarcity cannot be remedied; they can only be palliated. No trade deserves more the full protection of the law, and no trade requires it so much; because no trade is so much exposed to popular odium.

The corn merchant is odious to the populace, In years of scarcity the inferior ranks of people impute their distress to the avarice of the corn merchant, who becomes the object of their hatred and indignation. Instead of making profit upon such occasions, therefore, he is often in danger of being utterly ruined, and of having his magazines plundered and destroyed by their violence. It is in years of scarcity, however, when prices are high, that the corn merchant expects to make his principal profit. He is generally in contract with some farmers to furnish him for a certain number of years with a certain quantity of corn at a certain price. This contract price is settled according to what is supposed to be the moderate and reasonable, that is, the ordinary or average price, which, before the late years of scarcity, was commonly about eight-and-twenty shillings for the quarter of wheat, and for that of other grain in proportion. In years of scarcity, therefore, the corn merchant buys a great part of his corn for the ordinary price, and sells it for a much higher. That this extraordinary profit, however, is no more than sufficient to put his trade upon a fair level with other trades, and to compensate the many losses which he sustains upon other occasions, both from the perishable nature of the commodity itself, and from the frequent and unforeseen fluctuations of its price, seems evident enough, from this single circumstance, that great fortunes are as seldom made in this as in any other trade. The popular odium, however, which attends it in years of scarcity, the only *and this deters respectable people from entering the trade.* years in which it can be very profitable, renders people of character and fortune averse to enter into it. It is abandoned to an inferior set of dealers; and millers, bakers, mealmen, and meal factors, together with a number of wretched hucksters, are almost the only middle people that, in the home market, come between the grower and the consumer.

This popular odium was encouraged by legislation. The ancient policy of Europe, instead of discountenancing this popular odium against a trade so beneficial to the public, seems, on the contrary, to have authorised and encouraged it.

By the 5th and 6th of Edward VI. cap. 14. it was enacted, That whoever should buy any corn or grain[1] with intent to sell it again, should be reputed an unlawful engrosser, and should, for the first fault suffer two months imprisonment, and forfeit the value of the corn; for the second, suffer six months imprisonment, and forfeit double the value; and for the third, be set in the pillory, suffer imprisonment during the king's pleasure, and forfeit all his goods and chattels. The ancient policy of most other parts of Europe was no better than that of England.

Many restraints were imposed on traders. Our ancestors seem to have imagined that the people would buy their corn cheaper of the farmer than of the corn merchant, who, they were afraid, would require, over and above the price which he paid to the farmer, an exorbitant profit to himself. They endeavoured, therefore, to annihilate his trade altogether. They even endeavoured to hinder as much as possible any middle man of any kind from coming in between the grower and the consumer; and this was the meaning of the many restraints which they imposed upon the trade of those whom they called kidders or carriers of corn, a trade which nobody was allowed to exercise without a licence ascertaining his qualifications as a man of probity and fair dealing.[2] The authority of three justices of the peace was, by the statute of Edward VI. necessary, in order to grant this licence. But even this restraint was afterwards thought insufficient, and by a statute of Elizabeth,[3] the privilege of granting it was confined to the quarter-sessions.

Endeavours were made to force the farmers to be retailers, though manufacturers were forbidden to be so. The ancient policy of Europe endeavoured in this manner to regulate agriculture, the great trade of the country, by maxims quite different from those which it established with regard to manufactures, the great trade of the towns. By leaving the farmer no other customers but either the consumers or their immediate factors,[4] the kidders and carriers of corn, it endeavoured to force

[1] ['Any corn growing in the fields, or any other corn or grain, butter, cheese, fish or other dead victuals whatsoever'. But grain was exempted when below certain prices, *e.g.*, wheat, 6s. 8d. the quarter.]

[2] [This and the preceding sentence are misleading. The effect of the provisions quoted in the preceding paragraph would have been to 'annihilate altogether' the trade of the corn merchant if they had been left unqualified. To avoid this consequence 5 and 6 Ed. VI., c. 14, § 7, provides that badgers, laders, kidders or carriers may be licensed to buy corn with the intent to sell it again in certain circumstances. So that the licensing of kidders was a considerable alleviation, not, as the text suggests, an aggravation.]

[3] [5 Eliz., c. 12, § 4.]

[4] [Ed. 1 reads 'the consumer or his immediate factors'. It should be noticed that under 5 and 6 Edward VI., c. 14, § 7, the kidder might sell in 'open fair or market' as well as to consumers privately.]

him to exercise the trade, not only of a farmer, but of a corn merchant or corn retailer. On the contrary, it in many cases prohibited the manufacturer from exercising the trade of a shopkeeper, or from selling his own goods by retail. It meant by the one law to promote the general interest of the country, or to render corn cheap, without, perhaps, its being well understood how this was to be done. By the other it meant to promote that of a particular order of men, the shopkeepers, who would be so much undersold by the manufacturer, it was supposed, that their trade would be ruined if he was allowed to retail at all.

The manufacturer, however, though he had been allowed to keep a shop, and to sell his own goods by retail, could not have undersold the common shopkeeper. Whatever part of his capital he might have placed in his shop, he must have withdrawn it from his manufacture. In order to carry on his business on a level with that of other people, as he must have had the profit of a manufacturer on the one part, so he must have had that of a shopkeeper upon the other. Let us suppose, for example, that in the particular town where he lived, ten per cent. was the ordinary profit both of manufacturing and shopkeeping stock; he must in this case have charged upon every piece of his own goods which he sold in his shop, a profit of twenty per cent. When he carried them from his workhouse to his shop, he must have valued them at the price for which he could have sold them to dealer or shopkeeper, who would have bought them by wholesale. If he valued them lower, he lost a part of the profit of his manufacturing capital. When again he sold them from his shop, unless he got the same price at which a shopkeeper would have sold them, he lost a part of the profit of his shopkeeping capital. Though he might appear, therefore, to make a double profit upon the same piece of goods, yet as these goods made successively a part of two distinct capitals, he made but a single profit upon the whole capital employed about them; and if he made less than this profit, he was a loser, or did not employ his whole capital with the same advantage as the greater part of his neighbours.

What the manufacturer was prohibited to do, the farmer was in some measure enjoined to do; to divide his capital between two different employments; to keep one part of it in his granaries and stack yard, for supplying the occasional demands of the market; and to employ the other in the cultivation of his land. But as he could not afford to employ the latter for less than the ordinary profits of farming stock, so he could as little afford to employ the former for less than the ordinary profits of mercantile stock. Whether the stock which really carried on the business of the corn merchant belonged to the person who was called a farmer, or to the person who was called a corn merchant, an equal profit was in both cases requisite, in order to indemnify its owner for employing it in this manner; in order to put his business upon a level with other trades, and in order to hinder him from having an interest to change it as soon as possible for some other. The farmer, therefore, who was thus forced to exercise the trade of a corn merchant, could not afford to sell his corn cheaper than any other corn merchant would have been obliged to do in the case of a free competition.

The dealer confined to one branch of business can sell cheaper. The dealer who can employ his whole stock in one single branch of business, has an advantage of the same kind with the workman who can employ his whole labour in one single operation. As the latter acquires a dexterity which enables him, with the same two hands, to perform a much greater quantity of work; so the former acquires so easy and ready a method of transacting his business, of buying and disposing of his goods, that with the same capital he can transact a much greater quantity of business. As the one can commonly afford his work a good deal cheaper, so the other can commonly afford his goods somewhat cheaper than if his stock and attention were both employed about a greater variety of objects. The greater part of manufacturers could not afford to retail their own goods so cheap as a vigilant and active shopkeeper, whose sole business it was to buy them by wholesale, and to retail them again. The greater part of farmers could still less afford to retail their own corn, to supply the inhabitants of a town, at perhaps four or five miles distance from the greater part of them, so cheap as a vigilant and active corn merchant, whose sole business it was to purchase corn by wholesale, to collect it into a great magazine, and to retail it again.

Laws preventing the manufacturer from being a shopkeeper and compelling the farmer to be a corn merchant were both impolitic and unjust, but the latter was the most pernicious, The law which prohibited the manufacturer from exercising the trade of a shopkeeper, endeavoured to force this division in the employment of stock to go on faster than it might otherwise have done. The law which obliged the farmer to exercise the trade of a corn merchant, endeavoured to hinder it from going on so fast. Both laws were evident violations of natural liberty, and therefore unjust; and they were both too as impolitic as they were unjust. It is the interest of every society, that things of this kind should never either be forced or obstructed. The man who employs either his labour or his stock in a greater variety of ways than his situation renders necessary, can never hurt his neighbour by underselling him. He may hurt himself, and he generally does so. Jack of all trades will never be rich, says the proverb. But the law ought always to trust people with the care of their own interest, as in their local situations they must generally be able to judge better of it than the legislator can do. The law, however, which obliged the farmer to exercise the trade of a corn merchant, was by far the most pernicious of the two.

by obstructing the improvement of land. It obstructed not only that division in the employment of stock which is so advantageous to every society, but it obstructed likewise the improvement and cultivation of the land. By obliging the farmer to carry on two trades instead of one, it forced him to divide his capital into two parts, of which one only could be employed in cultivation. But if he had been at liberty to sell his whole crop to a corn merchant as fast as he could thresh it out, his whole capital might have returned immediately to the land, and have been employed in buying more cattle, and hiring more servants, in order to improve and cultivate it better. But by being obliged to sell his corn by retail, he was obliged to keep a great part of his capital in his granaries and stack yard through the year, and could not, therefore, cultivate so well as with the same capital he might otherwise have done. This law, therefore, necessarily obstructed the improvement of the land, and, instead of tending to render corn cheaper, must have tended to render it scarcer, and therefore dearer, than it would otherwise have been.

Corn merchants support the farmers just as wholesale dealers support the manufacturers. After the business of the farmer, that of the corn merchant is in reality the trade which, if properly protected and encouraged, would contribute the most to the raising of corn. It would support the trade of the farmer, in the same manner as the trade of the wholesale dealer supports that of the manufacturer.

Wholesale dealers allow manufacturers to devote their whole capital to manufacturing. The wholesale dealer, by affording a ready market to the manufacturer, by taking his goods off his hand as fast as he can make them, and by sometimes even advancing their price to him before he has made them, enables him to keep his whole capital, and sometimes even more than his whole capital, constantly employed in manufacturing, and consequently to manufacture a much greater quantity of goods than if he was obliged to dispose of them himself to the immediate consumers, or even to the retailers. As the capital of the wholesale merchant too is generally sufficient to replace that of many manufacturers, this intercourse between him and them interests the owner of a large capital to support the owners of a great number of small ones, and to assist them in those losses and misfortunes which might otherwise prove ruinous to them.

So corn merchants should allow farmers to devote their whole capital to cultivation. An intercourse of the same kind universally established between the farmers and the corn merchants, would be attended with effects equally beneficial to the farmers. They would be enabled to keep their whole capitals, and even more than their whole capitals, constantly employed in cultivation. In case of any of those accidents, to which no trade is more liable than theirs, they would find in their ordinary customer, the wealthy corn merchant, a person who had both an interest to support them, and the ability to do it, and they would not, as at present, be entirely dependent upon the forbearance of their landlord, or the mercy of his steward. Were it possible, as perhaps it is not, to establish this intercourse universally, and all at once, were it possible to turn all at once the whole farming stock of the kingdom to its proper business, the cultivation of land, withdrawing it from every other employment into which any part of it may be at present diverted, and were it possible, in order to support and assist upon occasion the operations of this great stock, to provide all at once another stock almost equally great, it is not perhaps very easy to imagine how great, how extensive, and how sudden would be the improvement which this change of circumstances would alone produce upon the whole face of the country.

Accordingly the statute of Edward VI. endeavoured to annihilate a trade which is the best palliative and preventative of a dearth. The statute of Edward VI., therefore, by prohibiting as much as possible any middle man from coming in between the grower and the consumer, endeavoured to annihilate a trade, of which the free exercise is not only the best palliative of the inconveniences of a dearth, but the best preventative of that calamity: after the trade of the farmer, no trade contributing so much to the growing of corn as that of the corn merchant.

Its provisions were moderated by later statutes down to 15 Car. II., c. 7,

The rigour of this law was afterwards softened by several subsequent statutes, which successively permitted the engrossing of corn when the price of wheat should not exceed twenty, twenty-four, thirty-two, and forty shillings the quarter.[1] At last, by the 15th of Charles II. c. 7. the engrossing or buying of corn in order to sell it again, as long as the price of wheat did not exceed forty-eight shillings the quarter, and that of other grain in proportion, was declared lawful to all persons not being forestallers, that is, not selling again in the same market within three months.[2] All the freedom which the trade of the inland corn dealer has ever yet enjoyed, was bestowed upon it by this statute. The statute of the twelfth of the present king, which repeals almost all the other ancient laws against engrossers and forestallers, does not repeal the restrictions of this particular statute, which therefore still continue in force.[3]

which is absurd, as it supposes,

This statute, however, authorises in some measure two very absurd popular prejudices.

(1) that engrossing is likely to be hurtful after a certain price has been reached.

First, it supposes that when the price of wheat has risen so high as forty-eight shillings the quarter, and that of other grain in proportion, corn is likely to be so engrossed as to hurt the people. But from what has been already said, it seems evident enough that corn can at no price be so engrossed by the inland dealers as to hurt the people: and forty-eight shillings the quarter besides, though it may be considered as a very high price, yet in years of scarcity it is a price which frequently takes place immediately after harvest, when scarce any part of the new crop can be sold off, and when it is impossible even for ignorance to suppose that any part of it can be so engrossed as to hurt the people.

(2) that forestalling is likely to be hurtful after a certain price has been reached.

Secondly, it supposes that there is a certain price at which corn is likely to be forestalled, that is, bought up in order to be sold again soon after in the same market, so as to hurt the people. But if a merchant ever buys up corn, either going to a particular market or in a

---

[1] [Diligent search has hitherto failed to discover these statutes.]

[2] [§ 4 incorrectly quoted. The words are 'not forestalling nor selling the same in the same market within three months'. Under 5 and 6 Ed. VI., c. 14, a person buying and selling again 'in any fair or market holden or kept in the same place or in any other fair or market within four miles' was a regrator, while a forestaller was one who bought or contracted to buy things on their way to market, or made any motion for enhancing the price of such things or preventing them going to market.]

[3] [12 Geo. III., c. 71, repeals 5 and 6 Ed. VI., c. 14, but does not mention 15 Car. II., c. 7, which is purely permissive. If 15 Car. II., c. 7, remained of any force in this respect

particular market, in order to sell it again soon after in the same market, it must be because he judges that the market cannot be so liberally supplied through the whole season as upon that particular occasion, and that the price, therefore, must soon rise. If he judges wrong in this, and if the price does not rise, he not only loses the whole profit of the stock which he employs in this manner, but a part of the stock itself, by the expence and loss which necessarily attend[1] the storing and keeping of corn. He hurts himself, therefore, much more essentially than he can hurt even the particular people whom he may hinder from supplying themselves upon that particular market day, because they may afterwards supply themselves just as cheap upon any other market day. If he judges right, instead of hurting the great body of the people, he renders them a most important service. By making them feel the inconveniencies of a dearth somewhat earlier than they otherwise might do, he prevents their feeling them afterwards so severely as they certainly would do, if the cheapness of price encouraged them to consume faster than suited the real scarcity of the season. When the scarcity is real, the best thing that can be done for the people is to divide the inconveniencies of it as equally as possible through all the different months and weeks, and days of the year. The interest of the corn merchant makes him study to do this exactly as he can: and as no other person can have either the same interest, or the same knowledge, or the same abilities to do it so exactly as he, this most important operation of commerce ought to be trusted entirely to him; or, in other words, the corn trade, so far at least as concerns the supply of the home market, ought to be left perfectly free.

The fear of engrossing and forestalling is as groundless as that of witchcraft.   The popular fear of engrossing and forestalling may be compared to the popular terrors and suspicions of witchcraft. The unfortunate wretches accused of this latter crime were not more innocent of the misfortunes imputed to them, than those who have been accused of the former. The law which put an end to all prosecutions against witchcraft, which put it out of any man's power to gratify his own malice by accusing his neighbour of that imaginary crime, seems effectually to have put an end to those fears and suspicions, by taking away the great cause which encouraged and supported them. The law which should restore entire freedom to the inland trade of corn,

---

it must have been merely in consequence of the common law being unfavourable to forestalling.]   [1] [Eds. 1 and 2 read 'attends'.]

would probably prove as effectual to put an end to the popular fears of engrossing and forestalling.

Still, the 15 Car. II., c. 7, is the best of the corn laws, as it gives the inland corn trade all the freedom it possesses. The 15th of Charles II. c. 7. however, with all its imperfections, has perhaps contributed more both to the plentiful supply of the home market, and to the increase of tillage, than any other law in the statute book. It is from this law that the inland corn trade has derived all the liberty and protection which it has ever yet enjoyed; and both the supply of the home market, and the interest of tillage, are much more effectually promoted by the inland, than either by the importation or exportation trade.

The inland trade is much more important than the foreign. The proportion of the average quantity of all sorts of grain imported into Great Britain to that of all sorts of grain consumed, it has been computed by the author of the tracts upon the corn trade, does not exceed that of one to five hundred and seventy. For supplying the home market, therefore, the importance of the inland trade must be to that of the importation trade as five hundred and seventy to one.[1]

The average quantity of all sorts of grain exported from Great Britain does not, according to the same author, exceed the one-and-thirtieth part of the annual produce.[2] For the encouragement of tillage, therefore, by providing a market for the home produce, the importance of the inland trade must be to that of the exportation trade as thirty to one.

I have no great faith in political arithmetic, and I mean not to warrant the exactness of either of these computations. I mention them only in order to show of how much less consequence, in the opinion of the most judicious and experienced persons, the foreign trade of corn is than the home trade. The great cheapness of corn in the years immediately preceding the establishment of the bounty, may perhaps, with reason, be ascribed in some measure to the operation of this statute of Charles II., which had been enacted about five-and twenty years before, and which had therefore full time to produce its effect.

A very few words will sufficiently explain all that I have to say concerning the other three branches of the corn trade.

---

[1] [Charles Smith, *Three Tracts on the Corn Trade and Corn Laws*, 2nd ed., 1766, p. 145. The figures have been already quoted above, vol. i., p. 483.]

[2] ['The export is bare one thirty-second part of the consumption, one thirty-third part of the growth exclusive of seed, one thirty-sixth part of the growth including the seed.'—*Ibid.*, p. 144; quoted above, p. 14.]

II. The Importer, whose trade benefits the people and does not really hurt the farmers and country gentlemen.

II. The trade of the merchant importer of foreign corn for home consumption, evidently contributes to the immediate supply of the home market, and must so far be immediately beneficial to the great body of the people. It tends, indeed, to lower somewhat the average money price of corn, but not to diminish its real value, or the quantity of labour which it is capable of maintaining. If importation was at all times free, our farmers and country gentlemen would, probably, one year with another, get less money for their corn than they do at present, when importation is at most times in effect prohibited; but the money which they got would be of more value, would buy more goods of all other kinds, and would employ more labour. Their real wealth, their real revenue, therefore, would be the same as at present, though it might be expressed by a smaller quantity of silver; and they would neither be disabled nor discouraged from cultivating corn as much as they do at present. On the contrary, as the rise in the real value of silver, in consequence of lowering the money price of corn, lowers somewhat the money price of all other commodities, it gives the industry of the country, where it takes place, some advantage in all foreign markets, and thereby tends to encourage and increase that industry. But the extent of the home market for corn must be in proportion to the general industry of the country where it grows, or to the number of those who produce something else, and therefore have something else, or what comes to the same thing, the price of something else, to give in exchange for corn. But in every country the home market, as it is the nearest and most convenient, so is it likewise the greatest and most important market for corn. That rise in the real value of silver, therefore, which is the effect of lowering the average money price of corn, tends to enlarge the greatest and most important market for corn, and thereby to encourage, instead of discouraging, its growth.

The Act of 2 Car. II., c. 13, imposed very high duties on importation

By the 22d of Charles II. c. 13. the importation of wheat, whenever the price in the home market did not exceed fifty-three shillings and four pence the quarter, was subjected to a duty of sixteen shillings the quarter; and to a duty of eight shillings whenever the price did not exceed four pounds.[1] The former of these two prices

---

[1] [This was not the first law of its kind. 3 Ed. IV., c. 2, was enacted because 'the labourers and occupiers of husbandry within this realm of England be daily grievously

has, for more than a century past, taken place only in times of very great scarcity; and the latter has, so far as I know, not taken place at all. Yet, till wheat had risen above this latter price, it was by this statute subjected to a very high duty; and till it had risen above the former, to a duty which amounted to a prohibition. The importation of other sorts of grain was restrained at rates, and by duties, in proportion to the value of the grain, almost equally[1] high.[2] Subsequent laws still further increased those duties.

endamaged by bringing of corn out of other lands and parts into this realm of England, when corn of the growing of this realm is at a low price,' and forbids importation of wheat when not over 6s. 8d., rye when not over 4s. and barley when not over 3s. the quarter. This Act was repealed by 21 Jac. I., c. 28, and 15 Car. II., c. 7, imposed a duty of 5s. 4d. on imported wheat, 4s. on rye, 2s. 8d. on barley, 2s. on buckwheat, 1s. 4d. on oats and 4s. on pease and beans, when the prices at the port of importation did not exceed for wheat, 48s.; barley and buckwheat, 28s.; oats, 13s. 4d.; rye, pease and beans, 32s. per quarter.]

[1] [Ed. 1 reads 'restrained by duties proportionably'.]

[2] Before the 13th of the present king, the following were the duties payable upon the importation of the different sorts of grain:

Grain.	Duties.			Duties.	Duties.
Beans to 28s. per qr.	19s. 10d. after	till 40s.	-	16s. 8d. then	12d.
Barley to 28s.	19s. 10d.		32s.	- 16s.	12d.
Malt is prohibited by the annual Malt-tax Bill.					
Oats to 16s.	5s. 10d. after				9½d.
Pease to 40s.	16s. 0d. after				9¾d.
Rye to 36s.	19s. 10d. till	40s.	-	16s. 8d. then	12d.
Wheat to 44s.	21s. 9d. till	53s. 4d.	-	17s. then	8s.

till 4l. and after that about 1s. 4d.

Buck wheat to 32s. per qr. to pay 16s.

These different duties were imposed, partly by the 22nd of Charles II. in place of the Old Subsidy, partly by the New Subsidy, by the One-third and Two-thirds Subsidy, and by the Subsidy 1747. [The table of duties in this note is an exact copy of that in Charles Smith, Three Tracts on the Corn Trade, 2nd ed., 1766, p. 83. That author professes to have taken the figures from 'Mr. Saxby, in his Book of Rates' (i.e., Henry Saxby, The British Customs, containing an Historical and Practical Account of each branch of that Revenue, 1757, pp. 111-114), but besides rounding off Saxby's fractions of a penny in an inaccurate and inconsistent manner, he has miscopied the second duty on barley, the first on pease and the third on wheat. The 'Old Subsidy' consisted of the 5 per cent. or 1s. poundage imposed by 12 Car. II., c. 4, on the values attributed to the various goods by the 'Book of Rates' annexed to the Act. According to this, imported beans, barley and malt were to be rated at 26s. 8d. the quarter when the actual price at the place of importation did not exceed 28s. When the actual price was higher than that they were to be rated at 5s. the quarter. Oats and pease were to be rated at 4s. the quarter. Rye when not over 36s. was to be rated at 26s. 8d., and when over that price at 5s. Wheat when not over 44s. was to be rated at 40s., and when over that price at 6s. 8d.

So under the Old Subsidy:

Beans, barley and malt at prices up to 28s. were to pay 1s. 4d., and when above that price 3d.

Oats and pease to pay 2·4d.

Rye up to 36s. to pay 1s. 4d., and when above, 3d.

Wheat up to 44s. to pay 2s., and when above, 4d.

The Act 22 Car. II., c. 13, took off these duties and substituted the following scheme:

Beans to 40s. to pay 16s., and above that price, 3d.

but its operation was generally suspended in years of scarcity. The distress which, in years of scarcity, the strict execution of those laws might have brought[1] upon the people, would probably have been very great. But, upon such occasions, its execution was generally suspended by temporary statutes,[2] which permitted, for a limited time, the importation of foreign corn. The necessity of these temporary statutes sufficiently demonstrates the impropriety of this general one.

Restraint was necessary on account of the bounty. These restraints upon importation, though prior to the establishment of the bounty, were dictated by the same spirit, by the same principles, which afterwards enacted that regulation. How hurtful soever in themselves, these or some other restraints upon importation became necessary in consequence of that regulation. If, when wheat was either below forty-eight shillings the quarter, or not much above it, foreign corn could have been imported either duty free, or upon paying only a small duty, it might have been exported again, with the benefit of the bounty, to the great loss of the public revenue, and to the entire perversion of the institution, of which the object was to extend the market for the home growth, not that for the growth of foreign countries.

Barley and malt to 32s. to pay 16s., and above, 3d.
Oats to 16s. to pay 5s. 4d., and above, 2·4d.
Pease and rye the same as beans.
Wheat to 53s. 4d. to pay 16s., then to 80s. to pay 8s., and above that price, 4d.
Buckwheat to 32s. to pay 16s.

But 9 and 10 Will. III., c. 23, imposed a 'New Subsidy' exactly equal to the Old, so that duties equal to those of 12 Car. II., c. 4, were superimposed on those of 22 Car. II., c. 13. By 2 and 3 Ann., c. 9, an additional third, and by 3 and 4 Ann., c. 5, an additional two-thirds of the Old Subsidy were imposed, and by 21 Geo. II., c. 2, another amount equal to the Old Subsidy ('the impost 1747') was further imposed. So between 1747 and 1773 the duties were those of 22 Car. II., c. 13, *plus* three times those of 12 Car. II., c. 4. This gives the following scheme:

Beans to 28s. pay 20s. and after till 40s. pay 16s. 9d. then 1s.
Barley to 28s. pays 20s. and after till 32s. pays 16s. 9d. then 1s.
Oats to 16s. pay 5s. 11·2d. and then pay 9·6d.
Pease to 40s. pay 16s. 7·2d. and then pay 9·6d.
Rye to 36s. pays 20s. and after till 40s. pays 16s. 9d. then 1s.
Wheat to 44s. pays 22s. and after till 53s. 4d. pays 17s. then 9s. till 80s. and after that 1s. 4d.

Saxby's figures are slightly less, as they take into account a 5 per cent. discount obtainable on all the subsidies except one. The note appears first in ed. 2.]

[1] [Eds. 1 and 2 do not contain 'subsequent laws still further increased those duties,' and read 'the distress which in years of scarcity the strict execution of this statute might have brought'.]

[2] [These do not seem to have been numerous. There were cases in 1757 and 1766. See the table in Charles Smith, *Three Tracts upon the Corn Trade and Corn Laws*, 2nd ed., pp. 44, 45.]

III. The Exporter, whose trade indirectly contributes to the plentiful supply of the home market.

III. The trade of the merchant exporter of corn for foreign consumption, certainly does not contribute directly to the plentiful supply of the home market. It does so, however, indirectly. From whatever source this supply may be usually drawn, whether from home growth or from foreign importation, unless more corn is either usually grown, or usually imported into the country, than what is usually consumed in it, the supply of the home market can never be very plentiful. But unless the surplus can, in all ordinary cases, be exported, the growers will be careful never to grow more, and the importers never to import more, than what the bare consumption of the home market requires. That market will very seldom be overstocked; but it will generally be understocked, the people, whose business it is to supply it, being generally afraid lest their goods should be left upon their hands. The prohibition of exportation limits the improvement and cultivation of the country to what the supply of its own inhabitants requires. The freedom of exportation enables it to extend cultivation[1] for the supply of foreign nations.

Liberty of exportation was made complete in 1700,

By the 12th of Charles II. c. 4. the exportation of corn was permitted whenever the price of wheat did not exceed forty shillings the quarter, and that of other grain in proportion.[2] By the 15th of the same prince,[3] this liberty was extended till the price of wheat exceeded forty-eight shillings the quarter; and by the 22d,[4] to all higher prices. A poundage, indeed, was to be paid to the king upon such exportation. But all grain was rated so low in the book of rates, that this poundage amounted only upon wheat to a shilling, upon oats to four pence, and upon all other grain to six pence the quarter.[5] By the 1st of William and Mary,[6] the act which established the bounty, this

---

[1] [Eds. 1 and 2 read 'extend its cultivation'.]

[2] [Earlier statutes are 15 Hen. VI., c. 2; 20 Hen. VI., c. 6; 23 Hen. VI., c. 6; 1 and 2 P. and M., c. 5, 5 Eliz., c. 5, § 26; 13 Eliz., c. 13; and 1 Jac., c. 25, §§ 26, 27. The preamble of the first of these says 'by the law it was ordained that no man might carry nor bring corn out of the realm of England without the King's licence, for cause whereof farmers and other men which use manurement of their land may not sell their corn but of a bare price to the great damage of all the realm'. Exportation was therefore legalised without licence when grain was above certain prices.]

[3] [C. 7.]   [4] [C. 13.]

[5] [The 'Book of Rates' (see above, p. 44, note) rated wheat for export at 20s., oats at 6s. 8d., and other grain at 10s. the quarter, and the duty was a shilling in the pound on these values.]

[6] [1 W. and M., c. 12. The bounty was to be given 'without taking or requiring anything for custom'.]

small duty was virtually taken off whenever the price of wheat did not exceed forty-eight shillings the quarter; and by the 11th and 12th of William III. c. 20. it was expressly taken off at all higher prices.

The trade of the merchant exporter was, in this manner, not only encouraged by a bounty, but rendered much more free than that of the inland dealer. By the last of these statutes, corn could be engrossed at any price for exportation; but it could not be engrossed for inland sale, except when the price did not exceed forty-eight shillings the quarter.[1] The interest of the inland dealer, however,

though the interest of the exporter sometimes differs from that of the people of his country. it has already been shown, can never be opposite to that of the great body of the people. That of the merchant exporter may, and in fact sometimes is. If, while his own country labours under a dearth, a neighbouring country should be afflicted with a famine, it might be his interest to carry corn to the latter country in such quantities as might very much aggravate the calamities of the dearth. The plentiful supply of the home market was not the direct object of those statutes; but, under the pretence of encouraging agriculture, to raise the money price of corn as high as possible, and thereby to occasion, as much as possible, a constant dearth in the home market. By the discouragement of importation, the supply of that market, even in times of great scarcity, was confined to the home growth; and by the encouragement of exportation, when the price was so high as forty-eight shillings the quarter, that market was not, even in times of considerable scarcity, allowed to enjoy the whole of that growth. The temporary laws, prohibiting for a limited time the exportation of corn, and taking off for a limited time the duties upon its importation, expedients to which Great Britain has been obliged so frequently to have recourse,[2] sufficiently demonstrate the impropriety of her general system. Had that system been good, she would not so frequently have been reduced to the necessity of departing from it.

The bad policy of some great countries may sometimes render it necessary for small countries to restrain exportation. Were all nations to follow the liberal system of free exportation and free importation, the different states into which a great continent was divided would so far resemble the different provinces of a great empire. As among the different provinces of

---

[1] [Because as to inland sale 15 Car. II., c. 7 (above, p. 40), remained in force.]

[2] [The Acts prohibiting exportation were much more numerous than the others. See above, p. 45, note 2, and the table in Charles Smith there referred to.]

a great empire the freedom of the inland trade appears, both from reason and experience, not only the best palliative of a dearth, but the most effectual preventative of a famine; so would the freedom of the exportation and importation trade be among the different states into which a great continent was divided. The larger the continent, the easier the communication through all the different parts of it, both by land and by water, the less would any one particular part of it ever be exposed to either of these calamities, the scarcity of any one country being more likely to be relieved by the plenty of some other. But very few countries have entirely adopted this liberal system. The freedom of the corn trade is almost every where more or less restrained, and, in many countries, is confined by such absurd regulations, as frequently aggravate the unavoidable misfortune of a dearth, into the dreadful calamity of a famine. The demand of such countries for corn may frequently become so great and so urgent, that a small state in their neighbourhood, which happened at the same time to be labouring under some degree of dearth, could not venture to supply them without exposing itself to the like dreadful calamity. The very bad policy of one country may thus render it in some measure dangerous and imprudent to establish what would otherwise be the best policy in another. The unlimited freedom of exportation, however, would be much less dangerous in great states, in which the growth being much greater, the supply could seldom be much affected by any quantity of corn that was likely to be exported. In a Swiss canton, or in some of the little states of Italy, it may, perhaps, sometimes be necessary to restrain the exportation of corn. In such great countries as France or England it scarce ever can. To hinder, besides, the farmer from sending his goods at all times to the best market, is evidently to sacrifice the ordinary laws of justice to an idea of public utility, to a sort of reasons of state; an act of legislative authority which ought to be exercised only, which can be pardoned only in cases of the most urgent necessity. The price at which the exportation of corn is prohibited, if it is ever to be prohibited, ought always to be a very high price.

The corn laws are like the laws on religion. The laws concerning corn may every where be compared to the laws concerning religion. The people feel themselves so much interested in what relates either to their subsistence in this life, or to their happiness in a life to come, that government must yield to their prejudices, and, in order to preserve the public tranquillity, establish that system which they approve of. It is upon this account, perhaps, that we so seldom find a reasonable system established with regard to either of those two capital objects.

IV. The Merchant Carrier, whose trade contributes to the plentiful supply of the home market. IV. The trade of the merchant carrier, or of the importer of foreign corn in order to export it again, contributes to the plentiful supply of the home market. It is not indeed the direct purpose of his trade to sell his corn there. But he will generally be willing to do so, and even for a good deal less money than he might expect in a foreign market; because he saves in this manner the expence of loading and unloading, of freight and insurance. The inhabitants of the country which, by means of the carrying trade, becomes the magazine and storehouse for the supply of other countries, can very seldom be in want themselves. Though the carrying trade might thus contribute to reduce the average money price of corn in the home market, it would not thereby lower its real value. It would only raise somewhat the real value of silver.

British law in effect prohibited the carrying trade in corn. The carrying trade was in effect prohibited in Great Britain, upon all ordinary occasions, by the high duties upon the importation of foreign corn, of the greater part of which there was no drawback;[1] and upon extraordinary occasions, when a scarcity made it necessary to suspend those duties by temporary statutes, exportation was always prohibited. By this system of laws, therefore, the carrying trade was in effect prohibited upon all occasions.

The prosperity of Great Britain is not due to the corn bounty, but to the security of enjoying the fruits of labour. That system of laws, therefore, which is connected with the establishment of the bounty, seems to deserve no part of the praise which has been bestowed upon it. The improvement and prosperity of Great Britain, which has been so often ascribed to those laws, may very easily be accounted for by other causes. That security which the laws in Great Britain give to every man that he shall enjoy the fruits of his own labour, is alone sufficient to make any country flourish, notwithstanding these and twenty other absurd regulations of commerce; and this security was perfected by the revolution, much about the same time that the bounty was established. The natural effort of every individual to better his own condition, when suffered to exert itself with freedom and security,

[1] [Ed. 1 does not contain 'of the greater part of which there was no drawback'.]

is so powerful a principle, that it is alone, and without any assistance, not only capable of carrying on the society to wealth and prosperity, but of surmounting a hundred impertinent obstructions with which the folly of human laws too often incumbers its operations; though the effect of these obstructions is always more or less either to encroach upon its freedom, or to diminish its security. In Great Britain industry is perfectly secure; and though it is far from being perfectly free, it is as free or freer than in any other part of Europe.

That the greatest prosperity has been subsequent proves nothing; Though the period of the greatest prosperity and improvement of Great Britain, has been posterior to that system of laws which is connected with the bounty, we must not upon that account impute it to those laws. It has been posterior likewise to the national debt. But the national debt has most assuredly not been the cause of it.

Spain and Portugal are poorer than Great Britain because their bad policy is more effectual and not counteracted by general liberty and security. Though the system of laws which is connected with the bounty, has exactly the same tendency with the police of Spain and Portugal; to lower somewhat the value of the precious metals in the country where it takes place;[1] yet Great Britain is certainly one of the richest countries in Europe, while Spain and Portugal are perhaps among the most beggarly. This difference of situation, however, may easily be accounted for from two different causes. First, the tax in Spain, the prohibition in Portugal of exporting gold and silver,[2] and the vigilant police which watches over the execution of those laws, must, in two very poor countries, which between them import annually upwards of six millions sterling,[3] operate, not only more directly, but much more forcibly in reducing the value of those metals there, than the corn laws can do in Great Britain. And, secondly, this bad policy is not in those countries counter-balanced by the general liberty and security of the people. Industry is there neither free nor secure, and the civil and ecclesiastical governments of both Spain and Portugal, are such as would alone be sufficient to perpetuate their present state of poverty, even though their regulations of commerce were as wise as the greater part of them are absurd and foolish.

The 13 Geo. III., c. 43, The 13th of the present king, c. 43. seems to have established a new system with regard to the corn

---

[1] [According to the argument above, p. 19.]
[2] [See above, p. 17.]   [3] [Above, vol. i., pp. 231–233.]

laws, in many respects better than the ancient one, but in one or two respects[1] perhaps not quite so good.

opens the home market at lower prices, By this statute the high duties upon importation for home consumption are taken off so soon as the price of middling wheat rises to forty-eight shillings the quarter; that of middling rye, pease or beans, to thirty-two shillings; that of barley to twenty-four shillings; and that of oats to sixteen shillings; and instead[2] of them a small duty is imposed of only six-pence upon the quarter of wheat, and upon that of other grain in proportion. With regard to all these different sorts of grain, but particularly with regard to wheat, the home market is thus opened to foreign supplies at prices considerably lower than before.[3]

stops the bounty earlier, By the same statute the old bounty of five shillings upon the exportation of wheat ceases so soon as the price rises to forty-four shillings the quarter, instead of forty-eight, the price at which it ceased before; that of two shillings and six-pence upon the exportation of barley ceases so soon as the price rises to twenty-two shillings, instead of twenty-four, the price at which it ceased before; that of two shillings and six-pence upon the exportation of oatmeal ceases so soon as the price rises to fourteen shillings, instead of fifteen, the price at which it ceased before. The bounty upon rye is reduced from three shillings and six-pence to three shillings, and it ceases so soon as the price rises to twenty-eight shillings, instead of thirty-two, the price at which it ceased before.[4] If bounties are as improper as I have endeavoured to prove them to be, the sooner they cease, and the lower they are, so much the better.

and admits corn for re-export duty free; The same statute permits, at the lowest prices, the importation of corn, in order to be exported again, duty free, provided it is in the meantime lodged in a warehouse under the joint locks of the king and the importer.[5] This liberty,

---

[1] [Ed. 1 reads 'in one respect'.]

[2] [Ed. 1 reads only 'By this statute the high duties upon importation for home consumption are taken off as soon as the price of wheat is so high as forty-eight shillings the quarter, and instead'.]

[3] [In place of this sentence ed. 1 reads 'The home market is in this manner not so totally excluded from foreign supplies as it was before.']

[4] [Ed. 1 reads (from the beginning of the paragraph) 'By the same statute the old bounty of five shillings upon the quarter of wheat ceases when the price rises so high as forty-four shillings, and upon that of other grain in proportion. The bounties too upon the coarser sorts of grain are reduced somewhat lower than they were before, even at the prices at which they take place.']

[5] [Ed. 1 reads 'The same statute permits at all prices the importation of corn in order to be exported again, duty free; provided it is in the meantime lodged in the king's warehouse.']

indeed, extends to no more than twenty-five of the different ports of Great Britain. They are, however, the principal ones, and there may not, perhaps, be warehouses proper for this purpose in the greater part of the others.[1]

which are
improvements,

So far this law seems evidently an improvement upon the ancient system.

but it gives a
bounty on the export
of oats,

But by the same law a bounty of two shillings the quarter is given for the exportation of oats whenever the price does not exceed fourteen shillings.
No bounty had ever been given before for the exportation of this grain, no more than for that of peas or beans.[2]

and prohibits expor-
tation of grain at
prices much too low.

By the same law too, the exportation of wheat is prohibited so soon as the price rises to forty-four shillings the quarter; that of rye so soon as it rises to twenty-eight shillings; that of barley so soon as it rises to twenty-two shillings; and that of oats so soon as they rise to fourteen shillings. Those several prices seem all of them a good deal too low, and there seems to be an impropriety, besides, in prohibiting exportation altogether at those precise prices at which that bounty, which was given in order to force it, is withdrawn.[3] The bounty ought certainly either to have been withdrawn at a much lower price, or exportation ought to have been allowed at a much higher.

It is as good a law
as can be expected
at present.

So far, therefore, this law seems to be inferior to the ancient system. With all its imperfections, however, we may perhaps say of it what was said of the laws of Solon, that, though not the best in itself, it is the best which the interests, prejudices, and temper of the times would admit of. It may perhaps in due time prepare the way for a better.[4]

---

[1] [Ed. 1 contains an additional sentence, 'Some provision is thus made for the establishment of the carrying trade.']

[2] [This paragraph is not in ed. 1.]

[3] [Ed. 1 reads (from the beginning of the paragraph) 'But by the same law exportation is prohibited as soon as the price of wheat rises to forty-four shillings the quarter, and that of other grain in proportion. The price seems to be a good deal too low, and there seems to be an impropriety besides in stopping exportation altogether at the very same price at which that bounty which was given in order to force it is withdrawn.']

[4] [These two sentences are not in ed. 1.]

CHAPTER VI

Of Treaties of Commerce

Treaties of commerce are advantageous to the favoured, When a nation binds itself by treaty either to permit the entry of certain goods from one foreign country which it prohibits from all others, or to exempt the goods of one country from duties to which it subjects those of all others, the country, or at least the merchants and manufacturers of the country, whose commerce is so favoured, must necessarily derive great advantage from the treaty. Those merchants and manufacturers enjoy a sort of monopoly in the country which is so indulgent to them. That country becomes a market both more extensive and more advantageous for their goods: more extensive, because the goods of other nations being either excluded or subjected to heavier duties, it takes off a greater quantity of theirs: more advantageous, because the merchants of the favoured country, enjoying a sort of monopoly there, will often sell their goods for a better price than if exposed to the free competition of all other nations.

but disadvantageous to the favouring country. Such treaties, however, though they may be advantageous to the merchants and manufacturers of the favoured, are necessarily disadvantageous to those of the favouring country. A monopoly is thus granted against them to a foreign nation; and they must frequently buy the foreign goods they have occasion for, dearer than if the free competition of other nations was admitted. That part of its own produce with which such a nation purchases foreign goods, must consequently be sold cheaper, because when two things are exchanged for one another, the cheapness of the one is a necessary consequence, or rather is the same thing with the dearness of the other. The exchangeable value of its annual produce, therefore, is likely to be diminished by every such treaty. This diminution, however, can scarce amount to any positive loss, but only to a lessening of the gain which it might otherwise make. Though it sells its goods cheaper than it otherwise might do, it will not probably sell them for less than they cost; nor, as in the case of bounties, for a price which will not replace the capital employed in bringing them to market, together with the ordinary profits of stock. The trade could not go on long if it did. Even the favouring country, therefore, may still gain by the trade, though less than if there was a free competition.

Treaties have been concluded with the object of obtaining a favourable balance of trade, Some treaties of commerce, however, have been supposed advantageous upon principles very different from these; and a commercial country has sometimes granted a monopoly of this kind against itself to certain goods of a foreign nation, because it expected that in the whole commerce between them, it would annually sell more than it would buy, and that a balance in gold and silver would be annually returned to it. It is upon this principle that the treaty of commerce between England and Portugal, concluded in 1703, by Mr. Methuen, has been so much commended.[1] The following is a *e.g., the Methuen treaty,* literal translation[2] of that treaty, which consists of three articles only.

ART. I

His sacred royal majesty of Portugal promises, both in his own name, and that of his successors, to admit, for ever hereafter, into Portugal, the woollen cloths, and the rest of the woollen manufactures of the British, as was accustomed, till they were prohibited by the law; nevertheless upon this condition:

ART. II

That is to say, that her sacred royal majesty of Great Britain shall, in her own name, and that of her successors, be obliged, for ever hereafter, to admit the wines of the growth of Portugal into Britain: so that at no time, whether there shall be peace or war between the kingdoms of Britain and France, any thing more shall be demanded for these wines by the name of custom or duty, or by whatsoever other title, directly or indirectly, whether they shall be imported

---

[1] [*E.g.*, in the *British Merchant*, 1721, Dedication to vol. iii.]

[2] [With three small exceptions, 'British' for 'Britons' and 'law' for 'laws' in art. I, and 'for' instead of 'from' before 'the like quantity or measure of French wine,' the translation is identical with that given in *A Collection of all the Treaties of Peace, Alliance and Commerce between Great Britain and other Powers from the Revolution in 1688 to the Present Time*, 1772, vol. i., pp. 61, 62.]

into Great Britain in pipes or hogsheads, or other casks, than what shall be demanded for the like quantity or measure of French wine, deducting or abating a third part of the custom or duty. But if at any time this deduction or abatement of customs, which is to be made as aforesaid, shall in any manner be attempted and prejudiced, it shall be just and lawful for his sacred royal majesty of Portugal, again to prohibit the woollen cloths, and the rest of the British woollen manufactures.

ART. III

The most excellent lords the plenipotentiaries promise and take upon themselves that their above-named masters shall ratify this treaty; and within the space of two months the ratifications shall be exchanged.

which is evidently advantageous to Portugal and disadvantageous to Great Britain. By this treaty the crown of Portugal becomes bound to admit the English woollens upon the same footing as before the prohibition; that is, not to raise the duties which had been paid before that time. But it does not become bound to admit them upon any better terms than those of any other nation, of France or Holland for example. The crown of Great Britain, on the contrary, becomes bound to admit the wines of Portugal, upon paying only two-thirds of the duty, which is paid for those of France, the wines most likely to come into competition with them. So far this treaty, therefore, is evidently advantageous to Portugal, and disadvantageous to Great Britain.

Portugal sends much gold to England; It has been celebrated, however, as a masterpiece of the commercial policy of England. Portugal receives annually from the Brazils a greater quantity of gold than can be employed in its domestic commerce, whether in the shape of coin or of plate. The surplus is too valuable to be allowed to lie idle and locked up in coffers, and as it can find no advantageous market at home, it must, notwithstanding any prohibition, be sent abroad, and exchanged for something for which there is a more advantageous market at home. A large share of it comes annually to England, in return either for English goods, or for those of other European nations that receive their returns through England. Mr. Baretti was informed that the weekly packet-boat from Lisbon brings, one week with another, more than fifty thousand pounds in gold to England.[1] The sum had probably been exaggerated. It would amount to more than two millions six hundred thousand pounds a year, which is more than the Brazils are supposed to afford.[2]

at one time nearly the whole of this gold was said to be on account of other European nations, Our merchants were some years ago out of humour with the crown of Portugal. Some privileges which had been granted them, not by treaty, but by the free grace of that crown, at the solicitation, indeed, it is probable, and in return for much greater favours, defence and protection, from the crown of Great Britain, had been either infringed or revoked. The people, therefore, usually most interested in celebrating the Portugal trade, were then rather disposed to represent it as less advantageous than it had commonly been imagined. The far greater part, almost the whole, they pretended, of this annual importation of gold, was not on account of Great Britain, but of other European nations; the fruits and wines of Portugal annually imported into Great Britain nearly compensating the value of the British goods sent thither.

but even if it were not so, the trade would not be more valuable than another of equal magnitude. Let us suppose, however, that the whole was on account of Great Britain, and that it amounted to a still greater sum than Mr. Baretti seems to imagine: this trade would not, upon that account, be more advantageous than any other in which, for the same value sent out, we received an equal value of consumable goods in return.

Most of the gold must be sent abroad again and exchanged for goods, and it would be better to buy the goods direct with home produce instead of buying gold in Portugal. It is but a very small part of this importation which, it can be supposed, is employed as an annual addition either to the plate or to the coin of the kingdom. The rest must all be sent abroad and exchanged for consumable goods of some kind or other. But if those consumable goods were purchased directly with the produce of English industry, it would be more for the advantage of England, than first to purchase with that produce the gold of Portugal, and afterwards

---

[1] [Joseph Baretti, *Journey from London to Genoa, through England, Portugal, Spain and France*, 3rd ed., 1770, vol. i., pp. 95, 96, but the amount stated is not so large as in the text above: it is 'often' from 'thirty to fifty and even sixty thousand pounds,' and not 'one week with another' but 'almost every week'. The gold all came in the packet boat because it, as a war vessel, was exempt from search.—Raynal, *Histoire philosophique*, Amsterdam ed. 1773, tom. iii., pp. 413, 414.]

[2] [Above, vol. i., pp. 232, 233.]

to purchase with that gold those consumable goods. A direct foreign trade of consumption is always more advantageous than a round-about one;[1] and to bring the same value of foreign goods to the home market, requires a much smaller capital in the one way[2] than in the other. If a smaller share of its industry, therefore, had been employed in producing goods fit for the Portugal market, and a greater in producing those fit for the other markets, where those consumable goods for which there is a demand in Great Britain are to be had, it would have been more for the advantage of England. To procure both the gold, which it wants for its own use, and the consumable goods, would, in this way, employ a much smaller capital than at present. There would be a spare capital, therefore, to be employed for other purposes, in exciting an additional quantity of industry, and in raising a greater annual produce.

Britain would find little difficulty in procuring gold even if excluded from trade with Portugal. Though Britain were entirely excluded from the Portugal trade, it could find very little difficulty in procuring all the annual supplies of gold which it wants, either for the purposes of plate, or of coin, or of foreign trade. Gold, like every other commodity, is always somewhere or another to be got for its value by those who have that value to give for it. The annual surplus of gold in Portugal, besides, would still be sent abroad, and though not carried away by Great Britain, would be carried away by some other nation, which would be glad to sell it again for its price, in the same manner as Great Britain does at present. In buying gold of Portugal, indeed, we buy it at the first hand; whereas, in buying it of any other nation, except Spain, we should buy it at the second, and might pay somewhat dearer. This difference, however, would surely be too insignificant to deserve the public attention.

It is said that all our gold comes from Portugal, but if it did not come from Portugal it would come from other countries. Almost all our gold, it is said, comes from Portugal. With other nations the balance of trade is either against us, or not much in our favour. But we should remember, that the more gold we import from one country, the less we must necessarily import from all others. The effectual demand for gold, like that for every other commodity, is in every country limited to a certain quantity. If nine-tenths of this quantity are imported from one country, there remains a tenth only to be imported from all others.

[1] [Above, vol. i., p. 391.]
[2] [Ed. 1 does not contain 'way'.]

The more gold besides that is annually imported from some particular countries, over and above what is requisite for plate and for coin, the more must necessarily be exported to some others; and the more that most insignificant object of modern policy, the balance of trade, appears to be in our favour with some particular countries, the more it must necessarily appear to be against us with many others.

If the attempt of France and Spain to exclude British ships from Portuguese ports had been successful, it would have been an advantage to England. It was upon this silly notion, however, that England could not subsist without the Portugal trade, that, towards the end of the late war,[1] France and Spain, without pretending either offence or provocation, required the king of Portugal to exclude all British ships from his ports, and for the security of this exclusion, to receive into them French or Spanish garrisons. Had the king of Portugal submitted to those ignominious terms which his brother-in-law the king of Spain proposed to him, Britain would have been freed from a much greater inconveniency than the loss of the Portugal trade, the burden of supporting a very weak ally, so unprovided of every thing for his own defence, that the whole power of England, had it been directed to that single purpose, could scarce perhaps have defended him for another campaign. The loss of the Portugal trade would, no doubt, have occasioned a considerable embarrassment to the merchants at that time engaged in it, who might not, perhaps, have found out, for a year or two, any other equally advantageous method of employing their capitals; and in this would probably have consisted all the inconveniency which England could have suffered from this notable piece of commercial policy.

The great importation of gold and silver is for foreign trade. The great annual importation of gold and silver is neither for the purpose of plate nor of coin, but of foreign trade. A round-about foreign trade of consumption can be carried on more advantageously by means of these metals than of almost any other goods. As they are the universal instruments of commerce, they are more readily received in return for all commodities than any other goods; and on account of their small bulk and great value, it costs less to transport them backward and forward from one place to another than almost any other sort of merchandize, and they lose less of their value by being so transported. Of all the commodities, therefore, which are bought in one

[1] [In 1762.]

foreign country, for no other purpose but to be sold or exchanged again for some other goods in another, there are none so convenient as gold and silver. In facilitating all the different round-about foreign trades of consumption which are carried on in Great Britain, consists the principal advantage of the Portugal trade; and though it is not a capital advantage, it is, no doubt, a considerable one.

Very little is required for plate and coin. That any annual addition which, it can reasonably be supposed, is made either to the plate or to the coin of the kingdom, could require but a very small annual importation of gold and silver, seems evident enough; and though we had no direct trade with Portugal, this small quantity could always, somewhere or another, be very easily got.

New gold plate is mostly made from old. Though the goldsmiths trade be very considerable in Great Britain, the far greater part of the new plate which they annually sell, is made from other old plate melted down; so that the addition annually made to the whole plate of the kingdom cannot be very great, and could require but a very small annual importation.

New coin is mostly made from old, as there is a profit on melting good coin. It is the same case with the coin. Nobody imagines, I believe, that even the greater part of the annual coinage, amounting, for ten years together, before the late reformation of the gold coin,[1] to upwards of eight hundred thousand pounds a year in gold,[2] was an annual addition to the money before current in the kingdom. In a country where the expence of the coinage is defrayed by the government, the value of the coin, even when it contains its full standard weight of gold and silver, can never be much greater than that of an equal quantity of those metals uncoined; because it requires only the trouble of going to the mint, and the delay perhaps of a few weeks, to procure for any quantity of uncoined gold and silver an equal quantity of those metals in coin. But, in every country, the greater part of the current coin is almost always more or less worn, or otherwise degenerated from its standard. In Great Britain it was, before the late reformation, a good deal so, the gold being more than two per cent. and the silver more than eight per cent. below its standard weight, But if forty-four guineas and a half, containing their full standard weight, a pound weight of gold, could purchase very little more than a pound weight of uncoined gold, forty-four guineas and a half wanting a part of their weight could not purchase a pound

---

[1] [See above, vol. i., p. 46.]   [2] [Above, vol. i., p. 321, note.]

weight, and something was to be added in order to make up the deficiency. The current price of gold bullion at market, therefore, instead of being the same with the mint price, or 46 l. 14 s. 6 d. was then about 47 l. 14 s. and sometimes about forty-eight pounds. When the greater part of the coin, however, was in this degenerate condition, forty-four guineas and a half, fresh from the mint, would purchase no more goods in the market than any other ordinary guineas, because when they came into the coffers of the merchant, being confounded with other money, they could not afterwards be distinguished without more trouble than the difference was worth. Like other guineas they were worth no more than 46 l. 14 s. 6 d. If thrown into the melting pot, however, they produced, without any sensible loss, a pound weight of standard gold, which could be sold at any time for between 47 l. 14 s. and 48 l. either in gold or silver, as fit for all the purposes of coin as that which had been melted down. There was an evident profit, therefore, in melting down new coined money, and it was done so instantaneously, that no precaution of government could prevent it. The operations of the mint were, upon this account, somewhat like the web of Penelope; the work that was done in the day was undone in the night. The mint was employed, not so much in making daily additions to the coin, as in replacing the very best part of it which was daily melted down.

A seignorage raises the value of coin above that of bullion of equal weight, Were the private people, who carry their gold and silver to the mint, to pay themselves for the coinage, it would add to the value of those metals in the same manner as the fashion does to that of plate. Coined gold and silver would be more valuable than uncoined. The seignorage, if it was not exorbitant, would add to the bullion the whole value of the duty; because, the government having every where the exclusive privilege of coining, no coin can come to market cheaper than they think proper to afford it. If the duty was exorbitant indeed, that is, if it was very much above the real value of the labour and expence requisite for coinage, false coiners, both at home and abroad, might be encouraged, by the great difference between the value of bullion and that of coin, to pour in so great a quantity of counterfeit money as might reduce the value of the government money. In France, however, though the seignorage is eight per cent. no sensible inconveniency of this kind is found to arise from it. The dangers to which a false coiner is every where exposed, if he lives in the country of which he counterfeits the coin, and to which his agents or correspondents are exposed if he lives in a foreign country, are by far too great to be incurred for the sake of a profit of six or seven per cent.

as in France.   The seignorage in France raises the value of the coin higher than in proportion to the quantity of pure gold which it contains. Thus by the edict of January 1726, the[1] mint price of fine gold of twenty-four carats was fixed at seven hundred and forty livres nine sous and one denier one-eleventh, the mark of eight Paris ounces. The gold coin of France, making an allowance for the remedy of the mint, contains twenty-one carats and three-fourths of fine gold, and two carats one-fourth of alloy. The mark of standard gold, therefore, is worth no more than about six hundred and seventy-one livres ten deniers. But in France this mark of standard gold is coined into thirty Louis d'ors of twenty-four livres each, or into seven hundred and twenty livres. The coinage, therefore, increases the value of a mark of standard gold bullion, by the difference between six hundred and seventy-one livres ten deniers, and seven hundred and twenty livres; or by forty-eight livres nineteen sous and two deniers.

It diminishes or destroys the profit obtained by melting coin.   A seignorage will, in many cases, take away altogether, and will, in all cases, diminish the profit of melting down the new coin. This profit always arises from the difference between the quantity of bullion which the common currency ought to contain, and that which it actually does contain. If this difference is less than the seignorage, there will be loss instead of profit. If it is equal to the seignorage, there will neither be profit nor loss. If it is greater than the seignorage, there will indeed be some profit, but less than if there was no seignorage. If, before the late reformation of the gold coin, for example, there had been a seignorage of five per cent. upon the coinage, there would

---

[1] See Dictionaire des Monnoies, tom. ii. article Seigneurage, p. 489. par M. Abot de Bazinghen, Conseiller-Commissaire en la Cour des Monnoie sà Paris. [Ed. 1 reads erroneously 'tom. i.' The book is *Traité des Monnoies et de la jurisdiction de la Cour des Monnoies en forme de dictionnaire*, par M. Abot de Bazinghen, Conseiller-Commissaire en la Cour des Monnoies de Paris, 1764, and the page is not 489, but 589. Garnier, in his edition of the *Wealth of Nations*, vol. v., p. 234, says the book 'n'est guère qu'une compilation faite sans soin et sans discernement,' and explains that the mint price mentioned above remained in force a very short time. It having failed to bring bullion to the mint, much higher prices were successively offered, and when the *Wealth of Nations* was published the seignorage only amounted to about 3 per cent. On the silver coin it was then about 2 per cent., in place of the 6 per cent. stated by Bazinghen, p. 590.]

have been a loss of three per cent. upon the melting down of the gold coin. If the seignorage had been two per cent. there would have been neither profit nor loss. If the seignorage had been one per cent. there would have been a profit, but of one per cent. only instead of two per cent. Wherever money is received by tale, therefore, and not by weight, a seignorage is the most effectual preventative of the melting down of the coin, and, for the same reason, of its exportation. It is the best and heaviest pieces that are commonly either melted down or exported; because it is upon such that the largest profits are made.

The abolition of seignorage in England was probably due to the bank of England,
The law for the encouragement of the coinage, by rendering it duty-free, was first enacted, during the reign of Charles II.[1] for a limited time; and afterwards continued, by different prolongations, till 1769, when it was rendered perpetual.[2] The bank of England, in order to replenish their coffers with money, are frequently obliged to carry bullion to the mint; and it was more for their interest, they probably imagined, that the coinage should be at the expence of the government, than at their own. It was, probably, out of complaisance to this great company that the government agreed to render this law perpetual. Should the custom of weighing gold, however, come to be disused, as it is very likely to be on account of its inconveniency; should the gold coin of England come to be received by tale, as it was before the late recoinage, this great company may perhaps, find that they have upon this, as upon some other occasions, mistaken their own interest not a little.

but the bank would have lost nothing by a seignorage whether it equalled the depreciation,
Before the late recoinage, when the gold currency of England was two per cent. below its standard weight, as there was no seignorage, it was two per cent. below the value of that quantity of standard gold bullion which it ought to have contained. When this great company, therefore, bought gold bullion in order to have it coined, they were obliged to pay for it two per cent. more than it was worth after the coinage. But if there had been a seignorage of two per cent. upon the coinage, the common gold currency, though two per

---

[1] ['An act for encouraging of coinage,' 18 Car. II., c. 5. The preamble says, 'Whereas it is obvious that the plenty of current coins of gold and silver of this kingdom is of great advantage to trade and commerce; for the increase whereof, your Majesty in your princely wisdom and care hath been graciously pleased to bear out of your revenue half the charge of the coinage of silver money'.]

[2] [Originally enacted for five years, it was renewed by 25 Car. II., c. 8, for seven years, revived for seven years by 1 Jac. II., c. 7, and continued by various Acts till made perpetual by 9 Geo. III., c. 25.]

cent. below its standard weight, would notwithstanding have been equal in value to the quantity of standard gold which it ought to have contained; the value of the fashion compensating in this case the diminution of the weight. They would indeed have had the seignorage to pay, which being two per cent. their loss upon the whole transaction would have been two per cent. exactly the same, but no greater than it actually was.

exceeded it,   If the seignorage had been five per cent. and the gold currency only two per cent. below its standard weight, the bank would in this case have gained three per cent. upon the price of the bullion; but as they would have had a seignorage of five per cent. to pay upon the coinage, their loss upon the whole transaction would, in the same manner, have been exactly two per cent.

or fell short of it.   If the seignorage had been only one per cent. and the gold currency two per cent. below its standard weight, the bank would in this case have lost only one per cent. upon the price of the bullion; but as they would likewise have had a seignorage of one per cent. to pay, their loss upon the whole transaction would have been exactly two per cent. in the same manner as in all other cases.

Nor would it lose if there were no depreciation.   If there was a reasonable seignorage, while at the same time the coin contained its full standard weight, as it has done very nearly since the late re-coinage, whatever the bank might lose by the seignorage, they would gain upon the price of the bullion; and whatever they might gain upon the price of the bullion, they would lose by the seignorage. They would neither lose nor gain, therefore, upon the whole transaction, and they would in this, as in all the foregoing cases, be exactly in the same situation as if there was no seignorage.

A seignorage is paid by no one,   When the tax upon a commodity is so moderate as not to encourage smuggling, the merchant who deals in it, though he advances, does not properly pay the tax, as he gets it back in the price of the commodity. The tax is finally paid by the last purchaser or consumer. But money is a commodity with regard to which every man is a merchant. Nobody buys it but in order to sell it again; and with regard to it there is in ordinary cases no last purchaser or consumer. When the tax upon coinage, therefore, is so moderate as not to encourage false coining, though every body advances the tax, nobody finally pays it; because every body gets it back in the advanced value of the coin.

and could not have augmented the expense of the bank. A moderate seignorage, therefore, would not in any case augment the expence of the bank, or of any other private persons who carry their bullion to the mint in order to be coined, and the want of a moderate seignorage does not in any case diminish it. Whether there is or is not a seignorage, if the currency contains its full standard weight, the coinage costs nothing to any body, and if it is short of that weight, the coinage must always cost the difference between the quantity of bullion which ought to be contained in it, and that which actually is contained in it.

The government loses and nobody gains by the absence of seignorage. The government, therefore, when it defrays the expence of coinage, not only incurs some small expence, but loses some small revenue which it might get by a proper duty; and neither the bank nor any other private persons are in the smallest degree benefited by this useless piece of public generosity.

Supposing the coin should again become depreciated, a seignorage would preserve the bank from considerable loss. The directors of the bank, however, would probably be unwilling to agree to the imposition of a seignorage upon the authority of a speculation which promises them no gain, but only pretends to insure them from any loss. In the present state of the gold coin, and as long as it continues to be received by weight, they certainly would gain nothing by such a change. But if the custom of weighing the gold coin should ever go into disuse, as it is very likely to do, and if the gold coin should ever fall into the same state of degradation in which it was before the late recoinage, the gain, or more properly the savings of the bank, in consequence of the imposition of a seignorage, would probably be very considerable. The bank of England is the only company which sends any considerable quantity of bullion to the mint, and the burden of the annual coinage falls entirely, or almost entirely, upon it. If this annual coinage had nothing to do but to repair the unavoidable losses and necessary wear and tear[1] of the coin, it could seldom exceed fifty thousand or at most a hundred thousand pounds. But when the coin is degraded below its standard weight, the annual coinage must, besides this, fill up the large vacuities which exportation and the melting pot are continually making in the current coin. It was upon this account that during the ten or twelve years immediately preceding the late reformation of the gold coin, the

---

[1] [Ed. 1 reads 'tear and wear'.]

annual coinage amounted at an average to more than eight hundred and fifty thousand pounds.[1] But if there had been a seignorage of four or five per cent. upon the gold coin, it would probably, even in the state in which things then were, have put an effectual stop to the business both of exportation and of the melting pot. The bank, instead of losing every year about two and a half per cent. upon the bullion which was to be coined into more than eight hundred and fifty thousand pounds, or incurring an annual loss of more than twenty-one thousand two hundred and fifty pounds, would not probably have incurred the tenth part of that loss.

The saving to the government may be regarded as too trifling, but that of the bank is worth consideration. The revenue allotted by parliament for defraying the expence of the coinage is but fourteen thousand pounds a year,[2] and the real expence which it costs the government, or the fees of the officers of the mint, do not upon ordinary occasions, I am assured, exceed the half of that sum. The saving of so very small a sum, or even the gaining of another which could not well be much larger, are objects too inconsiderable, it may be thought, to deserve the serious attention of government. But the saving of eighteen or twenty thousand pounds a year in case of an event which is not improbable, which has frequently happened before, and which is very likely to happen again, is surely an object which well deserves the serious attention even of so great a company as the bank of England.

Some of the foregoing reasonings and observations might perhaps have been more properly placed in those chapters of the first book which treat of the origin and use of money, and of the difference between the real and the nominal price of commodities. But as the law for the encouragement of coinage derives its origin from those vulgar prejudices which have been introduced by the mercantile system; I judged it more proper to reserve them for this chapter. Nothing could be more agreeable to the spirit of that system than a sort of bounty upon the production of money, the very thing which, it supposes, constitutes the wealth of every nation. It is one of its many admirable expedients for enriching the country.

[1] [Above, p. 59.]
[2] [Under 19 Geo. II., c. 14, § 2, a maximum of £15,000 is prescribed.]

CHAPTER VII

Of Colonies

PART FIRST

Of the Motives for establishing new Colonies

The interest which occasioned the first settlement of the different European colonies in America and the West Indies, was not altogether so plain and distinct as that which directed the establishment of those of ancient Greece and Rome.

Greek colonies were sent out when the population grew too great at home. All the different states of ancient Greece possessed, each of them, but a very small territory, and when the people in any one of them multiplied beyond what that territory could easily maintain, a part of them were sent in quest of a new habitation in some remote and distant part of the world; the warlike neighbours who surrounded them on all sides, rendering it difficult for any of them to enlarge very much its territory at home. The colonies of the Dorians resorted chiefly to Italy and Sicily, which, in the times preceding the foundation of Rome, were inhabited by barbarous and uncivilized nations: those of the Ionians and Eolians, the two other great tribes of the Greeks, to Asia Minor and the islands of the Egean Sea, of which the inhabitants seem at that time to have been pretty much in the same state as those of Sicily and Italy. The mother city, though she considered the colony as a child, at all times entitled to great favour and assistance, and owing in return much gratitude and respect, yet considered it as an emancipated child, over whom she *The mother city claimed no authority.* pretended to claim no direct authority or jurisdiction. The colony settled its own form of government, enacted its own laws, elected its own magistrates, and made peace or war with its neighbours as an independent state, which had no occasion to wait for the approbation or consent of the mother city. Nothing can be more plain and distinct than the interest which directed every such establishment.

Rome, like most of the other ancient republics, was originally founded upon an Agrarian law, which divided the public territory in a certain proportion among the different citizens who composed the state. The course of human affairs, by marriage, by succession, and by alienation, necessarily deranged this original division, and frequently threw the lands, which had been allotted for the maintenance of many different families into the possession of a single person. To remedy this disorder, for such it was supposed to be, a law was made, restricting the quantity of land which any citizen could possess to five hundred jugera, about three hundred and fifty English acres. This law, however, though we read of its having been executed upon one or two occasions, was either neglected or evaded, and the inequality of fortunes went on continually increasing. The greater part of the citizens had no land, and without it the manners and customs of those times rendered it difficult for a freeman to maintain his independency. In the present times, though a poor man has no land of his own, if he has a little stock, he may either farm the lands of another, or he may carry on some little retail trade; and if he has no stock, he may find employment either as a country labourer, or as an artificer. But, among the ancient Romans, the lands of the rich were all cultivated by slaves, who wrought under an overseer, who was likewise a slave; so that a poor freeman had little chance of being employed either as a farmer or as a labourer. All trades and manufactures too, even the retail trade, were carried on by the slaves of the rich for the benefit of their masters, whose wealth, authority, and protection made it difficult for a poor freeman to maintain the competition against them. The citizens, therefore, who had no land, had scarce any other means of subsistence but the bounties of the candidates at the annual elections. The tribunes, when they had a mind to animate the people against the rich and the great, put them in mind of the ancient division of lands, and represented that law which restricted this sort of private property as the fundamental law of the republic. The people became clamorous to get land, and the rich and the great, we may believe, were perfectly determined not to give them any part of theirs. To satisfy them in some measure, therefore, they frequently proposed to send out a new colony. But conquering Rome was, even upon such occasions, under no necessity of turning out her citizens to seek their fortune, if one may say so, through the

wide world, without knowing where they were to settle. She assigned them lands generally in the conquered provinces of Italy,
where, being within the dominions of the republic, they could
never form any independent state; but were at best but a sort of
corporation, which, though it had the power of enacting bye-laws

they were
entirely subject
to the mother city.

for its own government, was at all times subject to
the correction, jurisdiction, and legislative authority
of the mother city. The sending out a colony of
this kind, not only gave some satisfaction to the people, but often
established a sort of garrison too in a newly conquered province, of
which the obedience might otherwise have been doubtful. A Roman
colony, therefore, whether we consider the nature of the establishment itself, or the motives for making it, was altogether different
from a Greek one. The words accordingly, which in the original
languages denote those different establishments, have very different
meanings. The Latin word (*Colonia*) signifies simply a plantation.
The Greek word (αποικια), on the contrary, signifies a separation of dwelling, a departure from home, a going out of the house.
But, though the Roman colonies were in many respects different
from the Greek ones, the interest which prompted to establish them
was equally plain and distinct. Both institutions derived their origin
either from irresistible necessity, or from clear and evident utility.

The utility of the
American colonies
is not so evident.

The establishment of the European colonies in
America and the West Indies arose from no necessity: and though the utility which has resulted
from them has been very great, it is not altogether so clear and
evident. It was not understood at their first establishment, and was
not the motive either of that establishment or of the discoveries
which gave occasion to it; and the nature, extent, and limits of that
utility are not, perhaps, well understood at this day.

The Venetians had
a profitable trade
in East India goods,

The Venetians, during the fourteenth and fifteenth
centuries, carried on a very advantageous commerce
in spiceries, and other East India goods, which they
distributed among the other nations of Europe. They purchased
them chiefly[1] in Egypt, at that time under the dominion of the
Mammeluks, the enemies of the Turks, of whom the Venetians
were the enemies; and this union of interest, assisted by the money
of Venice, formed such a connection as gave the Venetians almost
a monopoly of the trade.

[1] ['Chiefly' is not in ed. 1.]

which was envied by the Portuguese and led them to discover the Cape of Good Hope passage, The great profits of the Venetians tempted the avidity of the Portuguese. They had been endeavouring, during the course of the fifteenth century, to find out by sea a way to the countries from which the Moors brought them ivory and gold dust across the Desart. They discovered the Madeiras, the Canaries, the Azores, the Cape de Verd islands, the coast of Guinea, that of Loango, Congo, Angola, and Benguela,[1] and finally, the Cape of Good Hope. They had long wished to share in the profitable traffic of the Venetians, and this last discovery opened to them a probable prospect of doing so. In 1497, Vasco de Gama sailed from the port of Lisbon with a fleet of four ships, and, after a navigation of eleven months, arrived upon the coast of Indostan, and thus completed a course of discoveries which had been pursued with great steadiness, and with very little interruption, for near a century together.

while Columbus endeavoured to reach the East Indies by sailing westwards. Some years before this, while the expectations of Europe were in suspense about the projects of the Portuguese, of which the success appeared yet to be doubtful, a Genoese pilot formed the yet more daring project of sailing to the East Indies by the West. The situation of those countries was at that time very imperfectly known in Europe. The few European travellers who had been there had magnified the distance; perhaps through simplicity and ignorance, what was really very great, appearing almost infinite to those who could not measure it; or, perhaps, in order to increase somewhat more the marvellous of their own adventures in visiting regions so immensely remote from Europe. The longer the way was by the East, Columbus very justly concluded, the shorter it would be by the West. He proposed, therefore, to take that way, as both the shortest and the surest, and he had the good fortune to convince Isabella of Castile of the probability of his project. He sailed from the port of Palos in August 1492, near five years before the expedition of Vasco de Gama set out from Portugal, and, after a voyage of between two and three months, discovered first some of the small Bahama or Lucayan islands, and afterwards the great island of St. Domingo.

Columbus mistook the countries he found for the Indies. But the countries which Columbus discovered, either in this or in any of his subsequent voyages, had no resemblance to those which he had gone

---

[1] [Ed. 1 reads 'that of Congo, Angola and Loango'.]

in quest of. Instead of the wealth, cultivation and populousness of China and Indostan, he found, in St. Domingo, and in all the other parts of the new world which he ever visited, nothing but a country quite covered with wood, uncultivated, and inhabited only by some tribes of naked and miserable savages. He was not very willing, however, to believe that they were not the same with some of the countries described by Marco Polo, the first European who had visited, or at least had left behind him any description of China or the East Indies; and a very slight resemblance, such as that which he found between the name of Cibao, a mountain in St. Domingo, and that of Cipango, mentioned by Marco Polo, was frequently sufficient to make him return to this favourite prepossession, though contrary to the clearest evidence.[1] In his letters to Ferdinand and Isabella he called the countries which he had discovered, the Indies. He entertained no doubt but that they were the extremity of those which had been described by Marco Polo, and that they were not very distant from the Ganges, or from the countries which had been conquered by Alexander. Even when at last convinced that they were different, he still flattered himself that those rich countries were at no great distance, and in a subsequent voyage, accordingly, went in quest of them along the coast of Terra Firma, and towards the isthmus of Darien.

Hence the names East and West Indies. In consequence of this mistake of Columbus, the name of the Indies has stuck to those unfortunate countries ever since; and when it was at last clearly discovered that the new were altogether different from the old Indies, the former were called the West, in contradistinction to the latter, which were called the East Indies.

The countries discovered were not rich It was of importance to Columbus, however, that the countries which he had discovered, whatever they were, should be represented to the court of Spain as of very great consequence; and, in what constitutes the real riches of every country, the animal and vegetable productions of the soil, there was at that time nothing which could well justify such a representation of them.

in animals The Cori, something between a rat and a rabbit, and supposed by Mr. Buffon[2] to be the same with the Aperea of

---

[1] [P. F. X. de Charlevoix, *Histoire de l'Isle Espagnole ou de S. Domingue* ,1730, tom. i., p. 99.]
[2] [*Histoire Naturelle*, tom. xv. (1750), pp. 160, 162.]

Brazil, was the largest viviparous quadruped in St. Domingo. This species seems never to have been very numerous, and the dogs and cats of the Spaniards are said to have long ago almost entirely extirpated it, as well as some other tribes of a still smaller size.[1] These, however, together with a pretty large lizard, called the Ivana or Iguana,[2] constituted the principal part of the animal food which the land afforded.

or vegetables,   The vegetable food of the inhabitants, though from their want of industry not very abundant, was not altogether so scanty. It consisted in Indian corn, yams, potatoes, bananes, &c. plants which were then altogether unknown in Europe, and which have never since been very much esteemed in it, or supposed to yield a sustenance equal to what is drawn from the common sorts of grain and pulse, which have been cultivated in this part of the world time out of mind.

cotton being not then considered of great consequence.   The cotton plant indeed afforded the material of a very important manufacture, and was at that time to Europeans undoubtedly the most valuable of all the vegetable productions of those islands. But though in the end of the fifteenth century the muslins and other cotton goods of the East Indies were much esteemed in every part of Europe, the cotton manufacture itself was not cultivated in any part of it. Even this production, therefore, could not at that time appear in the eyes of Europeans to be of very great consequence.

So Columbus relied on the minerals.   Finding nothing either in the animals or vegetables of the newly discovered countries, which could justify a very advantageous representation of them, Columbus turned his view towards their minerals; and in the richness of the productions of this third kingdom, he flattered himself, he had found a full compensation for the insignificancy of those of the other two. The little bits of gold with which the inhabitants ornamented their dress, and which, he was informed, they frequently found in the rivulets and torrents that fell from the mountains, were sufficient to satisfy him that those mountains abounded with the richest gold mines. St. Domingo, therefore, was represented as a country abounding with gold, and, upon that account (according to the prejudices not only of the present times, but of those times), an inexhaustible source of real wealth to the crown and

[1] [Charlevoix, *Histoire de l'Isle Espagnole*, tom. i., pp. 35, 36.]
[2] [*Ibid.*, p. 27.]

kingdom of Spain. When Columbus, upon his return from his first voyage, was introduced with a sort of triumphal honours to the sovereigns of Castile and Arragon, the principal productions of the countries which he had discovered were carried in solemn procession before him. The only valuable part of them consisted in some little fillets, bracelets, and other ornaments of gold, and in some bales of cotton. The rest were mere objects of vulgar wonder and curiosity; some reeds of an extraordinary size, some birds of a very beautiful plumage, and some stuffed skins of the huge alligator and manati; all of which were preceded by six or seven of the wretched natives, whose singular colour and appearance added greatly to the novelty of the shew.

The Council of Castile was attracted by the gold, Columbus proposing that the government should have half the gold and silver discovered. In consequence of the representations of Columbus, the council of Castile determined to take possession of countries of which the inhabitants were plainly incapable of defending themselves. The pious purpose of converting them to Christianity sanctified the injustice of the project. But the hope of finding treasures of gold there, was the sole motive which prompted to undertake it; and to give this motive the greater weight, it was proposed by Columbus that the half of all the gold and silver that should be found there should belong to the crown. This proposal was approved of by the council.

This was an impossible tax and was soon reduced. As long as the whole or the far greater part of the gold, which the first adventurers imported into Europe, was got by so very easy a method as the plundering of the defenceless natives, it was not perhaps very difficult to pay even this heavy tax. But when the natives were once fairly stript of all that they had, which, in St. Domingo, and in all the other countries discovered by Columbus, was done completely in six or eight years, and when in order to find more it had become necessary to dig for it in the mines, there was no longer any possibility of paying this tax. The rigorous exaction of it, accordingly, first occasioned, it is said, the total abandoning of the mines of St. Domingo, which have never been wrought since. It was soon reduced therefore to a third; then to a fifth; afterwards to a tenth; and at last to a twentieth part of the gross produce of the gold mines.[1] The tax upon silver continued for a long time to be a fifth of the gross produce. It was reduced to a tenth only in the course of the

[1] [Above, vol. i., p. 190.]

present century.[1] But the first adventurers do not appear to have been much interested about silver. Nothing less precious than gold seemed worthy of their attention.

The subsequent Spanish enterprises were all prompted by the same motive. All the other enterprises of the Spaniards in the new world, subsequent to those of Columbus, seem to have been prompted by the same motive. It was the sacred thirst of gold that carried Oieda, Nicuessa, and Vasco Nugnes de Balboa, to the isthmus of Darien, that carried Cortez to Mexico, and Almagro and Pizzarro to Chili and Peru. When those adventurers arrived upon any unknown coast, their first enquiry was always if there was any gold to be found there; and according to the information which they received concerning this particular, they determined either to quit the country or to settle in it.

A prudent law-giver would not wish to encourage gold and silver mining, Of all those expensive and uncertain projects, however, which bring bankruptcy upon the greater part of the people who engage in them, there is none perhaps more perfectly ruinous than the search after new silver and gold mines. It is perhaps the most disadvantageous lottery in the world, or the one in which the gain of those who draw the prizes bears the least proportion to the loss of those who draw the blanks: for though the prizes are few and the blanks many, the common price of a ticket is the whole fortune of a very rich man. Projects of mining, instead of replacing the capital employed in them, together with the ordinary profits of stock, commonly absorb both capital and profit. They are the projects, therefore, to which of all others a prudent law-giver, who desired to increase the capital of his nation, would least chuse to give any extraordinary encouragement, or to turn towards them a greater share of that capital than what would go to them of its own accord. Such in reality is the absurd confidence which almost all men have in their own good fortune, that wherever there is the least probability of success, too great a share of it is apt to go to them of its own accord.

but people have always believed in an Eldorado. But though the judgment of sober reason and experience concerning such projects has always been extremely unfavourable, that of human avidity has commonly been quite otherwise. The same passion which has

---

[1] [Ed. 1 (in place of these two sentences) reads, 'The tax upon silver, indeed, still continues to be a fifth of the gross produce.' Cp. above, vol. i., p. 189.]

suggested to so many people the absurd idea of the philosopher's stone, has suggested to others the equally absurd one of immense rich mines of gold and silver. They did not consider that the value of those metals has, in all ages and nations, arisen chiefly from their scarcity, and that their scarcity has arisen from the very small quantities of them which nature has any where deposited in one place, from the hard and intractable substances with which she has almost every where surrounded those small quantities, and consequently from the labour and expence which are every where necessary in order to penetrate to and get at them. They flattered themselves that veins of those metals might in many places be found as large and as abundant as those which are commonly found of lead, or copper, or tin, or iron. The dream of Sir Walter Raleigh concerning the golden city and country of Eldorado,[1] may satisfy us, that even wise men are not always exempt from such strange delusions. More than a hundred years after the death of that great man, the Jesuit Gumila was still convinced of the reality of that wonderful country, and expressed with great warmth, and I dare to say, with great sincerity, how happy he should be to carry the light of the gospel to a people who could so well reward the pious labours of their missionary.[2]

In this case expectations were to some extent realised, so far as the Spaniards were concerned, In the countries first discovered by the Spaniards, no gold or silver mines are at present known which are supposed to be worth the working. The quantities of those metals which the first adventurers are said to have found there, had probably been very much magnified, as well as the fertility of the mines which were wrought immediately after the first discovery. What those adventurers were reported to have found, however, was sufficient to inflame the avidity of all their countrymen. Every Spaniard who sailed to

[1] ['That mighty, rich and beautiful empire of Guiana, and . . . that great and golden city which the Spaniards call El Dorado.'—Ralegh's *Works*, ed. Thomas Birch, 1751, vol. ii., p. 141.]

[2] [P. Jos. Gumilla, *Histoire naturelle civile et géographique de l'Orénoque, etc.*, traduite par M. Eidous, 1758, tom. ii., pp. 46, 117, 131, 132, 137, 138, but the sentiment is apparently attributed to the author, who is described on the title page as 'de la compagnie de Jésus, supérieur des missions de l'Orénoque,' on the strength of a mistranslation of the French or possibly the original Spanish. If 'Dieu permit' were mistranslated 'God permit,' the following passage from pp. 137, 138 would bear out the text: 'On cherchait une vallée ou un territoire dont les rochers et les pierres étaient d'or, et les Indiens pour flatter la cupidité des Espagnols, et les éloigner en même temps de chez eux, leur peignaient avec les couleurs les plus vives l'or dont ce pays abondait pour se débarrasser plutôt de ces hôtes incommodes, et Dieu permit que les Espagnols ajoutassent foi à ces rapports, pour qu'ils découvrissent un plus grand nombre de provinces, et que la lumière de l'Évangile pût s'y répandre avec plus de facilité.']

America expected to find an Eldorado. Fortune too did upon this what she has done upon very few other occasions. She realized in some measure the extravagant hopes of her votaries, and in the discovery and conquest of Mexico and Peru (of which the one happened about thirty, the other about forty years after the first expedition of Columbus), she presented them with something not very unlike that profusion of the precious metals which they sought for.

A project of commerce to the East Indies, therefore, gave occasion to the first discovery of the West. A project of conquest gave occasion to all the establishments of the Spaniards in those newly discovered countries. The motive which excited them to this conquest was a project of gold and silver mines; and a course of accidents, which no human wisdom could foresee, rendered this project much more successful than the undertakers had any reasonable grounds for expecting.

but the other nations were not so successful. The first adventurers of all the other nations of Europe, who attempted to make settlements in America, were animated by the like chimerical views; but they were not equally successful. It was more than a hundred years after the first settlement of the Brazils, before any silver, gold, or diamond mines were discovered there. In the English, French, Dutch, and Danish colonies, none have ever yet been discovered; at least none that are at present supposed to be worth the working. The first English settlers in North America, however, offered a fifth of all the gold and silver which should be found there to the king, as a motive for granting them their patents. In the patents to Sir Walter Raleigh, to the London and Plymouth companies, to the council of Plymouth, &c. this fifth was accordingly reserved to the crown. To the expectation of finding gold and silver mines, those first settlers too joined that of discovering a north-west passage to the East Indies. They have hitherto been disappointed in both.

PART SECOND

Causes of the Prosperity of new Colonies

The colony of a civilized nation which takes possession either of a waste country, or of one so thinly inhabited, that the natives easily give place to the new settlers, advances more rapidly to wealth and greatness than any other human society.

Colonists take out knowledge and regular government, The colonists carry out with them a knowledge of agriculture and of other useful arts, superior to what can grow up of its own accord in the course of many centuries among savage and barbarous nations. They carry out with them too the habit of subordination, some notion of the regular government which takes place in their own country, of the system of laws which supports[1] it, and of a regular administration of justice; and they naturally establish something of the same kind in the new settlement. But among savage and barbarous nations, the natural progress of law and government is still slower than the natural progress of arts, after law and government have been so far *land is plentiful and cheap,* established, as is necessary for their protection. Every colonist gets more land than he can possibly cultivate. He has no rent, and scarce any taxes to pay. No landlord shares with him in its produce, and the share of the sovereign is commonly but a trifle. He has every motive to render as great as possible a produce, which is thus to be almost entirely his own. But his land is commonly so extensive, that with all his own industry, and with all the industry of other people whom he can get to employ, he can seldom make it produce the tenth part of what it is capable of producing. He is eager, therefore, to collect labourers from all quarters, and to reward them with the most liberal wages. *wages are high,* but those liberal wages, joined to the plenty and cheapness of land, soon make those labourers leave him, in order to become landlords themselves, and to reward, with equal liberality, other labourers, who soon leave them for the same reason that they left their first master. The liberal reward of labour encourages marriage. The children, during the tender years of infancy, are *and children are taken care of and are profitable.* well fed and properly taken care of, and when they are grown up, the value of their labour greatly overpays their maintenance. When arrived at maturity, the high price of labour, and the low price of land, enable them to establish themselves in the same manner as their fathers did before them.

Population and improvement, which mean wealth and greatness, are encouraged. In other countries, rent and profit eat up wages, and the two superior orders of people oppress the inferior one. But in new colonies, the interest of the two superior orders obliges them to treat the inferior one with more generosity and humanity; at least, where

---

[1] [Eds. 1–4 reads 'support'.]

that inferior one is not in a state of slavery. Waste lands of the greatest natural fertility, are to be had for a trifle. The increase of revenue which the proprietor, who is always the undertaker, expects from their improvement constitutes his profit; which in these circumstances is commonly very great. But this great profit cannot be made without employing the labour of other people in clearing and cultivating the land; and the disproportion between the great extent of the land and the small number of the people, which commonly takes place in new colonies, makes it difficult for him to get this labour. He does not, therefore, dispute about wages, but is willing to employ labour at any price. The high wages of labour encourage population. The cheapness and plenty of good land encourage improvement, and enable the proprietor to pay those high wages. In those wages consists almost the whole price of the land; and though they are high, considered as the wages of labour, they are low, considered as the price of what is so very valuable. What encourages the progress of population and improvement, encourages that of real wealth and greatness.

The progress of the Greek colonies was very rapid. The progress of many of the ancient Greek colonies towards wealth and greatness, seems accordingly, to have been very rapid. In the course of a century or two, several of them appear to have rivalled, and even to have surpassed their mother cities. Syracuse and Agrigentum in Sicily, Tarentum and Locri in Italy, Ephesus and Miletus in Lesser Asia, appear by all accounts to have been at least equal to any of the cities of ancient Greece. Though posterior in their establishment, yet all the arts of refinement, philosophy, poetry, and eloquence, seem to have been cultivated as early, and to have been improved as highly in them, as in any part of the mother country. The schools of the two oldest Greek philosophers, those of Thales and Pythagoras, were established, it is remarkable, not in ancient Greece, but the one in an Asiatic, the other in an Italian colony.[1] All those colonies had established themselves in countries inhabited by savage and barbarous nations, who easily gave place to the new settlers. They had plenty of good land, and as they were altogether independent of the mother city, they were at liberty to manage their own affairs in the way that they judged was most suitable to their own interest.

[Miletus and Crotona.]

That of the Roman colonies much less so. The history of the Roman colonies is by no means so brilliant. Some of them, indeed, such as Florence, have in the course of many ages, and after the fall of the mother city, grown up to be considerable states. But the progress of no one of them seems ever to have been very rapid. They were all established in conquered provinces, which in most cases had been fully inhabited before. The quantity of land assigned to each colonist was seldom very considerable, and as the colony was not independent, they were not always at liberty to manage their own affairs in the way that they judged was most suitable to their own interest.

The American colonies have had plenty of land and not very much interference from their mother countries. In the plenty of good land, the European colonies established in America and the West Indies resemble, and even greatly surpass, those of ancient Greece. In their dependency upon the mother state, they resemble those of ancient Rome; but their great distance from Europe has in all of them alleviated more or less the effects of this dependency. Their situation has placed them less in the view and less in the power of their mother country. In pursuing their interest their own way, their conduct has, upon many occasions, been overlooked, either because not known or not understood in Europe; and upon some occasions it has been fairly suffered and submitted to, because their distance rendered it difficult to restrain it. Even the violent and arbitrary government of Spain has, upon many occasions, been obliged to recall or soften the orders which had been given for the government of her[1] colonies, for fear of a general insurrection. The progress of all the European colonies in wealth, population, and improvement, has accordingly been very great.

The progress of the Spanish colonies, Mexico and Peru, has been very considerable. The crown of Spain, by its share of the gold and silver, derived some revenue from its colonies, from the moment of their first establishment. It was a revenue too, of a nature to excite in human avidity the most extravagant expectations of still greater riches. The Spanish colonies, therefore, from the moment of their first establishment, attracted very much the attention of their mother country; while those of the other European nations were for a long time in a great measure neglected. The former did not, perhaps, thrive the better in consequence of this attention; nor the latter the worse

[1] [Ed. 1 reads 'its'.]

in consequence of this neglect. In proportion to the extent of the country which they in some measure possess, the Spanish colonies are considered as less populous and thriving than those of almost any other European nation. The progress even of the Spanish colonies, however, in population and improvement, has certainly been very rapid and very great. The city of Lima, founded since the conquest, is represented by Ulloa, as containing fifty thousand inhabitants near thirty years ago.[1] Quito, which had been but a miserable hamlet of Indians, is represented by the same author as in his time equally populous.[2] Gemelli Carreri, a pretended traveller, it is said, indeed, but who seems every where to have written upon extreme good information, represents the city of Mexico as containing a hundred thousand inhabitants;[3] a number which, in spite of all the exaggerations of the Spanish writers, is, probably, more than five times greater than what it contained in the time of Montezuma. These numbers exceed greatly those of Boston, New York, and Philadelphia, the three greatest cities of the English colonies. Before the conquest of the Spaniards there were no cattle fit for draught either in Mexico or Peru. The lama was their only beast of burden, and its strength seems to have been a good deal inferior to that of a common ass. The plough was unknown among them. They were ignorant of the use of iron. They had no coined money, nor any established instrument of commerce of any kind. Their commerce was carried on by barter. A sort of wooden spade was their principal instrument of agriculture. Sharp stones served them for knives and hatchets to cut with; fish bones and the hard sinews of certain animals served them for needles to sew with; and these seem to have been their principal instruments of trade.[4] In this state of things, it seems impossible, that either of these empires could have been so much improved or so well cultivated as at present, when they are plentifully furnished with all sorts of European cattle, and when the use of iron, of the plough, and of many of the arts of Europe, has been introduced among them. But the populousness of every country must be in proportion to the degree of its improvement and cultivation. In spite of the cruel destruction of the natives which followed the conquest, these two great empires are, probably,

---

[1] [See above, vol. i., p. 226.]

[2] [Juan and Ulloa, *Voyage historique*, tom. i., p. 229.]

[3] [In Awnsham and John Churchill's *Collection of Voyages and Travels*, 1704, vol. iv., p. 508.]

[4] [Cp. above, vol. i., pp. 225, 226.

more populous now than they ever were before: and the people are surely very different; for we must acknowledge, I apprehend, that the Spanish creoles are in many respects superior to the ancient Indians.

The Portuguese colony of Brazil is very populous. After the settlements of the Spaniards, that of the Portugueze in Brazil is the oldest of any European nation in America. But as for a long time after the first discovery, neither gold nor silver mines were found in it, and as it afforded, upon that account, little or no revenue to the crown, it was for a long time in a great measure neglected; and during this state of neglect, it grew up to be a great and powerful colony. While Portugal was under the dominion of Spain, Brazil was attacked by the Dutch, who got possession of seven of the fourteen provinces into which it is divided. They expected soon to conquer the other seven, when Portugal recovered its independency by the elevation of the family of Braganza to the throne. The Dutch then, as enemies to the Spaniards, became friends to the Portugueze, who were likewise the enemies of the Spaniards. They agreed, therefore, to leave that part of Brazil, which they had not conquered, to the king of Portugal, who agreed to leave that part which they had conquered to them, as a matter not worth disputing about with such good allies. But the Dutch Government soon began to oppress the Portugueze colonists, who, instead of amusing themselves with complaints, took arms against their new masters, and by their own valour and resolution, with the connivance, indeed, but without any avowed assistance from the mother country, drove them out of Brazil. The Dutch, therefore, finding it impossible to keep any part of the country to themselves, were contented that it should be entirely restored to the crown of Portugal.[1] In this colony there are said to be more than six hundred thousand people,[2] either Portugueze or descended from Portugueze, creoles, mulattoes, and a mixed race between Portugueze and Brazilians. No one colony in America is supposed to contain so great a number of people of European extraction.

When Spain declined, various countries obtained a footing in America. Towards the end of the fifteenth, and during the greater part of the sixteenth century, Spain and Portugal were the two great naval powers upon the ocean: for though the commerce of Venice

---

[1] [Raynal, *Histoire philosophique*, Amsterdam ed., 1773, tom. iii., pp. 347–352.]
[2] [*Ibid.*, tom. iii., p. 424.]

extended to every part of Europe, its fleets had scarce ever sailed beyond the Mediterranean. The Spaniards, in virtue of the first discovery, claimed all America as their own; and though they could not hinder so great a naval power as that of Portugal from settling in Brazil, such was, at that time, the terror of their name, that the greater part of the other nations of Europe were afraid to establish themselves in any other part of that great continent. The French, who attempted to settle in Florida, were all murdered by the Spaniards.[1] But the declension of the naval power of this latter nation, in consequence of the defeat or miscarriage of, what they called, their Invincible Armada, which happened towards the end of the sixteenth century, put it out of their power to obstruct any longer the settlements of the other European nations. In the course of the seventeenth century, therefore, the English, French, Dutch, Danes, and Swedes, all the great nations who had any ports upon the ocean, attempted to make some settlements in the new world.

The Swedish colony of New Jersey was prospering when swallowed up by New York. The Swedes established themselves in New Jersey; and the number of Swedish families still to be found there, sufficiently demonstrates, that this colony was very likely to prosper, had it been protected by the mother country. But being neglected by Sweden it was soon swallowed up by the Dutch colony of New York, which again, in 1674,[2] fell under the dominion of the English.

The Danish colonies of St. Thomas and Santa Cruz have been very prosperous since the exclusive company was dissolved. The small islands of St. Thomas and Santa Cruz are the only countries in the new world that have ever been possessed by the Danes. These little settlements too were under the government of an exclusive company, which had the sole right, both of purchasing the surplus produce of the colonists, and of supplying them with such goods of other countries as they wanted, and which, therefore, both in its purchases and sales, had not only the power of oppressing them, but the greatest temptation to do so. The government of an exclusive company of merchants is, perhaps, the worst of all governments for any country whatever. It was not, however, able to stop altogether the progress of these colonies, though it rendered it more slow and languid. The late king of

---

[1] [Raynal, tom. vi., p. 8.]
[2] [A mistake for 1664.]

Denmark dissolved this company, and since that time the prosperity of these colonies has been very great.

The Dutch colony of Surinam is prosperous though still under an exclusive company. The Dutch settlements in the West, as well as those in the East Indies, were originally put under the government of an exclusive company. The progress of some of them, therefore, though it has been considerable, in comparison with that of almost any country that has been long peopled and established, has been languid and slow in comparison with that of the greater part of new colonies. The colony of Surinam, though very considerable, is still inferior to the greater part of the sugar colonies of the other European nations. The colony of Nova Belgia, now divided into the two provinces of New York and New Jersey, would probably have soon become considerable too, even though it had remained under the government of the Dutch. The plenty and cheapness of good land are such powerful causes of prosperity, that the very worst government is scarce capable of checking altogether the efficacy of their operation. The great distance too from the mother country would enable the colonists to evade more or less, by smuggling, the monopoly which the company enjoyed against them. At present the company allows all Dutch ships to trade to Surinam upon paying two and a half per cent. upon the value of their cargo for a licence; and only reserves to itself exclusively the direct trade from Africa to America, which consists almost entirely in the slave trade. This relaxation in the exclusive privileges of the company, is probably the principal cause of that degree of prosperity which that colony at present enjoys. Curaçoa and Eustatia, the two principal islands belonging to the Dutch, are free ports open to the ships of all nations; and this freedom, in the midst of better colonies whose ports are open to those of one nation only, has been the great cause of the prosperity of those two barren islands.

The French colony of Canada has shown rapid progress since the dissolution of the exclusive company. The French colony of Canada was, during the greater part of the last century, and some part of the present, under the government of an exclusive company. Under so unfavourable an administration its progress was necessarily very slow in comparison with that of other new colonies; but it became much more rapid when this company was dissolved after the fall of what is called the Mississippi scheme. When the English got possession of this country, they found in it near double the number of inhabitants which father Charlevoix had assigned to it between twenty and thirty years before.[1] That jesuit had travelled over the whole country, and had no inclination to represent it as less considerable than it really was.

St. Domingo, in spite of various obstacles, and the other French sugar colonies, are very thriving. The French colony of St. Domingo was established by pirates and free-booters, who, for a long time, neither required the protection, nor acknowledged the authority of France; and when that[2] race of banditti became so far citizens as to acknowledge this authority, it was for a long time necessary to exercise it with very great gentleness. During this period the population and improvement of this colony increased very fast. Even the oppression of the exclusive company, to which it was for some time subjected, with all the other colonies of France, though it no doubt retarded, had not been able to stop its progress altogether. The course of its prosperity returned as soon as it was relieved from that oppression. It is now the most important of the sugar colonies of the West Indies, and its produce is said to be greater than that of all the English sugar colonies put together. The other sugar colonies of France are in general all very thriving.

But the progress of the English colonies has been the most rapid. But there are no colonies of which the progress has been more rapid than that of the English in North America.

Plenty of good land, and liberty to manage their own affairs their own way, seem to be the two great causes of the prosperity of all new colonies.

They have not so much good land as the Spanish and Portuguese, but their institutions are more favourable to its improvement. In the plenty of good land the English colonies of North America, though, no doubt, very abundantly provided, are, however, inferior to those of the Spaniards and Portuguese, and not superior to some of those possessed by the French before the late war. But the political institutions of the English colonies have been more favourable to the improvement and cultivation of this land, than those of any of the other three nations.

(1) The engrossing of uncultivated land has been more restrained. First, the engrossing of uncultivated land, though it has by no means been prevented altogether, has been more restrained in the English colonies than

---

[1] [P. F. X. de Charlevoix, *Histoire et description générale de la Nouvelle France, avec le journal historique d'un voyage dans l'Amérique Septentrionnale*, 1744, tom. ii., p. 390, speaks of a population of 20,000 to 25,000 in 1713. Raynal says in 1753 and 1758 the population, excluding troops and Indians, was 91,000.—*Histoire philosophique*, Amsterdam ed., 1773, tom. vi., p. 137.]   [2] [Ed. 1 reads 'the'.]

in any other. The colony law which imposes upon every proprietor the obligation of improving and cultivating, within a limited time, a certain proportion of his lands, and which, in case of failure, declares those neglected lands grantable to any other person; though it has not, perhaps, been very strictly executed, has, however, had some effect.

(2) Primogeniture and entails are less prevalent and alienation more frequent. Secondly, in Pennsylvania there is no right of primogeniture, and lands, like moveables, are divided equally among all the children of the family. In three of the provinces of New England the oldest has only a double share, as in the Mosaical law. Though in those provinces, therefore, too great a quantity of land should sometimes be engrossed by a particular individual, it is likely, in the course of a generation or two, to be sufficiently divided again. In the other English colonies, indeed, the right of primogeniture takes place, as in the law of England. But in all the English colonies the tenure of the[1] lands, which are all held by free socage, facilitates alienation, and the grantee of any extensive tract of land, generally finds it for his interest to alienate, as fast as he can, the greater part of it, reserving only a small quit-rent. In the Spanish and Portugueze colonies, what is called the right of Majorazzo[2] takes place in the succession of all those great estates to which any title of honour is annexed. Such estates go all to one person, and are in effect entailed and unalienable. The French colonies, indeed, are subject to the custom of Paris, which, in the inheritance of land, is much more favourable to the younger children than the law of England. But, in the French colonies, if any part of an estate, held by the noble tenure of chivalry and homage, is alienated, it is, for a limited time, subject to the right of redemption, either by the heir of the superior or by the heir of the family; and all the largest estates of the country are held by such noble tenures, which necessarily embarrass alienation. But, in a new colony, a great uncultivated estate is likely to be much more speedily divided by alienation than by succession. The plenty and cheapness of good land, it has already been observed,[3] are the principal causes of the rapid prosperity of new colonies. The engrossing of land, in effect, destroys this plenty and cheapness.[4] The engrossing of uncultivated land, besides, is the greatest

---

[1] [Eds. 1 and 2 read 'their'.]
[2] Jus Majoratus. [Ed. 1 reads 'mayorazzo' in the text and 'mayoratus' in the note.]
[3] [Above, pp. 76, 77, and cp. vol. i., p. 104.]
[4] [This and the preceding sentence, beginning 'The plenty' are not in ed. 1.]

obstruction to its improvement. But the labour[1] that is employed
in the improvement and cultivation of land affords the greatest and
most valuable produce to the society. The produce of labour, in
this case,[2] pays not only its own wages, and the profit of the stock
which employs it, but the rent of the land too upon which it is
employed. The labour of the English colonists, therefore, being
more employed in the improvement and cultivation of land, is
likely to afford a greater and more valuable produce, than that of
any of the other three nations, which, by the engrossing of land, is
more or less diverted towards other employments.

(3) *Taxes are*   Thirdly, the labour of the English colonists is not
more moderate.   only likely to afford a greater and more valuable
produce, but, in consequence of the moderation of their taxes, a
greater proportion of this produce belongs to themselves, which they
may store up and employ in putting into motion a still greater
quantity of labour. The English colonists have never yet contributed
any thing towards the defence of the mother country, or towards
the support of its civil government. They themselves, on the contrary, have hitherto been defended almost entirely at the expence
of the mother country. But the expence of fleets and armies is out
of all proportion greater than the necessary expence of civil government. The expence of their own civil government has always been
very moderate. It has generally been confined to what was necessary
for paying competent salaries to the governor, to the judges, and to
some other officers of police, and for maintaining a few of the most
useful public works. The expence of the civil establishment of
Massachusett's Bay, before the commencement of the present[3] disturbances, used to be but about 18,000 l. a year. That of New
Hampshire and Rhode Island 3,500 l. each. That of Connecticut
4,000 l. That of New York and Pennsylvania 4,500 l. each. That of
New Jersey 1,200 l. That of Virginia and South Carolina 8,000 l.
each. The civil establishments of Nova Scotia and Georgia are partly
supported by an annual grant of parliament. But Nova Scotia pays,
besides, about 7,000 l. a year towards the public expences of the
colony; and Georgia about 2,500 l. a year. All the different civil

---

[1] [Ed. 1 reads 'The engrossing, however, of uncultivated land, it has already been
observed, is the greatest obstruction to its improvement and cultivation, and the
labour'.]

[2] [Ed. 1 reads 'Its produce in this case'.]

[3] [All eds. read 'present' here and on p. 98, but 'late' on p. 90. See above, vol. i.,
p. 524, note, and below, p. 475.]

establishments in North America, in short, exclusive of those of Maryland and North Carolina, of which no exact account has been got, did not, before the commencement of the present disturbances, cost the inhabitants above 64,700 l. a year;[1] an ever-memorable example at how small an expence three millions of people may not only be governed, but well governed. The most important part of the expence of government, indeed, that of defence and protection, has constantly fallen upon the mother country. The ceremonial too of the civil government in the colonies, upon the reception of a new governor, upon the opening of a new assembly, &c. though sufficiently decent, is not accompanied with any expensive pomp or parade. Their ecclesiastical government is conducted upon a plan equally frugal. Tithes are unknown among them; and their clergy, who are far from being numerous, are maintained either by moderate stipends, or by the voluntary contributions of the people. The power of Spain and Portugal, on the contrary, derives some support from the taxes levied upon their colonies. France, indeed, has never drawn any considerable revenue from its colonies, the taxes which it levies upon them being generally spent among them. But the colony government of all these three nations is conducted upon a much more expensive plan, and is accompanied with a much more expensive ceremonial. The sums spent upon the reception of a new viceroy of Peru, for example, have frequently been enormous.[2] Such ceremonials are not only real taxes paid by the rich colonists upon those particular occasions, but they serve to introduce among them the habit of vanity and expence upon all other occasions. They are not only very grievous occasional taxes, but they contribute to establish perpetual taxes of the same kind still more grievous; the ruinous taxes of private luxury and extravagance. In the colonies of all those three nations too, the ecclesiastical government is extremely oppressive. Tithes take place in all of them, and are levied with the utmost rigour in those of Spain and Portugal. All of them besides are oppressed with a numerous race of mendicant friars, whose beggary being not only licensed, but consecrated by religion, is a most grievous tax upon the poor people, who are most carefully taught that it is a duty to give, and a very great sin to refuse them their charity. Over and above all this, the clergy are, in all of them, the greatest engrossers of land.

[1] [The figures are evidently from the 'very exact account' quoted below, p. 475.]

[2] [Juan and Ulloa, *Voyage historique*, tom. i., pp. 437-441, give a lurid account of the magnificence of the ceremonial.]

(4) The trade monopoly of the mother country has been less oppressive, Fourthly, in the disposal of their surplus produce, or of what is over and above their own consumption, the English colonies have been more favoured, and have been allowed a more extensive market, than those of any other European nation. Every European nation has endeavoured more or less to monopolize to itself the commerce of its colonies, and, upon that account, has prohibited the ships of foreign nations from trading to them, and has prohibited them from importing European goods from any foreign nation. But the manner in which this monopoly has been exercised in different nations has been very different.

since there has been no exclusive company with its interest to buy the produce of the colonies as cheap as possible, Some nations have given up the whole commerce of their colonies to an exclusive company, of whom the colonies were obliged to buy all such European goods as they wanted, and to whom they were obliged to sell the whole of their own surplus produce. It was the interest of the company, therefore, not only to sell the former as dear, and to buy the latter as cheap as possible, but to buy no more of the latter, even at this low price, than what they could dispose of for a very high price in Europe. It was their interest, not only to degrade in all cases the value of the surplus produce of the colony, but in many cases to discourage and keep down the natural increase of its quantity. Of all the expedients that can well be contrived to stunt the natural growth of a new colony, that of an exclusive company is undoubtedly the most effectual. This, however, has been the policy of Holland, though their company, in the course of the present century, has given up in many respects the exertion of their exclusive privilege. This too was the policy of Denmark till the reign of the late king. It has occasionally been the policy of France, and of late, since 1755, after it had been abandoned by all other nations, on account of its absurdity, it has become the policy of Portugal with regard at least to two of the principal provinces of Brazil, Fernambuco and Marannon.[1]

nor any restriction of commerce to a particular port and to particular licensed ships, Other nations, without establishing an exclusive company, have confined the whole commerce of their colonies to a particular port of the mother country, from whence no ship was allowed to sail, but either in a fleet and at a particular season, or, if single, in

---

[1] [Maranon in 1755 and Fernambuco four years later.—Raynal, *Histoire philosophique*, Amsterdam ed., 1773, tom. iii., p. 402.]

consequence of a particular licence, which in most cases was very well paid for. This policy opened, indeed, the trade of the colonies to all the natives of the mother country, provided they traded from the proper port, at the proper season, and in the proper vessels. But as all the different merchants, who joined their stocks in order to fit out those licensed vessels, would find it for their interest to act in concert, the trade which was carried on in this manner would necessarily be conducted very nearly upon the same principles as that of an exclusive company. The profit of those merchants would be almost equally exorbitant and oppressive. The colonies would be ill supplied, and would be obliged both to buy very dear, and to sell very cheap. This, however, till within these few years, had[1] always been the policy of Spain, and the price of all European goods, accordingly, is said to have been[2] enormous in the Spanish West Indies. At Quito, we are told by Ulloa, a pound of iron sold for about four and six-pence, and a pound of steel for about six and nine-pence sterling.[3] But it is chiefly in order to purchase European goods, that the colonies part with their own produce. The more, therefore, they pay for the one, the less they really get for the other, and the dearness of the one is the same thing with the cheapness of the other. The policy of Portugal is in this respect the same as the ancient policy of Spain,[4] with regard to all its colonies, except Fernambuco and Marannon, and with regard to these it has lately adopted a still worse.

but freedom for every subject to trade with every port in the mother country,   Other nations leave the trade of their colonies free to all their subjects, who may carry it on from all the different ports of the mother country, and who have occasion for no other licence than the common dispatches of the customhouse. In this case the number and dispersed situation of the different traders renders it impossible for them to enter into any general combination, and their competition is sufficient to hinder them from making very exorbitant profits. Under so liberal a policy the colonies are enabled both to sell their own produce and to buy the goods of Europe at a reasonable price. But since the dissolution of the Plymouth company, when our colonies were but in their infancy, this has always been the policy of England. It has generally too been that of France, and has been

---

[1] [Ed. 1 reads 'This, however, has'.]   [2] [Ed. 1 reads 'said to be'.]
[3] [Iron sometimes at 100 écus the quintal and steel at 150.—Juan and Ulloa, *Voyage historique*, tom. i., p. 252.]
[4] [Ed. 1 reads 'the same as that of Spain'.]

uniformly so since the dissolution of what, in England, is commonly called their Mississippi company. The profits of the trade, therefore, which France and England carry on with their colonies, though no doubt somewhat higher than if the competition was free to all other nations, are, however, by no means exorbitant; and the price of European goods accordingly is not extravagantly high in the greater part of the colonies of either of those nations.

and freedom to export everything but the enumerated commodities to other places besides the mother country. In the exportation of their own surplus produce too, it is only with regard to certain commodities that the colonies of Great Britain are confined to the market of the mother country. These commodities having been enumerated in the act of navigation and in some other subsequent acts, have upon that account been called *enumerated commodities*.[1] The rest are called *non-enumerated*; and may be exported directly to other countries, provided it is in British or Plantation ships, of which the owners and three-fourths of the mariners are British subjects.

Some most important productions are not enumerated, Among the non-enumerated commodities are some of the most important productions of America and the West Indies; grain of all sorts, lumber, salt provisions, fish, sugar, and rum.

as grain, Grain is naturally the first and principal object of the culture of all new colonies. By allowing them a very extensive market for it, the law encourages them to extend this culture much beyond the consumption of a thinly inhabited country, and thus to provide beforehand an ample subsistence for a continually increasing population.

timber, In a country quite covered with wood, where timber consequently is of little or no value, the expence of clearing the ground is the principal obstacle to improvement. By allowing the colonies a very extensive market for their lumber, the law endeavours to facilitate improvement by raising the price of a commodity which would otherwise be of little value, and thereby enabling them to make some profit of what would otherwise be mere expence.

cattle, In a country neither half-peopled nor half cultivated, cattle naturally multiply beyond the consumption of the inhabitants, and are often upon that account of little or no value.

---

[1] [The commodities originally enumerated in 12 Car. II., c. 18, § 18, were sugar, tobacco, cotton-wool, indigo, ginger, fustic and other dyeing woods.]

But it is necessary, it has already been shewn,[1] that the price of cattle should bear a certain proportion to that of corn before the greater part of the lands of any country can be improved. By allowing to American cattle, in all shapes, dead and alive, a very extensive market, the law endeavours to raise the value of a commodity of which the high price is so very essential to improvement. The good effects of this liberty, however, must be somewhat diminished by the 4th of George III. c. 15. which puts hides and skins among the enumerated commodities, and thereby tends to reduce the value of American cattle.

fish,   To increase the shipping and naval power of Great Britain, by the extension of the fisheries of our colonies, is an object which the legislature seems to have had almost constantly in view. Those fisheries, upon this account, have had all the encouragement which freedom can give them, and they have flourished accordingly. The New England fishery in particular was, before the late[2] disturbances, one of the most important, perhaps in the world. The whale-fishery which, notwithstanding an extravagant bounty, is in Great Britain carried on to so little purpose, that in the opinion of many people (which I do not, however, pretend to warrant) the whole produce does not much exceed the value of the bounties which are annually paid for it, is in New England carried on without any bounty to a very great extent. Fish is one of the principal articles with which the North Americans trade to Spain, Portugal, and the Mediterranean.

sugar,   Sugar was originally an enumerated commodity which could be exported only to Great Britain. But in 1731, upon a representation of the sugar-planters, its exportation was permitted to all parts of the world.[3] The restrictions,[4] however, with which this liberty was granted, joined to the high price of sugar in Great Britain, have rendered it, in a great measure, ineffectual. Great Britain and her colonies still continue to be almost the sole market for all the sugar produced in the British plantations. Their consumption increases so fast, that, though in consequence of the increasing improvement of Jamaica, as well as of the Cedel Islands,[5] the impor-

---

[1] [Above, vol. i., pp. 165, 166, 244, 245.]   [2] [See above, p. 85, note 3.]

[3] [There seems to be some mistake here. The true date is apparently 1739, under the Act 12 Geo. II., c. 30.]

[4] [Ships not going to places south of Cape Finisterre were compelled to call at some port in Great Britain.]

[5] [Garnier, in his note to this passage, tom. iii., p. 323, points out that the islands ceded by the peace of Paris in 1763 were only Grenada and the Grenadines, but that the

tation of sugar has increased very greatly within these twenty years, the exportation to foreign countries is said to be not much greater than before.

and rum.   Rum is a very important article in the trade which the Americans carry on to the coast of Africa, from which they bring back negroe slaves in return.

Grain, meat and fish would have competed too strongly with British produce if forced into the British market.   If the whole surplus produce of America in grain of all sorts, in salt provisions, and in fish, had been put into the enumeration, and thereby forced into the market of Great Britain, it would have interfered too much with the produce of the industry of our own people. It was probably not so much from any regard to the interest of America, as from a jealousy of this interference, that those important commodities have not only been kept out of the enumeration, but that the importation into Great Britain of all grain, except rice, and of salt provisions, has, in the ordinary state of the law, been prohibited.

Originally non-enumerated commodities could be exported to any part of the world. Recently they have been confined to countries south of Cape Finisterre.   The non-enumerated commodities could originally be exported to all parts of the world. Lumber and rice, having been once put into the enumeration, when they were afterwards taken out of it, were confined, as to the European market, to the countries that lie south of Cape Finisterre.[1] By the 6th of George III. c. 52. all non-enumerated commodities were subjected to the like restriction. The parts of Europe which lie south of Cape Finisterre, are not manufacturing countries, and we were less jealous of the colony ships carrying home from them any manufactures which could interfere with our own.

The enumerated commodities are (1) commodities not produced at all in the mother country, and (2) commodities of which only a small part of the supply is produced in the mother country.   The enumerated commodities are of two sorts: first, such as are either the peculiar produce of America, or as cannot be produced, or at least are not produced, in the mother country. Of this kind are, melasses, coffee, cacao-nuts, tobacco, pimento, ginger, whale-fins, raw silk, cotton-wool, beaver, and other peltry of America, indigo, fustic, and other dying woods: secondly, such as are not the peculiar produce of America, but which are and may be produced in the

term here includes the other islands won during the war, St. Vincent, Dominica and Tobago, which are mentioned below, p. 481.]

[1] [Rice was put in by 3 and 4 Ann, c. 5, and taken out by 3 Geo. II., c. 28; timber was taken out by 5 Geo. III., c. 45.]

mother country, though not in such quantities as to supply the greater part of her demand, which is principally supplied from foreign countries. Of this kind are all naval stores, masts, yards, and bowsprits, tar, pitch, and turpentine, pig and bar iron, copper ore, hides and skins, pot and pearl ashes. The largest importation of commodities of the first kind could not discourage the growth or interfere with the sale of any part of the produce of the mother country. By confining them to the home market, our merchants, it was expected, would not only be enabled to buy them cheaper in the Plantations, and consequently to sell them with a better profit at home, but to establish between the Plantations and foreign countries an advantageous carrying trade, of which Great Britain was necessarily to be the center or emporium, as the European country into which those commodities were first to be imported. The importation of commodities of the second kind might be so managed too, it was supposed, as to interfere, not with the sale of those of the same kind which were produced at home, but with that of those which were imported from foreign countries; because, by means of proper duties, they might be rendered always somewhat dearer than the former, and yet a good deal cheaper than the latter. By confining such commodities to the home market, therefore, it was proposed to discourage the produce, not of Great Britain, but of some foreign countries with which the balance of trade was believed to be unfavourable to Great Britain.

On the importation of naval stores to Great Britain a bounty was given. The prohibition of exporting from the colonies, to any other country but Great Britain, masts, yards, and bowsprits, tar, pitch, and turpentine, naturally tended to lower the price of timber in the colonies, and consequently to increase the expence of clearing their lands, the principal obstacle to their improvement. But about the beginning of the present century, in 1703, the pitch and tar company of Sweden endeavoured to raise the price of their commodities to Great Britain, by prohibiting their exportation, except in their own ships, at their own price, and in such quantities as they thought proper.[1] In order to counteract this notable piece of mercantile policy, and to render herself as much as possible independent, not only of Sweden, but of all the other northern powers, Great Britain gave a bounty upon the importation of naval stores from America[2] and the effect of this

[1] [Anderson, *Commerce*, A.D. 1703.]
[2] [Details are given below, p. 162, in a chapter not contained in eds. 1 and 2.]

bounty was to raise the price of timber in America, much more than the confinement to the home market could lower it; and as both regulations were enacted at the same time, their joint effect was rather to encourage than to discourage the clearing of land in America.

American pig iron is exempt from duty. Though pig and bar iron too have been put among the enumerated commodities, yet as, when imported from America, they are exempted from considerable duties to which they are subject when imported from any other country,[1] the one part of the regulation contributes more to encourage the erection of furnaces in America, than the other to discourage it. There is no manufacture which occasions so great a consumption of wood as a furnace, or which can contribute so much to the clearing of a country over-grown with it.

These regulations have raised the value of timber and thus helped to clear the country. The tendency of some of these regulations to raise the value of timber in America, and thereby to facilitate the clearing of the land, was neither, perhaps, intended nor understood by the legislature. Though their beneficial effects, however, have been in this respect accidental, they have not upon that account been less real.

Freedom of trade prevails between the British American colonies and the British West Indies. The most perfect freedom of trade is permitted between the British colonies of America and the West Indies, both in the enumerated and in the non-enumerated commodities. Those colonies are now become so populous and thriving, that each of them finds in some of the others a great and extensive market for every part of its produce. All of them taken together, they make a great internal market for the produce of one another.

British liberality does not extend to refined manufactures. The liberality of England, however, towards the trade of her colonies has been confined chiefly to what concerns the market for their produce, either in its rude state, or in what may be called the very first stage of manufacture. The more advanced or more refined manufactures even of the colony produce, the merchants and manufacturers of Great Britain chuse to reserve to themselves, and have prevailed upon the legislature to prevent their establishment in the colonies, sometimes by high duties, and sometimes by absolute prohibitions.

Manufactured sugar is subject to heavy duty. While, for example, Muskovado sugars from the British plantations, pay upon importation only 6 s. 4 d. the hundred weight ; white sugars pay

[1] [23 Geo. II., c. 29.]

1 l. 1 s. 1 d.; and refined, either double or single, in loaves 4 l. 2 s. 5 d. $\frac{8}{20}$. When those high duties were imposed, Great Britain was the sole, and she still continues to be the principal market to which the sugars of the British colonies could be exported. They amounted, therefore, to a prohibition, at first of claying or refining sugar for any foreign market, and at present of claying or refining it for the market, which takes off, perhaps, more than nine-tenths of the whole produce. The manufacture of claying or refining sugar accordingly, though it has flourished in all the sugar colonies of France, has been little cultivated in any of those of England, except for the market of the colonies themselves. While Grenada was in the hands of the French, there was a refinery of sugar, by claying at least, upon almost every plantation. Since it fell into those of the English, almost all works of this kind have been given up, and there are at present, October 1773, I am assured, not above two or three remaining in the island. At present, however, by an indulgence of the custom-house, clayed or refined sugar, if reduced from loaves into powder, is commonly imported as Muskovado.

Steel furnaces and slit-mills may not be erected in the colonies. While Great Britain encourages in America the manufactures of pig and bar iron, by exempting them from duties to which the like commodities are subject when imported from any other country, she imposes an absolute prohibition upon the erection of steel furnaces and slit-mills in any of her American plantations.[1] She will not suffer her colonists to work in those more refined manufactures even for their own consumption; but insists upon their purchasing of her merchants and manufacturers all goods of this kind which they have occasion for.

Hats, wools and woollen goods produced in America may not be carried in bulk from province to province. She prohibits the exportation from one province to another by water, and even the carriage by land upon horseback or in a cart, of hats, of wools and woollen goods,[2] of the produce of America; a regulation which effectually prevents the establishment of any manufacture of such commodities for distant sale, and confines the industry of her colonists in this way to such coarse and household manufactures, as a private family commonly makes for

[1] [23 Geo. II., c. 29. Anderson, *Commerce*, A.D. 1750.]
[2] [Hats under 5 Geo. II., c. 22; wools under 10 and 11 W. III., c. 10. See Anderson, *Commerce*, A.D. 1732 and 1699.]

its own use, or for that of some of its neighbours in the same province.

Such prohibitions, To prohibit a great people, however, from making
though a violation all that they can of every part of their own produce,
of sacred rights, or from employing their stock and industry in the
have not as yet
been very hurtful. way that they judge most advantageous to themselves, is a manifest violation of the most sacred rights of mankind.
Unjust, however, as such prohibitions may be, they have not
hitherto been very hurtful to the colonies. Land is still so cheap, and,
consequently, labour so dear among them, that they can import
from the mother country, almost all the more refined or more
advanced manufactures cheaper than they could make them for
themselves. Though they had not, therefore, been prohibited from
establishing such manufactures, yet in their present state of improvement, a regard to their own interest would, probably, have prevented them from doing so. In their present state of improvement,
those prohibitions, perhaps, without cramping their industry, or
restraining it from any employment to which it would have gone
of its own accord, are only impertinent badges of slavery imposed
upon them, without any sufficient reason, by the groundless jealousy
of the merchants and manufacturers of the mother country. In
a more advanced state they might be really oppressive and
insupportable.

The importation Great Britain too, as she confines to her own
into Great Britain market some of the most important productions of
of various colonial the colonies, so in compensation she gives to some
productions is
encouraged either by of them an advantage in that market ; sometimes
abatement of duties by imposing higher duties upon the like produc-
or by bounties. tions when imported from other countries, and sometimes by
giving bounties upon their importation from the colonies. In the
first way she gives an advantage in the home-market to the sugar,
tobacco, and iron of her own colonies, and in the second to their
raw silk, to their hemp and flax, to their indigo, to their naval-
stores, and to their building-timber.[1] This second way of encouraging the colony produce by bounties upon importation, is, so far
as I have been able to learn, peculiar to Great Britain. The first is
not. Portugal does not content herself with imposing higher duties
upon the importation of tobacco from any other country, but
prohibits it under the severest penalties.

[1] [Details are given below, pp. 162–165, in a chapter which was not in eds. 1 and 2.]

In regard to im-
ports from Europe
the British colonies
have had more
liberal treatment
than those of other
countries,

With regard to the importation of goods from Europe, England has likewise dealt more liberally with her colonies than any other nation.

Great Britain allows a part, almost always the half, generally a larger portion, and sometimes the whole of the duty which is paid upon the importation of foreign goods, to be drawn back upon their exportation to any foreign country.[1] No independent foreign country, it was easy to foresee, would receive them if they came to it loaded with the heavy duties to which almost all foreign goods are subjected on their importation into Great Britain. Unless, therefore, some part of those duties was drawn back upon exportation, there was an end of the carrying trade; a trade so much favoured by the mercantile system.

drawbacks being
allowed,

Our colonies, however, are by no means independent foreign countries; and Great Britain having assumed to herself the exclusive right of supplying them with all goods from Europe, might have forced them (in the same manner as other countries have done their colonies) to receive such goods, loaded with all the same duties which they paid in the mother country. But, on the contrary, till 1763, the same drawbacks were paid upon the exportation of the greater part of foreign goods to our colonies as to any independent foreign country. In 1763, indeed, by the 4th of Geo. III. c. 15. this indulgence was a good deal abated, and it was enacted, 'That no part of the duty called the old subsidy should be drawn back for any goods of the growth, production, or manufacture of Europe or the East Indies, which should be exported from this kingdom to any British colony or plantation in America; wines, white callicoes and muslins excepted.'[2] Before this law, many different sorts of foreign goods might have been bought cheaper in the plantations than in the mother country; and some may still.

owing to the advice
of interested
merchants.

Of the greater part of the regulations concerning the colony trade, the merchants who carry it on, it must be observed, have been the principal advisers. We must not wonder, therefore, if, in the greater part of them, their interest has been more considered than either that of the colonies or that of the mother country. In their exclusive privilege

---

[1] [Above, pp. 3–7.]
[2] [The quotation is not quite *verbatim*. The provision is referred to above, p. 7, where, however, see note.]

of supplying the colonies with all the goods which they wanted from Europe, and of purchasing all such parts of their surplus produce as could not interfere with any of the trades which they themselves carried on at home, the interest of the colonies was sacrificed to the interest of those merchants. In allowing the same drawbacks upon the re-exportation of the greater part of European and East India goods to the colonies, as upon their re-exportation to any independent country, the interest of the mother country was sacrificed to it, even according to the mercantile ideas of that interest. It was for the interest of the merchants to pay as little as possible for the foreign goods which they sent to the colonies, and consequently, to get back as much as possible of the duties which they advanced upon their importation into Great Britain. They might thereby be enabled to sell in the colonies, either the same quantity of goods with a greater profit, or a greater quantity with the same profit, and, consequently, to gain something either in the one way or the other. It was, likewise, for the interest of the colonies to get all such goods as cheap and in as great abundance as possible. But this might not always be for the interest of the mother country. She might frequently suffer both in her revenue, by giving back a great part of the duties which had been paid upon the importation of such goods; and in her manufactures, by being undersold in the colony market, in consequence of the easy terms upon which foreign manufactures could be carried thither by means of those drawbacks. The progress of the linen manufacture of Great Britain, it is commonly said, has been a good deal retarded by the drawbacks upon the re-exportation of German linen to the American colonies.

But though the policy of Great Britain with regard to the trade of her colonies has been dictated by the same mercantile spirit as that of other nations, it has, however, upon the whole, been less illiberal and oppressive than that of any of them.

Except in regard to foreign trade the English colonies have complete liberty. In every thing, except their foreign trade, the liberty of the English colonists to manage their own affairs their own way is complete. It is in every respect equal to that of their fellow-citizens at home, and is secured in the same manner, by an assembly of the representatives of the people, who claim the sole right of imposing taxes for the support of the colony government. The authority of this assembly over-awes the executive power, and neither the meanest nor the most obnoxious colonist, as long as he obeys the law, has any thing to fear from the resentment, either of the governor, or of any other civil or military officer in the province. The colony assemblies, though like the house of commons in England, they are not always a very equal representation of the people, yet they approach more nearly to that character; and[1] as the executive power either has not the means to corrupt them, or, on account of the support which it receives from the mother country, is not under the necessity of doing so, they are perhaps in general more influenced by the inclinations of their constituents. The councils, which, in the colony legislatures, correspond to the house of lords in Great Britain, are not composed of an hereditary nobility. In some of the colonies, as in three of the governments of New England, those councils are not appointed by the king, but chosen by the representatives of the people. In none of the English colonies is there any hereditary nobility. In all of them, indeed, as in all other free countries, the descendant of an old colony family is more respected than an upstart of equal merit and fortune: but he is only more respected, and he has no privileges by which he can be troublesome to his neighbours. Before the commencement of the present disturbances, the colony assemblies had not only the legislative, but a part of the executive power. In Connecticut and Rhode Island, they elected the governor.[2] In the other colonies they appointed the revenue officers who collected the taxes imposed by those respective assemblies, to whom those officers were immediately responsible. There is more equality, therefore, among the English colonists than among the inhabitants of the mother country. Their manners are more republican, and their governments, those of three of the provinces of New England in particular, have hitherto been more republican too.

The absolute governments of Spain, of Portugal, and in a less degree of France, are even more violent in the colonies than at home. The absolute governments of Spain, Portugal, and France, on the contrary, take place in their colonies; and the discretionary powers which such governments commonly delegate to all their inferior officers are, on account of the great distance, naturally exercised there with more than ordinary

[1] [Ed. 1 does not contain the words 'they approach more nearly to that character; and'.]

[2] [The Board of Trade and Plantations, in a report to the House of Commons in 1732, insisted on this democratic character of the government of some of the colonies, and mentioned the election of governor by Connecticut and Rhode Island: the report is quoted in Anderson, *Commerce*, A.D. 1732.]

violence. Under all absolute governments there is more liberty in the capital than in any other part of the country. The sovereign himself can never have either interest or inclination to pervert the order of justice, or to oppress the great body of the people. In the capital his presence over-awes more or less all his inferior officers, who in the remoter provinces, from whence the complaints of the people are less likely to reach him, can exercise their tyranny with much more safety. But the European colonies in America are more remote than the most distant provinces of the greatest empires which had ever been known before. The government of the English colonies is perhaps the only one which, since the world began, could give perfect security to the inhabitants of so very distant a province. The administration of the French colonies, however, has always been conducted with more gentleness and moderation than that of the Spanish and Portuguese. This superiority of conduct is suitable both to the character of the French nation, and to what forms the character of every nation, the nature of their government, which, though arbitrary and violent in comparison with that of Great Britain, is legal and free in comparison with those of Spain and Portugal.

The sugar colonies of France are more prosperous than the English because they are not discouraged from refining, and slaves are better managed, It is in the progress of the North American colonies, however, that the superiority of the English policy chiefly appears. The progress of the sugar colonies of France has been at least equal, perhaps superior, to that of the greater part of those of England; and yet the sugar colonies of England enjoy a free government nearly of the same kind with that which takes place in her colonies of North America. But the sugar colonies of France are not discouraged, like those of England, from refining their own sugar; and, what is of still greater importance, the genius of their government naturally introduces a better management of their negro slaves.

absolute government being more favourable to the slaves than republican, In all European colonies the culture of the sugar-cane is carried on by negro slaves. The constitution of those who have been born in the temperate climate of Europe could not, it is supposed, support the labour of digging the ground under the burning sun of the West Indies; and the culture of the sugar-cane, as it is managed at present, is all hand labour, though, in the opinion of many, the drill plough might be introduced into it with great advantage. But, as the profit and success of the cultivation which is carried on by means of cattle, depend very much upon the good management of those cattle; so the profit and success of that which is carried on by slaves, must depend equally upon the good management of those slaves; and in the good management of their slaves the French planters, I think it is generally allowed, are superior to the English. The law, so far as it gives some weak protection to the slave against the violence of his master, is likely to be better executed in a colony where the government is in a great measure arbitrary, than in one where it is altogether free. In every country where the unfortunate law of slavery is established, the magistrate, when he protects the slave, intermeddles in some measure in the management of the private property of the master; and, in a free country, where the master is perhaps either a member of the colony assembly, or an elector of such a member, he dare not do this but with the greatest caution and circumspection. The respect which he is obliged to pay to the master, renders it more difficult for him to protect the slave. But in a country where the government is in a great measure arbitrary, where it is usual for the magistrate to intermeddle even in the management of the private property of individuals, and to send them, perhaps, a lettre de cachet if they do not manage it according to his liking, it is much easier for him to give some protection to the slave; and common humanity naturally disposes him to do so. The protection of the magistrate renders the slave less contemptible in the eyes of his master, who is thereby induced to consider him with more regard, and to treat him with more gentleness. Gentle usage renders the slave not only more faithful, but more intelligent, and therefore, upon a double account, more useful. He approaches more to the condition of a free servant, and may possess some degree of integrity and attachment to his master's interest, virtues which frequently belong to free servants, but which never can belong to a slave, who is treated as slaves commonly are in countries where the master is perfectly free and secure.

as may be seen in Roman history. That the condition of a slave is better under an arbitrary than under a free government, is, I believe, supported by the history of all ages and nations. In the Roman history, the first time we read of the magistrate interposing to protect the slave from the violence of his master, is under the emperors. When Vedius Pollio, in the presence of Augustus, ordered one of his slaves, who had committed a slight fault, to be cut into pieces and thrown into his fish-pond in order to feed his fishes, the emperor commanded him, with indignation, to emancipate immediately, not only that slave, but all the others that belonged to him.[1] Under the republic no magistrate could have had authority enough to protect the slave, much less to punish the master.

The superiority of the French sugar colonies is the more remarkable inasmuch as they have accumulated their own stock. The stock, it is to be observed, which has improved the sugar colonies of France, particularly the great colony of St. Domingo, has been raised almost entirely from the gradual improvement and cultivation of those colonies. It has been almost altogether the produce of the soil and of the industry[2] of the colonists, or, what comes to the same thing, the price of that produce gradually accumulated by good management, and employed in raising a still greater produce. But the stock which has improved and cultivated the sugar colonies of England has, a great part of it, been sent out from England, and has by no means been altogether the produce of the soil and industry of the colonists.[3] The prosperity of the English sugar colonies has been, in a great measure, owing to the great riches of England, of which a part has overflowed, if one may say so, upon those colonies. But the prosperity of the sugar colonies of France has been entirely owing to the good conduct of the colonists, which must therefore have had some superiority over that of the English; and this superiority has been remarked in nothing so much as in the good management of their slaves.

The policy of Europe has done nothing for the prosperity of the colonies. Such have been the general outlines of the policy of the different European nations with regard to their colonies.

The policy of Europe, therefore, has very little to boast of, either in the original establishment, or, so far as concerns their internal government,[4] in the subsequent prosperity of the colonies of America.

---

[1] [The story is told in the same way in *Lectures*, p. 97, but Seneca, *De ira*, lib. iii., cap. 40, and Dio Cassius, *Hist.*, lib. liv., cap. 23, say, not that Augustus ordered all the slaves to be emancipated, but that he ordered all the goblets on the table to be broken. Seneca says the offending slave was emancipated. Dio does not mention emancipation.]

[2] [Ed. 1 reads 'and industry'.]

[3] [The West India merchants and planters asserted, in 1775, that there was capital worth £60,000,000 in the sugar colonies and that half of this belonged to residents in Great Britain.—See the Continuation of Anderson's *Commerce*, A.D. 1775.]

[4] [Eds. 1 and 2 do not contain the words 'so far as concerns their in ernal government'.]

Folly and injustice directed the first project. Folly and injustice seem to have been the principles which presided over and directed the first project of establishing those colonies; the folly of hunting after gold and silver mines, and the injustice of coveting the possession of a country whose harmless natives, far from having ever injured the people of Europe, had received the first adventurers with every mark of kindness and hospitality.

The more respectable adventurers of later times were sent out by the disorder and injustice of European governments. The adventurers, indeed, who formed some of the later establishments, joined, to the chimerical project of finding gold and silver mines, other motives more reasonable and more laudable; but even these motives do very little honour to the policy of Europe.

The English puritans, restrained[1] at home, fled for freedom to America, and established there the four governments of New England. The English catholics, treated with much greater injustice,[2] established that of Maryland; the Quakers, that of Pennsylvania. The Portuguese Jews, persecuted by the inquisition, stript of their fortunes, and banished to Brazil, introduced, by their example, some sort of order and industry among the transported felons and strumpets, by whom that colony was originally peopled, and taught them the culture of the sugar-cane.[3] Upon all these different occasions it was, not the wisdom and policy, but the disorder and injustice of the European governments, which peopled and cultivated America.

To the actual establishment of the colonies the governments of Europe contributed little, In effectuating some of the most important of these establishments, the different governments of Europe had as little merit as in projecting them. The conquest of Mexico was the project, not of the council of Spain, but of a governor of Cuba;[4] and it was effectuated by the spirit of the bold adventurer[5] to whom it was entrusted, in spite of every thing which that governor, who soon repented of having trusted such a person, could do to thwart it. The conquerors of Chili and Peru, and of almost all the other Spanish settlements upon the continent of America, carried out with them no other public encouragement, but a general permission to make settlements and conquests in the name of the king of Spain. Those adventures were

---

[1] [Ed. 1 reads 'persecuted'.]   [2] [Ed. 1 reads 'with equal injustice'.]
[3] [Raynal, *Histoire philosophique*, Amsterdam ed., 1773, tom. iii., pp. 323, 324, 326, 327. Justamond's English trans., vol. ii., p. 442.]
[4] [Velasquez.]   [5] [Cortez.]

all at the private risk and expence of the adventurers. The government of Spain contributed scarce any thing to any of them. That of England contributed as little towards effectuating the establishment of some of its most important colonies in North America.

and discouraged rather than encouraged them after they were established. When those establishments were effectuated, and had become so considerable as to attract the attention of the mother country, the first regulations which she made with regard to them had always in view to secure to herself the monopoly of their commerce; to confine their market, and to enlarge her own at their expence, and, consequently, rather to damp and discourage, than to quicken and forward the course of their prosperity. In the different ways in which this monopoly has been exercised, consists one of the most essential differences in the policy of the different European nations with regard to their colonies. The best of them all, that of England, is only somewhat less illiberal and oppressive than that of any of the rest.

Europe has done nothing except provide the men who founded the colonies. In what way, therefore, has the policy of Europe contributed either to the first establishment, or to the present grandeur of the colonies of America? In one way, and in one way only, it has contributed a good deal. *Magna virûm Mater!*[1] It bred and formed the men who were capable of atchieving such great actions, and of laying the foundation of so great an empire; and there is no other quarter of the world of which the policy is capable of forming, or has ever actually and in fact formed such men. The colonies owe to the policy of Europe the education and great views of their active and enterprising founders; and some of the greatest and most important of them, so far as concerns their internal government,[2] owe to it scarce any thing else.

PART THIRD

Of the Advantages which Europe has derived from the Discovery of America, and from that of a Passage to the East Indies by the Cape of Good Hope

The advantages derived by Europe Such are the advantages which the colonies of America have derived from the policy of Europe.

---

[1] ['Salve magna parens frugum, Saturnia tellus, Magna virum.'—Virgil, *Georg*, ii., 173–174.]

[2] [Eds. 1 and 2 do not contain the words 'so far as concerns their internal government'. Cp. above, p. 101, note 4.]

from America are (1) the advantages of Europe in general, and (2) the advantages of the particular countries which have colonies. What are those which Europe has derived from the discovery and colonization of America?

Those advantages may be divided, first into the general advantages which Europe, considered as one great country, has derived from those great events; and, secondly, into the particular advantages which each colonizing country has derived from the colonies which particularly belong to it, in consequence of the authority or dominion which it exercises over them.

(1) The general advantages to Europe are, The general advantages which Europe, considered as one great country, has derived from the discovery and colonization of America, consist, first, in the increase of its enjoyments; and secondly, in the augmentation of its industry.

(a) an increase of enjoyments, The surplus produce of America, imported into Europe, furnishes the inhabitants of this great continent with a variety of commodities which they could not otherwise have possessed, some for conveniency and use, some for pleasure, and some for ornament, and thereby contributes to increase their enjoyments.

(b) an augmentation of industry not only in the countries which trade with America directly, The discovery and colonization of America, it will readily be allowed, have contributed to augment the industry, first, of all the countries which trade to it directly; such as Spain, Portugal, France, and England; and, secondly, of all those which, without trading to it directly, send, through the medium of other countries, goods to it of their own produce; such as Austrian Flanders, and some provinces of Germany, which, through the medium of the countries before mentioned, send to it a considerable quantity of linen and other goods. All such countries have evidently gained a more extensive market for their surplus produce, and must consequently have been encouraged to increase its quantity.

but also in other countries which do not send their produce to America, But, that those great events should likewise have contributed to encourage the industry of countries, such as Hungary and Poland, which may never, perhaps, have sent a single commodity of their own produce to America, is not, perhaps, altogether so evident. That those events have done so, however, cannot be doubted. Some part of the produce of America is consumed in Hungary and Poland, and there is some demand there for the sugar, chocolate, and tobacco, of that new quarter of the world. But those commodities must be purchased with something which is either the produce of the industry of Hungary and Poland, or with something which had been purchased with some part of that produce. Those commodities of America are new values, new equivalents, introduced into Hungary and Poland to be exchanged there for the surplus produce of those countries. By being carried thither they create a new and more extensive market for that surplus produce. They raise its value, and thereby contribute to encourage its increase. Though no part of it may ever be carried to America, it may be carried to other countries which purchase it with a part of their share of the surplus produce of America; and it may find a market by means of the circulation of that trade which was originally put into motion by the surplus produce of America.

or even receive any produce from America. Those great events may even have contributed to increase the enjoyments, and to augment the industry of countries which, not only never sent any commodities to America, but never received any from it. Even such countries may have received a greater abundance of other commodities from countries of which the surplus produce had been augmented by means of the American trade. This greater abundance, as it must necessarily have increased their enjoyments, so it must likewise have augmented their industry. A greater number of new equivalents of some kind or other must have been presented to them to be exchanged for the surplus produce of that industry. A more extensive market must have been created for that surplus produce, so as to raise its value, and thereby encourage its increase. The mass of commodities annually thrown into the great circle of European commerce, and by its various revolutions annually distributed among all the different nations comprehended within it, must have been augmented by the whole surplus produce of America. A greater share of this greater mass, therefore, is likely to have fallen to each of those nations, to have increased their enjoyments, and augmented their industry.

The exclusive trade of the mother countries reduces the enjoyments and industry of all Europe and America, especially the latter. The exclusive trade of the mother countries tends to diminish, or, at least, to keep down below what they would otherwise rise to, both the enjoyments and industry of all those nations in general, and of the American colonies in particular. It is a dead weight upon the action of one of the great springs which puts into motion a great part of the business of mankind. By rendering the colony produce dearer in all other countries, it lessens its consumption, and thereby cramps the industry of the colonies, and both the enjoyments and the industry of all other countries, which both enjoy less when they pay more for what they enjoy, and produce less when they get less for what they produce. By rendering the produce of all other countries dearer in the colonies, it cramps, in the same manner, the industry of all other countries, and both the enjoyments and the industry of the colonies. It is a clog which, for the supposed benefit of some particular countries, embarrasses the pleasures, and encumbers the industry of all other countries; but of the colonies more than of any other. It not[1] only excludes, as much as possible, all other countries from one particular market; but it confines, as much as possible, the colonies to one particular market: and the difference is very great between being excluded from one particular market, when all others are open, and being confined to one particular market, when all others are shut up. The surplus produce of the colonies, however, is the original source of all that increase of enjoyments and industry which Europe derives from the discovery and colonization of America; and the exclusive trade of the mother countries tends to render this source much less abundant than it otherwise would be.

(2) The particular advantages of the colonising countries are (a) the common advantages derived from provinces, (b) the peculiar advantages derived from provinces in America: The particular advantages which each colonizing country derives from the colonies which particularly belong to it, are of two different kinds; first, those common advantages which every empire derives from the provinces subject to its dominion; and, secondly, those peculiar advantages which are supposed to result from provinces of so very peculiar a nature as the European colonies of America.

(a) the common advantages are contributions of military forces and revenue, The common advantages which every empire derives from the provinces subject to its dominion, consist, first, in the military force which they furnish for its defence; and, secondly, in the revenue which they furnish for the support of its civil government. The Roman colonies furnished occasionally both the one and the other. The Greek colonies, sometimes, furnished a military force; but

---

[1] ['Not' appears first in ed. 3 and seems to have been inserted in error. The other countries are only excluded from a particular market, but the colonies are confined to one.]

seldom any revenue.[1] They seldom acknowledged themselves subject to the dominion of the mother city. They were generally her allies in war, but very seldom her subjects in peace.

but none of the colonies have ever furnished military force, The European colonies of America have never yet furnished any military force for the defence of the mother country. Their military force has never yet been sufficient for their own defence; and in the different wars in which the mother countries have been engaged, the defence of their colonies has generally occasioned a very considerable distraction of the military force of those countries. In this respect, therefore, all the European colonies have, without exception, been a cause rather of weakness than of strength to their respective mother countries.

and the colonies of Spain and Portugal alone have contributed revenue. The colonies of Spain and Portugal only have contributed any revenue towards the defence of the mother country, or the support of her civil government.[2] The taxes which have been levied upon those of other European nations, upon those of England in particular, have seldom been equal to the expence laid out upon them in time of peace, and never sufficient to defray that which they occasioned in time of war. Such colonies, therefore, have been a source of expence and not of revenue to their respective mother countries.

(b) the exclusive trade is the sole peculiar advantage. The advantages of such colonies to their respective mother countries, consist altogether in those peculiar advantages which are supposed to result from provinces of so very peculiar a nature as the European colonies of America; and the exclusive trade, it is acknowledged, is the sole source of all those peculiar advantages.

The exclusive trade of each country is a disadvantage to the other countries, In consequence of this exclusive trade, all that part of the surplus produce of the English colonies, for example, which consists in what are called enumerated commodities,[3] can be sent to no other country but England. Other countries must afterwards buy it of her. It must be cheaper therefore in England than it can be in any other country, and must contribute more to increase the enjoyments of England than those of any other country. It must likewise contribute more to encourage her industry. For all those parts of her own surplus produce which England exchanges for those enumerated commodities, she must get a better price than any other countries can get for the like parts

---

[1] [There is an example of revenue being furnished in Xenophon, *Anab.*, V., v., 7, 10.]
[2] [Above, p. 86.]   [3] [Above, p. 89.]

of theirs, when they exchange them for the same commodities. The manufactures of England, for example, will purchase a greater quantity of the sugar and tobacco of her own colonies, than the like manufactures of other countries can purchase of that sugar and tobacco. So far, therefore, as the manufactures of England and those of other countries are both to be exchanged for the sugar and tobacco of the English colonies, this superiority of price gives an encouragement to the former, beyond what the latter can in these circumstances enjoy. The exclusive trade of the colonies, therefore, as it diminishes, or, at least, keeps down below what they would otherwise rise to, both the enjoyments and the industry of the countries which do not possess it; so it gives an evident advantage to the countries which do possess it over those other countries.

rather than an advantage to that country, This advantage, however, will, perhaps, be found to be rather what may be called a relative than an absolute advantage; and to give a superiority to the country which enjoys it, rather by depressing the industry and produce of other countries, than by raising those of that particular country above what they would naturally rise to in the case of a free trade.

e.g., England gets tobacco cheaper than France, but not cheaper than it would if there were no exclusive trade. The tobacco of Maryland and Virginia, for example, by means of the monopoly which England enjoys of it, certainly comes cheaper to England than it can do to France, to whom England commonly sells a considerable part of it. But had France, and all other European countries been, at all times, allowed a free trade to Maryland and Virginia, the tobacco of those colonies might, by this time, have come cheaper than it actually does, not only to all those other countries, but likewise to England. The produce of tobacco, in consequence of a market so much more extensive than any which it has hitherto enjoyed, might, and probably would, by this time, have been so much increased as to reduce the profits of a tobacco plantation to their natural level with those of a corn plantation, which, it is supposed, they are still somewhat above.[1] The price of tobacco might, and probably would, by this time, have fallen somewhat lower than it is at present. An equal quantity of the commodities either of England, or of those other countries, might have purchased in Maryland and Virginia a greater quantity of tobacco than it can do at present, and, consequently,

[1] [Above, vol. i., p. 175.]

have been sold there for so much a better price. So far as that weed, therefore, can, by its cheapness and abundance, increase the enjoyments or augment the industry either of England or of any other country, it would, probably, in the case of a free trade, have produced both these effects in somewhat a greater degree than it can do at present. England, indeed, would not in this case have had any advantage over other countries. She might have bought the tobacco of her colonies somewhat cheaper, and, consequently, have sold some of her own commodities somewhat dearer than she actually does. But she could neither have bought the one cheaper nor sold the other dearer than any other country might have done. She might, perhaps, have gained an absolute, but she would certainly have lost a relative advantage.

To subject other countries to this disadvantage England has made two sacrifices. In order, however, to obtain this relative advantage in the colony trade, in order to execute the invidious and malignant project of excluding as much as possible other nations from any share in it, England, there are very probable reasons for believing, has not only sacrificed a part of the absolute advantage which she, as well as every other nation, might have derived from that trade, but has subjected herself both to an absolute and to a relative disadvantage in almost every other branch of trade.

The withdrawal of foreign capital from the colony trade raised profits in it and drew capital from other British trades and thereby raised profits in them, When, by the act of navigation,[1] England assumed to herself the monopoly of the colony trade, the foreign capitals which had before been employed in it were necessarily withdrawn from it. The English capital, which had before carried on but a part of it, was now to carry on the whole. The capital which had before supplied the colonies with but a part of the goods which they wanted from Europe, was now all that was employed to supply them with the whole. But it could not supply them with the whole, and the goods with which it did supply them were necessarily sold very dear. The capital which had before bought but a part of the surplus produce of the colonies, was now all that was employed to buy the whole. But it could not buy the whole at any thing near the old price, and, therefore, whatever it did buy it necessarily bought very cheap. But in an employment of capital in which the merchant sold very dear and bought very cheap, the profit must have been very great, and much above the

---

[1] [Above, vol. i., pp. 485-487.]

ordinary level of profit in other branches of trade. This superiority
of profit in the colony trade could not fail to draw from other
branches of trade a part of the capital which had before been
employed in them. But this revulsion of capital, as it must have
gradually increased the competition of capitals in the colony trade,
so it must have gradually diminished that competition in all those
other branches of trade; as it must have gradually lowered the profits
of the one, so it must have gradually raised those of the other, till
the profits of all came to a new level, different from and somewhat
higher than that at which they had been before.

and continues to do so. This double effect, of drawing capital from all
other trades, and of raising the rate of profit some-
what higher than it otherwise would have been at all trades, was
not only produced by this monopoly upon its first establishment,
but has continued to be produced by it ever since.

The colony trade has increased faster than the whole British capital, First, this monopoly has been continually drawing
capital from all other trades to be employed in that
of the colonies.

Though the wealth of Great Britain has increased very much
since the establishment of the act of navigation, it certainly has not
increased in the same proportion as that of the colonies. But the
foreign trade of every country naturally increases in proportion to
its wealth, its surplus produce in proportion to its whole produce;
and Great Britain having engrossed to herself almost the whole of
what may be called the foreign trade of the colonies, and her
capital not having increased in the same proportion as the extent of
that trade, she could not carry it on without continually withdrawing from other branches of trade some part of the capital which had
before been employed in them, as well as withholding from them
a great deal more which would otherwise have gone to them. Since
the establishment of the act of navigation, accordingly, the colony
trade has been continually increasing, while many other branches
of foreign trade, particularly of that to other parts of Europe, have
been continually decaying. Our manufactures for foreign sale,
instead of being suited, as before the act of navigation, to the
neighbouring market of Europe, or to the more distant one of the
countries which lie round the Mediterranean sea, have, the greater
part of them, been accommodated to the still more distant one of
the colonies, to the market in which they have the monopoly, rather
than to that in which they have many competitors. The causes of

decay in other branches of foreign trade, which, by Sir Matthew Decker,[1] and other writers, have been sought for in the excess and improper mode of taxation, in the high price of labour, in the increase of luxury, &c. may all be found in the over-growth of the colony trade. The mercantile capital of Great Britain, though very great, yet not being infinite; and though greatly increased since the act of navigation, yet not being increased in the same proportion as the colony trade, that trade could not possibly be carried on without withdrawing some part of that capital from other branches of trade, nor consequently without some decay of those other branches.

and the colonial monopoly has merely changed the direction of British trade.   England, it must be observed, was a great trading country, her mercantile capital was very great and likely to become still greater and greater every day, not only before the act of navigation had established the monopoly of the colony trade, but before that trade was very considerable. In the Dutch war, during the government of Cromwel, her navy was superior to that of Holland; and in that which broke out in the beginning of the reign of Charles II. it was at least equal, perhaps superior, to the united navies of France and Holland. Its superiority, perhaps, would scarce appear greater in the present times; at least if the Dutch navy was to bear the same proportion to the Dutch commerce now which it did then. But this great naval power could not, in either of those wars, be owing to the act of navigation. During the first of them the plan of that act had been but just formed; and though before the breaking out of the second it had been fully enacted by legal authority; yet no part of it could have had time to produce any considerable effect, and least of all that part which established the exclusive trade to the colonies. Both the colonies and their trade were inconsiderable then in comparison of what they are now. The island of Jamaica was an unwholesome desert, little inhabited, and less cultivated. New York and New Jersey were in the possession of the Dutch: the half of St. Christopher's in that of the French. The island of Antigua, the two Carolinas, Pensylvania, Georgia, and Nova Scotia, were not planted. Virginia, Maryland, and New England were planted; and though they were very thriving colonies, yet there was not, perhaps, at that time, either in Europe or America, a single person who

---

[1] [*Essay on the Causes of the Decline of the Foreign Trade, consequently of the Value of the Lands of Britain and on the means to restore both*, 2nd ed., 1750, pp. 28–36, *et passim*.]

foresaw or even suspected the rapid progress which they have since made in wealth, population and improvement. The island of Barbadoes, in short, was the only British colony of any consequence of which the condition at that time bore any resemblance to what it is at present. The trade of the colonies, of which England, even for some time after the act of navigation, enjoyed but a part (for the act of navigation was not very strictly executed till several years after it was enacted), could not at that time be the cause of the great trade of England, nor of the great naval power which was supported by that trade. The trade which at that time supported that great naval power was the trade of Europe, and of the countries which lie round the Mediterranean sea. But the share which Great Britain at present enjoys of that trade could not support any such great naval power. Had the growing trade of the colonies been left free to all nations, whatever share of it might have fallen to Great Britain, and a very considerable share would probably have fallen to her, must have been all an addition to this great trade of which she was before in possession. In consequence of the monopoly, the increase of the colony trade has not so much occasioned an addition to the trade which Great Britain had before, as a total change in its direction.

The monopoly has kept the rate of profit in British trade higher than it naturally would have been,　Secondly, this monopoly has necessarily contributed to keep up the rate of profit in all the different branches of British trade higher than it naturally would have been, had all nations been allowed a free trade to the British colonies.

The monopoly of the colony trade, as it necessarily drew towards that trade a greater proportion of the capital of Great Britain than what would have gone to it of its own accord; so by the expulsion of all foreign capitals it necessarily reduced the whole quantity of capital employed in that trade below what it naturally would have been in the case of a free trade. But, by lessening the competition of capitals in that branch of trade, it necessarily raised the rate of profit[1] in that branch. By lessening too the competition of British capitals in all other branches of trade, it necessarily raised the rate of British profit in all those other branches. Whatever may have been, at any particular period, since the establishment of the act of navigation, the state or extent of the mercantile capital of Great Britain, the monopoly of the colony trade must, during the con-

---

[1] [Ed. 1 reads 'rate of the profit'.]

tinuance of that state, have raised the ordinary rate of British profit higher than it otherwise would have been both in that and in all the other branches of British trade. If, since the establishment of the act of navigation, the ordinary rate of British profit has fallen considerably, as it certainly has, it must have fallen still lower, had not the monopoly established by that act contributed to keep it up.

and this puts the country at a disadvantage in the trades of which she has no monopoly, But whatever raises in any country the ordinary rate of profit higher than it otherwise would be, necessarily subjects that country both to an absolute and to a relative disadvantage in every branch of trade of which she has not the monopoly.

making her buy less and sell less, It subjects her to an absolute disadvantage: because in such branches of trade her merchants cannot get this greater profit, without selling dearer than they otherwise would do both the goods of foreign countries which they import into their own, and the goods of their own country which they export to foreign countries. Their own country must both buy dearer and sell dearer; must both buy less and sell less; must both enjoy less and produce less, than she otherwise would do.

and enabling other countries to undersell her in foreign markets. It subjects her to a relative disadvantage; because in such branches of trade it sets other countries which are not subject to the same absolute disadvantage, either more above her or less below her than they otherwise would be. It enables them both to enjoy more and to produce more in proportion to what she enjoys and produces. It renders their superiority greater or their inferiority less than it otherwise would be. By raising the price of her produce above what it otherwise would be, it enables the merchants of other countries to undersell her in foreign markets, and thereby to justle her out of almost all those branches of trade, of which she has not the monopoly.

High-profits raise the price of manufactures more than high wages. Our merchants frequently complain of the high wages of British labour as the cause of their manufactures being undersold in foreign markets; but they are silent about the high profits of stock. They complain of the extravagant gain of other people; but they say nothing of their own. The high profits of British stock, however, may contribute towards raising the price of British manufactures in many cases as much, and in some perhaps more, than the high wages of British labour.[1]

---

[1] [This passage is much the same as that which concludes bk. i., ch. ix., above, vol. i., p. 110; but this is the original, as the other was not in ed. 1.]

So British capital has been taken from European and Mediterranean trade, It is in this manner that the capital of Great Britain, one may justly say, has partly been drawn and partly been driven from the greater part of the different branches of trade of which she has not the monopoly; from the trade of Europe in particular, and from that of the countries which lie round the Mediterranean sea.

partly attracted by high profit in the colony trade, It has partly been drawn from those branches of trade; by the attraction of superior profit in the colony trade in consequence of the continual increase of that trade, and of the continual insufficiency of the capital which had carried it on one year to carry it on the next.

partly driven out by foreign competition. It has partly been driven from them; by the advantage which the high rate of profit, established in Great Britain, gives to other countries, in all the different branches of trade of which Great Britain has not the monopoly.

While raising British profit, the monopoly has lowered foreign profits. As the monopoly of the colony trade has drawn from those other branches a part of the British capital which would otherwise have been employed in them, so it has forced into them many foreign capitals which would never have gone to them, had they not been expelled from the colony trade. In those other branches of trade it has diminished the competition of British capitals, and thereby raised the rate of British profit higher than it otherwise would have been. On the contrary, it has increased the competition of foreign capitals, and thereby sunk the rate of foreign profit lower than it otherwise would have been. Both in the one way and in the other it must evidently have subjected Great Britain to a relative disadvantage in all those other branches of trade.

The colony trade is supposed to be more advantageous than others, The colony trade, however, it may perhaps be said, is more advantageous to Great Britain than any other; and the monopoly, by forcing into that trade a greater proportion of the capital of Great Britain than what would otherwise have gone to it, has turned that capital into an employment more advantageous to the country than any other which it could have found.

but trade with a neighbouring country is more advantageous than with a distant one, and The most advantageous employment of any capital to the country to which it belongs, is that which maintains there the greatest quantity of productive labour, and increases the most the annual produce *a direct trade is more advantageous than a round-about,* of the land and labour of that country. But the quantity of productive labour which any capital employed in the foreign trade of consumption can maintain, is exactly in proportion, it has been shewn in the second book,[1] to the frequency of its returns. A capital of a thousand pounds, for example, employed in a foreign trade of consumption, of which the returns are made regularly once in the year, can keep in constant employment, in the country to which it belongs, a quantity of productive labour equal to what a thousand pounds can maintain there for a year. If the returns are made twice or thrice in the year, it can keep in constant employment a quantity of productive labour equal to what two or three thousand pounds can maintain there for a year. A foreign trade of consumption carried on with a neighbouring,[2] is, upon this account, in general, more advantageous than one carried on with a distant country; and for the same reason a direct foreign trade of consumption, as it has likewise been shewn in the second book,[3] is in general more advantageous than a round-about one.

while the monopoly has forced capital into (1) a distant and (2) a round-about trade. But the monopoly of the colony trade, so far as it has operated upon the employment of the capital of Great Britain, has in all cases forced some part of it from a foreign trade of consumption carried on with a neighbouring,[4] to one carried on with a more distant country, and in many cases from a direct foreign trade of consumption to a round-about one.

(1) The trade with America and the West Indies is distant and the returns peculiarly infrequent. First, the monopoly of the colony trade has in all cases forced some part of the capital of Great Britain from a foreign trade of consumption carried on with a neighbouring, to one carried on with a more distant country.

It has, in all cases, forced some part of that capital from the trade with Europe, and with the countries which lie round the Mediterranean sea, to that with the more distant regions of America and the West Indies, from which the returns are necessarily less frequent, not only on account of the greater distance, but on account of the peculiar circumstances of those countries. New colonies, it has already been observed, are always understocked. Their capital is

---

[1] [Above, vol. i., p. 390.]
[2] [Ed. 1 reads 'with a neighbouring country'.]
[3] [Above, vol. i., p. 391.]
[4] [Ed. 1 reads 'with a neighbouring country'.]

always much less than what they could employ with great profit and advantage in the improvement and cultivation of their land. They have a constant demand, therefore, for more capital than they have of their own; and, in order to supply the deficiency of their own, they endeavour to borrow as much as they can of the mother country, to whom they are, therefore, always in debt. The most common way in which the colonists contract this debt, is not by borrowing upon bond of the rich people of the mother country, though they sometimes do this too, but by running as much in arrear to their correspondents, who supply them with goods from Europe, as those correspondents will allow them. Their annual returns frequently do not amount to more than a third, and sometimes not to so great a proportion of what they owe. The whole capital, therefore, which their correspondents advance to them is seldom returned to Britain in less than three, and sometimes not in less than four or five years. But a British capital of a thousand pounds, for example, which is returned to Great Britain only once in five years, can keep in constant employment only one-fifth part of the British industry which it could maintain if the whole was returned once in the year; and, instead of the quantity of industry which a thousand pounds could maintain for a year, can keep in constant employment the quantity only which two hundred pounds can maintain for a year. The planter, no doubt, by the high price which he pays for the goods from Europe, by the interest upon the bills which he grants at distant dates, and by the commission upon the renewal of those which he grants at near dates, makes up, and probably more than makes up, all the loss which his correspondent can sustain by this delay. But, though he may make up the loss of his correspondent, he cannot make up that of Great Britain. In a trade of which the returns are very distant, the profit of the merchant may be as great or greater than in one in which they are very frequent and near; but the advantage of the country in which he resides, the quantity of productive labour constantly maintained there, the annual produce of the land and labour must always be much less. That the returns of the trade to America, and still more those of that to the West Indies, are, in general, not only more distant, but more irregular, and more uncertain too, than those of the trade to any part of Europe, or even of the countries which lie round the Mediterranean sea, will readily be allowed, I imagine, by every body who has any experience of those different branches of trade.

(2) *It is also largely a round-about trade.* Secondly, the monopoly of the colony trade has, in many cases, forced some part of the capital of Great Britain from a direct foreign trade of consumption, into a round-about one.

Among the enumerated commodities which can be sent to no other market but Great Britain, there are several of which the quantity exceeds very much the consumption of Great Britain, and of which a part, therefore, must be exported to other countries. But this cannot be done without forcing some part of the capital of Great Britain into a round-about foreign trade of consumption. Maryland and Virginia, for example, send annually to Great Britain upwards of ninety-six thousand hogsheads of tobacco, and the consumption of Great Britain is said not to exceed fourteen thousand.[1] Upwards of eighty-two thousand hogsheads, therefore, must be exported to other countries, to France, to Holland, and to the countries which lie round the Baltic and Mediterranean seas. But, that part of the capital of Great Britain which brings those eighty-two thousand hogsheads to Great Britain, which re-exports them from thence to those other countries, and which brings back from those other countries to Great Britain either goods or money in return, is employed in a round-about foreign trade of consumption; and is necessarily forced into this employment in order to dispose of this great surplus. If we would compute in how many years the whole of this capital is likely to come back to Great Britain, we must add to the distance of the American returns that of the returns from those other countries. If, in the direct foreign trade of consumption which we carry on with America, the whole capital employed frequently does not come back in less than three or four years; the whole capital employed in this round-about one is not likely to come back in less than four or five. If the one can keep in constant employment but a third or a fourth part of the domestic industry which could be maintained by a capital returned once in the year, the other can keep in constant employment but a fourth or a fifth part of that industry. At some of the outports a credit is commonly given to those foreign correspondents to whom they export their tobacco. At the port of London, indeed, it is commonly sold for ready money. The rule is, *Weigh and pay*. At the port of London, therefore, the final returns of the whole round-about trade are more distant than the returns from America by the

[1] [These figures are given above, vol. i., p. 395; vol. ii., p. 4.]

time only which the goods may lie unsold in the warehouse; where, however, they may sometimes lie long enough.[1] But, had not the colonies been confined to the market of Great Britain for the sale of their tobacco, very little more of it would probably have come to us than what was necessary for the home consumption. The goods which Great Britain purchases at present for her own consumption with the great surplus of tobacco which she exports to other countries, she would, in this case, probably have purchased with the immediate produce of her own industry, or with some part of her own manufactures. That produce, those manufactures, instead of being almost entirely suited to one great market, as at present, would probably have been fitted to a great number of smaller markets. Instead of one great round-about foreign trade of consumption, Great Britain would probably have carried on a great number of small direct foreign trades of the same kind. On account of the frequency of the returns, a part, and probably but a small part; perhaps not above a third or a fourth, of the capital which at present carries on this great round-about trade, might have been sufficient to carry on all those small direct ones, might have kept in constant employment an equal quantity of British industry, and have equally supported the annual produce of the land and labour of Great Britain. All the purposes of this trade being, in this manner, answered by a much smaller capital, there would have been a large spare capital to apply to other purposes; to improve the lands, to increase the manufactures, and to extend the commerce of Great Britain; to come into competition at least with the other British capitals employed in all those different ways, to reduce the rate of profit in them all, and thereby to give to Great Britain, in all of them, a superiority over other countries still greater than what she at present enjoys.[2]

The monopoly has also forced part of the capital of Great Britain into a carrying trade, The monopoly of the colony trade too has forced some part of the capital of Great Britain from all foreign trade of consumption to a carrying trade; and, consequently, from supporting more or less the industry of Great Britain, to be employed altogether in supporting partly that of the colonies, and partly that of some other countries.

The goods, for example, which are annually purchased with the

---

[1] [These four sentences beginning with 'At some of the outports' are not in ed. 1.]
[2] [Ed. 1 reads 'possesses'.]

great surplus of eighty-two thousand hogsheads of tobacco annually re-exported from Great Britain, are not all consumed in Great Britain. Part of them, linen from Germany and Holland, for example, is returned to the colonies for their particular consumption. But, that part of the capital of Great Britain which buys the tobacco with which this linen is afterwards bought, is necessarily withdrawn from supporting the industry of Great Britain, to be employed altogether in supporting, partly that of the colonies, and partly that of the particular countries who pay for this tobacco with the produce of their own industry.

and makes her whole industry and commerce less secure owing to its being driven into one channel. The monopoly of the colony trade besides, by forcing towards it a much greater proportion of the capital of Great Britain than what would naturally have gone to it, seems to have broken altogether that natural balance which would otherwise have taken place among all the different branches of British industry. The industry of Great Britain, instead of being accommodated to a great number of small markets, has been principally suited to one great market. Her commerce, instead of running in a great number of small channels, has been taught to run principally in one great channel. But the whole system of her industry and commerce has thereby been rendered less secure; the whole state of her body politic less healthful, than it otherwise would have been. In her present condition, Great Britain resembles one of those unwholesome bodies in which some of the vital parts are overgrown, and which, upon that account, are liable to many dangerous disorders scarce incident to those in which all the parts are more properly proportioned. A small stop in that great blood-vessel, which has been artificially swelled beyond its natural dimensions, and through which an unnatural proportion of the industry and commerce of the country has been forced to circulate, is very likely to bring on the most dangerous disorders upon the whole body politic. The expectation of a rupture with the colonies, accordingly, has struck the people of Great Britain with more terror than they ever felt for a Spanish armada, or a French invasion. It was this terror, whether well or ill grounded, which rendered the repeal of the stamp act,[1] among the merchants at least, a popular measure. In the total exclusion from the colony market, was it to last only for a few years, the greater part of our merchants used to fancy that they

---

[1] [Ed. 1 places 'a popular measure' here.]

foresaw an entire stop to their trade; the greater part of our master manufacturers, the entire ruin of their business; and the greater part of our workmen, an end of their employment. A rupture with any of our neighbours upon the continent, though likely too to occasion some stop or interruption in the employments of some of all these different orders of people, is foreseen, however, without any such general emotion. The blood, of which the circulation is stopt in some of the smaller vessels, easily disgorges itself into the greater, without occasioning any dangerous disorder; but, when it is stopt in any of the greater vessels, convulsions, apoplexy, or death, are the immediate and unavoidable consequences. If but one of those overgrown manufactures, which by means either of bounties or of the monopoly of the home and colony markets, have been artificially raised up to an unnatural height, finds some small stop or interruption in its employment, it frequently occasions a mutiny and disorder alarming to government, and embarrassing even to the deliberations of the legislature. How great, therefore, would be the disorder and confusion, it was thought, which must necessarily be occasioned by a sudden and entire stop in the employment of so great a proportion of our principal manufacturers?

The gradual relaxation of the monopoly is desirable.   Some moderate and gradual relaxation of the laws which give to Great Britain the exclusive trade to the colonies, till it is rendered in a great measure free, seems to be the only expedient which can, in all future times,[1] deliver her from this danger, which can enable her or even force her to withdraw some part of her capital from this overgrown employment, and to turn it, though with less profit, towards other employments; and which, by gradually diminishing one branch of her industry and gradually increasing all the rest, can by degrees restore all the different branches of it to that natural, healthful, and proper proportion which perfect liberty necessarily establishes, and which perfect liberty can alone preserve. To open the colony trade all at once to all nations, might not only occasion some transitory inconveniency, but a great permanent loss to the greater part of those whose industry or capital is at present engaged in it. The sudden loss of the employment even of the ships which import the eighty-two thousand hogsheads of tobacco, which are over and above the consumption of Great Britain, might alone be felt very sensibly. Such are the unfortunate effects of all the regulations of the

[1] [Ed. 1 does not contain 'in all future times'.]

mercantile system! They not only introduce very dangerous disorders into the state of the body politic, but disorders which it is often difficult to remedy, without occasioning, for a time at least, still greater disorders. In what manner, therefore, the colony trade ought gradually to be opened; what are the restraints which ought first, and what are those which ought last to be taken away; or in what manner the natural system of perfect liberty and justice ought gradually to be restored, we must leave to the wisdom of future statesmen and legislators to determine.

The present exclusion from the trade with the twelve provinces would have been more severely felt but for five transitory circumstances. Five different events, unforeseen and unthought of, have very fortunately concurred to hinder Great Britain from feeling, so sensibly as it was generally expected she would, the total exclusion which has now taken place for more than a year (from the first of December, 1774)[1] from a very important branch of the colony trade, that of the twelve associated provinces of North America. First, those colonies, in preparing themselves for their non-importation agreement, drained Great Britain completely of all the commodities which were fit for their market: secondly, the extraordinary demand of the Spanish Flota[2] has, this year, drained Germany and the North of many commodities, linen in particular, which used to come into competition, even in the British market, with the manufactures of Great Britain: thirdly, the peace between Russia and Turkey,[3] has occasioned an extraordinary demand from the Turkey market, which, during the distress of the country, and while a Russian fleet was cruizing in the Archipelago, had been very poorly supplied: fourthly, the demand of the North of Europe for the manufactures of Great Britain, has been increasing from year to year for some time past: and, fifthly, the late partition[4] and consequential pacification of Poland, by opening the market of that great country, have this year added an extraordinary demand from thence to the increasing demand of the North. These events

---

[1] [The date at which the non-importation agreement began to operate.]

[2] ['For the greater security of the valuable cargoes sent to America, as well as for the more easy prevention of fraud, the commerce of Spain with its colonies is carried on by fleets which sail under strong convoys. These fleets, consisting of two squadrons, one distinguished by the name of the "Galeons," the other by that of the "Flota," are equipped annually. Formerly they took their departure from Seville; but as the port of Cadiz has been found more commodious, they have sailed from it since the year 1720.'—W. Robertson, *History of America*, bk. viii.; in *Works*, 1825, vol. vii., p. 372.]

[3] [By the treaty of Kainardji, 1774.]

[4] [In 1773.]

are all, except the fourth, in their nature transitory and accidental, and the exclusion from so important a branch of the colony trade, if unfortunately it should continue much longer, may still occasion some degree of distress. This distress, however, as it will come on gradually, will be felt much less severely than if it had come on all at once; and, in the mean time, the industry and capital of the country may find a new employment and direction, so as to prevent this distress[1] from ever rising to any considerable height.

The monopoly is bad,   The monopoly of the colony trade, therefore, so far as it has turned towards that trade a greater proportion of the capital of Great Britain than what would otherwise have gone to it, has in all cases turned it, from a foreign trade of consumption with a neighbouring, into one with a more distant country; in many cases, from a direct foreign trade of consumption, into a round-about one; and in some cases, from all foreign trade of consumption, into a carrying trade. It has in all cases, therefore, turned it, from a direction in which it would have maintained a greater quantity of productive labour, into one, in which it can maintain a much smaller quantity. By suiting, besides, to one particular market only, so great a part of the industry and commerce of Great Britain, it has rendered the whole state of that industry and commerce more precarious and less secure, than if their produce had been accommodated to a greater variety of markets.

but the trade itself is good.   We must carefully distinguish between the effects of the colony trade and those of the monopoly of that trade. The former are always and necessarily beneficial; the latter always and necessarily hurtful. But the former are so beneficial, that the colony trade, though subject to a monopoly, and notwithstanding the hurtful effects of that monopoly, is still upon the whole beneficial, and greatly beneficial; though a good deal less so than it otherwise would be.

The trade in its natural state increases the productive labour of Great Britain.   The effect of the colony trade in its natural and free state, is to open a great, though distant market for such parts of the produce of British industry as may exceed the demand of the markets nearer home, of those of Europe, and of the countries which lie round the Mediterranean sea. In its natural and free state, the colony trade, without drawing from those markets any part of the produce which had ever been sent to them, encourages Great Britain to increase the

---

[1] [Ed. 1 reads 'prevent it'.]

surplus continually, by continually presenting new equivalents to be exchanged for it. In its natural and free state, the colony trade tends to increase the quantity of productive labour in Great Britain, but without altering in any respect the direction of that which had been employed there before. In the natural and free state of the colony trade, the competition of all other nations would hinder the rate of profit from rising above the common level either in the new market, or in the new employment. The new market, without drawing any thing from the old one, would create, if one may say so, a new produce for its own supply; and that new produce would constitute a new capital for carrying on the new employment, which in the same manner would draw nothing from the old one.

The monopoly diminishes it. The monopoly of the colony trade, on the contrary, by excluding the competition of other nations, and thereby raising the rate of profit both in the new market and in the new employment, draws produce from the old market and capital from the old employment. To augment our share of the colony trade beyond what it otherwise would be, is the avowed purpose of the monopoly. If our share of that trade were to be no greater with, than it would have been without the monopoly, there could have been no reason for establishing the monopoly. But whatever forces into a branch of trade of which the returns are slower and more distant than those of the greater part of other trades, a greater proportion of the capital of any country, than what of its own accord would go to that branch, necessarily renders the whole quantity of productive labour annually maintained there, the whole annual produce of the land and labour of that country, less than they otherwise would be. It keeps down the revenue of the inhabitants of that country, below what it would naturally rise to, and thereby diminishes their power of accumulation. It not only hinders, at all times, their capital from maintaining so great a quantity of productive labour as it would otherwise maintain, but it hinders it from increasing so fast as it would otherwise increase, and consequently from maintaining a still greater quantity of productive labour.

The natural good effects of the trade more than counterbalance the bad effects of the monopoly. The natural good effects of the colony trade, however, more than counterbalance to Great Britain the bad effects of the monopoly, so that, monopoly and all together, that trade, even as it is carried on at present, is not only advantageous, but greatly

advantageous. The new market and the new employment[1] which
are opened by the colony trade, are of much greater extent than
that portion of the old market and of the old employment which is
lost by the monopoly. The new produce and the new capital which
has been created, if one may say so, by the colony trade, maintain
in Great Britain a greater quantity of productive labour, than what
can have been thrown out of employment by the revulsion of
capital from other trades of which the returns are more frequent.
If the colony trade, however, even as it is carried on at present, is
advantageous to Great Britain, it is not by means of the monopoly,
but in spite of the monopoly.

The colonies offer a market for the manufactured rather than the rude produce of Europe, It is rather for the manufactured than for the rude
produce of Europe, that the colony trade opens a
new market. Agriculture is the proper business of
all new colonies; a business which the cheapness of
land renders more advantageous than any other.
They abound, therefore, in the rude produce of land, and instead of
importing it from other countries, they have generally a large
surplus to export. In new colonies, agriculture either draws hands
from all other employments, or keeps them from going to any
other employment. There are few hands to spare for the necessary,
and none for the ornamental manufactures. The greater part of the
manufactures of both kinds, they find it cheaper to purchase of
other countries than to make for themselves. It is chiefly by encouraging the manufactures of Europe, that the colony trade indirectly
encourages its agriculture. The manufacturers of Europe, to whom
that trade gives employment, constitute a new market for the produce of the land; and the most advantageous of all markets; the
home market for the corn and cattle, for the bread and butcher's-
meat of Europe; is thus greatly extended by means of the trade to
America.

but the monopoly has not main- tained the manu- factures of Spain and Portugal, But that the monopoly of the trade of populous
and thriving colonies is not alone sufficient to estab-
lish, or even to maintain manufactures in any
country, the examples of Spain and Portugal
sufficiently demonstrate. Spain and Portugal were manufacturing
countries before they had any considerable colonies. Since they had
the richest and most fertile in the world, they have both ceased
to be so.

---

[1] [Eds. 1 and 2 read 'and employment'.]

where the bad effects of the monopoly have nearly overbalanced the good effects of the trade.

In Spain and Portugal, the bad effects of the monopoly, aggravated by other causes, have, perhaps, nearly overbalanced[1] the natural good effects of the colony trade. These causes seem to be, other monopolies of different kinds; the degradation of the value of gold and silver below what it is in most other countries; the exclusion from foreign markets by improper taxes upon exportation, and the narrowing of the home market, by still more improper taxes upon the transportation of goods from one part of the country to another; but above all, that irregular and partial administration of justice, which often protects the rich and powerful debtor from the pursuit of his injured creditor, and which makes the industrious part of the nation afraid to prepare goods for the consumption of those haughty and great men, to whom they dare not refuse to sell upon credit, and from whom they are altogether uncertain of repayment.

In England the good effects of the trade have greatly counteracted the bad effects of the monopoly.

In England, on the contrary, the natural good effects of the colony trade, assisted by other causes, have in a great measure conquered the bad effects of the monopoly. These causes seem to be, the general liberty of trade, which, notwithstanding some restraints, is at least equal, perhaps superior, to what it is in any other country; the liberty of exporting, duty free, almost all sorts of goods which are the produce of domestic industry, to almost any foreign country; and what, perhaps, is of still greater importance, the unbounded liberty of transporting them from any one part of our own country to any other, without being obliged to give any account to any public office, without being liable to question or examination of any kind; but above all, that equal and impartial administration of justice which renders the rights of the meanest British subject respectable to the greatest, and which, by securing to every man the fruits of his own industry, gives the greatest and most effectual encouragement to every sort of industry.

The trade has benefited British manufactures in spite of the monopoly, not in consequence of it.

If the manufactures of Great Britain, however, have been advanced, as they certainly have, by the colony trade, it has not been by means of the monopoly of that trade, but in spite of the monopoly. The effect of the monopoly has been, not to

[1] [Ed. 1 reads 'have entirely conquered'.]

augment the quantity, but to alter the quality and shape of a part of the manufactures of Great Britain, and to accommodate to a market, from which the returns are slow and distant, what would otherwise have been accommodated to one from which the returns are frequent and near. Its effect has consequently been to turn a part of the capital of Great Britain from an employment in which it would have maintained a greater quantity of manufacturing industry, to one in which it maintains a much smaller, and thereby to diminish, instead of increasing, the whole quantity of manufacturing industry maintained in Great Britain.

The monopoly of the colony trade, therefore, like all the other mean and malignant expedients of the mercantile system, depresses the industry of all other countries, but chiefly that of the colonies, without in the least increasing, but on the contrary diminishing, that of the country in whose favour it is established.

The monopoly reduces wages in the mother country, The monopoly hinders the capital of that country, whatever may at any particular time be the extent of that capital, from maintaining so great a quantity of productive labour as it would otherwise maintain, and from affording so great a revenue to the industrious inhabitants as it would otherwise afford. But as capital can be increased only by savings from revenue, the monopoly, by hindering it from affording so great a revenue as it would otherwise afford, necessarily hinders it from increasing so fast as it would otherwise increase, and consequently from maintaining a still greater quantity of productive labour, and affording a still greater revenue to the industrious inhabitants of that country. One great original source of revenue, therefore, the wages of labour, the monopoly must necessarily have rendered at all times less abundant than it otherwise would have been.

raises profits, and thereby tends to lower rents and the price of land. By raising the rate of mercantile profit, the monopoly discourages the improvement of land. The profit of improvement depends upon the difference between what the land actually produces, and what, by the application of a certain capital, it can be made to produce. If this difference affords a greater profit than what can be drawn from an equal capital in any mercantile employment, the improvement of land will draw capital from all mercantile employments. If the profit is less, mercantile employments will draw capital from the improvement of land. Whatever therefore raises the rate of mercantile profit, either lessens the superiority or increases the inferiority of the profit of improvement; and in the one case hinders capital from going to improvement, and in the other draws capital from it. But by discouraging improvement, the monopoly necessarily retards the natural increase of another great original source of revenue, the rent of land. By raising the rate of profit too, the monopoly necessarily keeps up the market rate of interest higher than it otherwise would be. But the price of land in proportion to the rent which it affords, the number of years purchase which is commonly paid for it, necessarily falls as the rate of interest rises, and rises as the rate of interest falls. The monopoly, therefore, hurts the interest of the landlord two different ways, by retarding the natural increase, first, of his rent, and secondly, of the price which he would get for his land in proportion to the rent which it affords.

It reduces the absolute amount of profit, The monopoly, indeed, raises the rate of mercantile profit, and thereby augments somewhat the gain of our merchants. But as it obstructs the natural increase of capital, it tends rather to diminish than to increase the sum total of the revenue which the inhabitants of the country derive from the profits of stock; a small profit upon a great capital generally affording a greater revenue than a great profit upon a small one. The monopoly raises the rate of profit, but it hinders the sum of profit from rising so high as it otherwise would do.

thus rendering all the original sources of revenue less abundant. All the original sources of revenue, the wages of labour, the rent of land, and the profits of stock, the monopoly renders much less abundant than they otherwise would be. To promote the little interest of one little order of men in one country, it hurts the interest of all other orders of men in that country, and of all men in all other countries.

More fatal still, it destroys parsimony. It is solely by raising the ordinary rate of profit that the monopoly either has proved or could prove advantageous to any one particular order of men. But besides all the bad effects to the country in general, which have already been mentioned as necessarily resulting from a high rate of profit; there is one more fatal, perhaps, than all these put together, but which, if we may judge from experience, is inseparably connected with it. The high rate of profit seems every where to destroy that parsimony which in other circumstances is natural to the character of the merchant. When profits are high, that sober virtue seems to be superfluous, and expensive luxury to suit better the affluence of his

situation. But the owners of the great mercantile capitals are necessarily the leaders and conductors of the whole industry of every
nation, and their example has a much greater influence upon the
manners of the whole industrious part of it than that of any other
order of men. If his employer is attentive and parsimonious, the
workman is very likely to be so too; but if the master is dissolute
and disorderly, the servant who shapes his work according to the
pattern which his master prescribes to him, will shape his life too
according to the example which he sets him. Accumulation is thus
prevented in the hands of all those who are naturally the most disposed to accumulate; and the funds destined for the maintenance of
productive labour receive no augmentation from the revenue of
those who ought naturally to augment them the most. The capital
of the country, instead of increasing, gradually dwindles away, and
the quantity of productive labour maintained in it grows every day
less and less. Have the exorbitant profits of the merchants of Cadiz
and Lisbon augmented the capital of Spain and Portugal? Have they
alleviated the poverty, have they promoted the industry of those
two beggarly countries? Such has been the tone of mercantile
expence in those two trading cities, that those exorbitant profits, far
from augmenting the general capital of the country, seem scarce
to have been sufficient to keep up the capitals upon which they were
made. Foreign capitals are every day intruding themselves, if I may
say so, more and more into the trade of Cadiz and Lisbon. It is to
expel those foreign capitals from a trade which their own[1] grows
every day more and more insufficient for carrying on, that the
Spaniards and Portuguese endeavour every day to straiten more and
more the galling bands of their absurd monopoly. Compare the
mercantile manners of Cadiz and Lisbon with those of Amsterdam,
and you will be sensible how differently the conduct and character
of merchants are affected by the high and by the low profits of
stock. The merchants of London, indeed, have not yet generally
become such magnificent lords as those of Cadiz and Lisbon; but
neither are they in general such attentive and parsimonious burghers
as those of Amsterdam. They are supposed, however, many of them,
to be a good deal richer than the greater part of the former, and
not quite so rich as many of the latter. But the rate of their profit
is commonly much lower than that of the former, and a good deal
higher than that of the latter. Light come light go, says the proverb;

---

[1] [Ed. 1 reads 'own capital'.]

and the ordinary tone of expence seems every where to be regulated, not so much according to the real ability of spending, as to the supposed facility of getting money to spend.

It is thus that the single advantage which the monopoly procures to a single order of men, is in many different ways hurtful to the general interest of the country.

The policy of the monopoly is a policy of shopkeepers. To found a great empire for the sole purpose of raising up a people of customers, may at first sight appear a project fit only for a nation of shopkeepers. It is, however, a project altogether unfit for a nation of shopkeepers; but extremely fit for a nation whose government is influenced by shopkeepers. Such statesmen, and such statesmen only,[1] are capable of fancying that they will find some advantage in employing the blood and treasure of their fellow-citizens, to found and maintain[2] such an empire. Say to a shopkeeper, Buy me a good estate, and I shall always buy my clothes at your shop, even though I should pay somewhat dearer than what I can have them for at other shops; and you will not find him very forward to embrace your proposal. But should any other person buy you such an estate, the shopkeeper would be much obliged to your benefactor if he would enjoin you to buy all your clothes at his shop. England purchased for some of her subjects, who found themselves uneasy at home, a great estate in a distant country. The price, indeed, was very small, and instead of thirty years purchase, the ordinary price of land in the present times, it amounted to little more than the expence of the different equipments which made the first discovery, reconnoitred the coast, and took a fictitious possession of the country. The land was good and of great extent, and the cultivators having plenty of good ground to work upon, and being for some time at liberty to sell their produce where they pleased, became in the course of little more than thirty or forty years (between 1620 and 1660) so numerous and thriving a people, that the shopkeepers and other traders of England wished to secure to themselves the monopoly of their custom. Without pretending, therefore, that they had paid any part, either of the original purchase-money, or of the subsequent expence of improvement, they petitioned the parliament that the cultivators of America might

---

[1] [Ed. 1 reads 'extremely fit for a nation that is governed by shopkeepers. Such sovereigns and such sovereigns only'.]

[2] [Ed. 1 reads 'their subjects, to found and to maintain'.]

for the future be confined to their shop; first, for buying all the goods which they wanted from Europe; and, secondly, for selling all such parts of their own produce as those traders might find it convenient to buy. For they did not find it convenient to buy every part of it. Some parts of it imported into England might have interfered with some of the trades which they themselves carried on at home. Those particular parts of it, therefore, they were willing that the colonists should sell where they could; the farther off the better; and upon that account proposed that their market should be confined to the countries south of Cape Finisterre. A clause in the famous act of navigation established this truly shopkeeper proposal into a law.

The expenditure of Great Britain on the colonies has all been laid out to support the monopoly, and is enormous. The maintenance of this monopoly has hitherto been the principal, or more properly perhaps the sole end and purpose of the dominion which Great Britain assumes over her colonies. In the exclusive trade, it is supposed, consists the great advantage of provinces, which have never yet afforded either revenue or military force for the support of the civil government, or the defence of the mother country. The monopoly is the principal badge of their dependency, and it is the sole fruit which has hitherto been gathered from that dependency. Whatever expence Great Britain has hitherto laid out in maintaining this dependency, has really been laid out in order to support this monopoly. The expence of the ordinary peace establishment of the colonies amounted, before the commencement of the present disturbances, to the pay of twenty regiments of foot; to the expence of the artillery, stores, and extraordinary provisions with which it was[1] necessary to supply them; and to the expence of a very considerable naval force which was constantly kept up, in order to guard, from the smuggling vessels of other nations, the immense coast of North America, and that of our West Indian islands. The whole expence of this peace establishment was a charge upon the revenue of Great Britain, and was, at the same time, the smallest part of what the dominion of the colonies has cost the mother country. If we would know the amount of the whole, we must add to the annual expence of this peace establishment the interest of the sums which, in consequence of her considering her colonies as provinces subject to her dominion, Great Britain has upon different occasions laid out upon their defence. We must add

[1] [Ed. 1 reads 'is' here and one line lower down.]

to it, in particular, the whole expence of the late war, and a great part of that of the war which preceded it.[1] The late war was altogether a colony quarrel, and the whole expence of it, in whatever part of the world it may have been laid out, whether in Germany or the East Indies, ought justly to be stated to the account of the colonies. It amounted to more than ninety millions sterling, including not only the new debt which was contracted, but the two shillings in the pound additional land tax, and the sums which were every year borrowed from the sinking fund. The Spanish war which began in 1739, was principally a colony quarrel. Its principal object was to prevent the search of the colony ships which carried on a contraband trade with the Spanish main. This whole expence is, in reality, a bounty which has been given in order to support a monopoly. The pretended purpose of it was to encourage the manufactures, and to increase the commerce of Great Britain. But its real effect has been to raise the rate of mercantile profit, and to enable our merchants to turn into a branch of trade, of which the returns are more slow and distant than those of the greater part of other trades, a greater proportion of their capital than they otherwise would have done; two events which if a bounty could have prevented, it might perhaps have been very well worth while to give such a bounty.

Under the present system of management, therefore, Great Britain derives nothing but loss from the dominion which she assumes over her colonies.

A voluntary separation would be very advantageous. To propose that Great Britain should voluntarily give up all authority over her colonies, and leave them to elect their own magistrates, to enact their own laws, and to make peace and war as they might think proper, would be to propose such a measure as never was, and never will be adopted, by any nation in the world. No nation ever voluntarily gave up the dominion of any province, how troublesome soever it might be to govern it, and how small soever the revenue which it afforded might be in proportion to the expence which it occasioned. Such sacrifices, though they might frequently be agreeable to the interest, are always mortifying to the pride of every nation, and what is perhaps of still greater consequence, they are always contrary to the private interest of the governing part of it, who would thereby be deprived of the disposal of many places of trust and profit, of many opportunities of acquiring wealth and distinction,

---

[1] [Ed. 1 reads 'and a great part of that which preceded it'.]

which the possession of the most turbulent, and, to the great body of the people, the most unprofitable province seldom fails to afford. The most visionary enthusiast would scarce be capable of proposing such a measure, with any serious hopes at least of its ever being adopted. If it was adopted, however, Great Britain would not only be immediately freed from the whole annual expence of the peace establishment of the colonies, but might settle with them such a treaty of commerce as would effectually secure to her a free trade, more advantageous to the great body of the people, though less so to the merchants, than the monopoly which she at present enjoys. By thus parting good friends, the natural affection of the colonies to the mother country, which, perhaps, our late dissensions have well nigh extinguished, would quickly revive. It might dispose them not only to respect, for whole centuries together, that treaty of commerce which they had concluded with us at parting, but to favour us in war as well as in trade, and, instead of turbulent and factious subjects, to become our most faithful, affectionate, and generous allies; and the same sort of parental affection on the one side, and filial respect on the other, might revive between Great Britain and her colonies, which used to subsist between those of ancient Greece and the mother city from which they descended.

The colonies do not furnish nearly sufficient revenue to make them advantageous. In order to render any province advantageous to the empire to which it belongs, it ought to afford, in time of peace, a revenue to the public sufficient not only for defraying the whole expence of its own peace establishment, but for contributing its proportion to the support of the general government of the empire. Every province necessarily contributes, more or less, to increase the expence of that general government. If any particular province, therefore, does not contribute its share towards defraying this expence, an unequal burden must be thrown upon some other part of the empire. The extraordinary revenue too which every province affords to the public in time of war, ought, from parity of reason, to bear the same proportion to the extraordinary revenue of the whole empire which its ordinary revenue does in time of peace. That neither the ordinary nor extraordinary revenue which Great Britain derives from her colonies, bears this proportion to the whole revenue of the British empire, will readily be allowed. The monopoly, it has been supposed, indeed, by increasing the private revenue of the people of Great Britain, and thereby enabling them to pay greater taxes, compensates the deficiency of the public revenue of the colonies. But this monopoly, I have endeavoured to show, though a very grievous tax upon the colonies, and though it may increase the revenue of a particular order of men in Great Britain, diminishes instead of increasing that of the great body of the people; and consequently diminishes instead of increasing the ability of the great body of the people to pay taxes. The men too whose revenue the monopoly increases, constitute a particular order, which it is both absolutely impossible to tax beyond the proportion of other orders, and extremely impolitic even to attempt to tax beyond that proportion, as I shall endeavour to shew in the following book.[1] No particular resource, therefore, can be drawn from this particular order.

The colonies may be taxed either by their own assemblies, or by the parliament of Great Britain.

The colonial assemblies will never vote enough, That the colony assemblies can ever be so managed as to levy upon their constituents a public revenue sufficient, not only to maintain at all times their own civil and military establishment, but to pay their proper proportion of the expence of the general government of the British empire, seems not very probable. It was a long time before even the parliament of England, though placed immediately under the eye of the sovereign, could be brought under such a system of management, or could be rendered sufficiently liberal in their grants for supporting the civil and military establishments even of their own country. It was only by distributing among the particular members of parliament, a great part either of the offices, or of the disposal of the offices arising from this civil and military establishment, that such a system of management could be established even with regard to the parliament of England. But the distance of the colony assemblies from the eye of the sovereign, their number, their dispersed situation, and their various constitutions, would render it very difficult to manage them in the same manner, even though the sovereign had the same means of doing it; and those means are wanting. It would be absolutely impossible to distribute among all the leading members of all the colony assemblies such a share, either of the offices or of the disposal of the offices arising from the general government of the British empire, as to dispose them to give up their popularity at home, and to tax their constituents for the support of that general government, of which

[1] [Below, p. 375.]

almost the whole emoluments were to be divided among people who were strangers to them. The unavoidable ignorance of administration, besides, concerning the relative importance of the different members of those different assemblies, the offences which must frequently be given, the blunders which must constantly be committed in attempting to manage them in this manner, seems[1] to render such a system of management altogether impracticable with regard to them.

and have no knowledge of what is required. The colony assemblies, besides, cannot be supposed the proper judges of what is necessary for the defence and support of the whole empire. The care of that defence and support is not entrusted to them. It is not their business, and they have no regular means of information concerning it. The assembly of a province, like the vestry of a parish, may judge very properly concerning the affairs of its own particular district; but can have no proper means of judging concerning those of the whole empire. It cannot even judge properly concerning the proportion which its own province bears to the whole empire; or concerning the relative degree of its wealth and importance, compared with the other provinces; because those other provinces are not under the inspection and superintendency of the assembly of a particular province. What is necessary for the defence and support of the whole empire, and in what proportion each part ought to contribute, can be judged of only by that assembly which inspects and superintends the affairs of the whole empire.

It has been proposed that parliament should tax the colonies by requisition, It has been proposed, accordingly, that the colonies should be taxed by requisition, the parliament of Great Britain determining the sum which each colony ought to pay, and the provincial assembly assessing and levying it in the way that suited best the circumstances of the province. What concerned the whole empire would in this way be determined by the assembly which inspects and superintends the affairs of the whole empire; and the provincial affairs of each colony might still be regulated by its own assembly. Though the colonies should in this case have no representatives in the British parliament, yet, if we may judge by experience, there is no probability that the parliamentary requisition would be unreasonable. The parliament of England has not upon any occasion shown the smallest disposition to overburden those parts of the

---

[1] [Ed. 1 reads 'seem'.]

empire which are not represented in parliament. The islands of Guernsey and Jersey, without any means of resisting the authority of parliament, are more lightly taxed than any part of Great Britain. Parliament in attempting to exercise its supposed right, whether well or ill grounded, of taxing the colonies, has never hitherto demanded of them any thing which even approached to a just proportion to what was paid by their fellow-subjects at home If the contribution of the colonies, besides, was to rise or fall in proportion to the rise or fall of the land tax, parliament could not tax them without taxing at the same time its own constituents, and the colonies might in this case be considered as virtually represented in parliament.

as the King of France taxes some of his provinces, Examples are not wanting of empires in which all the different provinces are not taxed, if I may be allowed the expression, in one mass; but in which the sovereign regulates the sum which each province ought to pay, and in some provinces assesses and levies it as he thinks proper; while in others, he leaves it to be assessed and levied as the respective states of each province shall determine. In some provinces of France, the king not only imposes what taxes he thinks proper, but assesses and levies them in the way he thinks proper. From others he demands a certain sum, but leaves it to the states of each province to assess and levy that sum as they think proper. According to the scheme of taxing by requisition, the parliament of Great Britain would stand nearly in the same situation towards the colony assemblies, as the king of France does towards the states of those provinces which still enjoy the privilege of having states of their own, the provinces of France which are supposed to be the best governed.

but parliament has not sufficient authority, But though, according to this scheme, the colonies could have no just reason to fear that their share of the public burdens should ever exceed the proper proportion to that of their fellow-citizens at home; Great Britain might have just reason to fear that it never would amount to that proper proportion. The parliament of Great Britain has not for some time past had the same established authority in the colonies, which the French king has in those provinces of France which still enjoy the privilege of having states of their own. The colony assemblies, if they were not very favourably disposed (and unless more skilfully managed than they ever have been hitherto, they are not very likely to be so), might still find many pretences for evading or rejecting the most reasonable requisitions of parliament. A French war breaks out, we shall suppose; ten millions must immediately be raised, in order to defend the seat of the empire. This sum must be borrowed upon the credit of some parliamentary fund mortgaged for paying the interest. Part of this fund parliament proposes to raise by a tax to be levied in Great Britain, and part of it by a requisition to all the different colony assemblies of America and the West Indies. Would people readily advance their money upon the credit of a fund, which partly depended upon the good humour of all those assemblies, far distant from the seat of the war, and sometimes, perhaps, thinking themselves not much concerned in the event of it? Upon such a fund no more money would probably be advanced than what the tax to be levied in Great Britain might be supposed to answer for. The whole burden of the debt contracted on account of the war would in this manner fall, as it always has done hitherto, upon Great Britain; upon a part of the empire, and not upon the whole empire. Great Britain is, perhaps, since the world began, the only state which, as it has extended its empire, has only increased its expence without once augmenting its resources. Other states have generally disburdened themselves upon their subject and subordinate provinces of the most considerable part of the expence of defending the empire. Great Britain has hitherto suffered her subject and subordinate provinces to disburden themselves upon her of almost this whole expence. In order to put Great Britain upon a footing of equality with her own colonies, which the law has hitherto supposed to be subject and subordinate, it seems necessary, upon the scheme of taxing them by parliamentary requisition, that parliament should have some means of rendering its requisitions immediately effectual, in case the colony assemblies should attempt to evade or reject them; and what those means are, it is not very easy to conceive, and it has not yet been explained.

and resistance breaks out.   Should the parliament of Great Britain, at the same time, be ever fully established in the right of taxing the colonies, even independent of the consent of their own assemblies, the importance of those assemblies would from that moment be at an end, and with it, that of all the leading men of British America. Men desire to have some share in the management of public affairs chiefly on account of the importance which it gives them. Upon the power which the greater part of the leading men, the natural aristocracy of every country, have of preserving or defending their respective importance, depends the stability and duration of every system of free government. In the attacks which those leading men are continually making upon the importance of one another, and in the defence of their own, consists the whole play of domestic faction and ambition. The leading men of America, like those of all other countries, desire to preserve their own importance. They feel, or imagine, that if their assemblies, which they are fond of calling parliaments, and of considering as equal in authority to the parliament of Great Britain, should be so far degraded as to become the humble ministers and executive officers of that parliament, the greater part of their own importance would be at an end. They have rejected, therefore, the proposal of being taxed by parliamentary requisition, and like other ambitious and high-spirited men, have rather chosen to draw the sword in defence of their own importance.

Representation in parliament in proportion to taxation should be offered. Towards the declension of the Roman republic, the allies of Rome, who had borne the principal burden of defending the state and extending the empire, demanded to be admitted to all the privileges of Roman citizens. Upon being refused, the social war broke out. During the course of that war Rome granted those privileges to the greater part of them, one by one, and in proportion as they detached themselves from the general confederacy. The parliament of Great Britain insists upon taxing the colonies; and they refuse to be taxed by a parliament in which they are not represented. If to each colony, which should detach itself from the general confederacy, Great Britain should allow such a number of representatives as suited the proportion of what it contributed to the public revenue of the empire, in consequence of its being subjected to the same taxes, and in compensation admitted to the same freedom of trade with its fellow-subjects at home; the number of its representatives to be augmented as the proportion of its contribution might afterwards augment; a new method of acquiring importance, a new and more dazzling object of ambition would be presented to the leading men of each colony. Instead of piddling for the little prizes which are to be found in what may be called the paltry raffle of colony faction; they might then hope, from the presumption which men naturally have in their own ability and good fortune, to draw some of the great prizes which sometimes come from the wheel of the great state lottery of British politics. Unless this or some other method

Otherwise it seems is fallen upon, and there seems to be none more
hopeless to expect obvious than this, of preserving the importance and
submission, of gratifying the ambition of the leading men of
America, it is not very probable that they will ever voluntarily
submit to us; and we ought to consider that the blood which must
be shed in forcing them to do so, is, every drop of it, the blood
either of those who are, or of those whom we wish to have for our
fellow-citizens. They are very weak who flatter themselves that, in
the state to which things have come, our colonies will be easily
conquered by force alone. The persons who now govern the resolutions of what they call their continental congress, feel in themselves
at this moment a degree of importance which, perhaps, the greatest
subjects in Europe scarce feel. From shopkeepers, tradesmen, and
attornies, they are become statesmen and legislators, and are
employed in contriving a new form of government for an extensive
empire, which, they flatter themselves, will become, and which,
indeed, seems very likely to become, one of the greatest and most
formidable that ever was in the world. Five hundred different
people, perhaps, who in different ways act immediately under the
continental congress; and five hundred thousand, perhaps, who act
under those five hundred, all feel in the same manner a proportionable rise in their own importance. Almost every individual of the
governing party in America, fills, at present in his own fancy, a
station superior, not only to what he had ever filled before, but to
what he had ever expected to fill; and unless some new object of
ambition is presented either to him or to his leaders, if he has the
ordinary spirit of a man, he will die in defence of that station.

and resistance will It is a remark of the president Henaut, that we now
be as obstinate as read with pleasure the account of many little trans-
that of Paris. actions of the Ligue, which when they happened
were not perhaps considered as very important pieces of news. But
every man then, says he, fancied himself of some importance; and
the innumerable memoirs which have come down to us from those
times were, the greater part of them, written by people who took
pleasure in recording and magnifying events in which, they flattered
themselves, they had been considerable actors.[1] How obstinately the

[1] ['Aucun des règnes précédents n'a fourni plus de volumes, plus d'anecdotes, plus
d'estampes, plus de pièces fugitives, etc. Il y a dans tout cela bien des choses inutiles;
mais comme Henri III. vivait au milieu de son peuple, aucun détail des actions de sa
vie n'a échappé à la curiosité; et comme Paris était le théâtre des principaux événements

city of Paris upon that occasion defended itself, what a dreadful famine it supported rather than submit to the best and afterwards[1] the most beloved of all the French kings, is well known. The greater part of the citizens, or those who governed the greater part of them, fought in defence of their own importance, which they foresaw was to be at an end whenever the ancient government should be re-established. Our colonies, unless they can be induced to consent to a union, are very likely to defend themselves against the best of all mother countries, as obstinately as the city of Paris did against one of the best of kings.

The discovery of representation makes the case different from that of Rome and Italy. The idea of representation was unknown in ancient times. When the people of one state were admitted to the right of citizenship in another, they had no other means of exercising that right but by coming in a body to vote and deliberate with the people of that other state. The admission of the greater part of the inhabitants of Italy to the privileges of Roman citizens, completely ruined the Roman republic. It was no longer possible to distinguish between who was and who was not a Roman citizen. No tribe could know its own members. A rabble of any kind could be introduced into the assemblies of the people, could drive out the real citizens, and decide upon the affairs of the republic as if they themselves had been such. But though America were[2] to send fifty or sixty new representatives to parliament, the door-keeper of the house of commons could not find any great difficulty in distinguishing between who was and who was not a member. Though the Roman constitution, therefore, was necessarily ruined by the union of Rome with the allied states of Italy, there is not the least probability that the British constitution would be hurt by the union of Great Britain with her colonies. That constitution, on the contrary, would be completed by it, and seems to be imperfect without it. The assembly which deliberates and decides concerning the affairs of every part of the empire, in order to be properly informed, ought certainly to have representatives from every part of it. That this union, however, could be easily effectuated, or that difficulties and great difficulties

de la ligue, les bourgeois qui y avaient la plus grande part, conservaient soigneusement les moindres faits qui se passaient sous leurs yeux; tout ce qu'ils voyaient leur paraissait grand, parce qu'ils y participaient, et nous sommes curieux, sur parole, de faits dont la plupart ne faisaient peut-être pas alors une grande nouvelle dans le monde.'—C. J. F. Hénault, *Nouvel Abrégé chronologique de l'histoire de France*, nouv. éd., 1768, p. 473, A.D. 1589.]

[1] [Eds. 4 and 5 erroneously insert 'to' here.]   [2] [Eds. 1–3 read 'was'.]

might not occur in the execution, I do not pretend. I have yet heard of none, however, which appear insurmountable. The principal perhaps arise, not from the nature of things, but from the prejudices and opinions of the people both on this and on the other side of the Atlantic.

The American representatives could be managed. We, on this side the water, are afraid lest the multitude of American representatives should overturn the balance of the constitution, and increase too much either the influence of the crown on the one hand, or the force of the democracy on the other. But if the number of American representatives were[1] to be in proportion to the produce of American taxation, the number of people to be managed would increase exactly in proportion to the means of managing them; and the means of managing, to the number of people to be managed. The monarchical and democratical parts of the constitution would, after the union, stand exactly in the same degree of relative force with regard to one another as they had done before.

The Americans would not be oppressed. The people on the other side of the water are afraid lest their distance from the seat of government might expose them to many oppressions. But their representatives in parliament, of which the number ought from the first to be considerable, would easily be able to protect them from all oppression. The distance could not much weaken the dependency of the representative upon the constituent, and the former would still feel that he owed his seat in parliament, and all the consequence which he derived from it, to the good-will of the latter. It would be the interest of the former, therefore, to cultivate that good-will by complaining, with all the authority of a member of the legislature, of every outrage which any civil or military officer might be guilty of in those remote parts of the empire. The distance of America from the seat of government, besides, the natives[2] of that country might flatter themselves, with some appearance of reason too, would not be of very long continuance. Such has hitherto been the rapid progress of that country in wealth, population and improvement, that in the course of little more than a century, perhaps, the produce of American might exceed that of British taxation. The seat of the empire would then naturally remove itself to that part of the empire which contributed most to the general defence and support of the whole.

---

[1] [Eds. 1–3 read 'was'.]   [2] [Ed. 1 reads 'nations'.]

The discovery of America and the Cape passage are the greatest events in history: the misfortunes of the natives of the East and West Indies may be temporary, so the results may be beneficial to all.

The discovery of America, and that of a passage to the East Indies by the Cape of Good Hope, are the two greatest and most important events recorded in the history of mankind.[1] Their consequences have already been very great: but, in the short period of between two and three centuries which has elapsed since these discoveries were made, it is impossible that the whole extent of their consequences can have been seen. What benefits, or what misfortunes to mankind may hereafter result from those great events, no human wisdom can foresee. By uniting, in some measure, the most distant parts of the world, by enabling them to relieve one another's wants, to increase one another's enjoyments, and to encourage one another's industry, their general tendency would seem to be beneficial. To the natives, however, both of the East and West Indies, all the commercial benefits which can have resulted from those events have been sunk and lost in the dreadful misfortunes which they have occasioned. These misfortunes, however, seem to have arisen rather from accident than from any thing in the nature of those events themselves. At the particular time when these discoveries were made, the superiority of force happened to be so great on the side of the Europeans, that they were enabled to commit with impunity every sort of injustice in those remote countries. Hereafter, perhaps, the natives of those countries may grow stronger, or those of Europe may grow weaker, and the inhabitants of all the different quarters of the world may arrive at that equality of courage and force which, by inspiring mutual fear, can alone overawe the injustice of independent nations into some sort of respect for the rights of one another. But nothing seems more likely to establish this equality of force than that mutual communication of knowledge and of all sorts of improvements which an extensive commerce from all countries to all countries naturally, or rather necessarily, carries along with it.

Meantime the discovery has exalted the mercantile system.

In the mean time one of the principal effects of those discoveries has been to raise the mercantile system to a degree of splendour and glory which it

[1] [Raynal begins his *Histoire philosophique* with the words 'Il n'y a point eu d'événement aussi intéressant pour l'espèce humaine en général et pour les peuples de l'Europe en particulier, que la découverte du nouveau monde et le passage aux Indes par le Cap de Bonne-Espérance. Alors a commencé une révolution dans le commerce, dans la puissance des nations, dans les mœurs, l'industrie et le gouvernement de tous les peuples.']

could never otherwise have attained to. It is the object of that system to enrich a great nation rather by trade and manufactures than by the improvement and cultivation of land, rather by the industry of the towns than by that of the country. But, in consequence of those discoveries, the commercial towns of Europe, instead of being the manufacturers and carriers for but a very small part of the world (that part of Europe which is washed by the Atlantic ocean, and the countries which lie round the Baltic and Mediterranean seas), have now become the manufacturers for the numerous and thriving cultivators of America, and the carriers, and in some respects the manufacturers too, for almost all the different nations of Asia, Africa, and America. Two new worlds have been opened to their industry, each of them much greater and more extensive than the old one, and the market of one of them growing still greater and greater every day.

The countries which possess America and trade to the East Indies appear to get all the advantage, but this is not the case. The countries which possess the colonies of America, and which trade directly to the East Indies, enjoy, indeed, the whole shew and splendour of this great commerce. Other countries, however, notwithstanding all the invidious restraints by which it is meant to exclude them, frequently enjoy a greater share of the real benefit of it. The colonies of Spain and Portugal, for example, give more real encouragement to the industry of other countries than to that of Spain and Portugal. In the single article of linen alone the consumption of those colonies amounts, it is said, but I do not pretend to warrant the quantity, to more than three millions sterling a year. But this great consumption is almost entirely supplied by France, Flanders, Holland, and Germany. Spain and Portugal furnish but a small part of it. The capital which supplies the colonies with this great quantity of linen is annually distributed among, and furnishes a revenue to the inhabitants of those other countries. The profits of it only are spent in Spain and Portugal, where they help to support the sumptuous profusion of the merchants of Cadiz and Lisbon.

The monopoly regulations sometimes harm the country which establishes them more than others. Even the regulations by which each nation endeavours to secure to itself the exclusive trade of its own colonies, are frequently more hurtful to the countries in favour of which they are established than to those against which they are established. The unjust oppression of the industry of other countries falls back, if I may say so, upon the heads of the oppressors, and crushes their industry more than it does that of those other countries. By those regulations, for example, the merchant of Hamburgh must send the linen which he destines for the American market to London, and he must bring back from thence the tobacco which he destines for the German market; because he can neither send the one directly to America, nor bring back the other directly from thence. By this restraint he is probably obliged to sell the one somewhat cheaper, and to buy the other somewhat dearer than he otherwise might have done; and his profits are probably somewhat abridged by means of it. In this trade, however, between Hamburgh and London, he certainly receives the returns of his capital much more quickly than he could possibly have done in the direct trade to America, even though we should suppose, what is by no means the case, that the payments of America were as punctual as those of London. In the trade, therefore, to which those regulations confine the merchant of Hamburgh, his capital can keep in constant employment a much greater quantity of German industry than it possibly could have done in the trade from which he is excluded. Though the one employment, therefore, may to him perhaps be less profitable than the other, it cannot be less advantageous to his country. It is quite otherwise with the employment into which the monopoly naturally attracts, if I may say so, the capital of the London merchant. That employment may, perhaps, be more profitable to him than the greater part of other employments, but, on account of the slowness of the returns, it cannot be more advantageous to his country.

The mother countries have engrossed only the expense and inconveniencies of possessing colonies. After all the unjust attempts, therefore, of every country in Europe to engross to itself the whole advantage of the trade of its own colonies, no country has yet been able to engross to itself any thing but the expence of supporting in time of peace and of defending in time of war the oppressive authority which it assumes over them. The inconveniencies resulting from the possession of its colonies, every country has engrossed to itself completely. The advantages resulting from their trade it has been obliged to share with many other countries.

The monopoly of American trade is a dazzling object. At first sight, no doubt, the monopoly of the great commerce of America, naturally seems to be an acquisition of the highest value. To the undiscerning eye of giddy ambition, it naturally presents itself amidst the confused scramble of politics and war, as a very dazzling object to fight for. The dazzling splendour of the object, however, the immense greatness of the commerce, is the very quality which renders the monopoly of it hurtful, or which makes one employment, in its own nature necessarily less advantageous to the country than the greater part of other employments, absorb a much greater proportion of the capital of the country than what would otherwise have gone to it.

The stock of a country naturally seeks the employment most advantageous to the country, The mercantile stock of every country, it has been shewn in the second book,[1] naturally seeks, if one may say so, the employment most advantageous to that country. If it is employed in the carrying trade, the country to which it belongs becomes the emporium of the goods of all the countries whose trade that stock carries on. But the owner of that stock necessarily wishes to dispose of as great a part of those goods as he can at home. He thereby saves himself the trouble, risk, and expence, of exportation, and he will upon that account be glad to sell them at home, not only for a much smaller price, but with somewhat a smaller profit than he might expect to make by sending them abroad. He naturally, therefore, endeavours as much as he can to turn his carrying trade into a foreign trade of consumption. If his stock again is employed in a foreign trade of consumption, he will, for the same reason, be glad to dispose of at home as great a part as he can of the home goods, which he collects in order to export to some foreign market, and he will thus endeavour, as much as he can, to turn his foreign trade of consumption into a home trade. The mercantile stock of every

preferring the near to the more distant employments, country naturally courts in this manner the near, and shuns the distant employment; naturally courts the employment in which the returns are frequent, and shuns that in which they are distant and slow; naturally courts the employment in which it can maintain the greatest quantity of productive labour in the country to which it belongs, or in which its owner resides, and shuns that in which it can maintain there the smallest quantity. It naturally courts the employment which in ordinary cases is most advantageous, and shuns that which in ordinary cases is least advantageous to that country.

unless profits are higher in the more But if in any of those distant employments, which in ordinary cases are less advantageous to the

---

[1] [Above, vol. i., pp. 381, 396.]

*distant, which indi-
cates that the more
distant employment
is necessary.* country, the profit should happen to rise somewhat higher than what is sufficient to balance the natural preference which is given to nearer employments, this superiority of profit will draw stock from those nearer employments, till the profits of all return to their proper level. This superiority of profit, however, is a proof that, in the actual circumstances of the society, those distant employments are somewhat under-stocked in proportion to other employments, and that the stock of the society is not distributed in the properest manner among all the different employments carried on in it. It is a proof that something is either bought cheaper or sold dearer than it ought to be, and that some particular class of citizens is more or less oppressed either by paying more or by getting less than what is suitable to that equality, which ought to take place, and which naturally does take place among all the different classes of them. Though the same capital never will maintain the same quantity of productive labour in a distant as in a near employment, yet a distant employment may be as necessary for the welfare of the society as a near one; the goods which the distant employment deals in being necessary, perhaps, for carrying on many of the nearer employments. But if the profits of those who deal in such goods are above their proper level, those goods will be sold dearer than they ought to be, or somewhat above their natural price, and all those engaged in the nearer employments will be more or less oppressed by this high price. Their interest, therefore, in this case requires that some stock should be withdrawn from those nearer employments, and turned towards that distant one,[1] in order to reduce its profits to their proper level, and the price of the goods which it deals in to their natural price. In this extraordinary case, the public interest requires that some stock should be withdrawn from those employments which in ordinary cases are more advantageous, and turned towards one which in ordinary cases is less advantageous to the public: and in this extraordinary case, the natural interests and inclinations of men coincide as exactly with the public interest as in all other ordinary cases, and lead them to withdraw stock from the near, and to turn it towards the distant employment.

*If too much goes to
any employment,
profit falls in that
employment and* It is thus that the private interests and passions of individuals naturally dispose them to turn their stock towards the employments which in ordinary

---

[1] [Ed. 1 reads 'distant employment'.]

the proper distribution is soon restored. cases are most advantageous to the society. But if from this natural preference they should turn too much of it towards those employments, the fall of profit in them and the rise of it in all others immediately dispose them to alter this faulty distribution. Without any intervention of law, therefore, the private interests and passions of men naturally lead them to divide and distribute the stock of every society, among all the different employments carried on in it, as nearly as possible in the proportion which is most agreeable to the interest of the whole society.

The mercantile system disturbs this distribution, especially in regard to American and Indian trade. All the different regulations of the mercantile system, necessarily derange more or less this natural and most advantageous distribution of stock. But those which concern the trade to America and the East Indies derange it perhaps more than any other; because the trade to those two great continents absorbs a greater quantity of stock than any two other branches of trade. The regulations, however, by which this derangement is effected in those two different branches of trade are not altogether the same. Monopoly is the great engine of both; but it is a different sort of monopoly. Monopoly of one kind or another, indeed, seems to be the sole engine of the mercantile system.

The Portuguese attempted at first to exclude all other nations from trading in the Indian Seas, and the Dutch still exclude all other nations from trade with the Spice Islands. In the trade to America every nation endeavours to engross as much as possible the whole market of its own colonies, by fairly excluding all other nations from any direct trade to them. During the greater part of the sixteenth century, the Portugueze endeavoured to manage the trade to the East Indies in the same manner, by claiming the sole right of sailing in the Indian seas, on account of the merit of having first found out the road to them. The Dutch still continue to exclude all other European nations from any direct trade to their spice islands. Monopolies of this kind are evidently established against all other European nations, who are thereby not only excluded from a trade to which it might be convenient for them to turn some part of their stock, but are obliged to buy the goods which that trade deals in somewhat dearer, than if they could import them themselves directly from the countries which produce them.

Now the principal ports are open, but But since the fall of the power of Portugal, no European nation has claimed the exclusive right of *each country has established an exclusive company.* sailing in the Indian seas, of which the principal ports are now open to the ships of all European nations. Except in Portugal,[1] however, and within these few years in France,[2] the trade to the East Indies has in every European country been subjected to an exclusive company. Monopolies of this kind are properly established against the very nation which erects them. The greater part of that nation are thereby not only excluded from a trade to which it might be convenient for them to turn some part of their stock, but are obliged to buy the goods which that trade deals in, somewhat dearer than if it was open and free to all their countrymen. Since the establishment of the English East India company, for example, the other inhabitants of England, over and above being excluded from the trade, must have paid in the price of the East India goods which they have consumed, not only for all the extraordinary profits which the company may have made upon those goods in consequence of their monopoly, but for all the extraordinary waste which the fraud and abuse, inseparable from the management of the affairs of so great a company, must necessarily have occasioned. The absurdity of this second kind of monopoly, therefore, is much more manifest than that of the first.

Both these kinds of monopolies derange more or less the natural distribution of the stock of the society: but they do not always derange it in the same way.

Monopolies of the American kind always attract, but monopolies of exclusive companies sometimes attract, sometimes repel stock. Monopolies of the first kind always attract to the particular trade in which they are established, a greater proportion of the stock of the society than what would go to that trade of its own accord. Monopolies of the second kind may sometimes attract stock towards the particular trade in which they are established, and sometimes repel it from that trade according to different circumstances. In poor countries they naturally attract towards that trade more stock than would otherwise go to it. In rich countries they naturally repel from it a good deal of stock which would otherwise go to it.

In poor countries they attract, Such poor countries as Sweden and Denmark, for example, would probably have never sent a single ship to the East Indies, had not the trade been subjected to an

---

[1] [See below, p. 149.]

[2] [The monopoly of the French East India Company was abolished in 1769.—See the Continuation of Anderson's *Commerce*, 1801, vol. iv., p. 128.]

exclusive company. The establishment of such a company necessarily encourages adventurers. Their monopoly secures them against
all competitors in the home market, and they have the same chance
for foreign markets with the traders of other nations. Their monopoly shows them the certainty of a great profit upon a considerable
quantity of goods, and the chance of a considerable profit upon a
great quantity. Without such extraordinary encouragement, the
poor traders of such poor countries would probably never have
thought of hazarding their small capitals in so very distant and
uncertain an adventure as the trade to the East Indies must naturally
have appeared to them.

in rich they repel.   Such a rich country as Holland, on the contrary,
would probably, in the case of a free trade, send many more ships
to the East Indies than it actually does. The limited stock of the
Dutch East India company[1] probably repels from that trade many
great mercantile capitals which would otherwise go to it. The mercantile capital of Holland is so great that it is, as it were, continually
overflowing, sometimes into the public funds of foreign countries,
sometimes into loans to private traders and adventurers of foreign
countries, sometimes into the most round-about foreign trades of
consumption, and sometimes into the carrying trade. All near
employments being completely filled up, all the capital which can
be placed in them with any tolerable profit being already placed
in them, the capital of Holland necessarily flows towards the
most distant employments. The trade to the East Indies, if it were[2]
altogether free, would probably absorb the greater part of this re-
dundant capital. The East Indies offer a market both for the manufactures of Europe and for the gold and silver as well as for several
other productions of America, greater and more extensive than both
Europe and America put together.

Both effects are   Every derangement of the natural distribution of
hurtful.   stock is necessarily hurtful to the society in which
it takes place; whether it be by repelling from a particular trade the
stock which would otherwise go to it, or by attracting towards a
particular trade that which would not otherwise come to it. If,
without any exclusive company, the trade of Holland to the East
Indies would be greater than it actually is, that country must suffer

---

[1] [Raynal, *Histoire philosophique*, ed. Amsterdam, 1773, tom. i., p. 203, gives the
original capital as 6,459,840 florins.]
[2] [Eds. 1–3 read 'if it was'.]

a considerable loss by part of its capital being excluded from the employment most convenient for that part. And in the same manner, if, without an exclusive company, the trade of Sweden and Denmark to the East Indies would be less than it actually is, or, what perhaps is more probable, would not exist at all, those two countries must likewise suffer a considerable loss by part of their capital being drawn into an employment which must be more or less unsuitable to their present circumstances. Better for them, perhaps, in their present circumstances, to buy East India goods of other nations, even though they should pay somewhat dearer, than to turn so great a part of their small capital to so very distant a trade, in which the returns are so very slow, in which that capital can maintain so small a quantity of productive labour at home, where productive labour is so much wanted, where so little is done, and where so much is to do.

A country which cannot trade to the East Indies without an exclusive company should not trade there. Though without an exclusive company, therefore, a particular country should not be able to carry on any direct trade to the East Indies, it will not from thence follow that such a company ought to be established there, but only that such a country ought not in these circumstances to trade directly to the East Indies. That such companies are not in general necessary for carrying on the East India trade, is sufficiently demonstrated by the experience of the Portugueze, who enjoyed almost the whole of it for more than a century together without any exclusive company.

The idea that the large capital of a company is necessary is fallacious. No private merchant, it has been said, could well have capital sufficient to maintain factors and agents in the different ports of the East Indies, in order to provide goods for the ships which he might occasionally send thither; and yet, unless he was able to do this, the difficulty of finding a cargo might frequently make his ships lose the season for returning, and the expence of so long a delay would not only eat up the whole profit of the adventure, but frequently occasion a very considerable loss. This argument, however, if it proved any thing at all, would prove that no one great branch of trade could be carried on without an exclusive company, which is contrary to the experience of all nations. There is no great branch of trade in which the capital of any one private merchant is sufficient, for carrying on all the subordinate branches which must be carried on, in order to carry on the principal one.[1] But when a nation is ripe for any great branch of trade, some merchants naturally turn their capitals towards the principal, and some towards the subordinate branches of it; and though all the different branches of it are in this manner carried on, yet it very seldom happens that they are all carried on by the capital of one private merchant. If a nation, therefore, is ripe for the East India trade, a certain portion of its capital will naturally divide itself among all the different branches of that trade. Some of its merchants will find it for their interest to reside in the East Indies, and to employ their capitals there in providing goods for the ships which are to be sent out by other merchants who reside in Europe. The settlements which different European nations have obtained in the East Indies, if they were taken from the exclusive companies to which they at present belong, and put under the immediate protection of the sovereign, would render this residence both safe and easy, at least to the merchants of the particular nations to whom those settlements belong. If at any particular time that part of the capital of any country which of its own accord tended and inclined, if I may say so, towards the East India trade, was not sufficient for carrying on all those different branches of it, it would be a proof that, at that particular time, that country was not ripe for that trade, and that it would do better to buy for some time, even at a higher price, from other European nations, the East India goods it had occasion for, than to import them itself directly from the East Indies. What it might lose by the high price of those goods could seldom be equal to the loss which it would sustain by the distraction of a large portion of its capital from other employments more necessary, or more useful, or more suitable to its circumstances and situation, than a direct trade to the East Indies.

There are not numerous and thriving colonies in Africa and the East Indies, as in America. Though the Europeans possess many considerable settlements both upon the coast of Africa and in the East Indies, they have not yet established in either of those countries such numerous and thriving colonies as those in the islands and continent of America. Africa, however, as well as several of the countries comprehended under the general name of the East Indies, are inhabited by barbarous nations. But those nations were by no means so weak and defenceless as the miserable and helpless Americans; and in proportion to the natural fertility of the countries which they inhabited,

---

[1] [Ed. 1 reads 'the principal branch'.]

they were besides much more populous. The most barbarous nations either of Africa or of the East Indies were shepherds; even the Hottentots were so.[1] But the natives of every part of America, except Mexico and Peru, were only hunters; and the difference is very great between the number of shepherds and that of hunters whom the same extent of equally fertile territory can maintain. In Africa and the East Indies, therefore, it was more difficult to displace the natives, and to extend the European plantations over the greater part of the lands of the original inhabitants. The genius of exclusive companies, besides, is unfavourable, it has already been observed,[2] to the growth of new colonies, and has probably been the principal cause of the little progress which they have made in the East Indies. The Portugueze carried on the trade both to Africa and the East Indies without any exclusive companies, and their settlements at Congo, Angola, and Benguela on the coast of Africa, and at Goa in the East Indies, though much depressed by superstition and every sort of bad government, yet bear some faint resemblance to the colonies of America, and are partly inhabited by Portugueze who have been established there for several generations. The Dutch settlements at the Cape of Good Hope and at Batavia, are at present the most considerable colonies which the Europeans have established either in Africa or in the East Indies, and both these[3] settlements are peculiarly fortunate in their situation. The Cape of Good Hope was inhabited by a race of people almost as barbarous and quite as incapable of defending themselves as the natives of America. It is besides the half-way house, if one may say so, between Europe and the East Indies, at which almost every European ship makes some stay both in going and returning. The supplying of those ships with every sort of fresh provisions, with fruit and sometimes with wine, affords alone a very extensive market for the surplus produce of the colonists. What the Cape of Good Hope is between Europe and every part of the East Indies, Batavia is between the principal countries of the East Indies. It lies upon the most frequented road from Indostan to China and Japan, and is nearly about mid-way upon that road. Almost all the ships too that sail between Europe and China touch at Batavia; and it is, over and above all this, the center and principal mart of what is called the country trade of the

---

[1] [Raynal, *Histoire philosophique*, 1773, tom. i., p. 178.]
[2] [Above, pp. 87, 88.]
[3] [Ed. 1 reads 'those'.]

East Indies; not only of that part of it which is carried on by Europeans, but of that which is carried on by the native Indians; and vessels navigated by the inhabitants of China and Japan, of Tonquin, Malacca, Cochin-China, and the island of Celebes, are frequently to be seen in its port. Such advantageous situations have enabled those two colonies to surmount all the obstacles which the oppressive genius of an exclusive company may have occasionally opposed to their growth. They have enabled Batavia to surmount the additional disadvantage of perhaps the most unwholesome climate in the world.

The Dutch exclusive company destroys spices and nutmeg trees, The English and Dutch companies, though they have established no considerable colonies, except the two above mentioned, have both made considerable conquests in the East Indies. But in the manner in which they both govern their new subjects, the natural genius of an exclusive company has shown itself most distinctly. In the spice islands the Dutch are said to[1] burn all the spiceries which a fertile season produces beyond what they expect to dispose of in Europe with such a profit as they think sufficient. In the islands where they have no settlements, they give a premium to those who collect the young blossoms and green leaves of the clove and nutmeg trees which naturally grow there, but which this savage[2] policy has now, it is said, almost completely extirpated. Even in the islands where they have settlements they have very much reduced, it is said, the number of those trees. If the produce even of their own islands was much greater than what suited their market, the natives, they suspect, might find means to convey some part of it to other nations; and the best way, they imagine, to secure their own monopoly, is to take care that no more shall grow than what they themselves carry to market. By different arts of oppression they have reduced *and has reduced the population of the Moluccas.* the population of several of the Moluccas nearly to the number which is sufficient to supply with fresh provisions and other necessaries of life their own insignificant garrisons, and such of their ships as occasionally come there for a cargo of spices. Under the government even of the Portugueze, however, those islands are said to have been tolerably *The English company has the same tendency.* well inhabited. The English company have not yet had time to establish in Bengal so perfectly destructive a system. The plan of their government, how-

---

[1] [Ed. 1 does not contain 'are said to'. The statement has already been twice made, vol. i., p. 177, and vol. ii., p. 31.]   [2] [Ed. 1 reads 'barbarous'.]

ever, has had exactly the same tendency. It has not been uncommon, I am well assured, for the chief, that is, the first clerk of a factory, to order a peasant to plough up a rich field of poppies, and sow it with rice or some other grain. The pretence was, to prevent a scarcity of provisions; but the real reason, to give the chief an opportunity of selling at a better price a large quantity of opium, which he happened then to have upon hand. Upon other occasions the order has been reversed; and a rich field of rice or other grain has been ploughed up, in order to make room for a plantation of poppies; when the chief foresaw that extraordinary profit was likely to be made by opium. The servants of the company have upon several occasions attempted to establish in their own favour the monopoly of some of the most important branches, not only of the foreign, but of the inland trade of the country. Had they been allowed to go on, it is impossible that they should not at some time or another have attempted to restrain the production of the particular articles of which they had thus usurped the monopoly, not only to the quantity which they themselves could purchase, but to that which they could expect to sell with such a profit as they might think sufficient. In the course of a century or two, the policy of the English company would in this manner have probably proved as completely destructive as that of the Dutch.

This destructive system is contrary to their interest as sovereigns, Nothing, however, can be more directly contrary to the real interest of those companies, considered as the sovereigns of the countries which they have conquered, than this destructive plan. In almost all countries the revenue of the sovereign is drawn from that of the people. The greater the revenue of the people, therefore, the greater the annual produce of their land and labour, the more they can afford to the sovereign. It is his interest, therefore, to increase as much as possible that annual produce. But if this is the interest of every sovereign, it is peculiarly so of one whose revenue, like that of the sovereign of Bengal, arises chiefly from a land-rent. That rent must necessarily be in proportion to the quantity and value of the produce, and both the one and the other must depend upon the extent of the market. The quantity will always be suited with more or less exactness to the consumption of those who can afford to pay for it, and the price which they will pay will always be in proportion to the eagerness of their competition. It is the interest of such a sovereign, therefore, to open the most extensive market for the produce of his country, to allow the most perfect freedom of commerce, in order to increase as much as possible the number and the competition of buyers; and upon this account to abolish, not only all monopolies, but all restraints upon the transportation of the home produce from one part of the country to another, upon its exportation to foreign countries, or upon the importation of goods of any kind for which it can be exchanged. He is in this manner most likely to increase both the quantity and value of that produce, and consequently of his own share of it, or of his own revenue.

but they prefer the transitory profits of the monopolist merchant to the permanent revenue of the sovereign. But a company of merchants are, it seems, incapable of considering themselves as sovereigns, even after they have become such. Trade, or buying in order to sell again, they still consider as their[1] principal business, and by a strange absurdity, regard the character of the sovereign as but an appendix to that of the merchant, as something which ought to be made subservient to it, or by means of which they may be enabled to buy cheaper in India, and thereby to sell with a better profit in Europe. They endeavour for this purpose to keep out as much as possible all competitors from the market of the countries which are subject to their government, and consequently to reduce, at least, some part of the surplus produce of those countries to what is barely sufficient for supplying their own demand, or to what they can expect to sell in Europe with such a profit as they may think reasonable. Their mercantile habits draw them in this manner, almost necessarily, though perhaps insensibly, to prefer upon all ordinary occasions the little and transitory profit of the monopolist to the great and permanent revenue of the sovereign, and would gradually lead them to treat the countries subject to their government nearly as the Dutch treat the Moluccas. It is the interest of the East India company considered as sovereigns, that the European goods which are carried to their Indian dominions, should be sold there as cheap as possible; and that the Indian goods which are brought from thence should bring there as good a price, or should be sold there as dear as possible. But the reverse of this is their interest as merchants. As sovereigns, their interest is exactly the same with that of the country which they govern. As merchants, their interest is directly opposite to that interest.[2]

---

[1] [Ed. 1 reads 'the'.]

[2] [Ed. 1 does not contain these four sentences beginning 'It is the interest'.]

The administration in India thinks only of buying cheap and selling dear, But if the genius of such a government, even as to what concerns its direction in Europe, is in this manner essentially and perhaps incurably faulty, that of its administration in India is still more so. That administration is necessarily composed of a council of merchants, a profession no doubt extremely respectable, but which in no country in the world carries along with it that sort of authority which naturally over-awes the people, and without force commands their willing obedience. Such a council can command obedience only by the military force with which they are accompanied, and their government is therefore necessarily military and despotical. Their proper business, however, is that of merchants. It is to sell, upon their masters account, the European goods consigned to them, and to buy in return Indian goods for the European market. It is to sell the one as dear and to buy the other as cheap as possible, and consequently to exclude as much as possible all rivals from the particular market where they keep their shop. The genius of the administration, therefore, so far as concerns the trade of the company, is the same as that of the direction. It tends to make government subservient to the interest of monopoly, and consequently to stunt the natural growth of some parts at least of the surplus produce of the country to what is barely sufficient for answering the demand of the company.

its members trade on their own account and cannot be prevented from doing so, All the members of the administration, besides, trade more or less upon their own account, and it is in vain to prohibit them from doing so. Nothing can be more completely foolish than to expect that the clerks of a great counting-house at ten thousand miles distance, and consequently almost quite out of sight, should, upon a simple order from their masters, give up at once doing any sort of business upon their own account, abandon for ever all hopes of making a fortune, of which they have the means in their hands, and content themselves with the moderate salaries which those masters allow them, and which, moderate as they are, can seldom be augmented, being commonly as large as the real profits of the company trade can afford. In such circumstances, to prohibit the servants of the company from trading upon their own account, can have scarce any other effect than to enable the superior servants, under pretence of executing their masters order, to oppress such of the inferior ones as have had the misfortune to fall under their displeasure. The servants

naturally endeavour to establish the same monopoly in favour
of their own private trade as of the public trade of the company. If
they are suffered to act as they could wish, they will establish this
monopoly openly and directly, by fairly prohibiting all other
people from trading in the articles in which they chuse to deal; and
this, perhaps, is the best and least oppressive way of establishing it.
But if by an order from Europe they are prohibited from doing this,
they will, notwithstanding, endeavour to establish a monopoly of
the same kind, secretly and indirectly, in a way that is much more
destructive to the country. They will employ the whole authority
of government, and pervert the administration of justice, in order
to harass and ruin those who interfere with them in any branch of
commerce which, by means of agents, either concealed, or at least
not publicly avowed, they may chuse to carry on. But the private

and this private
trade is more exten-
sive and harmful
than the public
trade of the
company.

trade of the servants will naturally extend to a much
greater variety of articles than the public trade of
the company. The public trade of the company
extends no further than the trade with Europe, and
comprehends a part only of the foreign trade of the
country. But the private trade of the servants may extend to all the
different branches both of its inland and foreign trade. The monopoly of the company can tend only to stunt the natural growth of
that part of the surplus produce which, in the case of a free trade,
would be exported to Europe. That of the servants tends to stunt
the natural growth of every part of the produce in which they chuse
to deal, of what is destined for home consumption, as well as of
what is destined for exportation; and consequently to degrade the
cultivation of the whole country, and to reduce the number of its
inhabitants. It tends to reduce the quantity of every sort of produce,
even that of the necessaries of life, whenever the servants of the company chuse to deal in them, to what those servants can both afford
to buy and expect to sell with such a profit as pleases them.[1]

The interest of the
servants is not, like
the real interest
of the company, the

From the nature of their situation too the servants
must be more disposed to support with rigorous
severity their own interest against that of the

[1] [Smith had in his library (see Bonar's *Catalogue*, p. 15) William Bolts, *Considerations
on India Affairs, particularly respecting the present state of Bengal and its Dependencies*,
ed. 1772. Pt. i., ch. xiv., of this is 'On the general modern trade of the English in Bengal;
on the oppressions and monopolies which have been the causes of the decline of trade,
the decrease of the revenues, and the present ruinous condition of affairs in Bengal'. At
p. 215 we find 'the servants of the Company . . . directly or indirectly monopolise
whatever branches they please of the internal trade of those countries'.]

same as that of the country. country which they govern, than their masters can be to support theirs. The country belongs to their masters, who cannot avoid having some regard for the interest of what belongs to them. But it does not belong to the servants. The real interest of their masters, if they were capable of understanding it, is the same with that of the country,[1] and it is from ignorance chiefly,[2] and the meanness of mercantile prejudice, that they ever oppress it. But the real interest of the servants is by no means the same with that of the country, and the most perfect information would not necessarily put an end to their oppressions. The regulations accordingly which have been sent out from Europe, though they have been frequently weak, have upon most occasions been well-meaning.[3] More intelligence and perhaps less good-meaning has sometimes appeared in those established by the servants in India. It is a very singular government in which every member of the administration wishes to get out of the country, and consequently to have done with the government, as soon as he can, and to whose interest, the day after he has left it and carried his whole fortune with him, it is perfectly indifferent though[4] the whole country was swallowed up by an earthquake.

---

[1] The interest of every proprietor of India Stock, however, is by no means the same with that of the country in the government of which his vote gives him some influence. See Book V. Chap. i. Part 3d. [This note appears first in ed. 3; ed. 2 has the following note: 'This would be exactly true if those masters never had any other interest but that which belongs to them as Proprietors of India stock. But they frequently have another of much greater importance. Frequently a man of great, sometimes even a man of moderate fortune, is willing to give thirteen or fourteen hundred pounds (the present price of a thousand pounds share in India stock) merely for the influence which he expects to acquire by a vote in the Court of Proprietors. It gives him a share, though not in the plunder, yet in the appointment of the plunderers of India; the Directors, though they make those appointments, being necessarily more or less under the influence of the Court of Proprietors, which not only elects them, but sometimes over-rules their appointments. A man of great or even a man of moderate fortune, provided he can enjoy this influence for a few years, and thereby get a certain number of his friends appointed to employments in India, frequently cares little about the dividend which he can expect from so small a capital, or even about the improvement or loss of the capital itself upon which his vote is founded. About the prosperity or ruin of the great empire, in the government of which that vote gives him a share, he seldom cares at all. No other sovereigns ever were, or from the nature of things ever could be, so perfectly indifferent about the happiness or misery of their subjects, the improvement or waste of their dominions, the glory or disgrace of their administration, as, from irresistible moral causes, the greater part of the Proprietors of such a mercantile Company are, and necessarily must be.' This matter with some slight alterations reappears in the portion of bk. v., chap. i., part iii., art. 1st, which was added in ed. 3 below, p. 275.]

[2] [Ed. 1 reads 'ignorance only'.]

[3] [Ed. 1 reads 'have commonly been well meaning'.]

[4] [Ed. 1 reads 'if'.]

The evils come from the system, not from the character of the men who administer it. I mean not, however, by any thing which I have here said, to throw any odious imputation upon the general character of the servants of the East India company, and much less upon that of any particular persons. It is the system of government, the situation in which they are[1] placed, that I mean to censure; not the character of those who have acted in it. They acted as their situation naturally directed, and they who have clamoured the loudest against them would, probably, not have acted better themselves. In war and negociation, the councils of Madras and Calcutta have upon several occasions conducted themselves with a resolution and decisive wisdom which would have done honour to the senate of Rome in the best days of that republic. The members of those councils, however, had been bred to professions very different from war and politics. But their situation alone, without education, experience, or even example, seems to have formed in them all at once the great qualities which it required, and to have inspired them both with abilities and virtues which they themselves could not well know that they possessed. If upon some occasions, therefore, it has animated them to actions of magnanimity which could not well have been expected from them, we should not wonder if upon others it has prompted them to exploits of somewhat a different nature.

Exclusive companies are nuisances. Such exclusive companies, therefore, are nuisances in every respect; always more or less inconvenient to the countries in which they are established, and destructive to those which have the misfortune to fall under their government.

[1] [Eds. 1 and 2 read 'were'.]

CHAPTER VIII

Conclusion of the Mercantile System[1]

The mercantile system discourages the exportation of materials of manufacture and instruments of trade.

Though the encouragement of exportation, and the discouragement of importation, are the two great engines by which the mercantile system proposes to enrich every country, yet with regard to some particular commodities, it seems to follow an opposite plan: to discourage exportation and to encourage importation. Its ultimate object, however, it pretends, is always the same, to enrich the country by an advantageous balance of trade. It discourages the exportation of the materials of manufacture, and of the instruments of trade, in order to give our own workmen an advantage, and to enable them to undersell those of other nations in all foreign markets: and by restraining, in this manner, the exportation of a few commodities, of no great price, it proposes to occasion a much

It encourages the importation of materials though not of instruments of trade.

greater and more valuable exportation of others. It encourages the importation of the materials of manufacture, in order that our own people may be enabled to work them up more cheaply, and thereby prevent a greater and more valuable importation of the manufactured commodities. I do not observe, at least in our Statute Book, any encouragement given to the importation of the instruments of trade. When manufactures have advanced to a certain pitch of greatness, the fabrication of the instruments of trade becomes itself the object of a great number of very important manufactures. To give any particular encouragement to the importation of such instruments, would interfere too much with the interest of those manufactures. Such importation, therefore, instead of being encouraged, has frequently been prohibited. Thus the importation of wool cards, except from Ireland, or when brought in as wreck or prize goods, was prohibited by the 3d of Edward IV.;[2] which

---

[1] [This chapter appears first in Additions and Corrections and ed. 3.
[2] [C. 4.]

prohibition was renewed by the 39th of Elizabeth,[1] and has been continued and rendered perpetual by subsequent laws.[2]

The importation of the materials of manufacture has sometimes been encouraged by an exemption from the duties to which other goods are subject, and sometimes by bounties.

Various materials *are exempt from* *customs duties.* The importation of sheep's wool from several different countries,[3] of cotton wool from all countries,[4] of undressed flax,[5] of the greater part of dying drugs,[6] of the greater part of undressed hides from Ireland or the British colonies,[7] of seal skins from the British Greenland fishery,[8] of pig and bar iron from the British colonies,[9] as well as of several other materials of manufacture, has been encouraged by an exemption from all duties, if properly entered at the customhouse. The private interest of our merchants and manufacturers may, perhaps, have extorted from the legislature these exemptions, as well as the greater part of our other commercial regulations. They are, however, perfectly just and reasonable, and if, consistently with the necessities of the state, they could be extended to all the other materials of manufacture, the public would certainly be a gainer.

Yarn, though a *manufactured article,* *is free from duty,* The avidity of our great manufacturers, however, has in some cases extended these exemptions a good deal beyond what can justly be considered as the rude materials of their work. By the 24 Geo. II. chap. 46. a small duty of only one penny the pound was imposed upon the importation of foreign brown linen yarn, instead of much higher duties to which it had been subjected before, viz. of sixpence the pound upon sail yarn, of one shilling the pound upon all French and Dutch yarn, and of two pounds thirteen shillings and fourpence upon the hundred weight of all spruce or Muscovia yarn.[10] But our manufacturers were not long satisfied with this reduction. By the 29th of the same king, chap. 15. the same law which gave a bounty upon the exportation of British and Irish linen of which the price did not

---

[1] [C. 14.]   [2] [3 Car. I., c. 4; 13 and 14 Car. II., c. 19.]
[3] [From Ireland, 12 Geo. II., c. 21; 26 Geo. II., c. 8. Spanish wool for clothing and Spanish felt wool.—Saxby, *British Customs*, p. 263.]
[4] [6 Geo. III., c. 52, § 20.]   [5] [4 Geo. II., c. 27.]
[6] [8 Geo. I., c. 15, § 10; see below, p. 174.]
[7] [9 Geo. III., c. 39, § 1, continued by 14 Geo. III., c. 86, § 11, and 21 Geo. III., c. 29, § 3.]
[8] [15 Geo. III., c. 31, § 10.]   [9] [Above, p. 93.]
[10] [Smith has here inadvertently given the rates at which the articles were valued in the 'Book of Rates,' 12 Car. II., c. 4, instead of the duties, which would be 20 per cent. on the rates. See below, pp. 409, 410.]

exceed eighteen pence the yard, even this small duty upon the importation of brown linen yarn was taken away. In the different operations, however, which are necessary for the preparation of linen yarn, a good deal more industry is employed, than in the subsequent operation of preparing linen cloth from linen yarn. To say nothing of the industry of the flax-growers and flax-dressers, three or four spinners, at least, are necessary, in order to keep one weaver in constant employment; and more than four-fifths of the whole quantity of labour, necessary for the preparation of linen

because the spinners are poor, unpro-tected people, and the master weavers are rich and powerful.

cloth, is employed in that of linen yarn; but our spinners are poor people, women commonly, scat-tered about in all different parts of the country, without support or protection. It is not by the sale of their work, but by that of the complete work of the weavers, that our great master manufacturers make their profits. As it is their interest to sell the complete manufacture as dear, so is it to buy the materials as cheap as possible. By extorting from the legislature bounties upon the exportation of their own linen, high duties upon the importation of all foreign linen, and a total pro-hibition of the home consumption of some sorts of French linen,[1] they endeavour to sell their own goods as dear as possible. By encouraging the importation of foreign linen yarn, and thereby bringing it into competition with that which is made by our own people, they endeavour to buy the work of the poor spinners as cheap as possible. They are as intent to keep down the wages of their own weavers, as the earnings of the poor spinners, and it is by no means for the benefit of the workman, that they endeavour either to raise the price of the complete work, or to lower that of the rude materials. [It is the industry which is carried on for the benefit of the rich and the powerful, that is principally encouraged by our mercantile system.] That which is carried on for the benefit of the poor and the indigent, is too often, either neglected, or oppressed.

This exemption and also the bounty on the exportation of linen are given by a temporary law.

Both the bounty upon the exportation of linen, and the exemption from duty upon the importation of foreign yarn, which were granted only for fifteen years, but continued by two different prolonga-tions,[2] expire with the end of the session of parliament which shall immediately follow the 24th of June 1786.

---

[1] [Above, vol. i., p. 496.]   [2] [10 Geo. III., c. 38, and 19 Geo. III., c. 27.]

Bounties on imported materials have been chiefly given to American produce, such as naval stores,

⌈The encouragement given to the importation of the materials of manufacture by bounties, has been principally confined to such as were imported from our American plantations.⌉

The first bounties of this kind were those granted, about the beginning of the present century, upon the importation of naval stores from America.[1] Under this denomination were comprehended timber fit for masts, yards, and bowsprits; hemp; tar, pitch, and turpentine. The bounty, however, of one pound the ton upon masting-timber, and that of six pounds the ton upon hemp, were extended to such as should be imported into England from Scotland.[2] Both these bounties continued without any variation, at the same rate, till they were severally allowed to expire; that upon hemp on the 1st of January 1741, and that upon masting-timber at the end of the session of parliament immediately following the 24th June 1781.

The bounties upon the importation of tar, pitch, and turpentine underwent, during their continuance, several alterations. Originally that upon tar was four pounds the ton; that upon pitch the same; and that upon turpentine, three pounds the ton. The bounty of four pounds the ton upon tar was afterwards confined to such as had been prepared in a particular manner; that upon other good, clean, and merchantable tar was reduced to two pounds four shillings the ton. The bounty upon pitch was likewise reduced to one pound; and that upon turpentine to one pound ten shillings the ton.[3]

colonial indigo,   The second bounty upon the importation of any of the materials of manufacture, according to the order of time, was that granted by the 21 Geo. II. chap. 30. upon the importation of indigo from the British plantations. When the plantation indigo was worth three-fourths of the price of the best French indigo, it was by this act entitled to a bounty of sixpence the pound. This bounty, which, like most others, was granted only for a limited time, was continued by several prolongations, but was reduced to four pence the pound.[4] It was allowed to expire with the end of the session of parliament which followed the 25th March 1781.

[1] [3 and 4 Ann, c. 10.—Anderson, *Commerce*, A.D. 1703.]

[2] [Masting-timber (and also tar, pitch and rosin), under 12 Ann, st. 1, c. 9, and masting-timber only under 2 Geo. II., c. 35, § 12. The encouragement of the growth of hemp in Scotland is mentioned in the preamble of 8 Geo. I., c. 12, and is presumably to be read into the enacting portion.]

[3] [8 Geo. I., c. 12; 2 Geo. II., c. 35, §§ 3, 11.]

[4] [3 Geo. III., c. 25.]

colonial hemp or undressed flax, The third bounty of this kind was that granted (much about the time that we were beginning sometimes to court and sometimes to quarrel with our American colonies) by the 4 Geo. III. chap. 26. upon the importation of hemp, or undressed flax, from the British plantations. This bounty was granted for twenty-one years, from the 24th June 1764, to the 24th June 1785. For the first seven years it was to be at the rate of eight pounds the ton, for the second at six pounds, and for the third at four pounds. It was not extended to Scotland, of which the climate (although hemp is sometimes raised there, in small quantities and of an inferior quality) is not very fit for that produce. Such a bounty upon the importation of Scotch flax into England would have been too great a discouragement to the native produce of the southern part of the united kingdom.

American wood, The fourth bounty of this kind, was that granted by the 5 Geo. III. chap. 45. upon the importation of wood from America. It was granted for nine years, from the 1st January 1766, to the 1st January 1775. During the first three years, it was to be for every hundred and twenty good deals, at the rate of one pound; and for every load containing fifty cubic feet of other squared timber at the rate of twelve shillings. For the second three years, it was for deals to be at the rate of fifteen shillings, and for other squared timber, at the rate of eight shillings; and for the third three years, it was for deals, to be at the rate of ten shillings, and for other squared timber, at the rate of five shillings.

colonial raw silk, The fifth bounty of this kind, was that granted by the 9 Geo. III. chap. 38. upon the importation of raw silk from the British plantations. It was granted for twenty-one years, from the 1st January 1770, to the 1st January 1791. For the first seven years it was to be at the rate of twenty-five pounds for every hundred pounds value; for the second, at twenty pounds; and for the third at fifteen pounds. The management of the silk-worm, and the preparation of silk, requires so much hand labour; and labour is so very dear in America, that even this great bounty, I have been informed, was not likely to produce any considerable effect.

colonial barrel staves, The sixth bounty of this kind, was that granted by 11 Geo. III. chap. 50. for the importation of pipe, hogshead, and barrel staves and heading from the British plantations. It was granted for nine years, from 1st January 1772, to the 1st January 1781. For the first three years, it was for a certain quantity of each, to be at the rate of six pounds; for the second three years, at four pounds; and for the third three years, at two pounds.

Irish hemp.   The seventh and last bounty of this kind, was that[1] granted by the 19 Geo. III. chap. 37. upon the importation of hemp from Ireland. It was granted in the same manner as that for the importation of hemp and undressed flax from America,[2] for twenty-one years, from the 24th June 1779, to the 24th June 1800. This term is divided, likewise, into three periods of seven years each; and in each of those periods, the rate of the Irish bounty is the same with that of the American. It does not, however, like the American bounty, extend to the importation of undressed flax. It would have been too great a discouragement to the cultivation of that plant in Great Britain. When this last bounty was granted, the British and Irish legislatures were not in much better humour with one another, than the British and American had been before. But this boon to Ireland, it is to be hoped, has been granted under more fortunate auspices, than all those to America.

These commodities were subject to duties when coming from foreign countries. It was alleged that the interest of the colonies and of the mother country was the same.   The same commodities upon which we thus gave bounties, when imported from America, were subjected to considerable duties when imported from any other country. The interest of our American colonies was regarded as the same with that of the mother country. Their wealth was considered as our wealth. Whatever money was sent out to them, it was said, came all back to us by the balance of trade, and we could never become a farthing the poorer, by any expence which we could lay out upon them. They were our own in every respect, and it was an expence laid out upon the improvement of our own property, and for the profitable employment of our own people. It is unnecessary, I apprehend, at present to say any thing further, in order to expose the folly of a system, which fatal experience has now sufficiently exposed. Had our American colonies really been a part of Great Britain, those bounties might have been considered as bounties upon production, and would still have been liable to all the objections to which such bounties are liable, but to no other.

The exportation of the materials of manufacture is sometimes discouraged by absolute prohibitions, and sometimes by high duties.

---

[1] [Additions and Corrections omits 'that'.]
[2] [The third bounty.]

The exportation of wool and live sheep is forbidden under heavy penalties, Our woollen manufacturers have been more successful than any other class of workmen, in persuading the legislature that the prosperity of the nation depended upon the success and extension of their particular business. They have not only obtained a monopoly against the consumers by an absolute prohibition of importing woollen cloths from any foreign country; but they have likewise obtained another monopoly against the sheep farmers and growers of wool, by a similar prohibition of the exportation of live sheep and wool. The severity of many of the laws which have been enacted for the security of the revenue is very justly complained of, as imposing heavy penalties upon actions which, antecedent to the statutes that declared them to be crimes, had always been understood to be innocent. But the cruellest of our revenue laws, I will venture to affirm, are mild and gentle, in comparison of some of those which the clamour of our merchants and manufacturers has extorted from the legislature, for the support of their own absurd and oppressive monopolies. Like the laws of Draco, these laws may be said to be all written in blood.

at one time mutilation and death, By the 8th of Elizabeth, chap. 3. the exporter of sheep, lambs or rams, was for the first offence to forfeit all his goods for ever, to suffer a year's imprisonment, and then to have his left hand cut off in a market town upon a market day, to be there nailed up; and for the second offence to be adjudged a felon, and to suffer death accordingly. To prevent the breed of our sheep from being propagated in foreign countries, seems to have been the object of this law. By the 13th and 14th of Charles II. chap. 18. the exportation of wool was made felony, and the exporter subjected to the same penalties and forfeitures as a felon.

but now twenty shillings for every sheep with forfeiture of the sheep and the owner's share in the ship, For the honour of the national humanity, it is to be hoped that neither of these statutes were ever executed. The first of them, however, so far as I know, has never been directly repealed, and Serjeant Hawkins seems to consider it as still in force.[1] It may however, perhaps, be considered as virtually repealed by the 12th of Charles II. chap. 32. sect. 3. which, without expressly taking away the penalties imposed by former statutes,[2] imposes a new

[1] [William Hawkins, *Treatise of the Pleas of the Crown*, 4th ed., 1762, bk. i., chap. 52.]

[2] [So far from doing so, it expressly provides that any greater penalties already prescribed shall remain in force.]

penalty, viz. That of twenty shillings for every sheep exported, or attempted to be exported, together with the forfeiture of the sheep and of the owner's share of the ship. The second of them was expressly repealed by the 7th and 8th of William III. chap. 28. sect. 4. By which it is declared that,

> Whereas the statute of the 13th and 14th of King Charles II. made against the exportation of wool, among other things in the said act mentioned, doth enact the same to be deemed felony; by the severity of which penalty the prosecution of offenders hath not been so effectually put in execution: Be it, therefore, enacted by the authority foresaid, that so much of the said act, which relates to the making the said offence felony, be repealed and made void.

and three shillings for every pound of wool, with other pains and penalties. The penalties, however, which are either imposed by this milder statute, or which, though imposed by former statutes, are not repealed by this one, are still sufficiently severe. Besides the forfeiture of the goods, the exporter incurs the penalty of three shillings for every pound weight of wool either exported or attempted to be exported, that is about four or five times the value. Any merchant or other person convicted of this offence is disabled from requiring any debt or account belonging to him from any factor or other person.[1] Let his fortune be what it will, whether he is, or is not able to pay those heavy penalties, the law means to ruin him completely. But as the morals of the great body of the people are not yet so corrupt as those of the contrivers of this statute, I have not heard that any advantage has ever been taken of this clause. If the person convicted of this offence is not able to pay the penalties within three months after judgment, he is to be transported for seven years, and if he returns before the expiration of that term, he is liable to the pains of felony, without benefit of clergy.[2] The owner of the ship knowing this offence forfeits all his interest in the ship and furniture. The master and mariners knowing this offence forfeit all their goods and chattels, and suffer three months imprisonment. By a subsequent statute the master suffers six months imprisonment.[3]

---

[1] [12 Car. II., c. 32.]

[2] [4 Geo. I., c. 11, § 6.]

[3] [Presumably the reference is to 10 and 11 W. III., c. 10, § 18, but this applies to the commander of a king's ship conniving at the offence, not to the master of the offending vessel.]

To prevent clan-destine exportation the inland commerce of wool is much hampered by restrictions, In order to prevent exportation, the whole inland commerce of wool is laid under very burdensome and oppressive restrictions. It cannot be packed in any box, barrel, cask, case, chest, or any other package, but only in packs of leather or pack-cloth, on which must be marked on the outside the words *wool* or *yarn*, in large letters not less than three inches long, on pain of for-feiting the same and the package, and three shillings for every pound weight, to be paid by the owner or packer.[1] It cannot be loaden on any horse or cart, or carried by land within five miles of the coast, but between sun-rising and sun-setting, on pain of forfeiting the same, the horses and carriages.[2] The hundred next adjoining to the sea coast, out of or through which the wool is carried or exported, forfeits twenty pounds, if the wool is under the value of ten pounds; and if of greater value, then treble that value, together with treble costs, to be sued for within the year. The execution to be against any two of the inhabitants, whom the sessions must reimburse, by an assessment on the other inhabitants, as in the cases of robbery. And if any person compounds with the hundred for less than this penalty, he is to be imprisoned for five years; and any other person may prosecute. These regulations take place through the whole kingdom.[3]

especially in Kent and Sussex, But in the particular counties of Kent and Sussex the restrictions are still more troublesome. Every owner of wool within ten miles of the sea-coast must give an account in writing, three days after shearing, to the next officer of the customs, of the number of his fleeces, and of the places where they are lodged. And before he removes any part of them he must give the like notice of the number and weight of the fleeces, and of the name and abode of the person to whom they are sold, and of the place to which it is intended they should be carried. No person within fifteen miles of the sea, in the said counties, can buy any wool, before he enters into bond to the king, that no part of the wool which he shall so buy shall be sold by him to any other person within fifteen miles of the sea. If any wool is found carrying towards the

---

[1] [12 Geo. II., c. 21, § 10.]

[2] [13 and 14 Car. II., c. 18, § 9, forbade removal of wool in any part of the country between 8 P.M. and 4 A.M. from March to September, and 5 P.M. and 7 A.M. from October to February. 7 and 8 W. III., c. 28, § 8, taking no notice of this, enacted the provision quoted in the text. The provision of 13 and 14 Car. II., c. 18, was repealed by 20 Geo. III., c. 55, which takes no notice of 7 and 8 W. III., c. 28.]

[3] [All these provisions are from 7 and 8 W. III., c. 28.]

sea-side in the said counties, unless it has been entered and security given as aforesaid, it is forfeited, and the offender also forfeits three shillings for every pound weight. If any person lays any wool, not entered as aforesaid, within fifteen miles of the sea, it must be seized and forfeited; and if, after such seizure, any person shall claim the same, he must give security to the Exchequer, that if he is cast upon trial he shall pay treble costs, besides all other penalties.[1]

and so also is the coasting trade. When such restrictions are imposed upon the inland trade, the coasting trade, we may believe, cannot be left very free. Every owner of wool who carrieth or causeth to be carried any wool to any port or place on the sea-coast, in order to be from thence transported by sea to any other place or port on the coast, must first cause an entry thereof to be made at the port from whence it is intended to be conveyed, containing the weight, marks, and number of the packages before he brings the same within five miles of that port; on pain of forfeiting the same, and also the horses, carts, and other carriages; and also of suffering and forfeiting, as by the other laws in force against the exportation of wool. This law, however, (1 Will. III. chap. 32.) is so very indulgent as to declare, that

> this shall not hinder any person from carrying his wool home from the place of shearing, though it be within five miles of the sea, provided that in ten days after shearing, and before he remove the wool, he do under his hand certify to the next officer of the customs, the true number of fleeces, and where it is housed; and do not remove the same, without certifying to such officer, under his hand, his intention so to do, three days before.[2]

Bond must be given that the wool to be carried coastways is to be landed at the particular port for which it is entered outwards; and if any part of it is landed without the presence of an officer, not only the forfeiture of the wool is incurred as in other goods, but the usual additional penalty of three shillings for every pound weight is likewise incurred.

The manufacturers alleged that English wool was superior to all others, which is entirely false. Our woollen manufacturers, in order to justify their demand of such extraordinary restrictions and regulations, confidently asserted, that English wool was of a peculiar quality, superior to that of any other country; that the wool of other countries could not, without

[9 and 10 W. III., c. 40.]   [2] [The quotation is not *verbatim*.]

some mixture of it, be wrought up into any tolerable manufacture; that fine cloth could not be made without it; that England, therefore, if the exportation of it could be totally prevented, could monopolize to herself almost the whole woollen trade of the world; and thus, having no rivals, could sell at what price she pleased, and in a short time acquire the most incredible degree of wealth by the most advantageous balance of trade. This doctrine, like most other doctrines which are confidently asserted by any considerable number of people, was, and still continues to be, most implicitly believed by a much greater number; by almost all those who are either unacquainted with the woollen trade, or who have not made particular enquiries. It is, however, so perfectly false, that English wool is in any respect necessary for the making of fine cloth, that it is altogether unfit for it. Fine cloth is made altogether of Spanish wool. English wool cannot be even so mixed with Spanish wool as to enter into the composition without spoiling and degrading, in some degree, the fabric of the cloth.[1]

These regulations have depressed the price of wool, as was desired,   ⌠It has been shown in the foregoing part of this work,[2] that the effect of these regulations has been to depress the price of English wool, not only below what it naturally would be in the present times, but very much below what it actually was in the time of Edward III. The price of Scots wool, when in consequence of the union it became subject to the same regulations, is said to have fallen about one half. It is observed by the very accurate and intelligent author of the Memoirs of Wool, the Reverend Mr. John Smith, that the price of the best English wool in England is generally below what wool of a very inferior quality commonly sells for in the market of Amsterdam.[3] To depress the price of this commodity below what may be called its natural and proper price, was the avowed purpose of those regulations; and there seems to be no doubt of their having produced the effect that was expected from them. ⌡

but this has not much reduced the quantity of wool grown,   This reduction of price, it may perhaps be thought, by discouraging the growing of wool, must have reduced very much the annual produce of that commodity, though not below what it formerly was, yet below

---

[1] ['It is well known that the real very superfine cloth everywhere must be entirely of Spanish wool.'—Anderson, *Commerce*, A.D. 1669.]

[2] [Above, vol. i., pp. 256, 257.]

[3] [*Chronicon Rusticum-Commerciale; or Memoirs of Wool*, etc., 1767, vol. ii., p. 418, note.]

what, in the present state of things, it probably would have been, had it, in consequence of an open and free market, been allowed to rise to the natural and proper price. I am, however, disposed to believe, that the quantity of the annual produce cannot have been much, though it may perhaps have been a little, affected by these regulations. The growing of wool is not the chief purpose for which the sheep farmer employs his industry and stock. He expects his profit, not so much from the price of the fleece, as from that of the carcase; and the average or ordinary price of the latter, must even, in many cases, make up to him whatever deficiency there may be in the average or ordinary price of the former. It has been observed in the foregoing part of this work, that

Whatever regulations tend to sink the price, either of wool or of raw hides, below what it naturally would be, must, in an improved and cultivated country, have some tendency to raise the price of butchers meat. The price both of the great and small cattle which are fed on improved and cultivated land, must be sufficient to pay the rent which the landlord, and the profit which the farmer has reason to expect from improved and cultivated land. If it is not, they will soon cease to feed them. Whatever part of this price, therefore, is not paid by the wool and the hide, must be paid by the carcase. The less there is paid for the one, the more must be paid for the other. In what manner this price is to be divided upon the different parts of the beast, is indifferent to the landlords and farmers, provided it is all paid to them. In an improved and cultivated country, therefore, their interest as landlords and farmers cannot be much affected by such regulations, though their interest as consumers may, by the rise in the price of provisions.[1]

According to this reasoning, therefore, this degradation in the price of wool is not likely, in an improved and cultivated country, to occasion any diminution in the annual produce of that commodity; except so far as, by raising the price of mutton, it may somewhat diminish the demand for, and consequently the production of, that particular species of butchers meat. Its effect, however, even in this way, it is probable, is not very considerable.

nor its quality,   But though its effect upon the quantity of the annual

---

[1] [Above, vol. i., p. 259.]

produce may not have been very considerable, its effect upon the quality, it may perhaps be thought, must necessarily have been very great. The degradation in the quality of English wool, if not below what it was in former times, yet below what it naturally would have been in the present state of improvement and cultivation, must have been, it may perhaps be supposed, very nearly in proportion to the degradation of price. As the quality depends upon the breed, upon the pasture, and upon the management and cleanliness of the sheep, during the whole progress of the growth of the fleece, the attention to these circumstances, it may naturally enough be imagined, can never be greater than in proportion to the recompence which the price of the fleece is likely to make for the labour and expence which that attention requires. It happens, however, that the goodness of the fleece depends, in a great measure, upon the health, growth, and bulk of the animal; the same attention which is necessary for the improvement of the carcase, is, in some respects, sufficient for that of the fleece. Notwithstanding the degradation of price, English wool is said to have been improved considerably during the course even of the present century. The improvement might perhaps have been greater if the price had been better; but the lowness of price, though it may have obstructed, yet certainly it has not altogether prevented that improvement.

so that the growers of wool have been less hurt than might have been expected. The violence of these regulations, therefore, seems to have affected neither the quantity nor the quality of the annual produce of wool so much as it might have been expected to do (though I think it probable that it may have affected the latter a good deal more than the former); and the interest of the growers of wool, though it must have been hurt in some degree, seems, upon the whole, to have been much less hurt than could well have been imagined.

Though prohibition of exportation cannot be justified, a duty on the exportation of wool might furnish revenue with little inconvenience. These considerations, however, will not justify the absolute prohibition of the exportation of wool.[1] But they will fully justify the imposition of a considerable tax upon that exportation.

To hurt in any degree the interest of any one order of citizens, for no other purpose but to promote that of some other, is evidently contrary to that justice and equality of treatment which the sovereign owes to all the different orders of his subjects. But the prohibition certainly hurts, in some

[1] [Additions and Corrections reads 'the wool'.]

degree, the interest of the growers of wool, for no other purpose but to promote that of the manufacturers.

Every different order of citizens is bound to contribute to the support of the sovereign or commonwealth. A tax of five, or even of ten shillings upon the exportation of every tod of wool, would produce a very considerable revenue to the sovereign. It would hurt the interest of the growers somewhat less than the prohibition, because it would not probably lower the price of wool quite so much. It would afford a sufficient advantage to the manufacturer, because, though he might not buy his wool altogether so cheap as under the prohibition, he would still buy it, at least, five or ten shillings cheaper than any foreign manufacturer could buy it, besides saving the freight and insurance, which the other would be obliged to pay. It is scarce possible to devise a tax which could produce any considerable revenue to the sovereign, and at the same time occasion so little inconveniency to any body.

The prohibition, notwithstanding all the penalties which guard it, does not prevent the exportation of wool. It is exported, it is well known, in great quantities. The great difference between the price in the home and that in the foreign market, presents such a temptation to smuggling, that all the rigour of the law cannot prevent it. This illegal exportation is advantageous to nobody but the smuggler. A legal exportation subject to a tax, by affording a revenue to the sovereign, and thereby saving the imposition of some other, perhaps, more burdensome and inconvenient taxes, might prove advantageous to all the different subjects of the state.

The exportation of fuller's earth has been subjected to the same penalties as the exportation of wool. The exportation of fuller's earth, or fuller's clay, supposed to be necessary for preparing and cleansing the woollen manufactures, has been subjected to nearly the same penalties as the exportation of wool.[1] Even tobacco-pipe clay, though acknowledged to be different from fuller's clay, yet, on account of their resemblance, and because fuller's clay might sometimes be exported as tobacco-pipe clay, has been laid under the same prohibitions and penalties.[2]

The exportation of raw hides is forbidden, By the 13th and 14th of Charles II. chap. 7. the exportation, not only of raw hides, but of tanned leather, except in the shape of boots, shoes, or

[1] [12 Car. II., c. 32; 13 and 14 Car. II., c. 18.]

[2] [13 and 14 Car. II., c. 18, § 8. The preamble to the clause alleges that 'great quantities of fuller's earth or fulling clay are daily carried and exported under the colour of tobacco-pipe clay'.]

slippers, was prohibited;[1] and the law gave a monopoly to our boot-makers and shoe-makers, not only against our graziers, but against our tanners. By subsequent statutes, our tanners have got themselves exempted from this monopoly, upon paying a small tax of only one shilling on the hundred weight of tanned leather, weighing one hundred and twelve pounds.[2] They have obtained likewise the drawback of two-thirds of the excise duties imposed upon their commodity, even when exported without further manufacture. All manufactures of leather may be exported duty free; and the exporter is besides entitled to the drawback of the whole duties of excise.[3] Our graziers still continue subject to the old monopoly. Graziers separated from one another, and dispersed through all the different corners of the country, cannot, without great difficulty, combine together for the purpose either of imposing monopolies upon their fellow-citizens, or of exempting themselves from such as may have been imposed upon them by other people.[4] Manufac-turers of all kinds, collected together in numerous bodies in all great *horns,*   cities, easily can. Even the horns of cattle are pro-hibited to be exported;[5] and the two insignificant trades of the horner and comb-maker enjoy, in this respect, a monopoly against the graziers.

woollen yarn and worsted, white cloths, watch cases, etc., also Restraints, either by prohibitions or by taxes, upon the exportation of goods which are partially, but not completely manufactured, are not peculiar to the manufacture of leather. As long as any thing remains to be done, in order to fit any commodity for immediate use and consumption, our manufacturers think that they themselves ought to have the doing of it. Woollen yarn and worsted are prohibited to be exported under the same penalties as wool.[6] Even white cloths are subject to a duty upon exportation,[7] and our dyers have so far obtained a

---

[1] [The preamble says that 'notwithstanding the many good laws before this time made and still in force, prohibiting the exportation of leather . . . by the cunning and subtlety of some persons and the neglect of others who ought to take care thereof; there are such quantities of leather daily exported to foreign parts that the price of leather is grown to those excessive rates that many artificers working leather cannot furnish themselves with sufficient store thereof for the carrying on of their trades, and the poor sort of people are not able to buy those things made of leather which of necessity they must make use of'.]

[2] [20 Car. II., c. 5; 9 Ann., c. 6, § 4.]

[3] [9 Ann., c. 11, § 39, explained by 10 Ann., c. 26, § 6, and 12 Ann., st. 2, c. 9, § 64.]

[4] [Above, vol. i., p. 141.]

[5] [Except under certain conditions by 4 Ed. IV., c. 8; wholly by 7 Jac. I., c. 14, § 4.]

[6] [Under 13 and 14 Car. II., c. 18, and 7 and 8 W. III., c. 28; above, p. 166.]

[7] [See below, next page.]

monopoly against our clothiers. Our clothiers would probably have been able to defend themselves against it, but it happens that the greater part of our principal clothiers are themselves likewise dyers. Watch-cases, clock-cases, and dial-plates for clocks and watches, have been prohibited to be exported.[1] Our clock-makers and watch-makers are, it seems, unwilling that the price of this sort of workmanship should be raised upon them by the competition of foreigners.

some metals. By some old statutes of Edward III., Henry VIII., and Edward VI.,[2] the exportation of all metals was prohibited. Lead and tin were alone excepted; probably on account of the great abundance of those metals; in the exportation of which, a considerable part of the trade of the kingdom in those days consisted. For the encouragement of the mining trade, the 5th of William and Mary, chap. 17. exempted from this prohibition, iron, copper, and mundic metal made from British ore. The exportation of all sorts of copper bars, foreign as well as British, was afterwards permitted by the 9th and 10th of William III. chap. 26.[3] The exportation of unmanufactured brass, of what is called gun-metal, bell-metal, and shroff-metal, still continues to be prohibited. Brass manufactures of all sorts may be exported duty free.[4]

On various other materials of manufacture considerable export duties are imposed. The exportation of the materials of manufacture, where it is not altogether prohibited, is in many cases subjected to considerable duties.

By the 8th George I. chap. 15., the exportation of all goods, the produce or manufacture of Great Britain, upon which any duties had been imposed by former statutes, was rendered duty free. The following goods, however, were excepted: Alum, lead, lead ore, tin, tanned leather, copperas, coals, wool cards, white woollen cloths, lapis calaminaris, skins of all sorts, glue, coney hair or wool, hares wool, hair of all sorts, horses, and litharge of lead. If you except horses, all these are either materials of manufacture, or incomplete manufactures (which may be considered as materials for still further manufacture), or instruments of trade. This statute

---

[1] [9 and 10 W. III., c. 28, professedly to prevent frauds.]

[2] [The preamble to the Act next quoted in the text mentions 28 Ed. III., c. 5 (iron); 33 Hen. VIII., c. 7 (brass, copper, etc.), and 2 and 3 Ed. VI., c. 37 (bell-metal, etc.).]

[3] [This Act is not printed in the ordinary collections, but the provision referred to is in Pickering's index, *s.v.* Copper, and the clause is recited in a renewing Act, 12 Ann., st. 1, c. 18.]

[4] [Under the general Act, 8 Geo. I., c. 15, mentioned immediately below.]

leaves them subject to all the old duties which had ever been imposed upon them, the old subsidy and one per cent. outwards.[1]

By the same statute a great number of foreign drugs for dyers' use, are exempted from all duties upon importation. Each of them, however, is afterwards subjected to a certain duty, not indeed a very heavy one, upon exportation.[2] Our dyers, it seems, while they thought it for their interest to encourage the importation of those drugs, by an exemption from all duties, thought it likewise for their interest to throw some small discouragement upon their exportation. The avidity, however, which suggested this notable piece of mercantile ingenuity, most probably disappointed itself of its object. It necessarily taught the importers to be more careful than they might otherwise have been, that their importation should not exceed what was necessary for the supply of the home market. The home market was at all times likely to be more scantily supplied; the commodities were at all times likely to be somewhat dearer there than they would have been, had the exportation been rendered as free as the importation.

Gum senega has a peculiar history and is subject to a large export duty, By the above-mentioned statute, gum senega, or gum arabic, being among the enumerated dying drugs, might be imported duty free. They were subjected, indeed, to a small poundage duty, amounting only to three pence in the hundredweight upon their re-exportation. France enjoyed, at that time, an exclusive trade to the country most productive of those drugs, that which lies in the neighbourhood of the Senegal; and the British market could not be easily supplied by the immediate importation of them from the place of growth. By the 25th Geo. II.[3] therefore, gum senega was allowed to be imported (contrary to the general dispositions of the act of navigation), from any part of Europe. As the law, however, did not mean to encourage this species of trade, so contrary to the general principles of the mercantile policy of England, it imposed a duty of ten shillings the hundred weight upon such importation, and no part of this duty was to be afterwards drawn back upon its exportation. The successful war which began in 1755 gave Great Britain the same exclusive trade to those countries which France had enjoyed before.[4]

---

[1] [12 Car. II., c. 4, § 2, and 14 Car. II., c. 11, § 35. The 1 per cent. was due on goods exported to ports in the Mediterranean beyond Malaga, unless the ship had sixteen guns and other warlike equipment. See Saxby, *British Customs*, pp. 48, 51.]

[2] [Sixpence in the pound on the values at which they are rated in the Act.]

[3] [C. 32.]   [4] [Anderson, *Commerce*, A.D. 1758.]

Our manufacturers, as soon as the peace was made, endeavoured to avail themselves of this advantage, and to establish a monopoly in their own favour, both against the growers, and against the importers of this commodity. By the 5th Geo. III. therefore, chap. 37. the exportation of gum senega from his majesty's dominions in Africa was confined to Great Britain, and was subjected to all the same restrictions, regulations, forfeitures and penalties, as that of the enumerated commodities of the British colonies in America and the West Indies. Its importation, indeed, was subjected to a small duty of six-pence the hundred weight, but its re-exportation was subjected to the enormous duty of one pound ten shillings the hundred weight. It was the intention of our manufacturers that the whole produce of those countries should be imported into Great Britain, and in order that they themselves might be enabled to buy it at their own price, that no part of it should be exported again, but at such an expence as would sufficiently discourage that exportation. Their avidity, however, upon this, as well as upon many other occasions, disappointed itself of its object. This enormous duty presented such a temptation to smuggling, that great quantities of this commodity were clandestinely exported, probably to all the manufacturing countries of Europe, but particularly to Holland, not only from Great Britain but from Africa. Upon this account,[1] by the 14 Geo. III. chap. 10. this duty upon exportation was reduced to five shillings the hundred weight.

beaver skins exported are charged seven pence, In the book of rates, according to which the old subsidy was levied, beaver skins were estimated at six shillings and eight-pence a-piece, and the different subsidies and imposts, which before the year 1722 had been laid upon their importation, amounted to one-fifth part of the rate, or to sixteen-pence upon each skin;[2] all of which, except half the old subsidy, amounting only to two-pence, was drawn back upon exportation.[3] This duty upon the importation of so important a material of manufacture had been thought too high, and, in the year 1722, the rate was reduced to two shillings and six-pence, which reduced the duty upon importation to six-pence, and of this only one half was to be drawn back upon exportation.[4] The same

---

[1] [As is stated in the preamble.]

[2] [The facts are given in the preamble to 8 Geo. I., c. 15, § 13. The old subsidy, the new, the one-third and the two-thirds subsidies account for 1s., and the additional impost for 4d.]

[3] [See above, p. 4.]   [4] 8 Geo. I., c. 15. [The year should be 1721.]

successful war put the country most productive of beaver under the dominion of Great Britain, and beaver skins being among the enumerated commodities, their exportation from America was consequently confined to the market of Great Britain. Our manufacturers[1] soon bethought themselves of the advantage which they might make of this circumstance, and in the year 1764,[2] the duty upon the importation of beaver-skin was reduced to one penny, but the duty upon exportation was raised to seven-pence each skin, without any drawback of the duty upon importation. By the same law, a duty of eighteen pence the pound was imposed upon the exportation of beaver-wool or combs, without making any alteration in the duty upon the importation of that commodity, which when imported by British and in British shipping, amounted at that time to between four-pence and five-pence the piece.

and coals five shillings a ton.   Coals may be considered both as a material of manufacture and as an instrument of trade. Heavy duties, accordingly, have been imposed upon their exportation, amounting at present (1783) to more than five shillings the ton, or to more than fifteen shillings the chaldron, Newcastle measure; which is in most cases more than the original value of the commodity at the coal pit, or even at the shipping port for exportation.

The exportation of the instruments of trade is commonly prohibited.   The exportation, however, of the instruments of trade, properly so called, is commonly restrained, not by high duties, but by absolute prohibitions. Thus by the 7th and 8th of William III. chap. 20. sect. 8. the exportation of frames or engines for knitting gloves or stockings is prohibited under the penalty, not only of the forfeiture of such frames or engines, so exported, or attempted to be exported, but of forty pounds, one half to the king, the other to the person who shall inform or sue for the same. In the same manner by the 14th Geo. III. chap. 71. the exportation to foreign parts, of any utensils made use of in the cotton, linen, woollen and silk manufactures, is prohibited under the penalty, not only of the forfeiture of such utensils, but of two hundred pounds, to be paid by the person who shall offend in this manner, and likewise of two hundred pounds to be paid by the master of the ship who shall knowingly suffer such utensils to be loaded on board his ship.

---

[1] [*I.e.* the hatters.]
[2] [4 Geo. III., c. 9.]

Similarly it is a grave offence to entice an artificer abroad, When such heavy penalties were imposed upon the exportation of the dead instruments of trade, it could not well be expected that the living instrument, the artificer, should be allowed to go free. Accordingly, by the 5 Geo. I. chap. 27. the person who shall be convicted of enticing any artificer of, or in any of the manufactures of Great Britain, to go into any foreign parts, in order to practise or teach his trade, is liable for the first offence to be fined in any sum not exceeding one hundred pounds, and to three months imprisonment, and until the fine shall be paid; and for the second offence, to be fined in any sum at the discretion of the court, and to imprisonment for twelve months, and until the fine shall be paid. By the 23 Geo. II. chap. 13. this penalty is increased for the first offence to five hundred pounds for every artificer so enticed, and to twelve months imprisonment, and until the fine shall be paid; and for the second offence, to one thousand pounds, and to two years imprisonment, and until the fine shall be paid.

By the former of those two statutes, upon proof that any person has been enticing any artificer, or that any artificer has promised or contracted to go into foreign parts for the purposes aforesaid, such artificer may be obliged to give security at the discretion of the court, that he shall not go beyond the seas, and may be committed to prison until he give such security.

and the artificer who exercises or teaches his trade abroad may be ordered to return. If any artificer has gone beyond the seas, and is exercising or teaching his trade in any foreign country, upon warning being given to him by any of his majesty's ministers or consuls abroad, or by one of his majesty's secretaries of state for the time being, if he does not, within six months after such warning, return into this realm, and from thenceforth abide and inhabit continually within the same, he is from thenceforth declared incapable of taking any legacy devised to him within this kingdom, or of being executor or administrator to any person, or of taking any lands within this kingdom by descent, devise, or purchase. He likewise forfeits to the king, all his lands, goods and chattels, is declared an alien in every respect, and is put out of the king's protection.[1]

It is unnecessary, I imagine, to observe, how contrary such regulations are to the boasted liberty of the subject, of which we affect to be so very jealous; but which, in this case, is so plainly sacrificed to the futile interests of our merchants and manufacturers.

---

[1] [Under the same statute, 5 Geo. I., c. 27.]

The object is to depress the manufactures of our neighbours. The laudable motive of all these regulations, is to extend our own manufactures, not by their own improvement, but by the depression of those of all our neighbours, and by putting an end, as much as possible, to the troublesome competition of such odious and disagreeable rivals. Our master manufacturers think it reasonable, that they themselves should have the monopoly of the ingenuity of all their countrymen. Though by restraining, in some trades, the number of apprentices which can be employed at one time, and by imposing the necessity of a long apprenticeship in all trades, they endeavour, all of them, to confine the knowledge of their respective employments to as small a number as possible; they are unwilling, however, that any part of this small number should go abroad to instruct foreigners.

The mercantile system absurdly considers production and not consumption to be the end of industry and commerce. Consumption is the sole end and purpose of all production; and the interest of the producer ought to be attended to, only so far as it may be necessary for promoting that of the consumer. The maxim is so perfectly self-evident, that it would be absurd to attempt to prove it. But in the mercantile system, the interest of the consumer is almost constantly sacrificed to that of the producer; and it seems to consider production, and not consumption, as the ultimate end and object of all industry and commerce.

Restraints on importation of competing commodities sacrifice the interest of the consumer to the producer, In the restraints upon the importation of all foreign commodities which can come into competition with those of our own growth, or manufacture, the interest of the home-consumer is evidently sacrificed to that of the producer. It is altogether for the benefit of the latter, that the former is obliged to pay that enhancement of price which this monopoly almost always occasions.

and so do bounties on exportation It is altogether for the benefit of the producer that bounties are granted upon the exportation of some of his productions. The home-consumer is obliged to pay, first, the tax which is necessary for paying the bounty, and secondly, the still greater tax which necessarily arises from the enhancement of the price of the commodity in the home market.

and the provisions of the Methuen treaty, By the famous treaty of commerce with Portugal,[1] the consumer is prevented by high duties from purchasing of a neighbouring country, a commodity

[1] [Above, p. 54.]

which our own climate does not produce, but is obliged to purchase it of a distant country, though it is acknowledged, that the commodity of the distant country is of a worse quality than that of the near one. The home-consumer is obliged to submit to this inconveniency, in order that the producer may import into the distant country some of his productions upon more advantageous terms than he would otherwise have been allowed to do. The consumer, too, is obliged to pay, whatever enhancement in the price of those very productions, this forced exportation may occasion in the home market.

but the most extravagant case of all is that of the management of the American and West Indian colonies. But in the system of laws which has been established for the management of our American and West Indian colonies, the interest of the home-consumer has been sacrificed to that of the producer with a more extravagant profusion than in all our other commercial regulations. A great empire has been established for the sole purpose of raising up a nation of customers who should be obliged to buy from the shops of our different producers, all the goods with which these could supply them. For the sake of that little enhancement of price which this monopoly might afford our producers, the home-consumers have been burdened with the whole expence of maintaining and defending that empire. For this purpose, and for this purpose only, in the two last wars, more than two hundred millions have been spent, and a new debt of more than a hundred and seventy millions has been contracted over and above all that had been expended for the same purpose in former wars. The interest of this debt alone is not only greater than the whole extraordinary profit, which, it ever could be pretended, was made by the monopoly of the colony trade, but than the whole value of that trade, or than the whole value of the goods, which at an average have been annually exported to the colonies.

The contrivers of the whole mercantile system are the producers and especially the merchants and manufacturers. It cannot be very difficult to determine who have been the contrivers of this whole mercantile system; not the consumers, we may believe, whose interest has been entirely neglected; but the producers, whose interest has been so carefully attended to; and among this latter class our merchants and manufacturers have been by far the principal architects. In the mercantile regulations, which have been taken notice of in this chapter, the interest of our manufacturers has been most peculiarly attended to; and the interest, not so much of the consumers, as that of some other sets of producers, has been sacrificed to it.[1]

[1] [This chapter appears first in Additions and Corrections and ed. 3, and is doubtless largely due to Smith's appointment in 1778 to the Commissionership of Customs (Rae, *Life of Adam Smith*, p. 320). He had in his library W. Sims and R. Frewin, *The Rates of Merchandise*, 1782 (see Bonar, *Catalogue*, p. 27), and probably had access to earlier works, such as Saxby's *British Customs*, 1757, which give the duties, etc., at earlier periods as well as references to the Acts of Parliament regulating them.]

CHAPTER IX

Of the Agricultural Systems, or of those Systems of Political Œconomy, which Represent the Produce of Land as either the Sole or the Principal Source of the Revenue and Wealth of Every Country

The agricultural system will require less lengthy explanation than the mercantile system. The agricultural systems of political œconomy will not require so long an explanation as that which I have thought it necessary to bestow upon the mercantile or commercial system.

That system which represents the produce of land as the sole source of the revenue and wealth of every country has, so far as I know, never been adopted by any nation, and it at present exists only in the speculations of a few men of great learning and ingenuity in France.[1] It would not, surely, be worth while to examine at great length the errors of a system which never has done, and probably never will do any harm in any part of the world. I shall endeavour to explain, however, as distinctly as I can, the great outlines of this very ingenious system.

Colbert adopted the mercantile system and favoured town industry, Mr. Colbert, the famous minister of Lewis XIV. was a man of probity, of great industry and knowledge of detail; of great experience and acuteness in the examination of public accounts, and of abilities, in short, every way fitted for introducing method and good order into the collection and expenditure of the public revenue. That minister had unfortunately embraced all the prejudices of the mercantile system, in its nature and essence a system of restraint and regulation,

[1] [The Économistes or Physiocrats. Quesnay, Mirabeau and Mercier de la Rivière are mentioned below, pp. 193, 200.]

and such as could scarce fail[1] to be agreeable to a laborious and plod-
ding man of business, who had been accustomed to regulate
the different departments of public offices, and to establish the
necessary checks and controuls for confining each to its proper
sphere. The industry and commerce of a great country he endeavoured to regulate upon the same model as the departments of a
public office; and instead of allowing every man to pursue his own
interest his own way, upon the liberal plan of equality, liberty and
justice, he bestowed upon certain branches of industry extraordinary privileges, while he laid others under as extraordinary restraints. He was not only disposed, like other European ministers,
to encourage more the industry of the towns than that of the country; but, in order to support the industry of the towns, he was
willing even to depress and keep down that of the country. In order
to render provisions cheap to the inhabitants of the towns, and
thereby to encourage manufactures and foreign commerce, he prohibited altogether the exportation of corn, and thus excluded the
inhabitants of the country from every foreign market for by far the
most important part of the produce of their industry. This prohibition, joined to the restraints imposed by the ancient provincial
laws of France upon the transportation of corn from one province
to another, and to the arbitrary and degrading taxes which are
levied upon the cultivators in almost all the provinces, discouraged
and kept down the agriculture of that country very much below
the state to which it would naturally have risen in so very fertile a
soil and so very happy a climate. This state of discouragement and
depression was felt more or less in every different part of the country,
and many different inquiries were set on foot concerning the causes
of it. One of those causes appeared to be the preference given, by
the institutions of Mr. Colbert, to the industry of the towns above
that of the country.

with the result that the French philosophers who support the agricultural system undervalue town industry. If the rod be bent too much one way, says the
proverb, in order to make it straight you must bend
it as much the other. The French philosophers,
who have proposed the system which represents
agriculture as the sole source of the revenue and
wealth of every country, seem to have adopted this proverbial
maxim; and as in the plan of Mr. Colbert the industry of the towns

---

[1] [Ed. 1 places a full stop at 'mercantile system' and continues 'That system, in its
nature and essence a system of restraint and regulation, could scarce fail'.]

was certainly over-valued in comparison with that of the country; so in their system it seems to be as certainly under-valued.

There are three classes in their system:
(1) proprietors,
(2) cultivators,
and (3) artificers, manufacturers and merchants.

The different orders of people who have ever been supposed to contribute in any respect towards the annual produce of the land and labour of the country, they divide into three classes. The first is the class of the proprietors of land. The second is the class of the cultivators, of farmers and country labourers, whom they honour with the peculiar appellation of the productive class. The third is the class of artificers, manufacturers and merchants, whom they endeavour to degrade by the humiliating appellation[1] of the barren or unproductive class.

Proprietors contribute to production by expenses on improvement of land,

The class of proprietors contributes to the annual produce by the expence which they may occasionally lay out upon the improvement of the land, upon the buildings, drains, enclosures and other ameliorations, which they may either make or maintain upon it, and by means of which the cultivators are enabled, with the same capital, to raise a greater produce, and consequently to pay a greater rent. This advanced rent may be considered as the interest or profit due to the proprietor upon the expence or capital which he thus employs in the improvement of his land. Such expences are in this system called ground expences (depenses foncieres).

cultivators, by original and annual expenses of cultivation.

The cultivators or farmers contribute to the annual produce by what are in this system called the original and annual expences (depenses primitives et depenses annuelles) which they lay out upon the cultivation of the land. The original expenses consist in the instruments of husbandry, in the stock of cattle, in the seed, and in the maintenance of the farmer's family, servants and cattle, during at least a great part of the first year of his occupancy, or till he can receive some return from the land. The annual expences consist in the seed, in the wear and tear[2] of the instruments of husbandry, and in the annual maintenance of the farmer's servants and cattle, and of his family

[1] [But, see below, p. 189, where the usefulness of the class is said to be admitted. In his exposition of physiocratic doctrine, Smith does not appear to follow any particular book closely. His library contained Du Pont's *Physiocratie, ou constitution naturelle du gouvernement le plus avantageux au genre humain,* 1768 (see Bonar, *Catalogue,* p. 92), and he refers lower down to La Rivière, *L'ordre naturel et essentiel des sociétés politiques,* 1767, but he probably relied largely on his recollection of conversations in Paris; see Rae, *Life of Adam Smith,* pp. 215–222.]

[2] [Ed. 1 reads 'tear and wear'.]

too, so far as any part of them can be considered as servants employed in cultivation. That part of the produce of the land which remains to him after paying the rent, ought to be sufficient, first, to replace to him within a reasonable time, at least during the term of his occupancy, the whole of his original expences, together with the ordinary profits of stock; and, secondly, to replace to him annually the whole of his annual expences, together likewise with the ordinary profits of stock. Those two sorts of expences are two capitals which the farmer employs in cultivation; and unless they are regularly restored to him, together with a reasonable profit, he cannot carry on his employment upon a level with other employments; but, from a regard to his own interest, must desert it as soon as possible, and seek some other.[1] That part of the produce of the land which is thus necessary for enabling the farmer to continue his business, ought to be considered as a fund sacred to cultivation, which if the landlord violates, he necessarily reduces[2] the produce of his own land, and in a few years not only disables the farmer from paying this racked rent, but from paying the reasonable rent which he might otherwise have got for his land. The rent which properly belongs to the landlord, is no more than the neat produce which remains after paying in the completest manner all the necessary expences which must be previously laid out in order to raise the gross, or the whole produce. It is because the labour of the cultivators, over and above paying completely all those necessary expences, affords a neat produce of this kind, that this class of people are in this system peculiarly distinguished by the honourable appellation of the productive class. Their original and annual expences are for the same reason called, in this system, productive expences, because, over and above replacing their own value, they occasion the annual reproduction of this neat produce.

These expenses should be free from all taxation. The ground expences, as they are called, or what the landlord lays out upon the improvement of his land, are in this system too honoured with the appellation of productive expences. Till the whole of those expences, together with the ordinary profits of stock, have been completely repaid to him by the advanced rent which he gets from his land, that advanced rent ought to be regarded as sacred and inviolable, both by the church and by the king; ought to be subject neither to tithe nor to taxation. If it is otherwise, by discouraging the improvement

---

[1] [Ed. 1 reads 'some other employment'.] [2] [Ed. 1 reads 'degrades'.]

W.N. II—G

of land, the church discourages the future increase of her own tithes, and the king the future increase of his own taxes. As in a well-ordered state of things, therefore, those ground expences, over and above reproducing in the completest manner their own value, occasion likewise after a certain time a reproduction of a neat produce, they are in this system considered as productive expences.

All other expenses The ground expences of the landlord, however, *and orders of people* together with the original and the annual expences *are unproductive,* of the farmer, are the only three sorts of expences which in this system are considered as productive. All other expences and all other orders of people, even those who in the common apprehensions of men are regarded as the most productive, are in this account of things represented as altogether barren and unproductive.

artificers and Artificers and manufacturers, in particular, whose *manufacturers in* industry, in the common apprehensions of men, *particular, and the* increases so much the value of the rude produce of *expense of* *employing them:* land, are in this system represented as a class of people altogether barren and unproductive. Their labour, it is said, replaces only the stock which employs them, together with its ordinary profits. That stock consists in the materials, tools, and wages, advanced to them by their employer; and is the fund destined for their employment and maintenance. Its profits are the fund destined for the maintenance of their employer. Their employer, as he advances to them the stock of materials, tools and wages necessary for their employment, so he advances to himself what is necessary for his own maintenance, and this maintenance he generally proportions to the profit which he expects to make by the price of their work. Unless its price repays to him the maintenance which he advances to himself, as well as the materials, tools and wages which he advances to his workmen, it evidently does not repay to him[1] the whole expence which he lays out upon it. The profits of manufacturing stock, therefore, are not, like the rent of land, a neat produce which remains after completely repaying the whole expence which must be laid out in order to obtain them. The stock of the farmer yields him a profit as well as that of the master manufacturer; and it yields a rent likewise to another person, which that of the master manufacturer does not. The expence, therefore, laid out in employing and maintaining artificers and manufacturers,

---

[1] [Ed. 1 reads 'repay him'.]

does no more than continue, if one may say so, the existence of its own value, and does not produce any new value. It is therefore altogether a barren and unproductive expence. The expence, on the contrary, laid out in employing farmers and country labourers, over and above continuing the existence of its own value, produces a new value, the rent of the landlord. It is therefore a productive expence.

mercantile stock also. Mercantile stock is equally barren and unproductive with manufacturing stock. It only continues the existence of its own value, without producing any new value. Its profits are only the repayment of the maintenance which its employer advances to himself during the time that he employs it, or till he receives the returns of it. They are only the repayment of a part of the expence which must be laid out in employing it.

The labour of artificers and manufacturers adds nothing to the value of the annual produce. The labour of artificers and manufacturers never adds any thing to the value of the whole annual amount of the rude produce of the land. It adds indeed greatly to the value of some particular parts of it. But the consumption which in the mean time it occasions of other parts, is precisely equal to the value which it adds to those parts; so that the value of the whole amount is not, at any one moment of time, in the least augmented by it. The person who works the lace of a pair of fine ruffles for example, will sometimes raise the value of perhaps a pennyworth of flax to thirty pounds sterling. But though at first sight he appears thereby to multiply the value of a part of the rude produce about seven thousand and two hundred times, he in reality adds nothing to the value of the whole annual amount of the rude produce. The working of that lace costs him perhaps two years labour. The thirty pounds which he gets for it when it is finished, is no more than the repayment of the subsistence which he advances to himself during the two years that he is employed about it. The value which, by every day's, month's, or year's labour, he adds to the flax, does no more than replace the value of his own consumption during that day, month, or year. At no moment of time, therefore, does he add any thing to the value of the whole annual amount of the rude produce of the land: the portion of that produce which he is continually consuming, being always equal to the value which he is continually producing. The extreme poverty of the greater part of the persons employed in this expensive, though trifling manufacture, may satisfy us that the price of their work does not in ordinary cases exceed the value of their subsistence. It is otherwise with the work of farmers and country labourers. The rent of the landlord is a value, which, in ordinary cases, it is continually producing, over and above replacing, in the most complete manner, the whole consumption, the whole expence laid out upon the employment and maintenance both of the workmen and of their employer.

Artificers, manufacturers and merchants can augment revenue only by privation. Artificers, manufacturers and merchants, can augment the revenue and wealth of their society, by parsimony only; or, as it is expressed in this system, by privation, that is, by depriving themselves of a part of the funds destined for their own subsistence. They annually reproduce nothing but those funds. Unless, therefore, they annually save some part of them, unless they annually deprive themselves of the enjoyment of some part of them, the revenue and wealth of their society can never be in the smallest degree augmented by means of their industry. Farmers and country labourers, on the contrary, may enjoy completely the whole funds destined for their own subsistence, and yet augment at the same time the revenue and wealth of their society. Over and above what is destined[1] for their own subsistence, their industry annually affords a neat produce, of which the augmentation necessarily augments the revenue and wealth of their society. Nations, therefore, which, like France or England, consist in a great measure of proprietors and cultivators, can be enriched by industry and enjoyment. Nations, on the contrary, which, like Holland and Hamburgh, are composed chiefly of merchants, artificers and manufacturers, can grow rich only through parsimony and privation. As the interest of nations so differently circumstanced, is very different, so is likewise the common character of the people. In those of the former kind, liberality, frankness, and good fellowship, naturally make a part of that common character. In the latter, narrowness, meanness, and a selfish disposition, averse to all social pleasure and enjoyment.

The unproductive class is maintained at the expense of the other two, The unproductive class, that of merchants, artificers and manufacturers, is maintained and employed altogether at the expence of the two other classes, of that of proprietors, and of that of cultivators. They furnish it both with the materials of its work and with the fund of its subsistence, with the corn and cattle which it consumes while it is em-

---

[1] [Ed. 1 reads 'above the funds destined'.]

ployed about that work. The proprietors and cultivators finally pay both the wages of all the workmen of the unproductive class, and the profits of all their employers. Those workmen and their employers are properly the servants of the proprietors and cultivators. They are only servants who work without doors, as menial servants work within. Both the one and the other, however, are equally maintained at the expence of the same masters. The labour of both is equally unproductive. It adds nothing to the value of the sum total of the rude produce of the land. Instead of increasing the value of that sum total, it is a charge and expence which must be paid out of it.

but is useful to them,   The unproductive class, however, is not only useful, but greatly useful to the other two classes. By means of the industry of merchants, artificers and manufacturers, the proprietors and cultivators can purchase both the foreign goods and the manufactured produce of their own countty which they have occasion for, with the produce of a much smaller quantity of their own labour, than what they would be obliged to employ, if they were to attempt, in an awkward and unskilful manner, either to import the one, or to make the other for their own use. By means of the unproductive class, the cultivators are delivered from many cares which would otherwise distract their attention from the cultivation of land. The superiority of produce, which, in consequence of this undivided attention, they are enabled to raise, is fully sufficient to pay the whole expence which the maintenance and employment of the unproductive class costs either the proprietors, or themselves. The industry of merchants, artificers and manufacturers, though in its own nature altogether unproductive, yet contributes in this manner indirectly to increase the produce of the land. It increases the productive powers of productive labour, by leaving it at liberty to confine itself to its proper employment, the cultivation of land; and the plough goes frequently the easier and the better by means of the labour of the man whose business is most remote from the plough.

and it is not their interest to discourage its industry;   It can never be the interest of the proprietors and cultivators to restrain or to discourage in any respect the industry of merchants, artificers and manufacturers. The greater the liberty which this unproductive class enjoys, the greater will be the competition in all the different trades which compose it, and the cheaper will the other two classes be supplied, both with foreign goods and with the manufactured produce of their own country.

nor is it ever the interest of the un-productive class to oppress the others. It can never be the interest of the unproductive class to oppress the other two classes. It is the surplus produce of the land, or what remains after deducting the maintenance, first, of the cultivators, and afterwards, of the proprietors, that maintains and employs the unproductive class. The greater this surplus, the greater must likewise be the maintenance and employment of that class.[1] The establishment of perfect justice, of perfect liberty, and of perfect equality, is the very simple secret which most effectually secures the highest degree of prosperity to all the three classes.

Mercantile states similarly are main-tained at the expence of landed states, The merchants, artificers and manufacturers of those mercantile states which, like Holland and Hamburgh, consist chiefly of this unproductive class, are in the same manner maintained and employed altogether at the expence of the proprietors and cultivators of land. The only difference is, that those proprietors and cultivators are, the greater part of them, placed at a most inconvenient distance from the merchants, artificers and manufacturers whom they supply with the materials of their work and the fund of their subsistence, are the inhabitants of other countries, and the subjects of other governments.

but are greatly useful to them, Such mercantile states, however, are not only useful, but greatly useful to the inhabitants of those other countries. They fill up, in some measure, a very important void, and supply the place of the merchants, artificers and manufacturers, whom the inhabitants of those countries ought to find at home, but whom, from some defect in their policy, they do not find at home.

and it is not the interest of landed nations to discourage their industry by high duties. It can never be the interest of those landed nations, if I may call them so, to discourage or distress the industry of such mercantile states, by imposing high duties upon their trade, or upon the commodities which they furnish. Such duties, by rendering those commodities dearer, could serve only to sink the real value of the surplus produce of their own land, with which, or, what comes to the same thing, with the price of which, those commodities are purchased. Such duties could serve only to discourage the increase of that surplus produce, and consequently the improvement and

---

[1] [Ed. 1 reads 'the greater must likewise be its maintenance and employment'.]

cultivation of their own land. The most effectual expedient, on the contrary, for raising the value of that surplus produce, for encouraging its increase, and consequently the improvement and cultivation of their own land, would be to allow the most perfect freedom to the trade of all such mercantile nations.

Freedom of trade would in due time supply artificers, etc., at home, This perfect freedom of trade would even be the most effectual expedient for supplying them, in due time, with all the artificers, manufacturers and merchants, whom they wanted at home, and for filling up in the properest and most advantageous manner that very important void which they felt there.

in consequence of the increase of their capital, which would first employ manufacturers, The continual increase of the surplus produce of their land, would, in due time, create a greater capital than what could be employed with the ordinary rate of profit in the improvement and cultivation of land; and the surplus part of it would naturally turn itself to the employment of artificers and manufacturers at home. But those artificers and manufacturers, finding at home both the materials of their work and the fund of their subsistence, might immediately, even with much less art and skill, be able to work as cheap as the like artificers and manufacturers of such mercantile states, who had both to bring from a great[1] distance. Even though, from want of art and skill, they might not for some time be able to work as cheap, yet, finding a market at home, they might be able to sell their work there as cheap as that of the artificers and manufacturers of such mercantile states, which could not be brought to that market but from so great a distance; and as their art and skill improved, they would soon be able to sell it cheaper. The artificers and manufacturers of such mercantile states, therefore, would immediately be rivalled in the market of those landed nations, and soon after undersold and justled out of it altogether. The cheapness of the manufactures of those landed nations, in consequence of the gradual improvements of art and skill, would, in due time, extend their sale beyond the home market, and carry them to many foreign markets, from which they would in the same manner gradually justle out many of the manufactures of such mercantile nations.

and afterwards overflow into foreign trade. This continual increase both of the rude and manufactured produce of those landed nations would in due time create a greater capital than

[1] [Misprinted 'greater' in ed. 5.]

could, with the ordinary rate of profit, be employed either in agriculture or in manufactures. The surplus of this capital would naturally turn itself to foreign trade, and be employed in exporting, to foreign countries, such parts of the rude and manufactured produce of its own country, as exceeded the demand of the home market. In the exportation of the produce of their own country, the merchants of a landed nation would have an advantage of the same kind over those of mercantile nations, which its artificers and manufacturers had over the artificers and manufacturers of such nations; the advantage of finding at home that cargo, and those stores and provisions, which the others were obliged to seek for at a distance. With inferior art and skill in navigation, therefore, they would be able to sell that cargo as cheap in foreign markets as the merchants of such mercantile nations; and with equal art and skill they would be able to sell it cheaper. They would soon, therefore, rival those mercantile nations in this branch of foreign trade,[1] and in due time would justle them out of it altogether.

Freedom of trade therefore is best for introducing manufactures and foreign trade.   According to this liberal and generous system, therefore, the most advantageous method in which a landed nation can raise up artificers, manufacturers and merchants of its own, is to grant the most perfect freedom of trade to the artificers, manufacturers and merchants of all other nations. It thereby raises the value of the surplus produce of its own land, of which the continual increase gradually establishes a fund, which in due time necessarily raises up all the artificers, manufacturers and merchants whom it has occasion for.

High duties and prohibitions sink the value of agricultural produce, raise mercantile and manufacturing profit,   When a landed nation, on the contrary, oppresses either by high duties or by prohibitions the trade of foreign nations, it necessarily hurts its own interest in two different ways. First, by raising the price of all foreign goods and of all sorts of manufactures, it necessarily sinks the real value of the surplus produce of its own land, with which, or, what comes to the same thing, with the price of which, it purchases those foreign goods and manufactures. Secondly, by giving a sort of monopoly of the home market to its own merchants, artificers and manufacturers, it raises the rate of mercantile and manufacturing profit in proportion to that of agricultural profit, and consequently either draws from agriculture a

---

[1] [Ed. 1 reads 'of their foreign trade'.]

part of the capital which had before been employed in it, or hinders from going to it a part of what would otherwise have gone to it. This policy, therefore, discourages agriculture in two different ways; first, by sinking the real value of its produce, and thereby lowering the rate of its profit; and, secondly, by raising the rate of profit in all other employments. Agriculture is rendered less advantageous, and trade and manufactures more advantageous than they otherwise would be; and every man is tempted by his own interest to turn, as much as he can, both his capital and his industry from the former to the latter employments.

and could only raise up manufacturers and merchants prematurely. Though, by this oppressive policy, a landed nation should be able to raise up artificers, manufacturers and merchants of its own, somewhat sooner than it could do by the freedom of trade; a matter, however, which is not a little doubtful; yet it would raise them up, if one may say so, prematurely, and before it was perfectly ripe for them. By raising up too hastily one species of industry, it would depress another more valuable species of industry. By raising up too hastily a species of industry which only replaces the stock which employs it, together with the ordinary profit, it would depress a species of industry which, over and above replacing that stock with its profit, affords likewise a neat produce, a free rent to the landlord. It would depress productive labour, by encouraging too hastily that labour which is altogether barren and unproductive.

The distribution of the produce of land is represented in the Economical Table. In what manner, according to this system, the sum total of the annual produce of the land is distributed among the three classes above mentioned, and in what manner the labour of the unproductive class does no more than replace the value of its own consumption, without increasing in any respect the value of that sum total, is represented by Mr. Quesnai, the very ingenious and profound author of this system, in some arithmetical formularies. The first of these formularies, which by way of eminence he peculiarly distinguishes by the name of the Œconomical Table,[1] represents the manner in which he supposes this distribution takes place, in a state of the most perfect liberty, and therefore of the highest prosperity; in a state where the annual produce is such as to afford the greatest possible neat produce, and where each class enjoys its proper share

[1] [See François Quesnay, *Tableau Œconomique*, 1758, reproduced in facsimile for the British Economic Association, 1894.]

of the whole annual produce. Some subsequent formularies represent the manner, in which, he supposes, this distribution is made in different states of restraint and regulation; in which, either the class of proprietors, or the barren and unproductive class, is more favoured than the class of cultivators, and in which, either the one or the other encroaches more or less upon the share which ought properly to belong to this productive class. Every such encroachment, every violation of that natural distribution, which the most perfect liberty would establish, must, according to this system, necessarily degrade more or less, from one year to another, the value and sum total of the annual produce, and must necessarily occasion a gradual declension in the real wealth and revenue of the society; a declension of which the progress must be quicker or slower, according to the degree of this encroachment, according as that natural distribution, which the most perfect liberty would establish, is more or less violated. Those subsequent formularies represent the different degrees of declension, which, according to this system, correspond to the different degrees in which this natural distribution of things is violated.

Nations can prosper in spite of hurtful regulations. Some speculative physicians seem to have imagined that the health of the human body could be preserved only by a certain precise regimen of diet and exercise, of which every, the smallest, violation necessarily occasioned some degree of disease or disorder proportioned to the degree of the violation. Experience, however, would seem to show, that the human body frequently preserves, to all appearance at least,[1] the most perfect state of health under a vast variety of different regimens; even under some which are generally believed to be very far from being perfectly wholesome. But the healthful state of the human body, it would seem, contains in itself some unknown principle of preservation, capable either of preventing or of correcting in many respects, the bad effects even of a very faulty regimen. Mr. Quesnai, who was himself a physician, and a very speculative physician, seems to have entertained a notion of the same kind concerning the political body, and to have imagined that it would thrive and prosper only under a certain precise regimen, the exact regimen of perfect liberty and perfect justice. He seems not to have considered that in the political body, the natural effort which every man is continually making to better his own condition, is a principle

[1] [Ed. 1 reads 'at least to all appearance'.]

of preservation capable of preventing and correcting, in many respects, the bad effects of a political œconomy, in some degree both partial and oppressive. Such a political œconomy, though it no doubt retards more or less, is not always capable of stopping altogether the natural progress of a nation towards wealth and prosperity, and still less of making it go backwards. If a nation could not prosper without the enjoyment of perfect liberty and perfect justice, there is not in the world a nation which could ever have prospered. In the political body, however, the wisdom of nature has fortunately made ample provision for remedying many of the bad effects of the folly and injustice of man; in the same manner as it has done in the natural body, for remedying those of his sloth and intemperance.

The system is wrong in representing artificers, etc., as unproductive, since,   The capital error of this system, however, seems to lie in its representing the class of artificers, manufacturers and merchants, as altogether barren and unproductive. The following observations may serve to show the impropriety of this representation.

(1) they reproduce at least their annual consumption and continue the capital which employs them,   First, this class, it is acknowledged, reproduces annually the value of its own annual consumption, and continues, at least, the existence of the stock or capital which maintains and employs it. But upon this account alone the denomination of barren or unproductive should seem to be very improperly applied to it. We should not call a marriage barren or unproductive, though it produced only a son and a daughter, to replace the father and mother, and though it did not increase the number of the human species, but only continued it as it was before. Farmers and country labourers, indeed, over and above the stock which maintains and employs them, reproduce annually a neat produce, a free rent to the landlord. As a marriage which affords three children is certainly more productive than one which affords only two; so the labour of farmers and country labourers is certainly more productive than that of merchants, artificers and manufacturers. The superior produce of the one class, however, does not render the other barren or unproductive.

(2) they are not like menial servants,   Secondly, it seems, upon this account, altogether improper to consider artificers, manufacturers and merchants, in the same light as menial servants. The labour of menial servants does not continue the existence of the fund which maintains and employs them. Their maintenance and employment is

altogether at the expence of their masters, and the work which they perform is not of a nature to repay that expence. That work consists in services which perish generally in the very instant of their performance, and does not fix or realize itself in any vendible commodity which can replace the value of their wages and maintenance. The labour, on the contrary, of artificers, manufacturers and merchants, naturally does fix and realize itself in some such vendible commodity. It is upon this account that, in the chapter in which I treat of productive and unproductive labour,[1] I have classed artificers, manufacturers and merchants, among the productive labourers, and menial servants among the barren or unproductive.

(3) their labour increases the real revenue of the society, Thirdly, it seems, upon every supposition, improper to say, that the labour of artificers, manufacturers and merchants, does not increase the real revenue of the society. Though we should suppose, for example, as it seems to be supposed in this system, that the value of the daily, monthly, and yearly consumption of this class was exactly equal to that of its daily, monthly, and yearly production; yet it would not from thence follow that its labour added nothing to the real revenue, to the real value of the annual produce of the land and labour of the society. An artificer, for example, who, in the first six months after harvest, executes ten pounds worth of work, though he should in the same time consume ten pounds worth of corn and other necessaries, yet really adds the value of ten pounds to the annual produce of the land and labour of the society. While he has been consuming a half yearly revenue of ten pounds worth of corn and other necessaries, he has produced an equal value of work capable of purchasing, either to himself or to some other person, an equal half yearly revenue. The value, therefore, of what has been consumed and produced during these six months is equal, not to ten, but to twenty pounds. It is possible, indeed, that no more than ten pounds worth of this value, may ever have existed at any one moment of time. But if the ten pounds worth of corn and other necessaries, which were consumed by the artificer, had been consumed by a soldier or by a menial servant, the value of that part of the annual produce which existed at the end of the six months, would have been ten pounds less than it actually is in consequence of the labour of the artificer. Though the value of what the artificer produces, therefore, should not at any one

[1] [Bk. ii., ch. iii., vol. i., pp. 351–371.]

moment of time be supposed greater than the value he consumes, yet at every moment of time the actually existing value of goods in the market is, in consequence of what he produces, greater than it otherwise would be.

When the patrons of this system assert, that the consumption of artificers, manufacturers and merchants, is equal to the value of what they produce, they probably mean no more than that their revenue, or the fund destined for their consumption, is equal to it. But if they had expressed themselves more accurately, and only asserted, that the revenue of this class was equal to the value of what they produced, it might readily have occurred to the reader, that what would naturally be saved out of this revenue, must necessarily increase more or less the real wealth of the society. In order, therefore, to make out something like an argument, it was necessary that they should express themselves as they have done; and this argument, even supposing things actually were as it seems to presume them to be, turns out to be a very inconclusive one.

(4) for augmenting annual produce parsimony is just as much required from farmers as from them, Fourthly, farmers and country labourers can no more augment, without parsimony, the real revenue, the annual produce of the land and labour of their society, than artificers, manufacturers and merchants. The annual produce of the land and labour of any society can be augmented only in two ways; either, first, by some improvement in the productive powers of the useful labour actually maintained within it; or, secondly, by some increase in the quantity of that labour.

The improvement in the productive powers of useful labour depend, first, upon the improvement in the ability of the workman; and, secondly, upon that of the machinery with which he works. But the labour of artificers and manufacturers, as it is capable of being more subdivided, and the labour of each workman reduced to a greater simplicity of operation, than that of farmers and country labourers, so it is likewise capable of both these sorts of improvement in a much higher degree.[1] In this respect, therefore, the class of cultivators can have no sort of advantage over that of artificers and manufacturers.

The increase in the quantity of useful labour actually employed within any society, must depend altogether upon the increase of the capital which employs it; and the increase of that capital again must

---

[1] See Book I. Chap. I. [vol. i., pp. 9-10].

be exactly equal to the amount of the savings from the revenue, either of the particular persons who manage and direct the employment of that capital, or of some other persons who lend it to them. If merchants, artificers and manufacturers are, as this system seems to suppose, naturally more inclined to parsimony and saving than proprietors and cultivators, they are, so far, more likely to augment the quantity of useful labour employed within their society, and consequently to increase its real revenue, the annual produce of its land and labour.

and (5) trade and manufactures can procure that subsistence which the system regards as the only revenue. Fifthly and lastly, though the revenue of the inhabitants of every country was supposed to consist altogether, as this system seems to suppose, in the quantity of subsistence which their industry could procure to them; yet, even upon this supposition, the revenue of a trading and manufacturing country must, other things being equal, always be much greater than that of one without trade or manufactures. By means of trade and manufactures, a greater quantity of subsistence can be annually imported into a particular country than what its own lands, in the actual state of their cultivation, could afford. The inhabitants of a town, though they frequently possess no lands of their own, yet draw to themselves by their industry such a quantity of the rude produce of the lands of other people as supplies them, not only with the materials of their work, but with the fund of their subsistence. What a town always is with regard to the country in its neighbourhood, one independent state or country may frequently be with regard to other independent states or countries. It is thus that Holland draws a great part of its subsistence from other countries; live cattle from Holstein and Jutland, and corn from almost all the different countries of Europe. A small quantity of manufactured produce purchases a great quantity of rude produce. A trading and manufacturing country, therefore, naturally purchases with a small part of its manufactured produce a great part of the rude produce of other countries; while, on the contrary, a country without trade and manufactures is generally obliged to purchase, at the expence of a great part of its rude produce, a very small part of the manufactured produce of other countries. The one exports what can subsist and accommodate but a very few, and imports the subsistence and accommodation of a great number. The other exports the accommodation and subsistence of a great number, and imports that of a very few only. The inhabitants of the one must always enjoy a much greater quantity of subsistence than what their own lands, in the actual state of their cultivation, could afford. The inhabitants of the other must always enjoy a much smaller quantity.

In spite of its errors the system has been valuable. This system, however, with all its imperfections, is, perhaps, the nearest approximation to the truth that has yet been published upon the subject of political œconomy, and is upon that account well worth the consideration of every man who wishes to examine with attention the principles of that very important science. Though in representing the labour which is employed upon land as the only productive labour, the notions which it inculcates are perhaps too narrow and confined; yet in representing the wealth of nations as consisting, not in the unconsumable riches of money, but in the consumable goods annually reproduced by the labour of the society; and in representing perfect liberty as the only effectual expedient for rendering this annual reproduction the greatest possible, its doctrine seems to be in every respect as just as it is generous and liberal. Its followers are very numerous; and as men are fond of paradoxes, and of appearing to understand what surpasses the comprehension of ordinary people, the paradox which it maintains, concerning the unproductive nature of manufacturing labour, has not perhaps contributed a little to increase the number of its admirers. They have for some years past made a pretty considerable sect, distinguished in the French republic of letters by the name of, The Œconomists. Their works have certainly been of some service to their country; not only by bringing into general discussion, many subjects which had never been well examined before, but by influencing in some measure the public administration in favour of agriculture. It has been in consequence of their representations, accordingly, that the agriculture of France has been delivered from several of the oppressions which it before laboured under. The term during which such a lease can be granted, as will be valid against every future purchaser or proprietor of the land, has been prolonged from nine to twenty-seven years.[1] The ancient provincial restraints upon the transportation of corn from one province of the kingdom to another, have been entirely taken away, and the liberty of exporting it to all foreign countries, has been established as the common law of the kingdom in all ordinary cases.[2] This sect, in their works, which are very

[1] [Above, vol. i., p. 416.]   [2] [Above, vol. i., p. 220, and vol. ii., p. 12.]

numerous, and which treat not only of what is properly called
Political Œconomy, or of the nature and causes of the wealth of
nations, but of every other branch of the system of civil government, all follow implicitly, and without any sensible variation, the
doctrine of Mr. Quesnai. There is upon this account little variety
in the greater part of their works. The most distinct and best connected account of this doctrine is to be found in a little book written
by Mr. Mercier de la Riviere, sometime Intendant of Martinico,
intitled, The natural and essential Order of Political Societies.[1] The
admiration of this whole sect for their master, who was himself a
man of the greatest modesty and simplicity, is not inferior to that of
any of the ancient philosophers for the founders of their respective
systems.

There have been, since the world began [says a very diligent
and respectable author, the Marquis de Mirabeau], three great
inventions which have principally given stability to political
societies, independent of many other inventions which have
enriched and adorned them. The first, is the invention of writing,
which alone gives human nature the power of transmitting,
without alteration, its laws, its contracts, its annals, and its discoveries. The second, is the invention of money, which binds
together all the relations between civilized societies. The third, is
the Œconomical Table, the result of the other two, which com-
pletes them both by perfecting their object; the great discovery
of our age, but of which our posterity will reap the benefit.[2]

Some nations have   As the political œconomy of the nations of modern
favoured agriculture; Europe, has been more favourable to manufactures
and foreign trade, the industry of the towns, than to agriculture, the

---

[1] [*L'ordre naturel et essentiel des sociétés politiques*, 1767, a quarto of 511 pages, seems,
as G. Schelle (*Du Pont de Nemours et l'ecole physiocratique*, 1888, p. 46, note) remarks,
not entitled to be called a 'little book,' but Smith may have been thinking of the edition
in two vols., 12mo, 1767, nominally printed 'à Londres chez Jean Nourse, libraire'.]

[2] ['Trois grandes inventions principales ont fondé stablement les sociétés, indépen-
damment de tant d'autres qui les ont ensuite dotées et décorées. Ces trois sont, 1°
L'invention de l'écriture, qui seule donne à l'humanité le pouvoir de transmettre, sans
altération, ses lois, ses pactes, ses annales et ses découvertes. 2° Celle de la monnaie, qui
lie tous les rapports entre les sociétés policées. La troisième enfin, qui est due à notre
âge, et dont nos neveux profiteront, est un dérivé des deux autres, et les complette
également en perfectionnant leur objet: c'est la découverte du Tableau économique,
qui devenant désormais le truchement universel, embrasse, et accorde toutes les
portions ou quotités correlatives, qui doivent entrer dans tous les calculs généraux de
l'ordre économique.'—*Philosophie Rurale ou économie générale et politique de l'agriculture,
pour servir de suite à l'Ami des Hommes*, Amsterdam, 1766, tom. i., pp. 52, 53.]

industry of the country; so that of other nations has followed a different plan, and has been more favourable to agriculture than to manufactures and foreign trade.

China, for example. The policy of China favours agriculture more than all other employments.[1] In China, the condition of a labourer is said to be as much superior to that of an artificer; as in most parts of Europe, that of an artificer is to that of a labourer. In China, the great ambition of every man is to get possession of some little bit of land, either in property or in lease; and leases are there said to be granted upon very moderate terms, and to be sufficiently secured to the lessees. The Chinese have little respect for foreign trade. Your beggarly commerce! was the language in which the Mandarins of Pekin used to talk to Mr. de Lange,[2] the Russian envoy, concerning it.[3] Except with Japan, the Chinese carry on, themselves, and in their own bottoms, little or no foreign trade; and it is only into one or two ports of their kingdom that they even admit the ships of foreign nations. Foreign trade, therefore, is, in China, every way confined within a much narrower circle than that to which it would naturally extend itself, if more freedom was allowed to it, either in their own ships, or in those of foreign nations.

China is itself of very great extent, but more foreign trade would be advantageous to it. Manufactures, as in a small bulk they frequently contain a great value, and can upon that account be transported at less expence from one country to another than most parts[4] of rude produce, are, in almost all countries, the principal support of foreign trade. In countries, besides, less extensive and less favourably circumstanced for interior commerce than China, they generally require the support of foreign trade. Without an extensive foreign market, they could not well flourish, either in countries so moderately extensive as to afford but a narrow home market; or in countries where the communication between one province and another was so difficult, as to render it impossible for the goods of any particular place to enjoy the whole of that home market which the country could afford. The perfection of manufacturing industry, it must be remembered,

---

[1] [Du Halde, *Description Géographique, etc., de la Chine,* tom. ii., p. 64.]

[2] [Ed. 1 reads 'Mr. Langlet'.]

[3] See the Journal of Mr. De Lange in Bell's Travels, vol. ii. p. 258, 276 and 293. [*Travels from St. Petersburg in Russia to Diverse Parts of Asia,* by John Bell of Antermony, Glasgow, 1763. The mandarins requested the Russians to cease 'from importuning the council about their beggarly commerce,' p. 293. Smith was a subscriber to this book. The note is not in ed. 1.]

[4] [Ed. 1 reads 'sorts'.]

depends altogether upon the division of labour; and the degree to which the division of labour can be introduced into any manufacture, is necessarily regulated, it has already been shown,[1] by the extent of the market. But the great extent of the empire of China, the vast multitude of its inhabitants, the variety of climate, and consequently of productions in its different provinces, and the easy communication by means of water carriage between the greater part of them, render the home market of that country of so great extent, as to be alone sufficient to support very great manufactures, and to admit of very considerable subdivisions of labour. The home market of China is, perhaps, in extent, not much inferior to the market of all the different countries of Europe put together.[2] A more extensive foreign trade, however, which to this great home market added the foreign market of all the rest of the world; especially if any considerable part of this trade was carried on in Chinese ships; could scarce fail to increase very much the manufactures of China, and to improve very much the productive powers of its manufacturing industry. By a more extensive navigation, the Chinese would naturally learn the art of using and constructing themselves all the different machines made use of in other countries, as well as the other[3] improvements of art and industry which are practised in all the different parts of the world. Upon their present plan they have little opportunity of improving themselves by the example of any other nation; except that of the Japanese.

Egypt and the Gentoo government of Indostan favoured agriculture. The policy of ancient Egypt too, and that of the Gentoo government of Indostan, seem to have favoured agriculture more than all other employments.

The people were divided into castes in these countries. Both in ancient Egypt and[4] Indostan, the whole body of the people was divided into different casts or tribes, each of which was confined, from father to son, to a particular employment or class of employments. The son of a priest was necessarily a priest; the son of a soldier, a soldier; the son of a labourer, a labourer; the son of a weaver, a weaver; the son of a taylor, a taylor; &c. In both countries, the cast of the priests held the highest rank, and that of the soldiers the next; and

---

[1] [Above, vol. i., pp. 21–27.]

[2] [Quesnay went further than this: 'L'historien dit que le commerce qui se fit dans l'intérieur de la Chine est si grand que celui de l'Europe ne peut pas lui être comparé.'—*Oeuvres*, ed. Oncken, 1888, p. 603.]

[3] [Ed. 1 reads 'as well as all the other'.]   [4] [Ed. 1 reads 'and in'.]

in both countries, the cast of the farmers and labourers was superior to the casts of merchants and manufacturers.

Irrigation was attended to there. The government of both countries was particularly attentive to the interest of agriculture. The works constructed by the ancient sovereigns of Egypt for the proper distribution of the waters of the Nile were famous in antiquity; and the ruined remains of some of them are still the admiration of travellers. Those of the same kind which were constructed by the ancient sovereigns of Indostan, for the proper distribution of the waters of the Ganges as well as of many other rivers, though they have been less celebrated, seem to have been equally great. Both countries, accordingly, though subject occasionally to dearths, have been famous for their great fertility. Though both were extremely populous, yet, in years of moderate plenty, they were both able to export great quantities of grain to their neighbours.

Egypt and India were dependent on other nations for foreign trade. The ancient Egyptians had a superstitious aversion to the sea; and as the Gentoo religion does not permit its followers to light a fire, nor consequently to dress any victuals upon the water, it in effect prohibits them from all distant sea voyages. Both the Egyptians and Indians must have depended almost altogether upon the navigation of other nations for the exportation of their surplus produce; and this dependency, as it must have confined the market, so it must have discouraged the increase of this surplus produce. It must have discouraged too the increase of the manufactured produce more than that of the rude produce. Manufactures require a much more extensive market than the most important parts of the rude produce of the land. A single shoemaker will make more than three hundred pairs of shoes in the year; and his own family will not perhaps wear out six pairs. Unless therefore he has the custom of at least fifty such families as his own, he cannot dispose of the whole produce of his own labour. The most numerous class of artificers will seldom, in a large country, make more than one in fifty or one in a hundred of the whole number of families contained in it. But in such large countries as France and England, the number of people employed in agriculture has by some authors been computed at a half, by others at a third, and by no author that I know of, at less than a fifth of the whole inhabitants of the country. But as the produce of the agriculture of both France and England is, the far greater part of it, consumed at home, each person employed in it must, according to these computations, require little more than the custom of one, two, or, at most, of[1] four such families as his own, in order to dispose of the whole produce of his own labour. Agriculture, therefore, can support itself under the discouragement of a confined market, much better than manufactures. In both ancient Egypt and Indostan, indeed, the confinement of the foreign market was in some measure compensated by the conveniency of many inland navigations, which opened, in the most advantageous manner, the whole extent of the home market to every part of the produce of every different district of those countries. The great extent of Indostan too rendered the home market of that country very great, and sufficient to support a great variety of manufactures. But the small extent of ancient Egypt, which was never equal to England, must at all times have rendered the home market of that country too narrow for supporting any great variety of manufactures. Bengal, accordingly, the province of Indostan which commonly exports the greatest quantity of rice, has always been more remarkable for the exportation of a great variety of manufactures, than for that of its grain. Ancient Egypt, on the contrary, though it exported some manufactures, fine linen in particular, as well as some other goods, was always most distinguished for its great exportation of grain. It was long the granary of the Roman empire.

The land tax gave eastern sovereigns a particular interest in agriculture. The sovereigns of China, of ancient Egypt, and of the different kingdoms into which Indostan has at different times been divided, have always derived the whole, or by far the most considerable part, of their revenue from some sort of land-tax or land-rent. This land-tax or land-rent, like the tithe in Europe, consisted in a certain proportion, a fifth, it is said, of the produce of the land, which was either delivered in kind, or paid in money, according to a certain valuation, and which therefore varied from year to year according to all the variations of the produce. It was natural therefore, that the sovereigns of those countries should be particularly attentive to the interests of agriculture, upon the prosperity or declension of which immediately depended the yearly increase or diminution of their own revenue.[2]

Ancient Greece and Rome discouraged manufactures and foreign trade, and The policy of the ancient republics of Greece, and that of Rome, though it honoured agriculture more than manufactures or foreign trade, yet seems

---

[1] [Ed. 1 does not contain 'of'.]
[2] [Below, p. 363.]

carried on manu-
factures only by
slave labour, which
is expensive.

rather to have discouraged the latter employments, than to have given any direct or intentional encouragement to the former. In several of the ancient states of Greece, foreign trade was prohibited altogether; and in several others the employments of artificers and manufacturers were considered as hurtful to the strength and agility of the human body, as rendering it incapable of those habits which their military and gymnastic exercises endeavoured to form in it, and as thereby disqualifying it more or less for[1] undergoing the fatigues and encountering the dangers of war. Such occupations were considered as fit only for slaves, and the free citizens of the state were prohibited from exercising them.[2] Even in those states where no such prohibition took place, as in Rome and Athens, the great body of the people were in effect excluded from all the trades which are now commonly exercised by the lower sort of the inhabitants of towns. Such trades were, at Athens and Rome, all occupied by the slaves of the rich, who exercised them for the benefit of their masters, whose wealth, power, and protection, made it almost impossible for a poor freeman to find a market for his work, when it came into competition with that of the slaves of the rich. Slaves, however, are very seldom inventive; and all the most important improvements, either in machinery, or in the[3] arrangement and distribution of work, which facilitate and abridge labour, have been the discoveries of freemen. Should a slave propose any improvement of this kind, his master would be very apt to consider the proposal as the suggestion of laziness, and of a desire to save his own labour at the master's expence. The poor slave, instead of reward, would probably meet with much abuse, perhaps with some punishment. In the manufactures carried on by slaves, therefore, more labour must generally have been employed to execute the same quantity of work, than in those carried on by freemen. The work of the former must, upon that account, generally have been dearer than that of the latter. The Hungarian mines, it is remarked by Mr. Montesquieu, though not richer,[4] have always been wrought with less expence, and therefore with more profit, than the Turkish mines in their neighbourhood. The Turkish mines are wrought by slaves; and the arms of those slaves are the only machines which the Turks have ever thought of employing. The Hungarian mines are wrought by freemen, who

[1] [Ed. 1 reads 'from'.]
[2] [Montesquieu, *Esprit des lois*, liv. iv., chap. 8.]
[3] [Ed. 1 reads 'that'.]
[4] [Ed. 1 reads 'more rich'.]

employ a great deal of machinery, by which they facilitate and abridge their own labour.[1] From the very little that is known about the price of manufactures in the times of the Greeks and Romans, it would appear that those of the finer sort were excessively dear. Silk sold for its weight in gold. It was not, indeed, in those times a European manufacture; and as it was all brought from the East Indies, the distance of the carriage may in some measure account for the greatness of the price. The price, however, which a lady, it is said, would sometimes pay for a piece of very fine linen, seems to have been equally extravagant; and as linen was always either a European, or, at farthest, an Egyptian manufacture, this high price can be accounted for only by the great expence of the labour which must have been employed about it, and the expence of this labour again could arise from nothing but the awkwardness of the machinery which it made use of. The price of fine woollens too, though not quite so extravagant, seems however to have been much above that of the present times. Some cloths, we are told by Pliny, dyed in a particular manner, cost a hundred denarii, or three pounds six shillings and eight pence the pound weight.[2] Others dyed in another manner cost a thousand denarii the pound weight, or thirty-three pounds six shillings and eight pence. The Roman pound, it must be remembered, contained only twelve of our avoirdupois ounces. This high price, indeed, seems to have been principally owing to the dye. But had not the cloths themselves been much dearer than any which are made in the present times, so very expensive a dye would not probably have been bestowed upon them. The disproportion would have been too great between the value of the accessory and that of the principal. The price mentioned by the same[3] author of some Triclinaria, a sort of woollen pillows or cushions made use of to lean upon as they reclined upon their couches at table, passes all credibility; some of them being said to have cost more than thirty thousand, others more than three hundred thousand pounds. This high price too is not said to have arisen from the dye. In the dress of the people of fashion of both sexes, there seems to have been much less variety, it is observed by Dr. Arbuthnot, in ancient than in modern times;[4] and the very

[1] [Lectures, p. 231; Montesquieu, Esprit des lois, liv. xv., chap. 8.]
[2] Plin. [H.N.] l. ix. c. 39.
[3] Plin. [H.N.] l. viii. c. 48. [Neither this nor the preceding note is in ed. 1.]
[4] [John Arbuthnot, Tables of Ancient Coins, Weights and Measures, 2nd ed., 1754, pp. 142–145.]

little variety which we find in that of the ancient statues confirms his observation. He infers from this, that their dress must upon the whole have been cheaper than ours: but the conclusion does not seem to follow. When the expence of fashionable dress is very great, the variety must be very small. But when, by the improvements in the productive powers of manufacturing art and industry, the expence of any one dress comes to be very moderate, the variety will naturally be very great. The rich not being able to distinguish themselves by the expence of any one dress, will naturally endeavour to do so by the multitude and variety of their dresses.

Everything which raises the price of manufactures discourages agriculture, The greatest and most important branch of the commerce of every nation, it has already been observed,[1] is that which is carried on between the inhabitants of the town and those of the country. The inhabitants of the town draw from the country the rude produce which constitutes both the materials of their work and the fund of their subsistence; and they pay for this rude produce by sending back to the country a certain portion of it manufactured and prepared for immediate use. The trade which is carried on between those two different sets of people, consists ultimately in a certain quantity of rude produce exchanged for a certain quantity of manufactured produce. The dearer the latter, therefore, the cheaper the former; and whatever tends in any country to raise the price of manufactured produce, tends to lower that of the rude produce of the land, and thereby to discourage agriculture. The smaller the quantity of manufactured produce which any given quantity of rude produce, or, what comes to the same thing, which the price of any given quantity of rude produce is capable of purchasing, the smaller the exchangeable value[2] of that given quantity of rude produce; the smaller the encouragement which either the landlord has to increase its quantity by improving, or the farmer by cultivating the land. Whatever, besides, tends to diminish in any country the number of artificers and manufacturers, tends to diminish the home market, the most important of all markets for the rude produce of the land, and thereby still further to discourage agriculture.

and this is done by systems which restrain manufactures and foreign trade. Those systems, therefore, which preferring agriculture to all other employments, in order to promote it, impose restraints upon manufactures and foreign trade, act contrary to the very end which they propose, and

---

[1] [Above, vol. i., p. 401.]　　　　　　　　[2] [Ed. 1 reads 'real value'.]

indirectly discourage that very species of industry which they mean to promote. They are so far, perhaps, more inconsistent than even the mercantile system. That system, by encouraging manufactures and foreign trade more than agriculture, turns a certain portion of the capital of the society from supporting a more advantageous, to support a less advantageous species of industry. But still it really and in the end encourages that species of industry which it means to promote. Those agricultural systems, on the contrary, really and in the end discourage their own favourite species of industry.

So all systems of encouragements and restraints retard the progress of society. It is thus that every system which endeavours, either, by extraordinary encouragements, to draw towards a particular species of industry a greater share of the capital of the society than what would naturally go to it; or, by extraordinary restraints, to force from a particular species of industry some share of the capital which would otherwise be employed in it; is in reality subversive of the great purpose which it means to promote. It retards, instead of accelerating, the progress of the society towards real wealth and greatness; and diminishes, instead of increasing, the real value of the annual produce of its land and labour.

The system of natural liberty leaves the sovereign only three duties: (1) the defence of the country; (2) the administration of justice, and (3) the maintenance of certain public works. All systems either of preference or of restraint, therefore, being thus completely taken away, the obvious and simple system of natural liberty establishes itself of its own accord. Every man, as long as he does not violate the laws of justice, is left perfectly free to pursue his own interest his own way, and to bring both his industry and capital into competition with those of any other man, or order of men. The sovereign is completely discharged from a duty, in the attempting to perform which he must always be exposed to innumerable delusions, and for the proper performance of which no human wisdom or knowledge could ever be sufficient; the duty of superintending the industry of private people, and of directing it towards the employments most suitable to the interest of the society. According to the system of natural liberty, the sovereign has only three duties to attend to; three duties of great importance, indeed, but plain and intelligible to common understandings: first, the duty of protecting the society from the violence and invasion of other independent societies; secondly, the duty of protecting, as far as possible, every member of the society from the injustice or oppression of every other member of it, or the duty of establishing an exact administration of justice; and, thirdly, the duty of erecting and maintaining certain public works and certain public institutions, which it can never be for the interest of any individual, or small number of individuals, to erect and maintain; because the profit could never repay the expence to any individual or small number of individuals, though it may frequently do much more than repay it to a great society.

The next book will treat of the necessary expenses of the sovereign, the methods of contribution towards the expenses of the whole society, and the causes and effects of public debts. The proper performance of those several duties of the sovereign necessarily supposes a certain expence; and this expence again necessarily requires a certain revenue to support it. In the following book, therefore, I shall endeavour to explain; first, what are the necessary expences of the sovereign or commonwealth; and which of those expences ought to be defrayed by the general contribution of the whole society; and which of them, by that of some particular part only, or of some particular members of the society: secondly, what are the different methods in which the whole society may be made to contribute towards defraying the expences incumbent on the whole society, and what are the principal advantages and inconveniencies of each of those methods: and, thirdly, what are the reasons and causes which have induced almost all modern governments to mortgage some part of this revenue, or to contract debts, and what have been the effects of those debts upon the real wealth, the annual produce of the land and labour of the society. The following book, therefore, will naturally be divided into three chapters.

BOOK V

Of the Revenue of the Sovereign or Commonwealth

CHAPTER I

Of the Expences of the Sovereign or Commonwealth

PART I

Of the Expence of Defence

The expense of a military force is different at different periods. The first duty of the sovereign, that of protecting the society from the violence and invasion of other independent societies, can be performed only by means of a military force. But the expence both of preparing this military force in time of peace, and of employing it in time of war, is very different in the different states of society, in the different periods of improvement.

Among hunters it costs nothing. Among nations of hunters, the lowest and rudest state of society, such as we find it among the native tribes of North America, every man is a warrior as well as a hunter. When he goes to war, either to defend his society, or to revenge the injuries which have been done to it by other societies, he maintains himself by his own labour, in the same manner as when he lives at home. His society, for in this state of things there is properly neither sovereign nor commonwealth, is at no sort of expence, either to prepare him for the field, or to maintain him while he is in it.[1]

When shepherds go to war the whole nation moves with its property Among nations of shepherds, a more advanced state of society, such as we find it among the Tartars and Arabs, every man is, in the same manner, a warrior. Such nations have commonly no fixed habitation, but live, either in tents, or in a sort of covered waggons which are easily transported from place to place. The whole tribe or nation changes its situation according to the different seasons of the year, as well as according to other accidents. When its herds and flocks have consumed the forage of one part of the country, it removes to

[1] [*Lectures*, p. 14.]

213

another, and from that to a third. In the dry season, it comes down
to the banks of the rivers; in the wet season it retires to the upper
country. When such a nation goes to war, the warriors will not
trust their herds and flocks to the feeble defence of their old men,
their women and children, and their old men, their women and
children, will not be left behind without defence and without subsistence. The whole nation, besides, being accustomed to a wandering life, even in time of peace, easily takes the field in time of war.
Whether it marches as an army, or moves about as a company of
herdsmen, the way of life is nearly the same, though the object proposed by it be[1] very different. They all go to war together, therefore,
and every one does as well as he can. Among the Tartars, even the
women have been frequently known to engage in battle. If they
conquer, whatever belongs to the hostile tribe is the recompence of
the victory. But if they are vanquished, all is lost, and not only their
herds and flocks, but their women and children, become the booty
of the conqueror. Even the greater part of those who survive the
action are obliged to submit to him for the sake of immediate subsistence. The rest are commonly dissipated and dispersed in the
desart.

and the sovereign   The ordinary life, the ordinary exercises of a Tar-
is at no expense.   tar or Arab, prepare him sufficiently for war. Running, wrestling, cudgel-playing, throwing the javelin, drawing the
bow, &c. are the common pastimes of those who live in the open
air, and are all of them the images of war. When a Tartar or Arab
actually goes to war, he is maintained, by his own herds and flocks
which he carries with him, in the same manner as in peace. His
chief or sovereign, for those nations have all chiefs or sovereigns, is
at no sort of expence in preparing him for the field; and when he is
in it, the chance of plunder is the only pay which he either expects
or requires.

Shepherds are far   An army of hunters can seldom exceed two or three
more formidable   hundred men. The precarious subsistence which the
than hunters.   chace affords could seldom allow a greater number
to keep together for any considerable time. An army of shepherds,
on the contrary, may sometimes amount to two or three hundred
thousand. As long as nothing stops their progress, as long as they
can go on from one district, of which they have consumed the
forage, to another which is yet entire; there seems to be scarce any

[1] [Ed. 1 reads 'is'.]

limit to the number who can march on together. A nation of hunters can never be formidable to the civilized nations in their neighbourhood. A nation of shepherds may. Nothing can be more contemptible than an Indian war in North America. Nothing, on the contrary, can be more dreadful than a Tartar invasion has frequently been in Asia. The judgment of Thucydides,[1] that both Europe and Asia could not resist the Scythians united, has been verified by the experience of all ages. The inhabitants of the extensive, but defenceless plains of Scythia or Tartary, have been frequently united under the dominion of the chief of some conquering horde or clan; and the havoc and devastation of Asia have always signalized their union. The inhabitants of the inhospitable desarts of Arabia, the other great nation of shepherds, have never been united but once; under Mahomet and his immediate successors.[2] Their union, which was more the effect of religious enthusiasm than of conquest, was signalized in the same manner. If the hunting nations of America should ever become shepherds, their neighbourhood would be much more dangerous to the European colonies than it is at present.

Husbandmen with little commerce and only household manufactures are easily converted into soldiers, and it seldom costs the sovereign anything to prepare them for the field, In a yet more advanced state of society, among those nations of husbandmen who have little foreign commerce, and no other manufactures but those coarse and houshold ones which almost every private family prepares for its own use; every man, in the same manner, either is a warrior, or easily becomes such. They who live by agriculture generally pass the whole day in the open air, exposed to all the inclemencies of the seasons. The hardiness of their ordinary life prepares them for the fatigues of war, to some of which their necessary occupations bear a great[3] analogy. The necessary occupation of a ditcher prepares him to work in the trenches, and to fortify a camp as well as to enclose a field. The ordinary pastimes of such husbandmen are the same as those of shepherds, and are in the same manner the images of war. But as husbandmen have less leisure than shepherds, they are not so frequently employed in those pastimes. They are soldiers, but soldiers not quite so much masters of their exercise. Such as they are, however, it seldom costs the sovereign or commonwealth any expence to prepare them for the field.

[1] [What Thucydides says (ii., 97) is that no European or Asiatic nation could resist the Scythians if they were united. Ed. I reads here and on next page 'Thucidides'.]

[2] [*Lectures*, pp. 20, 21.]

[3] [Ed. I reads 'a good deal of'.]

or to maintain them when they have taken the field. Agriculture, even in its rudest and lowest state, supposes a settlement; some sort of fixed habitation which cannot be abandoned without great loss. When a nation of mere husbandmen, therefore, goes to war, the whole people cannot take the field together. The old men, the women and children, at least, must remain at home to take care of the habitation. All the men of the military age, however, may take the field, and, in small nations of this kind, have frequently done so. In every nation the men of the military age are supposed to amount to about a fourth or a fifth[1] part of the whole body of the people. If the campaign too should begin after seed-time, and end before harvest, both the husbandman and his principal labourers can be spared from the farm without much loss. He trusts that the work which must be done in the mean time can be well enough executed by the old men, the women and the children. He is not unwilling, therefore, to serve without pay during a short[2] campaign, and it frequently costs the sovereign or commonwealth as little to maintain him in the field as to prepare him for it. The citizens of all the different states of ancient Greece seem to have served in this manner till after the second Persian war; and the people of Peloponesus till after the Peloponesian war. The Peloponesians, Thucydides observes, generally left the field in the summer, and returned home to reap the harvest.[3] The Roman people under their kings, and during the first ages of the republic, served in the same manner.[4] It was not till the siege of Veii, that they, who staid at home, began to contribute something towards maintaining those who went to war.[5] In the European monarchies, which were founded upon the ruins of the Roman empire, both before and for some time after the establishment of what is properly called the feudal law, the great lords, with all their immediate dependents, used to serve the crown at their own expence. In the field, in the same manner as at home, they maintained themselves by their own revenue, and not by any stipend or pay which they received from the king upon that particular occasion.

Later it becomes necessary to pay those who take the field, In a more advanced state of society, two different causes contribute to render it altogether impossible that they, who take the field, should maintain themselves at their own expence. Those two causes are, the progress of manufactures, and the improvement in the art of war.

---

[1] [Ed. 1 reads 'or fifth'.]
[3] [VII., 27.]   [4] [Livy, v., 2.]
[2] [Ed. 1 reads 'so short a'.]
[5] [Livy, iv., 59 *ad fin.*]

since artificers and manufacturers must be maintained by the public when away from their work, Though a husbandman should be employed in an expedition, provided it begins after seed-time and ends before harvest, the interruption of his business will not always occasion any considerable diminution of his revenue. Without the intervention of his labour, nature does herself the greater part of the work which remains to be done. But the moment that an artificer, a smith, a carpenter, or a weaver, for example, quits his workhouse, the sole source of his revenue is completely dried up. Nature does nothing for him, he does all for himself. When he takes the field, therefore, in defence of the public, as he has no revenue to maintain himself, he must necessarily be maintained by the public. But in a country of which a great part of the inhabitants are artificers and manufacturers, a great part of the people who go to war must be drawn from those classes, and must therefore be maintained by the public as long as they are employed in its service.

and the greater length of campaigns makes service without pay too heavy a burden even for husbandmen. When the art of war too has gradually grown up to be a very intricate and complicated science, when the event of war ceases to be determined, as in the first ages of society, by a single irregular skirmish or battle, but when the contest is generally spun out through several different campaigns, each of which lasts during the greater part of the year; it becomes universally necessary that the public should maintain those who serve the public in war, at least while they are employed in that service. Whatever in time of peace might be the ordinary occupation of those who go to war, so very tedious and expensive a service would otherwise be by far too heavy a burden upon them. After the second Persian war, accordingly, the armies of Athens seem to have been generally composed of mercenary troops; consisting, indeed, partly of citizens, but partly too of foreigners; and all of them equally hired and paid at the expence of the state. From the time of the siege of Veii, the armies of Rome received pay for their service during the time which they remained in the field.[1] Under the feudal governments the military service both of the great lords and of their immediate dependents was, after a certain period, universally exchanged for a payment in money, which was employed to maintain those who served in their stead.

[1] [Above, p. 216.]

The possible pro-portion of soldiers to the rest of the population is much smaller in civilised times.

The number of those who can go to war, in propor-tion to the whole number of the people, is neces-sarily much smaller in a civilized, than in a rude state of society. In a civilized society, as the soldiers are maintained altogether by the labour of those who are not soldiers, the number of the former can never[1] exceed what the latter can maintain, over and above maintaining, in a manner suitable to their respective stations, both themselves and the other officers of government, and law, whom they are obliged to maintain. In the little agrarian states of ancient Greece, a fourth or a fifth part of the whole body of the people considered them-selves as soldiers, and would sometimes, it is said, take the field. Among the civilized nations of modern Europe, it is commonly computed, that not more than one hundredth part of the inhabi-tants of any country can be employed as soldiers, without ruin to the country which pays the expence of their service.[2]

The expense of preparing for the field was long inconsiderable.

The expence of preparing the army for the field seems not to have become considerable in any nation, till long after that of maintaining it in the field had devolved entirely upon the sovereign or commonwealth. In all the different republics of ancient Greece, to learn his military exercises, was a necessary part of education imposed by the state upon every free citizen. In every city there seems to have been a public field, in which, under the protection of the public magistrate, the young people were taught their different exercises by different masters. In this very simple institution, consisted the whole expence which any Grecian state seems ever to have been at, in preparing its citizens for war. In ancient Rome the exercises of the Campus Martius answered the same purpose with those of the Gymnasium in ancient Greece. Under the feudal governments, the many public ordinances that the citizens of every district should practise archery as well as several other military exercises, were intended for pro-moting the same purpose, but do not seem to have promoted it so well. Either from want of interest in the officers entrusted with the execution of those ordinances, or from some other cause, they appear to have been universally neglected; and in the progress of all those governments, military exercises seem to have gone gradually into disuse among the great body of the people.

[1] [Ed. 1 reads 'never can'.]
[2] [Ed. 1 reads 'at whose expence they are employed'. Repeated all but *verbatim* below, p. 296.]

Soldiers were not a distinct class in Greece and Rome, nor at first in feudal times. In the republics of ancient Greece and Rome, during the whole period of their existence, and under the feudal governments for a considerable time after their first establishment, the trade of a soldier was not a separate, distinct trade, which constituted the sole or principal occupation of a particular class of citizens. Every subject of the state, whatever might be the ordinary trade or occupation by which he gained his livelihood, considered himself, upon all ordinary occasions, as fit likewise to exercise the trade of a soldier, and upon many extraordinary occasions as bound to exercise it.

But as war becomes more complicated, division of labour becomes necessary to carry the art to perfection. The art of war, however, as it is certainly the noblest of all arts, so in the progress of improvement it necessarily becomes one of the most complicated among them. The state of the mechanical, as well as of some other arts, with which it is necessarily connected, determines the degree of perfection to which it is capable of being carried at any particular time. But in order to carry it to this degree of perfection, it is necessary that it should become the sole or principal occupation of a particular class of citizens, and the division of labour is as necessary for the improvement of this, as of every other art. Into other arts the division of labour is naturally introduced by the prudence of individuals, who find that they promote their private interest better by confining themselves to a particular trade, than by exercising a great number. But it is the wisdom of the state only which can render the trade of a soldier a particular trade separate and distinct from all others. A private citizen who, in time of profound peace, and without any particular encouragement from the public, should spend the greater part of his time in military exercises, might, no doubt, both improve himself very much in them, and amuse himself very well; but he certainly would not promote his own interest. It is the wisdom of the state only which can render it for his interest to give up the greater part of his time to this peculiar occupation: and states have not always had this wisdom, even when their circumstances had become such, that the preservation of their existence required that they should have it.

As society advances the people become unwarlike. A shepherd has a great deal of leisure; a husbandman, in the rude state of husbandry, has some; an artificer or manufacturer has none at all. The first may, without any loss, employ a great deal of his time in martial exercises; the second may employ some part of it; but the last cannot employ a single hour in them without some loss, and his attention to his own interest naturally leads him to neglect them altogether. Those improvements in husbandry too, which the progress of arts and manufactures necessarily introduces, leave the husbandman as little leisure as the artificer. Military exercises come to be as much neglected by the inhabitants of the country as by those of the town, and the great body of the people becomes altogether unwarlike. That wealth, at the same time, which always follows the improvements of agriculture and manufactures, and which in reality is no more than the accumulated produce of those improvements, provokes the invasion of all their neighbours. An industrious, and upon that account a wealthy nation, is of all nations the most likely to be attacked; and unless the state takes some new measures for the public defence, the natural habits of the people render them altogether incapable of defending themselves.

There are only two methods of providing for defence, (1) to enforce military exercises and service, In these circumstances, there seem to be but two methods, by which the state can make any tolerable provision for the public defence.

It may either, first, by means of a very rigorous police, and in spite of the whole bent of the interest, genius and inclinations of the people, enforce the practice of military exercises, and oblige either all the citizens of the military age, or a certain number of them, to join in some measure the trade of a soldier to whatever other trade or profession they may happen to carry on.

or (2) to make the trade of the soldier a separate one: Or, secondly, by maintaining and employing a certain number of citizens in the constant practice of military exercises, it may render the trade of a soldier a particular trade, separate and distinct from all others.

in other words the establishment of a militia or a standing army. If the state has recourse to the first of those two expedients, its military force is said to consist in a militia; if to the second, it is said to consist in a standing army. The practice of military exercises is the sole or principal occupation of the soldiers of a standing army, and the maintenance or pay which the state affords them is the principal and ordinary fund of their subsistence. The practice of military exercises is only the occasional occupation of the soldiers of a militia, and they derive the principal and ordinary fund of their subsistence from some other occupation. In a militia, the character of the labourer, artificer, or tradesman, predominates over that of the soldier: in a standing army, that of the soldier predominates over every other character; and in this distinction seems to consist the essential difference between those two different species of military force.

Militias were anciently only exercised and not regimented. Militias have been of several different kinds. In some countries the citizens destined for defending the state, seem to have been exercised only, without being, if I may say so, regimented; that is, without being divided into separate and distinct bodies of troops, each of which performed its exercises under its own proper and permanent officers. In the republics of ancient Greece and Rome, each citizen, as long as he remained at home, seems to have practised his exercises either separately and independently, or with such of his equals as he liked best; and not to have been attached to any particular body of troops till he was actually called upon to take the field. In other countries, the militia has not only been exercised, but regimented. In England, in Switzerland, and, I believe, in every other country of modern Europe, where any imperfect military force of this kind has been established, every militia-man is, even in time of peace, attached to a particular body of troops, which performs its exercises under its own proper and permanent officers.

Fire-arms brought about the change by making dexterity less important, Before the invention of fire-arms, that army was superior in which the soldiers had, each individually, the greatest skill and dexterity in the use of their arms. Strength and agility of body were of the highest consequence, and commonly determined the fate of battles. But this skill and dexterity in the use of their arms, could be acquired only, in the same manner as fencing is[1] at present, by practising, not in great bodies, but each man separately, in a particular school, under a particular master, or with his own particular equals and companions. Since the invention of fire-arms, strength and agility of body, or even extraordinary dexterity and skill in the use of arms, though they are far from being of no consequence, are, however, of less consequence. The nature of the weapon, though it by no means puts the awkward upon a level with the skilful, puts him more nearly so than he ever was before. All the dexterity and skill, it is supposed, which are necessary for using it, can be well enough acquired by practising in great bodies.

[1] [Ed. 1 reads 'is acquired'.]

and discipline much more so. Regularity, order, and prompt obedience to command, are qualities which, in modern armies, are of more importance towards determining the fate of battles, than the dexterity and skill of the soldiers in the use of their arms. But the noise of fire-arms, the smoke, and the invisible death to which every man feels himself every moment exposed, as soon as he comes within cannon-shot, and frequently a long time before the battle can be well said to be engaged, must render it very difficult to maintain any considerable degree of this regularity, order, and prompt obedience, even in the beginning of a modern battle. In an ancient battle there was no noise but what arose from the human voice; there was no smoke, there was no invisible cause of wounds or death. Every man, till some mortal weapon actually did approach him, saw clearly that no such weapon was near him. In these circumstances, and among troops who had some confidence in their own skill and dexterity in the use of their arms, it must have been a good deal less difficult to preserve some degree of regularity and order, not only in the beginning, but through the whole progress of an ancient battle, and till one of the two armies was fairly defeated. But the habits of regularity, order, and prompt obedience to command, can be acquired only by troops which are exercised in great bodies.

A militia is always inferior to a standing army, A militia, however, in whatever manner it may be either disciplined or exercised, must always be much inferior to a well-disciplined and well-exercised standing army.

being less expert, The soldiers, who are exercised only once a week, or once a month, can never be so expert in the use of their arms, as those who are exercised every day, or every other day; and though this circumstance may not be of so much consequence in modern, as it was in ancient times, yet the acknowledged superiority of the Prussian troops, owing, it is said, very much to their superior expertness in their exercise, may satisfy us that it is, even at this day, of very considerable consequence.

and less well disciplined. The soldiers, who are bound to obey their officer only once a week or once a month, and who are at all other times at liberty to manage their own affairs their own way, without being in any respect accountable to him, can never be under the same awe in his presence, can never have the same disposition to ready obedience, with those whose whole life and conduct are every day directed by him, and who every day even rise and go to bed, or at least retire to their quarters, according to his orders. In what is called discipline, or in the habit of ready obedience, a militia must always be still more inferior to a standing army, than it may sometimes be in what is called the manual exercise, or in the management and use of its arms. But in modern war the habit of ready and instant obedience is of much greater consequence than a considerable superiority in the management of arms.

The best militias are those which go to war under the chieftains who rule in time of peace. Those militias which, like the Tartar or Arab militia, go to war under the same chieftains whom they are accustomed to obey in peace, are by far the best. In respect for their officers, in the habit of ready obedience, they approach nearest to standing armies. The highland militia, when it served under its own chieftains, had some advantage of the same kind. As the highlanders, however, were not wandering, but stationary shepherds, as they had all a fixed habitation, and were not, in peaceable times, accustomed to follow their chieftain from place to place; so in time of war they were less willing to follow him to any considerable distance, or to continue for any long time in the field. When they had acquired any booty they were eager to return home, and his authority was seldom sufficient to detain them. In point of obedience they were always much inferior to what is reported of the Tartars and Arabs. As the highlanders too, from their stationary life, spend less of their time in the open air, they were always less accustomed to military exercises, and were less expert in the use of their arms than the Tartars and Arabs are said to be.

A militia kept long enough in the field becomes a standing army. A militia of any kind, it must be observed, however, which has served for several successive campaigns in the field, becomes in every respect a standing army. The soldiers are every day exercised in the use of their arms, and, being constantly under the command of their officers, are habituated to the same prompt obedience which takes place in standing armies. What they were before they took the field, is of little importance. They necessarily become in every respect a standing army, after they have passed a few campaigns in it. Should the war in America drag out through another campaign,[1] the American militia may become in every respect a match for that

---

[1] [As ed. 1 was published at the beginning of March, 1776, this must have been written less than a year after the outbreak of the war, which lasted eight years.]

standing army, of which the valour appeared, in the last war,[1] at least not inferior to that of the hardiest veterans of France and Spain.

History shows the superiority of the standing army. This distinction being well understood, the history of all ages, it will be found, bears testimony to the irresistible superiority which a well-regulated standing army has over a militia.

That of Macedon defeated the Greek militias. One of the first standing armies of which we have any distinct account, in any well authenticated history, is that of Philip of Macedon. His frequent wars with the Thracians, Illyrians, Thessalians, and some of the Greek cities in the neighbourhood of Macedon, gradually formed his troops, which in the beginning were probably militia, to the exact discipline of a standing army. When he was at peace, which he was very seldom, and never for any long time together, he was careful not to disband that army. It vanquished and subdued, after a long and violent struggle, indeed, the gallant and well exercised militias of the principal republics of ancient Greece; and afterwards, with very little struggle, the effeminate and ill-exercised militia of the great Persian empire. The fall of the Greek republics and of the Persian empire, was the effect of the irresistible superiority which a standing army has over every sort of militia. It is the first great revolution in the affairs of mankind, of which history has preserved any distinct or circumstantial account.

In the wars of Carthage and Rome standing armies defeated militias. The fall of Carthage, and the consequent elevation of Rome, is the second. All the varieties in the fortune of those two famous republics may very well be accounted for from the same cause.

The Carthaginian standing army defeated the Roman militia in Italy From the end of the first to the beginning of the second Carthaginian war, the armies of Carthage were continually in the field, and employed under three great generals, who succeeded one another in the command; Amilcar, his son-in-law Asdrubal, and his son Annibal; first in chastising their own rebellious slaves, afterwards in subduing the revolted nations of Africa, and, lastly, in conquering the great kingdom of Spain. The army which Annibal led from Spain into Italy must necessarily, in those different wars, have been gradually formed to the exact discipline of a standing army. The Romans,

---

[1] [The Seven Years' War, 1756–1763. Ed. 1 reads 'of which in the last war the valour appeared'.]

in the mean time, though they had not been altogether at peace, yet they had not, during this period, been engaged in any war of very great consequence; and their military discipline, it is generally said, was a good deal relaxed. The Roman armies which Annibal encountered at Trebia, Thrasymenus and Cannæ, were militia opposed to a standing army. This circumstance, it is probable, contributed more than any other to determine the fate of those battles.

and Spain. The standing army which Annibal left behind him in Spain, had the like superiority over the militia which the Romans sent to oppose it, and in a few years, under the command of his brother, the younger Asdrubal, expelled them almost entirely from that country.

When the Roman militias became a standing army they defeated the Carthaginian standing army in Italy Annibal was ill supplied from home. The Roman militia, being continually in the field, became in the progress of the war a well disciplined and well exercised standing army; and the superiority of Annibal grew every day less and less. Asdrubal judged it necessary to lead the whole, or almost the whole of the standing army which he commanded in Spain, to the assistance of his brother in Italy. In this[1] march he is said to have been misled by his guides; and in a country which he did not know, was surprized and attacked by another standing army, in every respect equal or superior to his own, and was entirely defeated.

and the Carthaginian militia in Spain, and both standing army and militia in Africa. When Asdrubal had left Spain, the great Scipio found nothing to oppose him but a militia inferior to his own. He conquered and subdued that militia, and, in the course of the war, his own militia necessarily became a well-disciplined and well-exercised standing army. That standing army was afterwards carried to Africa, where it found nothing but a militia to oppose it. In order to defend Carthage it became necessary to recall the standing army of Annibal. The disheartened and frequently defeated African militia joined it, and, at the battle of Zama, composed the greater part of the troops of Annibal. The event of that day determined the fate of the two rival republics.

Thenceforward the Roman republic had standing armies, which found little resistance From the end of the second Carthaginian war till the fall of the Roman republic, the armies of Rome were in every respect standing armies. The standing army of Macedon made some resistance to

[1] ['This' is probably a misprint for 'his,' the reading of eds. 1–3.]

except from the standing army of Macedon. their arms. In the height of their grandeur, it cost them two great wars, and three great battles, to subdue that little kingdom; of which the conquest would probably have been still more difficult, had it not been for the cowardice of its last king. The militias of all the civilized nations of the ancient world, of Greece, of Syria, and of Egypt, made but a feeble resistance to the standing armies of Rome. The militias of some barbarous nations defended themselves much better. The Scythian or Tartar militia, which Mithridates drew from the countries north of the Euxine and Caspian seas, were the most formidable enemies whom[1] the Romans had to encounter after the second Carthaginian war. The Parthian and German militias too were always respectable, and, upon several occasions, gained very considerable advantages over the Roman armies. In general, however, and when the Roman armies were well commanded, they appear to have been very much superior; and if the Romans did not pursue the final conquest either of Parthia or Germany, it was probably because they judged, that it was not worth while to add those two barbarous countries to an empire which was already too large. The ancient Parthians appear to have been a nation of Scythian or Tartar extraction, and to have always retained a good deal of the manners of their ancestors. The ancient Germans were, like the Scythians or Tartars, a nation of wandering shepherds, who went to war under the same chiefs whom they were accustomed to follow in peace. Their militia was exactly of the same kind with that of the Scythians or Tartars, from whom too they were probably descended.

Under the emperors these armies degenerated into militias. Many different causes contributed to relax the discipline of the Roman armies. Its extreme severity was, perhaps, one of those causes. In the days of their grandeur, when no enemy appeared capable of opposing them, their heavy armour was laid aside as unnecessarily burdensome, their laborious exercises were neglected as unnecessarily toilsome. Under the Roman emperors besides, the standing armies of Rome, those particularly which guarded the German and Pannonian frontiers, became dangerous to their masters, against whom they used frequently to set up their own generals. In order to render them less formidable, according to some authors, Dioclesian, according to others, Constantine, first withdrew them from the frontier, where they had always before been encamped in great

[1] [Ed. 1 reads 'which'.]

bodies, generally of two or three legions each, and dispersed them in small bodies through the different provincial towns, from whence they were scarce ever removed, but when it became necessary to repel an invasion. Small bodies of soldiers quartered in trading and manufacturing towns, and seldom removed from those quarters, became themselves tradesmen, artificers, and manufacturers. The civil came to predominate over the military character; and the standing armies of Rome gradually degenerated into a corrupt, neglected, and undisciplined militia, incapable of resisting the attack of the German and Scythian militias, which soon afterwards invaded the western empire. It was only by hiring the militia of some of those nations to oppose to that of others, that the emperors were for some time able to defend themselves. The fall of the western empire is the third great revolution in the affairs of mankind, of which ancient history has preserved any distinct or circumstantial account. It was brought about by the irresistible superiority which the militia of a barbarous, has over that of a civilized nation; which the militia of a nation of shepherds, has over that of a nation of husbandmen, artificers, and manufacturers. The victories which have been gained by militias have generally been, not over standing armies, but over other militias in exercise and discipline inferior to themselves. Such were the victories which the Greek militia gained over that of the Persian empire; and such too were those which in later times the Swiss militia gained over that of the Austrians and Burgundians.

Militias were gradually superseded by standing armies in Western Europe. The military force of the German and Scythian nations who established themselves upon the ruins of the western empire, continued for some time to be of the same kind in their new settlements, as it had been in their original country. It was a militia of shepherds and husbandmen, which, in time of war, took the field under the command of the same chieftains whom it was accustomed to obey in peace. It was, therefore, tolerably well exercised, and tolerably well disciplined. As arts and industry advanced, however, the authority of the chieftains gradually decayed, and the great body of the people had less time to spare for military exercises. Both the discipline and the exercise of the feudal militia, therefore, went gradually to ruin, and standing armies were gradually introduced to supply the place of it. When the expedient of a standing army, besides, had once been adopted by one civilized nation, it became necessary that all its neighbours should follow the example. They soon found that their safety depended upon their doing so, and that their own militia was altogether incapable of resisting the attack of such an army.

A standing army does not lose its valour in time of peace, The soldiers of a standing army, though they may never have seen an enemy, yet have frequently appeared to possess all the courage of veteran troops, and the very moment that they took the field to have been fit to face the hardiest and most experienced veterans. In 1756, when the Russian army marched into Poland, the valour of the Russian soldiers did not appear inferior to that of the Prussians, at that time supposed to be the hardiest and most experienced veterans in Europe. The Russian empire, however, had enjoyed a profound peace for near twenty years before, and could at that time have very few soldiers who had ever seen an enemy. When the Spanish war broke out in 1739, England had enjoyed a profound peace for about eight and twenty years. The valour of her soldiers, however, far from being corrupted by that long peace, was never more distinguished than in the attempt upon Carthagena, the first unfortunate exploit of that unfortunate war. In a long peace the generals, perhaps, may sometimes forget their skill; but, where a well-regulated standing army has been kept up, the soldiers seem never to forget their valour.

and is the only safeguard of a civilised nation, When a civilized nation depends for its defence upon a militia, it is at all times exposed to be conquered by any barbarous nation which happens to be in its neighbourhood. The frequent conquests of all the civilized countries in Asia by the Tartars, sufficiently demonstrates[1] the natural superiority, which the militia of a barbarous, has over that of a civilized nation. A well-regulated standing army is superior to every militia. Such an army, as it can best be maintained by an opulent and civilized nation, so it can alone defend such a nation against the invasion of a poor and barbarous neighbour. It is only by means of a standing army, therefore, that the civilization of any country can be perpetuated, or even preserved for any considerable time.

also the only means of civilising a barbarous one. As it is only by means of a well-regulated standing army that a civilized country can be defended; so it is only by means of it, that a barbarous country can be suddenly and tolerably civilized. A standing army establishes, with an irresistible force, the law of the sovereign through

[1] [Almost certainly a misprint for 'demonstrate,' the reading of ed. 1.]

the remotest provinces of the empire, and maintains some degree of regular government in countries which could not otherwise admit of any. Whoever examines, with attention, the improvements which Peter the Great introduced into the Russian empire, will find that they almost all resolve themselves into the establishment of a well-regulated standing army. It is the instrument which executes and maintains all his other regulations. That degree of order and internal peace, which that empire has ever since enjoyed, is altogether owing to the influence of that army.

It is not unfavour- able to liberty. Men of republican principles have been jealous of a standing army as dangerous to liberty. It certainly is so, wherever the interest of the general and that of the principal officers are not necessarily connected with the support of the constitution of the state. The standing army of Cæsar destroyed the Roman republic. The standing army of Cromwel turned the long parliament out of doors.[1] But where the sovereign is himself the general, and the principal nobility and gentry of the country the chief officers of the army; where the military force is placed under the command of those who have the greatest interest in the support of the civil authority, because they have themselves the greatest share of that authority, a standing army can never be dangerous to liberty. On the contrary, it may in some cases be favourable to liberty.[2] The security which it gives to the sovereign renders unnecessary that troublesome jealousy, which, in some modern republics, seems to watch over the minutest actions, and to be at all times ready to disturb the peace of every citizen. Where the security of the magistrate, though supported by the principal people of the country, is endangered by every popular discontent; where a small tumult is capable of bringing about in a few hours a great revolution, the whole authority of government must be employed to suppress and punish every murmur and complaint against it. To a sovereign, on the contrary, who feels himself supported, not only by the natural aristocracy of the country, but by a well-regulated standing army, the rudest, the most groundless, and the most licentious remonstrances can give little disturbance. He can safely pardon or neglect them, and his consciousness of his own superiority naturally disposes him to do so. That degree of liberty which approaches to licentiousness can be tolerated only in countries where the

---

[1] [*Lectures*, p. 29. 'Cromwel,' which is Hume's spelling, appears first in ed. 4 here, but above, p. III, it is so spelt in all editions.]   [2] [*Lectures*, p. 263.]

sovereign is secured by a well-regulated standing army. It is in such countries only, that the public safety does not require, that the sovereign should be trusted with any discretionary power, for suppressing even the impertinent wantonness of this licentious liberty.

Defence thus grows more expensive. The first duty of the sovereign, therefore, that of defending the society from the violence and injustice of other independent societies, grows gradually more and more expensive, as the society advances in civilization. The military force of the society, which originally cost the sovereign no expence either in time of peace or in time of war, must, in the progress of improvement, first be maintained by him in time of war, and afterwards even in time of peace.

Fire-arms enhance the expense, The great change introduced into the art of war by the invention of fire-arms, has enhanced still further both the expence of exercising and disciplining any particular number of soldiers in time of peace, and that of employing them in time of war. Both their arms and their ammunition are become more expensive. A musquet is a more expensive machine than a javelin or a bow and arrows; a cannon or a mortar than a balista or a catapulta. The powder, which is spent in a modern review, is lost irrecoverably, and occasions a very considerable expence. The javelins and arrows which were thrown or shot in an ancient one, could easily be picked up again, and were besides of very little value. The cannon and the mortar are, not only much dearer, but much heavier machines than the balista or catapulta, and require a greater expence, not only to prepare them for the field, but to carry them to it. As the superiority of the modern artillery too, over that of the ancients is very great; it has become much more difficult, and consequently much more expensive, to fortify a town so as to resist even for a few weeks the attack of that superior artillery. In modern times many different causes contribute to render the defence of the society more expensive. The unavoidable effects of the natural progress of improvement have, in this respect, been a good deal enhanced by a great revolution in the art of war, to which a mere accident, the invention of gunpowder, seems to have given occasion.

and so give an advantage to rich nations, which is favourable to civilisation. In modern war the great expence of fire-arms gives an evident advantage to the nation which can best afford that expence; and consequently, to an opulent and civilized, over a poor and barbarous nation. In ancient times the opulent and civilized found it difficult to defend themselves against the poor and barbarous nations. In modern times the poor and barbarous find it difficult to defend themselves against the opulent and civilized. The invention of fire-arms, an invention which at first sight appears to be so pernicious, is certainly favourable both to the permanency and to the extension of civilization.[1]

PART II

Of the Expence of Justice

The expense of justice is different at different periods.

The second duty of the sovereign, that of pro-tecting, as far as possible, every member of the society from the injustice or oppression of every other member of it, or the duty of establishing an exact administra-tion of justice requires too very different degrees of expence in the different periods of society.

Civil government was first rendered necessary by the introduction of property.

Among nations of hunters, as there is scarce any property, or at least none that exceeds the value of two or three days labour; so there is seldom any established magistrate or any regular administra-tion of justice. Men who have no property can injure one another only in their persons or reputations. But when one man kills, wounds, beats, or defames another, though he to whom the injury is done suffers, he who does it receives no benefit. It is otherwise with the injuries to property. The benefit of the person who does the injury is often equal to the loss of him who suffers it. Envy, malice, or resentment, are the only passions which can prompt one man to injure another in his person or reputation. But the greater part of men are not very frequently under the influence of those passions; and the very worst men are so only occasionally. As their gratification too, how agreeable soever it may be to certain charac-ters, is not attended with any real or permanent advantage, it is in the greater part of men commonly restrained by prudential con-siderations. Men may live together in society with some tolerable

---

[1] [Hume, *History*, ed. of 1773, vol. ii., p. 432, says the 'furious engine,' artillery, 'though it seemed contrived for the destruction of mankind and the overthrow of empires, has in the issue rendered battles less bloody, and has given greater stability to civil societies,' but his reasons are somewhat different from those in the text above. This part of the chapter is evidently adapted from Part iv. 'Of Arms' in the *Lectures*, pp. 260–264, and the dissertation on the rise, progress and fall of militarism in Part i., pp. 26–34.]

degree of security, though there is no civil magistrate to protect them from the injustice of those passions. But avarice and ambition in the rich, in the poor the hatred of labour and the love of present ease and enjoyment, are the passions which prompt to invade property, passions much more steady in their operation, and much more universal in their influence. Wherever there is great property, there is great inequality. For one very rich man, there must be at least five hundred poor, and the affluence of the few supposes the indigence of the many. The affluence of the rich excites the indignation of the poor, who are often both driven by want, and prompted by envy, to invade his possessions. It is only under the shelter of the civil magistrate that the owner of that valuable property, which is acquired by the labour of many years, or perhaps of many successive generations, can sleep a single night in security. He is at all times surrounded by unknown enemies, whom, though he never provoked, he can never appease, and from whose injustice he can be protected only by the powerful arm of the civil magistrate continually held up to chastise it. The acquisition of valuable and[1] extensive property, therefore, necessarily requires the establishment of civil government. Where there is no property, or at least none that exceeds the value of two or three days labour, civil government is not so necessary.

Property strengthens the causes of subordination. Civil government supposes a certain subordination. But as the necessity of civil government gradually grows up with the acquisition of valuable property, so the principal causes which naturally introduce subordination gradually grow up with the growth of that valuable property.

There are four causes of subordination, The causes or circumstances which naturally introduce subordination, or which naturally, and antecedent to any civil institution, give some men some superiority over the greater part of their brethren, seem to be four in number.

(1) superiority of personal qualifications, The first of those causes or circumstances is the superiority of personal qualifications, of strength, beauty, and agility of body; of wisdom, and virtue, of prudence, justice, fortitude, and moderation of mind. The qualifications of the body, unless supported by those of the mind, can give little authority in any period of society. He is a very strong man, who, by mere strength of body, can force two weak ones to

[1] [Ed. 1 reads 'or'.]

obey him. The qualifications of the mind can alone give very great authority. They are, however, invisible qualities; always disputable, and generally disputed. No society, whether barbarous or civilized, has ever found it convenient to settle the rules of precedency of rank and subordination, according to those invisible qualities; but according to something that is more plain and palpable.

(2) *superiority of age,* The second of those causes or circumstances is the superiority of age. An old man, provided his age is not so far advanced as to give suspicion of dotage, is every where more respected than a young man of equal rank, fortune and abilities. Among nations of hunters, such as the native tribes of North America, age is the sole foundation of rank and precedency. Among them, father is the appellation of a superior; brother of an equal; and son, of an inferior. In the most opulent and civilized nations, age regulates rank among those who are in every other respect equal, and among whom, therefore, there is nothing else to regulate it. Among brothers and among sisters, the eldest always take place; and in the succession of the paternal estate every thing which cannot be divided, but must go entire to one person, such as a title of honour, is in most cases given to the eldest. Age is a plain and palpable quality which admits of no dispute.

(3) *superiority of fortune,* The third of those causes or circumstances is the superiority of fortune. The authority of riches, however, though great in every age of society, is perhaps greatest in the rudest age of society which admits of any considerable inequality of fortune. A Tartar chief, the increase of whose herds and flocks is sufficient to maintain a thousand men, cannot well employ that increase in any other way than in maintaining a thousand men. The rude state of his society does not afford him any manufactured produce, any trinkets or baubles of any kind, for which he can exchange that part of his rude produce which is over and above his own consumption. The thousand men whom he thus maintains, depending entirely upon him for their subsistence, must both obey his orders in war, and submit to his jurisdiction in peace. He is necessarily both their general and their judge, and his chieftainship is the necessary effect of the superiority of his fortune. In an opulent and civilized society, a man may possess a much greater fortune, and yet not be able to command a dozen of people. Though the produce of his estate may be sufficient to maintain, and may perhaps actually maintain, more than a thousand people, yet as those

people pay for every thing which they get from him, as he gives scarce any thing to any body but in exchange for an equivalent, there is scarce any body who considers himself as entirely dependent upon him, and his authority extends only over a few menial servants. The authority of fortune, however, is very great even in an opulent and civilized society. That it is much greater than that, either of age, or of personal qualities, has been the constant complaint of every period of society which admitted of any considerable inequality of fortune. The first period of society, that of hunters, admits of no such inequality. Universal poverty establishes there[1] universal equality, and the superiority, either of age, or of personal qualities, are the feeble, but the sole foundations of authority and subordination. There is therefore little or no authority or subordination in this period of society. The second period of society, that of shepherds, admits of very great inequalities of fortune, and there is no period in which the superiority of fortune gives so great authority to those who possess it. There is no period accordingly in which authority and subordination are more perfectly established. The authority of an Arabian scherif is very great; that of a Tartar khan altogether despotical.

and (4) superiority of birth. The fourth of those causes or circumstances is the superiority of birth. Superiority of birth supposes an ancient superiority of fortune in the family of the person who claims it. All families are equally ancient; and the ancestors of the prince, though they may be better known, cannot well be more numerous than those of the beggar. Antiquity of family means every where the antiquity either of wealth, or of that greatness which is commonly either founded upon wealth, or accompanied with it. Upstart greatness is every where less respected than ancient greatness.[2] The hatred of usurpers, the love of the family of an ancient monarch, are, in a great measure, founded upon the contempt which men naturally have for the former, and upon their veneration for the latter. As a military officer submits without reluctance to the authority of a superior by whom he has always been commanded, but cannot bear that his inferior should be set over his head; so men easily submit to a family to whom they and their ancestors have always submitted; but are fired with indignation when another family, in whom they had never acknowledged any such superiority, assumes a dominion over them.

---

[1] [Misprinted 'their' in eds. 4 and 5.]   [2] [*Lectures*, p. 10.]

The distinction of birth is not present among hunters,

The distinction of birth, being subsequent to the inequality of fortune, can have no place in nations of hunters, among whom all men, being equal in fortune, must likewise be very nearly equal in birth. The son of a wise and brave man may, indeed, even among them, be somewhat more respected than a man of equal merit who has the misfortune to be the son of a fool or a coward. The difference, however, will not be very great; and there never was, I believe, a great family in the world whose illustration was entirely derived from the inheritance of wisdom and virtue.

but always among shepherds.

The distinction of birth not only may, but always does take place among nations of shepherds. Such nations are always strangers to every sort of luxury, and great wealth can scarce ever be dissipated among them by improvident profusion. There are no nations accordingly who abound more in families revered and honoured on account of their descent from a long race of great and illustrious ancestors; because there are no nations among whom wealth is likely to continue longer in the same families.

Distinctions of birth and fortune are both most powerful among shepherds.

Birth and fortune are evidently the two circumstances which principally set one man above another. They are the two great sources of personal distinction, and are therefore the principal causes which naturally establish authority and subordination among men. Among nations of shepherds both those causes operate with their full force. The great shepherd or herdsman, respected on account of his great wealth, and of the great number of those who depend upon him for subsistence, and revered on account of the nobleness of his birth, and of the immemorial antiquity of his illustrious family, has a natural authority over all the inferior shepherds or herdsmen of his horde or clan. He can command the united force of a greater number of people than any of them. His military power is greater than that of any of them. In time of war they are all of them naturally disposed to muster themselves under his banner, rather than under that of any other person, and his birth and fortune thus naturally procure to him some sort of executive power. By commanding too the united force of a greater number of people than any of them, he is best able to compel any one of them who may have injured another to compensate the wrong. He is the person, therefore, to whom all those who are too weak to defend themselves naturally look up for protection. It is to him that they naturally complain of the injuries which they imagine have been done to them, and his interposition in such cases is more easily submitted to, even by the person complained of, than that of any other person would be. His birth and fortune thus naturally procure him some sort of judicial authority.

Among shepherds inequality of fortune arises and introduces civil government, It is in the age of shepherds, in the second period or society, that the inequality of fortune first begins to take place, and introduces among men a degree of authority and subordination which could not possibly exist before. It thereby introduces some degree of that civil government which is indispensably necessary for its own preservation: and it seems to do this naturally, and even independent of the consideration of that necessity. The consideration of that necessity comes no doubt afterwards to contribute very much to maintain and secure that authority and subordination. The rich, in particular, are necessarily interested to support that order of things, which can alone secure them in the possession of their own advantages. Men of inferior wealth combine to defend those of superior wealth in the possession of their property, in order that men of superior wealth may combine to defend them in the possession of theirs. All the inferior shepherds and herdsmen feel that the security of their own herds and flocks depends upon the security of those of the great shepherd or herdsman; that the maintenance of their lesser authority depends upon that of his greater authority, and that upon their subordination to him depends his power of keeping their inferiors in subordination to them. They constitute a sort of little nobility, who feel themselves interested to defend the property and to support the authority of their own little sovereign, in order that he may be able to defend their property and to support their authority. Civil government, so far as it is instituted for the security of property, is in reality instituted for the defence of the rich against the poor, or of those who have some property against those who have none at all.[1]

but the judicial authority was long a source of revenue rather than expense, The judicial authority of such a sovereign, however, far from being a cause of expence, was for a long time a source of revenue to him. The persons who applied to him for justice were always willing to pay for it, and a

[1] [*Lectures*, p. 15: 'Till there be property there can be no government, the very end of which is to secure wealth and to defend the rich from the poor.' Cp. Locke, *Civil Government*, § 94, 'government has no other end but the preservation of property'.]

present never failed to accompany a petition. After the authority of the sovereign too was thoroughly established, the person found guilty, over and above the satisfaction which he was obliged to make to the party, was likewise forced to pay an amercement to the sovereign. He had given trouble, he had disturbed, he had broke the peace of his lord the king, and for those offences an amercement was thought due. In the Tartar governments of Asia, in the governments of Europe which were founded by the German and Scythian nations who overturned the Roman empire, the administration of justice was a considerable source of revenue, both to the sovereign, and to all the lesser chiefs or lords who exercised under him any particular jurisdiction, either over some particular tribe or clan, or over some particular territory or district. Originally both the sovereign and the inferior chiefs used to exercise this jurisdiction in their own persons. Afterwards they universally found it convenient to delegate it to some substitute, bailiff, or judge. This substitute, however, was still obliged to account to his principal or constituent for the profits of the jurisdiction. Whoever reads the[1] instructions which were given to the judges of the circuit in the time of Henry II. will see clearly that those judges were a sort of itinerant factors, sent round the country for the purpose of levying certain branches of the king's revenue. In those days the administration of justice, not only afforded a certain revenue to the sovereign, but to procure this revenue seems to have been one of the principal advantages which he proposed to obtain by the administration of justice.

which produced great abuses,   This scheme of making the administration of justice subservient to the purposes of revenue, could scarce fail to be productive of several very gross abuses. The person, who applied for justice with a large present in his hand, was likely to get something more than justice; while he, who applied for it with a small one, was likely to get something less. Justice too might frequently be delayed, in order that this present might be repeated. The amercement, besides, of the person complained of, might frequently suggest a very strong reason for finding him in the wrong, even when he had not really been so. That such abuses were far from being uncommon, the ancient history of every country in Europe bears witness.

---

[1] They are to be found in Tyrrel's History of England. [*General History of England, both Ecclesiastical and Civil*, by James Tyrrell, vol. ii., 1700, pp. 576–579. The king is Richard I., not Henry II.]

whether the sov-
ereign exercised the
judicial authority
in person or by
deputy.

When the sovereign or chief exercised his judicial authority in his own person, how much soever he might abuse it, it must have been scarce possible to get any redress; because there could seldom be any body powerful enough to call him to account. When he exercised it by a bailiff, indeed, redress might sometimes be had. If it was for his own benefit only, that the bailiff had been guilty of any act of injustice, the sovereign himself might not always be unwilling to punish him, or to oblige him to repair the wrong. But if it was for the benefit of his sovereign, if it was in order to make court to the person who appointed him and who might prefer him, that he had committed any act of oppression, redress would upon most occasions be as impossible as if the sovereign had committed it himself. In all barbarous governments, accordingly, in all those ancient governments of Europe in particular, which were founded upon the ruins of the Roman empire, the administration of justice appears for a long time to have been extremely corrupt; far from being quite equal and impartial even under the best monarchs, and altogether profligate under the worst.

These abuses could
not be remedied so
long as the sovereign
depended only
on land revenue
and court fees,

Among nations of shepherds, where the sovereign or chief is only the greatest shepherd or herdsman of the horde or clan, he is maintained in the same manner as any of his vassals or subjects, by the increase of his own herds or flocks. Among those nations of husbandmen who are but just come out of the shepherd state, and who are not much advanced beyond that state; such as the Greek tribes appear to have been about the time of the Trojan war, and our German and Scythian ancestors when they first settled upon the ruins of the western empire; the sovereign or chief is, in the same manner, only the greatest landlord of the country, and is maintained, in the same manner as any other landlord, by a revenue derived from his own private estate, or from what, in modern Europe, was called the demesne of the crown. His subjects, upon ordinary occasions, contribute nothing to his support, except when, in order to protect them from the oppression of some of their fellow-subjects, they stand in need of his authority.[1] The presents which they make him upon such occasions, constitute the whole ordinary revenue, the whole of the emoluments which, except perhaps upon

---

[1] [Ed. 1 reads 'except when they stand in need of the interposition of his authority in order to protect them from the oppression of some of their fellow subjects'.]

some very extraordinary emergencies, he derives from his dominion over them. When Agamemnon, in Homer, offers to Achilles for his friendship the sovereignty of seven Greek cities, the sole advantage which he mentions as likely to be derived from it, was, that the people would honour him with presents.[1] As long as such presents, as long as the emoluments of justice, or what may be called the fees of court, constituted in this manner the whole ordinary revenue which the sovereign derived from his sovereignty, it could not well be expected, it could not even decently be proposed, that he should give them up altogether. It might, and it frequently was proposed, that he should regulate and ascertain them. But after they had been so regulated and ascertained, how to hinder a person who was all-powerful from extending them beyond those regulations, was still very difficult, not to say impossible. During the continuance of this state of things, therefore, the corruption of justice, naturally resulting from the arbitrary and uncertain nature of those presents, scarce admitted of any effectual remedy.

but when taxes became necessary, the people stipulated that no presents should be taken by judges. But when from different causes, chiefly from the continually increasing expence of defending the nation against the invasion of other nations, the private estate of the sovereign had become altogether insufficient for defraying the expence of the sovereignty; and when it had become necessary that the people should, for their own security, contribute towards this expence by taxes of different kinds, it seems to have been very commonly stipulated, that no present for the administration of justice should, under any pretence, be accepted either by the sovereign, or by his bailiffs and substitutes, the judges. Those presents, it seems to have been supposed, could more easily be abolished altogether, than effectually regulated and ascertained. Fixed salaries were appointed to the judges, which were supposed to compensate to them the loss of whatever might have been their share of the ancient emoluments of justice; as the taxes more than compensated to the sovereign the loss of his. Justice was then said to be administered gratis.

Justice is never administered gratis. Justice, however, never was in reality administered gratis in any country. Lawyers and attornies, at least, must always be paid by the parties; and, if they were not, they would perform their duty still worse than they actually perform it. The fees annually paid to lawyers and attornies amount, in every

[1] [*Iliad*, ix., 149–156, but the presents are not the 'sole advantage' mentioned.]

court, to a much greater sum than the salaries of the judges. The circumstance of those salaries being paid by the crown, can no-where much diminish the necessary expence of a law-suit. But it was not so much to diminish the expence, as to prevent the corruption of justice, that the judges were prohibited from receiving any present or fee from the parties.

The salaries of judges are a small part of the expense of civilised government,   The office of judge is in itself so very honourable, that men are willing to accept of it, though accompanied with very small emoluments. The inferior office of justice of peace, though attended with a good deal of trouble, and in most cases with no emoluments at all, is an object of ambition to the greater part of our country gentlemen. The salaries of all the different judges, high and low, together with the whole expence of the administration and execution of justice, even where it is not managed with very good œconomy, makes, in any civilized country, but a very inconsiderable part of the whole expence of government.

and might be defrayed by fees of court.   The whole expence of justice too might easily be defrayed by the fees of court; and, without exposing the administration of justice to any real hazard of corruption, the public revenue might thus be entirely discharged from a certain, though, perhaps, but a small incumbrance. It is difficult to regulate the fees of court effectually, where a person so powerful as the sovereign is to share in them, and to derive any considerable part of his revenue from them. It is very easy, where the judge is the principal person who can reap any benefit from them. The law can very easily oblige the judge to respect the regulation, though it might not always be able to make the sovereign respect it. Where the fees of court are precisely regulated and ascertained, where they are paid all at once, at a certain period of every process, into the hands of a cashier or receiver, to be by him distributed in certain known proportions among the different judges after the process is decided, and not till it is decided, there seems to be no more danger of corruption than where such fees are prohibited altogether. Those fees, without occasioning any considerable increase in the expence of a law-suit, might be rendered fully sufficient for defraying the whole expence of justice. By not being paid to the judges till the process was determined, they might be some incitement to the diligence of the court in examining and deciding it. In courts which consisted of a considerable number of judges, by proportioning the share of each judge to the number of hours and days which he had employed in examining the process, either in the court or in a committee by order of the court, those fees might give some encouragement to the diligence of each particular judge. Public services are never better performed than when their reward comes only in consequence of their being performed, and is proportioned to the diligence employed in performing them. In the different parliaments of France, the fees of court (called Epicès[1] and vacations) constitute the far greater part of the emoluments of the judges. After all deductions are made, the neat salary paid by the crown to a counsellor or judge in the parliament of Toulouse, in rank and dignity the second parliament of the kingdom, amounts only to a hundred and fifty livres, about six pounds eleven shillings sterling a year. About seven years ago[2] that sum was in the same place the ordinary yearly wages of a common footman. The distribution of those Epicès too is according to the diligence of the judges. A diligent judge gains a comfortable, though moderate, revenue by his office: An idle one gets little more than his salary. Those parliaments are perhaps, in many respects, not very convenient courts of justice; but they have never been accused; they seem never even to have been suspected of corruption.

The English courts were originally maintained by fees, and this led to their encroachments. The fees of court seem originally to have been the principal support of the different courts of justice in England. Each court endeavoured to draw to itself as much business as it could, and was, upon that account, willing to take cognizance of many suits which were not originally intended to fall under its jurisdiction. The court of king's bench, instituted for the trial of criminal causes only, took cognizance of civil suits; the plaintiff pretending that the defendant in not doing him justice, had been guilty of some trespass or misdemeanor. The court of exchequer, instituted for the levying of the king's revenue, and for enforcing the payment of such debts only as were due to the king, took cognizance of all other contract debts; the plaintiff alleging that he could not pay the king, because the defendant would not pay him. In consequence of such fictions it came, in many cases, to depend altogether upon the parties before what court they would chuse to have their cause tried; and each

---

[1] [The extraordinary accent here and seven lines lower down appears first in ed. 2.]

[2] [Smith was in Toulouse from February or March, 1764, to August, 1765.—Rae, *Life of Adam Smith*, pp. 174, 175, 188.]

court endeavoured, by superior dispatch and impartiality, to draw to itself as many causes as it could. The present admirable constitution of the courts of justice in England was, perhaps, originally in a great measure, formed by this emulation, which anciently took place between their respective judges; each judge endeavouring to give, in his own court, the speediest and most effectual remedy, which the law would admit, for every sort of injustice. Originally the courts of law gave damages only for breach of contract. The court of chancery, as a court of conscience, first took upon it to enforce the specific performance of agreements. When the breach of contract consisted in the non-payment of money, the damage sustained could be compensated in no other way than by ordering payment, which was equivalent to a specific performance of the agreement. In such cases, therefore, the remedy of the courts of law was sufficient. It was not so in others. When the tenant sued his lord for having unjustly outed him of his lease, the damages which he recovered were by no means equivalent to the possession of the land. Such causes, therefore, for some time, went all to the court of chancery, to the no small loss of the courts of law. It was to draw back such causes to themselves that the courts of law are said to have invented the artificial and fictitious writ of ejectment, the most effectual remedy for an unjust outer or dispossession of land.[1]

Courts might be maintained by a stamp duty on proceedings before them, but this would tempt them to multiply such proceedings. A stamp-duty upon the law proceedings of each particular court, to be levied by that court, and applied towards the maintenance of the judges and other officers belonging to it, might, in the same manner, afford a revenue sufficient for defraying the expence of the administration of justice, without bringing any burden upon the general revenue of the society. The judges indeed might, in this case, be under the temptation of multiplying unnecessarily the proceedings upon every cause, in order to increase, as much as possible, the produce of such a stamp-duty. It has been the custom in modern Europe to regulate, upon most occasions, the payment of the attornies and clerks of court, according to the number of pages which they had occasion to write; the court, however, requiring that each page should contain so many lines, and each line so many words. In order to increase their payment, the attornies and clerks have contrived to multiply words beyond all necessity, to the corruption of the law language

[1] [*Lectures*, p. 49. Above, vol. i., p. 415.]

of, I believe, every court of justice in Europe. A like temptation might perhaps occasion a like corruption in the form of law
proceedings.

Another way of securing independence would be to endow the courts with a revenue from property. But whether the administration of justice be so
contrived as to defray its own expence, or whether
the judges be maintained by fixed salaries paid to
them from some other fund, it does not seem
necessary that the person or persons entrusted with
the executive power should be charged with the management of
that fund, or with the payment of those salaries. That fund might
arise from the rent of landed estates, the management of each
estate being entrusted to the particular court which was to be maintained by it. That fund might arise even from the interest of a sum
of money, the lending out of which might, in the same manner, be
entrusted to the court which was to be maintained by it. A part,
though indeed but a small part, of the salary of the judges of the
court of session in Scotland, arises from the interest of a sum of
money. The necessary instability of such a fund seems, however, to
render it an improper one for the maintenance of an institution
which ought to last for ever.

The separation of the judicial from the executive power is due to the increase of executive business. The separation of the judicial from the executive
power seems originally to have arisen from the
increasing business of the society, in consequence of
its increasing improvement. The administration of
justice became so laborious and so complicated a
duty as to require the undivided attention of the persons to whom
it was entrusted. The person entrusted with the executive power,
not having leisure to attend to the decision of private causes himself, a deputy was appointed to decide them in his stead. In the progress of the Roman greatness, the consul was too much occupied
with the political affairs of the state, to attend to the administration
of justice. A prætor, therefore, was appointed to administer it in his
stead. In the progress of the European monarchies which were
founded upon the ruins of the Roman empire, the sovereigns and
the great lords came universally to consider the administration of
justice as an office, both too laborious and too ignoble for them to
execute in their own persons. They universally, therefore, discharged
themselves of it by appointing a deputy, bailiff, or judge.

The judicial should be not only separate When the judicial is united to the executive power,
it is scarce possible that justice should not frequently

but independent of the executive power.

be sacrificed to, what is vulgarly called, politics. The persons entrusted with the great interests of the state may, even without any corrupt views, sometimes imagine it necessary to sacrifice to those interests the rights of a private man. But upon the impartial administration of justice depends the liberty of every individual, the sense which he has of his own security. In order to make every individual feel himself perfectly secure in the possession of every right which belongs to him, it is not only necessary that the judicial should be separated from the executive power, but that it should be rendered as much as possible independent of that power. The judge should not be liable to be removed from his office according to the caprice of that power. The regular payment of his salary should not depend upon the good-will, or even upon the good œconomy of that power.

PART III

Of the Expence of public Works and public Institutions

The third duty of the sovereign is the erection and maintenance of those public works and institutions which are useful but not capable of bringing in a profit to individuals.

The third and last duty of the sovereign or commonwealth is that of erecting and maintaining those public institutions and those public works, which, though they may be in the highest degree advantageous to a great society, are, however, of such a nature, that the profit could never repay the expence to any individual or small number of individuals, and which it therefore cannot be expected that any individual or small number of individuals should erect or maintain. The performance of this duty requires too very different degrees of expence in the different periods of society.

These are chiefly institutions for facilitating commerce and promoting instruction.

After the public institutions and public works necessary for the defence of the society, and for the administration of justice, both of which have already been mentioned, the other works and institutions of this kind are chiefly those for facilitating the commerce of the society, and those for promoting the instruction of the people. The institutions for instruction are of two kinds; those for the education of the youth, and those for the instruction of people of all ages. The consideration of the manner in which the expence of those different sorts of public works and institutions may be most prop-

erly defrayed, will divide this third part of the present chapter into
three different articles.

ARTICLE I

*Of the public Works and Institutions for facilitating the Commerce of the
Society*

*And, first, of those which are necessary for facilitating Commerce in
general*[1]

*The expense of
such institutions
increases.*   That the erection and maintenance of the public
works which facilitate the commerce of any country, such as good roads, bridges, navigable canals,
harbours, &c. must require very different degrees of expence in the
different periods of society, is evident without any proof. The
expence of making and maintaining the public roads of any country
must evidently increase with the annual produce of the land and
labour of that country, or with the quantity and weight of the goods
which it becomes necessary to fetch and carry upon those roads.
The strength of a bridge must be suited to the number and weight
of the carriages, which are likely to pass over it. The depth and the
supply of water for a navigable canal must be proportioned to the
number and tunnage of the lighters, which are likely to carry goods
upon it; the extent of a harbour to the number of the shipping
which are likely to take shelter in it.

*The expense need
not be defrayed
from the general
public revenue,*   It does not seem necessary that the expence of those
public works should be defrayed from that public
revenue, as it is commonly called, of which the
collection and application are[2] in most countries assigned to the
executive power. The greater part of such public works may easily
be so managed, as to afford a particular revenue sufficient for defraying their own expence, without bringing any burden upon the
general revenue of the society.

*but may be raised
by tolls and other
particular charges.*   A highway, a bridge, a navigable canal, for example, may in most cases be both made and maintained
by a small toll upon the carriages which make use
of them: a harbour, by a moderate port-duty upon the tunnage of
the shipping which load or unload in it. The coinage, another

---

[1] [These two lines are not in eds. 1 and 2. See below, p. 253, note 2.]
[2] [Eds. 1–4 read 'is'; cp. below, p. 282, note 3.]

institution for facilitating commerce, in many countries, not only defrays its own expence, but affords a small revenue or seignorage to the sovereign. The post-office, another institution for the same purpose, over and above defraying its own expence, affords in almost all countries a very considerable revenue to the sovereign.

Tolls according to weight of carriages and capacity of boats are very equitable. When the carriages which pass over a highway or a bridge, and the lighters which sail upon a navigable canal, pay toll in proportion to their weight or their tunnage, they pay for the maintenance of those public works exactly in proportion to the wear and tear[1] which they occasion of them. It seems scarce possible to invent a more equitable way of maintaining such works. This tax or toll too, though it is advanced by the carrier, is finally paid by the consumer, to whom it must always be charged in the price of the goods. As the expence of carriage, however, is very much reduced by means of such public works, the goods, notwithstanding the toll, come cheaper to the consumer than they could otherwise have done; their price not being so much raised by the toll, as it is lowered by the cheapness of the carriage. The person who finally pays this tax, therefore, gains by the application, more than he loses by the payment of it. His payment is exactly in proportion to his gain. It is in reality no more than a part of that gain which he is obliged to give up in order to get the rest. It seems impossible to imagine a more equitable method of raising a tax.

If the tolls are higher on carriages of luxury, the rich contribute in an easy manner to the relief of the poor. When the toll upon carriages of luxury, upon coaches, post-chaises, &c. is made somewhat higher in proportion to their weight, than upon carriages of necessary use, such as carts, waggons, &c. the indolence and vanity of the rich is made to contribute in a very easy manner to the relief of the poor, by rendering cheaper the transportation of heavy goods to all the different parts of the country.

Roads and canals, etc., thus paid for cannot be made except where they are wanted. When high roads, bridges, canals, &c. are in this manner made and supported by the commerce which is carried on by means of them, they can be made only where that commerce requires them, and consequently where it is proper to make them. Their expence too, their grandeur and magnificence, must be suited to what that commerce can afford to pay. They must be made consequently as it

[1] [Ed. I reads 'tear and wear'.]

is proper to make them. A magnificent high road cannot be made through a desart country where there is little or no commerce, or merely because it happens to lead to the country villa of the intendant of the province, or to that of some great lord to whom the intendant finds it convenient to make his court. A great bridge cannot be thrown over a river at a place where nobody passes, or merely to embellish the view from the windows of a neighbouring palace: things which sometimes happen, in countries where works of this kind are carried on by any other revenue than that which they themselves are capable of affording.

Canals are better in the hands of private persons than of commissioners. In several different parts of Europe the toll or lockduty upon a canal is the property of private persons, whose private interest obliges them to keep up the canal. If it is not kept in tolerable order, the navigation necessarily ceases altogether, and along with it the whole profit which they can make by the tolls. If those tolls were put under the management of commissioners, who had themselves no interest in them, they might be less attentive to the maintenance of the works which produced them. The canal of Languedoc cost the king of France and the province upwards of thirteen millions of livres, which (at twenty-eight livres the mark of silver, the value of French money in the end of the last century) amounted to upwards of nine hundred thousand pounds sterling. When that great work was finished, the most likely method, it was found, of keeping it in constant repair was to make a present of the tolls to Riquet the engineer, who planned and conducted the work. Those tolls constitute at present a very large estate to the different branches of the family of that gentleman, who have, therefore, a great interest to keep the work in constant repair. But had those tolls been put under the management of commissioners, who had no such interest, they might perhaps have been dissipated in ornamental and unnecessary expences, while the most essential parts of the work were allowed to go to ruin.

But tolls on a high road cannot safely be made private property and must be committed to trustees. The tolls for the maintenance of a high road, cannot with any safety be made the property of private persons. A high road, though entirely neglected, does not become altogether impassable, though a canal does. The proprietors of the tolls upon a high road, therefore, might neglect altogether the repair of the road, and yet continue to levy very nearly the same tolls. It is proper, therefore, that the tolls for the maintenance of such work should be put under the management of commissioners or trustees.

The prevalence of complaints against British turnpike tolls is not remarkable. In Great Britain, the abuses which the trustees have committed in the management of those tolls, have in many cases been very justly complained of. At many turnpikes, it has been said, the money levied is more than double of what is necessary for executing, in the completest manner, the work which is often executed in a very slovenly manner, and sometimes not executed at all. The system of repairing the high roads by tolls of this kind, it must be observed, is not of very long standing. We should not wonder, therefore, if it has not yet been brought to that degree of perfection of which it seems capable.[1] If mean and improper persons are frequently appointed trustees; and if proper courts of inspection and account have not yet been established for controlling their conduct, and for reducing the tolls to what is barely sufficient for executing the work to be done by them; the recency of the institution both accounts and apologizes for those defects, of which, by the wisdom of parliament, the greater part may in due time be gradually remedied.

It has been proposed that the government should manage the turnpikes and make a revenue from them. The money levied at the different turnpikes in Great Britain is supposed to exceed so much what is necessary for repairing the roads, that the savings, which, with proper œconomy, might be made from it, have been considered, even by some ministers, as a very great resource which might at some time or another be applied to the exigencies of the state. Government, it has been said, by taking the management of the turnpikes into its own hands, and by employing the soldiers, who would work for a very small addition to their pay, could keep the roads in good order at a much less expence than it can be done by trustees, who have no other workmen to employ, but such as derive their whole subsistence from their wages. A great revenue, half a million, perhaps,[2] it has been pretended, might in this manner be gained without laying any new burden upon the people; and the turnpike roads might be made to contribute to the general expence of the state, in the same manner as the post-office does at present.

---

[1] [Ed. 1 reads 'seems to be capable'.]

[2] Since publishing the two first editions of this book, I have got good reasons to believe that all the turnpike tolls levied in Great Britain do not produce a neat revenue that amounts to half a million; a sum which, under the management of Government, would not be sufficient to keep in repair five of the principal roads in the kingdom. [This and the next note appear first in ed. 3.]

This plan is open to the following objections, That a considerable revenue might be gained in this manner, I have no doubt, though probably not near so much, as the projectors of this plan have supposed. The plan itself, however, seems liable to several very important objections.

(1) the tolls would be raised and become a great encumbrance to commerce, First, if the tolls which are levied at the turnpikes should ever be considered as one of the resources for supplying the exigencies of the state, they would certainly be augmented as those exigencies were supposed to require. According to the policy of Great Britain, therefore, they would probably be augmented very fast. The facility with which a great revenue could be drawn from them, would probably encourage administration to recur very frequently to this resource. Though it may, perhaps, be more than doubtful, whether half a million could by any œconomy be saved out of the present tolls, it can scarce be doubted but that a million might be saved out of them, if they were doubled; and perhaps two millions, if they were tripled.[1] This great revenue too might be levied without the appointment of a single new officer to collect and receive it. But the turnpike tolls being continually augmented in this manner, instead of facilitating the inland commerce of the country, as at present, would soon become a very great incumbrance upon it. The expence of transporting all heavy goods from one part of the country to another would soon be so much increased, the market for all such goods, consequently, would soon be so much narrowed, that their production would be in a great measure discouraged, and the most important branches of the domestic industry of the country annihilated altogether.

(2) a tax on carriages in proportion to weight falls principally on the poor, Secondly, a tax upon carriages in proportion to their weight, though a very equal tax when applied to the sole purpose of repairing the roads, is a very unequal one, when applied to any other purpose, or to supply the common exigencies of the state. When it is applied to the sole purpose above mentioned, each carriage is supposed to pay exactly for the wear and tear[2] which that carriage occasions of the roads. But when it is applied to any other purpose, each carriage is supposed to pay for more than that wear and tear, and contributes

---

[1] I have now good reasons to believe that all these conjectural sums are by much too large.

[2] [Ed. 1 reads here and two lines lower down 'tear and wear'.]

W.N. II—I

to the supply of some other exigency of the state. But as the turn-pike toll raises the price of goods in proportion to their weight, and not to their value, it is chiefly paid by the consumers of coarse and bulky, not by those of precious and light commodities. Whatever exigency of the state therefore this tax might be intended to supply, that exigency would be chiefly supplied at the expence of the poor, not of the rich; at the expence of those who are least able to supply it, not of those who are most able.

and (3) the roads would be neglected. Thirdly, if government should at any time neglect the reparation of the high roads, it would be still more difficult, than it is at present, to compel the proper application of any part of the turnpike tolls. A large revenue might thus be levied upon the people, without any part of it being applied to the only purpose to which a revenue levied in this manner ought ever to be applied. If the meanness and poverty of the trustees of turnpike roads render it sometimes difficult at present to oblige them to re-pair their wrong; their wealth and greatness would render it ten times more so in the case which is here supposed.

High roads are under the executive in France, In France, the funds destined for the reparation of the high roads are under the immediate direction of the executive power. Those funds consist, partly in a certain number of days labour[1] which the country people are in most parts of Europe obliged to give to the reparation of the high-ways; and partly in such a portion of the general revenue of the state as the king chuses to spare from his other expences.

and great post roads are generally good, but all the rest entirely neglected. By the ancient law of France, as well as by that of most other parts of Europe, the labour of the coun-try people[2] was under the direction of a local or provincial magistracy, which had no immediate dependency upon the king's council. But by the present practice both the labour of the country people, and whatever other fund the king may chuse to assign for the reparation of the high roads in any particular province or generality, are entirely under the management of the intendant; an officer who is appointed and removed by the king's council, who receives his orders from it, and is in constant correspondence with it. In the progress of despotism the authority of the executive power gradually absorbs that of every other power in the state, and assumes

---

[1] [Ed. 1 reads 'partly in the six days' labour'.]

[2] [Here and in the next sentence for 'the labour of the country people,' ed. 1 reads 'the six days' labour'.]

to itself the management of every branch of revenue which is destined for any public purpose. In France, however, the great post-roads, the roads which make the communication between the principal towns of the kingdom, are in general kept in good order; and in some provinces are even a good deal superior to the greater part of the turnpike roads of England. But what we call the cross-roads, that is, the far greater part of the roads in the country, are entirely neglected, and are in many places absolutely impassable for any heavy carriage. In some places it is even dangerous to travel on horseback, and mules are the only conveyance which can safely be trusted. The proud minister of an ostentatious court may frequently take pleasure in executing a work of splendour and magnificence, such as a great highway, which is frequently seen by the principal nobility, whose applauses not only flatter his vanity, but even contribute to support his interest at court. But to execute a great number of little works, in which nothing that can be done can make any great appearance, or excite the smallest degree of admiration in any traveller, and which, in short, have nothing to recommend them but their extreme utility, is a business which appears in every respect too mean and paultry to merit the attention of so great a magistrate. Under such an administration, therefore, such works are almost always entirely neglected.

The executive in China and other parts of Asia maintains both high roads and canals, it is said, in good condition, but this would not be the case in Europe.

In China, and in several other governments of Asia, the executive power charges itself both with the reparation of the high roads, and with the maintenance of the navigable canals. In the instructions which are given to the governor of each province, those objects, it is said, are constantly recommended to him, and the judgment which the court forms of his conduct is very much regulated by the attention which he appears to have paid to this part of his instructions. This branch of public police accordingly is said to be very much attended to in all those countries, but particularly in China, where the high roads, and still more the navigable canals, it is pretended, exceed very much every thing of the same kind which is known in Europe. The accounts of those works, however, which have been transmitted to Europe, have generally been drawn up by weak and wondering travellers; frequently by stupid and lying missionaries. If they had been examined by more intelligent eyes, and if the accounts of them had been reported by more faithful witnesses, they would not, perhaps, appear to be so wonderful. The account which Bernier gives of some works of this kind in Indostan, falls very much short of what had been reported of them by other travellers, more disposed to the marvellous than he was.[1] It may too, perhaps, be in those countries, as it is in France, where the great roads, the great communications which are likely to be the subjects of conversation at the court and in the capital, are attended to, and all the rest neglected. In China, besides, in Indostan, and in several other governments of Asia, the revenue of the sovereign arises almost altogether from a land-tax or land-rent, which rises or falls with the rise and[2] fall of the annual produce of the land. The great interest of the sovereign, therefore, his revenue, is in such countries necessarily and immediately connected with the cultivation of the land, with the greatness of its produce, and with the value of its produce. But in order to render that produce both as great and as valuable as possible, it is necessary to procure to it as extensive a market as possible, and consequently to establish the freest, the easiest, and the least expensive communication between all the different parts of the country; which can be done only by means of the best roads and the best navigable canals. But the revenue of the sovereign does not, in any part of Europe, arise chiefly from a land-tax or land-rent. In all the great kingdoms of Europe, perhaps, the greater part of it may ultimately depend upon the produce of the land: But that dependency is neither so immediate, nor so evident. In Europe, therefore, the sovereign does not feel himself so directly called upon to promote the increase, both in quantity and value, of the produce of the land, or, by maintaining good roads and canals, to provide the most extensive market for that produce. Though it should be true, therefore, what I apprehend is not a little doubtful, that in some parts of Asia this department of the public police is very properly managed by the executive power, there is not the least probability that, during the present state of things, it could be tolerably managed by that power in any part of Europe.

Public works of a local nature should be maintained by local revenue. Even those public works which are of such a nature that they cannot afford any revenue for maintaining themselves, but of which the conveniency is nearly confined to some particular place or district, are always better main-

---

[1] [*Voyages de François Bernier*, Amsterdam, 1710, can scarcely be said to discredit the ordinary eulogy of Indian roads and canals by an account of any particular works, but it does so by not mentioning them in places where it would be natural to do so if they had existed or been remarkable. See tom. ii., p. 249, 'les grandes rivières qui en ces quartiers n'ont ordinairement point de ponts'.]   [2] [Ed. 1 reads 'or'.]

tained by a local or provincial revenue, under the management of a
local and provincial administration, than by the general revenue of
the state, of which the executive power must always have the
management. Were the streets of London to be lighted and paved
at the expence of the treasury, is there any probability that they
would be so well lighted and paved as they are at present, or even at
so small an expence? The expence, besides, instead of being raised
by a local tax upon the inhabitants of each particular street, parish,
or district in London, would, in this case, be defrayed out of the
general revenue of the state, and would consequently be raised by a
tax upon all the inhabitants of the kingdom, of whom the greater
part derive no sort of benefit from the lighting and paving of the
streets of London.

*The abuses of local
administration are
small compared
with those of the
administration of
the general revenue.*
The abuses which sometimes creep into the local
and provincial administration of a local and provincial revenue, how enormous soever they may
appear, are in reality, however, almost always very
trifling, in comparison of those which commonly
take place in the administration and expenditure of the revenue of
a great empire. They are, besides, much more easily corrected.
Under the local or provincial administration of the justices of the
peace in Great Britain, the six days labour which the country people
are obliged to give to the reparation of the highways, is not always
perhaps very judiciously applied, but it is scarce ever exacted with
any circumstance of cruelty or oppression. In France, under the
administration of the intendants, the application is not always more
judicious, and the exaction is frequently the most cruel and oppressive. Such Corvées, as they are called, make one of the principal
instruments of tyranny by which those officers chastise any parish
or communeauté which has had the misfortune to fall under their
displeasure.[1]

Of the Public Works and Institutions which are necessary for facilitating particular Branches of Commerce[2]

*Some particular
institutions are
required to facilitate*
The object of the public works and institutions
above mentioned is to facilitate commerce in

[1] [Ed. 1 reads 'tyranny by which the intendant chastises any parish or communeauté
which has had the misfortune to fall under his displeasure'.]

[2] [This section (ending on p. 282) appears first in Additions and Corrections and
ed. 3.]

particular branches of commerce, as trade with barbarous nations requires forts, and trade with other nations requires ambassadors.

general. But in order to facilitate some particular branches of it, particular institutions are necessary, which again require a particular and extraordinary expence.

Some particular branches of commerce, which are carried on with barbarous and uncivilized nations, require extraordinary protection. An ordinary store or counting-house could give little security to the goods of the merchants who trade to the western coast of Africa. To defend them from the barbarous natives, it is necessary that the place where they are deposited, should be, in some measure, fortified. The disorders in the government of Indostan have been supposed to render a like precaution necessary even among that mild and gentle people; and it was under pretence of securing their persons and property from violence, that both the English and French East India Companies were allowed to erect the first forts which they possessed in that country. Among other nations, whose vigorous government will suffer no strangers to possess any fortified place within their territory, it may be necessary to maintain some ambassador, minister, or consul, who may both decide, according to their own customs, the differences arising among his own countrymen; and, in their disputes with the natives, may, by means of his public character, interfere with more authority, and afford them a more powerful protection, than they could expect from any private man. The interests of commerce have frequently made it necessary to maintain ministers in foreign countries, where the purposes, either of war or alliance, would not have required any. The commerce of the Turkey Company first occasioned the establishment of an ordinary ambassador at Constantinople.[1] The first English embassies to Russia arose altogether from commercial interests.[2] The constant interference which those interests necessarily occasioned between the subjects of the different states of Europe, has probably introduced the custom of keeping, in all neighbouring countries, ambassadors or ministers constantly resident even in the time of peace. This custom, unknown to ancient times, seems not to be older than the end of the fifteenth or beginning of the sixteenth century; that is, than the time when commerce first began to extend itself to the greater part of the nations of Europe, and when they first began to attend to its interests.

[1] [Anderson, *Commerce*, A.D. 1606.]   [2] [*Ibid.*, A.D. 1620, and cp. A.D. 1623.]

Branches of commerce which require extraordinary expense for their protection may reasonably bear a particular tax.

It seems not unreasonable, that the extraordinary expence, which the protection of any particular branch of commerce may occasion, should be defrayed by a moderate tax upon that particular branch; by a moderate fine, for example, to be paid by the traders when they first enter into it, or, what is more equal, by a particular duty of so much per cent. upon the goods which they either import into, or export out of, the particular countries with which it is carried on. The protection of trade in general, from pirates and free-booters, is said to have given occasion to the first institution of the duties of customs. But, if it was thought reasonable to lay a general tax upon trade, in order to defray the expence of protecting trade in general, it should seem equally reasonable to lay a particular tax upon a particular branch of trade, in order to defray the extraordinary expence of protecting that branch.

The proceeds of such taxes should be at the disposal of the executive, but have often been given to companies of merchants,

The protection of trade in general has always been considered as essential to the defence of the commonwealth, and, upon that account, a necessary part of the duty of the executive power. The collection and application of the general duties of customs, therefore, have always been left to that power. But the protection of any particular branch of trade is a part of the general protection of trade; a part, therefore, of the duty of that power; and if nations always acted consistently, the particular duties levied for the purposes of such particular protection, should always have been left equally to its disposal. But in this respect, as well as in many others, nations have not always acted consistently; and in the greater part of the commercial states of Europe, particular companies of merchants have had the address to persuade the legislature to entrust to them the performance of this part of the duty of the sovereign, together with all the powers which are necessarily connected with it.

which have always proved in the long run burdensome or useless.

These companies, though they may, perhaps, have been useful for the first introduction of some branches of commerce, by making, at their own expence, an experiment which the state might not think it prudent to make, have in the long-run proved, universally, either burdensome or useless, and have either mismanaged or confined the trade.

They are either regulated or joint-stock companies.

When those companies do not trade upon a joint stock, but are obliged to admit any person, properly qualified, upon paying a certain fine, and agreeing to submit to the regulations of the company, each member trading upon his own stock, and at his own risk, they are called regulated companies. When they trade upon a joint stock, each member sharing in the common profit or loss in proportion to his share in this stock, they are called joint stock companies.[1] Such companies, whether regulated or joint stock, sometimes have, and sometimes have not, exclusive privileges.

Regulated companies are like corporations of trades and act like them. Regulated companies resemble, in every respect, the corporations of trades, so common in the cities and towns of all the different countries of Europe; and are a sort of enlarged monopolies of the same kind. As no inhabitant of a town can exercise an incorporated trade, without first obtaining his freedom in the corporation, so in most cases no subject of the state can lawfully carry on any branch of foreign trade, for which a regulated company is established, without first becoming a member of that company. The monopoly is more or less strict according as the terms of admission are more or less difficult; and according as the directors of the company have more or less authority, or have it more or less in their power to manage in such a manner as to confine the greater part of the trade to themselves and their particular friends. In the most ancient regulated companies the privileges of apprenticeship were the same as in other corporations; and entitled the person who had served his time to a member of the company, to become himself a member, either without paying any fine, or upon paying a much smaller one than what was exacted of other people. The usual corporation spirit, wherever the law does not restrain it, prevails in all regulated companies. When they have been allowed to act according to their natural genius, they have always, in order to confine the competition to as small a number of persons as possible, endeavoured to subject the trade to many burdensome regulations. When the law has restrained them from doing this, they have become altogether useless and insignificant.

There are five existing regulated companies, The regulated companies for foreign commerce, which at present subsist in Great Britain, are, the ancient merchant adventurers company,[2] now commonly called the Hamburgh Company, the Russia[3] Company,

---

[1] [Sir Josiah Child, *New Discourse of Trade*, etc., chap. iii., divides companies into those in joint stock and those 'who trade not by a joint stock, but only are under a government and regulation'.]

[2] [The company or society of the Merchant Adventurers of England.]

[3] [Additions and Corrections reads 'Russian,' probably a misprint, though 'Russian,' which is incorrect, appears on the next page.]

the Eastland Company, the Turkey Company, and the African Company.

of which the Ham-   The terms of admission into the Hamburgh Com-
burg, Russian and   pany, are now said to be quite easy; and the directors
Eastland Companies
are merely useless.   either have it not in their power to subject the trade
to any burdensome restraint[1] or regulations, or, at least, have not of late exercised that power. It has not always been so. About the middle of the last century, the fine for admission was fifty, and at one time one hundred pounds,[2] and the conduct of the company was said to be extremely oppressive. In 1643, in 1645, and in 1661, the clothiers and free traders of the West of England complained of them to parliament, as of monopolists who confined the trade and oppressed the manufactures of the country.[3] Though those complaints produced no act of parliament, they had probably intimidated the company so far, as to oblige them to reform their conduct. Since that time, at least, there have[4] been no complaints against them. By the 10th and 11th of William III. c. 6.[5] the fine for admission into the Russian Company was reduced to five pounds; and by the 25th of Charles II. c. 7. that for admission into the Eastland Company, to forty shillings, while, at the same time, Sweden, Denmark and Norway, all the countries on the north side of the Baltic, were exempted from their exclusive charter.[6] The conduct of those companies had probably given occasion to those two acts of parliament. Before that time, Sir Josiah Child had represented both these and the Hamburgh Company as extremely oppressive, and imputed to their bad management the low state of the trade, which we at that time carried on to the countries comprehended within their respective charters.[7] But though such companies may not, in the present times, be very oppressive, they are certainly altogether useless. To be merely useless, indeed, is perhaps the highest eulogy which can ever justly be bestowed upon a regulated company;

---

[1] [Eds. 1–3 read 'restraints'.]

[2] [Anderson, *Commerce*, A.D. 1643: the fine was doubled in that year, being raised to £100 for Londoners and £50 for others.]

[3] [Anderson, *Commerce*, A.D. 1661, under which the other two years are also mentioned.]

[4] [Additions and Corrections and eds. 3 and 4 read 'has'. Smith very probably wrote 'there has been no complaint'.]

[5] [The preamble recites the history of the company.]

[6] [Anderson, *Commerce*, A.D. 1672.]

[7] [*New Discourse of Trade*, chap. iii., quoted by Anderson, *Commerce*, A.D. 1672. This part of the book was not published till long after 1672, but seems to have been written before the closing of the Exchequer in that year.]

and all the three companies above mentioned seem, in their present
state, to deserve this eulogy.

The Turkey Com-   The fine for admission into the Turkey Company,
pany is an oppressive was formerly twenty-five pounds for all persons
monopoly.   under twenty-six years of age, and fifty pounds for
all persons above that age. Nobody but mere merchants could be
admitted; a restriction which excluded all shop-keepers and retailers.[1] By a bye-law, no British manufactures could be exported
to Turkey but in the general ships of the company; and as those
ships sailed always from the port of London, this restriction confined the trade to that expensive[2] port, and the traders, to those who
lived in London and in its neighbourhood. By another bye-law, no
person living within twenty miles of London, and not free of the
city, could be admitted a member; another restriction, which,
joined to the foregoing, necessarily excluded all but the freemen of
London.[3] As the time for the loading and sailing of those general
ships depended altogether upon the directors, they could easily fill
them with their own goods and those of their particular friends, to
the exclusion of others, who, they might pretend, had made their
proposals too late. In this state of things, therefore, this company
was in every respect a strict and oppressive monopoly. Those
abuses gave occasion to the act of the 26th of George II. c. 18.
reducing the fine for admission to twenty pounds for all persons,
without any distinction of ages, or any restriction, either to mere
merchants, or to the freemen of London; and granting to all such
persons the liberty of exporting, from all the ports of Great Britain
to any port in Turkey, all British goods of which the exportation
was not prohibited; and of importing from thence all Turkish goods,
of which the importation was not prohibited, upon paying both the
general duties of customs, and the particular duties assessed for
defraying the necessary expences of the company; and submitting,
at the same time, to the lawful authority of the British ambassador
and consuls resident in Turkey, and to the bye-laws of the company duly enacted. To prevent any oppression by those bye-laws,
it was by the same act ordained, that if any seven members of the
company conceived themselves aggrieved by any bye-law which
should be enacted after the passing of this act, they might appeal to

[1] [Anderson, *Commerce*, A.D. 1605, 1643, 1753.]
[2] [Additions and Corrections reads 'extensive'.]
[3] [See the preamble to 26 Geo. II., c. 18.—Anderson, *Commerce*, A.D. 1753.]

the Board of Trade and Plantations (to the authority of which, a committee of the privy council has now succeeded), provided such appeal was brought within twelve months after the bye-law was enacted; and that if any seven members conceived themselves aggrieved by any bye-law which had been enacted before the passing of this act, they might bring a like appeal, provided it was within twelve months after the day on which this act was to take place. The experience of one year, however, may not always be sufficient to discover to all the members of a great company the pernicious tendency of a particular bye-law; and if several of them should afterwards discover it, neither the Board of Trade, nor the committee of council, can afford them any redress. The object, besides, of the greater part of the bye-laws of all regulated companies, as well as of all other corporations, is not so much to oppress those who are already members, as to discourage others from becoming so; which may be done, not only by a high fine, but by many other contrivances. The constant view of such companies is always to raise the rate of their own profit as high as they can; to keep the market, both for the goods which they export, and for those which they import, as much understocked as they can: which can be done only by restraining the competition, or by discouraging new adventurers from entering into the trade. A fine even of twenty pounds, besides, though it may not, perhaps, be sufficient to discourage any man from entering into the Turkey trade, with an intention to continue in it, may be enough to discourage a speculative merchant from hazarding a single adventure in it. In all trades, the regular established traders, even though not incorporated, naturally combine to raise profits, which are no-way so likely to be kept, at all times, down to their proper level, as by the occasional competition of speculative adventurers. The Turkey trade, though in some measure laid open by this act of parliament, is still considered by many people as very far from being altogether free. The Turkey Company contribute to maintain an ambassador and two or three consuls, who, like other public ministers, ought to be maintained altogether by the state, and the trade laid open to all his majesty's subjects. The different taxes levied by the company, for this and other corporation purposes, might afford a revenue much more than sufficient to enable the state to maintain such ministers.

Regulated companies are more unfit to maintain   Regulated companies, it was observed by Sir Josiah Child, though they had frequently supported

forts than joint-
stock companies,
public ministers, had never maintained any forts or garrisons in the countries to which they traded; whereas joint stock companies frequently had.[1] And in reality the former seem to be much more unfit for this sort of service than the latter. First, the directors of a regulated company have no particular interest in the prosperity of the general trade of the company, for the sake of which, such forts and garrisons are maintained. The decay of that general trade may even frequently contribute to the advantage of their own private trade; as by diminishing the number of their competitors, it may enable them both to buy cheaper, and to sell dearer. The directors of a joint stock company, on the contrary, having only their share in the profits which are made upon the common stock committed to their management, have no private trade of their own, of which the interest can be separated from that of the general trade of the company. Their private interest is connected with the prosperity of the general trade of the company; and with the maintenance of the forts and garrisons which are necessary for its defence. They are more likely, therefore, to have that continual and careful attention which that maintenance necessarily requires. Secondly, The directors of a joint stock company have always the management of a large capital, the joint stock of the company, a part of which they may frequently employ, with propriety, in building, repairing, and maintaining such necessary forts and garrisons. But the directors of a regulated company, having the management of no common capital, have no other fund to employ in this way, but the casual revenue arising from the admission fines, and from the corporation duties, imposed upon the trade of the company. Though they had the same interest, therefore, to attend to the maintenance of such forts and garrisons, they can seldom have the same ability to render that attention effectual. The maintenance of a public minister requiring scarce any attention, and but a moderate and limited expence, is a business much more suitable both to the temper and abilities of a regulated company.

but the African
company was
charged with this
duty.
Long after the time of Sir Josiah Child, however, in 1750, a regulated company was established, the present company of merchants trading to Africa, which was expressly charged at first with the maintenance of all the British forts and garrisons that lie between Cape Blanc and the Cape of Good Hope, and afterwards with that of those only which lie

---

[1] [*New Discourse of Trade*, chap. iii.]

between Cape Rouge and the Cape of Good Hope. The act which
establishes this company (the 23d of George II. c. 31.) seems to have
had two distinct objects in view; first, to restrain effectually the
oppressive and monopolizing spirit which is natural to the directors
of a regulated company; and secondly, to force them, as much as
possible to give an attention, which is not natural to them, towards
the maintenance of forts and garrisons.[1]

The statute estab-
lishing the company
endeavoured
ineffectually to
restrain the spirit of
monopoly,
For the first of these purposes, the fine for admission is limited to forty shillings. The company is
prohibited from trading in their corporate capacity,
or upon a joint stock; from borrowing money upon
common seal, or from laying any restraints upon
the trade which may be carried on freely from all places, and by all
persons being British subjects, and paying the fine. The government
is in a committee of nine persons who meet at London, but who are
chosen annually by the freemen of the company at London, Bristol
and Liverpool; three from each place. No committee-man can be
continued in office for more than three years together. Any committee-man might be removed by the Board of Trade and Plantations; now by a committee of council, after being heard in his own
defence. The committee are forbid to export negroes from Africa,
or to import any African goods into Great Britain. But as they are
charged with the maintenance of forts and garrisons, they may, for
that purpose, export from Great Britain to Africa, goods and stores
of different kinds. Out of the monies which they shall receive from
the company, they are allowed a sum not exceeding eight hundred
pounds for the salaries of their clerks and agents at London, Bristol
and Liverpool, the house-rent of their office at London, and all
other[2] expences of management, commission and agency in England. What remains of this sum, after defraying these different
expences, they may divide among themselves, as compensation for
their trouble, in what manner they think proper. By this constitution, it might have been expected, that the spirit of monopoly would
have been effectually restrained, and the first of these purposes
sufficiently answered. It would seem, however, that it had not.
Though by the 4th of George III. c. 20. the fort of Senegal, with all
its dependencies, had been vested in the company of merchants
trading to Africa, yet in the year following (by the 5th of George
III. c. 44.), not only Senegal and its dependencies, but the whole

[1] [Below, p. 266.]   [2] [Additions and Corrections reads 'all the other'.]

coast from the port of Sallee, in south Barbary, to Cape Rouge, was exempted from the jurisdiction of that company, was vested in the crown, and the trade to it declared free to all his majesty's subjects. The company had been suspected of restraining the trade, and of establishing some sort of improper monopoly. It is not, however, very easy to conceive how, under the regulations of the 23d George II. they could do so. In the printed debates of the House of Commons, not always the most authentic records of truth, I observe, however, that they have been accused of this. The members of the committee of nine being all merchants, and the governors and factors in their different forts and settlements being all dependent upon them, it is not unlikely that the latter might have given peculiar attention to the consignments and commissions of the former, which would establish a real monopoly.

and Parliament allots £13,000 a year to the company for forts, which sum they misapply. For the second of these purposes, the maintenance of the forts and garrisons, an annual sum has been allotted to them by parliament, generally about 13,000 l. For the proper application of this sum, the committee is obliged to account annually to the Cursitor Baron of Exchequer; which account is afterwards to be laid before parliament. But parliament, which gives so little attention to the application of millions, is not likely to give much to that of 13,000 l. a-year; and the Cursitor Baron of Exchequer, from his profession and education, is not likely to be profoundly skilled in the proper expence of forts and garrisons. The captains of his majesty's navy, indeed, or any other commissioned officers, appointed by the Board of Admiralty, may enquire into the condition of the forts and garrisons, and report their observations to that board. But that board seems to have no direct jurisdiction over the committee, nor any authority to correct those whose conduct it may thus enquire into; and the captains of his majesty's navy, besides, are not supposed to be always deeply learned in the science of fortification. Removal from an office, which can be enjoyed only for the term of three years, and of which the lawful emoluments, even during that term, are so very small, seems to be the utmost punishment to which any committee-man is liable, for any fault, except direct malversation, or embezzlement, either of the public money, or of that of the company; and the fear of that punishment can never be a motive of sufficient weight to force a continual and careful attention to a business, to which he has no other interest to attend. The committee are accused of having sent out bricks and stones from England for the reparation of Cape Coast Castle on the coast of Guinea, a business for which parliament had several times granted an extraordinary sum of money. These bricks and stones too, which had thus been sent upon so long a voyage, were said to have been of so bad a quality, that it was necessary to rebuild from the foundation the walls which had been repaired with them. The forts and garrisons which lie north of Cape Rouge, are not only maintained at the expence of the state, but are under the immediate government of the executive power; and why those which lie south of that Cape, and which too are, in part at least, maintained at the expence of the state, should be under a different government, it seems not very easy even to imagine a good reason. The protection of the Mediterranean trade was the original purpose or pretence of the garrisons of Gibraltar and Minorca, and the maintenance and government of those garrisons has always been, very properly, committed, not to the Turkey Company, but to the executive power. In the extent of its dominion consists, in a great measure, the pride and dignity of that power; and it is not very likely to fail in attention to what is necessary for the defence of that dominion. The garrisons at Gibraltar and Minorca, accordingly, have never been neglected; though Minorca has been twice taken, and is now probably lost for ever, that disaster was never even imputed to any neglect in the executive power. I would not, however, be understood to insinuate, that either of those expensive garrisons was ever, even in the smallest degree, necessary for the purpose for which they were originally dismembered from the Spanish monarchy. That dismemberment, perhaps, never served any other real purpose than to alienate from England her natural ally the King of Spain, and to unite the two principal branches of the house of Bourbon in a much stricter and more permanent alliance than the ties of blood could ever have united them.

Joint-stock companies differ from private partnerships: Joint stock companies, established either by royal charter or by act of parliament, differ in several respects, not only from regulated companies, but from private copartneries.

(1) withdrawals are by sale of shares; First, In a private copartnery, no partner, without the consent of the company, can transfer his share to another person, or introduce a new member into the company. Each member, however, may, upon proper warning, withdraw

from the copartnery, and demand payment from them of his share of the common stock. In a joint stock company, on the contrary, no member can demand payment of his share from the company; but each member can, without their consent, transfer his share to another person, and thereby introduce a new member. The value of a share in a joint stock is always the price which it will bring in the market; and this may be either greater or less, in any proportion, than the sum which its owner stands credited for in the stock of the company.

(2) liability is limited to the share held.   Secondly, In a private copartnery, each partner is bound for the debts contracted by the company to the whole extent of his fortune. In a joint stock company, on the contrary, each partner is bound only to the extent of his share.[1]

Such companies are managed by directors, who are negligent and profuse.   The trade of a joint stock company is always managed by a court of directors. This court, indeed, is frequently subject, in many respects, to the controul of a general court of proprietors. But the greater part of those proprietors seldom pretend to understand any thing of the business of the company; and when the spirit of faction happens not to prevail among them, give themselves no trouble about it, but receive contentedly such half yearly or yearly dividend, as the directors think proper to make to them. This total exemption from trouble and from risk, beyond a limited sum, encourages many people to become adventurers in joint stock companies, who would, upon no account, hazard their fortunes in any private copartnery. Such companies, therefore, commonly draw to themselves much greater stocks than any private copartnery can boast of. The trading stock of the South Sea Company, at one time, amounted to upwards of thirty-three millions eight hundred thousand pounds.[2] The divided capital of the Bank of England amounts, at present, to ten millions seven hundred and eighty thousand pounds.[3] The directors of such companies, however, being the managers rather of other people's money than of their own, it cannot well be expected, that they should watch over it with the same anxious vigilance with which the partners in a private copartnery frequently watch over

---

[1] [A joint-stock company here is an incorporated or chartered company. The common application of the term to other companies is later.]

[2] [Anderson, *Commerce*, A.D. 1723.]

[3] [It stood at this amount from 1746 to the end of 1781, but was then increased by a call of 8 per cent.—Anderson, *Commerce*, A.D. 1746, and (Continuation) A.D. 1781.]

their own. Like the stewards of a rich man, they are apt to consider attention to small matters as not for their master's honour, and very easily give themselves a dispensation from having it. Negligence and profusion, therefore, must always prevail, more or less, in the management of the affairs of such a company. It is upon this account that joint stock companies for foreign trade have seldom been able to maintain the competition against private adventurers. They have, accordingly, very seldom succeeded without an exclusive privilege; and frequently have not succeeded with one. Without an exclusive privilege they have commonly mismanaged the trade. With an exclusive privilege they have both mismanaged and confined it.

Some have and some have not exclusive privileges. The Royal African Company, the predecessors of the present African Company, had an exclusive privilege by charter; but as that charter had not been confirmed by act of parliament, the trade, in consequence of the declaration of rights, was, soon after the revolution, laid open to all his majesty's subjects.[1] The Hudson's Bay Company are, as to their legal rights, in the same situation as the Royal African Company.[2] Their exclusive charter has not been confirmed by act of parliament. The South Sea Company, as long as they continued to be a trading company, had an exclusive privilege confirmed by act of parliament; as have likewise the present United Company of Merchants trading to the East Indies.

The Royal African Company having lost exclusive privileges, failed. The Royal African Company soon found that they could not maintain the competition against private adventurers, whom, notwithstanding the declaration of rights, they continued for some time to call interlopers, and to persecute as such. In 1698, however, the private adventurers were subjected to a duty of ten per cent. upon almost all the different branches of their trade, to be employed by the company in the maintenance of their forts and garrisons. But, notwithstanding this heavy tax, the company were still unable to maintain the competition.[3] Their stock and credit gradually declined. In 1712, their debts had become so great, that a particular act of parliament was thought necessary, both for their security and for that of their creditors. It was enacted, that the resolution of two-thirds of these creditors in number and value, should bind the rest, both with regard to the time which should be allowed to the company for the

---

[1] [Anderson, *Commerce*, A.D. 1672 and A.D. 1698.]
[2] [*Ibid.*, A.D. 1670.]   [3] [*Ibid.*, A.D. 1698.]

payment of their debts; and with regard to any other agreement which it might be thought proper to make with them concerning those debts.[1] In 1730, their affairs were in so great disorder, that they were altogether incapable of maintaining their forts and garrisons, the sole purpose and pretext of their institution. From that year, till their final dissolution, the parliament judged it necessary to allow the annual sum of ten thousand pounds for that purpose.[2] In 1732, after having been for many years losers by the trade of carrying negroes to the West Indies, they at last resolved to give it up altogether; to sell to the private traders to America the negroes which they purchased upon the coast; and to employ their servants in a trade to the inland parts of Africa for gold dust, elephants teeth, dying drugs, &c. But their success in this more confined trade was not greater than in their former extensive one.[3] Their affairs continued to go gradually to decline, till at last, being in every respect a bankrupt company, they were dissolved by act of parliament, and their forts and garrisons vested in the present regulated company of merchants trading to Africa.[4] Before the erection of the Royal African Company, there had been three other joint stock companies successively established, one after another, for the African trade.[5] They were all equally unsuccessful. They all, however, had exclusive charters, which, though not confirmed by act of parliament, were in those days supposed to convey a real exclusive privilege.

The Hudson's Bay Company have been moderately successful, having in fact an exclusive trade and a very small number of proprietors. The Hudson's Bay Company, before their misfortunes in the late war, had been much more fortunate than the Royal African Company. Their necessary expence is much smaller. The whole number of people whom they maintain in their different settlements and habitations, which they have honoured with the name of forts, is said not to exceed a hundred and twenty persons.[6] This number, however, is sufficient to prepare beforehand the cargo of furs and other goods necessary for loading their ships, which, on account of the ice, can seldom remain above six or eight weeks in those seas. This advantage of having a cargo ready prepared, could not for several years be acquired by private

---

[1] [10 Ann., c. 27. Anderson, *Commerce*, A.D. 1712.]
[2] [*Ibid.*, A.D. 1730. The annual grant continued till 1746.]
[3] [*Ibid.*, A.D. 1733.]
[4] [23 Geo. II., c. 31; 25 Geo. II., c. 40; Anderson, *Commerce*, A.D. 1750, 1752; above, p. 261.]
[5] [Anderson, *Commerce*, A.D. 1618, 1631 *and* 1662.]
[6] [*Ibid.*, A.D. 1743, quoting Captain Christopher Middleton.]

adventurers, and without it there seems to be no possibility of trading to Hudson's Bay. The moderate capital of the company, which, it is said, does not exceed one hundred and ten thousand pounds,[1] may besides be sufficient to enable them to engross the whole, or almost the whole, trade and surplus produce of the miserable, though extensive country, comprehended within their charter. No private adventurers, accordingly, have ever attempted to trade to that country in competition with them. This company, therefore, have always enjoyed an exclusive trade in fact, though they may have no right to it in law. Over and above all this, the moderate capital of this company is said to be divided among a very small number of proprietors.[2] But a joint stock company, consisting of a small number of proprietors, with a moderate capital, approaches very nearly to the nature of a private copartnery, and may be capable of nearly the same degree of vigilance and attention. It is not to be wondered at, therefore, if in consequence of these different advantages, the Hudson's Bay Company had, before the late war, been able to carry on their trade with a considerable degree of success. It does not seem probable, however, that their profits ever approached to what the late Mr. Dobbs imagined them.[3] A much more sober and judicious writer, Mr. Anderson, author of The Historical and Chronological Deduction of Commerce, very justly observes, that upon examining the accounts which Mr. Dobbs himself has given for several years together, of their exports and imports, and upon making proper allowances for their extraordinary risk and expence, it does not appear that their profits deserve to be envied, or that they can much, if at all, exceed the ordinary profits of trade.[4]

The South Sea Company failed to make any profit by their annual ship to the Spanish West Indies, The South Sea Company never had any forts or garrisons to maintain, and therefore were entirely exempted from one great expence, to which other joint stock companies for foreign trade are subject. But they had an immense capital divided among an immense number of proprietors. It was naturally to be expected,

---

[1] [Anderson, *Commerce*, A.D. 1670.]

[2] ['Eight or nine private merchants do engross nine-tenth parts of the company's stock.' Anderson, *Commerce*, A.D. 1743, quoting from *An Account of the Countries Adjoining to Hudson's Bay . . . with an Abstract of Captain Middleton's Journal and Observations upon his Behaviour*, by Arthur Dobbs, Esq., 1744, p. 58.]

[3] [In his *Account*, pp. 3 and 58, he talks of 2,000 per cent., but this, of course, only refers to the difference between buying and selling prices.]

[4] [*Commerce*, A.D. 1743, but the examination is not nearly so comprehensive, nor the expression of opinion so ample as is suggested by the text.]

therefore, that folly, negligence, and profusion should prevail in the whole management of their affairs. The knavery and extravagance of their stock-jobbing projects are sufficiently known, and the explication of them would be foreign to the present subject. Their mercantile projects were not much better conducted. The first trade which they engaged in was that of supplying the Spanish West Indies with negroes, of which (in consequence of what was called the Assiento contract granted them by the treaty of Utrecht) they had the exclusive privilege. But as it was not expected that much profit could be made by this trade, both the Portugueze and French companies, who had enjoyed it upon the same terms before them, having been ruined by it, they were allowed, as compensation, to send annually a ship of a certain burden to trade directly to the Spanish West Indies.[1] Of the ten voyages which this annual ship was allowed to make, they are said to have gained considerably by one, that of the Royal Caroline in 1731, and to have been losers, more or less, by almost all the rest. Their ill success was imputed, by their factors and agents, to the extortion and oppression of the Spanish government; but was, perhaps, principally owing to the profusion and depredations of those very factors and agents; some of whom are said to have acquired great fortunes even in one year. In 1734, the company petitioned the king, that they might be allowed to dispose of the trade and tunnage of their annual ship, on account of the little profit which they made by it, and to accept of such equivalent as they could obtain from the king of Spain.[2]

lost £237,000 in their whale fishery, In 1724, this company had undertaken the whalefishery. Of this, indeed, they had no monopoly; but as long as they carried it on, no other British subjects appear to have engaged in it. Of the eight voyages which their ships made to Greenland, they were gainers by one, and losers by all the rest. After their eighth and last voyage, when they had sold their ships, stores, and utensils, they found that their whole loss, upon this branch, capital and interest included, amounted to upwards of two hundred and thirty-seven thousand pounds.[3]

and finally ceased to be a trading company. In 1722, this company petitioned the parliament to be allowed to divide their immense capital of more than thirty-three millions eight hundred thousand

---

[1] [Anderson, *Commerce*, A.D. 1713.]   [2] [*Ibid.*, A.D. 1731, 1732 and 1734.]
[3] [*Ibid.*, A.D. 1724 and 1732. But there was no successful voyage; the company were 'considerable losers in every one' of the eight years.]

pounds, the whole of which had been lent to government, into two equal parts: The one half, or upwards of sixteen millions nine hundred thousand pounds, to be put upon the same footing with other government annuities, and not to be subject to the debts contracted, or losses incurred, by the directors of the company, in the prosecution of their mercantile projects; the other half to remain, as before, a trading stock, and to be subject to those debts and losses. The petition was too reasonable not to be granted.[1] In 1733, they again petitioned the parliament, that three-fourths of their trading stock might be turned into annuity stock, and only one-fourth remain as trading stock, or exposed to the hazards arising from the bad management of their directors.[2] Both their annuity and trading stocks had, by this time, been reduced more than two millions each, by several different payments from government; so that this fourth amounted only to 3,662,784 l. 8 s. 6 d.[3] In 1748, all the demands of the company upon the king of Spain, in consequence of the Assiento contract, were, by the treaty of Aix-la-Chapelle, given up for what was supposed an equivalent. An end was put to their trade with the Spanish West Indies, the remainder of their trading stock was turned into an annuity stock, and the company ceased in every respect to be a trading company.[4]

They had competitors in the trade of the annual ship.   It ought to be observed, that in the trade which the South Sea Company carried on by means of their annual ship, the only trade by which it ever was expected that they could make any considerable profit, they were not without competitors, either in the foreign or in the home market. At Carthagena, Porto Bello, and La Vera Cruz, they had to encounter the competition of the Spanish merchants, who brought from Cadiz, to those markets, European goods, of the same kind with the outward cargo of their ship; and in England they had to encounter that of the English merchants, who imported from Cadiz goods of the Spanish West Indies, of the same kind with the inward cargo. The goods both of the Spanish and English merchants, indeed, were, perhaps, subject to higher duties. But the loss occasioned by the negligence, profusion, and malversation of the servants of the company, had probably been a tax much heavier than all those duties. That a joint stock company should be able to carry on

---

[1] [By 9 Geo. I., c. 6. Anderson, *Commerce*, A.D. 1723.]
[2] [This was done by 6 Geo. II., c. 28. *Ibid.*, A.D. 1733.]
[3] [*Ibid.*, A.D. 1732 and A.D. 1733.]
[4] [*Ibid.*, A.D. 1748 and A.D. 1750.]

successfully any branch of foreign trade, when private adventurers can come into any sort of open and fair competition with them, seems contrary to all experience.

The old East India Company, unable to support competition, The old English East India Company was established in 1600, by a charter from Queen Elizabeth. In the first twelve voyages which they fitted out for India, they appear to have traded as a regulated company, with separate stocks, though only in the general ships of the company. In 1612, they united into a joint stock.[1] Their charter was exclusive, and though not confirmed by act of parliament, was in those days supposed to convey a real exclusive privilege. For many years, therefore, they were not much disturbed by interlopers. Their capital which never exceeded seven hundred and forty-four thousand pounds,[2] and of which fifty pounds was a share,[3] was not so exorbitant, nor their dealings so extensive, as to afford either a pretext for gross negligence and profusion, or a cover to gross malversation. Notwithstanding some extraordinary losses, occasioned partly by the malice of the Dutch East India Company, and partly by other accidents, they carried on for many years a successful trade. But in process of time, when the principles of liberty were better understood, it became every day more and more doubtful how far a royal charter, not confirmed by act of parliament, could convey an exclusive privilege. Upon this question the decisions of the courts of justice were not uniform, but varied with the authority of government and the humours of the times. Interlopers multiplied upon them; and towards the end of the reign of Charles II. through the whole of that of James II. and during a part of that of William III. reduced them to great distress.[4] In 1698, a proposal was made to parliament of advancing two millions to government at eight per cent. provided the subscribers were erected into a new East India Company with exclusive privileges. The old East India Company offered seven hundred thousand pounds, nearly the amount of their capital, at four per cent. upon the same conditions. But such was at that time the state of public credit, that it was more convenient for government to borrow two millions at eight per cent. than seven

---

[1] ['Until this time the English East India trade was carried on by several separate stocks, making particular running-voyages; but in this year they united all into one general joint-capital stock.' Anderson, *Commerce*, A.D. 1612.]

[2] [*Ibid.*, A.D. 1693.]

[3] [*Ibid.*, A.D. 1676.]

[4] [*Ibid.*, A.D. 1681 and A.D. 1685.]

was superseded by the present company, hundred thousand pounds at four. The proposal of the new subscribers was accepted, and a new East India Company established in consequence. The old East India Company, however, had a right to continue their trade till 1701. They had, at the same time, in the name of their treasurer, subscribed, very artfully, three hundred and fifteen thousand pounds into the stock of the new. By a negligence in the expression of the act of parliament, which vested the East India trade in the subscribers to this loan of two millions, it did not appear evident that they were all obliged to unite into a joint stock.[1] A few private traders, whose subscriptions amounted only to seven thousand two hundred pounds, insisted upon the privilege of trading separately upon their own stocks and at their own risk.[2] The old East India Company had a right to a separate trade upon their old stock till 1701; and they had likewise, both before and after that period, a right, like that of other private traders, to a separate trade upon the three hundred and fifteen thousand pounds, which they had subscribed into the stock of the new company. The competition of the two companies with the private traders, and with one another, is said to have well nigh ruined both. Upon a subsequent occasion, in 1730, when a proposal was made to parliament for putting the trade under the management of a regulated company, and thereby laying it in some measure open, the East India Company, in opposition to this proposal, represented in very strong terms, what had been, at this time, the miserable effects, as they thought them, of this competition. In India, they said, it raised the price of goods so high, that they were not worth the buying; and in England, by overstocking the market, it sunk their price so low, that no profit could be made by them.[3] That by a more plentiful supply, to the great advantage and conveniency of the public, it must have reduced, very much, the price of India goods in the English market, cannot well be doubted; but that it should have raised very much their price in the Indian market, seems not very probable, as all the extraordinary demand which that competition could occasion, must have been but as a drop of water in the immense ocean of Indian commerce. The increase of demand, besides, though in the beginning it may sometimes raise the price of goods, never fails to lower it in the long run. It encourages production, and thereby increases the competition

---

[1] [The whole of this history is in Anderson, A.D. 1698.]
[2] [*Ibid.*, A.D. 1701.]   [3] [*Ibid.*, A.D. 1730.]

of the producers, who, in order to undersell one another, have re-course to new divisions of labour and new improvements of art, which might never otherwise have been thought of. The miserable effects of which the company complained, were the cheapness of consumption and the encouragement given to production, precisely the two effects which it is the great business of political œconomy to promote. The competition, however, of which they gave this doleful account, had not been allowed to be of long continuance. In 1702, the two companies, were, in some measure, united by an indenture tripartite, to which the queen was the third party;[1] and in 1708, they were, by act of parliament, perfectly consolidated into one company by their present name of the United Company of Merchants trading to the East Indies. Into this act it was thought worth while to insert a clause, allowing the separate traders to continue their trade till Michaelmas 1711, but at the same time empowering the directors, upon three years notice, to redeem their little capital of seven thousand two hundred pounds, and thereby to convert the whole stock of the company into a joint stock. By the same act, the capital of the company, in consequence of a new loan to government, was augmented from two millions to three millions two hundred thousand pounds.[2] In 1743, the company advanced another million to government. But this million being raised, not by a call upon the proprietors, but by selling annuities and contracting bond-debts, it did not augment the stock upon which the proprietors could claim a dividend. It augmented, however, their trading stock, it being equally liable with the other three millions two hundred thousand pounds to the losses sustained, and debts contracted, by the company in prosecution of their mercantile

which with exclusive privileges has traded successfully, projects. From 1708, or at least from 1711, this company, being delivered from all competitors, and fully established in the monopoly of the English commerce to the East Indies, carried on a successful trade, and from their profits made annually a moderate dividend to their

but has conquered large territories, proprietors. During the French war which began in 1741, the ambition of Mr. Dupleix, the French governor of Pondicherry, involved them in the wars of the Carnatic, and in the politics of the Indian princes. After many signal

---

[1] ['This coalition was made on the 22nd of July, 1702, by an indenture tripartite between the Queen and the said two companies.'—Anderson, *Commerce*, A.D. 1702.]

[2] [6 Ann., c. 17. Anderson, *Commerce*, A.D. 1708.]

successes, and equally signal losses, they at last lost Madras, at that time their principal settlement in India. It was restored to them by the treaty of Aix-la-Chapelle; and about this time the spirit of war and conquest seems to have taken possession of their servants in India, and never since to have left them. During the French war which began in 1755, their arms partook of the general good fortune of those of Great Britain. They defended Madras, took Pondicherry, recovered Calcutta, and acquired the revenues of a rich and extensive territory, amounting, it was then said, to upwards of three millions a-year. They remained for several years in quiet possession of this revenue: But in 1767, administration laid claim to their territorial acquisitions, and the revenue arising from them, as of right belonging to the crown; and the company, in compensation for this claim, agreed to pay to government four hundred thousand pounds a-year. They had before this gradually augmented their dividend from about six to ten per cent; that is, upon their capital of three millions two hundred thousand pounds, they had increased it by a hundred and twenty-eight thousand pounds, or had raised it from one hundred and ninety-two thousand, to three hundred and twenty thousand pounds a-year. They were attempting about this time to raise it still further, to twelve and a half per cent. which would have made their annual payments to their proprietors equal to what they had agreed to pay annually to government, or to four hundred thousand pounds a-year. But during the two years in which their agreement with government was to take place, they were restrained from any further increase of dividend by two successive acts of parliament,[1] of which the object was to enable them to make a speedier progress in the payment of their debts, which were at this time estimated at upwards of six or seven millions sterling. In 1769, they renewed their agreement with government for five years more, and stipulated, that during the course of that period they should be allowed gradually to increase their dividend to twelve and a half per cent.; never increasing it, however, more than one per cent. in one year. This increase of dividend, therefore, when it had risen to its utmost height, could augment their annual payments, to their proprietors and government together, but by six hundred and eight thousand pounds, beyond what they had been before their late territorial acquisitions. What the gross revenue of those territorial acquisitions was supposed to amount to, has already

---

[1] [7 Geo. III., c. 49, and 8 Geo. III., c. 11.]

been mentioned; and by an account brought by the Cruttenden East Indiaman in 1768, the nett revenue, clear of all deductions and military charges, was stated at two millions forty-eight thousand seven hundred and forty-seven pounds. They were said at the same time to possess another revenue, arising partly from lands, but chiefly from the customs established at their different settlements, amounting to four hundred and thirty-nine thousand pounds. The profits of their trade too, according to the evidence of their chairman before the House of Commons, amounted at this time to at least four hundred thousand pounds a-year; according to that of their accomptant, to at least five hundred thousand; according to the lowest account, at least equal to the highest dividend that was to be paid to their proprietors. So great a revenue might certainly have afforded an augmentation of six hundred and eight thousand pounds in their annual payments; and at the same time have left a large sinking fund sufficient for the speedy reduction of their debts. In 1773, however, their debts, instead of being reduced, were aug-
and mismanaged mented by an arrear to the treasury in the payment
them, of the four hundred thousand pounds, by another to the custom-house for duties unpaid, by a large debt to the bank for money borrowed, and by a fourth for bills drawn upon them from India, and wantonly accepted, to the amount of upwards of twelve hundred thousand pounds. The distress which these accumulated claims brought upon them, obliged them not only to reduce all at once their dividend to six per cent. but to throw themselves upon the mercy of government, and to supplicate, first, a release from the further payment of the stipulated four hundred thousand pounds a-year; and, secondly, a loan of fourteen hundred thousand, to save them from immediate bankruptcy. The great increase of their fortune had, it seems, only served to furnish their servants with a pretext for greater profusion, and a cover for greater malversation, than in proportion even to that increase in fortune.
so that Parliament The conduct of their servants in India, and the
has been obliged to general state of their affairs both in India and in
make alterations, Europe, became the subject of a parliamentary inquiry;[1] in consequence of which several very important alterations were made in the constitution of their government, both at home and abroad. In India their principal settlements of Madras, Bombay, and Calcutta, which had before been altogether indepen-

[1] [In 1772-3. Additions and Corrections and ed. 3 read 'subjects'.]

dent of one another, were subjected to a governor-general, assisted by a council of four assessors, parliament assuming to itself the first nomination of this governor and council who were to reside at Calcutta; that city having now become, what Madras was before, the most important of the English settlements in India. The court of the mayor of Calcutta, originally instituted for the trial of mercantile causes, which arose in the city and neighbourhood, had gradually extended its jurisdiction with the extension of the empire. It was now reduced and confined to the original purpose of its institution. Instead of it a new supreme court of judicature was established, consisting of a chief justice and three judges to be appointed by the crown. In Europe, the qualification necessary to entitle a proprietor to vote at their general courts was raised, from five hundred pounds, the original price of a share in the stock of the company, to a thousand pounds. In order to vote upon this qualification too, it was declared necessary that he should have possessed it, if acquired by his own purchase, and not by inheritance, for at least one year, instead of six months, the term requisite before. The court of twenty-four directors had before been chosen annually; but it was now enacted that each director should, for the future, be chosen for four years; six of them, however, to go out of office by rotation every year, and not to be capable of being re-chosen at the election of the six new directors for the ensuing year.[1] In consequence of these alterations, the courts, both of the proprietors and directors, it was expected, would be likely to act with more dignity and steadiness than they had usually done before. But it seems impossible, by any alterations, to render those courts, in any respect, fit to govern, or even to share in the government of a great empire; because the greater part of their members must always have too little interest in the prosperity of that empire, to give any serious attention to what may promote it. Frequently a man of great, sometimes even a man of small fortune, is willing to purchase a thousand pounds share in India stock, merely for the influence which he expects to acquire by a vote in the court of proprietors. It gives him a share, though not in the plunder, yet in the appointment of the plunderers of India; the court of directors, though they make that appointment, being necessarily more or less under the influence of the proprietors, who not only elect those directors, but sometimes over-rule the appointments of their servants in India. Provided he

[1] [13 Geo. III., c. 63.]

can enjoy this influence for a few years, and thereby provide for a certain number of his friends, he frequently cares little about the dividend; or even about the value of the stock upon which his vote is founded. About the prosperity of the great empire, in the government of which that vote gives him a share, he seldom cares at all. No other sovereigns ever were, or, from the nature of things, ever could be, so perfectly indifferent about the happiness or misery of their subjects, the improvement or waste of their dominions, the glory or disgrace of their administration; as, from irresistible moral causes, the greater part of the proprietors of such a mercantile company are, and necessarily must be. This indifference too was more likely to be increased than diminished by some of the new regulations which were made in consequence of the parliamentary inquiry. By a resolution of the House of Commons, for example, it was declared, that when the fourteen hundred thousand pounds lent to the company by government should be paid, and their bond-debts be reduced to fifteen hundred thousand pounds, they might then, and not till then, divide eight per cent. upon their capital; and that whatever remained of their revenues and neat profits at home, should be divided into four parts; three of them to be paid into the exchequer for the use of the public, and the fourth to be reserved as a fund, either for the further reduction of their bond-debts, or for the discharge of other contingent exigencies, which the company *which are not* might labour under.[1] But if the company were bad *likely to be of* stewards, and bad sovereigns, when the whole of *service.* their nett[2] revenue and profits belonged to themselves, and were at their own disposal, they were surely not likely to be better, when three-fourths of them were to belong to other people, and the other fourth, though to be laid out for the benefit of the company, yet to be so, under the inspection, and with the approbation, of other people.

They tend to It might be more agreeable to the company that *encourage waste,* their own servants and dependants should have either the pleasure of wasting, or the profit of embezzling whatever surplus might remain, after paying the proposed dividend of eight per cent., than that it should come into the hands of a set of people with whom those resolutions could scarce fail to set them, in some

---

[1] [*House of Commons Journals*, April 27, 1773.]
[2] [The spelling in other parts of the work is 'neat'. The Additions and Corrections read 'nett' both here and seven lines above. The discrepancy was obviously noticed in one case and not in the other.]

measure, at variance. The interest of those servants and dependants might so far predominate in the court of proprietors, as sometimes to dispose it to support the authors of depredations which had been committed in direct violation of its own authority. With the majority of proprietors, the support even of the authority of their own court might sometimes be a matter of less consequence, than the support of those who had set that authority at defiance.

and the company is now in greater distress than ever. The regulations of 1773, accordingly, did not put an end to the disorders of the company's government in India. Notwithstanding that, during a momentary fit of good conduct, they had at one time collected, into the treasury of Calcutta, more than three millions sterling; notwithstanding that they had afterwards extended, either their dominion, or their depredations over a vast accession of some of the richest and most fertile countries in India; all was wasted and destroyed. They found themselves altogether unprepared to stop or resist the incursion of Hyder Ali; and, in consequence of those disorders, the company is now (1784) in greater distress than ever; and, in order to prevent immediate bankruptcy, is once more reduced to supplicate the assistance of government. Different plans have been proposed by the different parties in parliament, for the better management of its affairs. And all those plans seem to agree in supposing, what was indeed always abundantly evident, that it is altogether unfit to govern its territorial possessions. Even the company itself seems to be convinced of its own incapacity so far, and seems, upon that account, willing to give them up to government.

Companies misuse the right of making peace and war. With the right of possessing forts and garrisons in distant and barbarous countries, is necessarily connected the right of making peace and war in those countries. The joint stock companies which have had the one right, have constantly exercised the other, and have frequently had it expressly conferred upon them. How unjustly, how capriciously, how cruelly they have commonly exercised it, is too well known from recent experience.

The grant of a temporary monopoly to a joint-stock company may sometimes be reasonable, but a perpetual monopoly creates an absurd tax. When a company of merchants undertake, at their own risk and expence, to establish a new trade with some remote and barbarous nation, it may not be unreasonable to incorporate them into a joint stock company, and to grant them, in case of their success, a monopoly of the trade for a certain number of years. It is the easiest and most natural way in which the state can recompense them for hazarding a dangerous and expensive experiment, of which the public is afterwards to reap the benefit. A temporary monopoly of this kind may be vindicated upon the same principles upon which a like monopoly of a new machine is granted to its inventor, and that of a new book to its author. But upon the expiration of the term, the monopoly ought certainly to determine; the forts and garrisons, if it was found necessary to establish any, to be taken into the hands of government, their value to be paid to the company, and the trade to be laid open to all the subjects of the state. By a perpetual monopoly, all the other subjects of the state are taxed very absurdly in two different ways; first, by the high price of goods, which, in the case of a free trade, they could buy much cheaper; and secondly, by their total exclusion from a branch of business, which it might be both convenient and profitable for many of them to carry on. It is for the most worthless of all purposes too that they are taxed in this manner. It is merely to enable the company to support the negligence, profusion, and malversation of their own servants, whose disorderly conduct seldom allows the dividend of the company to exceed the ordinary rate of profit in trades which are altogether free, and very frequently makes it fall even a good deal short of that rate. Without a monopoly, however, a joint stock company, it would appear from experience, cannot long carry on any branch of foreign trade. To buy in one market, in order to sell, with profit, in another, when there are many competitors in both; to watch over, not only the occasional variations in the demand, but the much greater and more frequent variations in the competition, or in the supply which that demand is likely to get from other people, and to suit with dexterity and judgment both the quantity and quality of each assortment of goods to all these circumstances, is a species of warfare of which the operations are continually changing, and which can scarce ever be conducted successfully, without such an unremitting exertion of vigilance and attention, as cannot long be expected from the directors of a joint stock company. The East India Company, upon the redemption of their funds, and the expiration of their exclusive privilege, have a right, by act of parliament, to continue a corporation with a joint stock, and to trade in their corporate capacity to the East Indies in common with the rest of their fellow-subjects. But in this situation, the superior vigilance and attention of private adventurers would, in all probability, soon make them weary of the trade.

A list of fifty-five companies with exclusive privileges for foreign trade which have failed has been collected by Abbé Morellet.

An eminent French author, of great knowledge in matters of political œconomy, the Abbé Morellet, gives a list of fifty-five joint stock companies for foreign trade, which have been established in different parts of Europe since the year 1600, and which, according to him, have all failed from mismanagement, notwithstanding they had exclusive privileges.[1] He has been misinformed with regard to the history of two or three of them, which were not joint stock companies and have not failed. But, in compensation, there have been several joint stock companies which have failed, and which he has omitted.

Only four trades can be well carried on by a company with no exclusive privilege, namely,

The only trades which it seems possible for a joint stock company to carry on successfully, without an exclusive privilege, are those, of which all the operations are capable of being reduced to what is called a routine, or to such a uniformity of method as admits of little or no variation. Of this kind is, first, the banking trade; secondly, the trade of insurance from fire, and from sea risk and capture in time of war; thirdly, the trade of making and maintaining a navigable cut or canal; and, fourthly, the similar trade of bringing water for the supply of a great city.

banking,

Though the principles of the banking trade may appear somewhat abstruse, the practice is capable of being reduced to strict rules. To depart upon any occasion from those rules, in consequence of some flattering speculation of extraordinary gain, is almost always extremely dangerous, and frequently fatal to the banking company which attempts it. But the constitution of joint stock companies renders them in general more tenacious of established rules than any private copartnery. Such companies, therefore, seem extremely well fitted for this trade. The principal banking companies in Europe, accordingly, are joint stock companies, many of which manage their trade very successfully without any exclusive privilege. The Bank of England has no other exclusive privilege, except that no other banking company in England shall consist of more than six persons.[2] The two banks of Edinburgh are joint stock companies without any exclusive privilege.

insurance,

The value of the risk, either from fire, or from loss by sea, or by capture, though it cannot, perhaps, be calculated very

---

[1] [*Examen de la réponse de M. N** [Necker] au Mémoire de M. l'Abbé Morellet, sur la Compagnie des Indes*: par l'auteur du Mémoire, 1769, pp. 35-38.] [2] [6 **Ann.**, c. 22.]

exactly, admits, however, of such a gross estimation as renders it, in some degree, reducible to strict rule and method. The trade of insurance, therefore, may be carried on successfully by a joint stock company, without any exclusive privilege. Neither the London Assurance, nor the Royal Exchange Assurance companies, have any such privilege.[1]

canal and aqueduct management and construction. When a navigable cut or canal has been once made, the management of it becomes quite simple and easy, and[2] is reducible to strict rule and method. Even the making of it is so, as it may be contracted for with undertakers at so much a mile, and so much a lock. The same thing may be said of a canal, an aqueduct, or a great pipe for bringing water to supply a great city. Such undertakings, therefore, may be, and accordingly frequently are, very successfully managed by joint stock companies without any exclusive privilege.

A joint stock company ought not to be established except for some purpose of remarkable utility, requiring a larger capital than can be provided by a private partnership. To establish a joint stock company, however, for any undertaking, merely because such a company might be capable of managing it successfully; or to exempt a particular set of dealers from some of the general laws which take place with regard to all their neighbours, merely because they might be capable of thriving if they had such an exemption, would certainly not be reasonable. To render such an establishment perfectly reasonable, with the circumstance of being reducible to strict rule and method, two other circumstances ought to concur. First, it ought to appear with the clearest evidence, that the undertaking is of greater and more general utility than the greater part of common trades; and secondly, that it requires a greater capital than can easily be collected into a private copartnery. If a moderate capital were[3] sufficient, the great utility of the undertaking would not be a sufficient reason for establishing a joint stock company; because, in this case, the demand for what it was to produce, would readily and easily be supplied by private adventurers. In the four trades above mentioned, both those circumstances concur.

These conditions are fulfilled by banking, The great and general utility of the banking trade when prudently managed, has been fully explained in the second book of this inquiry.[4] But a public

---

[1] [At least as against private persons, Anderson, *Commerce*, A.D. 1720.]
[2] [Eds. 4 and 5 insert 'it' here, by a misprint.]
[3] [Additions and Corrections and ed. 3 read 'was'.]
[4] [Above, vol. i., pp. 310–318.]

bank which is to support public credit, and upon particular emergencies to advance to government the whole produce of a tax, to the amount, perhaps, of several millions, a year or two before it comes in, requires a greater capital than can easily be collected into any private copartnery.

insurance, The trade of insurance gives great security to the fortunes of private people, and by dividing among a great many that loss which would ruin an individual, makes it fall light and easy upon the whole society. In order to give this security, however, it is necessary that the insurers should have a very large capital. Before the establishment of the two joint stock companies for insurance in London, a list, it is said, was laid before the attorney-general, of one hundred and fifty private insurers who had failed in the course of a few years.

canals and water works, That navigable cuts and canals, and the works which are sometimes necessary for supplying a great city with water, are of great and general utility; while at the same time they frequently require a greater expence than suits the fortunes of private people, is sufficiently obvious.

but not by anything else. Except the four trades above mentioned, I have not been able to recollect any other in which all the three circumstances, requisite for rendering reasonable the establishment of a joint stock company, concur. The English copper company of London, the lead smelting company, the glass grinding company, have not even the pretext of any great or singular utility in the object which they pursue; nor does the pursuit of that object seem to require any expence unsuitable to the fortunes of many private men. Whether the trade which those companies carry on, is reducible to such strict rule and method as to render it fit for the management of a joint stock company, or whether they have any reason to boast of their extraordinary profits, I do not pretend to know. The mine-adventurers company has been long ago bankrupt.[1] A share in the stock of the British Linen Company of Edinburgh sells, at present, very much below par, though less so than it did some years ago. The joint stock companies, which are established for the public-spirited purpose of promoting some particular manufacture, over and above managing their own affairs ill, to the diminution of the general stock of the society, can in other respects scarce ever fail to do more harm than good. Notwithstanding the

[1] [Anderson, *Commerce,* A.D. 1690, 1704, 1710, 1711.]

most upright intentions, the unavoidable partiality of their directors to particular branches of the manufacture, of which the undertakers mislead and impose upon them, is a real discouragement to the rest, and necessarily breaks, more or less, that natural proportion which would otherwise establish itself between judicious industry and profit, and which, to the general industry of the country, is of all encouragements the greatest and the most effectual.[1]

ARTICLE II

Of the Expence of the Institutions for the Education of Youth[2]

Institutions for education may also be made to furnish their own expense, The institutions for the education of the youth may, in the same manner, furnish a revenue sufficient for defraying their own expence. The fee or honorary which the scholar pays to the master naturally constitutes a revenue of this kind.

or may be endowed. Even where the reward of the master does not arise altogether from this natural revenue, it still is not necessary that it should be derived from that general revenue of the society, of which the collection and application are,[3] in most countries, assigned to the executive power. Through the greater part of Europe, accordingly, the endowment of schools and colleges makes either no charge upon that general revenue, or but a very small one. It every where arises chiefly from some local or provincial revenue, from the rent of some landed estate, or from the interest of some sum of money allotted and put under the management of trustees for this particular purpose, sometimes by the sovereign himself, and sometimes by some private donor.

Have endowments really promoted useful education? Have those public endowments contributed in general to promote the end of their institution? Have they contributed to encourage the diligence, and to improve the abilities of the teachers? Have they directed the course of education towards objects more useful, both to the individual and to the public, than those to which it would naturally have gone of its own accord? It should not seem very difficult to give at least a probable answer to each of those questions.

---

[1] [This section, beginning on p. 253, appears first in Additions and Corrections and ed. 3.]

[2] [Ed. 1 reads 'the youth' as in the first line of the text.]

[3] [Eds. 1–4 read 'is'.]

Exertion is always in proportion to its necessity. In every profession, the exertion of the greater part of those who exercise it, is always in proportion to the necessity they are under of making that exertion. This necessity is greatest with those to whom the emoluments of their profession are the only source from which they expect their fortune, or even their ordinary revenue and subsistence. In order to acquire this fortune, or even to get this subsistence, they must, in the course of a year,[1] execute a certain quantity of work of a known value; and, where the competition is free, the rivalship of competitors, who are all endeavouring to justle one another out of employment, obliges every man to endeavour to execute his work with a certain degree of exactness. The greatness of the objects which are to be acquired by success in some particular professions may, no doubt, sometimes animate the exertion of a few men of extraordinary spirit and ambition. Great objects, however, are evidently not necessary in order to occasion the greatest exertions. Rivalship and emulation render excellency, even in mean professions, an object of ambition, and frequently occasion the very greatest exertions. Great objects, on the contrary, alone and unsupported by the necessity of application, have seldom been sufficient to occasion any considerable exertion. In England, success in the profession of the law leads to some very great objects of ambition; and yet how few men, born to easy fortunes, have ever in this country been eminent in that profession?

Endowments diminish the necessity of application, The endowments of schools and colleges have necessarily diminished more or less the necessity of application in the teachers. Their subsistence, so far as it arises from their salaries, is evidently derived from a fund altogether independent of their success and reputation in their particular professions.

which is not entirely removed where the teacher receives part of his emoluments from fees, In some universities the salary makes but a part, and frequently but a small part of the emoluments of the teacher, of which the greater part arises from the honoraries or fees of his pupils. The necessity of application, though always more or less diminished, is not in this case entirely taken away.[2] Reputation in his profession is still of some importance to him, and he still has some dependency

---

[1] [Ed. 1 reads 'the year'.]

[2] [Rae, *Life of Adam Smith*, p. 48, thinks Smith's salary at Glasgow may have been about £70 with a house, and his fees near £100.]

upon the affection, gratitude, and favourable report of those who have attended upon his instructions; and these favourable sentiments he is likely to gain in no way so well as by deserving them, that is by the abilities and diligence with which he discharges every part of his duty.

but is entirely absent when his whole revenue arises from endowments. In other universities the teacher is prohibited from receiving any honorary or fee from his pupils, and his salary constitutes the whole of the revenue which he derives from his office. His interest is, in this case, set as directly in opposition to his duty as it is possible to set it. It is the interest of every man to live as much at his ease as he can; and if his emoluments are to be precisely the same, whether he does, or does not perform some very laborious duty, it is certainly his interest, at least as interest is vulgarly understood, either to neglect it altogether, or, if he is subject to some authority which will not suffer him to do this, to perform it in as careless and slovenly a manner as that authority will permit. If he is naturally active and a lover of labour, it is his interest to employ that activity in any way, from which he can derive some advantage, rather than in the performance of his duty, from which he can derive none.

Members of a college or university are indulgent to their fellow members. If the authority to which he is subject resides in the body corporate, the college, or university, of which he himself is a member, and in which the greater part of the other members are, like himself, persons who either are, or ought to be teachers; they are likely to make a common cause, to be all very indulgent to one another, and every man to consent that his neighbour may neglect his duty, provided he himself is allowed to neglect his own. In the university of Oxford, the greater part of the public professors have, for these many years, given up altogether even the pretence of teaching.

External control is ignorant and capricious. If the authority to which he is subject resides, not so much in the body corporate of which he is a member, as in some other extraneous persons, in the bishop of the diocese for example; in the governor of the province; or, perhaps, in some minister of state; it is not indeed in this case very likely that he will be suffered to neglect his duty altogether. All that such superiors, however, can force him to do, is to attend upon his pupils a certain number of hours, that is, to give a certain number of lectures in the week or in the year. What those lectures shall be, must still depend upon the diligence of the teacher; and that diligence is likely to be proportioned to the motives which he has for exerting it. An extraneous jurisdiction of this kind, besides, is liable to be exercised both ignorantly and capriciously. In its nature it is arbitrary and discretionary, and the persons who exercise it, neither attending upon the lectures of the teacher themselves, nor perhaps understanding the sciences which it is his business to teach, are seldom capable of exercising it with judgment. From the insolence of office too they are frequently indifferent how they exercise it, and are very apt to censure or deprive him of his office wantonly, and without any just cause. The person subject to such jurisdiction is necessarily degraded by it, and, instead of being one of the most respectable, is rendered one of the meanest and most contemptible persons in the society. It is by powerful protection only that he can effectually guard himself against the bad usage to which he is at all times exposed; and this protection he is most likely to gain, not by ability or diligence in his profession, but by obsequiousness to the will of his superiors, and by being ready, at all times, to sacrifice to that will the rights, the interest, and the honour of the body corporate of which he is a member. Whoever has attended for any considerable time to the administration of a French university, must have had occasion to remark the effects which naturally result from an arbitrary and extraneous jurisdiction of this kind.

To compel young men to attend a university has a bad effect on the teachers.
The privileges of graduates are thus like apprenticeship.

Whatever forces a certain number of students to any college or university, independent of the merit or reputation of the teachers, tends more or less to diminish the necessity of that merit or reputation. The privileges of graduates in arts, in law, physic[1] and divinity, when they can be obtained only by residing a certain number of years in certain universities, necessarily force a certain number of students to such universities, independent of the merit or reputation of the teachers. The privileges of graduates are a sort of statutes of apprenticeship, which have contributed to the improvement of education, just as the[2] other statutes of apprenticeship have to that of arts and manufactures.

Scholarships, The charitable foundations of scholarships, exhibitions, bursaries, &c. necessarily attach a certain number of

---

[1] [Eds. 1 and 2 read 'in physic'.]
[2] [Ed. 1 does not contain 'the'.]

students to certain colleges, independent altogether of the merit of those particular colleges. Were the students upon such charitable foundations left free to chuse what college they liked best, such liberty might perhaps contribute to excite some emulation among
regulations against migration, different colleges. A regulation, on the contrary, which prohibited even the independent members of every particular college from leaving it, and going to any other, without leave first asked and obtained of that which they meant to abandon, would tend very much to extinguish that emulation.

and assignment of students to particular tutors are equally pernicious. If in each college the tutor or teacher, who was to instruct each student in all arts and sciences, should not be voluntarily chosen by the student, but appointed by the head of the college; and if, in case of neglect, inability, or bad usage, the student should not be allowed to change him for another, without leave first asked and obtained; such a regulation would not only tend very much to extinguish all emulation among the different tutors of the same college, but to diminish very much in all of them the necessity of diligence and of attention to their respective pupils. Such teachers, though very well paid by their students, might be as much disposed to neglect them, as those who are not paid by them at all, or who have no other recompence but their salary.

Where such regulations prevail a teacher may avoid or suppress all visible signs of disapprobation on the part of his pupils. If the teacher happens to be a man of sense, it must be an unpleasant thing to him to be conscious, while he is lecturing his students, that he is either speaking or reading nonsense, or what is very little better than nonsense. It must too be unpleasant to him to observe that the greater part of his students desert his lectures; or perhaps attend upon them with plain enough marks of neglect, contempt, and derision. If he is obliged, therefore, to give a certain number of lectures, these motives alone, without any other interest, might dispose him to take some pains to give tolerably good ones. Several different expedients, however may be fallen upon, which will effectually blunt the edge of all those incitements to diligence. The teacher, instead of explaining to his pupils himself the science in which he proposes to instruct them, may read some book upon it; and if this book is written in a foreign and dead language, by interpreting it to them into their own; or, what would give him still less trouble, by making them interpret it to him, and by now and then making an occasional remark upon it, he may flatter himself that he is giving a lecture. The slightest degree of knowledge and application will enable him to do this, without exposing himself to contempt or derision, or saying any thing that is really foolish, absurd, or ridiculous. The discipline of the college, at the same time, may enable him to force all his pupils to the most regular attendance upon this sham-lecture, and to maintain the most decent and respectful behaviour during the whole time of the performance.

University and college discipline is contrived for the ease of the teachers, and quite unnecessary if the teachers are tolerably diligent. The discipline of colleges and universities is in general contrived, not for the benefit of the students, but for the interest, or more properly speaking, for the ease of the masters. Its object is, in all cases, to maintain the authority of the master, and whether he neglects or performs his duty, to oblige the students, in all cases to behave to him as if he performed it with the greatest diligence and ability. It seems to presume perfect wisdom and virtue in the one order, and the greatest weakness and folly in the other. Where the masters, however, really perform their duty, there are no examples, I believe, that the greater part of the students ever neglect theirs. No discipline is ever requisite to force attendance upon lectures which are really worth the attending, as is well known wherever any such lectures are given. Force and restraint may, no doubt, be in some degree requisite in order to oblige children, or very young boys, to attend to those parts of education which it is thought necessary for them to acquire during that early period of life; but after twelve or thirteen years of age, provided the master does his duty, force or restraint can scarce ever be necessary to carry on any part of education. Such is the generosity of the greater part of young men, that, so far from being disposed to neglect or despise the instructions of their master, provided he shows some serious intention of being of use to them, they are generally inclined to pardon a great deal of incorrectness in the performance of his duty, and sometimes even to conceal from the public a good deal of gross negligence.

The parts of education that are not conducted by public institutions are better taught. Those parts of education, it is to be observed, for the teaching of which there are no public institutions, are generally the best taught. When a young man goes to a fencing or a dancing school, he does not indeed always learn to fence or to dance very well; but he seldom fails of learning to fence or to dance. The good effects of the riding school are not commonly so evident. The expence of a riding school is so great, that in most places it is a public institution. The three most essential parts of literary education, to read, write, and account, it still continues to be more common to acquire in private than in public schools; and it very seldom happens that any body fails of acquiring them to the degree in which it is necessary to acquire them.

English public schools, where the teachers depend more upon fees, are less corrupt than the universities. In England the public schools are much less corrupted than the universities. In the schools the youth are taught, or at least may be taught, Greek and Latin; that is, every thing which the masters pretend to teach, or which, it is expected, they should teach. In the universities the youth neither are taught, nor always can find any proper means of being taught, the sciences, which it is the business of those incorporated bodies to teach. The reward of the schoolmaster in most cases depends principally, in some cases almost entirely, upon the fees or honoraries of his scholars. Schools have no exclusive privileges. In order to obtain the honours of graduation, it is not necessary that a person should bring a certificate of his having studied a certain number of years at a public school. If upon examination he appears to understand what is taught there, no questions are asked about the place where he learnt it.

What the universities teach badly would not be commonly taught at all but for them. The parts of education which are commonly taught in universities, it may, perhaps, be said are not very well taught. But had it not been for those institutions they would not have been commonly taught at all, and both the individual and the public would have suffered a good deal from the want of those important parts of education.

They were originally instituted for the education of churchmen in theology; The present universities of Europe were originally, the greater part of them, ecclesiastical corporations; instituted for the education of churchmen. They were founded by the authority of the pope, and were so entirely under his immediate protection, that their members, whether masters or students, had all of them what was then called the benefit of clergy, that is, were exempted from the civil jurisdiction of the countries in which their respective universities were situated, and were amenable only to the ecclesiastical tribunals. What was taught in the greater part of those universities was suitable to the end of their institution, either theology, or something that was merely preparatory to theology.

for this Latin was necessary, When christianity was first established by law, a corrupted Latin had become the common language of all the western parts of Europe. The service of the church accordingly, and the translation of the Bible which was read in churches, were both in that corrupted Latin; that is, in the common language of the country. After the irruption of the barbarous nations who overturned the Roman empire, Latin gradually ceased to be the language of any part of Europe. But the reverence of the people naturally preserves the established forms and ceremonies of religion, long after the circumstances which first introduced and rendered them reasonable are no more. Though Latin, therefore, was no longer understood any where by the great body of the people, the whole service of the church still continued to be performed in that language. Two different languages were thus established in Europe, in the same manner as in ancient Egypt; a language of the priests, and a language of the people; a sacred and a profane; a learned and an unlearned language. But it was necessary that the priests should understand something of that sacred and learned language in which they were to officiate; and the study of the Latin language therefore made, from the beginning, an essential part of university education.

but not Greek or Hebrew, which were introduced by the Reformation. It was not so with that either of the Greek, or of the Hebrew language. The infallible decrees of the church had pronounced the Latin translation of the Bible, commonly called the Latin Vulgate, to have been equally dictated by divine inspiration, and therefore of equal authority with the Greek and Hebrew originals. The knowledge of those two languages, therefore, not being indispensably requisite to a churchman, the study of them did not for a long time make a necessary part of the common course of university education. There are some Spanish universities, I am assured, in which the study of the Greek language has never yet made any part of that course. The first reformers found the Greek text of the new testament, and even the Hebrew text of the old, more favourable to their opinions, than the vulgate translation, which, as might naturally be supposed, had been gradually accommodated to support the doctrines of the catholic church. They set themselves, therefore, to expose the many errors of that translation, which the Roman catholic clergy were thus put under the necessity of defending or explaining. But this could not well be done without some knowledge of the original languages, of which the study was therefore gradually introduced into the greater part of universities; both of those which embraced, and of those which rejected, the doctrines of the reformation. The Greek language was connected with every part of that classical learning, which, though at first principally cultivated by catholics and Italians, happened to come into fashion much about the same time that the doctrines of the reformation were set on foot. In the greater part of universities, therefore, that language was taught previous to the study of philosophy, and as soon as the student had made some progress in the Latin. The Hebrew language having no connection with classical learning, and, except the holy scriptures, being the language of not a single book in any esteem, the study of it did not commonly commence till after that of philosophy, and when the student had entered upon the study of theology.

Greek and Latin continue to be a considerable part of university education. Originally the first rudiments both of the Greek and Latin languages were taught in universities, and in some universities they still continue to be so.[1] In others it is expected that the student should have previously acquired at least the rudiments of one or both of those languages, of which the study continues to make every where a very considerable part of university education.

There are three branches of Greek philosophy, The ancient Greek philosophy was divided into three great branches; physics, or natural philosophy; ethics, or moral philosophy; and logic. This general division seems perfectly agreeable to the nature of things.

(1) physics or natural philosophy, The great phenomena of nature, the revolutions of the heavenly bodies, eclipses, comets; thunder, lightning, and other extraordinary meteors; the generation, the life, growth, and dissolution of plants and animals; are objects which, as they necessarily excite the wonder, so they naturally[2] call forth the curiosity, of mankind to enquire into their causes. Superstition first attempted to satisfy this curiosity, by referring all those wonderful appearances to the immediate agency of the gods. Philosophy afterwards endeavoured to account for them, from more familiar causes, or from such as mankind were better acquainted with, than the agency of the gods. As those great phenomena are the first objects of human curiosity, so the science which pretends to explain them must naturally have been the first branch of philosophy that was cultivated. The first philosophers, accordingly, of whom history

---

[1] [Ed. I reads 'and they still continue to be so in some universities'.]
[2] ['Necessarily' and 'naturally' are transposed in ed. I.]

has preserved any account, appear to have been natural philosophers. (2) *ethics or moral philosophy,* In every age and country of the world men must have attended to the characters, designs, and actions of one another, and many reputable rules and maxims for the conduct of human life, must have been laid down and approved of by common consent. As soon as writing came into fashion, wise men or those who fancied themselves such, would naturally endeavour to increase the number of those established and respected maxims, and to express their own sense of what was either proper or improper conduct, sometimes in the more artificial form of apologues, like what are called the fables of Æsop; and sometimes in the more simple one of apophthegms, or wise sayings, like the Proverbs of Solomon, the verses of Theognis and Phocyllides, and some part of the works of Hesiod. They might continue in this manner for a long time merely to multiply the number of those maxims of prudence and morality, without even attempting to arrange them in any very distinct or methodical order, much less to connect them together by one or more general principles, from which they were all deducible, like effects from their natural causes. The beauty of a systematical arrangement of different observations connected by a few common principles, was first seen in the rude essays of those ancient times towards a system of natural philosophy. Something of the same kind was afterwards attempted in morals. The maxims of common life were arranged in some methodical order, and connected together by a few common principles, in the same manner as they had attempted to arrange and connect the phenomena of nature. The science which pretends to investigate and explain those connecting principles, is what is properly called moral philosophy. *and (3) logic.* Different authors gave different systems both of natural and moral philosophy. But the arguments by which they supported those different systems, far from being always demonstrations, were frequently at best but very slender probabilities, and sometimes mere sophisms, which had no other foundation but the inaccuracy and ambiguity of common language. Speculative systems have in all ages of the world been adopted for reasons too frivolous to have determined the judgment of any man of common sense, in a matter of the smallest pecuniary interest. Gross sophistry has scarce ever had any influence upon the opinions of mankind, except in matters of philosophy and speculation; and in these it has frequently had the greatest. The patrons of each system of natural and moral philosophy naturally endeavoured to expose the weakness of the arguments adduced to support the systems which were opposite to their own. In examining those arguments, they were necessarily led to consider the difference between a probable and a demonstrative argument, between a fallacious and a conclusive one; and Logic, or the science of the general principles of good and bad reasoning, necessarily arose out of the observations which a scrutiny of this kind gave occasion to. Though in its origin, posterior both to physics and to ethics, it was commonly taught, not indeed in all, but in the greater part of the ancient schools of philosophy, previously to either of those sciences. The student, it seems to have been thought, ought to understand well the difference between good and bad reasoning, before he was led to reason upon subjects of so great importance.

Philosophy was afterwards divided into five branches, This ancient division of philosophy into three parts was in the greater part of the universities of Europe, changed for another into five.

Metaphysics or pneumatics were added to physics, In the ancient philosophy, whatever was taught concerning the nature either of the human mind or of the Deity, made a part of the system of physics. Those beings, in whatever their essence might be supposed to consist, were parts of the great system of the universe, and parts too productive of the most important effects. Whatever human reason could either conclude, or conjecture, concerning them, made, as it were, two chapters, though no doubt two very important ones, of the science which pretended to give an account of the origin and revolutions of the great system of the universe. But in the universities of Europe, where philosophy was taught only as subservient to theology, it was natural to dwell longer upon these[1] two chapters than upon any other of the science. They were[2] gradually more and more extended, and were divided into many inferior chapters, till at last the doctrine of spirits, of which so little can be known, came to take up as much room in the system of philosophy as the doctrine of bodies, of which so much can be known. The doctrines concerning those two subjects were considered as making two distinct sciences. What are called Metaphysics or Pneumatics were set in opposition to Physics, and were cultivated[3] not only as the more sublime, but, for the purposes of a particular profession,

[1] [Ed. 1 reads 'those'.]   [2] [Ed. 1 reads 'Those two chapters were'.]
[3] [Ed. 1 reads 'What was called Metaphysics or Pneumatics was set in opposition to Physics, and was cultivated'.]

as the more useful science of the two. The proper subject of experiment and observation, a subject in which a careful attention is capable of making so many useful discoveries, was almost entirely neglected. The subject in which, after a few very simple and almost obvious truths, the most careful attention can discover nothing but obscurity and uncertainty, and can consequently produce nothing but subtleties and sophisms, was greatly cultivated.

and gave rise to Ontology. When those two sciences had thus been set in opposition to one another, the comparison between them naturally gave birth to a third, to what was called Ontology, or the science which treated of the qualities and attributes which were common to both the subjects of the other two sciences. But if subtleties and sophisms composed the greater part of the Metaphysics or Pneumatics of the schools, they composed the whole of this cobweb science of Ontology, which was likewise sometimes called Metaphysics.

Moral philosophy degenerated into casuistry and an ascetic morality, Wherein consisted the happiness and perfection of a man, considered not only as an individual, but as the member of a family, of a state, and of the great society of mankind, was the object which the ancient moral philosophy proposed to investigate. In that philosophy the duties of human life were treated of as subservient to the happiness and perfection of human life. But when moral, as well as natural philosophy, came to be taught only as subservient to theology, the duties of human life were treated of as chiefly subservient to the happiness of a life to come. In the ancient philosophy the perfection of virtue was represented as necessarily productive, to the person who possessed it, of the most perfect happiness in this life. In the modern philosophy it was frequently represented as generally, or rather as almost always inconsistent with any degree of happiness in this life; and heaven was to be earned only by penance and mortification, by the austerities and abasement of a monk; not by the liberal, generous, and spirited conduct of a man. Casuistry and an ascetic morality made up, in most cases, the greater part of the moral philosophy of the schools. By far the most important of all the different branches of philosophy, became in this manner by far the most corrupted.

the order being (1) logic, (2) ontology, (3) pneumatology, Such, therefore, was the common course of philosophical education in the greater part of the universities in[1] Europe. Logic was taught first: Ontology

[1] [Ed. 1 reads 'of'.]

(4) a debased moral philosophy,
(5) physics.

came in the second place: Pneumatology, comprehending the doctrine concerning the nature of the human soul and of the Deity, in the third: In the fourth followed a debased system of moral philosophy, which was considered as immediately connected with the doctrines of Pneumatology, with the immortality of the human soul, and with the rewards and punishments which, from the justice of the Deity, were to be expected in a life to come: A short and superficial system of Physics usually concluded the course.

University education was thus made less likely to produce men of the world.

The alterations which the universities of Europe thus introduced into the ancient course of philosophy, were all meant for the educaiton of ecclesiastics, and to render it a more proper introduction to the study of theology. But the additional quantity of subtlety and sophistry; the casuistry and the ascetic morality which those alterations introduced into it, certainly did not render it more proper for the education of gentlemen or men of the world, or more likely either to improve the understanding, or to mend the heart.

This course is still taught in most universitites with more or less diligence.

This course of philosophy is what still continues to be taught in the greater part of the universities of Europe; with more or less diligence, according as the constitution of each particular university happens to render diligence more or less necessary to the teachers. In some of the richest and best endowed universities, the tutors content themselves with teaching a few unconnected shreds and parcels of this corrupted course; and even these they commonly teach very negligently and superficially.

Few improvements in philosophy have been made by universities, and fewest by the richest universities.

The improvements which, in modern times, have been made in several different branches of philosophy, have not, the greater part of them, been made in universities; though some no doubt have. The greater part of universities have not even been very forward to adopt those improvements, after they were made; and several of those learned societies have chosen to remain, for a long time, the sanctuaries in which exploded systems and obsolete prejudices found shelter and protection, after they had been hunted out of every other corner of the world. In general, the richest and best endowed universities have been the slowest in adopting those improvements, and the most averse to permit any considerable change in the established plan of education. Those improvements were more easily introduced into some of the poorer universities, in which the teachers, depending upon their reputation for the greater part of their subsistence, were obliged to pay more attention to the current opinions of the world.[1]

In spite of all this the universities drew to themselves the education of gentlemen and men of fortune, But though the public schools and universities of Europe were originally intended only for the education of a particular profession, that of churchmen; and though they were not always very diligent in instructing their pupils even in the sciences which were supposed necessary for that profession, yet they gradually drew to themselves the education of almost all other people, particularly of almost all gentlemen and men of fortune. No better method, it seems, could be fallen upon of spending, with any advantage, the long interval between infancy and that period of life at which men begin to apply in good earnest to the real business of the world, the business which is to employ them during the remainder of their days. The greater part of what is taught in schools and universities, however, does not seem to be the most proper preparation for that business.

but in England it is becoming more usual to send young men to travel abroad, a plan so absurd that nothing but the discredit of the universities could have brought it into repute. In England, it becomes every day more and more the custom to send young people to travel in foreign countries immediately upon their leaving school, and without sending them to any university. Our young people, it is said, generally return home much improved by their travels. A young man who goes abroad at seventeen or eighteen, and returns home at one and twenty, returns three or four years older than he was when he went abroad; and at that age it is very difficult not to improve a good deal in three or four years. In the course of his travels, he generally acquires some knowledge of one or two foreign languages; a knowledge, however, which is seldom sufficient to enable him either to speak or write them with propriety. In other respects, he commonly returns home more conceited, more unprincipled, more dissipated, and more incapable of any serious application either to study or to business, than he could well have become in so short a time, had he lived at home. By travelling so very young, by spending in the most frivolous dissipation the most precious years of his life, at a distance from the inspection and

[1] [Above, p. 283.]

controul of his parents and relations, every useful habit, which the earlier parts of his education might have had some tendency to form in him, instead of being rivetted and confirmed, is almost necessarily either weakened or effaced. Nothing but the discredit into which the universities are allowing themselves to fall, could ever have brought into repute so very absurd a practice as that of travelling at this early period of life. By sending his son abroad, a father delivers himself, at least for some time, from so disagreeable an object as that of a son unemployed, neglected, and going to ruin before his eyes.

Such have been the effects of some of the modern institutions for education.

Different plans and different institutions for education seem to have taken place in other ages and nations.

In Greece the state directed education in gymnastics and music. In the republics of ancient Greece, every free citizen was instructed, under the direction of the public magistrate, in gymnastic exercises and in music. By gymnastic exercises it was intended to harden his body, to sharpen his courage, and to prepare him for the fatigues and dangers of war; and as the Greek militia was, by all accounts, one of the best that ever was in the world, this part of their public education must have answered completely the purpose for which it was intended. By the other part, music, it was proposed, at least by the philosophers and historians who have given us an account of those institutions, to humanize the mind, to soften the temper, and to dispose it for performing all the social and moral duties both of public and private life.

The Romans had the Campus Martius, resembling the gymnasium, but no music. They were none the worse for its absence. In ancient Rome the exercises of the Campus Martius answered the same purpose as those of the Gymnazium in ancient Greece,[1] and they seem to have answered it equally well. But among the Romans there was nothing which corresponded to the musical education of the Greeks. The morals of the Romans, however, both in private and public life, seem to have been, not only equal, but, upon the whole, a good deal superior to those of the Greeks. That they were superior in private life, we have the express testimony of Polybius[2] and of Dionysius of Halicarnassus,[3] two authors well acquainted with both nations; and the whole

[1] [Repeated all but *verbatim* from above, p. 218.]   [2] [*Hist.*, vi., 56; xviii., 34.]
[3] [*Ant. Rom.*, ii., xxiv. to xxvii,. esp. xxvi.]

tenor of the Greek and Roman history bears witness to the
superiority of the public morals of the Romans. The good temper
and moderation of contending factions seems to be the most essential circumstance in the public morals of a free people. But the
factions of the Greeks were almost always violent and sanguinary;
whereas, till the time of the Gracchi, no blood had ever been shed
in any Roman faction; and from the time of the Gracchi the
Roman republic may be considered as in reality dissolved. Notwithstanding, therefore, the very respectable authority of Plato,[1] Aristotle,[2] and Polybius,[3] and notwithstanding the very ingenious
reasons by which Mr. Montesquieu endeavours to support that
authority,[4] it seems probable that the musical education of the
Greeks had no great effect in mending their morals, since, without
any such education, those of the Romans were upon the whole
superior. The respect of those ancient sages for the institutions of
their ancestors, had probably disposed them to find much political
wisdom in what was, perhaps, merely an ancient custom, continued,
without interruption, from the earliest period of those societies, to
the times in which they had arrived at a considerable degree of
refinement. Music and dancing are the great amusements of almost
all barbarous nations, and the great accomplishments which are
supposed to fit any man for entertaining his society. It is so at this
day among the negroes on the coast of Africa. It was so among the
ancient Celtes, among the ancient Scandinavians, and, as we may
learn from Homer, among the ancient Greeks in the times preceding the Trojan war.[5] When the Greek tribes had formed themselves into little republics, it was natural that the study of those
accomplishments should, for a long time, make a part of the public
and common education of the people.

The teachers of military exercises and music were not paid or appointed by the state. The masters who instructed the young people
either in music or in military exercises, do not seem
to have been paid, or even appointed by the state,
either in Rome or even in Athens, the Greek republic of whose laws and customs we are the best informed. The
state required that every free citizen should fit himself for defending
it in war, and should, upon that account, learn his military exercises.
But it left him to learn them of such masters as he could find, and

---

[1] [*Repub.*, iii., 400–401.] [2] [*Politics*, 1340 a.] [3] [*Hist.*, iv., 20.]
[4] [*Esprit des lois*, liv. iv., chap. viii., where Plato, Aristotle and Polybius are quoted.]
[5] [*Iliad*, xiii., 137; xviii., 494, 594; *Odyssey*, i., 152; viii., 265; xviii., 304; xxiii., 134.]

it seems to have advanced nothing for this purpose, but a public field or place of exercise, in which he should practise and perform them.

Reading, writing and arithmetic were taught privately.   In the early ages both of the Greek and Roman republics, the other parts of education seem to have consisted in learning to read, write, and account according to the arithmetic of the times. These accomplishments the richer citizens seem frequently to have acquired at home, by the assistance of some domestic pedagogue, who was generally, either a slave, or a freed-man; and the poorer citizens, in the schools of such masters as made a trade of teaching for hire. Such parts of education, however, were abandoned altogether to the care of the parents or guardians of each individual. It does not appear that the state ever assumed any inspection or direction of them. By a law of Solon, indeed, the children were acquitted from maintaining those parents in their old age,[1] who had neglected to instruct them in some profitable trade or business.[2]

Philosophical education was independent of the state.   In the progress of refinement, when philosophy and rhetoric came into fashion, the better sort of people used to send their children to the schools of philosophers and rhetoricians, in order to be instructed in these fashionable sciences. But those schools were not supported by the public. They were for a long time barely tolerated by it. The demand for philosophy and rhetoric was for a long time so small, that the first professed teachers of either could not find constant employment in any one city, but were obliged to travel about from place to place. In this manner lived Zeno of Elea, Protagoras, Gorgias, Hippias, and many others. As the demand increased, the schools both of philosophy and rhetoric became stationary; first in Athens, and afterwards in several other cities. The state, however, seems never to have encouraged them further than by assigning to some of them a particular place to teach in, which was sometimes done too by private donors. The state seems to have assigned the Academy to Plato, the Lyceum to Aristotle, and the Portico to Zeno of Citta, the founder of the Stoics. But Epicurus bequeathed his gardens to his own school. Till about the time of Marcus Antoninus, however, no teacher appears to have had any salary from the public, or to have had any other emoluments, but what arose from the honor-

---

[1] [Ed. 1 places 'those parents' here.]
[2] [Plutarch, *Life of Solon*, quoted by Montesquieu, *Esprit des Lois*, liv. xxvi., ch. v.]

aries or fees of his scholars. The bounty which that philosophical emperor, as we learn from Lucian, bestowed upon one of[1] the teachers of philosophy, probably lasted no longer than his own life. There was nothing equivalent to the privileges of graduation, and to have attended any of those schools was not necessary, in order to be permitted to practise any particular trade or profession. If the opinion of their own utility could not draw scholars to them, the law neither forced any body to go to them, nor rewarded any body for having gone to them. The teachers had no jurisdiction over their pupils, nor any other authority besides that natural authority, which superior virtue and abilities never fail to procure from young people towards those who are entrusted with any part of their education.

No public institutions for teaching law existed at Rome, where law was first developed into an orderly system. At Rome, the study of the civil law made a part of the education, not of the greater part of the citizens, but of some particular families. The young people, however, who wished to acquire knowledge in the law, had no public school to go to, and had no other method of studying it, than by frequenting the company of such of their relations and friends, as were supposed to understand it. It is perhaps worth while to remark, that though the laws of the twelve tables were, many of them, copied from those of some ancient Greek republics, yet law never seems to have grown up to be a science in any republic of ancient Greece. In Rome it became a science very early, and gave a considerable degree of illustration to those citizens who had the reputation of understanding it. In the republics of ancient Greece, particularly in Athens, the ordinary courts of justice consisted of numerous, and therefore disorderly, bodies of people, who frequently decided almost at random, or as clamour, faction and party spirit happened to determine. The ignominy of an unjust decision, when it was to be divided among five hundred, a thousand, or fifteen hundred people (for some of their courts were so very numerous), could not fall very heavy upon any individual. At Rome, on the contrary, the principal courts of justice consisted either of a single judge, or of a small number of judges, whose characters, especially as they deliberated always in public, could not fail to be very much affected by any rash or unjust decision. In doubtful cases, such courts, from

---

[1] [The words 'one of' do not occur in eds. 1 and 2. They are perhaps a misprint for 'some of' or a misreading suggested by a failure to understand that 'his own life' is that of Marcus Antoninus. See Lucian, *Eunuchus*, iii.]

their anxiety to avoid blame, would naturally endeavour to shelter themselves under the example, or precedent, of the judges who had sat before them, either in the same, or in some other court. This attention to practice and precedent, necessarily formed the Roman law into that regular and orderly system in which it has been delivered down to us; and the like attention has had the like effects upon the laws of every other country where such attention has taken place. The superiority of character in the Romans over that of the Greeks, so much remarked by Polybius and Dionysius of Halicarnassus,[1] was probably more owing to the better constitution of their courts of justice, than to any of the circumstances to which those authors ascribe it. The Romans are said to have been particularly distinguished for their superior respect to an oath. But the people who were accustomed to make oath only before some diligent and well-informed court of justice, would naturally be much more attentive to what they swore, than they who were accustomed to do the same thing before mobbish and disorderly assemblies.

The ancient system was more successful than the modern, which corrupts public teaching and stifles private. The abilities, both civil and military, of the Greeks and Romans, will readily be allowed to have been, at least, equal to those of any modern nation. Our prejudice is perhaps rather to overrate them. But except in what related to military exercises, the state seems to have been at no pains to form those great abilities: for I cannot be induced to believe, that the musical education of the Greeks could be of much consequence in forming them. Masters, however, had been found, it seems, for instructing the better sort of people among those nations in every art and science in which the circumstances of their society rendered it necessary or convenient for them to be instructed. The demand for such instruction produced, what it always produces, the talent for giving it; and the emulation which an unrestrained competition never fails to excite, appears to have brought that talent to a very high degree of perfection. In the attention which the ancient philosophers excited, in the empire which they acquired over the opinions and principles of their auditors, in the faculty which they possessed of giving a certain tone and character to the conduct and conversation of those auditors; they appear to have been much superior to any modern teachers. In modern times, the diligence of public teachers is more or less corrupted by the circumstances, which render them more or

---

[1] [Above, p. 296.]

less independent of their success and reputation in their particular professions. Their salaries too put the private teacher, who would pretend to come into competition with them, in the same state with a merchant who attempts to trade without a bounty, in competition with those who trade with a considerable one. If he sells his goods at nearly the same price, he cannot have the same profit, and poverty and beggary at least, if not bankruptcy and ruin will infallibly be his lot. If he attempts to sell them much dearer, he is likely to have so few customers that his circumstances will not be much mended. The privileges of graduation, besides, are in many countries necessary, or at least extremely convenient to most men of learned professions; that is, to the far greater part of those who have occasion for a learned education. But those privileges can be obtained only by attending the lectures of the public teachers. The most careful attendance upon the ablest instructions of any private teacher, cannot always give any title to demand them. It is from these different causes that the private teacher of any of the sciences which are commonly taught in universities, is in modern times generally considered as in the very lowest order of men of letters. A man of real abilities can scarce find out a more humiliating or a more unprofitable employment to turn them to. The endowments of schools and colleges have, in this manner, not only corrupted the diligence of public teachers, but have rendered it almost impossible to have any good private ones.

If there were no public institutions for education nothing except what was useful would be taught. Were there no public institutions for education, no system, no science would be taught for which there was not some demand; or which the circumstances of the times did not render it either necessary, or convenient, or at least fashionable, to learn. A private teacher could never find his account in teaching, either an exploded and antiquated system of a science acknowledged to be useful, or a science universally believed to be a mere useless and pedantic heap of sophistry and nonsense. Such systems, such sciences, can subsist no where, but in those incorporated societies for education whose prosperity and revenue are in a great measure independent of their reputation, and altogether independent of their industry. Were there no public institutions for education, a gentleman, after going through, with application and abilities, the most complete course of education which the circumstances of the times were supposed to afford, could not come into the world completely ignorant of every thing which is the common subject of conversation among gentlemen and men of the world.

Women's education is excellent in consequence of the absence of public institutions. There are no public institutions for the education of women, and there is accordingly nothing useless, absurd, or fantastical in the common course of their education. They are taught what their parents or guardians judge it necessary or useful for them to learn; and they are taught nothing else. Every part of their education tends evidently to some useful purpose; either to improve the natural attractions of their person, or to form their mind to reserve, to modesty, to chastity, and to œconomy; to render them both likely to become the mistresses of a family, and to behave properly when they have become such. In every part of her life a woman feels some conveniency or advantage from every part of her education. It seldom happens that a man, in any part of his life, derives any conveniency or advantage from some of the most laborious and troublesome parts of his education.

Ought the state to give no attention to education? Ought the public, therefore, to give no attention, it may be asked, to the education of the people? Or if it ought to give any, what are the different parts of education which it ought to attend to in the different orders of the people? and in what manner ought it to attend to them?

In some cases it ought, in others it need not. In some cases the state of the society necessarily places the greater part of individuals in such situations as naturally form in them, without any attention of government, almost all the abilities and virtues which that state requires, or perhaps can admit of. In other cases the state of the society does not place the greater part of individuals in such situations, and some attention of government is necessary in order to prevent the almost entire corruption and degeneracy of the great body of the people.

Division of labour destroys intellectual, social and martial virtues unless government takes pains to prevent it, In the progress of the division of labour, the employment of the far greater part of those who live by labour, that is, of the great body of the people, comes to be confined to a few very simple operations; frequently to one or two. But the understandings of the greater part of men are necessarily formed by their ordinary employments. The man whose whole life is spent in performing a few simple operations, of which the effects too are, perhaps, always the same, or very nearly the same, has no occasion to exert his understanding, or to exercise his invention in finding out expedients for removing difficulties which never occur. He naturally loses, therefore, the habit of such exertion, and generally becomes as stupid and ignorant as it is possible for a human creature to become. The torpor of his mind renders him, not only incapable of relishing or bearing a part in any rational conversation, but of conceiving any generous, noble, or tender sentiment, and consequently of forming any just judgment concerning many even of the ordinary duties of private life. Of the great and extensive interests of his country he is altogether incapable of judging; and unless very particular pains have been taken to render him otherwise, he is equally incapable of defending his country in war. The uniformity of his stationary life naturally corrupts the courage of his mind, and makes him regard with abhorrence the irregular, uncertain, and adventurous life of a soldier. It corrupts even the activity of his body, and renders him incapable of exerting his strength with vigour and perseverance, in any other employment than that to which he has been bred. His dexterity at his own particular trade seems, in this manner, to be acquired at the expence of his intellectual, social, and martial virtues. But in every improved and civilized society this is the state into which the labouring poor, that is, the great body of the people, must necessarily fall, unless government takes some pains to prevent it.

whereas in barbarous societies those virtues are kept alive by constant necessity. It is otherwise in the barbarous societies, as they are commonly called, of hunters, of shepherds, and even of husbandmen in that rude state of husbandry which precedes the improvement of manufactures, and the extension of foreign commerce. In such societies the varied occupations of every man oblige every man to exert his capacity, and to invent expedients for removing difficulties which are continually occurring. Invention is kept alive, and the mind is not[1] suffered to fall into that drowsy stupidity, which, in a civilized society, seems to benumb the understanding of almost all the inferior ranks of people. In those barbarous societies, as they are called, every man, it has already been observed, is a warrior. Every man too is in some measure a statesman, and can form a tolerable judgment concerning the interest of the society, and the conduct of those who govern it. How far their chiefs are good judges in peace, or good leaders in war, is obvious to the observation of almost

---

[1] [Ed. 1 reads 'the minds of men are not'.]

every single man among them. In such a society indeed, no man can well acquire that improved and refined understanding, which a few men sometimes possess in a more civilized state. Though in a rude society there is a good deal of variety in the occupations of every individual, there is not a great deal in those of the whole society. Every man does, or is capable of doing, almost every thing which any other man does, or is capable of doing. Every man has a considerable degree of knowledge, ingenuity, and invention; but scarce any man has a great degree. The degree, however, which is commonly possessed, is generally sufficient for conducting the whole simple business of the society. In a civilized state, on the contrary, though there is little variety in the occupations of the greater part of individuals, there is an almost infinite variety in those of the whole society. These varied occupations present an almost infinite variety of objects to the contemplation of those few, who, being attached to no particular occupation themselves, have leisure and inclination to examine the occupations of other people. The contemplation of so great a variety of objects necessarily exercises their minds in endless comparisons and combinations, and renders their understandings, in an extraordinary degree, both acute and comprehensive. Unless those few, however, happen to be placed in some very particular situations, their great abilities, though honourable to themselves, may contribute very little to the good government or happiness of their society. Notwithstanding the great abilities of those few, all the nobler parts of the human character may be, in a great measure, obliterated and extinguished in the great body of the people.

The education of the common people requires attention from the state more than that of people of rank and fortune, whose parents can look after their interests, and who spend their lives in varied occupations chiefly intellectual, The education of the common people requires, perhaps, in a civilized and commercial society, the attention of the public more than that of people of some rank and fortune. People of some rank and fortune are generally eighteen or nineteen years of age before they enter upon that particular business, profession, or trade, by which they propose to distinguish themselves in the world. They have before that full time to acquire, or at least to fit themselves for afterwards acquiring, every accomplishment which can recommend them to the public esteem, or render them worthy of it. Their parents or guardians are generally sufficiently anxious that they should be so accomplished, and are, in most cases, willing enough to lay out the expence which is necessary for that purpose. If they are not always properly educated, it is seldom from the want of expence laid out upon their education; but from the improper application of that expence. It is seldom from the want of masters; but from the negligence and incapacity of the masters who are to be had, and from the difficulty, or rather from the impossibility which there is, in the present state of things, of finding any better. The employments too in which people of some rank or fortune spend the greater part of their lives, are not, like those of the common people, simple and uniform. They are almost all of them extremely complicated, and such as exercise the head more than the hands. The understandings of those who are engaged in such employments can seldom grow torpid for[1] want of exercise. The employments of people of some rank and fortune, besides, are seldom such as harass them from morning to night. They generally have a good deal of leisure, during which they may perfect themselves in every branch either of useful or ornamental knowledge of which they may have laid the foundation, or for which they may have acquired some taste in the earlier part of life.

unlike the children of the poor. It is otherwise with the common people. They have little time to spare for education. Their parents can scarce afford to maintain them even in infancy. As soon as they are able to work, they must apply to some trade by which they can earn their subsistence. That trade too is generally so simple and uniform as to give little exercise to the understanding; while, at the same time, their labour is both so constant and so severe, that it leaves them little leisure and less inclination to apply to, or even to think of anything else.

The state can encourage or insist on the general acquirement of reading, writing, and arithmetic, But though the common people cannot, in any civilized society, be so well instructed as people of some rank and fortune, the most essential parts of education, however, to read, write, and account, can be acquired at so early a period of life, that the greater part even of those who are to be bred to the lowest occupations, have time to acquire them before they can be employed in those occupations. For a very small expence the public can facilitate, can encourage, and can even impose upon almost the whole body of the people, the necessity of acquiring those most essential parts of education.

---

[1] [Ed. 1 reads 'from'.]

by establishing parish schools, The public can facilitate this acquisition by establishing in every parish or district a little school, where children may be taught for a reward so moderate, that even a common labourer may afford it; the master being partly, but not wholly paid by the public; because, if he was wholly, or even principally paid by it, he would soon learn to neglect his business. In Scotland the establishment of such parish schools has taught almost the whole common people to read, and a very great proportion of them to write and account. In England the establishment of charity schools has had an effect of the same kind, though not so universally, because the establishment is not so universal. If in those little schools the books, by which the children are taught to read, were a little more instructive than they commonly are; and if, instead of a[1] little smattering of Latin, which the children of the common people are sometimes taught there, and which can scarce ever be of any use to them; they were instructed in the elementary parts of geometry and mechanics, the literary education of this rank of people would perhaps be as complete as it can be.[2] There is scarce a common trade which does not afford some opportunities of applying to it the principles of geometry and mechanics, and which would not therefore gradually exercise and improve the common people in those principles, the necessary introduction to the most sublime as well as to the most useful sciences.

giving prizes, The public can encourage the acquisition of those most essential parts of education by giving small premiums, and little badges of distinction, to the children of the common people who excel in them.

and requiring men to pass an examination before setting up in trade. The public can impose upon almost the whole body of the people the necessity of acquiring those most essential parts of education, by obliging every man to undergo an examination or probation in them before he can obtain the freedom in any corporation, or be allowed to set up any trade either in a village or town corporate.

In this way the Greeks and Romans maintained a martial spirit. It was in this manner, by facilitating the acquisition of their military and gymnastic exercises, by encouraging it, and even by imposing upon the whole body of the people the necessity of learning those exercises, that the Greek and Roman republics maintained the martial spirit of their respective citizens. They facilitated the acquisition of those

---

[1] [Ed. 1 reads 'the'.]   [2] [Ed. 1 reads 'as it is capable of being'.]

exercises by appointing a certain place for learning and practising them, and by granting to certain masters the privilege of teaching in that place. Those masters do not appear to have had either salaries or exclusive privileges of any kind. Their reward consisted altogether in what they got from their scholars; and a citizen who had learnt his exercises in the public Gymnasia, had no sort of legal advantage over one who had learnt them privately, provided the latter had learnt them equally well. Those republics encouraged the acquisition of those exercises, by bestowing little premiums and badges of distinction upon those who excelled in them. To have gained a prize in the Olympic, Isthmian or Nemæan games gave illustration, not only to the person who gained it, but to his whole family and kindred. The obligation which every citizen was under to serve a certain number of years, if called upon, in the armies of the republic, sufficiently imposed the necessity of learning those exercises without which he could not be fit for that service.

Martial spirit in the people would diminish both the necessary size and the danger of a standing army. That in the progress of improvement the practice of military exercises, unless government takes proper pains to support it, goes gradually to decay, and, together with it, the martial spirit of the great body of the people, the example of modern Europe sufficiently demonstrates. But the security of every society must always depend, more or less, upon the martial spirit of the great body of the people. In the present times, indeed, that martial spirit alone, and unsupported by a well-disciplined standing army, would not, perhaps, be sufficient for the defence and security of any society. But where every citizen had the spirit of a soldier, a smaller standing army would surely be requisite. That spirit, besides, would necessarily diminish very much the dangers to liberty, whether real or imaginary, which are commonly apprehended from a standing army. As it would very much facilitate the operations of that army against a foreign invader, so it would obstruct them as much if unfortunately they should ever be directed against the constitution of the state.

The Greek and Roman institutions were more effectual than modern militias, which only include a small portion of the people. The ancient institutions of Greece and Rome seem to have been much more effectual, for maintaining the martial spirit of the great body of the people, than the establishment of what are called the militias of modern times. They were much more simple. When they were once established, they executed themselves, and it required little or no attention from government to maintain them in the most perfect vigour. Whereas to maintain, even in tolerable execution, the complex regulations of any modern militia, requires the continual and painful attention of government, without which they are constantly falling into total neglect and disuse. The influence, besides, of the ancient institutions was much more universal. By means of them the whole body of the people was completely instructed in the use of arms. Whereas it is but a very small part of them who can ever be so instructed by the regulations of any modern militia; except, perhaps, that of Switzerland.

It is the duty of government to prevent the growth of cowardice,   But a coward, a man incapable either of defending or of revenging himself, evidently wants one of the most essential parts of the character of a man. He is as much mutilated and deformed in his mind as another is in his body, who is either deprived of some of its most essential members, or has lost the use of them.[1] He is evidently the more wretched and miserable of the two; because happiness and misery, which reside altogether in the mind, must necessarily depend more upon the healthful or unhealthful, the mutilated or entire state of the mind, than upon that of the body. Even though the martial spirit of the people were of no use towards the defence of the society, yet to prevent that sort of mental mutilation, deformity, and wretchedness, which cowardice necessarily involves in it, from spreading themselves through the great body of the people, would still deserve the most serious attention of government; in the same manner as it would deserve its most serious attention to prevent a leprosy or any other loathsome and offensive disease, though neither mortal nor dangerous, from spreading itself among them; though, perhaps, no other public good might result from such attention besides the prevention of so great a public evil.

gross ignorance and stupidity.   The same thing may be said of the gross ignorance and stupidity which, in a civilized society, seem so frequently to benumb the understandings of all the inferior ranks of people. A man without the proper use of the intellectual faculties of a man, is, if possible, more contemptible than even a coward, and seems to be mutilated and deformed in a still more essential part of the character of human nature. Though the state was to derive no advantage from the instruction of the inferior ranks of people, it would still deserve its attention that they should not be altogether

[1] [Ed. 1 reads 'the use of those members'.]

uninstructed. The state, however, derives no inconsiderable advantage from their instruction. The more they are instructed, the less liable they are to the delusions of enthusiasm and superstition, which, among ignorant nations, frequently occasion the most dreadful disorders. An instructed and intelligent people besides, are always more decent and orderly than an ignorant and stupid one. They feel themselves, each individually, more respectable, and more likely to obtain the respect of their lawful superiors, and they are therefore more disposed to respect those superiors. They are more disposed to examine, and more capable of seeing through, the interested complaints of faction and sedition, and they are, upon that account, less apt to be misled into any wanton or unnecessary opposition to the measures of government. In free countries, where the safety of government depends very much upon the favourable judgment which the people may form of its conduct, it must surely be of the highest importance that they should not be disposed to judge rashly or capriciously concerning it.

ARTICLE III

Of the Expence of the Institutions for the Instruction of People of all Ages

These institutions are chiefly for religious instruction. Religious like other teachers are more vigorous if unestablished and unendowed.
The institutions for the instruction of people of all ages are chiefly those for religious instruction. This is a species of instruction of which the object is not so much to render the people good citizens in this world, as to prepare them for another and a better world in a life to come. The teachers of the doctrine which contains this instruction, in the same manner as other teachers, may either depend altogether for their subsistence upon the voluntary contributions of their hearers; or they may derive it from some other fund to which the law of their country may entitle them; such as a landed estate, a tythe or land tax, an established salary or stipend. Their exertion, their zeal and industry, are likely to be much greater in the former situation than in the latter. In this respect the teachers of new religions have always had a considerable advantage in attacking those ancient and established systems of which the clergy, reposing themselves upon their benefices, had neglected to keep up the fervour of faith and devotion in the great body of the people; and having given themselves up to

indolence, were become altogether incapable of making any vigorous exertion in defence even of their own establishment. The clergy of an established and well-endowed religion frequently become men of learning and elegance, who possess all the virtues of gentlemen, or which can recommend them to the esteem of gentlemen; but they are apt gradually to lose the qualities, both good and bad, which gave them authority and influence with the inferior ranks of people, and which had perhaps been the original causes of the success and establishment of their religion. Such a clergy, when attacked by a set of popular and bold, though perhaps stupid and ignorant enthusiasts, feel themselves as perfectly defenceless as the indolent, effeminate, and full-fed nations of the southern parts of Asia, when they were invaded by the active, hardy, and hungry Tartars of the North. Such a clergy, upon such an emergency, have commonly no other resource than to call upon the civil magistrate to persecute, destroy, or drive out their adversaries, as disturbers of the public peace. It was thus that the Roman catholic clergy called upon the civil magistrate to persecute the protestants; and the church of England, to persecute the dissenters; and that in general every religious sect, when it has once enjoyed for a century or two the security of a legal establishment, has found itself incapable of making any vigorous defence against any new sect which chose to attack its doctrine or discipline. Upon such occasions the advantage in point of learning and good writing may sometimes be on the side of the established church. But the arts of popularity, all the arts of gaining proselytes, are constantly on the side of its adversaries. In England those arts have been long neglected by the well-endowed clergy of the established church, and are at present chiefly cultivated by the dissenters and by the methodists. The independent provisions, however, which in many places have been made for dissenting teachers, by means of voluntary subscriptions, of trust rights, and other evasions of the law, seem very much to have abated the zeal and activity of those teachers. They have many of them become very learned, ingenious, and respectable men; but they have in general ceased to be very popular preachers. The methodists, without half the learning of the dissenters, are much more in vogue.

The inferior clergy of the Church of Rome are more   In the church of Rome, the industry and zeal of the inferior clergy are[1] kept more alive by the powerful

---

[1] [Eds. 1–3 read 'is'.]

stimulated by self-interest than those of any established Protestant Church. motive of self-interest, than perhaps in any established protestant church. The parochial clergy derive, many of them, a very considerable part of their subsistence from the voluntary oblations of the people; a source of revenue which confession gives them many opportunities of improving. The mendicant orders derive their whole subsistence from such oblations. It is with them, as with the hussars and light infantry of some armies; no plunder, no pay. The parochial clergy are like those teachers whose reward depends partly upon their salary, and partly upon the fees or honoraries which they get from their pupils; and these must always depend more or less upon their industry and reputation. The mendicant orders are like those teachers whose subsistence depends altogether upon their industry. They are obliged, therefore, to use every art which can animate the devotion of the common people. The establishment of the two great mendicant orders of St. Dominic and St. Francis, it is observed by Machiavel,[1] revived, in the thirteenth and fourteenth centuries, the languishing faith and devotion of the catholic church. In Roman catholic countries the spirit of devotion is supported altogether by the monks and by the poorer parochial clergy. The great dignitaries of the church, with all the accomplishments of gentlemen and men of the world, and sometimes with those of men of learning, are careful enough to maintain the necessary discipline over their inferiors, but seldom give themselves any trouble about the instruction of the people.

Hume says the state may leave the promotion of some arts to individuals who benefit by them, Most of the arts and professions in a state [says by far the most illustrious philosopher and historian of the present age] are of such a nature, that, while they promote the interests of the society, they are also useful or agreeable to some individuals; and in that case, the constant rule of the magistrate, except, perhaps, on the first introduction of any art, is, to leave the profession to itself, and trust its encouragement to the individuals who reap the benefit of it. The artizans, finding their profits to rise by the favour of their customers, increase, as much as possible, their skill and industry; and as matters are not disturbed by any injudicious tampering, the commodity is always sure to be at all times nearly proportioned to the demand.

[1] [In 'Discourses on the First Decade of Titus Livius,' book iii., chap. i.]

others must be pro-
moted by the state; But there are also some callings, which, though useful and even necessary in a state, bring no advantage or pleasure to any individual, and the supreme power is obliged to alter its conduct with regard to the retainers of those professions. It must give them public encouragement in order to their subsistence; and it must provide against that negligence to which they will naturally be subject, either by annexing particular honours to the profession, by establishing a long subordination of ranks and a strict dependance, or by some other expedient. The persons employed in the finances, fleets,[1] and magistracy, are instances of this order of men.

it might be thought
that the teaching of
religion belonged
to the first class, It may naturally be thought, at first sight, that the ecclesiastics belong to the first class, and that their encouragement, as well as that of lawyers and physicians, may safely be entrusted to the liberality of individuals, who are attached to their doctrines, and who find benefit or consolation from their spiritual ministry and assistance. Their industry and vigilance will, no doubt, be whetted by such an additional motive; and their skill in the profession, as well as their address in governing the minds of the people, must receive daily increase, from their increasing practice, study, and attention.

but it does not,
because the inter-
ested zeal of the
clergy should be
discouraged. But if we consider the matter more closely, we shall find, that this interested diligence of the clergy is what every wise legislator will study to prevent; because, in every religion except the true, it is highly pernicious, and it has even a natural tendency to pervert the true, by infusing into it a strong mixture of superstition, folly, and delusion. Each ghostly practitioner, in order to render himself more precious and sacred in the eyes of his retainers, will inspire them with the most violent abhorrence of all other sects, and continually endeavour, by some novelty, to excite the languid devotion of his audience. No regard will be paid to truth, morals, or decency in the doctrines inculcated. Every tenet will be adopted that best suits the disorderly affections of the human frame. Customers will be drawn to each conventicle by new industry and address in practising on the passions and credulity of the populace. And in the end, the civil magistrate will find, that he has dearly paid for his pretended frugality, in saving a fixed establishment for the priests; and that in reality the

[1] [The original reads 'finances, armies, fleets'.]

most decent and advantageous composition, which he can make with the spiritual guides, is to bribe their indolence, by assigning stated salaries to their profession, and rendering it superfluous for them to be farther active, than merely to prevent their flock from straying in quest of new pastures. And in this manner ecclesiastical establishments, though commonly they arose at first from religious views, prove in the end advantageous to the political interests of society.[1]

Establishments and public endowments have not been due to reasoning like this, but to the needs of political faction. But whatever may have been the good or bad effects of the independent provision of the clergy; it has, perhaps, been very seldom bestowed upon them from any view to those effects. Times of violent religious controversy have generally been times of equally violent political faction. Upon such occasions, each political party has either found it, or imagined it, for its interest, to league itself with some one or other of the contending religious sects. But this could be done only by adopting, or at least by favouring, the tenets of that particular sect. The sect which had the good fortune to be leagued with the conquering party, necessarily shared in the victory of its ally, by whose favour and protection it was soon enabled in some degree to silence and subdue all its adversaries. Those adversaries had generally leagued themselves with the enemies of the conquering party, and were therefore the enemies of that party. The clergy of this particular sect having thus become complete masters of the field, and their influence and authority with the great body of the people being in its highest vigour, they were powerful enough to over-awe the chiefs and leaders of their own party, and to oblige the civil magistrate to respect their opinions and inclinations. Their first demand was generally, that he should silence and subdue all their adversaries; and their second, that he should bestow an independent provision on themselves. As they had generally contributed a good deal to the victory, it seemed not unreasonable that they should have some share in the spoil. They were weary, besides, of humouring the people, and of depending upon their caprice for a subsistence. In making this demand therefore they consulted their own ease and comfort, without troubling themselves about the effect which it might have in future times upon the influence and authority of their order. The civil magistrate,

[1] [Hume, *History*, chap. xxix., vol. iv., pp. 30, 31, in ed. of 1773, which differs verbally both from earlier and from later editions.]

who could comply with this demand only by giving them something which he would have chosen much rather to take, or to keep to himself, was seldom very forward to grant it. Necessity, however, always forced him to submit at last, though frequently not till after many delays, evasions, and affected excuses.

If politics had never called in the aid of religion, sects would have been so numerous that they would have learnt to tolerate each other, But if politics had never called in the aid of religion, had the conquering party never adopted the tenets of one sect more than those of another, when it had gained the victory, it would probably have dealt equally and impartially with all the different sects, and have allowed every man to chuse his own priest and his own religion as he thought proper. There would in this case, no doubt, have been a great multitude of religious sects. Almost every different congregation might probably have made a little sect by itself, or have entertained some peculiar tenets of its own. Each teacher would no doubt have felt himself under the necessity of making the utmost exertion, and of using every art both to preserve and to increase the number of his disciples. But as every other teacher would have felt himself under the same necessity, the success of no one teacher, or sect of teachers, could have been very great. The interested and active zeal of religious teachers can be dangerous and troublesome only where there is, either but one sect tolerated in the society, or where the whole of a large society is divided into two or three great sects; the teachers of each[1] acting by concert, and under a regular discipline and subordination. But that zeal must be altogether innocent where the society is divided into two or three hundred, or perhaps into as many thousand small sects, of which no one could be considerable enough to disturb the public tranquillity. The teachers of each sect, seeing themselves surrounded on all sides with more adversaries than friends, would be obliged to learn that candour and moderation which is so seldom to be found among the teachers of those great sects, whose tenets, being supported by the civil magistrate, are held in veneration by almost all the inhabitants of extensive kingdoms and empires, and who therefore see nothing round them but followers, disciples, and humble admirers. The teachers of each little sect, finding themselves almost alone, would be obliged to respect those of almost every other sect, and the concessions which they would mutually find it both convenient and agreeable to make to one another, might in

---

[1] [Ed. 1 reads 'of each sect'.]

time probably reduce the doctrine of the greater part of them to that pure and rational religion, free from every mixture of absurdity, imposture, or fanaticism, such as wise men have in all ages of the world wished to see established; but such as positive law has perhaps never yet established, and probably never will establish in any country: because, with regard to religion, positive law always has been, and probably always will be, more or less influenced by popular superstition and enthusiasm. This plan of ecclesiastical government, or more properly of no ecclesiastical government, was what the sect called Independents, a sect no doubt of very wild enthusiasts, proposed to establish in England towards the end of the civil war. If it had been established, though of a very unphilosophical origin, it would probably by this time have been productive of the most philosophical good temper and moderation with regard to every sort of religious principle. It has been established in Pensylvania, where, though the Quakers happen to be the most numerous,[1] the law in reality favours no one sect more than another, and it is there said to have been productive of this philosophical good temper and moderation.

and if they did not, their zeal could do no harm. But though this equality of treatment should not be productive of this good temper and moderation in all, or even in the greater part of the religious sects of a particular country; yet provided those sects were sufficiently numerous, and each of them consequently too small to disturb the public tranquillity, the excessive zeal of each[2] for its particular tenets could not well be productive of any very hurtful effects, but, on the contrary, of several good ones: and if the government was perfectly decided both to let them all alone, and to oblige them all to let alone one another, there is little danger that they would not of their own accord subdivide themselves fast enough, so as soon to become sufficiently numerous.

Of the two systems of morality, the strict or austere and the liberal or loose, the first is favoured by the common people, the second by people of fashion. In every civilized society, in every society where the distinction of ranks has once been completely established, there have been always two different schemes or systems of morality current at the same time; of which the one may be called the strict or austere; the other the liberal, or, if you will, the loose system. The former is generally admired and revered by the common people: the latter is commonly more

[1] [Ed. 1 reads 'the most numerous sect'.]   [2] [Ed. 1 reads 'of each sect'.]

esteemed and adopted by what are called people of fashion. The degree of disapprobation with which we ought to mark the vices of levity, the vices which are apt to arise from great prosperity, and from the excess of gaiety and good humour, seems to constitute the principal distinction between those two opposite schemes or systems. In the liberal or loose system, luxury, wanton and even disorderly mirth, the pursuit of pleasure to some degree of intemperance, the breach of chastity, at least in one of the two sexes, &c. provided they are not accompanied with gross indecency, and do not lead to falshood or injustice, are generally treated with a good deal of indulgence, and are easily either excused or pardoned altogether. In the austere system, on the contrary, those excesses are regarded with the utmost abhorrence and detestation. The vices of levity are always ruinous to the common people, and a single week's thoughtlessness and dissipation is often sufficient to undo a poor workman for ever, and to drive him through despair upon committing the most enormous crimes. The wiser and better sort of the common people, therefore, have always the utmost abhorrence and detestation of such excesses, which their experience tells them are so immediately fatal to people of their condition. The disorder and extravagance of several years, on the contrary, will not always ruin a man of fashion, and people of that rank are very apt to consider the power of indulging in some degree of excess as one of the advantages of their fortune, and the liberty of doing so without censure or reproach, as one of the privileges which belong to their station. In people of their own station, therefore, they regard such excesses with but a small degree of disapprobation, and censure them either very slightly or not at all.

Religious sects usually begin with the austere system, Almost all religious sects have begun among the common people, from whom they have generally drawn their earliest, as well as their most numerous proselytes. The austere system of morality has, accordingly, been adopted by those sects almost constantly, or with very few exceptions; for there have been some. It was the system by which they could best recommend themselves to that order of people to whom they first proposed their plan of reformation upon what had been before established. Many of them, perhaps the greater part of them, have even endeavoured to gain credit by refining upon this austere system, and by carrying it to some degree of folly and extravagance; and this excessive rigour has frequently recommended them more than any thing else to the respect and veneration of the common people.

and in small reli-gious sects morals are regular and even disagreeably rig-orous and unsocial. A man of rank and fortune is by his station the distinguished member of a great society, who attend to every part of his conduct, and who thereby oblige him to attend to every part of it himself. His authority and consideration depend very much upon the respect which this society bears to him. He dare not do any thing which would disgrace or discredit him in it, and he is obliged to a very strict observation of that species of morals, whether liberal or austere, which the general consent of this society prescribes to persons of his rank and fortune. A man of low condition, on the contrary, is far from being a distinguished member of any great society. While he remains in a country village his conduct may be attended to, and he may be obliged to attend to it himself. In this situation, and in this situation only, he may have what is called a character to lose. But as soon as he comes into a great city, he is sunk in obscurity and darkness. His conduct is observed and attended to by nobody, and he is therefore very likely to neglect it himself, and to abandon himself to every sort of low profligacy and vice. He never emerges so effectually from this obscurity, his conduct never excites so much the attention of any respectable society, as by his becoming the member of a small religious sect. He from that moment acquires a degree of consideration which he never had before. All his brother sectaries are, for the credit of the sect, interested to observe his conduct, and if he gives occasion to any scandal, if he deviates very much from those austere morals which they almost always require of one another, to punish him by what is always a very severe punishment, even where no civil effects attend it, expulsion or excommunication from the sect. In little religious sects, accordingly, the morals of the common people have been almost always remarkably regular and orderly; generally much more so than in the established church. The morals of those little sects, indeed, have frequently been rather disagreeably rigorous and unsocial.

There are two possible remedies, There are two very easy and effectual remedies, however, by whose joint operation the state might, without violence, correct whatever was unsocial or disagreeably rigorous in the morals of all the little sects into which the country was divided.

(1) the requirement of a knowledge of science and philosophy from candidates for professions and offices; The first of those remedies is the study of science and philosophy, which the state might render almost universal among all people of middling or more than middling rank and fortune; not by giving salaries to teachers in order to make them negligent and idle, but by instituting some sort of probation, even in the higher and more difficult sciences, to be undergone by every person before he was permitted to exercise any liberal profession, or before he could be received as a candidate for any honourable office of trust or profit. If the state imposed upon this order of men the necessity of learning, it would have no occasion to give itself any trouble about providing them with proper teachers. They would soon find better teachers for themselves than any whom the state could provide for them. Science is the great antidote to the poison of enthusiasm and superstition; and where all the superior ranks of people were secured from it, the inferior ranks could not be much exposed to it.

and (2) the encouragement of public diversions. The second of those remedies is the frequency and gaiety of public diversions. The state, by encouraging, that is by giving entire liberty to all those who for their own interest would attempt, without scandal or indecency, to amuse and divert the people by painting, poetry, music, dancing; by all sorts of dramatic representations and exhibitions, would easily dissipate, in the greater part of them, that melancholy and gloomy humour which is almost always the nurse of popular superstition and enthusiasm. Public diversions have always been the objects of dread and hatred, to all the fanatical promoters of those popular frenzies. The gaiety and good humour which those diversions inspire were altogether inconsistent with that temper of mind, which was fittest for their purpose, or which they could best work upon. Dramatic representations besides, frequently exposing their artifices to public ridicule, and sometimes even to public execration, were upon that account, more than all other diversions, the objects of their peculiar abhorrence.

Where no one religion was favoured the sovereign would not require to influence the teachers of religion, In a country where the law favoured the teachers of no one religion more than those of another, it would not be necessary that any of them should have any particular or immediate dependency upon the sovereign or executive power; or that he should have any thing to do, either in appointing, or in dismissing them from their offices. In such a situation he would have no occasion to give himself any concern about them, further than to keep the peace among them, in the same manner as among the rest of his subjects; that is, to hinder them from persecuting, abusing, or oppressing one another. But it is quite otherwise in countries where there is an established or governing religion. The sovereign can in this case never be secure, unless he has the means of influencing in a considerable degree the greater part of the teachers of that religion.

as he must where there is an established church, The clergy of every established church constitute a great incorporation. They can act in concert, and pursue their interest upon one plan and with one spirit, as much as if they were under the direction of one man; and they are frequently too under such direction. Their interest as an incorporated body is never the same with that of the sovereign, and is sometimes directly opposite to it. Their great interest is to maintain their authority with the people; and this authority depends upon the supposed certainty and importance of the whole doctrine which they inculcate, and upon the supposed necessity of adopting every part of it with the most implicit faith, in order to avoid eternal misery. Should the sovereign have the imprudence to appear either to deride or doubt himself of the most trifling part of their doctrine, or from humanity attempt to protect those who did either the one or the other, the punctilious honour of a clergy who have no sort of dependency upon him, is immediately provoked to proscribe him as a profane person, and to employ all the terrors of religion in order to oblige the people to transfer their allegiance to some more orthodox and obedient prince. Should he oppose any of their pretensions or usurpations, the danger is equally great. The princes who have dared in this manner to rebel against the church, over and above this crime of rebellion, have generally been charged too with the additional crime of heresy, notwithstanding their solemn protestations of their faith and humble submission to every tenet which she thought proper to prescribe to them. But the authority of religion is superior to every other authority. The fears which it suggests conquer all other fears. When the authorised teachers of religion propagate through the great body of the people doctrines subversive of the authority of the sovereign, it is by violence only, or by the force of a standing army, that he can maintain his authority. Even a standing army cannot in this case give him any lasting security; because if the soldiers are not foreigners, which can seldom be the case, but drawn from the great body of the people, which must almost always be the case, they are likely to be soon corrupted by those very doctrines. The revolutions which the turbulence of the Greek clergy was continually occasioning at Constantinople, as long as the eastern empire subsisted; the convulsions which, during the course of several centuries, the turbulence of the Roman clergy was continually occasioning in every part of Europe, sufficiently demonstrate how precarious and insecure must always be the situation of the sovereign who has no proper means of influencing the clergy of the established and governing religion of his country.

since he cannot directly oppose the doctrines of the clergy. Articles of faith, as well as all other spiritual matters, it is evident enough, are not within the proper department of a temporal sovereign, who, though he may be very well qualified for protecting, is seldom supposed to be so for instructing the people. With regard to such matters, therefore, his authority can seldom be sufficient to counterbalance the united authority of the clergy of the established church. The public tranquillity, however, and his own security, may frequently depend upon the doctrines which they may think proper to propagate concerning such matters. As he can seldom directly oppose their decision, therefore, with proper weight and authority, it is necessary that he should be able to influence it; and he can influence it only by the fears and expectations which he may excite in the greater part of the individuals of the order. Those fears and expectations may consist in the fear of deprivation or other punishment, and in the expectation of further preferment.

The clergy hold their benefices for life, and violence used against them would be ineffectual; so management must be resorted to. In all Christian churches the benefices of the clergy are a sort of freeholds which they enjoy, not during pleasure, but during life, or good behaviour. If they held them by a more precarious tenure, and were liable to be turned out upon every slight disobligation either of the sovereign or of his ministers, it would perhaps be impossible for them to maintain their authority with the people, who would then consider them as mercenary dependents upon the court, in the sincerity of whose instructions they could no longer have any confidence. But should the sovereign attempt irregularly, and by violence, to deprive any number of clergymen of their freeholds, on account, perhaps, of their having propagated with more than ordinary zeal, some factious or seditious doctrine, he would only render, by such persecution, both them and their doctrine ten times more popular, and therefore ten times more troublesome and dangerous than they had been before. Fear is in almost all cases a wretched instrument of government, and ought in particular never to be employed against any order of men who have the smallest pretensions to independency. To attempt to terrify them, serves only to irritate their bad humour, and to confirm them in an opposition which more gentle usage perhaps might easily induce them, either to soften, or to lay aside altogether. The violence which the French government usually employed in order to oblige all their parliaments, or sovereign courts of justice, to enregister any unpopular edict, very seldom succeeded. The means commonly employed, however, the imprisonment of all the refractory members, one would think were forcible enough. The princes of the house of Stewart sometimes employed the like means in order to influence some of the members of the parliament of England; and they generally found them equally intractable. The parliament of England is now managed in another manner; and a very small experiment, which the duke of Choiseul made about twelve years ago upon the parliament of Paris, demonstrated sufficiently that all the parliaments of France might have been managed still more easily in the same manner. That experiment was not pursued. For though management and persuasion are always the easiest and the safest instruments of government, as force and violence are the worst and the most dangerous, yet such, it seems, is the natural insolence of man, that he almost always disdains to use the good instrument, except when he cannot or dare not use the bad one. The French government could and durst use force, and therefore disdained to use management and persuasion. But there is no order of men, it appears, I believe, from the experience of all ages, upon whom it is so dangerous, or rather so perfectly ruinous, to employ force and violence, as upon the respected clergy of any established church. The rights, the privileges, the personal liberty of every individual ecclesiastic, who is upon good terms with his own order, are, even in the most despotic governments, more respected than those of any other person of nearly equal rank and fortune. It is so in every gradation of despotism, from that of the gentle and mild government of Paris, to that of the violent and furious government of Constantinople. But though this order of men can scarce ever be forced, they may be managed as easily as any other; and the security of the sovereign, as well as the public tranquillity, seems to depend very much upon the means which he has of managing them, and those means seem to consist altogether in the preferment which he has to bestow upon them.

Bishops were originally elected by the clergy and people, afterwards by the clergy alone, In the ancient constitution of the Christian church,[1] the bishop of each diocese was elected by the joint votes of the clergy and of the people of the episcopal city. The people did not long retain their right of election; and while they did retain it, they almost always acted under the influence of the clergy, who in such spiritual matters appeared to be their natural guides. The clergy, however, soon grew weary of the trouble of managing them, and found it easier to elect their own bishops themselves. The abbot, in the same manner, was elected by the monks of the monastery, at least in the greater part of abbacies. All the inferior ecclesiastical benefices comprehended within the diocese were collated by the bishop, who bestowed them upon such ecclesiastics as he thought proper. All church preferments were in this manner in the disposal of the church. The sovereign, though he might have some indirect influence in those elections, and though it was sometimes usual to ask both his consent to elect, and his approbation of the election, yet had no direct or sufficient means of managing the clergy. The ambition of every clergyman naturally led him to pay court, not so much to his sovereign, as to his own order, from which only he could expect preferment.

still later to a large extent by the Pope. Through the greater part of Europe the Pope gradually drew to himself first the collation of almost all bishoprics and abbacies, or of what were called Consistorial benefices, and afterwards, by various machinations and pretences, of the greater part of inferior benefices comprehended within each diocese; little more being left to the bishop than what was barely necessary to give him a decent authority with his own clergy. By this arrangement the condition of the sovereign was still worse than it had been before. The clergy of all the different countries of Europe were thus formed into a sort of spiritual army, dispersed in different quarters, indeed, but of which all the movements and operations could now be directed by one head, and conducted upon one uniform plan. The clergy of each particular country might be considered as a particular detachment of that army, of which the operations could easily be supported and seconded by all

---

[1] [Ed. 1 reads 'Roman catholic church'.]

the other detachments quartered in the different countries round about. Each detachment was not only independent of the sovereign of the country in which it was quartered, and by which it was maintained, but dependent upon a foreign sovereign, who could at any time turn its arms against the sovereign of that particular country, and support them by the arms of all the other detachments.

This, joined with the great wealth of the clergy, rendered them exceedingly formidable. Those arms were the most formidable that can well be imagined. In the ancient state of Europe, before the establishment of arts and manufactures, the wealth of the clergy gave them the same sort of influence over the common people, which that of the great barons gave them over their respective vassals, tenants, and retainers. In the great landed estates, which the mistaken piety both of princes and private persons had bestowed upon the church, jurisdictions were established of the same kind with those of the great barons; and for the same reason. In those great landed estates, the clergy, or their bailiffs, could easily keep the peace without the support or assistance either of the king or of any other person; and neither the king nor any other person could keep the peace there without the support and assistance of the clergy. The jurisdictions of the clergy, therefore, in their particular baronies or manors, were equally independent, and equally exclusive of the authority of the king's courts, as those of the great temporal lords. The tenants of the clergy were, like those of the great barons, almost all tenants at will, entirely dependent upon their immediate lords, and therefore liable to be called out at pleasure, in order to fight in any quarrel in which the clergy might think proper to engage them. Over and above the rents of those estates, the clergy possessed, in the tythes, a very large portion of the rents of all the other estates in every kingdom of Europe. The revenues arising from both those species of rents were, the greater part of them, paid in kind, in corn, wine, cattle, poultry, &c. The quantity exceeded greatly what the clergy could themselves consume; and there were neither arts nor manufactures for the produce of which they could exchange the surplus. The clergy could derive advantage from this immense surplus in no other way than by employing it, as the great barons employed the like surplus of their revenues, in the most profuse hospitality, and in the most extensive charity. Both the hospitality and the charity of the ancient clergy, accordingly, are said to have been very great. They not only maintained almost the whole poor of every kingdom, but many knights and gentlemen had frequently no other means of subsistence than by travelling about from monastery to monastery, under pretence of devotion, but in reality to enjoy the hospitality of the clergy. The retainers of some particular prelates were often as numerous as those of the greatest lay-lords; and the retainers of all the clergy taken together were, perhaps, more numerous than those of all the lay-lords. There was always much more union among the clergy than among the lay-lords. The former were under a regular discipline and subordination to the papal authority. The latter were under no regular discipline or subordination, but almost always equally jealous of one another, and of the king. Though the tenants and retainers of the clergy, therefore, had both together been less numerous than those of the great lay-lords, and their tenants were probably much less numerous, yet their union would have rendered them more formidable. The hospitality and charity of the clergy too, not only gave them the command of a great temporal force, but increased very much the weight of their spiritual weapons. Those virtues procured them the highest respect and veneration among all the inferior ranks of people, of whom many were constantly, and almost all occasionally, fed by them. Every thing belonging or related to so popular an order, its possessions, its privileges, its doctrines, necessarily appeared sacred in the eyes of the common people, and every violation of them, whether real or pretended, the highest act of sacrilegious wickedness and profaneness. In this state of things, if the sovereign frequently found it difficult to resist the confederacy of a few of the great nobility, we cannot wonder that he should find it still more so to resist the united force of the clergy of his own dominions, supported by that of the clergy of all the neighbouring dominions. In such circumstances the wonder is, not that he was sometimes obliged to yield, but that he ever was able to resist.

Benefit of clergy and other privileges were the natural result. The privileges of the clergy in those ancient times (which to us who live in the present times appear the most absurd), their total exemption from the secular jurisdiction, for example, or what in England was called the benefit of clergy; were the natural or rather the necessary consequences of this state of things. How dangerous must it have been for the sovereign to attempt to punish a clergyman for any crime whatever, if his own order were disposed to protect him, and to represent either the proof as insufficient for convicting so holy a man, or the punishment as too severe to be inflicted upon one whose person had been rendered sacred by religion? The sovereign could, in such circumstances, do no better than leave him to be tried by the ecclesiastical courts, who, for the honour of their own order, were interested to restrain, as much as possible, every member of it from committing enormous crimes, or even from giving occasion to such gross scandal as might disgust the minds of the people.

The Church of Rome in the Middle Ages was the most formidable combination against liberty, reason and happiness.   In the state in which things were through the greater part of Europe during the tenth, eleventh, twelfth, and thirteenth centuries, and for some time both before and after that period, the constitution of the church of Rome may be considered as the most formidable combination that ever was formed against the authority and security of civil government, as well as against the liberty, reason, and happiness of mankind, which can flourish only where civil government is able to protect them. In that constitution the grossest delusions of superstition were supported in such a manner by the private interests of so great a number of people as put them out of all danger from any assault of human reason: because though human reason might perhaps have been able to unveil, even to the eyes of the common people, some of the delusions of superstition; it could never have dissolved the ties of private interest. Had this constitution been attacked by no other enemies but the feeble efforts of human reason, it must have endured for ever. But that immense and well-built fabric, which all the wisdom and virtue of man could never have shaken, much less have overturned, was by the natural course of things, first weakened, and[1] afterwards in part destroyed, and is now likely, in the course of a few centuries more, perhaps, to crumble into ruins altogether.

Its power was destroyed by the improvement of arts, manufactures and commerce.   The gradual improvements of arts, manufactures, and commerce, the same causes which destroyed the power of the great barons, destroyed in the same manner, through the greater part of Europe, the whole temporal power of the clergy. In the produce of arts, manufactures, and commerce, the clergy, like the great barons, found something for which they could exchange their rude produce, and thereby discovered the means of spending their whole revenues upon their own persons, without giving any considerable share of them to other people. Their charity became gradually less

---

[1] [Ed. 1 does not contain 'and'.]

extensive, their hospitality less liberal or less profuse. Their retainers became consequently less numerous, and by degrees dwindled away altogether. The clergy too, like the great barons, wished to get a better rent from their landed estates, in order to spend it, in the same manner, upon the gratification of their own private vanity and folly. But this increase of rent could be got only by granting leases to their tenants, who thereby became in a great measure independent of them. The ties of interest, which bound the inferior ranks of people to the clergy, were in this manner gradually broken and dissolved. They were even broken and dissolved sooner than those which bound the same ranks of people to the great barons: because the benefices of the church being, the greater part of them, much smaller than the estates of the great barons, the possessor of each benefice was much sooner able to spend the whole of its revenue upon his own person. During the greater part of the fourteenth and fifteenth centuries the power of the great barons was, through the greater part of Europe, in full vigour. But the temporal power of the clergy, the absolute command which they had once had over the great body of the people, was very much decayed. The power of the church was by that time very nearly reduced through the greater part of Europe to what arose from her spiritual authority; and even that spiritual authority was much weakened when it ceased to be supported by the charity and hospitality of the clergy. The inferior ranks of people no longer looked upon that order, as they had done before, as the comforters of their distress, and the relievers of their indigence. On the contrary, they were provoked and disgusted by the vanity, luxury, and expence of the richer clergy, who appeared to spend upon their own pleasures what had always before been regarded as the patrimony of the poor.

The sovereigns endeavoured to deprive the Pope of the disposal of the great benefices, and succeeded, especially in France and England. In this situation of things, the sovereigns in the different states of Europe endeavoured to recover the influence which they had once had in the disposal of the great benefices of the church, by procuring to the deans and chapters of each diocese the restoration of their ancient right of electing the bishop, and to the monks of each abbacy that of electing the abbot. The re-establishing of this ancient order was the object of several statutes enacted in England during the course of the fourteenth century, particularly of what is called the statute of provisors;[1] and

---

[1] [These nine words are not in ed. 1.]

of the Pragmatic sanction established in France in the fifteenth century. In order to render the election valid, it was necessary that the sovereign should both consent to it before-hand, and afterwards approve of the person elected; and though the election was still supposed to be free, he had, however, all the indirect means which his situation necessarily afforded him, of influencing the clergy in his own dominions. Other regulations of a similar tendency were established in other parts of Europe. But the power of the pope in the collation of the great benefices of the church seems, before the reformation, to have been nowhere so effectually and so universally restrained as in France and England. The Concordat afterwards, in the sixteenth century, gave to the kings of France the absolute right of presenting to all the great, or what are called the consistorial[1] benefices of the Gallican church.[2]

Ever since the French clergy have been less devoted to the Pope.   Since the establishment of the Pragmatic sanction and of the Concordat, the clergy of France have in general shown less respect to the decrees of the papal court than the clergy of any other catholic country. In all the disputes which their sovereign has had with the pope, they have almost constantly taken party with the former. This independency of the clergy of France upon the court of Rome, seems to be principally founded upon the Pragmatic sanction and the Concordat. In the earlier periods of the monarchy, the clergy of France appear to have been as much devoted to the pope as those of any other country. When Robert, the second prince of the Capetian race, was most unjustly excommunicated by the court of Rome, his own servants, it is said, threw the victuals which came from his table to the dogs, and refused to taste any thing themselves which had been polluted by the contact of a person in his situation.[3] They were taught to do so, it may very safely be presumed, by the clergy of his own dominions.

So even before the Reformation the clergy had less power and inclination to disturb the state.   The claim of collating to the great benefices of the church, a claim in defence of which the court of Rome had frequently shaken, and sometimes over-turned the thrones of some of the greatest sovereigns in Christendom, was in this manner either restrained or modified, or given up altogether, in many different

---

[1] [Ed. 1 reads 'great and consistorial'.]

[2] [Daniel, *Histoire de France*, 1755, tom. vii., pp. 158, 159; tom. ix., p. 40.]

[3] ['Il ne lui resta que deux domestiques pour le servir et lui préparer à manger, encore faisaient-ils passer par le feu les plats où il mangeait, et les vases où il buvait pour les

parts of Europe, even before the time of the reformation. As the
clergy had now less influence over the people, so the state had more
influence over the clergy. The clergy therefore had both less power
and less inclination to disturb the state.

The Reformation The authority of the church of Rome was in this
doctrines were state of declension, when the disputes which gave
recommended to the birth to the reformation, began in Germany, and
common people by soon spread themselves through every part of
the zeal of their Europe. The new doctrines were every where re-
teachers,
ceived with a high degree of popular favour. They were propagated with all that enthusiastic zeal which commonly animates the
spirit of party, when it attacks established authority. The teachers of
those doctrines, though perhaps in other respects not more learned
than many of the divines who defended the established church,
seem in general to have been better acquainted with ecclesiastical
history, and with the origin and progress of that system of opinions
upon which the authority of the church was established, and they
had thereby some advantage in almost every dispute. The austerity
of their manners gave them authority with the common people,
who contrasted the strict regularity of their conduct with the disorderly lives of the greater part of their own clergy. They possessed
too in a much higher degree than their adverssaries, all the arts of
popularity and of gaining proselytes, arts which the lofty and
dignified sons of the church had long neglected, as being to them in
a great measure useless. The reason of the new doctrines recommended them to some, their novelty to many; the hatred and
contempt of the established clergy to a still greater number; but
the zealous, passionate, and fanatical, though frequently coarse and
rustic, eloquence with which they were almost every where inculcated, recommended them to by far the greatest number.

and enabled sove- The success of the new doctrines was almost every
reigns on bad where so great, that the princes who at that time
terms with Rome happened to be on bad terms with the court of
to overturn the Rome, were by means of them easily enabled, in
Church with ease,
their own dominions, to overturn the church, which, having lost
the respect and veneration of the inferior ranks of people, could
make scarce any resistance. The court of Rome had disobliged some

purifier, comme ayant été fouillés par un homme retranché de la communion des
fidèles.'—*Ibid.*, tom. iii., pp. 305–306. Hénault's account is similar, *Nouvel Abrégé
chronologique*, 1768, tom. i., p. 114, A.D. 996.]

of the smaller princes in the northern parts of Germany, whom it had probably considered as too insignificant to be worth the managing. They universally, therefore, established the reformation in their own dominions. The tyranny of Christiern II. and of Troll archbishop of Upsal, enabled Gustavus Vasa to expel them both from Sweden. The pope favoured the tyrant and the archbishop, and Gustavus Vasa found no difficulty in establishing the reformation in Sweden. Christiern II. was afterwards deposed from the throne of Denmark, where his conduct had rendered him as odious as in Sweden. The pope, however, was still disposed to favour him, and Frederic of Holstein, who had mounted the throne in his stead, revenged himself by following the example of Gustavus Vasa. The magistrates of Berne and Zurich, who had no particular quarrel with the pope, established with great ease the reformation in their respective cantons, where just before some of the clergy had, by an imposture somewhat grosser than ordinary, rendered the whole order both odious and contemptible.

while in countries the sovereigns of which were friendly to Rome the Reformation was suppressed or obstructed. In this critical situation of its affairs, the papal court was at sufficient pains to cultivate the friendship of the powerful sovereigns of France and Spain, of whom the latter was at that time emperor of Germany. With their assistance it was enabled, though not without great difficulty and much bloodshed, either to suppress altogether, or to obstruct very much the progress of the reformation in their dominions. It was well enough inclined too to be complaisant to the king of England. But from the circumstances of the times, it could not be so without giving offence to a still greater sovereign, Charles V. king of Spain and emperor of Germany. Henry VIII. accordingly, though he did not embrace himself the greater part of the doctrines of the reformation, was yet enabled, by their general prevalence,[1] to suppress all the monasteries, and to abolish the authority of the church of Rome in his dominions. That he should go so far, though he went no further, gave some satisfaction to the patrons of the reformation, who having got possession of the government in the reign of his son and successor, completed without any difficulty the work which Henry VIII. had begun.

In some countries the Reformation overturned both church and state. In some countries, as in Scotland, where the government was weak, unpopular, and not very firmly established, the reformation was strong enough to

---

[1] [Ed. 1 reads 'by the general prevalence of those doctrines'.]

overturn, not only the church, but the state likewise for attempting to support the church.

The followers of the Reformation had no common authority like the court of Rome, and divided into Lutherans and Calvinists.

Among the followers of the reformation, dispersed in all the different countries of Europe, there was no general tribunal, which, like that of the court of Rome, or an œcumenical council, could settle all disputes among them, and with irresistible authority prescribe to all of them the precise limits of orthodoxy. When the followers of the reformation in one country, therefore, happened to differ from their brethren in another, as they had no common judge to appeal to, the dispute could never be decided; and many such disputes arose among them. Those concerning the government of the church, and the right of conferring ecclesiastical benefices, were perhaps the most interesting to the peace and welfare of civil society. They gave birth accordingly to the two principal parties or sects among the followers of the reformation, the Lutheran and Calvinistic sects, the only sects among them, of which the doctrine and discipline have ever yet been established by law in any part of Europe.

The Lutherans and the Church of England preferred episcopacy, and gave the disposal of benefices to the sovereign and other lay patrons.

The followers of Luther, together with what is called the church of England, preserved more or less of the episcopal government, established subordination among the clergy, gave the sovereign the disposal of all the bishoprics, and other consistorial benefices within his dominions, and thereby rendered him the real head of the church; and without depriving the bishop of the right of collating to the smaller benefices within his diocese, they, even to those benefices, not only admitted, but favoured the right of presentation both in the sovereign and in all other lay patrons. This sytem of church government was from the beginning favourable to peace and good order, and to submission to the civil sovereign. It has never, accordingly, been the occasion of any tumult or civil commotion in any country in which it has once been established. The church of England in particular has always valued herself, with great reason, upon the unexceptionable loyalty of her principles. Under such a government the clergy naturally endeavour to recommend themselves to the sovereign, to the court, and to the nobility and gentry of the country, by whose influence they chiefly expect to obtain preferment. They pay court to those patrons, sometimes, no doubt, by the vilest flattery and assentation, but frequently too by cultivating all those arts which best deserve, and which are therefore most likely to gain them the esteem of people of rank and fortune; by their knowledge in all the different branches of useful and ornamental learning, by the decent liberality of their manners, by the social good humour of their conversation, and by their avowed contempt of those absurd and hypocritical austerities which fanatics inculate and pretend to practise, in order to draw upon themselves the veneration, and upon the greater part of men of rank and fortune, who avow that they do not practise them, the abhorrence of the common people. Such a clergy, however, while they pay their court in this manner to the higher ranks of life, are very apt to neglect altogether the means of maintaining their influence and authority with the lower. They are listened to, esteemed and respected by their superiors; but before their inferiors they are frequently incapable of defending, effectually and to the conviction of such hearers, their own sober and moderate doctrines against the most ignorant enthusiast who chuses to attack them.

Zwinglian Calvinists gave the right of election to the people, and established equality among the clergy. The followers of Zuinglius, or more properly those of Calvin, on the contrary, bestowed upon the people of each parish, whenever the church became vacant, the right of electing their own pastor; and established at the same time the most perfect equality among the clergy. The former part of this institution, as long as it remained in vigour, seems to have been productive of nothing but disorder and confusion, and to have tended equally to corrupt the morals both of the clergy and of the people. The latter part seems never to have had any effects but what were perfectly agreeable.

Election by the people gave rise to great disorders, As long as the people of each parish preserved the right of electing their own pastors, they acted almost always under the influence of the clergy, and generally of the most factious and fanatical of the order. The clergy, in order to preserve their influence in those popular elections, became, or affected to become, many of them, fanatics themselves, encouraged fanaticism among the people, and gave the preference almost always to the most fanatical candidate. So small a matter as the appointment of a parish priest occasioned almost always a violent contest, not only in one parish, but in all the neighbouring parishes, who seldom failed to take part[1] in the quarrel. When the

----

[1] [Eds. 1 and 2 read 'take party'.]

parish happened to be situated in a great city, it divided all the inhabitants into two parties; and when that city happened either to
constitute itself a little republic, or to be the head and capital of a
little republic, as is the case with many of the considerable cities in
Switzerland and Holland, every paltry dispute of this kind, over and
above exasperating the animosity of all their other factions, threat-
ened to leave behind it both a new schism in the church, and a new
faction in the state. In those small republics, therefore, the magistrate
very soon found it necessary, for the sake of preserving the public
peace, to assume to himself the right of presenting to all vacant

and after trial was   benefices. In Scotland, the most extensive country in
abolished in Scot-   which this presbyterian form of church government
land, though the   has ever been established, the rights of patronage
concurrence of the
people is still   were in effect abolished by the act which established
required.   presbytery in the beginning of the reign of William
III.[1] That act at least put it in the power of certain classes of people
in each parish, to purchase, for a very small price, the right of
electing their own pastor. The constitution which this act established was allowed to subsist for about two and twenty years, but
was abolished by the 10th of queen Anne, ch. 12. on account of the
confusions and disorders which this more popular mode of election
had almost every where occasioned.[2] In so extensive a country as
Scotland, however, a tumult in a remote parish was not so likely to
give disturbance to government, as in a smaller state. The 10th of
queen Anne restored the rights of patronage. But though in Scotland the law gives the benefice without any exception to the person
presented by the patron; yet the church requires sometimes (for she
has not in this respect been very uniform in her decisions) a certain
concurrence of the people, before she will confer upon the presentee
what is called the cure of souls, or the ecclesiastical jurisdiction in the
parish. She sometimes at least, from an affected concern for the
peace of the parish, delays the settlement till this concurrence can be
procured. The private tampering of some of the neighbouring
clergy, sometimes to procure, but more frequently to prevent this
concurrence, and the popular arts which they cultivate in order to

[1] [The 'Act concerning Patronages,' 53rd of the second session of the first parliament
of William and Mary, is doubtless meant, but this is a separate Act from the 'Act
ratifying the Confession of Faith and settling Presbyterian Church Government,' *Acts
of the Parliaments of Scotland*, 1822, vol. ix., pp. 133, 196.]
[2] [The preamble of the Act mentions 'the great hardship upon the patrons' as well as
the 'great heats and divisions'.]

enable them upon such occasions to tamper more effectually, are perhaps the causes which principally keep up whatever remains of the old fanatical spirit, either in the clergy or in the people of Scotland.

The equality of the Presbyterian clergy makes them independent and respectable. The equality which the presbyterian form of church government establishes among the clergy, consists, first, in the equality of authority or ecclesiastical jurisdiction; and, secondly, in the equality of benefice. In all presbyterian churches the equality of authority is perfect: that of benefice is not so. The difference, however, between one benefice and another, is seldom so considerable as commonly to tempt the possessor even of the small one[1] to pay court to his patron, by the vile arts of flattery and assentation, in order to get a better. In all the presbyterian churches, where the rights of patronage are thoroughly established, it is by nobler and better arts that the established clergy in general endeavour to gain the favour of their superiors; by their learning, by the irreproachable regularity of their life, and by the faithful and diligent discharge of their duty. Their patrons even frequently complain of the independency of their spirit, which they are apt to construe into ingratitude for past favours, but which at worst, perhaps, is seldom any more than that indifference which naturally arises from the consciousness that no further favours of the kind are ever to be expected. There is scarce perhaps to be found any where in Europe a more learned, decent, independent, and respectable set of men, than the greater part of the presbyterian clergy of Holland, Geneva, Switzerland, and Scotland.

The mediocrity of their benefices gives them influence with the common people. Where the church benefices are all nearly equal, none of them can be very great, and this mediocrity of benefice, though it may no doubt be carried too far, has, however, some very agreeable effects. Nothing but the most exemplary morals can give dignity to a man of small fortune. The vices of levity and vanity necessarily render him ridiculous, and are, besides, almost as ruinous to him as they are to the common people. In his own conduct, therefore, he is obliged to follow that system of morals which the common people respect the most. He gains their esteem and affection by that plan of life which his own interest and situation would lead him to follow. The common people look upon him with that kindness with which we naturally regard one who approaches somewhat to our own condition, but

[1] [Ed. 1 reads 'small benefice'.]

who, we think, ought to be in a higher. Their kindness naturally provokes his kindness. He becomes careful to instruct them, and attentive to assist and relieve them. He does not even despise the prejudices of people who are disposed to be so favourable to him, and never treats them with those contemptuous and arrogant airs which we so often meet with in the proud dignitaries of opulent and well-endowed churches. The presbyterian clergy, accordingly, have more influence over the minds of the common people than perhaps the clergy of any other established church. It is accordingly in presbyterian countries only that we ever find the common people converted, without persecution, completely, and almost to a man, to the established church.

It also enables the universities to draw on them for professors, who are thus the most eminent men of letters. In countries where church benefices are the greater part of them very moderate, a chair in a university is generally a better establishment than a church benefice. The universities have, in this case, the picking and chusing of their members from all the churchmen of the country, who, in every country, constitute by far the most numerous class of men of letters. Where church benefices, on the contrary, are many of them very considerable, the church naturally draws from the universities the greater part of their eminent men of letters; who generally find some patron who does himself honour by procuring them church preferment. In the former situation we are likely to find the universities filled with the most eminent men of letters that are to be found in the country. In the latter we are likely to find few eminent men among them, and those few among the youngest members of the society, who are likely too to be drained away from it, before they can have acquired experience and knowledge enough to be of much use to it. It is observed by Mr. de Voltaire, that father Porrée, a jesuit of no great eminence in the republic of letters, was the only professor they had ever had in France whose works were worth the reading.[1] In a country which has produced so many eminent men of letters, it must appear somewhat singular, that scarce one of them should have been a professor in a university. The famous Gassendi was, in the beginning of his life, a professor in the university of Aix. Upon the

---

[1] [Voltaire's expression is not quite so strong as it is represented. He says in the catalogue of writers in the *Siècle de Louis XIV.*, 'Porée (Charles), né en Normandie en 1675, Jésuite, du petit nombre des professeurs qui ont eu de la célébrité chez les gens du monde. Eloquent dans le goût de Sénèque, poëte et très bel esprit. Son plus grand mérite fut de faire aimer les lettres et la vertu à ses disciples. Mort en 1741.']

first dawning of his genius, it was represented to him, that by going into the church he could easily find a much more quiet and comfortable subsistence, as well as a better situation for pursuing his studies; and he immediately followed the advice. The observation of Mr. de Voltaire may be applied, I believe, not only to France, but to all other Roman catholic countries. We very rarely find, in any of them, an eminent man of letters who is a professor in a university, except, perhaps, in the professions of law and physic; professions from which the church is not so likely to draw them. After the church of Rome, that of England is by far the richest and best endowed church in Christendom. In England, accordingly, the church is continually draining the universities of all their best and ablest members; and an old college tutor, who is known and distinguished in Europe as an eminent man of letters, is as rarely to be found there as in any Roman catholic country. In Geneva, on the contrary, in the protestant cantons of Switzerland, in the protestant countries of Germany, in Holland, in Scotland, in Sweden, and Denmark, the most eminent men of letters whom those countries have produced, have, not all indeed, but the far greater part of them, been professors in universities. In those countries the universities are continually draining the church of all its most eminent men of letters.

Eminent men of letters in Greece and Rome were mostly teachers. It may, perhaps, be worth while to remark, that, if we except the poets, a few orators, and a few historians, the far greater part of the other eminent men of letters, both of Greece and Rome, appear to have been either public or private teachers; generally either of philosophy or of rhetoric. This remark will be found to hold true from the days of Lysias and Isocrates, of Plato and Aristotle, down to those of Plutarch and Epictetus, of Suetonius and Quintilian.[1] To impose upon any man the necessity of teaching, year after year, any particular branch of science, seems, in reality, to be the most effectual method for rendering him completely master of it himself. By being obliged to go every year over the same ground, if he is good for any thing, he necessarily becomes, in a few years, well acquainted with every part of it: and if upon any particular point he should form too

[1] [*Quaere* as to Suetonius. Ed. 1 continues here 'Several of those whom we do not know with certainty to have been public teachers appear to have been private tutors. Polybius, we know, was private tutor to Scipio Æmilianus; Dionysius of Halicarnassus, there are some probable reasons for believing, was so to the children of Marcus and Quintus Cicero.']

hasty an opinion one year, when he comes in the course of his lectures to re-consider the same subject the year thereafter, he is very likely to correct it.[1] As to be a teacher of science is certainly the natural employment of a mere man of letters; so is it likewise, perhaps, the education which is most likely to render him a man of solid learning and knowledge. The mediocrity of church benefices naturally tends to draw the greater part of men of letters, in the country where it takes place, to the employment in which they can be the most useful to the public, and, at the same time, to give them the best education, perhaps, they are capable of receiving. It tends to render their learnings both as solid as possible, and as useful as possible.

The revenue of the church except that part which arises from endowments is a branch of that of the state. The revenue of every established church, such parts of it excepted as may arise from particular lands or manors, is a branch, it ought to be observed, of the general revenue of the state, which is thus diverted to a purpose very different from the defence of the state. The tythe, for example, is a real land-tax, which puts it out of the power of the proprietors of land to contribute so largely towards the defence of the state as they otherwise might be able to do. The rent of land, however, is, according to some, the sole fund, and according to others, the principal fund, from which, in all great monarchies, the exigencies of the state must be ultimately supplied. The more of this fund that is given to the church, the less, it is evident, can be spared to the state. It may be laid down as a certain maxim, that, all other things being supposed equal, the richer the church, the poorer must necessarily be, either the sovereign on the one hand, or the people on the other; and in all cases, the less able must the state be to defend itself.

In some cantons of Switzerland, the old revenue of the church now maintains both church and state. In several protestant countries, particularly in all the protestant cantons of Switzerland, the revenue which anciently belonged to the Roman catholic church, the tythes and church lands, has been found a fund sufficient, not only to afford competent salaries to the established clergy, but to defray, with little or no addition, all the other expences of the state. The magistrates of the powerful canton of Berne, in particular, have accumulated out of the savings from this fund a very large sum, supposed to amount to several millions, part of which is deposited in a public treasure, and part is placed at

---

[1] [The *Lectures* leave little doubt that this is a fragment of autobiography.]

interest in what are called the public funds of the different indebted nations of Europe; chiefly in those of France and Great Britain. What may be the amount of the whole expence which the church, either of Berne, or of any other protestant canton, costs the state, I

The whole revenue of the Church of Scotland is a trifling amount, but that church produces all possible good effects.

do not pretend to know. By a very exact account it appears, that, in 1755, the whole revenue of the clergy of the church of Scotland, including their glebe or church lands, and the rent of their manses or dwelling-houses, estimated according to a rea-

sonable valuation, amounted only to 68,514 l. 1 s. 5 d. $\frac{1}{12}$. This very moderate revenue affords a decent subsistence to nine hundred and forty-four ministers. The whole expence of the church, including what is occasionally laid out for the building and reparation of churches, and of the manses of ministers, cannot well be supposed to exceed eighty or eighty-five thousand pounds a-year. The most opulent church in Christendom does not maintain better the uniformity of faith, the fervour of devotion, the spirit of order, regularity, and austere morals in the great body of the people, than this very poorly endowed church of Scotland. All the good effects, both civil and religious, which an established church can be supposed

This is also true in a still higher degree of the Swiss Protestant churches.

to produce, are produced by it as completely as by any other. The greater part of the protestant churches of Switzerland, which in general are not

better endowed than the church of Scotland, produce those effects in a still higher degree. In the greater part of the protestant cantons, there is not a single person to be found who does not profess himself to be of the established church. If he professes himself to be of any other, indeed, the law obliges him to leave the canton. But so severe, or rather indeed so oppressive a law, could never have been executed in such free countries, had not the diligence of the clergy before-hand converted to the established church the whole body of the people, with the exception of, perhaps, a few individuals only. In some parts of Switzerland, accordingly, where, from the accidental union of a protestant and Roman catholic country, the conversion has not been so complete, both religions are not only tolerated but established by law.

Large revenue is unsuitable to the office of clergymen.

The proper performance of every service seems to require that its pay or recompence should be, as exactly as possible, proportioned to the nature of the service. If any service is very much under-paid, it is very apt to suffer by the meanness and incapacity of the greater part of those who are employed in it. If it is very much over-paid, it is apt to suffer, perhaps, still more by their negligence and idleness. A man of a large revenue, whatever may be his profession, thinks he ought to live like other men of large revenues; and to spend a great part of his time in festivity, in vanity, and in dissipation. But in a clergyman this train of life not only consumes the time which ought to be employed in the duties of his function, but in the eyes of the common people destroys almost entirely that sanctity of character which can alone enable him to perform those duties with proper weight and authority.

PART IV

Of the Expence of supporting the Dignity of the Sovereign

The expense of supporting the dignity of the sovereign increases as the expenditure of the people increases, Over and above the expence[1] necessary for enabling the sovereign to perform his several duties, a certain expence is requisite for the support of his dignity. This expence varies both with the different periods of improvement, and with the different forms of government.

In an opulent and improved society, where all the different orders of people are growing every day more expensive in their houses, in their furniture, in their tables, in their dress, and in their equipage; it cannot well be expected that the sovereign should alone hold out against the fashion. He naturally, therefore, or rather necessarily becomes more expensive in all those different articles too. His dignity even seems to require that he should become so.

and is greater in a monarchy than in a republic. As in point of dignity, a monarch is more raised above his subjects than the chief magistrate of any republic is ever supposed to be above his fellow-citizens; so a greater expence is necessary for supporting that higher dignity. We naturally expect more splendor in the court of a king, than in the mansion-house of a doge or burgo-master.

CONCLUSION

The expense of defence and of maintaining the The expence of defending the society, and that of supporting the dignity of the chief magistrate, are

---

[1] [Ed. 5 reads 'expences,' but this seems to be a misprint or misreading suggested by the fact that several expenses have been mentioned.]

dignity of the sovereign should be paid by genera contribution. both laid out for the general benefit of the whole society. It is reasonable, therefore, that they should be defrayed by the general contribution of the whole society, all the different members contributing, as nearly as possible, in proportion to their respective abilities.

But the expense of justice may be defrayed by fees of court, The expence of the administration of justice too, may, no doubt, be considered as laid out for the benefit of the whole society. There is no impropriety, therefore, in its being defrayed by the general contribution of the whole society. The persons, however, who give occasion to this expence are those who, by their injustice in one way or another, make it necessary to seek redress or protection from the courts of justice. The persons again most immediately benefited by this expence, are those whom the courts of justice either restore to their rights, or maintain in their rights. The expence of the administration of justice, therefore, may very properly be defrayed by the particular contribution of one or other, or both of those two different sets of persons, according as different occasions may require, that is, by the fees of court. It cannot be necessary to have recourse to the general contribution of the whole society, except for the conviction of those criminals who have not themselves any estate or fund sufficient for paying those fees.

and expenses of local benefit ought to be defrayed by local revenue. Those local or provincial expences of which the benefit is local or provincial (what is laid out, for example, upon the police of a particular town or district) ought to be defrayed by a local or provincial revenue, and ought to be no burden upon the general revenue of the society. It is unjust that the whole society should contribute towards an expence of which the benefit is confined to a part of the society.

The expense of roads may not unjustly be defrayed by general contribution, but better by tolls. The expence of maintaining good roads and communications is, no doubt, beneficial to the whole society, and may, therefore, without any injustice, be defrayed by the general contribution of the whole society. This expence, however, is most immediately and directly beneficial to those who travel or carry goods from one place to another, and to those who consume such goods. The turnpike tolls in England, and the duties called peages in other countries, lay it altogether upon those two different sets of people, and thereby discharge the general revenue of the society from a very considerable burden.

The expense of education and religious instruction may also be defrayed by general contribution, but better by fees and voluntary contribution.

The expence of the institutions for education and religious instruction, is likewise, no doubt, beneficial to the whole society, and may, therefore, without injustice, be defrayed by the general contribution of the whole society. This expence, however, might perhaps with equal propriety, and even with some advantage, be defrayed altogether by those who receive the immediate benefit of such education and instruction, or by the voluntary contribution of those who think they have occasion for either the one or the other.

Any deficiencies in the revenue of institutions beneficial to the whole society must be made up by general contribution.

When the institutions or public works which are beneficial to the whole society, either cannot be maintained altogether, or are not maintained altogether by the contribution of such particular members of the society as are most immediately benefited by them, the deficiency must in most cases be made up by the general contribution of the whole society. The general revenue of the society, over and above defraying the expence of defending the society, and of supporting the dignity of the chief magistrate, must make up for the deficiency of many particular branches of revenue. The sources of this general or public revenue, I shall endeavour to explain in the following chapter.

CHAPTER II

Of the Sources of the General or Public Revenue of the Society

All revenue comes from one of two sources: (1) property belonging to the sovereign; (2) the revenue of the people. The revenue which must defray, not only the expence of defending the society and of supporting the dignity of the chief magistrate, but all the other necessary expences of government, for which the constitution of the state has not provided any particular revenue, may be drawn, either, first, from some fund which peculiarly belongs to the sovereign or commonwealth, and which is independent of the revenue of the people; or, secondly, from the revenue of the people.

PART I

Of the Funds or Sources of Revenue which may peculiarly belong to the Sovereign or Commonwealth

The property may be in stock or land. The funds or sources of revenue which may peculiarly belong to the sovereign or commonwealth must consist, either in stock, or in land.

Revenue from stock may be profit or interest. The sovereign, like any other owner of stock, may derive a revenue from it, either by employing it himself, or by lending it. His revenue is in the one case profit, in the other interest.

Tartar and Arabian chiefs make profit from herds and flocks, The revenue of a Tartar or Arabian chief consists in profit. It arises principally from the milk and increase of his own herds and flocks, of which he himself superintends the management, and is the principal shepherd or herdsman of his own horde or tribe. It is, however, in this earliest and rudest state of civil government only that profit has ever made the principal part of the public revenue of a monarchical state.

Hamburg from a wine cellar and apothecary's shop, and many states from banks

Small republics have sometimes derived a considerable revenue from the profit of mercantile projects. The republic of Hamburgh is said to do so from the profits of a public wine cellar and apothecary's shop.[1] The state cannot be very great of which the sovereign has leisure to carry on the trade of a wine merchant or apothecary. The profit of a public bank has been a source of revenue to more considerable states. It has been so not only to Hamburgh, but to Venice and Amsterdam. A revenue of this kind has even by some people been thought not below the attention of so great an empire as that of Great Britain. Reckoning the ordinary dividend of the bank of England at five and a half per cent. and its capital at ten millions seven hundred and eighty thousand pounds, the neat annual profit, after paying the expence of management, must amount, it is said, to five hundred and ninety-two thousand nine hundred pounds. Government, it is pretended, could borrow this capital at three per cent. interest, and by taking the management of the bank into its own hands, might make a clear profit of two hundred and sixty-nine thousand five hundred pounds a year. The orderly, vigilant, and parsimonious administration of such aristocracies as those of Venice and Amsterdam, is extremely proper, it appears from experience, for the management of a mercantile project of this kind. But whether such a government as that of England; which, whatever may be its virtues, has never been famous for good œconomy; which, in time of peace, has generally conducted itself with the slothful and negligent profusion that is perhaps natural to monarchies; and in time of war has constantly acted with all the thoughtless extravagance that democracies are apt to fall into; could be safely trusted with the management of such a project, must at least be a good deal more doubtful.

and post offices.   The post office is properly a mercantile project.

---

[1] See Memoires concernant les Droits & Impositions en Europe: tome i. page 73. This work was compiled by the order of the court for the use of a commission employed for some years past in considering the proper means for reforming the finances of France. The account of the French taxes, which takes up three volumes in quarto, may be regarded as perfectly authentic. That of those of other European nations was compiled from such informations as the French ministers at the different courts could procure. It is much shorter, and probably not quite so exact as that of the French taxes. [The book is by Moreau de Beaumont, Paris, 1768-9, 4 vols., 4to. The correct title of vol. i. is *Mémoires concernant les Impositions et Droits en Europe*; vols. ii.–iv. are *Mémoires concernant les Impositions et Droits*, 2de. Ptie., *Impositions et Droits en France*. Smith obtained his copy through Turgot, and attached great value to it, believing it to be very rare. See Bonar, *Catalogue*, p. 10.]

The government advances the expence of establishing the different offices, and of buying or hiring the necessary horses or carriages, and is repaid with a large profit by the duties upon what is carried. It is perhaps the only mercantile project which has been successfully managed by, I believe, every sort of government. The capital to be advanced is not very considerable. There is no mystery in the business. The returns are not only certain, but immediate.

But generally princes are unsuccessful as traders. Princes, however, have frequently engaged in many other mercantile projects, and have been willing, like private persons, to mend their fortunes by becoming adventurers in the common branches of trade. They have scarce ever succeeded. The profusion with which the affairs of princes are always managed, renders it almost impossible that they should. The agents of a prince regard the wealth of their master as inexhaustible; are careless at what price they buy; are careless at what price they sell; are careless at what expence they transport his goods from one place to another. Those agents frequently live with the profusion of princes, and sometimes too, in spite of that profusion, and by a proper method of making up their accounts, acquire the fortunes of princes. It was thus, as we are told by Machiavel, that the agents of Lorenzo of Medicis, not a prince of mean abilities, carried on his trade. The republic of Florence was several times obliged to pay the debt into which their extravagance had involved him. He found it convenient, accordingly, to give up the business of merchant, the business to which his family had originally owed their fortune, and in the latter part of his life to employ both what remained of that fortune, and the revenue of the state of which he had the disposal, in projects and expences more suitable to his station.[1]

The two characters are inconsistent. No two characters seem more inconsistent than those of trader and sovereign. If the trading spirit of the English East India company renders them very bad sovereigns; the spirit of sovereignty seems to have rendered them equally bad traders. While they were traders only, they managed their trade successfully, and were able to pay from their profits a moderate dividend to the proprietors of their stock. Since they became sovereigns, with a revenue which, it is said, was originally more than three millions sterling, they have been obliged to beg the extraordinary assistance of government in order to avoid immediate

[1] [*Hist. of Florence*, bk. viii., *ad fin.*]

bankruptcy.[1] In their former situation, their servants in India considered themselves as the clerks of merchants: in their present situation, those servants consider themselves as the ministers of sovereigns.

Treasure may be lent to subjects or foreign states: A state may sometimes derive some part of its public revenue from the interest of money, as well as from the profits of stock. If it has amassed a treasure, it may lend a part of that treasure, either to foreign states, or to its own subjects.

Berne lends to foreign states, The canton of Berne derives a considerable revenue by lending a part of its treasure to foreign states; that is, by placing it in the public funds of the different indebted nations of Europe, chiefly in those of France and England.[2] The security of this revenue must depend, first, upon the security of the funds in which it is placed, or upon the good faith of the government which has the management of them; and, secondly, upon the certainty or probability of the continuance of peace with the debtor nation. In the case of a war, the very first act of hostility, on the part of the debtor nation, might be the forfeiture of the funds of its creditor. This policy of lending money to foreign states is, so far as I know, peculiar to the canton of Berne.

Hamburg has a pawnshop, The city of Hamburgh[3] has established a sort of public pawn-shop, which lends money to the subjects of the state upon pledges at six per cent. interest. This pawn-shop or Lombard, as it is called, affords a revenue, it is pretended, to the state of a hundred and fifty thousand crowns, which, at four-and-sixpence the crown, amounts to 33,750 l. sterling.

Pennsylvania lent paper money on land security. The government of Pensylvania, without amassing any treasure, invented a method of lending, not money indeed, but what is equivalent to money, to its subjects. By advancing to private people, at interest, and upon land security to double the value, paper bills of credit to be redeemed fifteen years after their date, and in the mean time made transferrable from hand to hand like bank notes, and declared by act of assembly to be a legal tender in all payments from one inhabitant of the province to another, it raised a moderate revenue, which went a considerable way towards defraying an annual expence of about

---

[1] [Details are given above, p. 274, but that is in a passage which appears first in ed. 3.]
[2] [Above, p. 336.]
[3] See Memoires concernant les Droits & Impositions en Europe; tome i. p. 73.

4,500 l. the whole ordinary expence of that frugal and orderly government. The success of an expedient of this kind must have depended upon three different circumstances; first, upon the demand for some other instrument of commerce, besides gold and silver money; or upon the demand for such a quantity of consumable stock, as could not be had without sending abroad the greater part of their gold and silver money, in order to purchase it; secondly, upon the good credit of the government which made use of this expedient; and, thirdly, upon the moderation with which it was used, the whole value of the paper bills of credit never exceeding that of the gold and silver money which would have been necessary for carrying on their circulation, had there been no paper bills of credit. The same expedient was upon different occasions adopted by several other American colonies: but, from want of this moderation, it produced, in the greater part of them, much more disorder than conveniency.

No great revenue can be derived from such a source. The unstable and perishable nature of stock and credit, however, render them unfit to be trusted to, as the principal funds of that sure, steady and permanent revenue, which can alone give security and dignity to government. The government of no great nation, that was advanced beyond the shepherd state, seems ever to have derived the greater part of its public revenue from such sources.

Revenue from land is much more important, Land is a fund of a more stable and permanent nature; and the rent of public lands, accordingly, has been the principal source of the public revenue of many a great nation that was much advanced beyond the shepherd state. From the produce or rent of the public lands, the ancient republics of Greece and Italy derived, for a long time, the greater part of that revenue which defrayed the necessary expences of the commonwealth. The rent of the crown lands constituted for a long time the greater part of the revenue of the ancient sovereigns of Europe.

especially when war cost little, as in ancient Greece and Italy, War and the preparation for war, are the two circumstances which in modern times occasion the greater part of the necessary expence of all great states. But in the ancient republics of Greece and Italy every citizen was a soldier, who both served and prepared himself for service at his own expence. Neither of those two circumstances, therefore, could occasion any very considerable expence to the state. The rent of a very moderate landed estate might be fully sufficient for defraying all the other necessary expences of government.

and in feudal times, when all expenses were small. In the ancient monarchies of Europe, the manners and customs of the times sufficiently prepared the great body of the people for war; and when they took the field, they were, by the condition of their feudal tenures, to be maintained, either at their own expence, or at that of their immediate lords, without bringing any new charge upon the sovereign. The other expences of government were, the greater part of them, very moderate. The administration of justice, it has been shown, instead of being a cause of expence, was a source of revenue. The labour of the country people, for three days before and for three days after harvest, was thought a fund sufficient for making and maintaining all the bridges, highways, and other public works which the commerce of the country was supposed to require. In those days the principal expence of the sovereign seems to have consisted in the maintenance of his own family and houshold. The officers of his houshold, accordingly, were then the great officers of state. The lord treasurer received his rents. The lord steward and lord chamberlain looked after the expence of his family. The care of his stables was committed to the lord constable and the lord marshal. His houses were all built in the form of castles, and seem to have been the principal fortresses which he possessed. The keepers of those houses or castles might be considered as a sort of military governors. They seem to have been the only military officers whom it was necessary to maintain in time of peace. In these circumstances the rent of a great landed estate might, upon ordinary occasions, very well defray all the necessary expences of government.

The present rent of all the land in the country would not suffice for the ordinary expenditure In the present state of the greater part of the civilized monarchies of Europe, the rent of all the lands in the country, managed as they probably would be if they all belonged to one proprietor, would scarce perhaps amount to the ordinary revenue which they levy upon the people even in peaceable times. The ordinary revenue of Great Britain, for example, including not only what is necessary for defraying the current expence of the year, but for paying the interest of the public debts, and for sinking a part of the capital of those debts, amounts to upwards of ten millions a year. But the land tax, at four shillings in the pound, falls short of two millions a year. This land tax, as it is called, however, is supposed to be one-fifth, not only of the rent of all the land, but of that of all the houses, and of the interest of all the capital stock of Great Britain, that part of it only excepted which is either lent to the public, or employed as farming stock in the cultivation of land. A very considerable part of the produce of this tax arises from the rent of houses, and the interest of capital stock. The land-tax of the city of London, for example, at four shillings in the pound, amounts to 123,399 l. 6 s. 7 d. That of the city of Westminster, to 63,092 l. 1 s. 5 d. That of the palaces of Whitehall and St. James's, to 30,754 l. 6 s. 3 d.[1] A certain proportion of the land-tax is in the same manner assessed upon all the other cities and towns corporate in the kingdom, and arises almost altogether, either from the rent of houses, or from what is supposed to be the interest of trading and capital stock. According to the estimation, therefore, by which Great Britain is rated to the land-tax, the whole mass of revenue arising from the rent of all the lands, from that of all the houses, and from the interest of all the capital stock, that part of it only excepted which is either lent to the public, or employed in the cultivation of land, does not exceed ten millions sterling a year, the ordinary revenue which government levies upon the people even in peaceable times. The estimation by which Great Britain is rated to the land-tax is, no doubt, taking the whole kingdom at an average, very much below the real value; though in several particular counties and districts it is said to be nearly equal to that value. The rent of the lands alone, exclusive of that of houses, and of the interest of stock, has by many people been estimated at twenty millions, an estimation made in a great measure at random, and which, I apprehend, is as likely to be above as below the truth.[2]

but if the whole of the land of the country were under the extravagant management of the state, the rent would be much reduced, But if the lands of Great Britain, in the present state of their cultivation, do not afford a rent of more than twenty millions a year, they could not well afford the half most probably not the fourth part of that rent, if they all belonged to a single proprietor, and were put under the negligent, expensive, and oppressive management of his factors and agents. The crown lands of Great Britain do not at present afford the fourth part of the rent, which could probably be drawn from them if they were the property of private persons. If the crown lands were more extensive, it is probable they would be still worse managed.

[1] [The figures are those of the Land Tax Acts.]
[2] [See on these estimates Sir Robert Giffen, *Growth of Capital*, 1889, pp. 89, 90.]

and the revenue of
the people would
be reduced by a
still greater amount. The revenue which the great body of the people derives from land is in proportion, not to the rent, but to the produce of the land. The whole annual produce of the land of every country, if we except what is reserved for seed, is either annually consumed by the great body of the people, or exchanged for something else that is consumed by them. Whatever keeps down the produce of the land below what it would otherwise rise to, keeps down the revenue of the great body of the people, still more than it does that of the proprietors of land. The rent of land, that portion of the produce which belongs to the proprietors, is scarce anywhere in Great Britain supposed to be more than a third part of the whole produce. If the land, which in one state of cultivation affords a rent of ten millions sterling a year, would in another afford a rent of twenty millions; the rent being, in both cases, supposed a third part of the produce; the revenue of the proprietors would be less than it otherwise might be by ten millions a year only; but the revenue of the great body of the people would be less than it otherwise might be by thirty millions a year, deducting only what would be necessary for seed. The population of the country would be less by the number of people which thirty millions a year, deducting always the seed, could maintain, according to the particular mode of living and expence which might take place in the different ranks of men among whom the remainder was distributed.

The sale of crown
lands would benefit
both sovereign and
people. Though there is not at present, in Europe, any civilized state of any kind which derives the greater part of its public revenue from the rent of lands which are the property of the state; yet, in all the great monarchies of Europe, there are still many large tracts of land which belong to the crown. They are generally forest; and sometimes forest where, after travelling several miles, you will scarce find a single tree; a mere waste and loss of country in respect both of produce and population. In every great monarchy of Europe the sale of the crown lands would produce a very large sum of money, which, if applied to the payment of the public debts, would deliver from mortgage a much greater revenue than any which those lands have ever afforded to the crown. In countries where lands, improved and cultivated very highly, and yielding at the time of sale as great a rent as can easily be got from them, commonly sell at thirty years purchase; the unimproved, uncultivated, and low-rented crown lands

might well be expected to sell at forty, fifty or sixty years purchase. The crown might immediately enjoy the revenue which this great price would redeem from mortgage. In the course of a few years it would probably enjoy another revenue. When the crown lands had become private property, they would, in the course of a few years, become well-improved and well-cultivated. The increase of their produce would increase the population of the country, by augmenting the revenue and consumption of the people. But the revenue which the crown derives from the duties of customs and excise, would necessarily increase with the revenue and consumption of the people.

The revenue from crown lands costs the people more than any other. The revenue which, in any civilized monarchy, the crown derives from the crown lands, though it appears to cost nothing to individuals, in reality costs more to the society than perhaps any other equal revenue which the crown enjoys. It would, in all cases, be for the interest of the society to replace this revenue to the crown by some other equal revenue, and to divide the lands among the people, which could not well be done better, perhaps, than by exposing them to public sale.

Public parks, etc., are the only lands which should belong to the sovereign. Lands, for the purposes of pleasure and magnificence, parks, gardens, public walks, &c. possessions which are every where considered as causes of expence, not as sources of revenue, seem to be the only lands which, in a great and civilized monarchy, ought to belong to the crown.

The greater part of the sovereign's expense must be defrayed by taxes. Public stock and public lands, therefore, the two sources of revenue which may peculiarly belong to the sovereign or commonwealth, being both improper and insufficient funds for defraying the necessary expence of any great and civilized state; it remains that this expence must, the greater part of it, be defrayed by taxes of one kind or another; the people contributing a part of their own private revenue in order to make up a public revenue to the sovereign or commonwealth.

PART II

Of Taxes

Taxes may be intended to fall on rent, profit, or wages, or upon all The private revenue of individuals, it has been shewn in the first book of this Inquiry, arises ultimately from three different sources; Rent, Profit, *three sorts of revenue.* and Wages. Every tax must finally be paid from some one or other of those three different sorts of revenue, or from all of them indifferently. I shall endeavour to give the best account I can, first, of those taxes, which, it is intended, should fall upon rent; secondly, of those which, it is intended, should fall upon profit; thirdly, of those which, it is intended, should fall upon wages; and, fourthly, of those which, it is intended, should fall indifferently upon all those three different sources of private revenue. The particular consideration of each of these four different sorts of taxes will divide the second part of the present chapter into four articles, three of which will require several other subdivisions. Many of those taxes, it will appear from the following review, are not finally paid from the fund, or source of revenue, upon which it was intended they should fall.

There are four maxims with regard to taxes in general, Before I enter upon the examination of particular taxes, it is necessary to premise the four following maxims with regard to taxes in general.

(1) equality, I. The subjects of every state ought to contribute towards the support of the government, as nearly as possible, in proportion to their respective abilities; that is, in proportion to the revenue which they respectively enjoy under the protection of the state. The expence of government to the individuals of a great nation, is like the expence of management to the joint tenants of a great estate, who are all obliged to contribute in proportion to their respective interests in the estate. In the observation or neglect of this maxim consists, what is called the equality or inequality of taxation. Every tax, it must be observed once for all, which falls finally upon one only of the three sorts of revenue above mentioned, is necessarily unequal, in so far as it does not affect the other two. In the following examination of different taxes I shall seldom take much further notice of this sort of inequality, but shall, in most cases, confine my observations to that inequality which is occasioned by a particular tax falling unequally even upon that particular sort of private revenue which is affected by it.

(2) certainty, II. The tax which each individual is bound to pay ought to be certain, and not arbitrary. The time of payment, the manner of payment, the quantity to be paid, ought all to be clear and plain to the contributor, and to every other person. Where it is otherwise, every person subject to the tax is put more or less in the power of the tax-gatherer, who can either aggravate the tax upon

any obnoxious contributor, or extort, by the terror of such aggravation, some present or perquisite to himself. The uncertainty of taxation encourages the insolence and favours the corruption of an order of men who are naturally unpopular, even where they are neither insolent nor corrupt. The certainty of what each individual ought to pay is, in taxation, a matter of so great importance, that a very considerable degree of inequality, it appears, I believe, from the experience of all nations, is not near so great an evil as a very small degree of uncertainty.

(3) convenience of payment, III. Every tax ought to be levied at the time, or in the manner, in which it is most likely to be convenient for the contributor to pay it. A tax upon the rent of land or of houses, payable at the same term at which such rents are usually paid, is levied at the time when it is most likely to be convenient for the contributor to pay; or, when he is most likely to have wherewithal to pay. Taxes upon such consumable goods as are articles of luxury, are all finally paid by the consumer, and generally in a manner that is very convenient for him. He pays them by little and little, as he has occasion to buy the goods. As he is at liberty too, either to buy, or not to buy, as he pleases, it must be his own fault if he ever suffers any considerable inconveniency from such taxes.

and (4) economy in collection, IV. Every tax ought to be so contrived as both to take out and to keep out of the pockets of the people as little as possible, over and above what it brings into the public treasury of the state. A tax may either take out or keep out of the pockets of the people a great deal more than it brings into the public treasury, in the four following ways. First, the levying of it may require a great number of officers, whose salaries may eat up the greater part of the produce of the tax, and whose perquisites may impose another additional tax upon the people. Secondly, it may obstruct the industry of the people, and discourage them from applying to certain branches of business which might give maintenance and employment to great multitudes. While it obliges the people to pay, it may thus diminish, or perhaps destroy, some of the funds which might enable them more easily to do so. Thirdly, by the forfeitures and other penalties which those unfortunate individuals incur who attempt unsuccessfully to evade the tax, it may frequently ruin them, and thereby put an end to the benefit which the community might have received from the employment of their capitals. An injudicious tax offers a great temptation to smuggling.

But the penalties of smuggling must rise in proportion to the temptation. The law, contrary to all the ordinary principles of justice, first creates the temptation, and then punishes those who yield to it; and it commonly enhances the punishment too in proportion to the very circumstance which ought certainly to alleviate it, the temptation to commit the crime.[1] Fourthly, by subjecting the people to the frequent visits and the odious examination of the tax-gatherers, it may expose them to much unnecessary trouble, vexation, and oppression; and though vexation is not, strictly speaking, expence, it is certainly equivalent to the expence at which every man would be willing to redeem himself from it. It is in some one or other of these four different ways that taxes are frequently so much more burdensome to the people than they are beneficial to the sovereign.

which have recom-
mended themselves
to all nations.
The evident justice and utility of the foregoing maxims have recommended them more or less to the attention of all nations. All nations have endeavoured, to the best of their judgment, to render their taxes as equal as they could contrive; as certain, as convenient to the contributor, both in the time and in the mode of payment, and in proportion to the revenue which they brought to the prince, as little burdensome to the people.[2] The following short review of some of the principal taxes which have taken place in different ages and countries will show, that the endeavours of all nations have not in this respect been equally successful.

ARTICLE I

Taxes upon Rent. Taxes upon the Rent of Land

A tax on the rent
of land may be on
a constant or
variable valuation.
A tax upon the rent of land may either be imposed according to a certain canon, every district being valued at a certain rent, which valuation is not

---

[1] See Sketches of the History of Man [1774, by Henry Home, Lord Kames, vol. i.] page 474 & seq. [This author at the place quoted gives six 'general rules' as to taxation:

1. 'That wherever there is an opportunity of smuggling taxes ought to be moderate.'
2. 'That taxes expensive in the levying ought to be avoided.'
3. 'To avoid arbitrary taxes.'
4. 'To remedy' inequality of riches 'as much as possible, by relieving the poor and burdening the rich.'
5. 'That every tax which tends to impoverish the nation ought to be rejected with indignation.'
6. 'To avoid taxes that require the oath of party.']

[2] [In ed. 1 'as they could contrive' comes here instead of three lines earlier.

afterwards to be altered; or it may be imposed in such a manner as to vary with every variation in the real rent of the land, and to rise or fall with the improvement or declension of its cultivation.

If on a constant valuation it becomes unequal, like the British land tax.   A land-tax which, like that of Great Britain, is assessed upon each district according to[1] a certain invariable canon, though it should be equal at the time of its first establishment, necessarily becomes unequal in process of time, according to the unequal degrees of improvement or neglect in the cultivation of the different parts of the country. In England, the valuation according to which the different counties and parishes were assessed to the land-tax by the 4th of William and Mary was very unequal even at its first establishment. This tax, therefore, so far offends against the first of the four maxims above-mentioned. It is perfectly agreeable to the other three. It is perfectly certain. The time of payment for the tax, being the same as that for the rent, is as convenient as it can be to the contributor. Though the landlord is in all cases the real contributor, the tax is commonly advanced by the tenant, to whom the landlord is obliged to allow it in the payment of the rent. This tax is levied by a much smaller number of officers than any other which affords nearly the same revenue. As the tax upon each district does not rise with the rise of the rent, the sovereign does not share in the profits of the landlord's improvements. Those improvements sometimes contribute,[2] indeed, to the discharge of the other landlords of the district. But the aggravation of the tax, which this may sometimes occasion upon a particular estate, is always so very small, that it never can discourage those improvements,[3] nor keep down the produce of the land below what it would otherwise rise to. As it has no tendency to diminish the quantity, it can have none to raise the price of that produce. It does not obstruct the industry of the people. It subjects the landlord to no other inconveniency besides the unavoidable one of paying the tax.

Circumstances have made the constant valuation favourable to the British   The advantage, however, which the landlord has derived from the invariable constancy of the valuation by which all the lands of Great Britain are

---

[1] [Ed. 1 reads 'is imposed according to'. For the origin of the stereotyped assessment of the land tax, see Cannan, *Hist. of Local Rates in England*, 1896, pp. 114–119.]

[2] [Ed. 2 reads 'They contribute'.]

[3] [Ed. 1, beginning after 'the same revenue,' six lines higher up reads 'As the tax does not rise with the rise of the rent, the sovereign does not share in the profits of the landlord's improvements. The tax therefore does not discourage those improvements.']

landlords, the country having prospered and rents risen,
rated to the land-tax, has been principally owing to some circumstances altogether extraneous to the nature of the tax.

It has been owing in part to the great prosperity of almost every part of the country, the rents of almost all the estates of Great Britain having, since the time when this valuation was first established, been continually rising, and scarce any of them having fallen. The landlords, therefore, have almost all gained the difference between the tax which they would have paid, according to the present rent of their estates, and that which they actually pay according to the ancient valuation. Had the state of the country been different, had rents been gradually falling in consequence of the declension of cultivation, the landlords would almost all have lost this difference. In the state of things which has happened to take place since the revolution, the constancy of the valuation has been advantageous to the landlord and hurtful to the sovereign. In a different state of things it might have been advantageous to the sovereign and hurtful to the landlord.

and the value of money and silver remained uniform.
As the tax is made payable in money, so the valuation of the land is expressed in money. Since the establishment of this valuation the value of silver has been pretty uniform, and there has been no alteration in the standard of the coin either as to weight or fineness. Had silver risen considerably in its value, as it seems to have done in the course of the two centuries which preceded the discovery of the mines of America, the constancy of the valuation might have proved very oppressive to the landlord. Had silver fallen considerably in its value, as it certainly did for about a century at least after the discovery of those mines, the same constancy of valuation would have reduced very much this branch of the revenue of the sovereign. Had any considerable alteration been made in the standard of the money, either by sinking the same quantity of silver to a lower denomination, or by raising it to a higher; had an ounce of silver, for example, instead of being coined into five shillings and twopence, been coined, either into pieces which bore so low a denomination as two shillings and seven-pence, or into pieces which bore so high a one as ten shillings and four-pence, it would in the one case have hurt the revenue of the proprietor, in the other that of the sovereign.

The constancy of valuation might have been very
In circumstances, therefore, somewhat different from those which have actually taken place, this

inconvenient to one or other of the parties. constancy of valuation might have been a very great inconveniency, either to the contributors, or to the commonwealth. In the course of ages such circumstances, however, must, at some time or other, happen. But though empires, like all the other works of men, have all hitherto proved mortal, yet every empire aims at immortality. Every constitution, therefore, which it is meant should be as permanent as the empire itself, ought to be convenient, not in certain circumstances only, but in all circumstances; or ought to be suited, not to those circumstances which are transitory, occasional, or accidental, but to those which are necessary and therefore always the same.

The French economists recommend a tax varying with the rent. A tax upon the rent of land which varies with every variation of the rent, or which rises and falls according to the improvement or neglect of cultivation, is recommended by that sect of men of letters in France, who call themselves the œconomists, as the most equitable of all taxes. All taxes, they pretend, fall ultimately upon the rent of land, and ought therefore to be imposed equally upon the fund which must finally pay them. That all taxes ought to fall as equally as possible upon the fund which must finally pay them, is certainly true. But without entering into the disagreeable discussion of the metaphysical arguments by which they support their very ingenious theory, it will sufficiently appear, from the following review, what are the taxes which fall finally upon the rent of the land, and what are those which fall finally upon some other fund.

In the Venetian territory rented lands are taxed 10 per cent. and lands cultivated by the proprietor 8 per cent. In the Venetian territory all the arable lands which are given in lease to farmers are taxed at a tenth of the rent.[1] The leases are recorded in a public register which is kept by the officers of revenue in each province or district. When the proprietor cultivates his own lands, they are valued according to an equitable estimation, and he is allowed a deduction of one-fifth of the tax, so that for such lands he pays only eight instead of ten per cent. of the supposed rent.

Such a land tax is more equal but is not so certain, and is more troublesome and expensive than the British. A land-tax of this kind is certainly more equal than the land-tax of England. It might not, perhaps, be altogether so certain, and the assessment of the tax might frequently occasion a good deal more trouble to the landlord. It might too be a good deal more expensive in the levying.

[1] Memoires concernant les Droits [tom. i.] p. 240, 241.

The uncertainty and expense could be diminished. Such a system of administration, however, might perhaps be contrived as would, in a great measure, both prevent this uncertainty and moderate this expence.

Leases should be registered, The landlord and tenant, for example, might jointly be obliged to record their lease in a public register. Proper penalties might be enacted against concealing or misrepresenting any of the conditions; and if part of those penalties were to be paid to either of the two parties who informed against and convicted the other of such concealment or misrepresentation, it would effectually deter them from combining together in order to defraud the public revenue. All the conditions of the lease might be sufficiently known from such a record.

fines taxed higher than rent, Some landlords, instead of raising the rent, take a fine for the renewal of the lease. This practice is in most cases the expedient of a spendthrift, who for a sum of ready money sells a future revenue of much greater value. It is in most cases, therefore, hurtful to the landlord. It is frequently hurtful to the tenant, and it is always hurtful to the community. It frequently takes from the tenant so great a part of his capital, and thereby diminishes so much his ability to cultivate the land, that he finds it more difficult to pay a small rent than it would otherwise have been to pay a great one. Whatever diminishes his ability to cultivate, necessarily keeps down, below what it would otherwise have been, the most important part of the revenue of the community. By rendering the tax upon such fines a good deal heavier than upon the ordinary rent, this hurtful practice might be discouraged, to the no small advantage of all the different parties concerned, of the landlord, of the tenant, of the sovereign, and of the whole community.

conditions of cultivation should be discouraged by high valuation, Some leases prescribe to the tenant a certain mode of cultivation, and a certain succession of crops during the whole continuance of the lease. This condition, which is generally the effect of the landlord's conceit of his own superior knowledge (a conceit in most cases very ill founded), ought always to be considered as an additional rent; as a rent in service instead of a rent in money. In order to discourage the practice, which is generally a foolish one, this species of rent might be valued rather high, and consequently taxed somewhat higher than common money rents.

rents payable in kind should be valued high, Some landlords, instead of a rent in money, require a rent in kind, in corn, cattle, poultry, wine, oil, &c. others again require a rent in service. Such rents are always more hurtful to the tenant than beneficial to the landlord. They either take more or keep more out of the pocket of the former, than they put into that of the latter. In every country where they take place, the tenants are poor and beggarly, pretty much according to the degree in which they take place. By valuing, in the same manner, such rents rather high, and consequently taxing them somewhat higher than common money rents, a practice which is hurtful to the whole community might perhaps be sufficiently discouraged.

and an abatement given to landlords cultivating a certain extent of their land. When the landlord chose to occupy himself a part of his own lands, the rent might be valued according to an equitable arbitration of the farmers and landlords in the neighbourhood, and a moderate abatement of the tax might be granted to him, in the same manner as in the Venetian territory; provided the rent of the lands which he occupied did not exceed a certain sum. It is of importance that the landlord should be encouraged to cultivate a part of his own land. His capital is generally greater than that of the tenant, and with less skill he can frequently raise a greater produce. The landlord can afford to try experiments, and is generally disposed to do so. His unsuccessful experiments occasion only a moderate loss to himself. His successful ones contribute to the improvement and better cultivation of the whole country. It might be of importance, however, that the abatement of the tax should encourage him to cultivate to a certain extent only. If the landlords should, the greater part of them, be tempted to farm the whole of their own lands, the country (instead of sober and industrious tenants, who are bound by their own interest to cultivate as well as their capital and skill will allow them) would be filled with idle and profligate bailiffs, whose abusive management would soon degrade the cultivation, and reduce the annual produce of the land, to the diminution, not only of the revenue of their masters, but of the most important part of that of the whole society.

Such a system would free the tax from inconvenient uncertainty and encourage improvement. Such a system of administration might, perhaps, free a tax of this kind from any degree of uncertainty which could occasion either oppression or inconveniency to the contributor; and might at the same time serve to introduce into the common management of land such a plan or policy, as might contribute a good deal to the general improvement and good cultivation of the country.

The extra expense of levying the tax would be inconsiderable. The expence of levying a land-tax, which varied with every variation of the rent, would no doubt be somewhat greater than that of levying one which was always rated according to a fixed valuation. Some additional expence would necessarily be incurred both by the different register offices which it would be proper to establish in the different districts of the country, and by the different valuations which might occasionally be made of the lands which the proprietor chose to occupy himself. The expence of all this, however, might be very moderate, and much below what is incurred in the levying of many other taxes, which afford a very inconsiderable revenue in comparison of what might easily be drawn from a tax of this kind.

The value of improvements should be for a fixed term exempt from taxation, The discouragement which a variable land-tax of this kind might give to the improvement of land, seems to be the most important objection which can be made to it. The landlord would certainly be less disposed to improve, when the sovereign, who contributed nothing to the expence, was to share in the profit of the improvement. Even this objection might perhaps be obviated by allowing the landlord, before he began his improvement, to ascertain, in conjunction with the officers of revenue, the actual value of his lands, according to the equitable arbitration of a certain number of landlords and farmers in the neighbourhood, equally chosen by both parties; and by rating him according to this valuation for such a number of years, as might be fully sufficient for his complete indemnification. To draw the attention of the sovereign towards the improvement of the land, from a regard to the increase of his own revenue, is one of the principal advantages proposed by this species of land-tax. The term, therefore, allowed for the indemnification of the landlord, ought not to be a great deal longer than what was necessary for that purpose; lest the remoteness of the interest should discourage too much this attention. It had better, however, be somewhat too long than in any respect too short. No incitement to the attention of the sovereign can ever counterbalance the smallest discouragement to that of the landlord. The attention of the sovereign can be at best but a very general and vague consideration of what is likely to contribute to the better cultivation of the greater part of his dominions. The attention of the landlord is a particular and minute consideration of what is likely to be the most advantageous application of every inch of ground upon his estate. The principal attention of the sovereign ought to be to encourage, by every means in his power, the attention both of the landlord and of the farmer; by allowing both to pursue their own interest in their own way, and according to their own judgment; by giving to both the most perfect security that they shall enjoy the full recompence of their own industry; and by procuring to both the most extensive market for every part of their produce, in consequence of establishing the easiest and safest communications both by land and by water, through every part of his own dominions, as well as the most unbounded freedom of exportation to the dominions of all other princes.

and the tax would then be as little inconvenient as is possible. If by such a system of administration a tax of this kind could be so managed as to give, not only no discouragement, but, on the contrary, some encouragement to the improvement of land, it does not appear likely to occasion any other inconveniency to the landlord, except always the unavoidable one of being obliged to pay the tax.

It would adjust itself to all changes. In all the variations of the state of the society, in the improvement and in the declension of agriculture; in all the variations in the value of silver, and in all those in the standard of the coin, a tax of this kind would, of its own accord and without any attention of government, readily suit itself to the actual situation of things, and would be equally just and equitable in all those different changes. It would, therefore, be much more proper to be established as a perpetual and unalterable regulation, or as what is called a fundamental law of the commonwealth, than any tax which was always to be levied according to a certain valuation.

Some states make a survey and valuation for the land tax, Some states, instead of the simple and obvious expedient of a register of leases, have had recourse to the laborious and expensive one of an actual survey and valuation of all the lands in the country. They have suspected, probably, that the lessor and lessee, in order to defraud the public revenue, might combine to conceal the real terms of the lease. Doomsday-book seems to have been the result of a very accurate survey of this kind.

for example, Prussia, In the ancient dominions of the king of Prussia, the land-tax is assessed according to an actual survey and valuation, which is reviewed and altered from time to time.[1] According to that valuation, the lay proprietors pay from twenty to twenty-five per cent. of their revenue. Ecclesiastics from forty to forty-five per cent. The survey and valuation of Silesia was made *Silesia,* by order of the present king; it is said with great accuracy. According to that valuation, the lands belonging to the bishop of Breslaw are taxed at twenty-five per cent. of their rent. The other revenues of the ecclesiastics of both religions, at fifty per cent. The commanderies of the Teutonic order, and of that of Malta, at forty per cent. Lands held by a noble tenure, at thirty-eight and one-third per cent. Lands held by a base tenure, at thirty-five and one-third per cent.[2]

and Bohemia. The survey and valuation of Bohemia is said to have been the work of more than a hundred years. It was not perfected till after the peace of 1748, by the orders of the present empress queen.[3] The survey of the dutchy of Milan, which was begun in the time of Charles VI., was not perfected till after 1760. It is esteemed one of the most accurate that has ever been made. The survey of Savoy and Piedmont was executed under the orders of the late king of Sardinia.[4]

Under the Prussian land tax the church lands are taxed higher than the rest; in some states they are taxed lower than the rest. In the dominions of the king of Prussia the revenue of the church is taxed much higher than that of lay proprietors.[5] The revenue of the church is, the greater part of it, a burden upon the rent of land. It seldom happens that any part of it is applied towards the improvement of land; or is so employed as to contribute in any respect towards increasing the revenue of the great body of the people. His Prussian majesty had probably, upon that account, thought it reasonable, that it should contribute a good deal more towards relieving the exigencies of the state. In some countries the lands of the church are exempted from all taxes. In others they are taxed more lightly than other lands. In the dutchy of Milan, the lands which the church possessed before 1575, are rated to the tax at a third only of their value.[6]

Differences are often made between land held by noble and base tenures. In Silesia, lands held by a noble tenure are taxed three per cent. higher than those held by a base tenure. The honours and privileges of different

---

[1] Memoires concernant les Droits, &c. tome i. p. 114, 115, 116, &c.
[2] [*Ibid.*, pp. 117–119.]   [3] Id. p. 83, 84 [and 79].
[4] Id. p. 280, &c. also p. 287, &c. to 316.
[5] [As stated just above.]   [6] [*Mémoires*, tom. i., p. 282.]

kinds annexed to the former, his Prussian majesty had probably imagined, would sufficiently compensate to the proprietor a small aggravation of the tax; while at the same time the humiliating inferiority of the latter would be in some measure alleviated by being taxed somewhat more lightly. In other countries, the system of taxation, instead of alleviating, aggravates this inequality. In the dominions of the king of Sardinia, and in those provinces of France which are subject to what is called the real or predial taille, the tax falls altogether upon the lands held by a base tenure. Those held by a noble one are exempted.

A land tax assessed according to a general survey and valuation soon becomes unequal, A land-tax assessed according to a general survey and valuation, how equal soever it may be at first, must, in the course of a very moderate period of time, become unequal. To prevent its becoming so would require the continual and painful attention of government to all the variations in the state and produce of every different farm in the country. The governments of Prussia, of Bohemia, of Sardinia, and of the dutchy of Milan, actually exert an attention of this kind; an attention so unsuitable to the nature of government, that it is not likely to be of long continuance, and which, if it is continued, will probably in the long-run occasion much more trouble and vexation than it can possibly bring relief to the contributors.

as in Montauban. In 1666, the generality of Montauban was assessed to the Real or predial taille[1] according, it is said, to a very exact survey and valuation.[2] By 1727, this assessment had become altogether unequal. In order to remedy this inconveniency, government has found no better expedient than to impose upon the whole generality an additional tax of a hundred and twenty thousand livres. This additional tax is rated upon all the different districts subject to the taille according to the old assessment. But it is levied only upon those which in the actual state of things are by that assessment under-taxed, and it is applied to the relief of those which by the same assessment are over-taxed. Two districts, for example, one of which ought in the actual state of things to be taxed at nine hundred, the other at eleven hundred livres, are by the old assessment both taxed at a thousand livres. Both these districts are by the additional tax rated at eleven hundred livres each. But this additional tax is levied only upon the district under-charged, and it is applied

---

[1] [Misprinted 'tallie' here and six lines lower down in eds. 2–5.]
[2] Memoires concernant les Droits &c. tome ii. p. 139, &c. [pp. 145–147].

altogether to the relief of that over-charged, which consequently pays only nine hundred livres. The government neither gains nor loses by the additional tax, which is applied altogether to remedy the inequalities arising from the old assessment. The application is pretty much regulated according to the discretion of the intendant of the generality, and must, therefore, be in a great measure arbitrary.

Taxes which are proportioned, not to the Rent, but to the Produce of Land

Taxes on the produce are finally paid by the landlord,

Taxes upon the produce of land are in reality taxes upon the rent; and though they may be originally advanced by the farmer, are finally paid by the landlord. When a certain portion of the produce is to be paid away for a tax, the farmer computes, as well as he can, what the value of this portion is, one year with another, likely to amount to, and he makes a proportionable abatement in the rent which he agrees to pay to the landlord. There is no farmer who does not compute beforehand what the church tythe, which is a land-tax of this kind, is, one year with another, likely to amount to.

and are very unequal taxes,

The tythe, and every other land-tax of this kind, under the appearance of perfect equality, are very unequal taxes; a certain portion of the produce being, in different situations, equivalent to a very different portion of the rent. In some very rich lands the produce is so great, that the one half of it is fully sufficient to replace to the farmer his capital employed in cultivation, together with the ordinary profits of farming stock in the neighbourhood. The other half, or, what comes to the same thing, the value of the other half, he could afford to pay as rent to the landlord, if there was no tythe. But if a tenth of the produce is taken from him in the way of tythe, he must require an abatement of the fifth part of his rent, otherwise he cannot get back his capital with the ordinary profit. In this case the rent of the landlord, instead of amounting to a half, or five-tenths of the whole produce, will amount only to four-tenths of it. In poorer lands, on the contrary, the produce is sometimes so small, and the expence of cultivation so great, that it requires four-fifths of the whole produce to replace to the farmer his capital with the ordinary profit. In this case, though there was no tythe, the rent of the landlord could amount to no more than one-fifth or two-tenths of the whole produce. But if the farmer pays one-tenth of the produce in the way of tythe, he must require an equal abatement of the rent of the landlord, which will thus be reduced to one-tenth only of the whole produce. Upon the rent of rich lands, the tythe may sometimes be a tax of no more than one-fifth part, or four shillings in the pound; whereas upon that of poorer lands, it may sometimes be a tax of one-half, or of ten shillings in the pound.

which discourage both improvement and good cultivation. The tythe, as it is frequently a very unequal tax upon the rent, so it is always a great discouragement both to the improvements of the landlord and to the cultivation of the farmer. The one cannot venture to make the most important, which are generally the most expensive improvements; nor the other to raise the most valuable, which are generally too the most expensive crops; when the church, which lays out no part of the expence, is to share so very largely in the profit. The cultivation of madder was for a long time confined by the tythe to the United Provinces, which, being presbyterian countries, and upon that account exempted from this destructive tax, enjoyed a sort of monopoly of that useful dying drug against the rest of Europe. The late attempts to introduce the culture of this plant into England, have been made only in consequence of the statute which enacted that five shillings an acre should be received in lieu of all manner of tythe upon madder.[1]

They form the principal revenue of the state in many Asiatic countries, As through the greater part of Europe, the church, so in many different countries of Asia, the state, is principally supported by a land-tax, proportioned, not to the rent, but to the produce of the land. In China, the principal revenue of the sovereign consists in a tenth part of the produce of all the lands of the empire. This tenth part, however, is estimated so very moderately, that, in many provinces, it is said not to exceed a thirtieth part of the ordinary produce. The land-tax or land-rent which used to be paid to the Mahometan government of Bengal, before that country fell into the hands of the English East India company, is said to have amounted to about a fifth part of the produce. The land-tax of ancient Egypt is said likewise to have amounted to a fifth part.[2]

and are said to interest the sovereign in the In Asia, this sort of land-tax is said to interest the sovereign in the improvement and cultivation of

---

[1] [31 Geo. II., c. 12, continued by 5 Geo. III., c. 18.]   [2] [Genesis xlvii. 26.]

improvement and cultivation of land there. land.[1] The sovereigns of China, those of Bengal while under the Mahometan government, and those of ancient Egypt, are said accordingly to have been extremely attentive to the making and maintaining of good roads and navigable canals, in order to increase, as much as possible, both the quantity and value of every part of the produce of the land, by procuring to every part of it the most extensive market which their own dominions could afford. The tythe of the church is divided into such small portions, that no one of its proprietors can have any interest of this kind. The parson of a parish could never find his account in making a road or canal to a distant part of the country, in order to extend the market for the produce of his own particular parish. Such taxes, when destined for the maintenance of the state, have some advantages which may serve in some measure to balance their inconveniency. When destined for the maintenance of the church, they are attended with nothing but inconveniency.

They may be in kind or in money. Taxes upon the produce of land may be levied, either in kind; or, according to a certain valuation, in money.

Collection in kind is quite unsuitable for public revenue. The parson of a parish, or a gentleman of small fortune who lives upon his estate, may sometimes, perhaps, find some advantage in receiving, the one his tythe, and the other his rent, in kind. The quantity to be collected, and the district within which it is to be collected, are so small, that they both can oversee, with their own eyes, the collection and disposal of every part of what is due to them. A gentleman of great fortune, who lived in the capital, would be in danger of suffering much by the neglect, and more by the fraud of his factors and agents, if the rents of an estate in a distant province were to be paid to him in this manner. The loss of the sovereign, from the abuse and depredation of his tax-gatherers, would necessarily be much greater. The servants of the most careless private person are, perhaps, more under the eye of their master than those of the most careful prince; and a public revenue, which was paid in kind, would suffer so much from the mismanagement of the collectors, that a very small part of what was levied upon the people would ever arrive at the treasury of the prince. Some part of the public revenue of China, however, is said to be paid in this manner. The Mandarins and other tax-gatherers will, no doubt, find their advantage in continuing the practice of a

---

[1] [Above, p. 204.]

payment which is so much more liable to abuse than any payment in money.

A money tax on produce may be always the same or may vary with the market price of produce. A tax upon the produce of land which is levied in money, may be levied either according to a valuation which varies with all the variations of the market price; or according to a fixed valuation, a bushel of wheat, for example, being always valued at one and the same money price, whatever may be the state of the market. The produce of a tax levied in the former way, will vary only according to the variations in the real produce of the land according to the improvement or neglect of cultivation. The produce of a tax levied in the latter way will vary, not only according to the variations in the produce of the land, but according to both those in the value of the precious metals, and those in the quantity of those metals which is at different times contained in coin of the same denomination. The produce of the former will always bear the same proportion to the value of the real produce of the land. The produce of the latter may, at different times, bear very different proportions to that value.

When a certain sum of money is to be paid in compensation for the tax it becomes exactly like the English land tax. When, instead either of a certain portion of the produce of land, or of the price of a certain portion, a certain sum of money is to be paid in full compensation for all tax or tythe; the tax becomes, in this case, exactly of the same nature with the land-tax of England. It neither rises nor falls with the rent of the land. It neither encourages nor discourages improvement. The tythe in the greater part of those parishes which pay what is called a modus in lieu of all other tythe, is a tax of this kind. During the Mahometan government of Bengal, instead of the payment in kind of the fifth[1] part of the produce, a modus, and, it is said, a very moderate one, was established in the greater part of the districts or zemindaries of the country. Some of the servants of the East India company, under pretence of restoring the public revenue to its proper value, have, in some provinces, exchanged this modus for a payment in kind. Under their management this change is likely both to discourage cultivation, and to give new opportunities for abuse in the collection of the public revenue, which has fallen very much below what it was said to have been, when it first fell under the management of the company. The servants of the company may, perhaps, have

---

[1] [Eds. 1–4 read 'a fifth'.]

profited by this change, but at the expence, it is probable, both of
their masters and of the country.

Taxes upon the Rent of Houses

House rent consists   The rent of a house may be distinguished into two
of two parts,   parts, of which the one may very properly be called
the Building rent; the other is commonly called the Ground rent.

building rent,   The building rent is the interest or profit of the
capital expended in building the house. In order to put the trade of
a builder upon a level with other trades, it is necessary that this rent
should be sufficient, first, to pay him the same interest which he
would have got for his capital if he had lent it upon good security;
and, secondly, to keep the house in constant repair, or, what comes
to the same thing, to replace, within a certain term of years, the
capital which had been employed in building it. The building rent,
or the ordinary profit of building, is, therefore, every where regulated by the ordinary interest of money. Where the market rate of
interest is four per cent. the rent of a house which, over and above
paying the ground rent, affords six, or six and a half per cent. upon
the whole expence of building, may perhaps afford a sufficient profit
to the builder. Where the market rate of interest is five per cent., it
may perhaps require seven or seven and a half per cent. If, in proportion to the interest of money, the trade of the builder affords at any
time a much greater profit than this, it will soon draw so much
capital from other trades as will reduce the profit to its proper level.
If it affords at any time much less than this, other trades will soon
draw so much capital from it as will again raise that profit.

and ground rent.   Whatever part of the whole rent of a house is over
and above what is sufficient for affording this reasonable profit,
naturally goes to the ground-rent; and where the owner of the
ground and the owner of the building are two different persons, is,
in most cases, completely paid to the former. This surplus rent is the
price which the inhabitant of the house pays for some real or supposed advantage of the situation. In country houses, at a distance
from any great town, where there is plenty of ground to chuse
upon, the ground rent is scarce any thing, or no more than what the
ground which the house stands upon would pay if employed in
agriculture. In country villas in the neighbourhood of some great
town, it is sometimes a good deal higher; and the peculiar conve-

niency or beauty of situation is there frequently very well paid for. Ground rents are generally highest in the capital, and in those particular parts of it where there happens to be the greatest demand for houses, whatever be the reason of that demand, whether for trade and business, for pleasure and society, or for mere vanity and fashion.

A tax on house rent paid by the tenant falls partly on the inhabitant and partly on the owner of the ground,

A tax upon house-rent, payable by the tenant and proportioned to the whole rent of each house, could not, for any considerable time at least, affect the building rent. If the builder did not get his reasonable profit, he would be obliged to quit the trade; which, by raising the demand for building, would in a short time bring back his profit to its proper level with that of other trades. Neither would such a tax fall altogether upon the ground-rent; but it would divide itself in such a manner as to fall, partly upon the inhabitant of the house, and partly upon the owner of the ground.

as may be shown by an example.

Let us suppose, for example, that a particular person judges that he can afford for house-rent an expence of sixty pounds a year; and let us suppose too that a tax of four shillings in the pound, or of one-fifth, payable by the inhabitant, is laid upon house-rent. A house of sixty pounds rent will in this case cost him seventy-two pounds a year, which is twelve pounds more than he thinks he can afford. He will, therefore, content himself with a worse house, or a house of fifty pounds rent, which, with the additional ten pounds that he must pay for the tax, will make up the sum of sixty pounds a year, the expence which he judges he can afford; and in order to pay the tax he will give up a part of the additional conveniency which he might have had from a house of ten pounds a year more rent. He will give up, I say, a part of this additional conveniency; for he will seldom be obliged to give up the whole, but will, in consequence of the tax, get a better house for fifty pounds a year, than he could have got if there had been no tax. For as a tax of this kind, by taking away this particular competitor, must diminish the competition for houses of sixty pounds rent, so it must likewise diminish it for those of fifty pounds rent, and in the same manner for those of all other rents, except the lowest rent, for which it would for some time increase the competition. But the rents of every class of houses for which the competition was diminished, would necessarily be more or less reduced. As no part of this reduction, however, could, for any considerable time at least, affect the building rent; the whole of it must in the long-run necessarily fall upon the ground-rent. The final payment of this tax, therefore, would fall, partly upon the inhabitant of the house, who, in order to pay his share, would be obliged to give up a part of his conveniency; and partly upon the owner of the ground, who, in order to pay his share, would be obliged to give up a part of his revenue. In what proportion this final payment would be divided between them, it is not perhaps very easy to ascertain. The division would probably be very different in different circumstances, and a tax of this kind might, according to those different circumstances, affect very unequally both the inhabitant of the house and the owner of the ground.

On the inhabitants it would be an unequal tax, falling heaviest on the rich. The inequality with which a tax of this kind might fall upon the owners of different ground-rents, would arise altogether from the accidental inequality of this division. But the inequality with which it might fall upon the inhabitants of different houses would arise, not only from this, but from another cause. The proportion of the expence of house-rent to the whole expence of living, is different in the different degrees of fortune. It is perhaps highest in the highest degree, and it diminishes gradually through the inferior degrees, so as in general to be lowest in the lowest degree. The necessaries of life occasion the great expence of the poor. They find it difficult to get food, and the greater part of their little revenue is spent in getting it. The luxuries and vanities of life occasion the principal expence of the rich; and a magnificent house embellishes and sets off to the best advantage all the other luxuries and vanities which they possess. A tax upon house-rents, therefore, would in general fall heaviest upon the rich; and in this sort of inequality there would not, perhaps, be any thing very unreasonable. It is not very unreasonable that the rich should contribute to the public expence, not only in proportion to their revenue, but something more than in that proportion.

It would be like a tax on any other consumable commodity, it would be very much in proportion to men's whole expense, and it would produce considerable revenue. The rent of houses, though it in some respects resembles the rent of land, is in one respect essentially different from it. The rent of land is paid for the use of a productive subject. The land which pays it produces it. The rent of houses is paid for the use of an unproductive subject. Neither the house nor the ground which it stands upon produce any thing. The person who pays the rent, therefore, must draw it from some other source of revenue, distinct from and independent of this subject.[1] A tax upon the rent of houses, so far as it falls upon the inhabitants, must be drawn from the same source as the rent itself, and must be paid from their revenue, whether derived from the wages of labour, the profits of stock, or the rent of land. So far as it falls upon the inhabitants, it is one of those taxes which fall, not upon one only, but indifferently upon all the three different sources of revenue; and is in every respect of the same nature as a tax upon any other sort of consumable commodities. In general there is not, perhaps, any one article of expence or consumption by which the liberality or narrowness of a man's whole expence can be better judged of, than by his house-rent. A proportional tax upon this particular article of expence might, perhaps, produce a more considerable revenue than any which has hitherto been drawn from it in any part of Europe. If the tax indeed was very high, the greater part of people would endeavour to evade it, as much as they could, by contenting themselves with smaller houses, and by turning the greater part of their expence into some other channel.

The rent could be easily ascertained. Empty houses should be exempt, and houses occupied by their proprietor should be assessed at their letting value. The rent of houses might easily be ascertained with sufficient accuracy, by a policy of the same kind with that which would be necessary for ascertaining the ordinary rent of land. Houses not inhabited ought to pay no tax. A tax upon them would fall altogether upon the proprietor, who would thus be taxed for a subject which afforded him neither conveniency nor revenue. Houses inhabited by the proprietor ought to be rated, not according to the expence which they might have cost in building, but according to the rent which an equitable arbitration might judge them likely to bring, if leased to a tenant. If rated according to the expence which they may have cost in building, a tax of three or four shillings in the pound, joined with other taxes, would ruin almost all the rich and great families of this, and, I believe, of every other civilized country. Whoever will examine, with attention, the different town and country houses of some of the richest and greatest families in this country, will find that, at the rate of only six and a half, or seven per cent. upon the original expence of building, their house-rent is nearly equal to the whole neat rent of their estates. It is the accumulated expence of several successive generations, laid out upon objects of great beauty and magnificence,

[1] [Above, vol. i., p. 296.]

indeed; but, in proportion to what they cost, of very small exchangeable value.[1]

Ground rent is a still more proper subject of taxation than building rent, Ground-rents are a still more proper subject of taxation than the rent of houses. A tax upon ground-rents would not raise the rents of houses. It would fall altogether upon the owner of the ground-rent, who acts always as a monopolist, and exacts the greatest rent which can be got for the use of his ground. More or less can be got for it according as the competitors happen to be richer or poorer, or can afford to gratify their fancy for a particular spot of ground at a greater or smaller expence. In every country the greatest number of rich competitors is in the capital, and it is there accordingly that the highest ground-rents are always to be found. As the wealth of those competitors would in no respect be increased by a tax upon ground-rents, they would not probably be disposed to pay more for the use of the ground. Whether the tax was to be advanced by the inhabitant, or by the owner of the ground, would be of little importance. The more the inhabitant was obliged to pay for the tax, the less he would incline to pay for the ground; so that the final payment of the tax would fall altogether upon the owner of the ground-rent. The ground-rents of uninhabited houses ought to pay no tax.

as no discouragement is given to industry by the taxation of the rent of land. Both ground-rents and the ordinary rent of land are a species of revenue which the owner, in many cases, enjoys without any care or attention of his own. Though a part of this revenue should be taken from him in order to defray the expences of the state, no discouragement will thereby be given to any sort of industry. The annual produce of the land and labour of the society, the real wealth and revenue of the great body of the people, might be the same after such a tax as before. Ground-rents, and the ordinary rent of land, are, therefore, perhaps, the species of revenue which can best bear to have a peculiar tax imposed upon them.

Ground rents are even a more proper subject of taxation Ground-rents seem, in this respect, a more proper subject of peculiar taxation than even the ordinary

---

[1] Since the first publication of this book, a tax nearly upon the above-mentioned principles has been imposed. [This note appears first in ed. 3. The tax was first imposed by 18 Geo. III., c. 26, and was at the rate of 6d. in the pound on houses of £5 and under £50 annual value, and 1s. in the pound on houses of higher value, but by 19 Geo. III., c. 59, the rates were altered to 6d. in the pound on houses of £5 and under £20 annual value, 9d. on those of £20 and under £40, and 1s. on those of £40 and upwards.]

than ordinary land rents. rent of land. The ordinary rent of land is, in many cases, owing partly at least to the attention and good management of the landlord. A very heavy tax might discourage too much this attention and good management. Ground-rents, so far as they exceed the ordinary rent of land, are altogether owing to the good government of the sovereign, which, by protecting the industry either of the whole people, or of the inhabitants of some particular place, enables them to pay so much more than its real value for the ground which they build their houses upon; or to make to its owner so much more than compensation for the loss which he might sustain by this use of it. Nothing can be more reasonable than that a fund which owes its existence to the good government of the state, should be taxed peculiarly, or should contribute something more than the greater part of other funds, towards the support of that government.

Ground rents are nowhere separately taxed, but might be. Though, in many different countries of Europe, taxes have been imposed upon the rent of houses, I do not know of any in which ground-rents have been considered as a separate subject of taxation. The contrivers of taxes have, probably, found some difficulty in ascertaining what part of the rent ought to be considered as ground-rent, and what part ought to be considered as building-rent. It should not, however, seem very difficult to distinguish those two parts of the rent from one another.

House rent is legally liable to the British land tax. In Great Britain the rent of houses is supposed to be taxed in the same proportion as the rent of land, by what is called the annual land-tax. The valuation, according to which each different parish and district is assessed to this tax, is always the same. It was originally extremely unequal, and it still continues to be so. Through the greater part of the kingdom this tax falls still more lightly upon the rent of houses than upon that of land. In some few districts only, which were originally rated high, and in which the rents of houses have fallen considerably, the land-tax of three or four shillings in the pound, is said to amount to an equal proportion of the real rent of houses.[1] Untenanted houses, though by law subject to the tax, are, in most districts, exempted from it by the favour of the assessors; and this exemption sometimes occasions some little variation in the rate of particular houses, though that of the district is always the same. Improvements of rent, by

[1] [Ed. 1 reads 'the houses'.]

new buildings, repairs, &c.; go to the discharge of the district, which occasions still further variations in the rate of particular houses.[1]

In Holland there is a tax on the capital value of houses. In the province of Holland[2] every house is taxed at two and a half per cent. of its value, without any regard either to the rent which it actually pays, or to the circumstance of its being tenanted or untenanted. There seems to be a hardship in obliging the proprietor to pay a tax for an untenanted house, from which he can derive no revenue, especially so very heavy a tax. In Holland, where the market rate of interest does not exceed three per cent. two and a half per cent. upon the whole value of the house, must, in most cases, amount to more than a third of the building-rent, perhaps of the whole rent. The valuation, indeed, according to which the houses are rated, though very unequal, is said to be always below the real value. When a house is rebuilt, improved or enlarged, there is a new valuation, and the tax is rated accordingly.

House taxes in England have not been proportioned to the rent, The contrivers of the several taxes which in England have, at different times, been imposed upon houses, seem to have imagined that there was some great difficulty in ascertaining, with tolerable exactness, what was the real rent of every house. They have regulated their taxes, therefore, according to some more obvious circumstance, such as they had probably imagined would, in most cases, bear some proportion to the rent.

but first to the number of hearths, The first tax of this kind was hearth-money; or a tax of two shillings upon every hearth. In order to ascertain how many hearths were in the house, it was necessary that the tax-gatherer should enter every room in it. This odious visit rendered the tax odious. Soon after the revolution, therefore, it was abolished as a badge of slavery.

and later to the number of windows. The next tax of this kind was, a tax of two shillings upon every dwelling house inhabited. A house with ten windows to pay four shillings more. A house with twenty windows and upwards to pay eight shillings. This tax was afterwards so far altered, that houses with twenty windows, and with less than thirty, were ordered to pay ten shillings, and those with thirty windows and upwards to pay twenty shillings. The number of windows can, in most cases, be counted from the outside, and, in all cases, without entering every room in the house. The visit of the

---

[1] [Ed. 1 does not contain this sentence.]
[2] Memoires concernant les Droits, &c. [tom. i.], p. 223.

tax-gatherer, therefore, was less offensive in this tax than in the hearth-money.

The present window-tax augments gradually from 2d. per window to 2s. This tax was afterwards repealed, and in the room of it was established the window-tax, which has undergone too several alterations and augmentations. The window-tax, as it stands at present (January, 1775), over and above the duty of three shillings upon every house in England, and of one shilling upon every house in Scotland, lays a duty upon every window, which, in England, augments gradually from two-pence, the lowest rate, upon houses with not more than seven windows; to two shillings, the highest rate, upon houses with twenty-five windows and upwards.

Window taxes are objectionable, chiefly on the ground of inequality. The principal objection to all such taxes is their inequality, an inequality of the worst kind, as they must frequently fall much heavier upon the poor than upon the rich. A house of ten pounds rent in a country town may sometimes have more windows than a house of five hundred pounds rent in London; and though the inhabitant of the former is likely to be a much poorer man than that of the latter, yet so far as his contribution is regulated by the window-tax, he must contribute more to the support of the state. Such taxes are, therefore, directly contrary to the first of the four maxims above mentioned. They do not seem to offend much against any of the other three.

Taxes on houses lower rents. The natural tendency of the window-tax, and of all other taxes upon houses, is to lower rents. The more a man pays for the tax, the less, it is evident, he can afford to pay for the rent. Since the imposition of the window-tax, however, the rents of houses have upon the whole risen, more or less, in almost every town and village of Great Britain, with which I am acquainted. Such has been almost every where the increase of the demand for houses, that it has raised the rents more than the window-tax could sink them; one of the many proofs of the great prosperity of the country, and of the increasing revenue of its inhabitants. Had it not been for the tax, rents would probably have risen still higher.

ARTICLE II

Taxes upon Profit, or upon the Revenue arising from Stock

Profit is divided into interest and surplus over interest. The revenue or profit arising from stock naturally divides itself into two parts; that which pays the interest, and which belongs to the owner of the stock; and that surplus part which is over and above what is necessary for paying the interest.

The surplus is not taxable.　This latter part of profit is evidently a subject not taxable directly. It is the compensation, and in most cases it is no more than a very moderate compensation, for the risk and trouble of employing the stock. The employer must have this compensation, otherwise he cannot, consistently with his own interest, continue the employment. If he was taxed directly, therefore, in proportion to the whole profit, he would be obliged either to raise the rate of his profit, or to charge the tax upon the interest of money; that is, to pay less interest. If he raised the rate of his profit in proportion to the tax, the whole tax, though it might be advanced by him, would be finally paid by one or other of two different sets of people, according to the different ways in which he might employ the stock of which he had the management. If he employed it as a farming stock in the cultivation of land, he could raise the rate of his profit only by retaining a greater portion, or, what comes to the same thing, the price of a greater portion of the produce of the land; and as this could be done only by a reduction of rent, the final payment of the tax would fall upon the landlord. If he employed it as a mercantile or manufacturing stock, he could raise the rate of his profit only by raising the price of his goods; in which case the final payment of the tax would fall altogether upon the consumers of those goods. If he did not raise the rate of his profit, he would be obliged to charge the whole tax upon that part of it which was allotted for the interest of money. He could afford less interest for whatever stock he borrowed, and the whole weight of the tax would in this case fall ultimately upon the interest of money. So far as he could not relieve himself from the tax in the one way, he would be obliged to relieve himself in the other.

Interest at first sight seems as fit to be taxed as rent,　The interest of money seems at first sight a subject equally capable of being taxed directly as the rent of land. Like the rent of land, it is a neat produce which remains after completely compensating the whole risk and trouble of employing the stock. As a tax upon the rent of land cannot raise rents; because the neat produce which remains after replacing the stock of the farmer, together with his reasonable profit, cannot be greater after the tax than before it; so, for the same reason, a tax upon the interest of money could not raise the rate of interest;

the quantity of stock or money in the country, like the quantity of land, being supposed to remain the same after the tax as before it. The ordinary rate of profit, it has been shewn in the first book,[1] is every where regulated by the quantity of stock to be employed in proportion to the quantity of the employment, or of the business which must be done by it. But the quantity of the employment, or of the business to be done by stock, could neither be increased nor diminished by any tax upon the interest of money. If the quantity of the stock to be employed therefore, was neither increased nor diminished by it, the ordinary rate of profit would necessarily remain the same. But the portion of this profit necessary for compensating the risk and trouble of the employer, would likewise remain the same; that risk and trouble being in no respect altered. The residue, therefore, that portion which belongs to the owner of the stock, and which pays the interest of money, would necessarily remain the same too. At first sight, therefore, the interest of money seems to be a subject as fit to be taxed directly as the rent of land.

but it is not, since,   There are, however, two different circumstances which render the interest of money a much less proper subject of direct taxation than the rent of land.

(1) the amount received by an individual cannot be readily and exactly ascertained,   First, the quantity and value of the land which any man possesses can never be a secret, and can always be ascertained with great exactness. But the whole amount of the capital stock which he possesses is almost always a secret, and can scarce ever be ascertained with tolerable exactness. It is liable, besides, to almost continual variations. A year seldom passes away, frequently not a month, sometimes scarce a single day, in which it does not rise or fall more or less. An inquisition into every man's private circumstances, and an inquisition which, in order to accommodate the tax to them, watched overall the fluctuations of his fortune, would be a source of such continual and endless vexation as no people could support.

and (2) stock may be removed from the country imposing the tax.   Secondly, land is a subject which cannot be removed, whereas stock easily may. The proprietor of land is necessarily a citizen of the particular country in which his estate lies. The proprietor of stock is properly a citizen of the world, and is not necessarily attached to any particular

[1] [Chap. ix.]

country. He would be apt to abandon the country in which he was exposed to a vexatious inquisition, in order to be assessed to a burdensome tax, and would remove his stock to some other country where he could either carry on his business, or enjoy his fortune more at his ease. By removing his stock he would put an end to all the industry which it had maintained in the country which he left. Stock cultivates land; stock employs labour. A tax which tended to drive away stock from any particular country, would so far tend to dry up every source of revenue, both to the sovereign and to the society. Not only the profits of stock, but the rent of land and the wages of labour, would necessarily be more or less diminished by its removal.

Where such a tax exists it is levied on a loose and very low valuation, The nations, accordingly, who have attempted to tax the revenue arising from stock, instead of any severe inquisition of this kind, have been obliged to content themselves with some very loose, and, therefore, more or less arbitrary estimation. The extreme inequality and uncertainty of a tax assessed in this manner, can be compensated only by its extreme moderation, in consequence of which every man finds himself rated so very much below his real revenue, that he gives himself little disturbance though his neighbour should be rated somewhat lower.

as under the English land tax. By what is called the land-tax in England, it was intended that stock should be taxed in the same proportion as land. When the tax upon land was at four shillings in the pound, or at one-fifth of the supposed rent, it was intended that stock should be taxed at one-fifth of the supposed interest. When the present annual land-tax was first imposed, the legal rate of interest was six per cent. Every hundred pounds stock, accordingly, was supposed to be taxed at twenty-four shillings, the fifth part of six pounds. Since the legal rate of interest has been reduced to five per cent.[1] every hundred pounds stock is supposed to be taxed at twenty shillings only. The sum to be raised, by what is called the land-tax, was divided between the country and the principal towns. The greater part of it was laid upon the country; and of what was laid upon the towns, the greater part was assessed upon the houses. What remained to be assessed upon the stock or trade of the towns (for the stock upon the land was not meant to be taxed) was very much below the real value of that stock or trade. Whatever in-

[1] [Above, vol. i., pp. 99. 100.]

equalities, therefore, there might be in the original assessment, gave little disturbance. Every parish and district still continues to be rated for its land, its houses, and its stock, according to the original assessment; and the almost universal prosperity of the country, which in most places has raised very much the value of all these, has rendered those inequalities of still less importance now. The rate too upon each district continuing always the same, the uncertainty of this tax, so far as it might be assessed upon the stock of any individual, has been very much diminished, as well as rendered of much less consequence. If the greater part of the lands of England are not rated to the land-tax at half their actual value, the greater part of the stock of England is, perhaps, scarce rated at the fiftieth part of its actual value. In some towns the whole land-tax is assessed upon houses; as in Westminster, where stock and trade are free. It is otherwise in London.

Inquisition is avoided.   In all countries a severe inquisition into the circumstances of private persons has been carefully avoided.

At Hamburg each inhabitant privately assesses himself on oath.   At Hamburgh[1] every inhabitant is obliged to pay to the state, one-fourth per cent. of all that he possesses; and as the wealth of the people of Hamburgh consists principally in stock, this tax may be considered as a tax upon stock. Every man assesses himself, and, in the presence of the magistrate, puts annually into the public coffer a certain sum of money, which he declares upon oath to be one-fourth per cent. of all that he possesses, but without declaring what it amounts to, or being liable to any examination upon that subject.[2] This tax is generally supposed to be paid with great fidelity. In a small republic, where the people have entire confidence in their magistrates, are convinced of the necessity of the tax for the support of the state, and believe that it will be faithfully applied to that purpose, such conscientious and voluntary payment may sometimes be expected. It is not peculiar to the people of Hamburgh.

---

[1] Memoires concernant les Droits, tome i. p. 74.

[2] [The *Mémoires* only say 'La taille consiste dans le quart pour cent que tout habitant, sans exception, est obligé de payer de tout ce qu'il possède en meubles et immeubles. Il ne se fait aucune répartition de cette taille. Chaque bourgeois se cottise lui-même et porte son imposition à la maison de ville, et on n'exige autre chose de lui, sinon le serment qu'il est obligé de faire que ce qu'il paye forme véritablement ce qu'il doit acquitter.' But Lord Kames, *Sketches of the History of Man*, vol. i., p. 476, says, 'Every merchant puts privately into the public chest, the sum that, in his own opinion, he ought to contribute.']

W.N. II—N

In some Swiss cantons each man assesses himself publicly, The canton of Underwald[1] in Switzerland is frequently ravaged by storms and inundations, and[2] is thereby exposed to extraordinary expences. Upon such occasions the people assemble, and every one is said to declare with the greatest frankness what he is worth, in order to be taxed accordingly. At Zurich the law orders, that, in cases of necessity, every one should be taxed in proportion to his revenue; the amount of which, he is obliged to declare upon oath. They have no suspicion, it is said, that any of their fellow-citizens will deceive them. At Basil the principal revenue of the state arises from a small custom upon goods exported. All the citizens make oath that they will pay every three months all the taxes imposed by the law. All merchants and even all inn-keepers are trusted with keeping themselves the account of the goods which they sell either within or without the territory. At the end of every three months they send this account to the treasurer, with the amount of the tax computed at the bottom of it. It is not suspected that the revenue suffers by this confidence.[3]

which would be a hardship at Hamburg. To oblige every citizen to declare publicly upon oath the amount of his fortune, must not, it seems, in those Swiss cantons, be reckoned a hardship. At Hamburgh it would be reckoned the greatest. Merchants engaged in the hazardous projects of trade, all tremble at the thoughts of being obliged at all times to expose the real state of their circumstances. The ruin of their credit and the miscarriage of their projects, they foresee, would too often be the consequence. A sober and parsimonious people, who are strangers to all such projects, do not feel that they have occasion for any such concealment.

Holland once adopted the Hamburg practice. In Holland, soon after the exaltation of the late prince of Orange to the stadtholdership, a tax of two per cent. or the fiftieth penny, as it was called, was imposed upon the whole substance of every citizen. Every citizen assessed himself and paid his tax in the same manner as at Hamburgh; and it was in general supposed to have been paid with great fidelity. The people had at that time the greatest affection for their new government, which they had just established by a general insurrection. The tax was to be paid but once; in order to relieve the state in a particular exigency. It was, indeed, too heavy to be

---

[1] [Ed. 1 reads 'Underwold'.]   [2] [Ed. 5 adds 'it' here, doubtless a misprint.]
[3] Memoires concernant les Droits, tome i. p. 163, 166, 171. [The statements as to the confidence felt in these self-assessments are not taken from the *Mémoires*.]

permanent. In a country where the market rate of interest seldom exceeds three per cent., a tax of two per cent. amounts to thirteen shillings and fourpence in the pound upon the highest neat revenue which is commonly drawn from stock. It is a tax which very few people could pay without encroaching more or less upon their capitals. In a particular exigency the people may, from great public zeal, make a great effort, and give up even a part of their capital, in order to relieve the state. But it is impossible that they should continue to do so for any considerable time; and if they did, the tax would soon ruin them so completely as to render them altogether incapable of supporting the state.

On that occasion the tax was meant to be a tax on the capital. The tax upon stock imposed by the land-tax bill in England, though it is proportioned to the capital, is not intended to diminish or take away any part of at capital. It is meant only to be a tax upon the interest of money proportioned to that upon the rent of land; so that when the latter is at four shillings in the pound, the former may be at four shillings in the pound too. The tax at Hamburgh, and the still more moderate taxes of Underwald and Zurich, are meant, in the same manner, to be taxes, not upon the capital, but upon the interest or neat revenue of stock. That of Holland was meant to be a tax upon the capital.

Taxes upon the Profit of particular Employments

Taxes are sometimes imposed on particular profits, In some countries extraordinary taxes are imposed upon the profits of stock; sometimes when employed in particular branches of trade, and sometimes when employed in agriculture.

such as those on hawkers, pedlars, etc. Of the former kind are in England the tax upon hawkers and pedlars, that upon hackney coaches and chairs, and that which the keepers of ale-houses pay for a licence to retail ale and spirituous liquors. During the late war, another tax of the same kind was proposed upon shops.[1] The war having been undertaken, it was said, in defence of the trade of the country, the merchants, who were to profit by it, ought to contribute towards the support of it.

These fall not on the dealers but on the consumers of the goods, A tax, however, upon the profits of stock employed in any particular branch of trade, can never fall finally upon the dealers (who must in all ordinary

[1] [Proposed by Legge in 1759. See Dowell, *History of Taxation and Taxes in England*, 1884, vol. ii., p. 137.]

cases have their reasonable profit, and, where the competition is free, can seldom have more than that profit), but always upon the consumers, who must be obliged to pay in the price of the goods the tax which the dealer advances; and generally with some overcharge.

but when not proportioned to the trade of the dealer they oppress the small and favour the great dealer. A tax of this kind when it is proportioned to the trade of the dealer, is finally paid by the consumer, and occasions no oppression to the dealer. When it is not so proportioned, but is the same upon all dealers, though in this case too it is finally paid by the consumer, yet it favours the great, and occasions some oppression to the small dealer. The tax of five shillings a week upon every hackney coach, and that of ten shillings a year upon every hackney chair, so far as it is advanced by the different keepers of such coaches and chairs, is exactly enough proportioned to the extent of their respective dealings. It neither favours the great, nor oppresses the smaller dealer. The tax of twenty shillings a year for a licence to sell ale; of forty shillings for a licence to sell spirituous liquors; and of forty shillings more for a licence to sell wine, being the same upon all retailers, must necessarily give some advantage to the great, and occasion some oppression to the small dealers. The former must find it more easy to get back the tax in the price of their goods than the latter. The moderation of the tax, however, renders this inequality of less importance, and it may to many people appear not improper to give some discouragement to the multiplication of little ale-houses. The tax upon shops, it was intended, should be the same upon all shops. It could not well have been otherwise. It would have been impossible to proportion with tolerable exactness the tax upon a shop to the extent of the trade carried on in it, without such an inquisition as would have been altogether insupportable in a free country. If the tax had been considerable, it would have oppressed the small, and forced almost the whole retail trade into the hands of the great dealers. The competition of the former being taken away, the latter would have enjoyed a monopoly of the trade; and like all other monopolists would soon have combined to raise their profits much beyond what was necessary for the payment of the tax. The final payment, instead of falling upon the shopkeeper, would have fallen upon the consumer, with a considerable over-charge to the profit of the shopkeeper. For these reasons, the project of a tax upon shops was laid aside, and in the room of it was substituted the subsidy 1759.

The personal taille in France on the profits of agriculture is arbitrary and uncertain. What in France is called the personal taille is, perhaps, the most important tax upon the profits of stock employed in agriculture that is levied in any part of Europe.

In the disorderly state of Europe during the prevalence of the feudal government, the sovereign was obliged to content himself with taxing those who were too weak to refuse to pay taxes. The great lords, though willing to assist him upon particular emergencies, refused to subject themselves to any constant tax, and he was not strong enough to force them. The occupiers of land all over Europe were, the greater part of them, originally bond-men. Through the greater part of Europe they were gradually emancipated. Some of them acquired the property of landed estates which they held by some base or ignoble tenure, sometimes under the king, and sometimes under some other great lord, like the ancient copy-holders of England. Others, without acquiring the property, obtained leases for terms of years, of the lands which they occupied under their lord, and thus became less dependent upon him. The great lords seem to have beheld the degree of prosperity and independency which this inferior order of men had thus come to enjoy, with a[1] malignant and contemptuous indignation, and willingly consented that the sovereign should tax them.[2] In some countries this tax was confined to the lands which were held in property by an ignoble tenure; and, in this case, the taille was said to be real. The land-tax established by the late king of Sardinia, and the taille in the provinces of Languedoc, Provence, Dauphiné, and Brittany; in the generality of Montauban, and in the elections of Agen and Condom, as well as in some other districts of France, are taxes upon lands held in property by an ignoble tenure.[3] In other countries the tax was laid upon the supposed profits of all those who held in farm or lease lands belonging to other people, whatever might be the tenure by which the proprietor held them; and in this case the taille was said to be personal. In the greater part of those provinces of France, which are called the Countries of Elections, the taille is of this kind. The real taille, as it is imposed only upon a part of the lands of the country, is necessarily an unequal, but it is not always an arbitrary tax, though it is so upon some occasions. The personal taille, as it is intended to be proportioned to the profits of a certain

---

[1] [Ed. 1 does not contain 'a'.]   [2] [Above, vol. i., p. 417.]
[3] [Above, p. 361.]

class of people, which can only be guessed at, is necessarily both arbitrary and unequal.

The authority which assesses it is always ignorant of the real abilities of the contributors and often misled by friendship, party animosity and private resentment.

In France the personal taille at present (1775) annually imposed upon the twenty generalities, called the Countries of Elections, amounts to 40,107,239 livres, 16 sous.[1] The proportion in which this sum is assessed upon those different provinces, varies from year to year, according to the reports which are made to the king's council concerning the goodness or badness of the crops, as well as other circumstances, which may either increase or diminish their respective abilities to pay. Each generality is divided into a certain number of elections, and the proportion in which the sum imposed upon the whole generality is divided among those different elections, varies likewise from year to year, according to the reports made to the council concerning their respective abilities. It seems impossible that the council, with the best intentions, can ever proportion with tolerable exactness, either of those two assessments to the real abilities of the province or district upon which they are respectively laid. Ignorance and misinformation must always, more or less, mislead the most upright council. The proportion which each parish ought to support of what is assessed upon the whole election, and that which each individual ought to support of what is assessed upon his particular parish, are both in the same manner varied, from year to year, according as circumstances are supposed to require. These circumstances are judged of, in the one case, by the officers of the election; in the other by those of the parish; and both the one and the other are, more or less, under the direction and influence of the intendant. Not only ignorance and misinformation, but friendship, party animosity, and private resentment, are said frequently to mislead such assessors. No man subject to such a tax, it is evident, can ever be certain, before he is assessed of what he is to pay. He cannot even be certain after he is assessed. If any person has been taxed who ought to have been exempted; or if any person has been taxed beyond his proportion, though both must pay in the mean time, yet if they complain, and make good their complaints, the whole parish is reimposed next year in order to reimburse them. If any of the contributors become bankrupt or insolvent, the collector is obliged to advance his tax, and the whole parish is reimposed next yaer in

---

[1] Memoires concernant les Droits, &c. tome ii. p. 17.

order to reimburse the collector. If the collector himself should become bankrupt, the parish which elects him must answer for his conduct to the receiver-general of the election. But, as it might be troublesome for the receiver to prosecute the whole parish, he takes at his choice five or six of the richest contributors, and obliges them to make good what had been lost by the insolvency of the collector. The parish is afterwards reimposed in order to reimburse those five or six. Such reimpositions are always over and above the taille of the particular year in which they are laid on.

Taxes on the profits of agriculture do not, like those on profits of other trades, fall on the consumer, but on the landlord. When a tax is imposed upon the profits of stock in a particular branch of trade, the traders are all careful to bring no more goods to market than what they can sell at a price sufficient to reimburse them for advancing the tax. Some of them withdraw a part of their stocks from the trade, and the market is more sparingly supplied than before. The price of the goods rises, and the final payment of the tax falls upon the consumer. But when a tax is imposed upon the profits of stock employed in agriculture, it is not the interest of the farmers to withdraw any part of their stock from that employment. Each farmer occupies a certain quantity of land, for which he pays rent. For the proper cultivation of this land a certain quantity of stock is necessary; and by withdrawing any part of this necessary quantity, the farmer is not likely to be more able to pay either the rent or the tax. In order to pay the tax, it can never be his interest to diminish the quantity of his produce, nor consequently to supply the market more sparingly than before. The tax, therefore, will never enable him to raise the price of his produce, so as to[1] reimburse himself by throwing the final payment upon the consumer. The farmer, however, must have his reasonable profit as well as every other dealer, otherwise he must give up the trade. After the imposition of a tax of this kind, he can get this reasonable profit only by paying less rent to the landlord. The more he is obliged to pay in the way of tax, the less he can afford to pay in the way of rent. A tax of this kind imposed during the currency of a lease may, no doubt, distress or ruin the farmer. Upon the renewal of the lease it must always fall upon the landlord.

The discouragement to good cultivation caused by the personal taille In the countries where the personal taille takes place, the farmer is commonly assessed in proportion to the stock which he appears to employ in

---

[1] [Ed. 1 reads 'nor to'.]

injures the public, the farmer and the landlord. cultivation. He is, upon this account, frequently afraid to have a good team of horses or oxen, but endeavours to cultivate with the meanest and most wretched instruments of husbandry that he can. Such is his distrust in the justice of his assessors, that he counterfeits poverty, and wishes to appear scarce able to pay any thing for fear of being obliged to pay too much. By this miserable policy he does not, perhaps, always consult his own interest in the most effectual manner; and he probably loses more by the diminution of his produce than he saves by that of his tax. Though, in consequence of this wretched cultivation the market is, no doubt, somewhat worse supplied; yet the small rise of price which this may occasion, as it is not likely even to indemnify the farmer for the diminution of his produce, it is still less likely to enable him to pay more rent to the landlord. The public, the farmer, the landlord, all suffer more or less by this degraded cultivation. That the personal taille tends, in many different ways, to discourage cultivation, and consequently to dry up the principal source of the wealth of every great country, I have already had occasion to observe in the third book of this Inquiry.[1]

Per capita taxes on negro slaves fall on the landlords. What are called poll-taxes in the southern provinces of North America, and in the West Indian[2] islands, annual taxes of so much a head upon every negroe, are properly taxes upon the profits of a certain species of stock employed in agriculture. As the planters are, the greater part of them, both farmers and landlords, the final payment of the tax falls upon them in their quality of landlords without any retribution.

Poll taxes have been represented as badges of slavery, but, to the taxpayer every tax is a badge of liberty. Taxes of so much a head upon the bondmen employed in cultivation, seem anciently to have been common all over Europe. There subsists at present a tax of this kind in the empire of Russia. It is probably upon this account that poll-taxes of all kinds have often been represented as badges of slavery.[3] Every tax, however, is to the person who pays it a badge, not of slavery, but of liberty. It denotes that he is subject to government, indeed, but that, as he has some property, he cannot himself be the property of a master. A poll-tax upon slaves is altogether different from a poll-tax upon freemen. The latter is paid by the persons upon whom it is

---

[1] [Above, vol. i., p. 417.]   [2] [Ed. 1 reads 'West India'.]
[3] [E.g., by Montesquieu, *Esprit des lois,* liv. xiii., chap. xiv.]

imposed; the former by a different set of persons. The latter is either altogether arbitrary or altogether unequal, and in most cases is both the one and the other; the former, though in some respects unequal, different slaves being of different values, is in no respect arbitrary. Every master who knows the number of his own slaves, knows exactly what he has to pay. Those different taxes, however, being called by the same name, have been considered as of the same nature.

Taxes on menial servants are like taxes on consumable commodities. The taxes which in Holland are imposed upon men and maid servants, are taxes, not upon stock, but upon expence; and so far resemble the taxes upon consumable commodities. The tax of a guinea a head for every man servant, which has lately been imposed in Great Britain,[1] is of the same kind. It falls heaviest upon the middling rank. A man of two hundred a year may keep a single man servant. A man of ten thousand a year will not keep fifty. It does not affect the poor.[2]

Taxes on particular profits cannot affect interest. Taxes upon the profits of stock in particular employments can never affect the interest of money. Nobody will lend his money for less interest to those who exercise the taxed, than to those who exercise the untaxed employments. Taxes upon the revenue arising from stock in all employments, where the government attempts to levy them with any degree of exactness, will, in many cases, fall upon the interest of money. The Vingtieme, or twentieth penny, in France, is a tax of the same kind with what is called the land-tax in England, and is assessed, in the same manner, upon the revenue arising from land, houses, and stock. So far as it affects stock it is assessed, though not with great vigour, yet with much more exactness than that part of the land-tax of England which is imposed upon the same fund. It, in many cases, falls altogether upon the interest of money. Money is frequently sunk in France upon what are called Contracts for the constitution of a rent; that is, perpetual annuities redeemable at any time by the debtor upon repayment of the sum originally advanced, but of which this redemption is not exigible by the creditor except in particular cases. The Vingtieme seems not to have raised the rate of those annuities, though it is exactly levied upon them all.

---

[1] [17 Geo. III., c. 39.]
[2] [This paragraph is not in ed. 1.]

APPENDIX TO ARTICLES I AND II

Taxes upon the capital Value of Lands, Houses, and Stock

Taxes on the transmission of property often necessarily take a part of the capital value.

While property remains in the possession of the same person, whatever permanent taxes may have been imposed upon it, they have never been intended to diminish or take away any part of its capital value, but only some part of the revenue arising from it. But when property changes hands, when it is transmitted either from the dead to the living, or from the living to the living, such taxes have frequently been imposed upon it as necessarily take away some part of its capital value.

Transfers from the dead to the living and all transfers of immovable property can be taxed directly; transfers by way of loan of money have been taxed by stamp duties or duties on registration.

The transference of all sorts of property from the dead to the living, and that of immoveable property, of lands and houses, from the living to the living, are transactions which are in their nature either public and notorious, or such as cannot be long concealed. Such transactions, therefore, may be taxed directly. The transference of stock or moveable property, from the living to the living, by the lending of money, is frequently a secret transaction, and may always be made so. It cannot easily, therefore, be taxed directly. It has been taxed indirectly in two different ways; first, by requiring that the deed, containing the obligation to repay, should be written upon paper or parchment which had paid a certain stamp-duty, otherwise not to be valid; secondly, by requiring, under the like penalty of invalidity, that it should be recorded either in a public or secret register, and by imposing certain duties upon such registration. Stamp-duties and duties of registration have frequently been imposed likewise upon the deeds transferring property of all kinds from the dead to the living, and upon those transferring immoveable property from the living to the living, transactions which might easily have been taxed directly.

Transfers from the dead to the living were taxed by the Vicesima Hereditatum,

The Vicesima Hereditatum, the twentieth penny of inheritances, imposed by Augustus upon the ancient Romans, was a tax upon the transference of property from the dead to the living. Dion Cassius,[1]

[1] Lib. 55 [(25) quoted by Burman and Bouchaud]. See also Burman de Vectigalibus Pop. Rom. cap. xi. [in *Utriusque thesauri antiquitatum romanarum graecarumque nova supplementa* congesta ab Joanne Poleno, Venice, 1737, vol. i., p. 1032B] and Bouchaud de

the author who writes concerning it the least indistinctly, says, that it was imposed upon all successions, legacies, and donations, in case of death, except upon those to the nearest relations, and to the poor. *and the Dutch tax on successions.* Of the same kind is the Dutch tax upon successions.[1] Collateral successions are taxed, according to the degree of relation, from five to thirty per cent. upon the whole value of the succession. Testamentary donations, or legacies to collaterals, are subject to the like duties. Those from husband to wife, or from wife to husband, to the fifteenth[2] penny. The Luctuosa Hereditas, the mournful succession of ascendents to descendents, to the twentieth penny only. Direct successions, or those of descendents, to ascendents, pay no tax. The death of a father, to such of his children as live in the same house with him, is seldom attended with any increase, and frequently with a considerable diminution of revenue; by the loss of his industry, of his office, or of some life-rent estate; of which he may have been in possession. That tax would be cruel and oppressive which aggravated their loss by taking from them any part of his succession. It may, however, sometimes be otherwise with those children who, in the language of the Roman law, are said to be emancipated; in that of the Scotch law, to be forisfamiliated; that is, who have received their portion, have got families of their own, and are supported by funds separate and independent of those of their father. Whatever part of his succession might come to such children, would be a real addition to their fortune, and might therefore, perhaps, without more inconveniency than what attends all duties of this kind, be liable to some tax.

The feudal law taxed the transference of land, The casualties of the feudal law were taxes upon the transference of land, both from the dead to the living, and from the living to the living. In ancient times they constituted in every part of Europe one of the principal branches of the revenue of the crown.

by wardships and reliefs, The heir of every immediate vassal of the crown paid a certain duty, generally a year's rent, upon receiving the investiture of the estate. If the heir was a minor, the whole rents of the estate, during the continuance of the minority, devolved to the superior without any other charge, besides the

l'impôt du vingtieme sur les successions [*et de l'impôt sur les marchandises chez les Romains*; nouv. ed., 1772, pp. 10 *sqq.*]

[1] See Memoires concernant les Droits, &c. tome i. p. 225.

[2] [All eds. read 'fiftieth,' but the *Mémoires* say 'quinzième' and the 'only' in the next sentence shows that Smith intended to write 'fifteenth'.]

maintenance of the minor, and the payment of the widow's dower, when there happened to be a dowager upon the land. When the minor came to be of age, another tax, called Relief, was still due to the superior, which generally amounted likewise to a year's rent. A long minority, which in the present times so frequently disburdens a great estate of all its incumbrances, and restores the family to their ancient splendour, could in those times have no such effect. The waste, and not the disincumbrance of the estate, was the common effect of a long minority.

and fines on aliena-tion, which last still form a considerable branch of revenue in many countries. By the feudal law the vassal could not alienate without the consent of his superior, who generally extorted a fine or composition for granting it. This fine, which was at first arbitrary, came in many countries to be regulated at a certain portion of the price of the land. In some countries, where the greater part of the other feudal customs have gone into disuse, this tax upon the alienation of land still continues to make a very[1] considerable branch of the revenue of the sovereign. In the canton of Berne it is so high as a sixth part of the price of all noble fiefs; and a tenth part of that of all ignoble ones.[2] In the canton of Lucerne the tax upon the sale of lands is not universal, and takes place only in certain districts. But if any person sells his land, in order to remove out of the territory, he pays ten per cent. upon the whole price of the sale.[3] Taxes of the same kind upon the sale either of all lands, or of lands held by certain tenures, take place in many other countries, and make a more or less considerable branch of the revenue of the sovereign.

These taxes on the sale of land may be levied by stamps or duties on registration. Such transactions may be taxed indirectly, by means either of stamp-duties, or of duties upon registration; and those duties either may or may not be proportioned to the value of the subject which is transferred.

In Great Britain the duties are not proportioned to the value of the property. In Great Britain the stamp-duties are higher or lower, not so much according to the value of the property transferred (an eighteen penny or half crown stamp being sufficient upon a bond for the largest sum of money) as according to the nature of the deed. The highest do not exceed six pounds upon every sheet of paper, or skin of parchment; and these high duties fall chiefly upon grants

---

[1] [Ed. 1 does not contain 'very'.]
[2] Memoires concernant les Droits, &c. tome i. p. 154.   [2] Id. p. 157.

from the crown, and upon certain law proceedings, without any regard to the value of the subject. There are in Great Britain no duties on the registration of deeds or writings, except the fees of the officers who keep the register; and these are seldom more than a reasonable recompence for their labour. The crown derives no revenue from them.

In Holland some are proportioned and others not. In Holland[1] there are both stamp-duties and duties upon registration; which in some cases are, and in some are not proportioned to the value of the property transferred. All testaments must be written upon stamped paper of which the price is proportioned to the property disposed of, so that there are stamps which cost from three pence, or three stivers a sheet, to three hundred florins, equal to about twenty-seven pounds ten shillings of our money. If the stamp is of an inferior price to what the testator ought to have made use of, his succession is confiscated. This is over and above all their other taxes on succession. Except bills of exchange, and some other mercantile bills, all other deeds, bonds, and contracts, are subject to a stamp-duty. This duty, however, does not rise in proportion to the value of the subject. All sales of land and of houses, and all mortgages upon either, must be registered, and, upon registration, pay a duty to the state of two and a half per cent. upon the amount of the price or of the mortgage.[2] This duty is extended to the sale of all ships and vessels of more than two tons burthen, whether decked or undecked. These, it seems, are considered as a sort of houses upon the water. The sale of moveables, when it is ordered by a court of justice, is subject to the like duty of two and a half per cent.

In France different sets of officers collect the stamp duties and the registration duties. In France there are both stamp-duties and duties upon registration. The former are considered as a branch of the aides or excise, and in the provinces where those duties take place, are levied by the excise officers. The latter are considered as a branch of the domain of the crown, and are levied by a different set of officers.

Both stamps and registration duties are modern methods of taxation. Those modes of taxation, by stamp-duties and by duties upon registration, are of very modern invention. In the course of little more than a century, however, stamp-duties have, in Europe, become almost universal, and duties upon registration extremely common. There is no art

---

[1] Memoires concernant les Droits, &c. tome i. p. 223, 224, 225.
[2] [Ed. 1 reads 'or the mortgage'.]

which one government sooner learns of another, than that of draining money from the pockets of the people.

*Taxes on transfers
from the dead to the
living fall on the
person who acquires
the property;
taxes on sales of
land fall on the
seller;*
Taxes upon the transference of property from the
dead to the living, fall finally as well as immediately
upon the person to whom the property is transferred. Taxes upon the sale of land fall altogether
upon the seller. The seller is almost always under
the necessity of selling, and must, therefore, take
such a price as he can get. The buyer is scarce ever under the necessity of buying, and will, therefore, only give[1] such a price as he
likes. He considers what the land will cost him in tax and price
together. The more he is obliged to pay in the way of tax, the less
he will be disposed to give in the way of price. Such taxes, therefore,
fall almost always upon a necessitous person, and must, therefore,
*taxes on the sale of
new buildings fall
on the buyer;*
be frequently very cruel and oppressive. Taxes
upon the sale of new-built houses, where the building is sold without the ground, fall generally upon
the buyer, because the builder must generally have his profit; otherwise he must give up the trade. If he advances the tax, therefore, the
buyer must generally repay it to him. Taxes upon the sale of old
*taxes on the sale
of old houses fall
on the seller;*
houses, for the same reason as those upon the sale
of land, fall generally upon the seller; whom in
most cases either conveniency or necessity obliges
to sell. The number of new-built houses that are annually brought
to market, is more or less regulated by the demand. Unless the
demand is such as to afford the builder his profit, after paying all
expences, he will build no more houses. The number of old houses
which happen at any time to come to market is regulated by accidents of which the greater part have no relation to the demand.
Two or three great bankruptcies in a mercantile town, will bring
*taxes on the sale
of ground rents fall
on the seller;*
many houses to sale, which must be sold for what
can be got for them. Taxes upon the sale of ground
rents fall altogether upon the seller; for the same
reason as those upon the sale of land. Stamp-duties, and duties upon
*taxes on loans fall
on the borrower;
taxes on law pro-
ceedings fall on the
suitors.*
the registration of bonds and contracts for borrowed
money, fall altogether upon the borrower, and, in
fact, are always paid by him. Duties of the same
kind upon law proceedings fall upon the suitors.
They reduce to both the capital value of the subject in dispute. The

[1][Ed. 1 reads 'give only'.]

more it costs to acquire any property, the less must be the neat[1] value of it when acquired.

All taxes on transfers, so far as they diminish the capital value, are unthrifty. All taxes upon the transference of property of every kind, so far as they diminish the capital value of that property, tend to diminish the funds destined for the maintenance of productive labour. They are all more or less unthrifty taxes that increase the revenue of the sovereign, which seldom maintains any but unproductive labourers; at the expence of the capital of the people, which maintains none but productive.

Even when proportioned to the value of the property they are unequal, because the frequency of transfer varies. They are certain, convenient and inexpensive. Such taxes, even when they are proportioned to the value of the property transferred, are still unequal; the frequency of transference not being always equal in property of equal value. When they are not proportioned to this value, which is the case with the greater part of the stamp-duties, and duties of registration, they are still more so. They are in no respect arbitrary, but are or may be in all cases perfectly clear and certain. Though they sometimes fall upon the person who is not very able to pay; the time of payment is in most cases sufficiently convenient for him. When the payment becomes due, he must in most cases have the money to pay. They are levied at very little expence, and in general subject the contributors to no other inconveniency besides always the unavoidable one of paying the tax.

French stamp-duties on transfers are not much complained of, but the registration duties (or Contrôle) are said to be arbitrary and uncertain. In France the stamp-duties are not much complained of. Those of registration, which they call the Contrôle, are. They give occasion, it is pretended, to much extortion in the officers of the farmers-general who collect the tax, which is in a great measure arbitrary and uncertain. In the greater part of the libels[2] which have been written against the present system of finances in France, the abuses of the Contrôle make a principal article. Uncertainty, however, does not seem to be necessarily inherent in the nature of such taxes. If the popular complaints are well founded, the abuse must arise, not so much from the nature of the tax, as from the want of precision and distinctness in the words of the edicts or laws which impose it.

---

[1] [Ed. 1 does not contain 'neat'.]

[2] [The word is used in its older sense, equivalent to the modern 'pamphlets'. See Murray, *Oxford English Dictionary, s.v.*]

Public registration of mortgages and all rights to immovable property is advantageous, but secret registers ought not to exist. The registration of mortgages, and in general of all rights upon immoveable property, as it gives great security both to creditors and purchasers, is extremely advantageous to the public. That of the greater part of deeds of other kinds is frequently inconvenient and even dangerous to individuals, without any advantage to the public. All registers which, it is acknowledged, ought to be kept secret, ought certainly never to exist. The credit of individuals ought certainly never to depend upon so very slender a security as the probity and religion of the inferior officers of revenue. But where the fees of registration have been made a source of revenue to the sovereign, register offices have commonly been multiplied without end, both for the deeds which ought to be registered, and for those which ought not. In France there are several different sorts of secret registers. This abuse, though not perhaps a necessary, it must be acknowledged, is a very natural effect of such taxes.

Many stamp-duties are duties on consumption. Such stamp-duties as those in England upon cards and dice, upon news-papers and periodical pamphlets, &c. are properly taxes upon consumption; the final payment falls upon the persons who use or consume such commodities. Such stamp-duties as those upon licences to retail ale, wine, and spirituous liquors, though intended, perhaps, to fall upon the profits of the retailers, are likewise finally paid by the consumers of those liquors. Such taxes, though called by the same name, and levied by the same officers and in the same manner with the stamp-duties above mentioned upon the transference of property, are however of a quite different nature, and fall upon quite different funds.

ARTICLE III

Taxes upon the Wages of Labour

A tax on wages must raise wages by rather more than the amount of the tax. The wages of the inferior classes of workmen, I have endeavoured to show in the first book, are every where necessarily regulated by two different circumstances; the demand for labour, and the ordinary or average price of provisions. The demand for labour, according as it happens to be either increasing, stationary, or declining; or to require an increasing, stationary, or declining population, regulates the subsistence of the labourer, and determines in what degree it shall be, either liberal, moderate, or scanty. The ordinary or average price of provisions determines the quantity of money which must be paid to the workman in order to enable him, one year with another, to purchase this liberal, moderate, or scanty subsistence. While the demand for labour and the price of provisions, therefore, remain the same, a direct tax upon the wages of labour can have no other effect than to raise them somewhat higher than the tax. Let us suppose, for example, that in a particular place the demand for labour and the price of provisions were such, as to render ten shillings a week the ordinary wages of labour; and that a tax of one-fifth, or four shillings in the pound, was imposed upon wages. If the demand for labour and the price of provisions remained the same, it would still be necessary that the labourer should in that place earn such a subsistence as could be bought only for ten shillings a week, or that after paying the tax he should have ten shillings a week free wages. But in order to leave him such free wages after paying such a tax, the price of labour must in that place soon rise, not to twelve shillings a week only, but to twelve and sixpence; that is, in order to enable him to pay a tax of one-fifth, his wages must necessarily soon rise, not one-fifth part only, but one-fourth. Whatever was the proportion of the tax, the wages of labour must in all cases rise, not only in that proportion, but in a higher proportion. If the tax, for example, was one-tenth, the wages of labour must necessarily soon rise, not one-tenth part only, but one-eighth.

The rise in the wages of manufacturing labour would be advanced by the employers and paid by the consumers, and the rise in agricultural wages advanced by the farmers and paid by the landlords. A direct tax upon the wages of labour, therefore, though the labourer might perhaps pay it out of his hand, could not properly be said to be even advanced by him; at least if the demand for labour and the average price of provisions remained the same after the tax as before it. In all such cases, not only the tax, but something more than the tax, would in reality be advanced by the person who immediately employed him. The final payment would in different cases fall upon different persons. The rise which such a tax might occasion in the wages of manufacturing labour would be advanced by the master manufacturer, who would both be entitled and obliged to charge it, with a profit, upon the price of his goods. The final payment of this rise of wages, therefore, together with the additional profit of the master manufacturer, would fall upon the consumer. The rise which such a tax might occasion in the wages of country labour would be advanced by the farmer, who, in order to maintain the same number of labourers as before, would be obliged to employ a greater capital. In order to get back this greater capital, together with the ordinary profits of stock, it would be necessary that he should retain a larger portion, or what comes to the same thing, the price of a larger portion, of the produce of the land, and consequently that he should pay less rent to the landlord. The final payment of this rise of wages, therefore, would in this case fall upon the landlord, together with the additional profit of the farmer who had advanced it. In all cases a direct tax upon the wages of labour must, in the long-run, occasion both a greater reduction in the rent of land, and a greater rise in the price of manufactured goods, than would have followed from the proper assessment of a sum equal to the produce of the tax, partly upon the rent of land, and partly upon consumable commodities.

The effect of the tax in raising wages is generally disguised by the fall in the demand for labour which it occasions. If direct taxes upon the wages of labour have not always occasioned a proportionable rise in those wages, it is because they have generally occasioned a considerable fall in the demand for labour. The declension of industry, the decrease of employment for the poor, the diminution of the annual produce of the land and labour of the country, have generally been the effects of such taxes. In consequence of them, however, the price of labour must always be higher than it otherwise would have been in the actual state of the demand: and this enhancement of price, together with the profit of those who advance it, must always be finally paid by the landlords and consumers.

A tax on agricultural wages raises prices no more than one on farmers' profits. A tax upon the wages of country labour does not raise the price of the rude produce of land in proportion to the tax;[1] for the same reason that a tax upon the farmer's profit does not raise that price in that proportion.[2]

Many countries have such taxes, e.g., France and Bohemia. Absurd and destructive as such taxes are, however, they take place in many countries. In France that part of the taille which is charged upon the industry of workmen and day-labourers in country villages, is properly a tax of this kind. Their wages are computed according to the common

---

[1] [Ed. 1 does not contain 'in proportion to the tax'.]
[2] [Ed. 1 does not contain 'in that proportion'.]

rate of the district in which they reside, and that they may be as little liable as possible to any over-charge, their yearly gains are estimated at no more than two hundred working days in the year.[1] The tax of each individual is varied from year to year according to different circumstances, of which the collector or the commissary, whom the intendant appoints to assist him, are the judges. In Bohemia, in consequence of the alteration in the system of finances which was begun in 1748, a very heavy tax is imposed upon the industry of artificers. They are divided into four classes. The highest class pay a hundred florins a year; which, at two-and-twenty-pence half-penny a florin, amounts to 9 l. 7 s. 6 d. The second class are taxed at seventy; the third at fifty; and the fourth, comprehending artificers in villages, and the lowest class of those in towns, at twenty-five florins.[2]

A tax on the recompense of the liberal professions, etc., would also raise that recompense, The recompence of ingenious artists and of men of liberal professions, I have endeavoured to show in the first book,[3] necessarily keeps a certain proportion to the emoluments of inferior trades. A tax upon this recompence, therefore, could have no other effect than to raise it somewhat higher than in proportion to the tax. If it did not rise in this manner, the ingenious arts and the liberal professions, being no longer upon a level with other trades, would be so much deserted that they would soon return to that level.

but a tax on government offices would not raise salaries. The emoluments of offices are not, like those of trades and professions, regulated by the free competition of the market, and do not, therefore, always bear a just proportion to what the nature of the employment requires. They are, perhaps, in most countries, higher than it requires; the persons who have the administration of government being generally disposed to reward both themselves and their immediate dependents rather more than enough. The emoluments of offices, therefore, can in most cases very well bear to be taxed. The persons, besides, who enjoy public offices, especially the more lucrative, are in all countries the objects of general envy; and a tax upon their emoluments, even though it should be somewhat higher than upon any other sort of revenue, is always a very popular tax. In England, for example, when by the land-tax every other sort of

---

[1] Memoires concernant les Droits, &c. tom. ii. p. 108.
[2] Id. tom. iii. [really i.] p. 87.   [3] [Above, vol. i., pp. 112–123.]

revenue was supposed to be[1] assessed at four shillings in the pound, it was very popular to lay a real tax of five shillings and sixpence in the pound upon the salaries of offices which exceeded a hundred pounds a year; the pensions of the younger branches of the royal family, the pay of the officers of the army and navy, and a few others less obnoxious to envy excepted.[2] There are in England no other direct taxes upon the wages of labour.

ARTICLE IV

Taxes which, it is intended, should fall indifferently upon every different Species of Revenue

These are capitation taxes and taxes on consumable commodities. The taxes which, it is intended, should fall indifferently upon every different species of revenue, are capitation taxes, and taxes upon consumable commodities. These must be paid indifferently from whatever revenue the contributors may possess; from the rent of their land, from the profits of their stock, or from the wages of their labour.

Capitation Taxes

Capitation taxes ostensibly proportioned to revenue are altogether arbitrary. Capitation taxes, if it is attempted to proportion them to the fortune or revenue of each contributor, become altogether arbitrary. The state of a man's fortune varies from day to day, and without an inquisition more intolerable than any tax, and renewed at least once every year, can only be guessed at. His assessment, therefore, must in most cases depend upon the good or bad humour of his assessors, and must, therefore, be altogether arbitrary and uncertain.

If proportioned to rank they are unequal. Capitation taxes, if they are proportioned not to the supposed fortune, but to the rank of each contributor, become altogether unequal; the degrees of fortune being frequently unequal in the same degree of rank.

---

[1] ['Was supposed to be' is equivalent to 'was nominally but not really'.]

[2] [Eds. 1 and 2 read 'a real tax of five shillings in the pound upon the salaries of offices which exceeded a hundred pounds a year; those of the judges and a few others less obnoxious to envy excepted.' Under 31 Geo. II., c. 22, a tax of 1s. in the pound was imposed on all offices worth more than £100 a year, naval and military offices excepted. The judges were not excepted, but their salaries were raised soon afterwards. See Dowell, *History of Taxation and Taxes*, vol. ii., pp. 135-136. The 6d. seems a mistake; the 5s. is arrived at by adding the 4s. land tax (which was 'real' in the case of offices) and the 1s.]

In the first case they are always grievous and in the second they are intolerable unless they are light.

Such taxes, therefore, if it is attempted to render them equal, become altogether arbitrary and uncertain; and if it is attempted to render them certain and not arbitrary, become altogether unequal. Let the tax be light or heavy, uncertainty is always a great grievance. In a light tax a considerable degree of inequality may be supported; in a heavy one it is altogether intolerable.

In the poll taxes of William III. assessment was chiefly according to rank.

In the different poll-taxes which took place in England during the reign of William III.[1] the contributors were, the greater part of them, assessed according to the degree of their rank; as dukes, marquisses, earls, viscounts, barons, esquires, gentlemen, the eldest and youngest sons of peers, &c. All shopkeepers and tradesmen worth more than three hundred pounds, that is, the better sort of them, were subject to the same assessment; how great soever might be the difference in their fortunes.[2] Their rank was more considered than their fortune. Several of those who in the first poll-tax were rated according to their supposed fortune, were afterwards rated according to their rank. Serjeants, attornies, and proctors at law, who in the first poll-tax were assessed at three shillings in the pound of their supposed income, were afterwards assessed as gentlemen.[3] In the assessment of a tax which was not very heavy, a considerable degree of inequality had been found less insupportable than any degree of uncertainty.

In France the assessment is by rank in the higher and by supposed fortune in the lower orders of people.

In the capitation which has been levied in France without any interruption since the beginning of the present century, the highest orders of people are rated according to their rank, by an invariable tariff; the lower orders of people, according to what is supposed to be their fortune, by an assessment which varies from year to year. The officers of the king's court, the judges and other officers in the superior courts of justice, the officers of the troops, &c.

[The first of these is under 1 W. and M., sess. 1, c. 13.]

[2] [1 W. and M., sess. 2, c. 7, § 2.]

[3] [Under 1 W. and M., c. 13, § 4, serjeants, attorneys and proctors, as well as certain other classes, were to pay 3s. in the pound on their receipts. Under 1 W. and M., sess. 2, c. 7, § 2, attorneys and proctors and others were to pay 20s. in addition to the sums already charged. Under 2 W. and M., sess. 1, c. 2, § 5, serjeants-at-law were to pay £15, apparently in addition to the 3s. in the pound. Under 3 W. and M., c. 6, the poundage charge does not appear at all. The alterations were doubtless made in order to secure certainty, but purely in the interest of the government, which desired to be certain of getting a fixed amount. Under the Land Tax Act of 8 and 9 W. III., c. 6, § 5, serjeants, attorneys, proctors, etc., are again charged to an income tax.]

are assessed in the first manner. The inferior ranks of people in the provinces are assessed in the second. In France the great easily submit to a considerable degree of inequality in a tax which, so far as it affects them, is not a very heavy one; but could not brook the arbitrary assessment of an intendant. The inferior ranks of people must, in that country, suffer patiently the usage which their superiors think proper to give them.

The French tax is more rigorously exacted than the English taxes were. In England the different poll-taxes never produced the sum which had been expected from them, or which, it was supposed, they might have produced, had they been exactly levied. In France the capitation always produces the sum expected from it. The mild government of England, when it assessed the different ranks of people to the poll-tax, contented itself with what that assessment happened to produce; and required no compensation for the loss which the state might sustain either by those who could not pay, or by those who would not pay (for there were many such), and who, by the indulgent execution of the law, were not forced to pay. The more severe government of France assesses upon each generality a certain sum, which the intendant must find as he can. If any province complains of being assessed too high, it may, in the assessment of next year, obtain an abatement proportioned to the over-charge of the year before. But it must pay in the mean time. The intendant, in order to be sure of finding the sum assessed upon his generality, was impowered to assess it in a larger sum, that the failure or inability of some of the contributors might be compensated by the over-charge of the rest; and till 1765, the fixation of this surplus assessment was left altogether to his discretion. In that year indeed the council assumed this power to itself. In the capitation of the provinces, it is observed by the perfectly well-informed author of the Memoirs upon the impositions in France, the proportion[1] which falls upon the nobility, and upon those whose privileges exempt them from the taille, is the least considerable. The largest falls upon those subject to the taille, who are assessed to the capitation at so much a pound of what they pay to that other tax.[2]

Capitation taxes on the lower orders of people are like taxes on wages. Capitation taxes, so far as they are levied upon the lower ranks of people, are direct taxes upon the wages of labour, and are attended with all the inconveniencies of such taxes.

---

[1] [Ed. 1 reads 'portion'.]   [2] [*Mémoires*, tom. ii., p. 421.]

They are inexpensive and afford a sure revenue.

Capitation taxes are levied at little expence; and, where they are rigorously exacted, afford a very sure revenue to the state. It is upon this account that in countries where the ease, comfort, and security of the inferior ranks of people are little attended to, capitation taxes are very common. It is in general, however, but a small part of the public revenue, which, in a great empire, has ever been drawn from such taxes; and the greatest sum which they have ever afforded, might always have been found in some other way much more convenient to the people.

Taxes upon consumable Commodities

The impossibility of taxation according to revenue has given rise to taxation according to expenditure on consumable commodities,

The impossibility of taxing the people, in proportion to their revenue, by any capitation, seems to have given occasion to the invention of taxes upon consumable commodities. The state not knowing how to tax, directly and proportionably, the revenue of its subjects, endeavours to tax it indirectly by taxing their expence, which, it is supposed, will in most cases be nearly in proportion to their revenue. Their expence is taxed by taxing the consumable commodities upon which it is laid out.

either necessaries or luxuries,

Consumable commodities are either necessaries or luxuries.

necessaries including all that creditable people of the lowest order cannot decently go without.

By necessaries I understand, not only the commodities which are indispensably necessary for the support of life, but whatever the custom of the country renders it indecent for creditable people, even of the lowest order, to be without. A linen shirt, for example, is, strictly speaking, not a necessary of life. The Greeks and Romans lived, I suppose, very comfortably, though they had no linen.[1] But in the present times, through the greater part of Europe, a creditable day-labourer would be ashamed to appear in public without a linen shirt, the want of which would be supposed to denote that disgraceful degree of poverty, which, it is presumed, no body can well fall into without extreme bad conduct. Custom, in the same manner, has rendered leather shoes a necessary of life in

---

[1] [Dr. John Arbuthnot, in his *Tables of Ancient Coins, Weights and Measures*, 2nd ed., 1754, p. 142, says that linen was not used among the Romans, at least by men, till about the time of Alexander Severus.]

England. The poorest creditable person of either sex would be ashamed to appear in public without them. In Scotland, custom has rendered them a necessary of life to the lowest order of men; but not to the same order of women, who may, without any discredit, walk about bare-footed. In France, they are necessaries neither to men nor to women; the lowest rank of both sexes appearing there publicly, without any discredit, sometimes in wooden shoes, and sometimes bare-footed. Under necessaries therefore, I comprehend, not only those things which nature, but those things which the established rules of decency have rendered necessary to the lowest rank of people. All other things I call luxuries; without meaning by this appellation, to throw the smallest degree of reproach upon the temperate use of them. Beer and ale, for example, in Great Britain, and wine, even in the wine countries, I call luxuries.[1] A man of any rank may, without any reproach, abstain totally from tasting such liquors. Nature does not render them necessary for the support of life; and custom nowhere renders it indecent to live without them.

What raises the price of subsistence must raise wages. As the wages of labour are every where regulated, partly by the demand for it, and partly by the average price of the necessary articles of subsistence; whatever raises this average price must necessarily raise those wages, so that the labourer may still be able to purchase that quantity of those necessary articles which the state of the demand for labour, whether increasing, stationary, or declining, requires that he should have.[2] A tax upon those articles necessarily raises their price somewhat higher than the amount of the tax, because the dealer who advances the tax, must generally get it back with a profit. Such a tax must, therefore, occasion a rise in the wages of labour proportionable to this rise of price.

So that a tax on necessaries, like a tax on wages, raises wages. It is thus that a tax upon the necessaries of life, operates exactly in the same manner as a direct tax upon the wages of labour. The labourer, though he may pay it out of his hand, cannot, for any considerable time at least, be properly said even to advance it. It must always in the long-run be advanced to him by his immediate employer in the advanced rate of his wages. His employer, if he is a manufacturer, will charge upon the price of his goods this rise of wages, together with a profit; so that the final payment of the tax, together with this over-

[1] [In *Lectures*, p. 179, and above in ed. i., vol. i., p. 488, note, beer seems to be regarded as a necessary of life rather than a luxury.]   [2] See Book I., Chap. 8.

charge, will fall upon the consumer. If his employer is a farmer, the final payment, together with a like over-charge, will fall upon the rent of the landlord.

Taxes on luxuries even if consumed by the poor have no such effect, It is otherwise with taxes upon what I call luxuries; even upon those of the poor. The rise in the price of the taxed commodities, will not necessarily occasion any rise in the wages of labour. A tax upon tobacco, for example, though a luxury of the poor as well as of the rich, will not raise wages. Though it is taxed in England at three times, and in France at fifteen times its original price, those high duties seem to have no effect upon the wages of labour. The same thing may be said of the taxes upon tea and sugar; which in England and Holland have become luxuries of the lowest ranks of people; and of those upon chocolate, which in Spain is said to have become so. The different taxes which in Great Britain have in the course of the present century been imposed upon spirituous liquors, are not supposed to have had any effect upon the wages of labour. The rise in the price of porter, occasioned by an additional tax of three shillings upon the barrel of strong beer,[1] has not raised the wages of common labour in London. These were about eighteen pence and twenty-pence a day before the tax, and they are not more now.

as they act like sumptuary laws, and so do not diminish the ability of the poor to bring up useful families, The high price of such commodities does not necessarily diminish the ability of the inferior ranks of people to bring up families. Upon the sober and industrious poor, taxes upon such commodities act as sumptuary laws, and dispose them either to moderate, or to refrain altogether from the use of superfluities which they can no longer easily afford. Their ability to bring up families, in consequence of this forced frugality, instead of being diminished, is frequently, perhaps, increased by the tax. It is the sober and industrious poor who generally bring up the most numerous families, and who principally supply the demand for useful labour. All the poor indeed are not sober and industrious, and the dissolute and disorderly might continue to indulge themselves in the use of such commodities after this rise of price in the same manner as before; without regarding the distress which this indulgence might bring upon their families. Such disorderly persons, however, seldom rear up numerous families; their children generally perishing from neglect, mismanagement, and the scantiness

[1] [1 Geo. III., c. 7.]

or unwholesomeness of their food. If by the strength of their constitution they survive the hardships to which the bad conduct of their parents exposes them; yet the example of that bad conduct commonly corrupts their morals; so that, instead of being useful to society by their industry, they become public nuisances by their vices and disorders. Though the advanced price of the luxuries of the poor, therefore, might increase somewhat the distress of such disorderly families, and thereby diminish somewhat their ability to bring up children; it would not probably diminish much the useful population of the country.

whereas a rise in the price of necessaries diminishes the ability of the poor to bring up useful families and supply the demand for labour.

Any rise in the average price of necessaries, unless it is compensated by a proportionable rise in the wages of labour, must necessarily diminish more or less the ability of the poor to bring up numerous families, and consequently to supply the demand for useful labour; whatever may be the state of that demand, whether increasing, stationary, or declining; or such as requires an increasing, stationary, or declining population.

Taxes on necessaries are contrary to the interest of the middle and superior ranks of people.

Taxes upon luxuries have no tendency to raise the price of any other commodities except that of the commodities taxed. Taxes upon necessaries, by raising the wages of labour, necessarily tend to raise the price of all manufactures, and consequently to diminish the extent of their sale and consumption. Taxes upon luxuries are finally paid by the consumers of the commodities taxed, without any retribution. They fall indifferently upon every species of revenue, the wages of labour, the profits of stock, and the rent of land. Taxes upon necessaries, so far as they affect the labouring poor, are finally paid, partly by landlords in the diminished rent of their lands, and partly by rich consumers, whether landlords or others, in the advanced price of manufactured goods; and always with a considerable over-charge. The advanced price of such manufactures as are real necessaries of life, and are destined for the consumption of the poor, of coarse woollens, for example, must be compensated to the poor by a farther advancement of their wages. The middling and superior ranks of people, if they understood their own interest, ought always to oppose all taxes upon the necessaries of life, as well as all direct taxes upon the wages of labour. The final payment of both the one and the other falls altogether upon themselves, and always with a considerable over-charge. They fall

heaviest upon the landlords, who always pay in a double capacity;
in that of landlords, by the reduction of their rent; and in that of rich
consumers, by the increase of their expence. The observation of Sir
Matthew Decker, that certain taxes are, in the price of certain goods,
sometimes repeated and accumulated four or five times, is perfectly
just with regard to taxes upon the necessaries of life. In the price of
leather, for example, you must pay, not only for the tax upon the
leather of your own shoes, but for a part of that upon those of the
shoe-maker and the tanner. You must pay too for the tax upon the
salt, upon the soap, and upon the candles which those workmen
consume while employed in your service, and for the tax upon the
leather, which the salt-maker, the soap-maker, and the candle-maker
consume while employed in their service.[1]

*The chief British
taxes on necessaries
are those on salt,
leather, soap and
candles,*   In Great Britain, the principal taxes upon the
necessaries of life are those upon the four commodities just now mentioned, salt, leather, soap, and
candles.

Salt is a very ancient and a very universal subject of taxation. It
was taxed among the Romans, and it is so at present in, I believe,
every part of Europe. The quantity annually consumed by any
individual is so small, and may be purchased so gradually, that
nobody, it seems to have been thought, could feel very sensibly
even a pretty heavy tax upon it. It is in England taxed at three
shillings and fourpence a bushel; about three times the original price
of the commodity. In some other countries the tax is still higher.
Leather is a real necessary of life. The use of linen renders soap such.
In countries where the winter nights are long, candles are a necessary instrument of trade. Leather and soap are in Great Britain taxed
at three halfpence a pound; candles at a penny;[2] taxes which, upon
the original price of leather, may amount to about eight or ten per
cent.; upon that of soap to about twenty or five and twenty per
cent.; and upon that of candles to about fourteen or fifteen per cent.;
taxes which, though lighter than that upon salt, are still very heavy.
As all those four commodities are real necessaries of life, such heavy
taxes upon them must increase somewhat the expence of the sober
and industrious poor, and must consequently raise more or less the
wages of their labour.

---

[1] [Leather is Decker's example, *Essay on the Decline of the Foreign Trade*, 2nd ed.,
1750, pp. 29, 30. See also p. 10.]
[2] [See Dowell, *History of Taxation and Taxes*, 1884, vol. iv., pp. 318, 322, 330.]

and also sea-borne coal. In a country where the winters are so cold as in Great Britain, fuel is, during that season, in the strictest sense of the word, a necessary of life, not only for the purpose of dressing victuals, but for the comfortable subsistence of many different sorts of workmen who work within doors; and coals are the cheapest of all fuel. The price of fuel has so important an influence upon that of labour, that all over Great Britain manufactures have confined themselves principally to the coal countries; other parts of the country, on account of the high price of this necessary article, not being able to work so cheap. In some manufactures, besides, coal is a necessary instrument of trade; as in those of glass, iron, and all other metals. If a bounty could in any case be reasonable, it might perhaps be so upon the transportation of coals from those parts of the country in which they abound, to those in which they are wanted. But the legislature, instead of a bounty, has imposed a tax of three shillings and three-pence a ton upon coal carried coastways;[1] which upon most sorts of coal is more than sixty per cent. of the original price at the coal-pit. Coals carried either by land or by inland navigation pay no duty. Where they are naturally cheap, they are consumed duty free: where they are naturally dear, they are loaded with a heavy duty.

Such taxes at any rate bring in revenue, which is more than can be said of the regulations of the corn trade, etc., which produce equally bad effects. Such taxes, though they raise the price of subsistence, and consequently the wages of labour, yet they afford a considerable revenue to government, which it might not be easy to find in any other way. There may, therefore, be good reasons for continuing them. The bounty upon the exportation of corn, so far as it tends in the actual state of tillage to raise the price of that necessary article, produces all the like bad effects; and instead of affording any revenue, frequently occasions a very great expence to government. The high duties upon the importation of foreign corn, which in years of moderate plenty amount to a prohibition; and the absolute prohibition of the importation either of live cattle or of salt provisions, which takes place in the ordinary state of the law, and which, on account of the scarcity, is at present suspended for a limited time with regard to Ireland and the British plantations,[2] have all the bad effects of taxes upon the necessaries of life, and produce no revenue to government. Nothing seems

[1] [Saxby, *British Customs*, p. 307. 8 Ann., c. 4; 9 Ann., c. 6.]
[2] [Above, vol. i., p. 443.]

necessary for the repeal of such regulations, but to convince the
public of the futility of that system in consequence of which they
have been established.

Much higher taxes on necessaries prevail in many other countries. There are taxes on bread,   Taxes upon the necessaries of life are much higher
in many other countries than in Great Britain.
Duties upon flour and meal when ground at the
mill, and upon bread when baked at the oven, take
place in many countries. In Holland the money price of the bread
consumed in towns is supposed to be doubled by means of such
taxes. In lieu of a part of them, the people who live in the country
pay every year so much a head, according to the sort of bread they
are supposed to consume. Those who consume wheaten bread, pay
three guilders fifteen stivers; about six shillings and ninepence half-
penny. These, and some other taxes of the same kind, by raising the
price of labour, are said to have ruined the greater part of the
manufactures of Holland.[1] Similar taxes, though not quite so heavy,
take place in the Milanese, in the states of Genoa, in the dutchy of
Modena, in the dutchies of Parma, Placentia, and Guastalla, and in
the ecclesiastical state. A French[2] author of some note has proposed
to reform the finances of his country, by substituting in the room
of the greater part of other taxes, this most ruinous of all taxes. There
is nothing so absurd, says Cicero, which has not sometimes been
asserted by some philosophers.[3]

and meat.   Taxes upon butchers meat are still more common
than those upon bread. It may indeed be doubted whether butchers
meat is any where a necessary of life. Grain and other vegetables,
with the help of milk, cheese, and butter, or oil, where butter is not
to be had, it is known from experience, can, without any butchers
meat, afford the most plentiful, the most wholesome, the most
nourishing, and the most invigorating diet. Decency no where
requires that any man should eat butchers meat, as it in most places
requires that he should wear a linen shirt or a pair of leather shoes.

A tax on a consumable commodity may be levied either   Consumable commodities, whether necessaries or
luxuries, may be taxed in two different ways. The

---

[1] Memoires concernant les Droits, &c. p. 210, 211 [and 233. See below, p. 438.]

[2] Le Reformateur. [Amsterdam, 1756. Garnier in his note on this passage, *Recherches*, etc., tom. iv., p. 387, attributes this work to Clicquot de Blervache, French Inspector-general of Manufactures and Commerce, 1766-90, but later authorities doubt or deny Clicquot's authorship. See Jules de Vroil, *Étude sur Clicquot-Blervache*, 1870, pp. xxxi-xxxiii.]

[3] [*De Divinatione*, ii., 58, 'Sed nescio quomodo nihil tam absurde dici potest quod non dicatur ab aliquo philosophorum.']

periodically from the consumer or once for all from the dealer when the consumer acquires it. consumer may either pay an annual sum on account of his using or consuming goods of a certain kind; or the goods may be taxed while they remain in the hands of the dealer, and before they are delivered to the consumer. The consumable goods which last a considerable time before they are consumed altogether, are most properly taxed in the one way. Those of which the consumption is either immediate or more speedy, in the other. The coach-tax and plate-tax are examples of the former method of imposing: the greater part of the other duties of excise and customs, of the latter.

The first method is best when the commodity is durable. A coach may, with good management, last ten or twelve years. It might be taxed, once for all, before it comes out of the hands of the coach-maker. But it is certainly more convenient for the buyer to pay four pounds a year for the privilege of keeping a coach, than to pay all at once forty or forty-eight pounds additional price to the coach-maker; or a sum equivalent to what the tax is likely to cost him during the time he uses the same coach. A service of plate, in the same manner, may last more than a century. It is certainly easier for the consumer to pay five shillings a year for every hundred ounces of plate, near one per cent. of the value, than to redeem this long annuity at five and twenty or thirty years purchase, which would enhance the price at least five and twenty or thirty per cent. The different taxes which affect houses are certainly more conveniently paid by moderate annual payments, than by a heavy tax of equal value upon the first building or sale of the house.

Sir M. Decker proposed to adapt it also to other commodities by issuing annual licences to consume them, but this would be liable to greater objections than the second and usual method. It was the well-known proposal of Sir Matthew Decker, that all commodities, even those of which the consumption is either immediate or very speedy, should be taxed in this manner; the dealer advancing nothing, but the consumer paying a certain annual sum for the licence to consume certain goods.[1] The object of his scheme was to promote all the different branches of foreign trade, particularly the carrying trade, by taking away all duties upon importation and exportation, and thereby enabling the merchant to employ his whole capital and credit in the purchase of goods and the freight of ships, no part of either being diverted towards the advancing of taxes. The project, however, of taxing, in this manner, goods of immediate or speedy

---

[1] [*Essay on the Causes of the Decline of the Foreign Trade,* 2nd ed., 1750, pp. 78–163.]

consumption, seems liable to the four following very important objections. First, the tax would be more unequal, or not so well proportioned to the expence and consumption of the different contributors, as in the way in which it is commonly imposed. The taxes upon ale, wine, and spirituous liquors, which are advanced by the dealers, are finally paid by the different consumers exactly in proportion to their respective consumption. But if the tax were[1] to be paid by purchasing a licence to drink those liquors, the sober would, in proportion to his consumption, be taxed much more heavily than the drunken consumer. A family which exercised great hospitality would be taxed much more lightly than one who[2] entertained fewer guests. Secondly, this mode of taxation, by paying for an annual, half-yearly, or quarterly licence to consume certain goods, would diminish very much one of the principal conveniences of taxes upon goods of speedy consumption; the piece-meal payment. In the price of three-pence halfpenny, which is at present paid for a pot of porter, the different taxes upon malt, hops, and beer, together with the extraordinary profit which the brewer charges for having advanced them, may perhaps amount to about three halfpence. If a workman can conveniently spare those three halfpence, he buys a pot of porter. If he cannot, he contents himself with a pint, and, as a penny saved is a penny got, he thus gains a farthing by his temperance. He pays the tax piece-meal, as he can afford to pay it, and when he can afford to pay it; and every act of payment is perfectly voluntary, and what he can avoid if he chuses to do so. Thirdly, such taxes would operate less as sumptuary laws. When the licence was once purchased, whether the purchaser drunk much or drunk little, his tax would be the same. Fourthly, if a workman were[3] to pay all at once, by yearly, half-yearly or quarterly payments, a tax equal to what he at present pays, with little or no inconveniency, upon all the different pots and pints of porter which he drinks in any such period of time, the sum might frequently distress him very much. This mode of taxation, therefore, it seems evident, could never, without the most grievous oppression, produce a revenue nearly equal to what is derived from the present mode without any oppression. In several countries, however, commodities of an immediate or very speedy consumption are taxed in this manner. In Holland, people pay so much a head for a licence to drink tea. I have already mentioned a tax upon bread,

---

[1] [Eds. 1–3 read 'was'.]
[2] [Eds. 1 and 2 read 'which'.]   [3] [Eds. 1–3 read 'was'.]

which, so far as it is consumed in farm-houses and country villages, is there levied in the same manner.

Excepting the four mentioned above, British excise duties fall chiefly on luxuries. The duties of excise are imposed chiefly upon goods of home produce destined for home consumption. They are imposed only upon a few sorts of goods of the most general use. There can never be any doubt either concerning the goods which are subject to those duties, or concerning the particular duty which each species of goods is subject to. They fall almost altogether upon what I call luxuries, excepting always the four duties above mentioned, upon salt, soap, leather, candles, and, perhaps, that upon green glass.

Customs were originally regarded as taxes on merchants' profits, The duties of customs are much more ancient than those of excise. They seem to have been called customs, as denoting customary payments which had been in use from time immemorial. They appear to have been originally considered as taxes upon the profits of merchants. During the barbarous times of feudal anarchy, merchants, like all the other inhabitants of burghs, were considered as little better than emancipated bondmen, whose persons were despised, and whose gains were envied. The great nobility, who had consented that the king should tallage the profits of their own tenants, were not unwilling that he should tallage likewise those of an order of men whom it was much less their interest to protect. In those ignorant times, it was not understood, that the profits of merchants are a subject not taxable directly; or that the final payment of all such taxes must fall, with a considerable over-charge, upon the consumers.

those of aliens being taxed more heavily. The gains of alien merchants were looked upon more unfavourably than those of English merchants. It was natural, therefore, that those of the former should be taxed more heavily than those of the latter.[1] This distinction between the duties upon aliens and those upon English merchants, which was begun from ignorance, has been continued from the spirit of monopoly, or in order to give our own merchants an advantage both in the home and in the foreign market.

So originally customs were imposed equally on all sorts of goods, and on exports as well as imports. With this distinction, the ancient duties of customs were imposed equally upon all sorts of goods, necessaries as well as luxuries, goods exported as well as goods imported. Why should the dealers in one sort of goods, it seems to have been thought,

[1] [Above, vol. i., pp. 487, 520.]

be more favoured than those in another? or why should the merchant exporter be more favoured than the merchant importer?

The first was that on wool and leather, and the second tonnage (on wine) and poundage (on all other goods). Subsidies were additions to poundage.
The ancient customs were divided into three branches. The first, and perhaps the most ancient of all those duties, was that upon wool and leather. It seems to have been chiefly or altogether an exportation duty. When the woollen manufacture came to be established in England, lest the king should lose any part of his customs upon wool by the exportation of woollen cloths, a like duty was imposed upon them. The other two branches were, first, a duty upon wine, which, being imposed at so much a ton, was called a tonnage; and, secondly, a duty upon all other goods, which, being imposed at so much a pound of their supposed value, was called a poundage. In the forty-seventh year of Edward III. a duty of sixpence in the pound was imposed upon all goods exported and imported, except wools, wool-fells, leather, and wines, which were subject to particular duties. In the fourteenth of Richard II. this duty was raised to one shilling in the pound; but three years afterwards, it was again reduced to sixpence. It was raised to eight-pence in the second year of Henry IV.; and in the fourth year of the same prince, to one shilling. From this time to the ninth year of William III. this duty continued at one shilling in the pound. The duties of tonnage and poundage were generally granted to the king by one and the same act of parliament, and were called the Subsidy of Tonnage and Poundage. The subsidy of poundage having continued for so long a time at one shilling in the pound, or at five per cent.; a subsidy came, in the language of the customs, to denote a general duty of this kind of five per cent. This subsidy, which is now called the Old Subsidy, still continues to be levied according to the book of rates established in the twelfth of Charles II. The method of ascertaining, by a book of rates, the value of goods subject to this duty, is said to be older than the time of James I.[1] The new subsidy imposed by the ninth and tenth of William III.[2] was an additional five per cent. upon the greater part of goods. The one-third and the two-third subsidy[3] made up between them another five per cent. of which they were proportionable parts. The subsidy of 1747[4] made a fourth five per

[1] [Gilbert, *Treatise on the Court of Exchequer*, 1758, p. 224, mentions a Book of Rates printed in 1586. Dowell, *History of Taxation and Taxes*, 1884, vol. i., pp. 146, 165, places the beginning of the system soon after 1558.]   [2] [C. 23.]

[3] [2 and 3 Ann., c. 9; 3 and 4 Ann., c. 5.]   [4] [21 Geo. II., c. 2.]

cent. upon the greater part of goods; and that of 1759,[1] a fifth upon some particular sorts of goods. Besides those five subsidies, a great variety of other duties have occasionally been imposed upon particular sorts of goods, in order sometimes to relieve the exigencies of the state, and sometimes to regulate the trade of the country, according to the principles of the mercantile system.

The prevalence of the principles of the mercantile system has led to the removal of nearly all the export duties, That system has come gradually more and more into fashion. The old subsidy was imposed indifferently upon exportation as well as importation. The four subsequent subsidies, as well as the other duties which have since been occasionally imposed upon particular sorts of goods, have, with a few exceptions, been laid altogether upon importation. The greater part of the ancient duties which had been imposed upon the exportation of the goods of home produce and manufacture, have either been enlightened or taken away altogether. In most cases they have been taken away. Bounties have even been given upon the exportation of some of them. Drawbacks too, sometimes of the whole, and, in most cases, of a part of the duties which are paid upon the importation of foreign goods, have been granted upon their exportation. Only half the duties imposed by the old subsidy upon importation are drawn back upon exportation: but the whole of those imposed by the latter[2] subsidies and other imposts are, upon the greater part of goods, drawn back in the same manner.[3] This growing favour of exportation, and discouragement of importation, have suffered only a few exceptions, which chiefly concern the materials of some manufactures. These, our merchants and manufacturers are willing should come as cheap as possible to themselves, and as dear as possible to their rivals and competitors in other countries. Foreign materials are, upon this account, sometimes allowed to be imported duty free; Spanish wool, for example, flax, and raw linen yarn. The exportation of the materials of home produce, and of those which are the particular[4] produce of our colonies, has sometimes been prohibited, and sometimes subjected to higher duties. The exportation of English wool has been prohibited.[5] That of beaver skins, of

---

[1] [32 Geo. II., c. 10, on tobacco, linen, sugar and other grocery, except currants, East India goods (except coffee and raw silk), brandy and other spirits (except colonial rum), and paper.]

[2] [Ed. 1 reads, more intelligibly, 'later'. Another example of this unfortunate change occurs below, p. 468.   [3] [Above, p. 4, written after the present passage.]

[4] [Eds. 1–3 read 'peculiar,' and 'particular' is perhaps a misprint.]

[5] [Above, pp. 165–169.]

beaver wool, and of gum Senega,[1] has been subjected to higher duties; Great Britain, by the conquest of Canada and Senegal, having got almost the monopoly of those commodities.

and has been unfavourable to the revenue of the state, That the mercantile system has not been very favourable to the revenue of the great body of the people, to the annual produce of the land and labour of the country, I have endeavoured to shew in the fourth book of this Inquiry. It seems not to have been more favourable to the revenue of the sovereign; so far at least as that revenue depends upon the duties of customs.

annihilating parts of it by prohibitions of importation, In consequence of that system, the importation of several sorts of goods has been prohibited altogether. This prohibition has in some cases entirely prevented, and in others has very much diminished the importation of those commodities, by reducing the importers to the necessity of smuggling. It has entirely prevented the importation of foreign woollens; and it has very much diminished that of foreign silks and velvets. In both cases it has entirely annihilated the revenue of customs which might have been levied upon such importation.

and reducing other parts by high duties. The high duties which have been imposed upon the importation of many different sorts of foreign goods, in order to discourage their consumption in Great Britain, have in many cases served only to encourage smuggling; and in all cases have reduced the revenue of the customs below what more moderate duties would have afforded. The saying of Dr. Swift, that in the arithmetic of the customs two and two, instead of making four, make some times only one,[2] holds perfectly true with regard to such heavy duties, which never could have been imposed, had not the mercantile system taught us, in many cases, to employ taxation as an instrument, not of revenue, but of monopoly.

---

[1] [Above, pp. 175, 176.]

[2] [Swift attributes the saying to an unnamed commissioner of customs. 'I will tell you a secret, which I learned many years ago from the commissioners of the customs in London: they said when any commodity appeared to be taxed above a moderate rate, the consequence was to lessen that branch of the revenue by one-half; and one of these gentlemen pleasantly told me that the mistake of parliaments on such occasions was owing to an error of computing two and two make four; whereas in the business of laying impositions, two and two never made more than one; which happens by lessening the import, and the strong temptation of running such goods as paid high duties, at least in this kingdom.'—'Answer to a Paper Called a Memorial of the Poor Inhabitants, Tradesmen and Labourers of the Kingdom of Ireland' (in *Works*, ed. Scott, 2nd ed., 1883, vol. vii., pp. 165–166). The saying is quoted from Swift by Hume in his *Essay on the Balance of Trade*, and by Lord Kames in his *Sketches of the History of Man*, 1774, vol. i., p. 474.]

Bounties and draw-
backs (great part
of which is
obtained by fraud)
and expenses of
management make
a large deduction
from the customs
revenue.

The bounties which are sometimes given upon the exportation of home produce and manufactures, and the drawbacks which are paid upon the re-exportation of the greater part of foreign goods, have given occasion to many frauds, and to a species of smuggling more destructive of the public revenue than any other. In order to obtain the bounty or drawback, the goods, it is well known, are sometimes shipped and sent to sea; but soon afterwards clandestinely relanded in some other part of the country. The defalcation of the revenue of customs occasioned by bounties and drawbacks, of which a great part are obtained fraudulently, is very great. The gross produce of the customs in the year which ended on the 5th of January 1755, amounted to 5,068,000 l. The bounties which were paid out of this revenue, though in that year there was no bounty upon corn, amounted to 167,800 l. The drawbacks which were paid upon debentures and certificates, to 2,156,800 l. Bounties and drawbacks together, amounted to 2,324,600 l. In consequence of these deductions the revenue of the customs amounted only to 2,743,400 l.: from which, deducting 287,900 l. for the expence of management in salaries and other incidents, the neat revenue of the customs for that year comes out to be 2,455,500 l. The expence of management amounts in this manner to between five and six per cent. upon the gross revenue of the customs, and to something more than ten per cent. upon what remains of that revenue, after deducting what is paid away in bounties and drawbacks.

In the customs
returns the imports
are minimised and
the exports
exaggerated.

Heavy duties being imposed upon almost all goods imported, our merchant importers smuggle as much, and make entry of as little as they can. Our merchant exporters, on the contrary, make entry of more than they export; sometimes out of vanity, and to pass for great dealers in goods which pay no duty; and sometimes to gain a bounty or a drawback. Our exports, in consequence of these different frauds, appear upon the customhouse books greatly to overbalance our imports; to the unspeakable comfort of those politicians who measure the national prosperity by what they call the balance of trade.

The customs are
very numerous and
much less perspic-
uous and distinct

All goods imported, unless particularly exempted, and such exemptions are not very numerous, are liable to some duties of custums. If any goods are *than the excise duties.* imported not mentioned in the book of rates, they are taxed at 4 s. 9$\frac{9}{20}$ d. for every twenty shillings value,[1] according to the oath of the importer, that is, nearly at five subsidies, or five poundage duties. The book of rates is extremely comprehensive, and enumerates a great variety of articles, many of them little used, and therefore not well known. It is upon this account frequently uncertain under what article a particular sort of goods ought to be classed, and consequently what duty they ought to pay. Mistakes with regard to this sometimes ruin the custom-house officer, and frequently occasion much trouble, expence, and vexation to the importer. In point of perspicuity, precision, and distinctness, therefore, the duties of customs are much inferior to those of excise.

They might with great advantage be confined to a few articles. In order that the greater part of the members of any society should contribute to the public revenue in proportion to their respective expence, it does not seem necessary that every single article of that expence should be taxed. The revenue, which is levied by the duties of excise, is supposed to fall as equally upon the contributors as that which is levied by the duties of customs; and the duties of excise are imposed upon a few articles only of the most general use and consumption. It has been the opinion of many people, that, by proper management, the duties of customs might likewise, without any loss to the public revenue, and with great advantage to foreign trade, be confined to a few articles only.

Foreign wines and brandies and East and West Indian products at present yield most of the customs revenue. The foreign articles, of the most general use and consumption in Great Britain, seem at present to consist chiefly in foreign wines and brandies; in some of the productions of America and the West Indies, sugar, rum, tobacco, cocoanuts, &c. and in some of those of the East Indies, tea, coffee, china-ware, spiceries of all kinds, several sorts of piece-goods, &c. These different articles afford, perhaps, at present, the greater part of the revenue which is drawn from the duties of customs. The taxes which at present subsist upon foreign manufactures, if you except those upon the few contained in the foregoing enumeration, have the greater part of them been imposed for the purpose, not of revenue, but of monopoly, or to give our own merchants an advantage in the home market. By removing all prohibitions, and by subjecting all foreign

---

[1] [Saxby, *British Customs*, p. 266.]

manufactures to such moderate taxes, as it was found from experience afforded upon each article the greatest revenue to the public,
our own workmen might still have a considerable advantage in the
home market, and many articles, some of which at present afford no
revenue to government, and others a very inconsiderable one, might
afford a very great one.

The yield of high duties is often less-ened by smuggling or diminished consumption. High taxes, sometimes by diminishing the consumption of the taxed commodities, and sometimes
by encouraging smuggling, frequently afford a
smaller revenue to government than what might
be drawn from more moderate taxes.

In the first case the only remedy is to lower the duty. When the diminution of revenue is the effect of the
diminution of consumption, there can be but one
remedy, and that is the lowering of the tax.

For smuggling the remedy is to lower the tax or increase the difficulty of smuggling. When the diminution of the revenue is the effect
of the encouragement given to smuggling, it may
perhaps be remedied in two ways; either by
diminishing the temptation to smuggle, or by
increasing the difficulty of smuggling. The temptation to smuggle
can be diminished only by the lowering of the tax; and the difficulty
of smuggling can be increased only by establishing that system of
administration which is most proper for preventing it.

Excise laws are more embarrassing to the smuggler than the customs. The excise laws, it appears, I believe, from experience, obstruct and embarrass the operations of the
smuggler much more effectually than those of the
customs. By introducing into the customs a system of administration as similar to that of the excise as the nature of the different duties
will admit, the difficulty of smuggling might be very much increased. This alteration, it has been supposed by many people, might
very easily be brought about.

If customs were confined to a few articles, a system of excise supervision of stores could be instituted. The importer of commodities liable to any duties
of customs, it has been said, might at his option be
allowed either to carry them to his own private
warehouse, or to lodge them in a warehouse provided either at his own expence or at that of the
public, but under the key of the customhouse officer, and never to
be opened but in his presence. If the merchant carried them to his
own private warehouse, the duties to be immediately paid, and
never afterwards to be drawn back; and that warehouse to be at all
times subject to the visit and examination of the customhouse

officer, in order to ascertain how far the quantity contained in it corresponded with that for which the duty had been paid. If he carried them to the public warehouse, no duty to be paid till they were taken out for home consumption. If taken out for exportation, to be duty-free; proper security being always given that they should be so exported. The dealers in those particular commodities, either by wholesale or retail, to be at all times subject to the visit and examination of the customhouse officer; and to be obliged to justify by proper certificates the payment of the duty upon the whole quantity contained in their shops or warehouses. What are called the excise-duties upon rum imported are at present levied in this manner, and the same system of administration might perhaps be extended to all duties upon goods imported; provided always that those duties were, like the duties of excise, confined to a few sorts of goods of the most general use and consumption. If they were extended to almost all sorts of goods, as at present, public warehouses of sufficient extent could not easily be provided, and goods of a very delicate nature, or of which the preservation required much care and attention, could not safely be trusted by the merchant in any warehouse but his own.

Great simplification without loss of revenue would then be secured, If by such a system of administration smuggling, to any considerable extent, could be prevented even under pretty high duties; and if every duty was occasionally either heightened or lowered according as it was most likely, either the one way or the other, to afford the greatest revenue to the state; taxation being always employed as an instrument of revenue and never of monopoly; it seems not improbable that a revenue, at least equal to the present neat revenue of the customs, might be drawn from duties upon the importation of only a few sorts of goods of the most general use and consumption; and that the duties of customs might thus be brought to the same degree of simplicity, certainty, and precision, as those of excise. What the revenue at present loses, by drawbacks upon the re-exportation of foreign goods which are afterwards relanded and consumed at home, would under this system be saved altogether. If to this saving, which would alone be very considerable, were[1] added the abolition of all bounties upon the exportation of home-produce; in all cases in which those bounties were not in reality drawbacks of some duties of excise which had before been advanced; it cannot well be doubted

---

[1] [Eds. 1–3 read 'was'.]

but that the neat revenue of customs might, after an alteration of this kind, be fully equal to what it had ever been before.

while the trade and manufactures of the country would gain greatly. If by such a change of system the public revenue suffered no loss, the trade and manufactures of the country would certainly gain a very considerable advantage. The trade in the commodities not taxed, by far the greatest number, would be perfectly free, and might be carried on to and from all parts of the world with every possible advantage. Among those commodities would be comprehended all the necessaries of life, and all the materials of manufacture. So far as the free importation of the necessaries of life reduced their average money price in the home market, it would reduce the money price of labour, but without reducing in any respect its real recompence. The value of money is in proportion to the quantity of the necessaries of life which it will purchase. That of the necessaries of life is altogether independent of the quantity of money which can be had for them. The reduction in the money price of labour would necessarily be attended with a proportionable one in that of all home-manufactures, which would thereby gain some advantage in all foreign markets. The price of some manufactures would be reduced in a still greater proportion by the free importation of the raw materials. If raw silk could be imported from China and Indostan duty-free, the silk manufacturers in England could greatly undersell those of both France and Italy. There would be no occasion to prohibit the importation of foreign silks and velvets. The cheapness of their goods would secure to our own workmen, not only the possession of the home, but a very great command of the foreign market. Even the trade in the commodities taxed would be carried on with much more advantage than at present. If those commodities were delivered out of the public warehouse for foreign exportation, being in this case exempted from all taxes, the trade in them would be perfectly free. The carrying trade in all sorts of goods would under this system enjoy every possible advantage. If those commodities were delivered out for home-consumption, the importer not being obliged to advance the tax till he had an opportunity of selling his goods, either to some dealer, or to some consumer, he could always afford to sell them cheaper than if he had been obliged to advance it at the moment of importation. Under the same taxes, the foreign trade of consumption even in the taxed commodities, might in this manner be carried on with much more advantage than it can at present.

Sir Robert Walpole's excise scheme was something of this kind so far as wine and tobacco are concerned.

It was the object of the famous excise scheme of Sir Robert Walpole to establish, with regard to wine and tobacco, a system not very unlike that which is here proposed. But though the bill which was then brought into parliament, comprehended those two commodities only; it was generally supposed to be meant as an introduction to a more extensive scheme of the same kind. Faction, combined with the interest of smuggling merchants, raised so violent, though so unjust, a clamour against that bill, that the minister thought proper to drop it; and from a dread of exciting a clamour of the same kind, none of his successors have dared to resume the project.

The duties on foreign luxuries fall chiefly on the middle and upper ranks.

The duties upon foreign luxuries imported for home-consumption, though they sometimes fall upon the poor, fall principally upon people of middling or more than middling fortune. Such are, for example, the duties upon foreign wines, upon coffee, chocolate, tea, sugar, &c.

Those on the luxuries of home produce fall on people of all ranks.

The duties upon the cheaper luxuries of home-produce destined for home-consumption, fall pretty equally upon people of all ranks in proportion to their respective expence. The poor pay the duties upon malt, hops, beer, and ale, upon their own consumption: The rich, upon both[1] their own consumption and that of their servants.

Taxes on the consumption of the inferior ranks are much more productive than those on the consumption of the rich.

The whole consumption of the inferior ranks of people, or of those below the middling rank, it must be observed, is in every country much greater, not only in quantity, but in value, than that of the middling and of those above the middling rank. The whole expence of the inferior is much greater than that of the superior ranks. In the first place, almost the whole capital of every country is annually distributed among the inferior ranks of people, as the wages of productive labour. Secondly, a great part of the revenue arising from both[2] the rent of land and[3] the profits of stock, is annually distributed among the same rank, in the wages and maintenance of menial servants, and other unproductive labourers. Thirdly, some part of the profits of stock belongs to the same rank, as a revenue arising from the employment of their small capitals. The amount of the profits annually made by small shop-

---

[1] [Ed. 1 reads 'both upon'.]
[2] [Ed. 1 reads 'both from'.]   [3] [Ed. 1 reads 'and from'.]

keepers, tradesmen, and retailers of all kinds, is every where very considerable, and makes a very considerable portion of the annual produce. Fourthly, and lastly, some part even of the rent of land belongs to the same rank; a considerable part to those who are somewhat below the middling rank, and a small part even to the lowest rank; common labourers sometimes possessing in property an acre or two of land. Though the expence of those inferior ranks of people, therefore, taking them individually, is very small, yet the whole mass of it, taking them collectively, amounts always to by much the largest portion of the whole expence of the society; what remains, of the annual produce of the land and labour of the country for the consumption of the superior ranks, being always much less, not only in quantity but in value. The taxes upon expence, therefore, which fall chiefly upon that of the superior ranks of people, upon the smaller portion of the annual produce, are likely to be much less productive than either those which fall indifferently upon the expence of all ranks, or even those which fall chiefly upon that of the inferior ranks; than either those which fall indifferently upon the whole annual produce, or those which fall chiefly upon the larger portion of it. The excise upon the materials and manufacture of home-made fermented and spirituous liquors is accordingly, of all the different taxes upon expence, by far the most productive; and this branch of the excise falls very much, perhaps principally, upon the expence of the common people. In the year which ended on the 5th of July 1775, the gross produce of this branch of the excise amounted to 3,341,837 l. 9 s. 9 d.[1]

But such taxes must never be on the necessary consumption of the inferior ranks. It must always be remembered, however, that it is the luxurious and not the necessary expence of the inferior ranks of people that ought ever to be taxed. The final payment of any tax upon their necessary expence would fall altogether upon the superior ranks of people; upon the smaller portion of the annual produce, and not upon the greater. Such a tax must in all cases either raise the wages of labour, or lessen the demand for it. It could not raise the wages of labour, without throwing the final payment of the tax upon the superior ranks of people. It could not lessen the demand for labour, without lessening the annual produce of the land and labour of the country, the fund from which all taxes must be finally paid. Whatever might be the state to which a tax of this kind reduced the demand for

---

[1] [Ed. 1 reads '£3,314,223 18s. 10¾d.']

labour, it must always raise wages higher than they otherwise would be in that state; and the final payment of this enhancement of wages must in all cases fall upon the superior ranks of people.

Liquors brewed or distilled for private use are exempt from excise, though a composition must be paid for malting. Fermented liquors brewed, and spirituous liquors distilled, not for sale, but for private use, are not in Great Britain liable to any duties of excise. This exemption, of which the object is to save private families from[1] the odious visit and examination of the tax-gatherer, occasions the burden of those duties to fall frequently much lighter upon the rich than upon the poor. It is not, indeed, very common to distil for private use, though it is done sometimes. But in the country, many middling and almost all rich and great families brew their own beer. Their strong beer, therefore, costs them eight shillings a barrel less than it costs the common brewer, who must have his profit upon the tax, as well as upon all the other expence which he advances. Such families, therefore, must drink their beer at least nine or ten shillings a barrel cheaper than any liquor of the same quality can be drunk by the common people, to whom it is every where more convenient to buy their beer, by little and little, from the brewery or the alehouse. Malt, in the same manner, that is made for the use of a private family, is not liable to the visit or examination of the tax-gatherer; but in this case the family must compound at seven shillings and sixpence a head for the tax. Seven shillings and sixpence are equal to the excise upon ten bushels of malt; a quantity fully equal to what all the different members of any sober family, men, women, and children, are at an average likely to consume. But in rich and great families, where country hospitality is much practised, the malt liquors consumed by the members of the family make but a small part of the consumption of the house. Either on account of this composition, however, or for other reasons, it is not near so common to malt as to brew for private use. It is difficult to imagine any equitable reason why those who either brew or distil for private use, should not be subject to a composition of the same kind.

It is said that a tax on malt smaller than the present taxes on malt, beer and ale taken together would bring in more revenue, A greater revenue than what is at present drawn from all the heavy taxes upon malt, beer, and ale, might be raised, it has frequently been said, by a much lighter tax upon malt; the opportunities of defrauding the revenue being much greater in a

---

[1] [Ed. 1 reads 'is not to expose private families to'.]

brewery than in a malt-house; and those who brew for private use being exempted from all duties or composition for duties, which is not the case with those who malt for private use.

In the porter brewery of London, a quarter of malt is commonly brewed into more than two barrels and a half, sometimes into three *and figures are* barrels of porter. The different taxes upon malt *quoted to prove it.* amount to six shillings a quarter; those upon strong beer and ale to eight shillings a barrel. In the porter brewery, therefore, the different taxes upon malt, beer, and ale, amount to between twenty-six and thirty shillings upon the produce of a quarter of malt. In the country brewery for common country sale, a quarter of malt is seldom brewed into less than two barrels of strong and one barrel of small beer; frequently into two barrels and a half of strong beer. The different taxes upon small beer amount to one shilling and four-pence a barrel. In the country brewery, therefore, the different

	l.	s.	d.
In 1772, the old malt-tax produced	722,023	11	11
The additional	356,776	7	9¾
In 1773, the old tax produced. . . .	561,627	3	7½
The additional	278,650	15	3¾
In 1774, the old tax produced. . . .	624,614	17	5¾
The additional	310,745	2	8½
In 1775, the old tax produced. . . .	657,357	—	8¼
The additional	323,785	12	6¼
	4)3,835,580	12	—¾
Average of these four years	958,895	3	—³⁄₁₆
In 1772, the country excise produced . . .	1,243,128	5	3
The London brewery	408,260	7	2¾
In 1773, the country excise	1,245,808	3	3
The London brewery	405,406	17	10½
In 1774, the country excise	1,246,373	14	5½
The London brewery	320,601	18	—¼
In 1775, the country excise	1,214,583	6	1
The London brewery	463,670	7	—¼
	4)6,547,832	19	2¼
Average of these four years	1,636,958	4	9½
To which adding the average malt tax, or . .	958,895	3	—³⁄₁₆
The whole amount of those different taxes comes out to be	2,595,853	7	9¹¹⁄₁₆
But by tripling the malt tax, or by raising it from six to eighteen shillings upon the quarter of malt, that single tax would produce	2,876,685	9	—⁹⁄₁₆
A sum which exceeds the foregoing by . . .	280,832	1	2¹⁴⁄₁₆

taxes upon malt, beer, and ale, seldom amount to less than twenty-three shillings and four-pence, frequently to twenty-six shillings, upon the produce of a quarter of malt. Taking the whole kingdom at an average, therefore, the whole amount of the duties upon malt, beer, and ale, cannot be estimated at less than twenty-four or twenty-five shillings upon the produce of a quarter of malt. But by taking off all the different duties upon beer and ale, and by tripling the malt-tax, or by raising it from six to eighteen shillings upon the quarter of malt, a greater revenue, it is said, might be raised by this single tax than what is at present drawn from all those heavier taxes.

Taxes on cyder and mum included in the old malt tax are counterbalanced by the 'country excise' duty on cyder, verjuice, vinegar and mead. Under the old malt tax, indeed, is comprehended a tax of four shillings upon the hogshead of cyder, and another of ten shillings upon the barrel of mum. In 1774, the tax upon cyder produced only 3083 l. 6 s. 8 d. It probably fell somewhat short of its usual amount; all the different taxes upon cyder having, that year, produced less than ordinary. The tax upon mum, though much heavier, is still less productive, on account of the smaller consumption of that liquor. But to balance whatever may be the ordinary amount of those two taxes; there is comprehended under what is called The country excise, first, the old excise of six shillings and eight-pence upon the hogshead of cyder; secondly, a like tax of six shillings and eight-pence upon the hogshead of verjuice; thirdly, another of eight shillings and nine-pence upon the hogshead of vinegar; and, lastly, a fourth tax of eleven-pence upon the gallon of mead or metheglin: the produce of those different taxes will probably much more than counterbalance that of the duties imposed, by what is called The annual malt tax upon cyder and mum.

If the malt tax were raised, it would be proper to reduce the excises on wines and spirits containing malt, Malt is consumed not only in the brewery of beer and ale, but in the manufacture of low wines and spirits. If the malt tax were[1] to be raised to eighteen shillings upon the quarter, it might be necessary to make some abatement in the different excises which are imposed upon those particular sorts of low wines and spirits of which malt makes any part of the materials. In what are called Malt spirits, it makes commonly but a third part of the materials; the other two-thirds being either raw barley, or one-third barley and one-third wheat. In the distillery of malt spirits, both the opportunity and the temptation to smuggle, are much greater than either

---

[1] [Eds. 1–3 read 'was'.]

in a brewery or in a malthouse; the opportunity, on account of the smaller bulk and greater value of the commodity; and the temptation, on account of the superior height of the duties, which amount to 3 s. 10$\frac{2}{3}$ d.[1] upon the gallon of spirits. By increasing the duties upon malt, and reducing those upon the distillery, both the opportunities and the temptation to smuggle would be diminished, which might occasion a still further augmentation of revenue.

but not so as to reduce the price of spirits.   It has for some time past been the policy of Great Britain to discourage the consumption of spirituous liquors, on account of their supposed tendency to ruin the health and to corrupt the morals of the common people. According to this policy, the abatement of the taxes upon the distillery ought not to be so great as to reduce, in any respect, the price of those liquors. Spirituous liquors might remain as dear as ever; while at the same time the wholesome and invigorating liquors of beer and ale might be considerably reduced in their price. The people might thus be in part relieved from one of the burdens of which they at present complain the most; while at the same time the revenue might be considerably augmented.

Dr. Davenant objects that the maltster's profits would be unfairly taxed, and the rent and profit of barley land reduced,   The objections of Dr. Davenant to this alteration in the present system of excise duties, seem to be without foundation. Those objections are, that the tax, instead of dividing itself as at present pretty equally upon the profit of the maltster, upon that of the brewer, and upon that of the retailer, would, so far as it affected profit, fall altogether upon that of the maltster; that the maltster could not so easily get back the amount of the tax in the advanced price of his malt, as the brewer and retailer in the advanced price of their liquor; and that so heavy a tax upon malt might reduce the rent and profit of barley land.[2]

---

[1] Though the duties directly imposed upon proof spirits amount only to 2s. 6d. per gallon, these added to the duties upon the low wines, from which they are distilled, amount to 3s. 10$\frac{2}{3}$d. Both low wines and proof spirits are, to prevent frauds, now rated according to what they gauge in the wash. [This note appears first in ed. 3; ed. 1 reads '2s. 6d.' in the text instead of '3s. 10$\frac{2}{3}$d.']

[2] [*Political and Commercial Works*, ed. Sir Charles Whitworth, 1771, vol. i., pp. 222, 223. But Davenant does not confine the effect of the existing tax to the maltster, the brewer and the retailer. The tax, he says, 'which seems to be upon malt, does not lie all upon that commodity, as is vulgarly thought. For a great many different persons contribute to the payment of this duty, before it comes into the Exchequer. First, the landlord, because of the excise, is forced to let his barley land at a lower rate; and, upon the same score, the tenant must sell his barley at a less price; then the maltster bears his share, for because of the duty, he must abate something in the price of his malt, or keep it; in a proportion it likewise affects the hop merchant, the cooper, the collier, and all

but the change would make malt liquors cheaper, and so be likely to increase the consumption,

No tax can ever reduce, for any considerable time, the rate of profit in any particular trade, which must always keep its level with other trades in the neighbourhood. The present duties upon malt, beer, and ale, do not affect the profits of the dealers in those commodities, who all get back the tax with an additional profit, in the enhanced price of their goods. A tax indeed may render the goods upon which it is imposed so dear as to diminish the consumption of them. But the consumption of malt is in malt liquors; and a tax of eighteen shillings upon the quarter of malt could not well render those liquors dearer than the different taxes, amounting to twenty-four or twenty-five shillings, do at present. Those liquors, on the contrary, would probably become cheaper, and the consumption of them would be more likely to increase than to diminish.

and the maltster could recover eighteen shillings as easily as the brewer at present recovers twenty-four or thirty and might be given longer credit.

It is not very easy to understand why it should be more difficult for the maltster to get back eighteen shillings in the advanced price of his malt, than it is at present for the brewer to get back twenty-four or twenty-five, sometimes thirty shillings, in that of his liquor. The maltster, indeed, instead of a tax of six shillings, would be obliged to advance one of eighteen shillings upon every quarter of malt. But the brewer is at present obliged to advance a tax of twenty-four or twenty-five, sometimes thirty shillings upon every quarter of malt which he brews. It could not be more inconvenient for the maltster to advance a lighter tax, that it is at present for the brewer to advance a heavier one. The maltster doth not always keep in his granaries a stock of malt which it will require a longer time to dispose of, than the stock of beer and ale which the brewer frequently keeps in his cellars. The former, therefore, may frequently get the returns of his money as soon as the latter. But whatever inconveniency might arise to the maltster from being obliged to advance a heavier tax, it[1] could easily be remedied by granting him a few months longer credit that is at present commonly given to the brewer.

trades that have relation to the commodity. The retailers and brewers bear likewise a great share, whose gains of necessity will be less, because of that imposition; and, lastly, it comes heaviest of all upon the consumers.' If the duty were put upon the maltster, it would be 'difficult for him to raise the price of a dear commodity a full $\frac{1}{2}$d. at once: so that he must bear the greatest part of the burden himself, or throw it upon the farmer, by giving less for barley, which brings the tax directly upon the land of England.']

[1] [Ed. 1 does not contain 'it'.]

The consumption of barley not being reduced, the rent and profit of barley land could not be reduced, as there is no monopoly. Nothing could reduce the rent and profit of barley land which did not reduce the demand for barley. But a change of system, which reduced the duties upon a quarter of malt brewed into beer and ale from twenty-four and twenty-five shillings to eighteen shillings, would be more likely to increase than diminish that demand. The rent and profit of barley land, besides, must always be nearly equal to those of other equally fertile and equally well cultivated land. If they were less, some part of the barley land would soon be turned to some other purpose; and if they were greater, more land would soon be turned to the raising of barley. When the ordinary price of any particular produce of land is at what may be called a monopoly price, a tax upon it necessarily reduces the rent and profit of the land which grows it. A tax upon the produce of those precious vineyards, of which the wine falls so much short of the effectual demand, that its price is always above the natural proportion to that of the produce of other equally fertile and equally well cultivated land, would necessarily reduce the rent and profit of those vineyards. The price of the wines being already the highest that could be got for the quantity commonly sent to market, it could not be raised higher without diminishing that quantity; and the quantity could not be diminished without still greater loss, because the lands could not be turned to any other equally valuable produce. The whole weight of the tax, therefore, would fall upon the rent and profit; properly upon the rent of the vineyard. When it has been proposed to lay any new tax upon sugar, our sugar planters have frequently complained that the whole weight of such taxes fell, not upon the consumer, but upon the producer; they never having been able to raise the price of their sugar after the tax, higher than it was before. The price had, it seems, before the tax been a monopoly price; and the argument adduced to shew that sugar was an improper subject of taxation, demonstrated, perhaps, that it was a proper one; the gains of monopolists, whenever they can be come at, being certainly of all subjects the most proper. But the ordinary price of barley has never been a monopoly price; and the rent and profit of barley land have never been above their natural proportion to those of other equally fertile and equally well cultivated land. The different taxes which have been imposed upon malt, beer and ale, have never lowered the price of barley; have never reduced the rent and profit of barley land. The price of malt to the brewer has constantly risen in proportion to the taxes imposed upon it; and those taxes, together with the different duties upon beer and ale, have constantly either raised the price, or what comes to the same thing, reduced the quality of those commodities to the consumer. The final payment of those taxes has fallen constantly upon the consumer, and not upon the producer.

The only sufferers would be those who brew for private use.   The only people likely to suffer by the change of system here proposed, are those who brew for their own private use. But the exemption, which this superior rank of people at present enjoy, from very heavy taxes which are paid by the poor labourer and artificer, is surely most unjust and unequal, and ought to be taken away, even though this change was never to take place. It has probably been the interest of this superior order of people, however, which has hitherto prevented a change of system that could not well fail both to increase the revenue and to relieve the people.

Tolls on goods carried from place to place affect prices unequally.   Besides such duties as those of customs and excise above-mentioned, there are several others which affect the price of goods more unequally and more indirectly. Of this kind are the duties which in French are called Péages, which in old Saxon times were called Duties of Passage, and which seem to have been originally established for the same purpose as our turnpike tolls, or the tolls upon our canals and navigable rivers, for the maintenance of the road or of the navigation. Those duties, when applied to such purposes, are most properly imposed according to the bulk or weight of the goods. As they were originally local and provincial duties, applicable to local and provincial purposes, the administration of them was in most cases entrusted to the particular town, parish, or lordship, in which they were levied; such communities being in some way or other supposed to be accountable for the application. The sovereign, who is altogether unaccountable, has in many countries assumed to himself the administration of those duties; and though he has in most cases enhanced very much the duty, he has in many entirely neglected the application. If the turnpike tolls of Great Britain should ever become one of the resources of government, we may learn, by the example of many other nations, what would probably be the consequence. Such tolls are no doubt finally paid by the consumer; but the consumer is not taxed in proportion to his expence when he pays, not according to the value, but according to the bulk or weight of what he consumes. When such duties are imposed, not according to the bulk or weight, but according to the supposed value of the goods, they become properly a sort of inland customs or excises, which obstruct very much the most important of all branches of commerce, the interior commerce of the country.

Some countries levy transit duties on foreign goods. In some small states duties similar to those passage duties are imposed upon goods carried across the territory, either by land or by water, from one foreign country to another. These are in some countries called transit-duties. Some of the little Italian states, which are situated upon the Po, and the rivers which run into it, derive some revenue from duties of this kind, which are paid altogether by foreigners, and which, perhaps, are[1] the only duties that one state can impose upon the subjects of another, without obstructing in any respect the industry or commerce of its own. The most important transit-duty in the world is that levied by the king of Denmark upon all merchant ships which pass through the Sound.

Taxes on luxuries do not reach absentees, but the fact that they are paid voluntarily recommends them. Such taxes upon luxuries as the greater part of the duties of customs and excise, though they all[2] fall indifferently upon every different species of revenue, and are paid finally, or without any retribution, by whoever consumes the commodities upon which they are imposed, yet they do not always fall equally or proportionably upon the revenue of every individual. As every man's humour regulates the degree of his consumption, every man contributes rather according to his humour than in proportion to his revenue; the profuse contribute more, the parsimonious less, than their proper proportion. During the minority of a man of great fortune, he contributes commonly very little, by his consumption, towards the support of that state from whose protection he derives a great revenue. Those who live in another country contribute nothing, by their consumption, towards the support of the government of that country, in which is situated the source of their revenue. If in this latter country there should be no land-tax, nor any considerable duty upon the transference either of moveable or of immoveable property, as is the case in Ireland, such absentees may derive a great revenue from the protection of a government to the support of which they do not contribute a single shilling. This inequality is likely to be greatest in a country of which the govern-

---

[1] [Ed. 1 reads 'are perhaps'.]   [2] [Ed. 1 does not contain 'all'.]

ment is in some respects subordinate and dependent upon that of some other. The people who possess the most extensive property in the dependent, will in this case generally chuse to live in the governing country. Ireland is precisely in this situation, and we cannot therefore wonder that the proposal of a tax upon absentees should be so very popular in that country. It might, perhaps, be a little difficult to ascertain either what sort, or what degree of absence would[1] subject a man to be taxed as an absentee, or at what precise time the tax should either begin or end. If you except, however, this very peculiar situation, any inequality in the contribution of individuals, which can arise from such taxes, is much more than compensated by the very circumstance which occasions that inequality; the circumstance that every man's contribution is altogether voluntary; it being altogether in his power either to consume or not to consume the commodity taxed. Where such taxes, therefore, are properly assessed and upon proper commodities, they are paid with less grumbling than any other. When they are advanced by the merchant or manufacturer, the consumer, who finally pays them, soon comes to confound them with the price of the commodities, and almost forgets that he pays any tax.

They are also certain, Such taxes are or may be perfectly certain, or may be assessed so as to leave no doubt concerning either what ought to be paid, or when it ought to be paid; concerning either the quantity or the time of payment. Whatever uncertainty there may sometimes be, either in the duties of customs in Great Britain, or in other duties of the same kind in other countries, it cannot arise from the nature of those duties, but from the inaccurate or unskilful manner in which the law that imposes them is expressed.

and payable at convenient times, Taxes upon luxuries generally are, and always may be, paid piece-meal, or in proportion as the contributors have occasion to purchase the goods upon which they are imposed. In the time and mode of payment they are, or may be, of all taxes the most convenient. Upon the whole, such taxes, therefore, are, perhaps, as agreeable to the three first of the four general maxims concerning taxation, as any other. They offend in every respect against the fourth.

but take much more from the people than they yield to the state, since Such taxes, in proportion to what they bring into the public treasury of the state, always take out or keep out of the pockets of the people more than

---

[1] [Ed. 1 reads 'should'.]

almost any other taxes. They seem to do this in all the four different ways in which it is possible to do it.

(1) the salaries and perquisites of customs and excise officers take a large proportion of what is collected;

First, the levying of such taxes, even when imposed in the most judicious manner, requires a great number of customhouse and excise officers, whose salaries and perquisites are a real tax upon the people, which brings nothing into the treasury of the state. This expence, however, it must be acknowledged, is more moderate in Great Britain than in most other countries. In the year which ended on the fifth of July 1775, the gross produce of the different duties, under the management of the commissioners of excise in England, amounted to 5,507,308 l. 18 s. 8¼ d.[1] which was levied at an expence of little more than five and a half per cent. From this gross produce, however, there must be deducted what was paid away in bounties and drawbacks upon the exportation of exciseable goods, which will reduce the neat produce below five millions.[2] The levying of the salt duty, an excise duty, but under a different management, is much more expensive. The neat revenue of the customs does not amount to two millions and a half, which is levied at an expence of more than ten per cent. in the salaries of officers, and other incidents. But the perquisites of customhouse officers are every where much greater than their salaries; at some ports more than double or triple those salaries. If the salaries of officers, and other incidents, therefore, amount to more than ten per cent. upon the neat revenue of the customs; the whole expence of levying that revenue may amount, in salaries and perquisites together, to more than twenty or thirty per cent. The officers of excise receive few or no perquisites: and the administration of that branch of the revenue being of more recent establishment, is in general less corrupted than that of the customs, into which length of time has introduced and authorised many abuses. By charging upon malt the whole revenue which is at present levied by the different duties upon malt and malt liquors, a saving, it is supposed, of more than fifty thousand pounds might be made in the annual expence of the excise. By confining the duties of customs to a few sorts of goods, and by levying those duties according to the excise laws, a much greater saving might probably be made in the annual expence of the customs.

---

[1] [Ed. 1 reads '£5,479,695 7s. 10d.']
[2] The neat produce of that year, after deducting all expenses and allowances, amounted to 4,975,652 l. 19 s. 6 d. [This note appears first in ed. 2.]

(2) particular branches of industry are discouraged; Secondly, such taxes necessarily occasion some obstruction or discouragement to certain branches of industry. As they always raise the price of the commodity taxed, they so far discourage its consumption, and consequently its production. If it is a commodity of home growth or manufacture, less labour comes to be employed in raising and producing it. If it is a foreign commodity of which the tax increases in this manner the price, the commodities of the same kind which are made at home may thereby, indeed, gain some advantage in the home market, and a greater quantity of domestic industry may thereby be turned toward preparing them. But though this rise of price in a foreign commodity may encourage domestic industry in one particular branch, it necessarily discourages that industry in almost every other. The dearer the Birmingham manufacturer buys his foreign wine, the cheaper he necessarily sells that part of his hardware with which, or, what comes to the same thing, with the price of which he buys it. That part of his hardware, therefore, becomes of less value to him, and he has less encouragement to work at it. The dearer the consumers in one country pay for the surplus produce of another, the cheaper they necessarily sell that part of their own surplus produce with which, or, what comes to the same thing, with the price of which they buy it. That part of their own surplus produce becomes of less value to them, and they have less encouragement to increase its quantity. All taxes upon consumable commodities, therefore, tend to reduce the quantity of productive labour below what it otherwise would be, either in preparing the commodities taxed, if they are home commodities; or in preparing those with which they are purchased, if they are foreign commodities. Such taxes too always alter, more or less, the natural direction of national industry, and turn it into a channel always different from, and generally less advantageous than that in which it would have run of its own accord.

(3) smuggling is encouraged; Thirdly, the hope of evading such taxes by smuggling gives frequent occasion to forfeitures and other penalties, which entirely ruin the smuggler; a person, who, though no doubt highly blameable for violating the laws of his country, is frequently incapable of violating those of natural justice, and would have been, in every respect, an excellent citizen, had not the laws of his country made that a crime which nature never meant to be so. In those corrupted governments where there is at least a

general suspicion of much unnecessary expence, and great misapplication of the public revenue, the laws which guard it are little respected. Not many people are scrupulous about smuggling, when, without perjury, they can find any easy and safe opportunity of doing so. To pretend to have any scruple about buying smuggled goods, though a manifest encouragement to the violation of the revenue laws, and to the perjury which almost always attends it, would in most countries be regarded as one of those pedantic pieces of hypocrisy which, instead of gaining credit with any body, serve only to expose the person who affects to practise them, to the suspicion of being a greater knave than most of his neighbours. By this indulgence of the public, the smuggler is often encouraged to continue a trade which he is thus taught to consider as in some measure innocent; and when the severity of the revenue laws is ready to fall upon him, he is frequently disposed to defend with violence, what he has been accustomed to regard as his just property. From being at first, perhaps, rather imprudent than criminal, he at last too often becomes one of the hardiest and most determined violators of the laws of society. By the ruin of the smuggler, his capital, which had before been employed in maintaining productive labour, is absorbed either in the revenue of the state or in that of the revenue-officer, and is employed in maintaining unproductive, to the diminution of the general capital of the society, and of the useful industry which it might otherwise have maintained.

and (4) vexation equivalent to expense is caused by the tax-gatherers' examinations and visits. Fourthly, such taxes, by subjecting at least the dealers in the taxed commodities to the frequent visits and odious examination of the tax-gatherers, expose them sometimes, no doubt, to some degree of oppression, and always to much trouble and vexation; and though vexation, as has already been said,[1] is not strictly speaking expence, it is certainly equivalent to the expence at which every man would be willing to redeem himself from it. The laws of excise, though more effectual for the purpose for which they were instituted, are, in this respect, more vexatious than those of the customs. When a merchant has imported goods subject to certain duties of customs, when he has paid those duties, and lodged the goods in his warehouse, he is not in most cases liable to any further trouble or vexation from the customhouse officer. It is otherwise with goods subject to duties of excise. The dealers have no respite

[1] [Above, p. 352.]

from the continual visits and examination of the excise officers. The duties of excise are, upon this account, more unpopular than those of the customs; and so are the officers who levy them. Those officers, it is pretended, though in general, perhaps, they do their duty fully as well as those of the customs; yet, as that duty obliges them to be frequently very troublesome to some of their neighbours, commonly contract a certain hardness of character which the others frequently have not. This observation, however, may very probably be the mere suggestion of fraudulent dealers, whose smuggling is either prevented or detected by their diligence.

Great Britain suffers less than other countries from these inconveniencies. The inconveniencies, however, which are, perhaps, in some degree inseparable from taxes upon consumable commodities, fall as light upon the people of Great Britain as upon those of any other country of which the government is nearly as expensive. Our state is not perfect, and might be mended; but it is as good or better than that of most of our neighbours.

Duties on commodities are sometimes repeated on each sale, as by the Spanish Alcavala, In consequence of the notion that duties upon consumable goods were taxes upon the profits of merchants, those duties have, in some countries, been repeated upon every successive sale of the goods. If the profits of the merchant importer or merchant manufacturer were taxed, equality seemed to require that those of all the middle buyers, who intervened between either of them and the consumer, should likewise be taxed. The famous Alcavala of Spain seems to have been established upon this principle. It was at first a tax of ten per cent., afterwards of fourteen per cent., and is at present of only six per cent. upon the sale of every sort of property, whether moveable or immoveable; and it is repeated every time the property is sold.[1] The levying of this tax requires a multitude of revenue-officers sufficient to guard the transportation of goods, not only from one province to another, but from one shop to another. It subjects, not

[1] Memoires concernant les Droits, &c. tom. i. p. 455. ['La première branche, connue sous la dénomination de Alcavala y Cientos, consiste dans un droit qui se perçoit sur toutes les choses mobiliaires et immobiliaires qui sont vendues, échangées et négociées: ce droit qui dans le principe avoit été fixé à quatorze pour cent a été depuis réduit à six pour cent.' The rest of the information is probably from Uztariz, *Theory and Practice of Commerce and Maritime Affairs*, trans. by John Kippax, 1751, chap. 96, *ad init.*, vol. ii., p. 236. 'It is so very oppressive as to lay 10 per cent. for the primitive Alcavala, and the four 1 per cents. annexed to it, a duty not only chargeable on the first sale, but on every future sale of goods, I am jealous, it is one of the principal engines, that contributed to the ruin of most of our manufactures and trade. For though these duties are not charged to the full in some places, a heavy tax is paid.']

only the dealers in some sorts of goods, but those in all sorts, every farmer, every manufacturer, every merchant and shop-keeper, to the continual visits and examination of the tax-gatherers. Through the greater part of a country in which a tax of this kind is established, nothing can be produced for distant sale. The produce of every part of the country must be proportioned to the consumption of the neighbourhood. It is to the Alcavala, accordingly, that Ustaritz imputes the ruin of the manufactures of Spain.[1] He might have imputed to it likewise the declension of agriculture, it being imposed not only upon manufactures, but upon the rude produce of the land.

and the 3 per cent. tax at Naples.   In the kingdom of Naples there is a similar tax of three per cent. upon the value of all contracts, and consequently upon that of all contracts of sale. It is both lighter than the Spanish tax, and the greater part of towns and parishes are allowed to pay a composition in lieu of it. They levy this composition in what manner they please, generally in a way that gives no interruption to the interior commerce of the place. The Neapolitan tax, therefore, is not near so ruinous as the Spanish one.

Great advantage is obtained by the uniformity of taxation in Great Britain.   The uniform system of taxation, which, with a few exceptions of no great consequence, takes place in all the different parts of the united kingdom of Great Britain, leaves the interior commerce of the country, the inland and coasting trade, almost entirely free. The inland trade is almost perfectly free, and the greater part of goods may be carried from one end of the kingdom to the other, without requiring any permit or let-pass, without being subject to question, visit, or examination from the revenue officers. There are a few exceptions, but they are such as can give no interruption to any important branch of the inland commerce of the country. Goods carried coastwise, indeed, require certificates or coast cockets. If you except coals, however, the rest are almost all duty-free. This freedom of interior commerce, the effect of the uniformity of the system of taxation, is perhaps one of the principal causes of the prosperity of Great Britain; every great country being necessarily the best and most extensive market for the greater part of the productions of its own industry. If the same freedom, in consequence of the same uniformity, could be extended to Ireland and the planta-

---

[1] [See the preceding note. Uztariz' opinion is quoted by Lord Kames, *Sketches of the History of Man*, 1774, vol. i., p. 516.]

tions, both the grandeur of the state and the prosperity of every part of the empire, would probably be still greater than at present.

In France the diversity of taxes in different provinces occasions many hindrances to internal trade,   In France, the different revenue laws which take place in the different provinces, require a multitude of revenue-officers to surround, not only the frontiers of the kingdom, but those of almost each particular province, in order either to prevent the importation of certain goods, or to subject it to the payment of certain duties, to the no small interruption of the interior commerce of the country. Some provinces are allowed to compound for the gabelle or salt-tax. Others are exempted from it altogether. Some provinces are exempted from the exclusive sale of tobacco, which the farmers-general enjoy through the greater part of the kingdom. The aids, which correspond to the excise in England, are very different in different provinces. Some provinces are exempted from them, and pay a composition or equivalent. In those in which they take place and are in farm, there are many local duties which do not extend beyond a particular town or district. The Traites, which correspond to our customs, divide the kingdom into three great parts; first, the provinces subject to the tarif of 1664, which are called the provinces of the five great farms, and under which are comprehended Picardy, Normandy, and the greater part of the interior provinces of the kingdom; secondly, the provinces subject to the tarif of 1667, which are called the provinces reckoned foreign, and under which are comprehended the greater part of the frontier provinces; and thirdly, those provinces which are said to be treated as foreign, or which, because they are allowed a free commerce with foreign countries, are in their commerce with the other provinces of France subjected to the same duties as other foreign countries. These are Alsace, the three bishopricks of Metz, Toul, and Verdun, and the three cities of Dunkirk, Bayonne, and Marseilles. Both in the provinces of the five great farms (called so on account of an ancient division of the duties of customs into five great branches, each of which was originally the subject of a particular farm, though they are now all united into one), and in those which are said to be reckoned foreign, there are many local duties which do not extend beyond a particular town or district. There are some such even in the provinces which are said to be treated as foreign, particularly in the city of Marseilles. It is unnecessary to observe how much, both the restraints upon the interior commerce of the country, and the number of the revenue officers must be multiplied, in order to guard the frontiers of those different provinces and districts, which are subject to such different systems of taxation.

and the commerce in wine is subject to particular restraints. Over and above the general restraints arising from this complicated system of revenue laws, the commerce of wine, after corn perhaps the most important production of France, is in the greater part of the provinces subject to particular restraints, arising from the favour which has been shewn to the vineyards of particular provinces and districts, above those of others. The provinces most famous for their wines, it will be found, I believe, are those in which the trade in that article is subject to the fewest restraints of this kind. The extensive market which such provinces enjoy, encourages good management both in the cultivation of their vineyards, and in the subsequent preparation of their wines.

Milan and Parma are still more absurdly managed. Such various and complicated revenue laws are not peculiar to France. The little dutchy of Milan is divided into six provinces, in each of which there is a different system of taxation with regard to several different sorts of consumable goods. The still smaller territories of the duke of Parma are divided into three or four, each of which has, in the same manner, a system of its own. Under such absurd management, nothing, but the great fertility of the soil and happiness of the climate, could preserve such countries from soon relapsing into the lowest state of poverty and barbarism.

The collection of taxes by government officers is much superior to letting the taxes to farm. Taxes upon consumable commodities may either be levied by an administration of which the officers are appointed by government and are immediately accountable to government, of which the revenue must in this case vary from year to year, according to the occasional variations in the produce of the tax; or they may be let in farm for a rent certain, the farmer being allowed to appoint his own officers, who, though obliged to levy the tax in the manner directed by the law, are under his immediate inspection, and are immediately accountable to him. The best and most frugal way of levying a tax can never be by farm. Over and above what is necessary for paying the stipulated rent, the salaries of the officers, and the whole expence of administration, the farmer must always draw from the produce of the tax a certain profit proportioned at least to the advance which he makes, to the risk which he runs, to the trouble which he is at, and to the knowledge and skill which it requires to manage so very complicated a concern. Government, by establishing an administration under their own immediate inspection, of the same kind with that which the farmer establishes, might at least save this profit, which is almost always exorbitant. To farm any considerable branch of the public revenue, requires either a great capital or a great credit; circumstances which would alone restrain the competition for such an undertaking to a very small number of people. Of the few who have this capital or credit, a still smaller number have the necessary knowledge or experience; another circumstance which restrains the competition still further. The very few, who are in condition to become competitors, find it more for their interest to combine together; to become co-partners instead of competitors, and when the farm is set up to auction, to offer no rent, but what is much below the real value. In countries where the public revenues are in farm, the farmers are generally the most opulent people. Their wealth would alone excite the public indignation, and the vanity which almost always accompanies such upstart fortunes, the foolish ostentation with which they commonly display that wealth, excites that indignation still more.

Farmers of taxes require sanguinary revenue laws. The farmers of the public revenue never find the laws too severe, which punish any attempt to evade the payment of a tax. They have no bowels for the contributors, who are not their subjects, and whose universal bankruptcy, if it should happen the day after their farm is expired, would not much affect their interest. In the greatest exigencies of the state, when the anxiety of the sovereign for the exact payment of his revenue is necessarily the greatest, they seldom fail to complain that without laws more rigorous than those which actually take place, it will be impossible for them to pay even the usual rent. In those moments of public distress their demands cannot be disputed. The revenue laws, therefore, become gradually more and more severe. The most sanguinary are always to be found in countries where the greater part of the public revenue is in farm. The mildest, in countries where it is levied under the immediate inspection of the sovereign. Even a bad sovereign feels more compassion for his people than can ever be expected from the farmers of his revenue. He knows that the permanent grandeur of his family depends upon the prosperity of his people, and he will never knowingly ruin that prosperity for the sake of any momentary interest of his own. It is otherwise with the farmers of his revenue, whose grandeur may frequently be the effect of the ruin, and not of the prosperity of his people.

Taxation by monopolies let to farm is even worse. A tax is sometimes, not only farmed for a certain rent,[1] but the farmer has, besides, the monopoly of the commodity taxed. In France, the duties[2] upon tobacco and salt are levied in this manner. In such cases the farmer, instead of one, levies two exorbitant profits upon the people; the profit of the farmer, and the still more exorbitant one of the monopolist. Tobacco being a luxury, every man is allowed to buy or not to buy as he chuses. But salt being a necessary, every man is obliged to buy of the farmer a certain quantity of it; because, if he did not buy this quantity of the farmer, he would, it is presumed, buy it of some smuggler. The taxes upon both commodities are exorbitant. The temptation to smuggle consequently is to many people irresistible, while at the same time the rigour of the law, and the vigilance of the farmer's officers, render the yielding to that temptation almost certainly ruinous. The smuggling of salt and tobacco sends every year several hundred people to the gallies, besides a very considerable number whom it sends to the gibbet. Those taxes levied in this manner yield a very considerable revenue to government. In 1767, the farm of tobacco was let for twenty-two millions five hundred and forty-one thousand two hundred and seventy-eight livres a year. That of salt, for thirty-six millions four hundred and ninety-two thousand four hundred and four livres. The farm in both cases was to commence in 1768, and to last for six years. Those who consider the blood of the people as nothing in comparison with the revenue of the prince, may perhaps approve of this method of levying taxes. Similar taxes and monopolies of salt and tobacco have been established in many other countries; particularly in the Austrian and Prussian dominions, and in the greater part of the states of Italy.

In France the three branches of revenue which are levied by government officers are much more economical. In France, the greater part of the actual revenue of the crown is derived from eight different sources; the taille, the capitation, the two vingtiemes, the gabelles, the aides, the traites, the domaine, and the farm of tobacco. The five last are, in the greater part of the provinces, under farm. The three first are every where levied by an administration under the immediate inspection and

----

[1] [Ed. 1 reads 'rent certain'.]   [2] [Ed. 1 reads 'the taxes'.]

direction of government, and it is universally acknowledged that, in proportion to what they take out of the pockets of the people, they bring more into the treasury of the prince than the other five, of which the administration is much more wasteful and expensive.

The taille and capitations should be abolished, the vingtièmes increased, the taxes on commodities made uniform, and farming abolished. The finances of France seem, in their present state, to admit of three very obvious reformations. First, by abolishing the taille and the capitation, and by encreasing the number of vingtiemes, so as to produce an additional revenue equal to the amount of those other taxes, the revenue of the crown might be preserved; the expence of collection might be much diminished; the vexation of the inferior ranks of people, which the taille and capitation occasion, might be entirely prevented; and the superior ranks might not be more burdened than the greater part of them are at present. The vingtieme, I have already observed,[1] is a tax very nearly of the same kind with what is called the land-tax of England. The burden of the taille, it is acknowledged, falls finally upon the proprietors of land; and as the greater part of the capitation is assessed upon those who are subject to the taille at so much a pound of that other tax, the final payment of the greater part of it must likewise fall upon the same order of people. Though the number of the vingtiemes, therefore, was increased so as to produce an additional revenue equal to the amount of both those taxes, the superior ranks of people might not be more burdened than they are at present. Many individuals no doubt would, on account of the great inequalities with which the taille is commonly assessed upon the estates and tenants of different individuals. The interest and opposition of such favoured subjects are the obstacles most likely to prevent this or any other reformation of the same kind. Secondly, by rendering the gabelle, the aides, the traites,[2] the taxes upon tobacco, all the different customs and excises, uniform in all the different parts of the kingdom, those taxes might be levied at much less expence, and the interior commerce of the kingdom might be rendered as free as that of England. Thirdly, and lastly, by subjecting all those taxes to an administration under the immediate inspection and direction of government, the exorbitant profits of the farmers general might be added to the revenue of the state. The opposition arising from the private interest of individuals, is likely to be as effectual for preventing the two last as the first mentioned scheme of reformation.

[1] [Above, p. 385.]　　　　[2] [Ed. 1 does not contain 'the traites'.]

The French system is in every respect inferior to the British. The French system of taxation seems, in every respect, inferior to the British. In Great Britain ten millions sterling are annually levied upon less than eight millions of people, without its being possible to say that any particular order is oppressed. From the collections of the Abbé Expilly,[1] and the observations of the author of the Essay upon the legislation and commerce of corn,[2] it appears probable, that France, including the provinces of Lorraine and Bar, contains about twenty-three or twenty-four millions of people; three times the number perhaps contained in Great Britain. The soil and climate of France are better than those of Great Britain. The country has been much longer in a state of improvement and cultivation, and is, upon that account, better stocked with all those things which it requires a long time to raise up and accumulate, such as great towns, and convenient and well-built houses, both in town and country. With these advantages, it might be expected that in France a revenue of thirty millions might be levied for the support of the state, with as little inconveniency as a revenue of ten millions is in Great Britain. In 1765 and 1766, the whole revenue paid into the treasury of France, according to the best, though, I acknowledge, very imperfect, accounts which I could get of it, usually run between 308 and 325 millions of livres; that is, it did not amount to fifteen millions sterling; not the half of what might have been expected, had the people contributed in the same proportion to their numbers as the people of Great Britain. The people of France, however, it is generally acknowledged, are much more oppressed by taxes than the people of Great Britain. France, however, is certainly the great empire in Europe which, after that of Great Britain, enjoys the mildest and most indulgent government.

In Holland heavy taxes on necessaries have ruined manufactures. In Holland the heavy taxes upon the necessaries of life have ruined, it is said, their principal manufactures,[3] and are likely to discourage gradually even

---

[1] [These estimates seem to have been quoted in England at the time, since the Continuation of Anderson's *Commerce*, under the year 1773, mentions 'the calculations of the Abbé D'Expilly published about this time in Paris,' which gave 8,661,381 births and 6,664,161 deaths as the number taking place in the nine years, 1754 to 1763, in France, inclusive of Lorraine and Bar. In his *Dictionnaire géographique, historique et politique des Gaules et de la France*, tom. v. (1768), *s.v.* Population, Expilly estimated the population at 22,014,357. See Levasseur, *La Population française*, tom. i., 1889, pp. 215 and 216 note.]

[2] [*Sur la législation et le commerce des grains* (by Necker), 1775, ch. viii., estimates the population at 24,181,333 by the method of multiplying the deaths by 31.]

[3] [Above, p. 405.]

their fisheries and their trade in ship-building. The taxes upon the necessaries of life are inconsiderable in Great Britain, and no manufacture has hitherto been ruined by them. The British taxes which bear hardest on manufactures are some duties upon the importation of raw materials, particularly upon that of raw silk. The revenue of the states general and of the different cities, however, is said to amount to more than five millions two hundred and fifty thousand pounds sterling; and as the inhabitants of the United Provinces cannot well be supposed to amount to more than a third part of those of Great Britain, they must, in proportion to their number, be much more heavily taxed.

But perhaps Holland has done the best possible. After all the proper subjects of taxation have been exhausted, if the exigencies of the state still continue to require new taxes, they must be imposed upon improper ones.[1] The taxes upon the necessaries of life, therefore, may be no impeachment of the wisdom of that republic, which, in order to acquire and to maintain its independency, has, in spite of its great frugality, been involved in such expensive wars as have obliged it to contract great debts. The singular countries of Holland and Zealand, besides, require a considerable expence even to preserve their existence, or to prevent their being swallowed up by the sea, which must have contributed to increase considerably the load of taxes in those two provinces. The republican form of government seems to be the principal support of the present grandeur of Holland. The owners of great capitals, the great mercantile families, have generally either some direct share, or some indirect influence, in the administration of that government. For the sake of the respect and authority which they derive from this situation, they are willing to live in a country where their capital, if they employ it themselves, will bring them less profit, and if they lend it to another, less interest; and where the very moderate revenue which they can draw from it will purchase less of the necessaries and conveniences of life than in any other part of Europe. The residence of such wealthy people necessarily keeps alive, in spite of all disadvantages, a certain degree of industry in the country. Any public calamity which should destroy the republican form of government, which should throw the whole administration into the hands of nobles and of soldiers, which should annihilate altogether the importance of those wealthy merchants, would soon render it

[1] [Below, p. 466.]

disagreeable to them to live in a country where they were no longer likely to be much respected. They would remove both their residence and their capital to some other country, and the industry and commerce of Holland would soon follow the capitals which supported them.

CHAPTER III

Of Public Debts

When expensive luxuries are unknown, persons with large revenue are likely to hoard savings. In that rude state of society which precedes the extension of commerce and the improvement of manufactures, when those expensive luxuries which commerce and manufactures can alone introduce, are altogether unknown, the person who possesses a large revenue, I have endeavoured to show in the third book of this Inquiry,[1] can spend or enjoy that revenue in no other way than by maintaining nearly as many people as it can maintain. A large revenue may at all times be said to consist in the command of a large quantity of the necessaries of life. In that rude state of things it is commonly paid in a large quantity of those necessaries, in the materials of plain food and coarse clothing, in corn and cattle, in wool and raw hides. When neither commerce nor manufactures furnish any thing for which the owner can exchange the greater part of those materials which are over and above his own consumption, he can do nothing with the surplus but feed and clothe nearly as many people as it will feed and clothe. A hospitality in which there is no luxury, and a liberality in which there is no ostentation, occasion, in this situation of things, the principal expences of the rich and the great. But these, I have likewise endeavoured to show in the same book,[2] are expences by which people are not very apt to ruin themselves. There is not, perhaps, any selfish pleasure so frivolous, of which the pursuit has not sometimes ruined even sensible men. A passion for cock-fighting has ruined many. But the instances, I believe, are not very numerous of people who have been ruined by a hospitality or liberality of this kind; though the hospitality of luxury and the liberality of ostentation have ruined many. Among our feudal ancestors, the long time during which estates used to continue in the same family, sufficiently demonstrates the general disposition of people to live within their income.

[1] [Above, vol. i., pp. 433, 434.]   [2] [Above, vol. i., p. 440.]

Though the rustic hospitality, constantly exercised by the great land-holders, may not, to us in the present times, seem consistent with that order, which we are apt to consider as inseparably connected with good œconomy, yet we must certainly allow them to have been at least so far frugal as not commonly to have spent their whole income. A part of their wool and raw hides they had generally an opportunity of selling for money. Some part of this money, perhaps, they spent in purchasing the few objects of vanity and luxury, with which the circumstances of the times could furnish them; but some part of it they seem commonly to have hoarded. They could not well indeed do any thing else but hoard whatever money they saved. To trade was disgraceful to a gentleman, and to lend money at interest, which at that time was considered as usury and prohibited by law, would have been still more so. In those times of violence and disorder, besides, it was convenient to have a hoard of money at hand, that in case they should be driven from their own home, they might have something of known value to carry with them to some place of safety. The same violence, which made it convenient to hoard, made it equally convenient to conceal the hoard. The frequency of treasure-trove, or of treasure found of which no owner was known, sufficiently demonstrates the frequency in those times both of hoarding and of concealing the hoard. Treasure-trove was then considered as an important branch of the revenue of the sovereign.[1] All the treasure-trove of the kingdom would scarce perhaps in the present times make an important branch of the revenue of a private gentleman of a good estate.

So the ancient sovereigns of Europe amassed treasures. The same disposition to save and to hoard prevailed in the sovereign, as well as in the subjects. Among nations to whom commerce and manufactures are little known, the sovereign, it has already been observed in the fourth book,[2] is in a situation which naturally disposes him to the parsimony requisite for accumulation. In that situation the expence even of a sovereign cannot be directed by that vanity which delights in the gaudy finery of a court. The ignorance of the times affords but few of the trinkets in which that finery consists. Standing armies are not then necessary, so that the expence even of a sovereign, like that of any other great lord, can be employed in scarce any thing but bounty to his tenants, and hospitality to his retainers. But bounty and hospitality very seldom lead to extravagance; though vanity

---

[1] [Cp. vol. i., p. 301.]   [2] [Above, vol. i., p. 468.]

almost always does.[1] All the ancient sovereigns of Europe accordingly, it has already been observed, had treasures. Every Tartar chief in the present times is said to have one.

When luxuries are introduced, the sovereign's expenditure equals his revenue in time of peace, In a commercial country abounding with every sort of expensive luxury, the sovereign, in the same manner as almost all the great proprietors in his dominions, naturally spends a great part of his revenue in purchasing those luxuries. His own and the neighbouring countries supply him abundantly with all the costly trinkets which compose the splendid, but insignificant pageantry of a court. For the sake of an inferior pageantry of the same kind, his nobles dismiss their retainers, make their tenants independent, and become gradually themselves as insignificant as the greater part of the wealthy burghers in his dominions. The same frivolous passions, which influence their conduct, influence his. How can it be supposed that he should be the only rich man in his dominions who is insensible to pleasures of this kind? If he does not, what he is very likely to do, spend upon those pleasures so great a part of his revenue as to debilitate very much the defensive power of the state, it cannot well be expected that he should not spend upon them all that part of it which is over and above what is necessary for supporting that defensive power. His ordinary expence becomes equal to his ordinary revenue, and it is well if it does not frequently exceed it. The amassing of treasure can no longer be expected, and when extraordinary exigencies require extraordinary expences, he must necessarily call upon his subjects for an extraordinary aid. The present and the late king of Prussia are the only great princes of Europe, who, since the death of Henry IV. of France in 1610, are supposed to have amassed any considerable treasure.[2] The parsimony which leads to accumulation has become almost as rare in republican as in monarchical governments. The Italian republics, the United Provinces of the Netherlands, are all in debt. The canton of Berne is the single republic in Europe which has amassed any considerable treasure.[3] The other Swiss republics have not. The taste for some sort of pageantry, for splendid buildings, at least, and other public ornaments, frequently prevails as much in the apparently sober senate-house of a little republic, as in the dissipated court of the greatest king.

---

[1] [Repeated *verbatim* from vol. i., p. 468.] [2] [Above, vol. i., p. 463.]
[3] [Above, p. 344.]

and in time of war he contracts debts. The want of parsimony in time of peace, imposes the necessity of contracting debt in time of war. When war comes, there is no money in the treasury but what is necessary for carrying on the ordinary expence of the peace establishment. In war an establishment of three or four times that expence becomes necessary for the defence of the state, and consequently a revenue three or four times greater than the peace revenue. Supposing that the sovereign should have, what he scarce ever has, the immediate means of augmenting his revenue in proportion to the augmentation of his expence, yet still the produce of the taxes, from which this increase of revenue must be drawn, will not begin to come into the treasury till perhaps ten or twelve months after they are imposed. But the moment in which war begins, or rather the moment in which it appears likely to begin, the army must be augmented, the fleet must be fitted out, the garrisoned towns must be put into a posture of defence; that army, that fleet, those garrisoned towns must be furnished with arms, ammunition, and provisions. An immediate and great expence must be incurred in that moment of immediate danger, which will not wait for the gradual and slow returns of the new taxes. In this exigency government can have no other resource but in borrowing.

The same causes which make borrowing necessary make it possible. The same commercial state of society which, by the operation of moral causes, brings government in this manner into the necessity of borrowing, produces in the subjects both an ability and an inclination to lend. If it commonly brings along with it the necessity of borrowing, it likewise brings along[1] with it the facility of doing so.

Merchants and manufacturers are able to lend, A country abounding with merchants and manufacturers, necessarily abounds with a set of people through whose hands not only their own capitals, but the capitals of all those who either lend them money, or trust them with goods, pass as frequently, or more frequently, than the revenue of a private man, who, without trade or business, lives upon his income, passes through his hands. The revenue of such a man can regularly pass through his hands only once in a year. But the whole amount of the capital and credit of a merchant, who deals in in a trade of which the returns are very quick, may sometimes pass through his hands two, three, or four times in a year. A country

[1] [Ed. 5 omits 'along,' doubtless by a misprint.]

abounding with merchants and manufacturers, therefore, necessarily abounds with a set of people who have it at all times in their power to advance, if they chuse to do so, a very large sum of money to government. Hence the ability in the subjects of a commercial state to lend.

and also willing.   Commerce and manufactures can seldom flourish long in any state which does not enjoy a regular administration of justice, in which the people do not feel themselves secure in the possession of their property, in which the faith of contracts is not supported by law, and in which the authority of the state is not supposed to be regularly employed in enforcing the payment of debts from all those who are able to pay. Commerce and manufactures, in short, can seldom flourish in any state in which there is not a certain degree of confidence in the justice of government. The same confidence which disposes great merchants and manufacturers, upon ordinary occasions, to trust their property to the protection of a particular government; disposes them, upon extraordinary occasions, to trust that government with the use of their property. By lending money to government, they do not even for a moment diminish their ability to carry on their trade and manufactures. On the contrary, they commonly augment it. The necessities of the state render government upon most occasions willing to borrow upon terms extremely advantageous to the lender. The security which it grants to the original creditor, is made transferable to any other creditor, and, from the universal confidence in the justice of the state, generally sells in the market for more than was originally paid for it. The merchant or monied man makes money by lending money to government, and instead of diminishing, increases his trading capital. He generally considers it as a favour, therefore, when the administration admits him to a share in the first subscription for a new loan. Hence the inclination or willingness in the subjects of a commercial state to lend.

A government dispenses itself from saving if it knows it can borrow,   The government of such a state is very apt to repose itself upon this ability and willingness of its subjects to lend it their money on extraordinary occasions. It foresees the facility of borrowing, and therefore dispenses itself from the duty of saving.

whereas if there is no possibility of borrowing, it feels it must save.   In a rude state of society there are no great mercantile or manufacturing capitals. The individuals, who hoard whatever money they can save, and who conceal their hoard, do so from a distrust of the justice of government, from a fear that if it was known that they had a hoard, and where that hoard was to be found, they would quickly be plundered. In such a state of things few people would be able, and no body would be willing, to lend their money to government on extraordinary exigencies. The sovereign feels that he must provide for such exigencies by saving, because he foresees the absolute impossibility of borrowing. This foresight increases still further his natural disposition to save.

Nations have begun to borrow without special security and have afterwards mortgaged particular funds. The progress of the enormous debts which at present oppress, and will in the long-run probably ruin, all the great nations of Europe, has been pretty uniform. Nations, like private men, have generally begun to borrow upon what may be called personal credit, without assigning or mortgaging any particular fund for the payment of the debt; and when this resource has failed them, they have gone on to borrow upon assignments or mortgages of particular funds.

The unfunded debt of Great Britain is contracted in the first way. What is called the unfunded debt of Great Britain, is contracted in the former of those two ways. It consists partly in a debt which bears, or is supposed to bear, no interest, and which resembles the debts that a private man contracts upon account; and partly in a debt which bears interest, and which resembles what a private man contracts upon his bill or promissory note. The debts which are due either for extraordinary services, or for services either not provided for, or not paid at the time when they are performed; part of the extraordinaries of the army, navy, and ordnance, the arrears of subsidies to foreign princes, those of seamen's wages, &c. usually constitute a debt of the first kind. Navy and Exchequer bills, which are issued sometimes in payment of a part of such debts and sometimes for other purposes, constitute a debt of the second kind; Exchequer bills bearing interest from the day on which they are issued, and navy bills six months after they are issued. The bank of England, either by voluntarily discounting those bills at their current value, or by agreeing with government for certain considerations to circulate Exchequer bills, that is, to receive them at par, paying the interest which happens to be due upon them, keeps up their value and facilitates their circulation, and thereby frequently enables government to contract a very large debt of this kind. In France, where there is no bank, the state bills (billets d'état[1]) have sometimes sold at sixty and seventy per cent. discount. During the great re-coinage in King William's time, when the bank of England thought proper to put a stop to its usual transactions, Exchequer bills and tallies are said to have sold from twenty-five to sixty per cent. discount;[2] owing partly, no doubt, to the supposed instability of the new government established by the Revolution, but partly too to the want of the support of the bank of England.

Mortgages of particular branches of revenue are either for a term of years, when money is said to be raised by anticipation, or in perpetuity, when it is said to be raised by funding. When this resource is exhausted, and it becomes necessary, in order to raise money, to assign or mortgage some particular branch of the public revenue for the payment of the debt, government has upon different occasions done this in two different ways. Sometimes it has made this assignment or mortgage for a short period of time only, a year, or a few years, for example; and sometimes for perpetuity. In the one case, the fund was supposed sufficient to pay, within the limited time, both principal and interest of the money borrowed. In the other, it was supposed sufficient to pay the interest only, or a perpetual annuity equivalent to the interest, government being at liberty to redeem at any time this annuity, upon paying back the principal sum borrowed. When money was raised in the one way, it was said to be raised by anticipation; when in the other, by perpetual funding, or, more shortly, by funding.

The annual land and malt taxes are always anticipated. In Great Britain the annual land and malt taxes are regularly anticipated every year, by virtue of a borrowing clause constantly inserted into the acts which impose them. The bank of England generally advances at an interest, which since the Revolution has varied from eight to three per cent. the sums for which those taxes are granted, and receives payment as their produce gradually comes in. If there is a deficiency, which there always is, it is provided for in the supplies of the ensuing year. The only considerable branch of the public revenue which yet remains unmortgaged is thus regularly spent before it

---

[1] See Examen des Reflexions politiques sur les Finances. [P. J. Duverney, *Examen du livre intitulé Réflexions politiques sur les finances et le commerce* (by Du Tot), tom. i., p. 225.]

[2] [James Postlethwayt, *History of the Public Revenue*, 1759, pp. 14, 15, mentions discounts of 25 and 55 per cent. The discount varied with the priority of the tallies and did not measure the national credit in general, but the probability of particular taxes bringing in enough to pay the amounts charged upon them. See also above, vol. i., p. 338.]

comes in. Like an improvident[1] spendthrift, whose pressing occasions will not allow him to wait for the regular payment of his revenue, the state is in the constant practice of borrowing of its own factors and agents, and of paying interest for the use of its own money.

Under William III. and Anne anticipations gave rise to deficiencies, In the reign of king William, and during a great part of that of queen Anne, before we had become so familiar as we are now with the practice of perpetual funding, the greater part of the new taxes were imposed but for a short period of time (for four, five, six, or seven years only), and a great part of the grants of every year consisted in loans upon anticipations of the produce of those taxes. The produce being frequently insufficient for paying within the limited term the principal and interest of the money borrowed, deficiencies arose, to make good which it became necessary to prolong the term.

and the term of the mortgage taxes was prolonged in 1697, In 1697, by the 8th of William III. c. 20. the deficiencies of several taxes were charged upon what was then called the first general mortgage or fund, consisting of a prolongation to the first of August, 1706, of several different taxes, which would have expired within a shorter term, and of which the produce was accumulated into one general fund. The deficiencies charged upon this prolonged term amounted to 5,160,459 l. 14 s. 9¼ d.[2]

in 1701, In 1701, those duties, with some others, were still further prolonged for the like purposes till the first of August, 1710, and were called the second general mortgage or fund.[3] The deficiencies charged upon it amounted to 2,055,999 l. 7 s. 11½ d.

in 1707, In 1707, those duties were still further prolonged, as a fund for new loans, to the first of August, 1712, and were called the third general mortgage or fund. The sum borrowed upon it was 983,254 l. 11 s. 9¼ d.

in 1708, In 1708, those duties were all (except the old subsidy of tonnage and poundage, of which one moiety only was made a part of this fund, and a duty upon the importation of Scotch linen, which had been taken off by the articles of union) still further continued, as a fund for new loans, to the first of August, 1714, and were called the fourth general mortgage or fund.[4] The sum borrowed upon it was 925,176 l. 9 s. 2¼ d.[5]

---

[1] [Ed. 1 reads 'unprovident,' as do all editions below, p. 450.]
[2] [Postlethwayt, *op. cit.*, p. 38. Ed. 5 misprints '9½d.']
[3] [*Ibid.*, p. 40.]   [4] [*Ibid.*, p. 59.]   [5] [*Ibid.*, pp. 63, 64.]

in 1709,　　　In 1709, those duties were all (except the old subsidy of tonnage and poundage, which was now left out of this fund altogether) still further continued for the same purpose to the first of August, 1716, and were called the fifth general mortgage or fund.[1] The sum borrowed upon it was 922,029 l. 6 s. 0 d.

and in 1710.　　　In 1710, those duties were again prolonged to the first of August, 1720, and were called the sixth general mortgage or fund.[2] The sum borrowed upon it was 1,296,552 l. 9 s. 11¾ d.

In 1711 the taxes were continued for ever and made into a fund for paying the interest on £9,177,968.　　　In 1711, the same duties (which at this time were thus subject to four different anticipations), together with several others, were continued for ever, and made a fund for paying the interest of the capital of the South Sea company, which had that year advanced to government, for paying debts and making good deficiencies, the sum of 9,177,967 l. 15 s. 4 d.;[3] the greatest loan which at that time had ever been made.

The only earlier taxes imposed in perpetuity to pay interest on debt were those for paying interest on the advances of the Bank and East India Company.　　　Before this period, the principal, so far as I have been able to observe, the only taxes which in order to pay the interest of a debt had been imposed for perpetuity, were those for paying the interest of the money which had been advanced to government by the Bank and East India Company, and of what it was expected would be advanced, but which was never advanced, by a projected land bank. The bank fund at this time amounted to 3,375,027 l. 17 s. 10½ d. for which was paid an annuity or interest of 206,501 l. 13 s. 5 d.[4] The East India fund amounted to 3,200,000 l. for which was paid an annuity or interest 160,000 l.;[5] the bank fund being at six per cent.,[6] the East India fund at five per cent. interest.

In 1715 several taxes were accumulated into the Aggregate Fund,　　　In 1715, by the first of George I. c. 12. the different taxes which had been mortgaged for paying the bank annuity, together with several others which by this act were likewise rendered perpetual, were accumulated into one common fund called The Aggregate Fund, which was charged, not only with the payments[7] of the bank annuity, but with several

---

[1] [Postlethwayt, *op. cit.*, p. 68.]　　[2] [*Ibid.*, p. 71.]　　　[3] [*Ibid.*, p. 311.]
[4] [*Ibid.*, pp. 301–303, and see above, vol. i., p. 339.]
[5] [*Ibid.*, pp. 319, 320.]
[6] [The odd £4,000 of the £206,501 13s. 5d. was for expenses of management. See above, vol. i., p. 339.]
[7] [Ed. 1 reads 'payment,' perhaps correctly.]

other annuities and burdens of different kinds. This fund was afterwards augmented by the third of George I. c. 8. and by the fifth of
George I. c. 3. and the different duties which were then added to it
were likewise rendered perpetual.[1]

and in 1717 several
others into the
General Fund.

In 1717, by the third of George I. c. 7.[2] several other
taxes were rendered perpetual, and accumulated
into another common fund, called The General
Fund, for the payment of certain annuities, amounting in the whole
to 724,849 l. 6 s. 10½ d.

Thus most of the
anticipated taxes
were made into a
fund for paying
interest only.

In consequence of those different acts, the greater
part of the taxes which before had been anticipated
only for a short term of years, were rendered perpetual as a fund for paying, not the capital, but the
interest only, of the money which had been borrowed upon them
by different successive anticipations.

When once become
familiar, perpetual
funding is preferred
to anticipation.

Had money never been raised but by anticipation,
the course of a few years would have liberated the
public revenue, without any other attention of
government besides that of not overloading the fund by charging
it with more debt than it could pay within the limited term, and of
not anticipating a second time before the expiration of the first
anticipation. But the greater part of European governments have
been incapable of those attentions. They have frequently overloaded
the fund even upon the first anticipation; and when this happened
not to be the case, they have generally taken care to overload it, by
anticipating a second and a third time before the expiration of the
first anticipation. The fund becoming in this manner altogether
insufficient for paying both principal and interest of the money
borrowed upon it, it became necessary to charge it with the interest
only, or a perpetual annuity equal to the interest, and such unprovident anticipations necessarily gave birth to the more ruinous practice of perpetual funding. But though this practice necessarily puts
off the liberation of the public revenue from a fixed period to one
so indefinite that it is not very likely ever to arrive; yet as a greater
sum can in all cases be raised by this new practice than by the old one
of anticipations, the former, when men have once become familiar
with it, has in the great exigencies of the state been universally preferred to the latter. To relieve the present exigency is always the

---

[1] [Postlethwayt, *History of the Public Revenue*, p. 305.]
[2] [This Act belongs to 1716, not 1717.]

object which principally interests those immediately concerned in the administration of public affairs. The future liberation of the public revenue, they leave to the care of posterity.

A fall in the market rate of interest led to a saving, which gave rise to the Sinking Fund. During the reign of queen Anne, the market rate of interest had fallen from six to five per cent., and in the twelfth year of her reign five per cent. was declared to be the highest rate which could lawfully be taken for money borrowed upon private security.[1] Soon after the greater part of the temporary taxes of Great Britain had been rendered perpetual, and distributed into the Aggregate, South Sea, and General Funds, the creditors of the public, like those of private persons, were induced to accept of five per cent. for the interest of their money,[2] which occasioned a saving of one per cent. upon the capital of the greater part of the debts which had been thus funded for perpetuity, or of one-sixth of the greater part of the annuities which were paid out of the three great funds above mentioned. This saving left a considerable surplus in the produce of the different taxes which had been accumulated into those funds, over and above what was necessary for paying the annuities which were now charged upon them, and laid the foundation of what has since been called the Sinking Fund. In 1717, it amounted to 323,434 l. 7 s. 7½ d.[3] In 1727, the interest of the greater part of the public debts was still further reduced to four per cent.;[4] and in 1753[5] and 1757, to three and a half and three per cent.; which reductions still further augmented the sinking fund.

A sinking fund facilitates the contraction of new debts. A sinking fund, though instituted for the payment of old, facilitates very much the contracting of new debts. It is a subsidiary fund always at hand to be mortgaged in aid of any other doubtful fund, upon which money is proposed to be raised in any exigency of the state. Whether the sinking fund of Great Britain has been more frequently applied to the one or to the other of those two purposes, will sufficiently appear by and by.

Money is also borrowed by terminable and life annuities. Besides those two methods of borrowing, by anticipations and by perpetual funding, there are two other methods, which hold a sort of middle place between them. These are, that of borrowing upon annuities

---

[1] [Above, vol. i., pp. 99, 100.]

[2] [In 1717, under the provisions of 3 Geo. I., c. 7. Postlethwayt, *History of the Public Revenue*, pp. 120, 145.]   [3] [Anderson, *Commerce*, A.D. 1717.]

[4] [*Ibid.*, A.D. 1727.]   [5] [This should be 1750. *Ibid.*, A.D. 1749.]

for terms of years, and that of borrowing upon annuities for lives.

Under William III. During the reigns of king William and queen Anne,
and Anne large sums large sums were frequently borrowed upon annui-
were borrowed ties for terms of years, which were sometimes
on annuities
for terms of years. longer and sometimes shorter. In 1693, an act was
passed for borrowing one million upon an annuity of fourteen per
cent.,[1] or of 140,000 l. a year, for sixteen years. In 1691, an act was
passed for borrowing a million upon annuities for lives, upon terms
which in the present times would appear very advantageous. But
the subscription was not filled up. In the following year[2] the deficiency was made good by borrowing upon annuities for lives at
fourteen per cent., or at little more than seven years purchase. In
1695, the persons who had purchased those annuities were allowed
to exchange them for others of ninety-six years, upon paying into
the Exchequer sixty-three pounds in the hundred; that is, the difference between fourteen per cent. for life, and fourteen per cent. for
ninety-six years, was sold for sixty-three pounds, or for four and a
half years purchase. Such was the supposed instability of government, that even these terms procured few purchasers. In the reign of
queen Anne, money was upon different occasions borrowed both
upon annuities for lives, and upon annuities for terms of thirty-two,
of eighty-nine, of ninety-eight, and of ninety-nine years. In 1719,
the proprietors of the annuities for thirty-two years were induced
to accept in lieu of them South Sea stock to the amount of eleven
and a half years purchase of the annuities, together with an additional
quantity of stock equal to the arrears which happened then to be
due upon them.[3] In 1720, the greater part of the other annuities for
terms of years both long and short were subscribed into the same
fund. The long annuities at that time amounted to 666,821 l.
8 s. 3½ d. a year.[4] On the 5th of January, 1775, the remainder of
them, or what was not subscribed at that time, amounted only to
136,453 l. 12 s. 8 d.

But little money During the two wars which begun in 1739 and in
was so borrowed 1755, little money was borrowed either upon
in the wars of the
middle of the annuities for terms of years, or upon those for lives.
eighteenth century, An annuity for ninety-eight or ninety-nine years,
most people
preferring a however, is worth nearly as much money as a
perpetual annuity, perpetuity, and should, therefore, one might think,

---

[1] [5 and 6 W. and M., c. 7.]   [2] [4 W. and M., c. 3.]
[3] [Anderson, *Commerce*, A.D. 1719.]   [4] [*Ibid.*, A.D. 1720.]

be a fund for borrowing nearly as much. But those who, in order to make family settlements, and to provide for remote futurity, buy into the public stocks, would not care to purchase into one of which the value was continually diminishing; and such people make a very considerable proportion both of the proprietors and purchasers of stock. An annuity for a long term of years, therefore, though its intrinsic value may be very nearly the same with that of a perpetual annuity, will not find nearly the same number of purchasers. The subscribers to a new loan, who mean generally to sell their subscription as soon as possible, prefer greatly a perpetual annuity redeemable by parliament, to an irredeemable annuity for a long term of years of only equal amount. The value of the former may be supposed always the same, or very nearly the same; and it makes, therefore, a more convenient transferable stock than the latter.

and annuities for terms and for lives were only given as premiums. During the two last mentioned wars, annuities, either for terms of years or for lives, were seldom granted but as premiums to the subscribers to a new loan, over and above the redeemable annuity or interest upon the credit of which the loan was supposed to be made. They were granted, not as the proper fund upon which the money was borrowed; but as an additional encouragement to the lender.

Tontines are preferred to annuities on separate lives, though they do not liberate the public revenue so quickly. Annuities for lives have occasionally been granted in two different ways; either upon separate lives, or upon lots of lives, which in French are called Tontines, from the name of their inventor. When annuities are granted upon separate lives, the death of every individual annuitant disburthens the public revenue so far as it was affected by his annuity. When annuities are granted upon tontines, the liberation of the public revenue does not commence till the death of all the annuitants comprehended in one lot, which may sometimes consist of twenty or thirty persons, of whom the survivors succeed to the annuities of all those who die before them; the last survivor succeeding to the annuities of the whole lot. Upon the same revenue more money can always be raised by tontines than by annuities for separate lives. An annuity, with a right of survivorship, is really worth more than an equal annuity for a separate life, and from the confidence which every man naturally has in his own good fortune, the principle upon which is founded the success of all lotteries, such an annuity generally sells for something more than it is worth. In countries where it is usual for government to raise money by granting annuities, tontines are upon this account generally preferred to annuities for separate lives. The expedient which will raise most money, is almost always preferred to that which is likely to bring about in the speediest manner the liberation of the public revenue.

In France a much greater proportion of the whole debt is in life annuities than in England; In France a much greater proportion of the public debts consists in annuities for lives than in England. According to a memoir presented by the parliament of Bordeaux to the king in 1764, the whole public debt of France is estimated at twenty-four hundred millions of livres; of which the capital for which annuities for lives had been granted, is supposed to amount to three hundred millions, the eighth part of the whole public debt. The annuities themselves are computed to amount to thirty millions a year, the fourth part of one hundred and twenty millions, the supposed interest of that whole debt. These estimations, I know very well, are not exact, but having been presented by so very respectable a body as approximations to the truth, they may, I apprehend, be considered as such. It is not the different degrees of anxiety in the two governments of France and England for the liberation of the public revenue, which occasions this difference in their respective modes of borrowing. It arises altogether from the different views and interests of the lenders.

the difference is due to the fact that in England the lenders are merchants, In England, the seat of government being in the greatest mercantile city in the world, the merchants are generally the people who advance money to government. By advancing it they do not mean to diminish, but, on the contrary, to increase their mercantile capitals; and unless they expected to sell with some profit their share in the subscription for a new loan, they never would subscribe. But if by advancing their money they were to purchase, instead of perpetual annuities, annuities for lives only, whether their own or those of other people, they would not always be so likely to sell them with a profit. Annuities upon their own lives they would always sell with loss; because no man will give for an annuity upon the life of another, whose age and state of health are nearly the same with his own, the same price which he would give for one upon his own. An annuity upon the life of a third person, indeed, is, no doubt, of equal value to the buyer and the seller; but its real value begins to diminish from the moment it is granted, and continues to do so more and more as long as it subsists. It can never, therefore, make so convenient a transferable stock as a perpetual annuity, of which the real value may be supposed always the same, or very nearly the same.

whereas in France they are persons engaged in the farming and collection of the taxes, who are chiefly bachelors. In France the seat of government not being in a great mercantile city, merchants do not make so great a proportion of the people who advance money to government. The people concerned in the finances, the farmers general, the receivers of the taxes which are not in farm, the court bankers, &c. make the greater part of those who advance their money in all public exigencies. Such people are commonly men of mean birth, but of great wealth, and frequently of great pride. They are too proud to marry their equals, and women of quality disdain to marry them. They frequently resolve, therefore, to live bachelors, and having neither any families of their own, nor much regard for those of their relations, whom they are not always very fond of acknowledging, they desire only to live in splendour during their own time, and are not unwilling that their fortune should end with themselves. The number of rich people, besides, who are either averse to marry, or whose condition of life renders it either improper or inconvenient for them to do so, is much greater in France than in England. To such people, who have little or no care for posterity, nothing can be more convenient than to exchange their capital for a revenue, which is to last just as long,[1] and no longer than they wish it to do.

The system of perpetual funding prevents the people from feeling distinctly the burden of war. The ordinary expence of the greater part of modern governments in time of peace being equal or nearly equal to their ordinary revenue, when war comes, they are both unwilling and unable to increase their revenue in proportion to the increase of their expence. They are unwilling, for fear of offending the people, who by so great and so sudden an increase of taxes, would soon be disgusted with the war; and they are unable, from not well knowing what taxes would be sufficient to produce the revenue wanted. The facility of borrowing delivers them from the embarrassment which this fear and inability would otherwise occasion. By means of borrowing they are enabled, with a very moderate increase of taxes, to raise, from year to year, money sufficient for carrying on the war, and by the practice of perpetual funding they are enabled, with the smallest possible increase of taxes, to raise annually the largest possible sum of money. In great empires the people who live in the

[1] [Ed. 1 reads 'just as long as'.]

capital, and in the provinces remote from the scene of action, feel, many of them, scarce any inconveniency from the war; but enjoy, at their ease, the amusement of reading in the newspapers the exploits of their own fleets and armies. To them this amusement compensates the small difference between the taxes which they pay on account of the war, and those which they had been accustomed to pay in time of peace. They are commonly dissatisfied with the return of peace, which puts an end to their amusement, and to a thousand visionary hopes of conquest and national glory, from a longer continuance of the war.

Their burdens are not reduced on the conclusion of peace. The return of peace, indeed, seldom relieves them from the greater part of the taxes imposed during the war. These are mortgaged for the interest of the debt contracted in order to carry it on. If, over and above paying the interest of this debt, and defraying the ordinary expence of government, the old revenue, together with the new taxes, produce some surplus revenue, it may perhaps be converted into a sinking fund for paying off the debt. But, in the first place, this sinking fund, even supposing it should be applied to no other purpose, is generally altogether inadequate for paying, in the course of any period during which it can reasonably be expected that peace should continue, the whole debt contracted during the war; and, in the second place, this fund is almost always applied to other purposes.

Any new taxes imposed are rarely sufficient to do more than pay the new interest. Sinking funds arise generally from reductions of interest, The new taxes were imposed for the sole purpose of paying the interest of the money borrowed upon them. If they produce more, it is generally something which was neither intended nor expected, and is therefore seldom very considerable. Sinking funds have generally arisen, not so much from any surplus of the taxes which was over and above what was necessary for paying the interest or annuity originally charged upon them, as from a subsequent reduction of that interest. That of Holland in 1655, and that of the ecclesiastical state in 1685, were both formed in this manner.[1] Hence the usual insufficiency of such funds.

and are constantly misapplied. During the most profound peace, various events occur which require an extraordinary expence, and government finds it always more convenient to defray this expence by misapplying the sinking fund than by imposing a new tax. Every

---

[1] [Anderson, *Commerce*, mentions these reductions under their dates, and recalls them in reference to the British reductions in 1717.]

new tax isi mmediately felt more or less by the people. It occasions always some murmur, and meets with some opposition. The more taxes may have been multiplied, the higher they may have been raised upon every different subject of taxation; the more loudly the people complain of every new tax, the more difficult it becomes to either to find out new subjects of taxation, or to raise much higher the taxes already imposed upon the old. A momentary suspension of the payment of debt is not immediately felt by the people, and occasions neither murmur nor complaint. To borrow of the sinking fund is always an obvious and easy expedient for getting out of the present difficulty. The more the public debts may have been accumulated, the more necessary it may have become to study to reduce them, the more dangerous, the more ruinous it may be to misapply any part of the sinking fund; the less likely is the public debt to be reduced to any considerable degree, the more likely, the more certainly is the sinking fund to be misapplied towards defraying all the extraordinary expences which occur in time of peace. When a nation is already overburdened with taxes, nothing but the necessities of a new war, nothing but either the animosity of national vengeance, or the anxiety for national security, can induce the people to submit, with tolerable patience, to a new tax. Hence the usual misapplication of the sinking fund.

The British debt had its origin in the war of 1688-97, In Great Britain, from the time that we had first recourse to the ruinous expedient of perpetual funding, the reduction of the public debt in time of peace, has never borne any proportion to its accumulation in time of war. It was in the war which began in 1688, and was concluded by the treaty of Ryswick in 1697, that the foundation of the present enormous debt of Great Britain was first laid.

which left a debt of twenty-one and a half millions. This was reduced by five millions in 1697-1701. On the 31st of December 1697, the public debts of Great Britain, funded and unfunded, amounted to 21,515,742 l. 13 s. 8½ d. A great part of those debts had been contracted upon short anticipations, and some part upon annuities for lives; so that before the 31st of December 1701, in less than four years, there had partly been paid off, and partly reverted to the public, the sum of 5,121,041 l. 12 s. 0¾ d.; a greater reduction of the public debt than has ever since been brought about in so short a period of time. The remaining debt, therefore, amounted only to 16,394,701 l. 1 s. 7¼ d.

From 1702 to 1722 the increase was thirty-nine millions, and from 1722 to 1739 the reduction was only eight and one-third millions. In the war which began in 1702, and which was concluded by the treaty of Utrecht, the public debts were still more accumulated. On the 31st of December 1714, they amounted to 53,681,076 l. 5 s. 6$\frac{1}{2}$ d. The subscription into the South Sea fund of the short and long[1] annuities increased the capital of the public debts, so that on the 31st of December 1722, it amounted to 55,282,978 l. 1 s. 3$\frac{5}{6}$ d. The reduction of the debt began in 1723, and went on so slowly that, on the 31st of December 1739, during seventeen years of profound peace, the whole sum paid off was no more than 8,328,354 l. 17 s. 11$\frac{3}{12}$ d. the capital of the public debt at that time amounting to 46,954,623 l. 3 s. 4$\frac{7}{12}$ d.

From 1739 to 1748 the increase was thirty-one and one-third millions. The Spanish war, which began in 1739, and the French war which soon followed it, occasioned a further increase of the debt, which, on the 31st of December 1748, after the war had been concluded by the treaty of Aix la Chapelle, amounted to 78,293,313 l. 1 s. 10$\frac{3}{4}$ d. The most profound peace of seventeen years continuance had taken no more than 8,328,354 l. 17 s. 11$\frac{3}{12}$ d. from it. A war of less than nine years continuance added 31,338,689 l. 18 s. 6$\frac{1}{6}$ d. to it.[2]

During the peace of 1748-55 the reduction was six millions, and the seven years' war added more than seventy-five. During the administration of Mr. Pelham, the interest of the public debt was reduced, or at least measures were taken for reducing it, from four to three per cent.;[3] the sinking fund was increased, and some part of the public debt was paid off. In 1755, before the breaking out of the late war, the funded debt of Great Britain amounted to 72,289,673 l.[4] On the 5th of January 1763, at the conclusion of the peace, the funded debt amounted to 122,603,336 l 8 s. 2$\frac{1}{4}$ d.[5] The unfunded debt has been stated at 13,927,589 l. 2 s. 2 d. But the expence occasioned by the war did not end with the conclusion of the peace;[6] so that though, on the 5th of January 1764, the funded debt was increased (partly by a new loan, and partly by funding a part of the unfunded debt)[7] to

---

[1] [Ed. 1 reads 'long and short'.]

[2] See James Postlethwaite's history of the public revenue. [Pp. 42, 143–145, 147, 224, 300. The reference covers the three paragraphs in the text above.]

[3] [Above, p. 451.]

[4] [*Present State of the Nation* (above, vol. i., p. 465), p. 28.]

[5] [Anderson, *Commerce*, postscript *ad init.*]

[6] ['But the expenses of the war did not cease with its operations.'—*Considerations* (see a few lines below), p. 4.]

[7] [*Ibid.*, p. 5.]

129,586,789 l. 10 s. 1¾ d.[1] there still remained (according to the very well informed author of the Considerations on the trade and finances of Great Britain[2]) an unfunded debt which was brought to account in that and the following year, of 9,975,017 l. 12 s. 2¹⁵⁄₄₄ d. In 1764, therefore, the public debt of Great Britain, funded and unfunded together, amounted, according to this author, to 139,561,807 l. 2 s. 4 d.[3] The annuities for lives too, which had been granted as premiums to the subscribers to the new loans in 1757, estimated at fourteen years purchase, were valued at 472,500 l.; and the annuities for long terms of years, granted as premiums likewise, in 1761 and 1762, estimated at 27½ years purchase, were valued at 6,826,875 l.[4] During a peace of about seven years continuance, the prudent and truly patriot administration of Mr. Pelham, was not able to pay off an old debt of six millions. During the war of nearly the same continuance, a new debt of more than seventy-five millions was contracted.

In the eleven years of peace before January 1775 the reduction was only ten and a half millions, and most of this was due to reductions of interest.

On the 5th of January 1775, the funded debt of Great Britain amounted to 124,996,086 l. 1 s. 6¼ d. The unfunded, exclusive of a large civil list debt, to 4,150,236 l. 3 s. 11⅞ d. Both together, to 129,146,322 l. 5 s. 6 d. According to this account the whole debt paid off during eleven years profound peace amounted only to 10,415,474 l. 16 s. 9⅞ d. Even this small reduction of debt, however, has not been all made from the savings out of the ordinary revenue of the state. Several extraneous sums, altogether independent of that ordinary revenue, have contributed towards it. Amongst[5] these we may reckon an additional shilling in the pound land tax for three years; the two millions received from the East India company, as indemnification for their territorial acquisitions; and the one hundred and ten thousand pounds received from the bank for the renewal of their charter. To these must be added several other sums, which, as they arose out of the late war, ought perhaps to be considered as deductions from the expences of it. The principal are,

---

[1] [The account is given in the Continuation of Anderson's *Commerce*, A.D. 1764, vol. iv., p. 58. in ed. of 1801. The '¾d.' should be '¼d.']

[2] [*Considerations on the Trade and Finances of this Kingdom and on the measures of administration with respect to those great national objects since the conclusion of the peace*, by Thomas Whately, 1766 (often ascribed to George Grenville), p. 22.]

[3] [This is the amount obtained by adding the two items mentioned, and is the reading of ed. 1. Eds. 2–5 all read '£139,516,807 2s. 4d.,' which is doubtless a misprint. The total is not given in *Considerations*.]

[4] [*Considerations*, p. 4.]　　　　　[5] [Ed. 1 reads 'Among'.]

	l.	s.	d.
The produce of French prizes	690,449	18	9
Composition for French prisoners	670,000	0	0
What has been received from the sale of the ceded islands[1]	95,500	0	0

Total, 1,455,949 18 9

If we add to this sum the balance of the earl of Chatham's and Mr. Calcraft's accounts, and other army savings of the same kind, together with what has been received from the bank, the East India company, and the additional shilling in the pound land tax; the whole must be a good deal more than five millions. The debt, therefore, which since the peace has been paid out of the savings from the ordinary revenue of the state, has not, one year with another, amounted to half a million a year. The sinking fund has, no doubt, been considerably augmented since the peace, by the debt which has been paid off, by the reduction of the redeemable four per cents. to three per cents., and by the annuities for lives which have fallen in, and, if peace were[2] to continue, a million, perhaps, might now be annually spared out of it towards the discharge of the debt. Another million, accordingly, was paid in the course of last year; but, at the same time, a large civil list debt was left unpaid, and we are now involved in a new war which, in its progress, may prove as expensive as any of our former wars.[3] The new debt which will probably be contracted before the end of the next campaign, may perhaps be nearly equal to all the old debt which has been paid off from the savings out of the ordinary revenue of the state. It would be altogether chimerical, therefore, to expect that the public debt should ever be completely discharged by any savings which are likely to be made from that ordinary revenue as it stands at present.

The opinion that the national debt is an additional capital is altogether erroneous. The public funds of the different indebted nations of Europe, particularly those of England, have by one author been represented as the accumulation of a great capital superadded to the other capital of the country, by means of which its trade is extended, its manufactures multiplied, and its lands cultivated and improved much beyond

---

[1] [Above, p. 90, note 5.]   [2] [Eds. 1–3 read 'was'.]

[3] It has proved more expensive than any of our former wars; and has involved us in an additional debt of more than one hundred millions. During a profound peace of eleven years, little more than ten millions of debt was paid; during a war of seven years, more than one hundred millions was contracted. [This note appears first in ed. 3.]

what they could have been by means of that other capital only.[1] He does not consider that the capital which the first creditors of the public advanced to government, was, from the moment in which they advanced it, a certain portion of the annual produce turned away from serving in the function of a capital, to serve in that of a revenue; from maintaining productive labourers to maintain unproductive ones, and to be spent and wasted, generally in the course of the year, without even the hope of any future reproduction. In return for the capital which they advanced they obtained, indeed, an annuity in the public funds in most cases of more than equal value. This annuity, no doubt, replaced to them their capital, and enabled them to carry on their trade and business to the same or perhaps to a greater extent than before; that is, they were enabled either to borrow of other people a new capital upon the credit of this annuity, or by selling it to get from other people a new capital of their own, equal or superior to that which they had advanced to government. This new capital, however, which they in this manner either bought or borrowed of other people, must have existed in the country before, and must have been employed as all capitals are, in maintaining productive labour. When it came into the hands of those who had advanced their money to government, though it was in some respects a new capital to them, it was not so to the country; but was only a capital withdrawn from certain employments in order to be turned towards others. Though it replaced to them what they had advanced to government, it did not replace it to the country. Had they not advanced this capital to government, there would have been in the country two capitals, two portions of the annual produce, instead of one, employed in maintaining productive labour.

When necessary expenditure is met by taxes, it only diverts unproductive labour from one unproductive employment to another.

When for defraying the expence of government a revenue is raised within the year from the produce of free or unmortgaged taxes, a certain portion of the revenue of private people is only turned away from maintaining one species of unproductive labour, towards maintaining another. Some part of what they pay in those taxes might no doubt have been

---

[1] [Garnier's note, *Recherches etc.*, tom. iv., p. 501, is 'Pinto: *Traité de la Circulation et du Crédit*,' a work published in 1771 ('Amsterdam'), 'par l'auteur de l'essai sur le luxe,' of which see esp. pp. 44, 45, 209–211. But an English essay of 1731 to the same effect is quoted by Melon, *Essai Politique sur le Commerce*, chap. xxiii., ed. of 1761, p. 296, and Melon seems to be referred to below, p. 463. Cp. *Lectures*, p. 210.]

accumulated into capital, and consequently employed in maintaining productive labour; but the greater part would probably have been spent and consequently employed in maintaining unproductive labour. The public expence, however, when defrayed in this manner, no doubt hinders more or less the further accumulation of new capital; but it does not necessarily occasion the destruction of any actually existing capital.

When it is met by borrowing, it diverts labour from productive to unproductive employment, and the only advantage is that people can continue to save more during the war, When the public expence is defrayed by funding, it is defrayed by the annual destruction of some capital which had before existed in the country; by the perversion of some portion of the annual produce which had before been destined for the maintenance of productive labour, towards that of unproductive labour. As in this case, however, the taxes are lighter than they would have been, had a revenue sufficient for defraying the same expence been raised within the year; the private revenue of individuals is necessarily less burdened, and consequently their ability to save and accumulate some part of that revenue into capital is a good deal less impaired. If the method of funding destroy[1] more old capital, it at the same time hinders less the accumulation or acquisition of new capital, than that of defraying the public expence by a revenue raised within the year. Under the system of funding, the frugality and industry of private people can more easily repair the breaches which the waste and extravagance of government may occasionally make in the general capital of the society.

which advantage disappears immediately peace is concluded. Under the other system, too, wars would be shorter and periods of peace longer. It is only during the continuance of war, however, that the system of funding has this advantage over the other system. Were the expence of war to be defrayed always by a revenue raised within the year, the taxes from which that extraordinary revenue was drawn would last no longer than the war. The ability of private people to accumulate, though less during the war, would have been greater during the peace than under the system of funding. War would not necessarily have occasioned the destruction of any old capitals, and peace would have occasioned the accumulation of many more new. Wars would in general be more speedily concluded, and less wantonly undertaken. The people feeling, during the continuance of the war, the

---

[1] [Eds. 1–3 read the indicative, 'destroys'.]

complete burden of it, would soon grow weary of it, and government, in order to humour them, would not be under the necessity of carrying it on longer than it was necessary to do so. The foresight of the heavy and unavoidable burdens of war would hinder the people from wantonly calling for it when there was no real or solid interest to fight for. The seasons during which the ability of private people to accumulate was somewhat impaired, would occur more rarely, and be of shorter continuance. Those on the contrary, during which that ability was in the highest vigour, would be of much longer duration than they can well be under the system of funding.

Moreover funding at length burdens the revenue so greatly that the ordinary peace expenditure exceeds that which would under the other system have been sufficient in war. When funding, besides, has made a certain progress, the multiplication of taxes which it brings along with it sometimes impairs as much the ability of private people to accumulate even in time of peace, as the other system would in time of war. The peace revenue of Great Britain amounts at present to more than ten millions a year. If free and unmortgaged, it might be sufficient, with proper management and without contracting a shilling of new debt, to carry on the most vigorous war. The private revenue of the inhabitants of Great Britain is at present as much encumbered in time of peace, their ability to accumulate is[1] as much impaired as it would have been in the time of the most expensive war, had the pernicious system of funding never been adopted.

The fact of part or the whole of the debt being held at home makes no difference. In the payment of the interest of the public debt, it has been said, it is the right hand which pays the left.[2] The money does not go out of the country. It is only a part of the revenue of one set of the inhabitants which is transferred to another; and the nation is not a farthing the poorer. This apology is founded altogether in the sophistry of the mercantile system, and after the long examination which I have already bestowed upon that system, it may perhaps be unnecessary to say any thing further about it. It supposes, besides, that the whole public debt is owing to the inhabitants of the country, which happens not to be true; the Dutch, as well as several other foreign nations, having a very considerable share in our public

---

[1] [Misprinted 'it' in ed. 5.]

[2] ['Les Dettes d'un État sont des dettes de la main droite à la main gauche, dont le corps ne se trouvera point affaibli, s'il a la quantité d'aliments nécessaires, et s'il sait les distribuer.'—Melon, *Essai politique sur le Commerce*, chap. xxiii., ed. of 1761, p. 296.]

funds. But though the whole debt were owing to the inhabitants of the country, it would not upon that account be less pernicious.

Land and capital, the two original sources of all revenue, are managed by landlords and owners of capital. Land and capital stock are the two original sources of all revenue both private and public. Capital stock pays the wages of productive labour, whether employed in agriculture, manufactures, or commerce. The management of those two original sources of revenue belongs to two different sets of people; the proprietors of land, and the owners or employers of capital stock.

Taxation may diminish or destroy the landlord's ability to improve his land, The proprietor of land is interested for the sake of his own revenue to keep his estate in as good condition as he can, by building and repairing his tenants houses, by making and maintaining the necessary drains and enclosures, and all those other expensive improvements which it properly belongs to the landlord to make and maintain. But by different land-taxes the revenue of the landlord may be so much diminished; and by different duties upon the necessaries and conveniences of life, that diminished revenue may be rendered of so little real value, that he may find himself altogether unable to make or maintain those expensive improvements. When the landlord, however, ceases to do his part, it is altogether impossible that the tenant should continue to do his. As the distress of the landlord increases, the agriculture of the country must necessarily decline.

and induce the owner of capital to remove it from the country. When, by different taxes upon the necessaries and conveniences of life, the owners and employers of capital stock find, that whatever revenue they derive from it, will not, in a particular country, purchase the same quantity of those necessaries and conveniences which an equal revenue would in almost any other, they will be disposed to remove to some other. And when, in order to raise those taxes, all or the greater part of merchants and manufacturers, that is, all or the greater part of the employers of great capitals, come to be continually exposed to the mortifying and vexatious visits of the tax-gatherers, this disposition to remove will soon be changed into an actual removal. The industry of the country will necessarily fall with the removal of the capital which supported it, and the ruin of trade and manufactures will follow the declension of agriculture.

The transference of the sources of revenue from the To transfer from the owners of those two great sources of revenue, land and capital stock, from the *owners of particular portions of them to the creditors of the public must occasion neglect of land and waste or removal of capital.*　persons immediately interested in the good condition of every particular portion of land, and in the good management of every particular portion of capital stock, to another set of persons (the creditors of the public, who have no such particular interest), the greater part of the revenue arising from either, must, in the long-run, occasion both the neglect of land, and the waste or removal of capital stock. A creditor of the public has no doubt a general interest in the prosperity of the agriculture, manufactures, and commerce of the country; and consequently in the good condition of its lands, and in the good management of its capital stock. Should there be any general failure or declension in any of these things, the produce of the different taxes might no longer be sufficient to pay him the annuity or interest which is due to him. But a creditor of the public, considered merely as such, has no interest in the good condition of any particular portion of land, or in the good management of any particular portion of capital stock. As a creditor of the public he has no knowledge of any such particular portion. He has no inspection of it. He can have no care about it. Its ruin may in some[1] cases be unknown to him, and cannot directly affect him.

The practice of funding has always enfeebled states.　The practice of funding has gradually enfeebled every state which has adopted it. The Italian republics seem to have begun it. Genoa and Venice, the only two remaining which can pretend to an independent existence, have both been enfeebled by it. Spain seems to have learned the practice from the Italian republics, and (its taxes being probably less judicious than theirs) it has, in proportion to its natural strength, been still more enfeebled. The debts of Spain are of very old standing. It was deeply in debt before the end of the sixteenth century, about a hundred years before England owed a shilling. France, notwithstanding all its natural resources, languishes under an oppressive load of the same kind. The republic of the United Provinces is as much enfeebled by its debts as either Genoa or Venice. Is it likely that in Great Britain alone a practice, which has brought either weakness or desolation into every other country, should prove altogether innocent?

The superiority of the British system　The system of taxation established in those different countries, it may be said, is inferior to that of

---

[1] [Ed. 1 reads 'most'.]

of taxation will not enable Britain to support an unlimited burden. England. I believe it is so. But it ought to be remembered, that when the wisest government has exhausted all the proper subjects of taxation, it must, in cases of urgent necessity, have recourse to improper ones.[1] The wise republic of Holland has upon some occasions been obliged to have recourse to taxes as inconvenient as the greater part of those of Spain. Another war begun before any considerable liberation of the public revenue had been brought about, and growing in its progress as expensive as the last war, may, from irresistible necessity, render the British system of taxation as oppressive as that of Holland, or even as that of Spain. To the honour of our present system of taxation, indeed, it has hitherto given so little embarrassment to industry, that, during the course even of the most expensive wars, the frugality and good conduct of individuals seem[2] to have been able by saving and accumulation, to repair all the breaches which the waste and extravagance of government had made in the general capital of the society. At the conclusion of the late war, the most expensive that Great Britain ever waged, her agriculture was as flourishing, her manufacturers as numerous and as fully employed, and her commerce as extensive, as they had ever been before. The capital, therefore, which supported all those different branches of industry, must have been equal to what it had ever been before. Since the peace, agriculture has been still further improved, the rents of houses have risen in every town and village of the country, a proof of the increasing wealth and revenue of the people; and the annual amount of the greater part of the old taxes, of the principal branches of the excise and customs in particular, has been continually increasing, an equally clear proof of an increasing consumption, and consequently of an increasing produce, which could alone support that consumption. Great Britain seems to support with ease, a burden which, half a century ago, nobody believed her capable of supporting. Let us not, however, upon this account rashly conclude that she is capable of supporting any burden; nor even be too confident that she could support, without great distress, a burden a little greater than what has already been laid upon her.

Bankruptcy is always the end of great accumulation of debt. When national debts have once been accumulated to a certain degree, there is scarce, I believe, a single instance of their having been fairly and completely paid. The liberation of the public revenue, if it has ever been

---

[1] [Above, p. 439.]   [2] [Eds. 1 and 2 read 'seems'.]

brought about at all, has always been brought about by a bankruptcy; sometimes by an avowed one, but always by a real one, though frequently by a pretended payment.[1]

Raising the coin has been the usual method of disguising bankruptcy though this expedient has much worse consequences than open bankruptcy. The raising of the denomination of the coin has been the most usual expedient by which a real public bankruptcy has been disguised under the appearance of a pretended payment. If a sixpence, for example, should either by act of parliament or royal proclamation be raised to the denomination of a shilling, and twenty sixpences to that of a pound sterling; the person who under the old denomination had borrowed twenty shillings, or near four ounces of silver, would, under the new, pay with twenty sixpences, or with something less than two ounces. A national debt of about a hundred and twenty-eight millions, nearly the capital of the funded and unfunded debt of Great Britain, might in this manner be paid with about sixty-four millions of our present money. It would indeed be a pretended payment only, and the creditors of the public would really be defrauded of ten shillings in the pound of what was due to them. The calamity too would extend much further than to the creditors of the public, and those of every private person would suffer a proportionable loss; and this without any advantage, but in most cases with a great additional loss, to the creditors of the public. If the creditors of the public indeed were generally much in debt to other people, they might in some measure compensate their loss by paying their creditors in the same coin in which the public had paid them. But in most countries the creditors of the public are, the greater part of them, wealthy people, who stand more in the relation of creditors than in that of debtors towards the rest of their fellow-citizens. A pretended payment of this kind, therefore, instead of alleviating, aggravates in most cases the loss of the creditors of the public; and without any advantage to the public, extends the calamity to a great number of other innocent people. It occasions a general and most pernicious subversion of the fortunes of private people; enriching in most cases the idle and profuse debtor at the expence of the industrious and frugal creditor, and transporting a great part of the national capital from the hands which were likely to increase and

[1] [Raynal says 'L'évidence autorise seulement à dire que les gouvernements qui pour le malheur des peuples ont adopté le détestable système des emprunts doivent tôt ou tard l'abjurer: et que l'abus qu'ils en ont fait les forceront vraisemblablement à être infidèles.'—*Histoire philosophique*, Amsterdam, 1773, tom. iv., p. 274.]

improve it, to those which are likely to dissipate and destroy it. When it becomes necessary for a state to declare itself bankrupt, in the same manner as when it becomes necessary for an individual to do so, a fair, open, and avowed bankruptcy is always the measure which is both least dishonourable to the debtor, and least hurtful to the creditor. The honour of a state is surely very poorly provided for, when, in order to cover the disgrace of a real bankruptcy, it has recourse to a juggling trick of this kind, so easily seen through, and at the same time so extremely pernicious.

It has been adopted by many states, including ancient Rome, Almost all states, however, ancient as well as modern, when reduced to this necessity, have, upon some occasions, played this very juggling trick. The Romans, at the end of the first Punic war, reduced the As, the coin or denomination by which they computed the value of all their other coins, from containing twelve ounces of copper to contain only two ounces: that is, they raised two ounces of copper to a denomination which had always before expressed the value of twelve ounces. The republic was, in this manner, enabled to pay the great debts which it had contracted with the sixth part of what it really owed. So sudden and so great a bankruptcy, we should in the present times be apt to imagine, must have occasioned a very violent popular clamour. It does not appear to have occasioned any. The law which enacted it was, like all other laws relating to the coin, introduced and carried through the assembly of the people by a tribune, and was probably a very popular law. In Rome, as in all the other ancient republics, the poor people were constantly in debt to the rich and the great, who, in order to secure their votes at the annual elections, used to lend them money at exorbitant interest, which, being never paid, soon accumulated into a sum too great either for the debtor to pay, or for any body else to pay for him. The debtor, for fear of a very severe execution, was obliged, without any further gratuity, to vote for the candidate whom the creditor recommended. In spite of all the laws against bribery and corruption, the bounty of the candidates, together with the occasional distributions of corn, which were ordered by the senate, were the principal funds from which, during the latter[1] times of the Roman republic, the poorer citizens derived their subsistence. To deliver themselves from this subjection to their creditors, the poorer citizens were continually calling out either for an entire abolition of

---

[1] [Eds. 1 and 2 read 'later'; cp. above, p. 410.]

debts, or for what they called New Tables; that is, for a law which should entitle them to a complete acquittance, upon paying only a certain proportion of their accumulated debts. The law which reduced the coin of all denominations to a sixth part of its former value, as it enabled them to pay their debts with a sixth part of what they really owed, was equivalent to the most advantageous new tables. In order to satisfy the people, the rich and the great were, upon several different occasions, obliged to consent to laws both for abolishing debts, and for introducing new tables; and they probably were induced to consent to this law, partly for the same reason, and partly that, by liberating the public revenue, they might restore vigour to that government of which they themselves had the principal direction. An operation of this kind would at once reduce a debt of a hundred and twenty-eight millions to twenty-one millions three hundred and thirty-three thousand three hundred and thirty-three pounds six shillings and eightpence. In the course of the second Punic war the As was still further reduced, first, from two ounces of copper to one ounce; and afterwards from one ounce to half an ounce; that is, to the twenty-fourth part of its original value.[1] By combining the three Roman operations into one, a debt of a hundred and twenty-eight millions of our present money, might in this manner be reduced all at once to a debt of five millions three hundred and thirty-three thousand three hundred and thirty-three pounds six shillings and eight-pence. Even the enormous debt of Great Britain might in this manner soon be paid.

and has led to the universal reduction of the value of the coin. By means of such expedients the coin of, I believe, all nations has been gradually reduced more and more below its original value, and the same nominal sum has been gradually brought to contain a smaller and a smaller quantity of silver.

Another expedient is to adulterate the coin, Nations have sometimes, for the same purpose, adulterated the standard of their coin; that is, have mixed a greater quantity of alloy in it. If in the pound weight of our silver coin, for example, instead of eighteen penny-weight, according to the present standard, there was mixed eight ounces of alloy; a pound sterling, or twenty shillings of such coin, would be worth little more than six shillings and eight-pence

---

[1] [This chapter of Roman history is based on a few sentences in Pliny, *H.N.*, lib. xxxiii., cap. iii. Modern criticism has discovered the facts to be not nearly so simple as they are represented in the text.]

of our present money. The quantity of silver contained in six shillings and eight-pence of our present money, would thus be raised very nearly to the denomination of a pound sterling. The adulteration of the standard has exactly the same effect with what the French call an augmentation, or a direct raising of the denomination of the coin.

but this is a treacherous fraud which occasions such indignation that it usually fails. An augmentation, or a direct raising of the denomination of the coin, always is, and from its nature must be, an open and avowed operation. By means of it pieces of a smaller weight and bulk are called by the same name which had before been given to pieces of a greater weight and bulk. The adulteration of the standard, on the contrary, has generally been a concealed operation. By means of it pieces were issued from the mint of the same denominations, and, as nearly as could be contrived, of the same weight, bulk, and appearance, with pieces which had been current before of much greater value. When king John of France,[1] in order to pay his debts, adulterated his coin, all the officers of his mint were sworn to secrecy. Both operations are unjust. But a simple augmentation is an injustice of open violence; whereas an adulteration is an injustice of treacherous fraud. This latter operation, therefore, as soon as it has been discovered, and it could never be concealed very long, has always excited much greater indignation than the former. The coin after any considerable augmentation has very seldom been brought back to its former weight; but after the greatest adulterations it has almost always been brought back to its former fineness. It has scarce ever happened that the fury and indignation of the people could otherwise be appeased.

It has been tried in England, Scotland and most other countries. In the end of the reign of Henry VIII. and in the beginning of that of Edward VI. the English coin was not only raised in its denomination, but adulterated in its standard. The like frauds were practised in Scotland during the minority of James VI. They have occasionally been practised in most other countries.

For the paying off or reduction of the British debt a very That the public revenue of Great Britain can ever[2] be completely liberated, or even that any consider-

---

[1] See Du Cange Glossary, voce Moneta; the Benedictine edition. [This gives a table of the alterations made in the coin and refers to Le Blanc. *Traité historique des Monnoyes de France*, 1792, in which the fact that the officers were adjured by their oaths to keep the matter secret is mentioned on p. 218, but the adjuration is also quoted in the more accessible Melon, *Essai politique sur le Commerce*, chap. xiii., ed. of 1761, p. 177.]

[2] [Misprinted 'never' in eds. 2–5.]

considerable
increase of revenue
or diminution of
expense is necessary.

able progress can ever be made towards that liberation, while the surplus of that revenue, or what is over and above defraying the annual expence of the peace establishment, is so very small, it seems altogether in vain to expect. That liberation, it is evident, can never be brought about without either some very considerable augmentation of the public revenue, or some equally considerable reduction of the public expence.

Alterations in
taxation might
increase the revenue
considerably, but
not sufficiently.

A more equal land tax, a more equal tax upon the rent of houses, and such alterations in the present system of customs and excise as those which have been mentioned in the foregoing chapter, might, perhaps, without increasing the burden of the greater part of the people, but only distributing the weight of it more equally upon the whole, produce a considerable augmentation of revenue. The most sanguine projector, however, could scarce flatter himself that any augmentation of this kind would be such as could give any reasonable hopes, either of liberating the public revenue altogether, or even of making such progress towards that liberation in time of peace, as either to prevent or to compensate the further accumulation of the public debt in the next war.

An extension of
taxation to Ireland
and the colonies
would afford a
larger increase.

By extending the British system of taxation to all the different provinces of the empire inhabited by people of either[1] British or European extraction, a much greater augmentation of revenue might be expected. This, however, could scarce, perhaps, be done, consistently with the principles of the British constitution, without admitting into the British parliament, or if you will into the states-general of the British empire, a fair and equal representation of all those different provinces, that of each province bearing the same proportion to the produce of its taxes, as the representation of Great Britain might bear to the produce of the taxes levied upon Great Britain. The private interest of many powerful individuals, the confirmed prejudices of great bodies of people seem, indeed, at present, to oppose to so great a change such obstacles as it may be very difficult, perhaps, altogether impossible, to surmount. Without, however, pretending to determine whether such a union be practicable or impracticable, it may not, perhaps, be improper, in a speculative work of this kind, to consider how far the British system of

[1] [Ed. 1 reads 'either of'.]

taxation might be applicable to all the different provinces of the empire; what revenue might be expected from it if so applied, and in what manner a general union of this kind might be likely to affect the happiness and prosperity of the different provinces comprehended within it. Such a speculation can at worst be regarded but as a new Utopia, less amusing certainly, but not more useless and chimerical than the old one.

The land-tax, the stamp-duties, and the different duties of customs and excise, constitute the four principal branches of the British taxes.

The land-tax could well be extended to Ireland, America and the West Indies. Ireland is certainly as able, and our American and West Indian plantations more able to pay a land-tax than Great Britain. Where the landlord is subject neither to tithe nor poors rate, he must certainly be more able to pay such a tax, than where he is subject to both those other burdens. The tithe, where there is no modus, and where it is levied in kind, diminishes more what would otherwise be the rent of the landlord, than a land-tax which really amounted to five shillings in the pound. Such a tithe will be found in most cases to amount to more than a fourth part of the real rent of the land, or of what remains after replacing completely the capital of the farmer, together with his reasonable profit. If all moduses and all impropriations were taken away, the complete church tithe of Great Britain and Ireland could not well be estimated at less than six or seven millions. If there was no tithe either in Great Britain or Ireland, the landlords could afford to pay six or seven millions additional land-tax, without being more burdened than a very great part of them are at present. America pays no tithe, and could therefore very well afford to pay a land-tax. The lands in America and the West Indies, indeed, are in general not tenanted nor[1] leased out to farmers. They could not therefore be assessed according to any rent-roll. But neither were the lands of Great Britain, in the 4th of William and Mary, assessed according to any rent-roll, but according to a very loose and inaccurate estimation. The lands in America might be assessed either in the same manner, or according to an equitable valuation in consequence of an accurate survey, like that which was lately made in the Milanese, and in the dominions of Austria, Prussia, and Sardinia.[2]

---

[1] [Ed. 1 reads 'or'.]
[2] [Above, pp. 353, 360, 361.]

Stamp duties could easily be extended. Stamp-duties, it is evident, might be levied without any variation in all countries where the forms of law process, and the deeds by which property both real and personal is transferred, are the same or nearly the same.

The extension of the customs would be of great advantage to all, as it would be accompanied by an extension of free trade. The extension of the custom-house laws of Great Britain to Ireland and the plantations, provided it was accompanied, as in justice it ought to be, with an extension of the freedom of trade, would be in the highest degree advantageous to both. All the invidious restraints which at present oppress the trade of Ireland, the distinction between the enumerated and non-enumerated commodities of America, would be entirely at an end.[1] The countries north of Cape Finisterre would be as open to every part of the produce of America, as those south of that Cape are to some parts of that produce at present. The trade between all the different parts of the British empire would, in consequence of this uniformity in the custom-house laws, be as free as the coasting trade of Great Britain is at present. The British empire would thus afford within itself an immense internal market for every part of the produce of all its different provinces. So great an extension of market would soon compensate both to Ireland and the plantations, all that they could suffer from the increase of the duties of customs.

Excise duties would require some variation, The excise is the only part of the British system of taxation, which would require to be varied in any respect according as it was applied to the different provinces of the empire. It might be applied to Ireland without any variation; the produce and consumption of that kingdom being exactly of the same nature with those of Great Britain. In its application to America and the West Indies, of which the produce and consumption are so very different from those of Great Britain, some modification might be necessary, in the same manner as in its application to the cyder and beer counties of England.

as for example in the case of American beer. A fermented liquor, for example, which is called beer, but which, as it is made of melasses, bears very little resemblance to our beer, makes a considerable part of the common drink of the people in America. This liquor, as it can be kept only for a few days, cannot, like our beer, be prepared and stored up for sale in great breweries; but every private family must brew it for their own use, in the same manner as they cook

[1] [Above, p. 89.]

their victuals. But to subject every private family to the odious
visits and examination of the tax-gatherers, in the same manner as
we subject the keepers of alehouses and the brewers for public sale,
would be altogether inconsistent with liberty. If for the sake of
equality it was thought necessary to lay a tax upon this liquor, it
might be taxed by taxing the material of which it is made, either at
the place of manufacture, or, if the circumstances of the trade rendered such an excise improper, by laying a duty upon its importation into the colony in which it was to be consumed. Besides the
duty of one penny a gallon imposed by the British parliament upon
the importation of melasses into America; there is a provincial tax
of this kind upon their importation into Massachusets Bay, in ships
belonging to any other colony, of eight-pence the hogshead; and
another upon their importation, from the northern colonies, into
South Carolina, of five-pence the gallon. Or if neither of these
methods was found convenient, each family might compound for
its consumption of this liquor, either according to the number of
persons of which it consisted, in the same manner as private families
compound for the malt-tax in England; or according to the different
ages and sexes of those persons, in the same manner as several
different taxes are levied in Holland; or nearly as Sir Matthew
Decker proposes that all taxes upon consumable commodities should
be levied in England.[1] This mode of taxation, it has already been
observed, when applied to objects of a speedy consumption, is not
a very convenient one. It might be adopted, however, in cases where
no better could be done.

Sugar, rum and tobacco could be made subject to excise. Sugar, rum, and tobacco, are commodities which
are no where necessaries of life, which are become
objects of almost universal consumption, and which
are therefore extremely proper subjects of taxation. If a union with
the colonies were[2] to take place, those commodities might be taxed
either before they go out of the hands of the manufacturer or
grower; or if this mode of taxation did not suit the circumstances of
those persons, they might be deposited in public warehouses both
at the place of manufacture, and at all the different ports of the
empire to which they might afterwards be transported, to remain
there, under the joint custody of the owner and the revenue officer,
till such time as they should be delivered out either to the consumer,
to the merchant retailer for home-consumption, or to the merchant

[1] [Above, pp. 406–407.]   [2] [Eds. 1–3 read 'was'.]

exporter, the tax not to be advanced till such delivery. When delivered out for exportation, to go duty free; upon proper security being given that they should really be exported out of the empire. These are perhaps the principal commodities with regard to which a union with the colonies might require some considerable change in the present system of British taxation.

The increase of revenue thus obtained, if proportionate to the increased population taxed, would yield six millions and a quarter to be applied in reduction of debt, and this sum would of course be a growing one.

What might be the amount of the revenue which this system of taxation extended to all the different provinces of the empire might produce, it must, no doubt, be altogether impossible to ascertain with tolerable exactness. By means of this system there is annually levied in Great Britain, upon less than eight millions of people, more than ten millions of revenue. Ireland contains more than two millions of people, and according to the accounts laid before the congress,[1] the twelve associated provinces of America contain more than three. Those accounts, however, may have been exaggerated, in order, perhaps, either to encourage their own people, or to intimidate those of this country, and we shall suppose therefore that our North American and West Indian colonies taken together contain no more than three millions; or that the whole British empire, in Europe and America, contains no more than thirteen millions of inhabitants. If upon less than eight millions of inhabitants this system of taxation raises a revenue of more than ten millions sterling; it ought upon thirteen millions of inhabitants to raise a revenue of more than sixteen millions two hundred and fifty thousand pounds sterling. From this revenue, supposing that this system could produce it, must be deducted, the revenue usually raised in Ireland and the plantations for defraying the expence of their respective civil governments. The expence of the civil and military establishment of Ireland, together with the interest of the public debt, amounts, at a medium of the two years which ended March 1775, to something less than seven hundred and fifty thousand pounds a year. By a very exact account[2] of the revenue of the principal colonies of America and the West Indies, it amounted, before the commencement of the present[3] disturbances, to a hundred and forty-one thousand eight hundred pounds. In this account,

---

[1] [Given in the Continuation of Anderson's *Commerce*, A.D. 1774, vol. iv., p. 178, in ed. of 1801.]　　　　　[2] [Above, p. 85.]

[3] [Ed. 1 reads 'late'; cp. above, vol. i., p. 524.]

however, the revenue of Maryland, of North Carolina, and of all our late acquisitions both upon the continent and in the islands, is omitted, which may perhaps make a difference of thirty or forty thousand pounds. For the sake of even numbers therefore, let us suppose that the revenue necessary for supporting the civil government of Ireland and the plantations, may amount to a million. There would remain consequently a revenue of fifteen millions two hundred and fifty thousand pounds, to be applied towards defraying the general expence of the empire, and towards paying the public debt. But if from the present revenue of Great Britain a million could in peaceable times be spared towards the payment of that debt, six millions two hundred and fifty thousand pounds could very well be spared from this improved revenue. This great sinking fund too might be augmented every year by the interest of the debt which had been discharged the year before, and might in this manner increase so very rapidly, as to be sufficient in a few years to discharge the whole debt, and thus to restore completely the at present debilitated and languishing vigour of the empire. In the mean time the people might be relieved from some of the most burdensome taxes; from those which are imposed either upon the necessaries of life, or upon the materials of manufacture. The labouring poor would thus be enabled to live better, to work cheaper, and to send their goods cheaper to market. The cheapness of their goods would increase the demand for them, and consequently for the labour of those who produced them. This increase in the demand for labour, would both increase the numbers and improve the circumstances of the labouring poor. Their consumption would increase, and together with it the revenue arising from all those articles of their consumption upon which the taxes might be allowed to remain.

Some necessary deductions from this estimate would be counter-balanced by additions resulting from a few simple alterations. The revenue arising from this system of taxation, however, might not immediately increase in proportion to the number of people who were subjected to it. Great indulgence would for some time be due to those provinces of the empire which were thus subjected to burthens to which they had not before been accustomed, and even when the same taxes came to be levied every where as exactly as possible, they would not every where produce a revenue proportioned to the numbers of the people. In a poor country the consumption of the principal commodities subject to the duties of customs and excise is very small; and in a thinly inhabited country the opportunities of smuggling are very great. The consumption of malt liquors among the inferior ranks of people in Scotland is very small, and the excise upon malt, beer, and ale, produces less there than in England in proportion to the numbers of the people and the rate of the duties, which upon malt is different on account of a supposed difference of quality. In these particular branches of the excise, there is not, I apprehend, much more smuggling in the one country than in the other. The duties upon the distillery, and the greater part of the duties of customs, in proportion to the numbers of people in the respective countries, produce less in Scotland than in England, not only on account of the smaller consumption of the taxed commodities, but of the much greater facility of smuggling. In Ireland, the inferior ranks of people are still poorer than in Scotland, and many parts of the country are almost as thinly inhabited. In Ireland, therefore, the consumption of the taxed commodities might, in proportion to the number of the people, be still less than in Scotland, and the facility of smuggling nearly the same. In America and the West Indies the white people even of the lowest rank are in much better circumstances than those of the same rank in England, and their consumption of all the luxuries in which they usually indulge themselves is probably much greater. The blacks, indeed, who make the greater part of the inhabitants both of the southern colonies upon the continent and of the West India[1] islands, as they are in a state of slavery, are, no doubt, in a worse condition than the poorest people either in Scotland or Ireland. We must not, however, upon that account, imagine that they are worse fed, or that their consumption of articles which might be subjected to moderate duties, is less than that even of the lower ranks of people in England. In order that they may work well, it is the interest of their master that they should be fed well and kept in good heart, in the same manner as it is his interest that his working cattle should be so. The blacks accordingly have almost every where their allowance of rum and of melasses or spruce beer, in the same manner as the white servants; and this allowance would not probably be withdrawn, though those articles should be subjected to moderate duties. The consumption of the taxed commodities, therefore, in proportion to the number of inhabitants, would probably be as great in America and the West Indies as in any part of the British empire. The opportunities of smuggling indeed, would be much greater; America, in proportion

---

[1] [Eds. 1 and 2 read 'West Indian'.]

to the extent of the country, being much more thinly inhabited than either Scotland or Ireland. If the revenue, however, which is at present raised by the different duties upon malt and malt liquors, were[1] to be levied by a single duty upon malt, the opportunity of smuggling in the most important branch of the excise would be almost entirely taken away: And if the duties of customs, instead of being imposed upon almost all the different articles of importation, were confined to a few of the most general use and consumption, and if the levying of those duties were subjected to the excise laws, the opportunity of smuggling, though not so entirely taken away, would be very much diminished. In consequence of those two, apparently, very simple and easy alterations, the duties of customs and excise might probably produce a revenue as great in proportion to the consumption of the most thinly inhabited province, as they do at present in proportion to that of the most populous.

The Americans have little gold and silver, The Americans, it has been said, indeed, have no gold or silver money; the interior commerce of the country being carried on by a paper currency, and the gold and silver which occasionally come among them being all sent to Great Britain in return for the commodities which they receive from us. But without gold and silver, it is added, there is no possibility of paying taxes. We already get all the gold and silver which they have. How is it possible to draw from them what they have not?

but this is the effect of choice, not necessity. The present scarcity of gold and silver money in America is not the effect of the poverty of that country, or of the inability of the people there to purchase those metals. In a country where the wages of labour are so much higher, and the price of provisions so much lower than in England, the greater part of the people must surely have wherewithal to purchase a greater quantity, if it were[2] either necessary or convenient for them to do so. The scarcity of those metals therefore, must be the effect of choice, and not of necessity.

It is for transacting either domestic or foreign business, that gold and silver money is either necessary or convenient

Paper is more convenient to the Americans for home trade, The domestic business of every country, it has been shewn in the second book of this Inquiry,[3] may, at least in peaceable times, be transacted by means of

---

[1] [Eds. 1–3 read 'was' here and five lines below.]   [2] [Eds. 1–3 read 'was'.]
[3] [Above, vol. i., pp. 309–315.]

a paper currency, with nearly the same degree of conveniency as by gold and silver money. It is convenient for the Americans, who could always employ with profit in the improvement of their lands a greater stock than they can easily get, to save as much as possible the expence of so costly an instrument of commerce as gold and silver, and rather to employ that part of their surplus produce which would be necessary for purchasing those metals, in purchasing the instruments of trade, the materials of clothing, several parts of household furniture, and the iron-work necessary for building and extending their settlements and plantations; in purchasing, not dead stock, but active and productive stock. The colony governments find it for their interest to supply the[1] people with such a quantity of paper-money as is fully sufficient and generally more than sufficient for transacting their domestic business. Some of those governments, that of Pennsylvania particularly, derive a revenue from lending this paper-money to their subjects at an interest of so much per cent. Others, like that of Massachusett's Bay, advance upon extraordinary emergencies a paper-money of this kind for defraying the public expence, and afterwards, when it suits the conveniency of the colony, redeem it at the depreciated value to which it gradually falls. In 1747[2] that colony paid, in this manner, the greater part of its public debts, with the tenth part of the money for which its bills had been granted. It suits the conveniency of the planters to save the expence of employing gold and silver money in their domestic transactions; and it suits the conveniency of the colony governments to supply them with a medium, which, though attended with some very considerable disadvantages, enables them to save that expence. The redundancy of paper-money necessarily banishes gold and silver from the domestic transactions of the colonies, for the same reason that it has banished those metals from the greater part of the domestic transactions in[3] Scotland; and in both countries it is not the poverty, but the enterprizing and projecting spirit of the people, their desire of employing all the stock which they can get as active and productive stock, which has occasioned this redundancy of paper-money.

while for their external trade they   In the exterior commerce which the different colonies carry on with Great Britain, gold and silver

---

[1] [Ed. 1 omits 'the'.]

[2] See Hutchinson's Hist. of Massachusett's Bay, Vol. II., page 436 & seq. [*History of the Colony of Massachusets Bay*, 2nd ed., 1765-8.]

[3] [Ed. 1 reads 'of'.]

use as much gold and silver as is necessary.

are more or less employed, exactly in proportion as they are more or less necessary. Where those metals are not necessary, they seldom appear. Where they are necessary, they are generally found

In the trade between Great Britain and Virginia and Maryland tobacco is a more convenient currency than gold and silver.

In the commerce between Great Britain and the tobacco colonies, the British goods are generally advanced to the colonists at a pretty long credit, and are afterwards paid for in tobacco, rated at a certain price. It is more convenient for the colonists to pay in tobacco than in gold and silver. It would be more convenient for any merchant to pay for the goods which his correspondents had sold to him in some other sort of goods which he might happen to deal in, than in money. Such a merchant would have no occasion to keep any part of his stock by him unemployed, and in ready money, for answering occasional demands. He could have, at all times, a larger quantity of goods in his shop or warehouse, and he could deal to a greater extent. But it seldom happens to be convenient for all the correspondents of a merchant to receive payment for the goods which they sell to him, in goods of some other kind which he happens to deal in. The British merchants who trade to Virginia and Maryland happen to be a particular set of correspondents, to whom it is more convenient to receive payment for the goods which they sell to those colonies in tobacco than in gold and silver. They expect to make a profit by the sale of the tobacco. They could make none by that of the gold and silver. Gold and silver, therefore, very seldom appear in the commerce between Great Britain and the tobacco colonies. Maryland and Virginia have as little occasion for those metals in their foreign as in their domestic commerce. They are said, accordingly, to have less gold and silver money than any other colonies in America. They are reckoned, however, as thriving, and consequently as rich, as any of their neighbours.

The northern colonies generally find the gold and silver necessary to pay the balance on their trade with Great Britain.

In the northern colonies, Pennsylvania, New York, New Jersey, the four governments of New England, &c. the value of their own produce which they export to Great Britain is not equal to that of the manufactures which they import for their own use, and for that of some of the other colonies to which they are the carriers. A balance, therefore, must be paid to the mother country in gold and silver, and this balance they generally find.

The sugar colonies generally find the gold and silver necessary to pay the balance to Great Britain which arises from the sugar planters being absentees.

In the sugar colonies the value of the produce annually exported to Great Britain is much greater than that of all the goods imported from thence. If the sugar and rum annually sent to the mother country were paid for in those colonies, Great Britain would be obliged to send out every year a very large balance in money, and the trade to the West Indies would, by a certain species of politicians, be considered as extremely disadvantageous. But it so happens, that many of the principal proprietors of the sugar plantations reside in Great Britain. Their rents are remitted to them in sugar and rum, the produce of their estates. The sugar and rum which the West India merchants purchase in those colonies upon their own account, are not equal in value to the goods which they annually sell there. A balance therefore must necessarily[1] be paid to them in gold and silver, and this balance too is generally found.

Any difficulties have not been proportionate to the size of the balances due,

The difficulty and irregularity of payment from the different colonies to Great Britain, have not been at all in proportion to the greatness or smallness of the balances which were respectively due from them. Payments have in general been more regular from the northern than from the tobacco colonies, though the former have generally paid a pretty large balance in money, while the latter have either paid[2] no balance, or a much smaller one. The difficulty of getting payment from our different sugar colonies has been greater or less in proportion, not so much to the extent of the balances respectively due from them, as to the quantity of uncultivated land which they contained; that is, to the greater or smaller temptation which the planters have been under of over-trading, or of undertaking the settlement and plantation of greater quantities of waste land than suited the extent of their capitals. The returns from the great island of Jamaica, where there is still much uncultivated land, have, upon this account, been in general more irregular and uncertain, than those from the smaller islands of Barbadoes, Antigua, and St. Christophers, which have for these many years been completely cultivated, and have, upon that account, afforded less field for the speculations of the planter. The new acquisitions of Grenada, Tobago, St. Vincents, and Dominica,[3] have opened a new field for speculations of this kind;

---

[1] [Ed. 1 reads 'must generally'.]   [2] [Ed. 1 reads 'paid either'.]
[3] [Above, p. 90, note 5.]

and the returns from those islands have of late been as irregular and uncertain as those from the great island of Jamaica.

and have arisen from unnecessary and excessive enterprise. It is not, therefore, the poverty of the colonies which occasions, in the greater part of them, the present scarcity of gold and silver money. Their great demand for active and productive stock makes it convenient for them to have as little dead stock as possible; and disposes them upon that account to content themselves with a cheaper, though less commodious instrument of commerce than gold and silver. They are thereby enabled to convert the value of that gold and silver into the instruments of trade, into the materials of clothing, into household furniture, and into the iron work necessary for building and extending their settlements and plantations. In those branches of business which cannot be transacted without gold and silver money, it appears, that they can always find the necessary quantity of those metals; and if they frequently do not find it, their failure is generally the effect, not of their necessary poverty, but of their unnecessary and excessive enterprize. It is not because they are poor that their payments are irregular and uncertain; but because they are too eager to become excessively rich. Though all that part of the produce of the colony taxes, which was over and above what was necessary for defraying the expence of their own civil and military establishments, were to be remitted to Great Britain in gold and silver, the colonies have abundantly wherewithal to purchase the requisite quantity of those metals. They would in this case be obliged, indeed, to exchange a part of their surplus produce, with which they now purchase active and productive stock, for dead stock. In transacting their domestic business they would be obliged to employ a costly instead of a cheap instrument of commerce; and the expence of purchasing this costly instrument might damp somewhat the vivacity and ardour of their excessive enterprize in the improvement of land. It might not, however, be necessary to remit any part of the American revenue in gold and silver. It might be remitted in bills drawn upon and accepted by particular merchants or companies in Great Britain, to whom a part of the surplus produce of America had been consigned, who would pay into the treasury the American revenue in money, after having themselves received the value of it in goods; and the whole business might frequently be transacted without exporting a single ounce of gold or silver[1] from America.

---

[1] [Ed. 1 reads 'gold and silver'.]

It is justice that Ireland and America should contribute to the discharge of the British debt.

It is not contrary to justice that both Ireland and America should contribute towards the discharge of the public debt of Great Britain. That debt has been contracted in support of the government established by the Revolution, a government to which the protestants of Ireland owe, not only the whole authority which they at present enjoy in their own country, but every security which they possess for their liberty, their property, and their religion; a government to which several of the colonies of America owe their present charters, and consequently their present constitution, and to which all the colonies of America owe the liberty, security, and property which they have ever since enjoyed. That public debt has been contracted in the defence, not of Great Britain alone, but of all the different provinces of the empire; the immense debt contracted in the late war in particular, and a great part of that contracted in the war before, were both properly contracted in defence of America.

Union would deliver Ireland from an oppressive aristocracy founded on religious and political prejudices.

By a union with Great Britain, Ireland would gain, besides the freedom of trade, other advantages much more important, and which would much more than compensate any increase of taxes that might accompany that union. By the union with England, the middling and inferior ranks of people in Scotland gained a complete deliverance from the power of an aristocracy which had always before oppressed them. By an union with Great Britain, the greater part of the people of all ranks in Ireland would gain an equally complete deliverance from a much more oppressive aristocracy; an aristocracy not founded, like that of Scotland, in the natural and respectable distinctions of birth and fortune; but in the most odious of all distinctions, those of religious and political prejudices; distinctions which, more than any other, animate both the insolence of the oppressors and the hatred and indignation of the oppressed, and which commonly render the inhabitants of the same country more hostile to one another than those of different countries ever are. Without a union with Great Britain, the inhabitants of Ireland are not likely for many ages to consider themselves as one people.

The colonies would be delivered from rancorous factions which are likely

No oppressive aristocracy has ever prevailed in the colonies. Even they, however, would, in point of happiness and tranquillity, gain considerably by a *to lead to bloodshed in case of separation from Great Britain.* union with Great Britain. It would, at least, deliver them from those rancorous and virulent factions which are inseparable from small democracies, and which have so frequently divided the affections of their people, and disturbed the tranquillity of their governments, in their form so nearly democratical. In the case of a total separation from Great Britain, which, unless prevented by a union of this kind, seems very likely to take place, those factions would be ten times more virulent than ever. Before the commencement of the present disturbances, the coercive power of the mother-country had always been able to restrain those factions from breaking out into any thing worse than gross brutality and insult. If that coercive power were[1] entirely taken away, they would probably soon break out into open violence and bloodshed. In all great countries which are united under one uniform government, the spirit of party commonly prevails less in the remote provinces than in the centre of the empire. The distance of those provinces from the capital, from the principal seat of the great scramble of faction and ambition, makes them enter less into the views of any of the contending parties, and renders them more indifferent and impartial spectators of the conduct of all. The spirit of party prevails less in Scotland than in England. In the case of a union it would probably prevail less in Ireland than in Scotland, and the colonies would probably soon enjoy a degree of concord and unanimity at present unknown in any part of the British empire. Both Ireland and the colonies, indeed, would be subjected to heavier taxes than any which they at present pay. In consequence, however, of a diligent and faithful application of the public revenue towards the discharge of the national debt, the greater part of those taxes might not be of long continuance, and the public revenue of Great Britain might soon be reduced to what was necessary for maintaining a moderate peace establishment.

East India with lighter taxes and less corrupt administration might yield an even larger addition of revenue. The territorial acquisitions of the East India company, the undoubted right of the crown, that is, of the state and people of Great Britain, might be rendered another source of revenue more abundant perhaps, than all those already mentioned. Those countries are represented as more fertile, more extensive; and, in proportion to their extent, much richer and more populous than Great Britain. In order to draw a great revenue from them, it would not

[1] [Eds. 1–3 read 'was'.]

probably be necessary, to introduce any new system of taxation into countries which are already sufficiently and more than sufficiently taxed. It might, perhaps, be more proper to lighten, than to aggravate, the burden of those unfortunate countries, and to endeavour to draw a revenue from them, not by imposing new taxes, but by preventing the embezzlement and misapplication of the greater part of those which they already pay.

If no such augmentation of revenue can be obtained Great Britain should reduce her expenses by ridding herself of the cost of the colonies in peace and war. If it should be found impracticable for Great Britain to draw any considerable augmentation of revenue from any of the resources above mentioned; the only resource which can remain to her is a diminution of her expence. In the mode of collecting, and in that of expending the public revenue; though in both there may be still room for improvement; Great Britain seems to be at least as œconomical as any of her neighbours. The military establishment which she maintains for her own defence in time of peace, is more moderate than that of any European state which can pretend to rival her either in wealth or in power. None of those articles, therefore, seem to admit of any considerable reduction of expence. The expence of the peace establishment of the colonies was, before the commencement of the present disturbances, very considerable, and is an expence which may, and if no revenue can be drawn from them, ought certainly to be saved altogether. This constant expence in time of peace, though very great, is insignificant in comparison with what the defence of the colonies has cost us in time of war. The last war, which was undertaken altogether on account of the colonies, cost Great Britain, it has already been observed, upwards of ninety millions.[1] The Spanish war of 1739 was principally undertaken on their account; in which, and in the French war that was the consequence of it, Great Britain spent upwards of forty millions, a great part of which ought justly to be charged to the colonies. In those two wars the colonies cost Great Britain much more than double the sum which the national debt amounted to before the commencement of the first of them. Had it not been for those wars that debt might, and probably would by this time, have been completely paid; and had it not been for the colonies, the former of those wars might not, and the latter certainly would not have been undertaken. It was because the colonies were supposed to be provinces of

[1] [Above, vol. i., p. 463.]

the British empire, that this expence was laid out upon them. But countries which contribute neither revenue nor military force towards the support of the empire, cannot be considered as provinces. They may perhaps be considered as appendages, as a sort of splendid and showy equipage of the empire. But if the empire can no longer support the expence of keeping up this equipage, it ought certainly to lay it down; and if it cannot raise its revenue in proportion to its expence, it ought, at least, to accommodate its expence to its revenue. If the colonies, notwithstanding their refusal to submit to British taxes, are still to be considered as provinces of the British empire, their defence in some future war may cost Great Britain as great an expence as it ever has done in any former war. The rulers of Great Britain have, for more than a century past, amused the people with the imagination that they possessed a great empire on the west side of the Atlantic. This empire, however, has hitherto existed in imagination only. It has hitherto been, not an empire, but the project of an empire; not a gold mine, but the project of a gold mine; a project which has cost, which continues to cost, and which, if pursued in the same way as it has been hitherto, is likely to cost, immense expence, without being likely to bring any profit; for the effects of the monopoly of the colony trade, it has been shewn,[1] are, to the great body of the people, mere loss instead of profit. It is surely now time that our rulers should either realize this golden dream, in which they have been indulging themselves, perhaps, as well as the people; or, that they should awake from it themselves, and endeavour to awaken the people. If the project cannot be completed, it ought to be given up. If any of the provinces of the British empire cannot be made to contribute towards the support of the whole empire, it is surely time that Great Britain should free herself from the expence of defending those provinces in time of war, and of supporting any part of their civil or military establishments in time of peace, and endeavour to accommodate her future views and designs to the real mediocrity of her circumstances.

[1] [Above, pp. 103–146.]

Appendix [1]

The two following Accounts are subjoined in order to illustrate and confirm what is said in the Fifth Chapter of the Fourth Book,[2] concerning the Tonnage bounty to the White Herring Fishery. The Reader, I believe, may depend upon the accuracy of both Accounts.

An Account of Busses fitted out in Scotland for Eleven Years, with the Number of Empty Barrels carried out, and the Number of Barrels of Herrings caught; also the Bounty at a Medium on each Barrel of Seasteeks, and on each Barre when fully packed.

Years	Number of Busses.	Empty Barrels carried out.	Barrels of Herrings caught.	Bounty paid on the Busses.		
				£.	s.	d.
1771	29	5948	2832	2085	0	0
1772	168	41316	22237	11055	7	6
1773	190	42333	42055	12510	8	6
1774	248	59303	56365	16952	2	6
1775	275	69144	52879	19315	15	0
1776	294	76329	51863	21290	7	6
1777	240	62679	43313	17592	2	6
1778	220	56390	40958	16316	2	6
1779	206	55194	29367	15287	0	0
1780	181	48315	19885	13445	12	6
1781	135	33992	16593	9613	12	6
Total,	2186	550943	378347	155463	11	0

Seasteeks 378347   Bounty at a medium for each barrel of seasteeks, ... £. 0 8 2¼
But a barrel of seasteeks being only reckoned two-
thirds of a barrel fully packed, one-third is deducted
⅓ deducted 126115⅔   which brings the bounty to . . £. 0 12 3¾

Barrels full
  packed, } 252231⅓

---

[1] [See above, p. 25.]
[2] [In Additions and Corrections this matter is printed in the text, and consequently the reading here is 'confirm what is said above'.]

Brought over—£. 0 12 3¾

And if the herrings are exported, there is besides a premium of 0 2 8

So that the bounty paid by Government in money for each
barrel, is . . . . £. 0 14 11¾
But if to this, the duty of the salt usually taken credit for
as expended in curing each barrel, which at a medium is of
foreign, one bushel and one-fourth of a bushel, at 10 s. a
bushel, be added, viz. 0 12 6

The bounty on each barrel would amount to . . . £. 1 7 5¾

If the herrings are cured with British salt, it will stand thus, viz.

Bounty as before . . . . £. 0 14 11¾
—but if to this bounty the duty on two bushels of Scots salt
at 1 s. 6 d. per bushel, supposed to be the quantity at a medium
used in curing each barrel is added, to wit,   . . .   0 3 0

The bounty on each barrel will amount to   . . . £. 0 17 11¾

And,

When buss herrings are entered for home consumption in
Scotland, and pay the shilling a barrel of duty, the bounty
stands thus, to wit as before . . . . . . £. 0 12 3¾
From which the 1 s. a barrel is to be deducted   . .   0 1 0

0 11 3¾

But to that there is to be added again, the duty of the
foreign salt used in curing a barrel of herrings, viz. . .   0 12 6

So that the premium allowed for each barrel of herrings
entered for home consumption is . . . . . £. 1 3 9¾

If the herrings are cured with British salt, it will stand as follows, viz.

Bounty on each barrel brought in by the busses as above . £. 0 12 3¾
From which deduct the 1 s. a barrel paid at the time they
are entered for home consumption 0 1 0

£. 0 11 3¾

But if to the bounty the duty on two bushels of Scots salt
at 1 s. 6 d. per bushel, supposed to be the quantity at a medium
used in curing each barrel, is added, to wit,   . . .   0 3 0

The premium for each barrel entered for home consumption will be . . . . £. 0 14 3¾

Though the loss of duties upon herrings exported cannot, perhaps, properly
be considered as bounty; that upon herrings entered for home consumption
certainly may.

An Account of the Quantity of Foreign Salt imported into Scotland, and of Scots Salt delivered Duty free from the Works there for the Fishery, from the 5th of April 1771 to the 5th of April 1782, with a Medium of both for one Year.

PERIOD.	Foreign Salt imported	Scots Salt delivered from the Works
	Bushels.	Bushels.
From the 5th of April 1771, to the 5th of April 1782.	936974	168226
Medium for one Year	$85179\frac{5}{11}$	$15293\frac{3}{11}$

It is to be observed that the Bushel of Foreign Salt weighs 84 lb. that of British Salt 56 lb. only.

Index I

SUBJECTS

[*This index is the original index, which appeared first in edition 3, with (in square brackets) additions by the present editor. It covers only the text and the author's notes. For books quoted in the editor's notes, readers should consult Index II.*]

three parts, 462; a great quantity of bullion alternately exported and imported for the purposes of foreign trade, 465; annual amount of these metals imported into Spain and Portugal, 466; the importation of, not the principal benefit derived from foreign trade, 468; the value of, how affected by the discovery of the American mines, 469; and by the passage round the Cape of Good Hope to the East Indies, 470; effect of the annual exportation of silver to the East Indies, 471; the commercial means pursued to increase the quantity of these metals in a country, 472, 496; bullion how received and paid at the bank of Amsterdam, 505; at what prices, 506, *note*; a trading country without mines, not likely to be exhausted by an annual exportation of these metals, 517

The value of, in Spain and Portugal, depreciated by restraining the exportation of them, ii. 17; are not imported for the purposes of plate or coin but for foreign trade, 58; the search after mines of, the most ruinous of all projects, 73; are valuable, because scarce, and difficult to be procured, 74

Gorgias, evidence of the wealth he acquired by teaching, i. 149

[Gottenburg, tea smuggled from, i. 228; company, 457]

Government, civil, indispensably necessary for the security of private property, ii. 232; subordination in society, by what means introduced, *ib.*; inequality of fortune introduces civil government for its preservation, 236; the administration of justice, a source of revenue in early times, 237; why government ought not to have the management of turnpikes, 248; nor of other public works, 252-3; [expense of, like that of a great estate, 350; soon learns the art of draining its subjects' pockets, 390;] want of parsimony during peace, imposes a necessity of contracting debts to carry on a war, 444; must support a regular administration of justice to cause manufactures and commerce to flourish, 445; origin of a national debt, 446; progression of public debts, *ib.*; war, why generally agreeable to the people, 456

Governors, political, the greatest spendthrifts in society, i. 367

[Gracchi, ii. 297]

[Grapes might be grown in Scotland at sufficient expense, i. 480]

Grasses, artificial, tend to reduce the price of butcher's meat, i. 168

Graziers, subject to monopolies obtained by manufacturers to their prejudice, ii. 173

Greece, [ancient, had no word for apprentice, i. 137; slavery harsher than in the middle ages, 411; cultivation of corn degenerated, *ib.*; citizens consisted of landed proprietors, 420; opulent and industrious, 427]

Foreign trade promoted [prohibited] in several of the antient states of, ii. 205; [trade and manufactures carried on by slaves, 205-6; citizens long served in war without pay, 216;] military exercises, a part of general education, 218; soldiers not a distinct profession in, 219; [individual military exercises, 220; militias defeated by Macedonian and Roman standing armies, 224-5; but had defeated Persian militia, 227; just beyond the shepherd stage at the Trojan war, 238;] course of education in the republics of, 296; the morals of the Greeks inferior to those of the Romans, *ib.*; [299-300; sanguinary factions, 297; exercises and elementary education, 297-8;] schools of the philosophers and rhetoricians, 298; law no science among the Greeks, 299; courts of justice, *ib.*; [abilities of people equal to those of modern nations, 300;] the martial spirit of the people, how supported, 307-8; [great men of letters were teachers, 235-6; public revenue largely obtained from state lands, 345]

[Greek clergy turbulent, ii. 320]

the trade of insurance may be successfully carried on by a joint stock company, ii. 280

Interest, landed, monied, and trading, distinguished, i. 373; [public, promoted by private, i. 145; ii. 477]

Interest for the use of money, the foundation of that allowance explained, i. 59; [varies with the rate of profit, 99;] historical view of the alterations of, in England, and other countries, 99–110; remarks on the high rates of, in Bengal, 105; and in China, 107; may be raised by defective laws, independent on the influence of wealth or poverty, ib.; the lowest ordinary rate of, must somewhat more than compensate occasional losses, ib.; the common relative proportion between interest and mercantile profits inquired into, 109; [stock lent at, 372–80;] was not lowered in consequence of the discovery of the American mines, 376; how the legal rate of, ought to be fixed, 379; consequences of its being fixed too high or too low, 379–80; the market rate of, regulates the price of land, 380

[As a source of public revenue, ii. 344; nominally subject to British land tax, 346;] whether a proper object of taxation, 375; [fall in the rate of, 377, 451]

[Invisible hand, i. 477]

[Ionians colonised Asia Minor and the Ægean, ii. 66]

Ireland [land not cultivated by factors, i. 176; supplies strong porters and beautiful prostitutes, fed on potatoes, to London, 179; exports salt meat, 254; may not export wool except to England, 256; may export raw hides to England duty free, 258; ii. 160; may export hides to other countries, i. 258; only lately allowed to export cattle to England, 443;] why never likely to furnish cattle to the prejudice of Great Britain, 481; [discharged soldiers and seamen may exercise any trade in, 493]

[Bounty on hemp imported into Britain, ii. 164;] the proposed absentee tax there considered, 426–7; [able to pay land tax, 472; extension of British custom duties to, proposed, 473;] ought in justice to contribute toward the discharge of the public debt of Great Britain, 483; expediency of a union with Great Britain, ib.; [would get rid of an oppressive aristocracy and a spirit of party, 484]

[Isabella of Castile, ii. 69]

Isocrates, the handsome income he made by teaching, i. 149; [man of letters also a teacher, ii. 335]

[Isthmian games, ii. 307]

Italy [corn chiefly imported during Roman prosperity, i. 168; question whether a new vineyard would be profitable, 172; olive plantations not to be envied by Britain, 178; not gone backward since discovery of America, 225; introduction of wind and water mills, 273; artistic genius decayed but monuments remain, 369; cultivation degenerated when abandoned to slaves, 411; prohibition of exportation and encouragement to importation of corn obstructed cultivation, 418–19; ancient inhabitants were proprietors, 420; cities became independent, 425; cities the first which commerce raised to opulence, 427; silks and velvets exchanged for corn of Poland, 428; breeding of silkworms introduced, 429;] the only great country in Europe, which has been cultivated and improved in every part by means of its foreign commerce, 444; [sober, though wine is cheap, 518]

[In little states restraint on export of corn may sometimes be necessary, ii. 48;] was originally colonized by the Dorians, 66; [Roman colonies, 67, 68, 78; Greek colonies, 77; school of philosophers in a Greek colony, ib.;

regulated, *ib.*; the different kinds of industry seldom dealt impartially with by any nation, 3; the division of labour considered, 7; this division increases the quantity of work, 11; instances in illustration, 16; from what principle the division of labour originates, 17; the divisibility of, governed by the market, 21; labour the real measure of the exchangeable value of commodities, 34; different kinds of, not easily estimated by immediate comparison, 35; is compared by the intermediate standard of money, 36; is an invariable standard for the value of commodities, 37; has a real, and a nominal price, 38; the quantity of labour employed on different objects, the only rule for exchanging them in the rude stages of society, 53; difference between the wages of labour and profits on stock, in manufactures, 54; the whole labour of a country never exerted, 61; is in every instance suited to the demand, 65; the effect of extraordinary calls for, 66–7; the deductions made from the produce of labour employed upon land, 73; why dearer in North America than in England, 78; is cheap in countries that are stationary, 80; the demand for, would continually decrease in a declining country, 82; the province of Bengal cited as an instance, *ib.*; is not badly paid for in Great Britain, *ib.*; an increasing demand for, favourable to population, 89; that of freemen cheaper to the employers than that of slaves, 90; the money price of, how regulated, 95; is liberally rewarded in new colonies, 103; common labour and skilful labour distinguished, 113–114; the free circulation of, from one employment to another, obstructed by corporation laws, 151; the unequal prices of, in different places, probably owing to the law of settlements, 157; can always procure subsistence on the spot where it is purchased, 163–4; the money price of, in different countries, how governed, 211; is set into motion by stock employed for profit, 277; the division of, depends on the accumulation of stock, 291; machines to facilitate labour, advantageous to society, 304; productive and unproductive, distinguished, 351; various orders of men specified, whose labour is unproductive, 352; unproductive labourers all maintained by revenue, 354; the price of, how raised by the increase of the national capital, 375; its price, though nominally raised, may continue the same, 377

Is liberally rewarded in new colonies, ii. 76; of artificers and manufacturers, never adds any value to the whole amount of the rude produce of the land, according to the French agricultural system of political œconomy, 186; this doctrine shewn to be erroneous, 196; the productive powers of labour, how to be improved, 197; [forced, 253, 346; division of, see Division of labour]

Labourers, useful and productive, every where proportioned to the capital stock on which they are employed, i. 2; share the produce of their labour, in most cases, with the owners of the stock on which they are employed, 55–6; their wages a continued subject of contest between them and their masters, 74; are seldom successful in their outrageous combinations, 75–6; the sufficiency of their earnings, a point not easily determined, 76; their wages sometimes raised by increase of work, 77; their demands limited by the funds destined for payment, *ib.*; are continually wanted in North America, 79; miserable condition of those in China, 80–1; are not ill paid in Great Britain, 82; if able to maintain their families in dear years, they must be at their ease in plentiful seasons, 83; a proof furnished in the complaints of their luxury, 87; why worse paid than artificers, 114; their interests strictly connected with the interests of the society, 277; labour the only source of their revenue, 294; effects of a life of labour on the understandings of the poor, ii. 302–3

Index II

AUTHORITIES

This index contains the names of authorities referred to in the editor's notes as well as in the author's notes and the text.

PRINTED IN GREAT BRITAIN BY
BUTLER AND TANNER LTD
FROME AND LONDON